Bocconi
University
Press

Andrea Beltratti

FINANCIAL MARKETS AND INVESTMENTS

Cover: Cristina Bernasconi, Milano
Typesetting: Alberto Bellanti, Milan

EGEA S.p.A.
Via Salasco, 5 – 20136 Milano
Tel. 02/5836.5751 – Fax 02/5836.5753
egea.edizioni@unibocconi.it – www.egeaeditore.it

First edition: January 2025

ISBN Domestic Edition 979-12-80623-38-6
ISBN International Edition 979-12- 81627-18-5
ISBN Digital Domestic Edition 978-88-238-8918-7
ISBN Digital International Edition 979-12- 81627-19-2

Table of contents

Introduction **1**

1 Financial markets **5**

1.1 Introduction 5
1.2 Markets, investors, contracts, management, and assets: an introduction 6
1.3 Financial instruments 10
1.3.1 Bonds 10
1.3.2 Stocks 11
1.3.3 Asset classes 12
1.3.4 Public and private assets 14
1.3.5 Corporate governance as an infrastructure for protecting financiers 16
1.4 Financial markets 17
1.4.1 Public firms 17
1.4.2 Primary and secondary markets 19
1.4.3 The cost and benefit of listing in stock markets 19
1.5 Uses and misuses of markets 20
1.5.1 What are financial markets used for? 20
1.5.2 Markets, business objectives, and investors 21
1.5.3 Critical issues in the use of markets 22
1.6 Collective investment vehicles 23
1.6.1 Mutual funds/UCITS 23
1.6.2 Exchange traded funds 26

2 Asset returns **29**

2.1 Introduction 29
2.2 The rate of return 29
2.2.1 Arithmetic returns 29
2.2.2 Logarithmic returns 31
2.3 Measuring risk in financial portfolios 32
2.3.1 The rate of return as a random variable 32
2.3.2 The probability function 32
2.3.3 Relevant intervals in the normal distribution 35

2.4 Unconditional probability distributions 37
2.4.1 The unconditional expected return and volatility 37
2.4.2 Skewness and kurtosis 38
2.4.3 The limits of normality 40
2.5 Long-run average excess returns 42
2.5.1 Indices 42
2.5.2 Empirical evidence 43
2.5.3 Compounded growth 46
2.5.4 Biases in stock indices 46
2.5.5 Interpretation of stock indices returns 47
2.5.6 Asymmetry in the distribution of returns 48
2.6 Conditional probability distributions 49
2.6.1 The conditional expectation 49
2.6.2 The conditional expectation of the rate of return 50
2.6.3 Computing the conditional mean: an example 53
2.6.4 Actual return, expected return, and shock 54
2.7 Value at Risk 55
2.7.1 What is the maximum potential loss? 55
2.7.2 What is VaR? 56
2.7.3 Computing VaR from volatility 57
2.7.4 The sensitivity of VaR to parameters 58
2.8 Estimating volatility 60
2.8.1 The VIX index 60
2.8.2 Conditional variance computation 61
2.8.3 The variance dynamics: an equivalent description 62
2.8.4 Unconditional non-normality and conditional variance 64
2.8.5 Evaluating the performance of a VaR model 64

3 Rational financial choices and the utility function 71
3.1 Introduction 71
3.2 Risk and uncertainty 72
3.3 The utility function 73
3.3.1 Expected utility 73
3.3.2 Utility functions and risk aversion 76
3.3.3 The CRRA utility function 77
3.3 The mean/variance utility function 79
3.3.1 Preferences over mean and variance 79
3.3.2 The indifference curve 82
3.4 The risk premium 85
3.5 Estimating risk aversion 86
3.5.1 Estimating risk aversion from surveys 86
3.5.2 Psychology, neuroscience and risk aversion 88

4 Behavioral finance **93**
4.1 Introduction 93
4.2 Behavioral finance 94
4.3 Examples of behavioral finance theories 96
4.3.1 Thinking, fast and slow 96
4.3.2 Heuristics (rules of thumb) 97
4.3.3 Loss avoidance 100
4.4 Human behavior and undesirable outcomes 104
4.4.1 Behavioral biases 105
4.4.2 Emotional biases 108
4.5 Typical mistakes in financial choice 111
4.5.1 Underinvesting in stocks 111
4.5.2 Excessive trading 112
4.5.3 Insufficient diversification 114
4.6 Solutions 114
4.6.1 Policy solutions 114
4.6.2 Financial education 115

5 Sovereign bonds **119**
5.1 Introduction 119
5.2 Bond price in secondary markets 119
5.2.1 Compound interest and present value 119
5.2.2 Invoice price and flat price 120
5.2.3 Price determination 121
5.2.4 The relationship between price and interest rate 122
5.2.5 The holding period return 123
5.2.6 The yield to maturity 126
5.3 The term structure of interest rates 127
5.3.1 The spot rate: definition 127
5.3.2 The term structure and bond pricing 127
5.3.3 The term structure of interest rates 128
5.3.4 The forward rate 131
5.4 Why does the term structure move over time? 132
5.4.1 The expectations theory of interest rates 132
5.4.2 Segmentation theory 133
5.4.3 The predictive power of the term structure 134

6 Risk and management of bond portfolios **141**
6.1 Introduction 141
6.2 Duration 141
6.2.1 Definition 141
6.2.2 Duration and maturity 142
6.2.3 Duration and rate risk 143
6.2.4 Convexity 144

6.3 Immunization 145
6.3.1 Duration, reinvestment risk, and price risk 145
6.3.2 Immunization 146
6.4 Corporate bonds 149
6.4.1 General features 149
6.4.2 Credit ratings 151
6.4.3 Probability of default and loss given default 151
6.4.4 Corporate bond returns 153
6.4.5 Corporate bond risk measurement 154

7 The expected return/risk trade-off and the benefits of diversification 159
7.1 Introduction 159
7.2 From individual assets to the portfolio 160
7.2.1 Portfolio return 160
7.2.2 Expected return and volatility with a risky and a risk-free asset 160
7.3 The capital allocation line 162
7.3.1 The relationship between expected return and risk 162
7.3.2 Leverage 164
7.4 The benefits of diversification 166
7.4.1 Two risky assets 166
7.4.2 The risk/reward trade-off for extreme values of the correlation coefficient 168
7.4.3 The general case for a two-risky-asset portfolio 170
7.4.4 Currency risk 173
7.5 The risk-free asset and two risky securities 174

8 The efficient frontier and the optimal portfolio 185
8.1 Introduction 185
8.2 Equally balanced portfolio 186
8.3 The Markowitz model 188
8.3.1 Portfolio optimization 188
8.3.2 Notation 188
8.3.3 Efficiency without a risk-free asset 189
8.3.4 Efficiency with a risk-free asset 192
8.4 The Markowitz model and investors' portfolios 198
8.4.1 The capital allocation line and the two-fund separation theorem 198
8.4.2 Qualitative investment implications 199
8.4.3 Choosing the optimal portfolio: graphical solution 200
8.4.4 Choosing the optimal portfolio: analytical solution 201
8.4.5 Reverse engineering the optimal portfolio solution 202
8.4.6 The Markowitz model and the democratization of finance 202
8.5 Wealth management: liabilities, time diversification, and non-traded assets 204

8.5.1 A general approach to hedging liabilities 204
8.5.2 Time diversification 206
8.5.3 Non-traded assets: the case of human capital 208
8.6 Asset management and the practice of portfolio optimization 209
8.6.1 Asset allocation terminology and benchmarks 209
8.6.2 Parameter estimation 210
8.6.3 Non-negativity constraints 211

9 The capital asset pricing model 217
9.1 Introduction 217
9.2 An asset marginal contribution to portfolio risk 217
9.3 The CAPM 221
9.3.1 Introduction: the Markowitz relation between risk and expected return 221
9.3.2 The equilibrium interpretation of the Markowitz relation between risk and expected return 222
9.3.3 The CAPM pricing equation 224
9.4 The index model 225
9.4.1 The index model and alpha 225
9.4.2 The index model and risk 226
9.5 Econometric testing of the CAPM 229
9.5.1 The index model and CAPM testing 229
9.5.2 CAPM testing: graphical analysis 229
9.5.3 CAPM testing: econometric analysis 231
9.5.4 Increasing the power of the test 233

10 Picking stocks and investing with style 239
10.1 Introduction 239
10.2 Alpha and small portfolios 240
10.2.1 Alphas 240
10.2.2 Undiversified alpha portfolios 240
10.3 Optimal selection of an active portfolio: the model by Treynor and Black 242
10.4 Long-short diversified portfolios 245
10.4.1 Searching for alpha 245
10.4.2 Building long-short portfolios 245
10.5 The most relevant anomalies/portfolio strategies 246
10.5.1 The size premium 246
10.5.2 The value premium 248
10.5.3 The momentum premium 249
10.5.4 The carry premium 250
10.5.5 The low-risk premium 251
10.5.6 The quality premium 252

10.5.7 Other anomalies 253
10.6 Why are there anomalies? 254
10.6.1 Rational risk premia 254
10.6.2 Behavioral errors 255
10.6.3 Agency issues 255
10.6.4 Lack of information 256
10.6.5 Inappropriate statistical methodologies 256
10.6.6 Transaction costs neglect 257
10.6.7 Leverage 257
10.7 Investment implications 258
10.7.1 Using anomalies 258
10.7.2 Hedge funds 259

11 Theory and practice of multifactor models 263
11.1 Introduction 263
11.2 The multifactor model and arbitrage 263
11.2.1 The multifactor model 264
11.2.2 Arbitrage and the pricing equation 264
11.2.3 Arbitrage with equal betas 265
11.2.4 Arbitrage with different betas 267
11.2.5 The APT pricing equation 268
11.2.6 Pricing individual stocks 269
11.3 Factor identification 270
11.3.1 Macroeconomic factors 270
11.3.2 Factor replicating portfolios 271
11.3.3 The Fama–French model 272
11.4 Application of the Fama–French model 274
11.4.1 Liquidity risk 274
11.4.2 Pricing in international markets 275
11.5 Performance evaluation 277
11.5.1 Introduction to performance evaluation 277
11.5.2 The index model and the CAPM 277
11.5.3 Performance evaluation and the Fama–French model 278
11.5.4 Evidence 279

12 Prices and values 285
12.1 Introduction 285
12.2 Valuation and infinite horizon 286
12.2.1 Value with a one-period horizon 286
12.2.2 Value with an infinite horizon 287
12.3 Gordon's model 288
12.3.1 Simplifying assumptions 288
12.3.2 Growth and earnings reinvestment 289

12.3.3 How much are growth opportunities worth? 291
12.4 The multi-phase model 291
12.5 Applications 293
12.5.1 The price–earnings ratio 293
12.5.2 The book-to-price ratio 295
12.5.3 Market value and expected return 296
12.5.4 The price-to-earnings ratio and expected return 297
12.6 Speculative bubbles 298
12.7 Fundamentals and unexpected returns 299

13 Market efficiency 305
13.1 Introduction 305
13.2 The definition of an efficient market 306
13.2.1 Characteristics of market efficiency 306
13.2.2 Why efficiency is important 306
13.2.3 Brief remarks on information efficiency 307
13.3 Efficiency tests 308
13.4 Valuation efficiency and return variance 308
13.4.1 Excess volatility 308
13.4.2 Asset pricing and consumption 310
13.5 Valuation efficiency and predictability of returns 311
13.5.1 Predictive regressions 311
13.5.2 Predictive regressions and market efficiency with a constant risk premium 312
13.5.3 The random walk 312
13.5.4 Predictability, efficiency, and time-varying risk premium 313
13.5.5 Prediction and alternative data 314
13.6 Valuation efficiency and price reactions 315
13.6.1 News and prices 315
13.6.2 Event studies 315
13.7 The equity premium 317
13.7.1 The equity premium and the mean/variance utility function 317
13.7.2 The equity premium and covariance with consumption 318
13.7.3 The equity premium puzzle 320
13.8 Psychological drivers of market prices 324
13.9 Risky arbitrage 326

14 Private assets 329
14.1 Introduction 329
14.2 Private assets 330
14.3 Private equity 331
14.4 Private debt 333
14.4.1 Private debt and business development companies 333
14.4.2 Why private debt 335
14.5 Real estate 336

14.5.1 How to invest in real estate 336
14.5.2 Indirect investment in real estate stocks 336
14.5.3 Funds and investment in real estate 337
14.6 Art 338
14.6.1 Art as an alternative asset 338
14.6.2 Investing in art 339
14.7 Performance evaluation of private assets 340
14.7.1 The internal rate of return 340
14.7.2 Other performance indicators 343
14.7.3 Value creation in private equity funds 344
14.8 Private market price indices 345
14.8.1 Why is it difficult to measure the performance of private markets? 345
14.8.2 Unsmoothing 345
14.8.3 Hedonic prices 346
14.8.4 Prices obtained from repeat sales 349
14.8.5 Long-term average returns for real estate 350
14.8.6 Long-term average returns for art investing 351
14.9 Alternative assets 352
14.9.1 Real estate and optimization 352
14.9.2 Does CAPM explain the expected return from real estate? 354
14.9.3 Real estate and optimization 355

15 Sustainability and ESG investing 359
15.1 Introduction 359
15.2 What is sustainability? 360
15.2.1 Sustainable development 360
15.2.2 Accounting for environmental and social goods and services 361
15.2.3 Challenges in accounting for environmental and social goods and services 362
15.3 CSR, ESG investing, and sustainability 363
15.3.1 CSR 363
15.3.2 SRI/ESG investing 364
15.3.3 Measurement and ratings 366
15.4 ESG investing, portfolio choice and risk premia 367
15.4.1 Preferences for ESG factors 367
15.4.2 ESG factors, asset demand, and risk premia 368
15.4.3 Expected returns, volatilities, and ESG factors 370
15.5 Finance and climate change 371
15.5.1 Climate change and financial risk 371
15.5.2 Climate change and risk premia 372
15.5.3 Climate change and real estate 374

Bibliography 377

Introduction

The word finance seems to have arisen from ideas of limits and boundaries. According to the Merriam-Webster dictionary, https://www.merriam-webster.com/wordplay/financial-word-origins, "the word fine comes from Anglo-French fin and Latin finis, both of which mean "end" or "boundary," and in its earliest uses in English, fine referred to various ends, limits, and boundaries. The modern-day financial meaning of the word actually dates to the 15th century and refers to a sum imposed as punishment for an offense. Up until the 19th century, however, fine was also used for a sum paid as compensation or for exemption from punishment—in other words, money paid to avoid punishment or imprisonment. A common expression was to make fine, which referred to the exemption from punishment or the release from captivity by paying a sum of money. The word finance also emerged in the 15th century but from Anglo-French finer, meaning "to end" as well as "to pay," and similarly in English referred to an end or payment. In the 18th century, the word came to refer to pecuniary resources and the management of funds".

The word "fine", in Italian, describes the goal, the purpose of an activity. Modern finance is not the end of a relationship between individuals, but the beginning of a formal association for a well-defined purpose. The cover of the book refers to the Ziggurath associated with ancient Mesopotamia (now mainly Iraq) appearing at around 2000 BCE. The motivation for the association between finance and ancient Mesopotamia has to do with the early examples of trade and its financing as discussed in the fascinating book by Professor Goetzmann (2016). The need to trade, to exchange things like grain and clay with precious metals, minerals, and wood from other regions was an early motivation for financing the construction and use of ships and most of all for writing financial contracts among traders to share resources and risks that would be too large for a single individual. Four thousand years ago finance was about goals and not about terminating contracts.

Finance includes a wide range of activities implemented by individual and institutional investors, financial institutions, corporations. These activities deal with two main purposes: managing a pool of financial wealth to purse specific goals and finding the needed resources to spend (on consumption or investment) before income is realized. In the second half of the last century finance studies were highly contaminated by mathematics and by statistics, also due to the availability of easy-to-use data in the context of increasing econometric sophistication, however, in the last couple of decades, there has been more attention to understand behavior on the part of individuals and institutions. This may be surprising considering advances in Big data and Artificial Intelligence, but there is no contradiction: improving processes and reducing costs magnifies the role of decision-makers who may spend more time in making decisions. Within corporations, finance is used more and more as a common language that is critical for dialogue among different functions and for strategic planning. However, even a final user in corporate finance or investment management needs to acquire basic technical knowledge which may facilitate the right interpretation of quantitative tools that are available off-the-shelf from a variety of platforms.

The book results from my experience of teaching undergraduate students at Bocconi University and executive programs at the SDA Bocconi School of Management. The guidelines that I have followed, in my courses and in this book, are as follows:

- discuss in a simple but rigorous way the most relevant models;
- present a balanced view of different theoretical positions when there is no academic consensus (for example on market efficiency);
- provide a guide for top down asset allocation, discussing relevant practical elements like parameter estimation and non-negativity constraints that are crucial for creating forward-looking portfolios;
- include in boxes several empirical examples that may help understanding the theory and introduce a few technical boxes (for example on issues like the origin of Markowitz model equations and the stochastic discount factor approach to value determination) that may be skipped by readers who are interested in applications and not on theory.

The result is a book that may be used mainly for undergraduate courses, even though the selection of topics, and the applied approach, may make it interesting also for Master of Science and Finance Executive programs. The undergraduate course that I have been teaching at Bocconi covers about 75% of the material in thirty-two classes lasting one and a half hour each. It is also possible to use the book for shorter courses, perhaps taught in the context of Master in Finance for executives or blocks of custom programs.

This book presents a selection of basic technical knowledge which will allow the reader to understand a wide range of topics, going from portfolio allocation to asset valuation, from expected return determination to basic knowledge of financial risk modelling, from understanding of market prices for liquid assets to basic concepts of private asset investment, with a final chapter on the investment implications of the new attention for sustainability.

The first chapter introduces the terminology and discusses the main types of asset classes and financial intermediaries. The second chapter proposes an unconventional choice: rather than introducing statistics and later applying it to financial problems, it is based on a close link between definitions and applications. This has the purpose of immediately raising the reader's attention in the context of issues related to risk modelling and understanding empirical evidence about long-run stock and bond returns. The third chapter is about describing preferences towards risk in the context of the traditional utility function. Most of the chapter uses the simple mean-variance utility function which, albeit academically poor, has the advantage of being intuitive and based on the two crucial parameters of expected return and volatility that are central in most practical applications. The fourth chapter discusses most recent research about the way investors actually behave rather than a description of how they should behave in theory. Behavioral finance borrows deeply from psychology and several references are made to experiments that have highlighted differences between the theory and practice of investment, at least for retail investors.

An unconventional choice also characterizes chapters five and six where we present a description of the bond market, introducing important definitions of the yield to maturity (also crucial for modern technique of performance evaluation surveyed in chapter fourteen), spot and forward rates, drivers of the term structure as well as basic tools for managing bond portfolios like duration and immunization. Chapters seven and eight deal with portfolio allocation, starting from the simple case of a risk-free and a risky asset that allows a simple derivation of the capital allocation line, and then complicating the picture by considering two risky assets. Some time is spent on the two risky asset case that is used for building the intuition about the benefits of diversification. The move to the general number of risky assets includes a detailed analysis of the Markowitz optimization model, followed by several discussions about the practical use of the model from the point of view of an investor pursuing a top down asset allocation.

Chapter nine uses the Markowitz model as a way to understand the equilibrium pricing implications of the portfolio diversification model through the Capital Asset Pricing Model (noting that the mathematics of the efficient frontier may be used to derive the CAPM even without an equilibrium approach), also presenting a description of the methodology for empirically testing the CAPM. The CAPM is at the same time one of the models most rejected by academic empirical analyses and most used in practical applications, for example for the cost of equity computation. Rejections of the CAMP have created a long literature on anomalies that has inspired many investors in their search for a return/ risk trade-off that is superior to that offered by the market. These are reviewed in chapter ten, while chapter eleven is about the more general theory based on arbitrage pricing (APT). Empirical models for expected return determination on diversified portfolios are then discussed as potentially consistent with the APT. Important applications are in alpha measurement and performance evaluation.

Chapter twelve is about pricing assets based on fundamentals. Changing expectations of fundamentals are a key driver of price volatility and a long debate tries to understand whether movements are rational and mainly depend on cash flow expectations and time-varying expected returns. Chapter thirteen uses the pricing models to discuss the fascinating topic of market efficiency, a reference point of extraordinary importance for economic growth and resource allocation in decentralized competitive markets. The different implications of efficiency for market prices and returns are introduced together with a survey of the main results deriving from the various tests. This fascinating debate has no definite conclusions but highlight a series of important points for corporations and investors. Chapter fourteen deals with private assets, that have become more and more central to the portfolios of many investors. Some investors are overexposed to private assets (for example households owning a house or entrepreneurs owning their company) and would benefit from diversification into public assets, but several other investors, mainly institutional, actively search for diversification into private assets. The case studies considered in the chapter concern private equity, private debt, and art. Chapter fifteen reconsiders several tools and issues that have been covered in the previous chapters and discusses them in the context of the debate about sustainability. This raises fascinating issues about the meaning of sustainability, the challenges associated with measuring it and the obstacles to achieving it (mainly in the form of non-traded assets and externalities), and the role of financial markets and intermediaries. Empirical results about the role of ESG investing for portfolio diversification and the pricing of environmental factors are also discussed.

I thank all the students who have provided useful comments over time, particularly those taking my Bocconi undergraduate courses in the last three decades and those attending my course at the Executive Master in Finance in the last eight years. The book is dedicated to them.

I thank EGEA for active collaboration during this project.

1 Financial markets

1.1 Introduction

Finance is a huge infrastructure allowing investors to hold diversified portfolios of financial contracts representing a variety of assets. We study this infrastructure from the point of view of asset owners, understanding the risk and return characteristic of the investment opportunity set and asking how they can best invest their wealth. This introduction provides an overall framework for thinking about the relation between assets and investors, starting from the way assets become financial securities associated with ownership rights over pieces of assets and their cash flows. Some assets are privately held by specific owners, while others are public and listed, enlarging investment opportunities for buyers and being sources of financing for sellers.

Financial markets provide advantages to buyers and sellers of listed securities, including the possibility to profitably invest savings and to select the best portfolio allocation. The productivity of individuals working for corporations magnifies the return on assets; sound diversification choices offer the possibility to improve the expected return/risk trade-off at the portfolio level. For the full and effective use of financial markets, it is necessary to have a stable and shared legal framework, a fair and rapid judicial system, and a corporate governance framework that is consistent with respect of property rights. The protection of creditors' and shareholders' rights incentivizes the purchase of financial securities and the associated risk-taking, contributing to the better allocation of resources and economic growth. Financial markets facilitate the separation of ownership and management and at the same time perform numerous other tasks: the best distribution of overall risk among different investors, the possibility of investing financial resources to manage the dynamics of consumption over time, the generation of information through pricing, and the allocation of system resources to companies that create more value for the community. The misuse of markets, by both investors and companies, significantly reduces the contribution of markets to economic growth.

Over time, investors have witnessed a dramatic growth in the available investment opportunity set, which also includes collective vehicles that trade listed assets such as mutual funds and exchange traded funds, and vehicles such as private equity funds and private debt funds dealing with private assets and making them investable. Such vehicles further improve the risk/return trade-off and increase the freedom to select portfolios that best suit the preferences of buyers.

1.2 Markets, investors, contracts, management, and assets: an introduction

The sophistication of the financial system is a benchmark to judge the degree of development of a modern economy. An efficient financial system including financial markets and financial intermediaries is an essential tool to improve the rate of growth through, among other things, better connections between savers and investors, leading to higher savings and investments, more data creation and processing to monitor the management of assets and create new information sources, and financial innovation. Levine (2005) surveys theoretical and empirical literatures on value creation in finance, while Shiller (2013) proposes a qualitative analysis of the different contributions made by finance professionals to economic growth (to "the good society"). Financial markets and financial intermediaries help investors own assets and create new value through economic growth. Figure 1.1 and Figure 1.2 sketch a few useful elements to understand the relations between asset owners and assets and at the same time represents an introduction to the topics explored in the next chapters.

Figure 1.1 The asset cycle

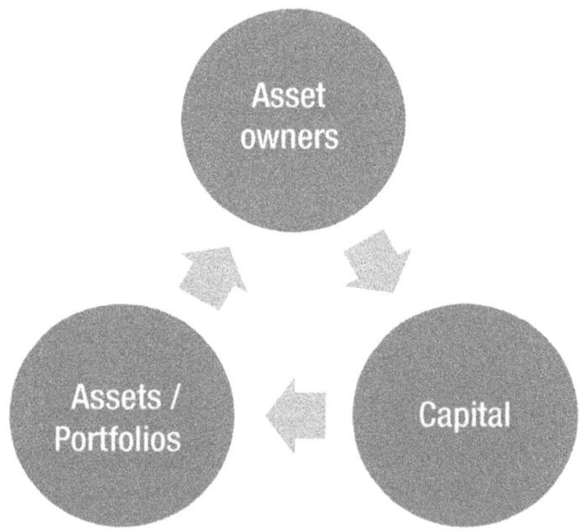

Figure 1.1 shows that capital is owned by someone and, when understood from the perspective of owners or investors (individuals and institutions), can be interpreted as an asset and included in portfolios. Asset owners make decisions that change the stock of capital over time, giving rise to a cycle. Figure 1.2 provides some more key elements characterizing the asset cycle.

Starting from the bottom right, asset owners are individuals and institutions characterized by a portfolio of assets. Their decisions about which assets should be owned depends upon several factors: they first need to understand what combinations of assets are the most efficient, considering parameters such as expected returns and risks, and then select their optimal portfolios based on their risk aversion, liabilities, goals, values, and personalities. Statman (2010) suggests that investors are

Figure 1.2 **From capital sources to asset ownership**

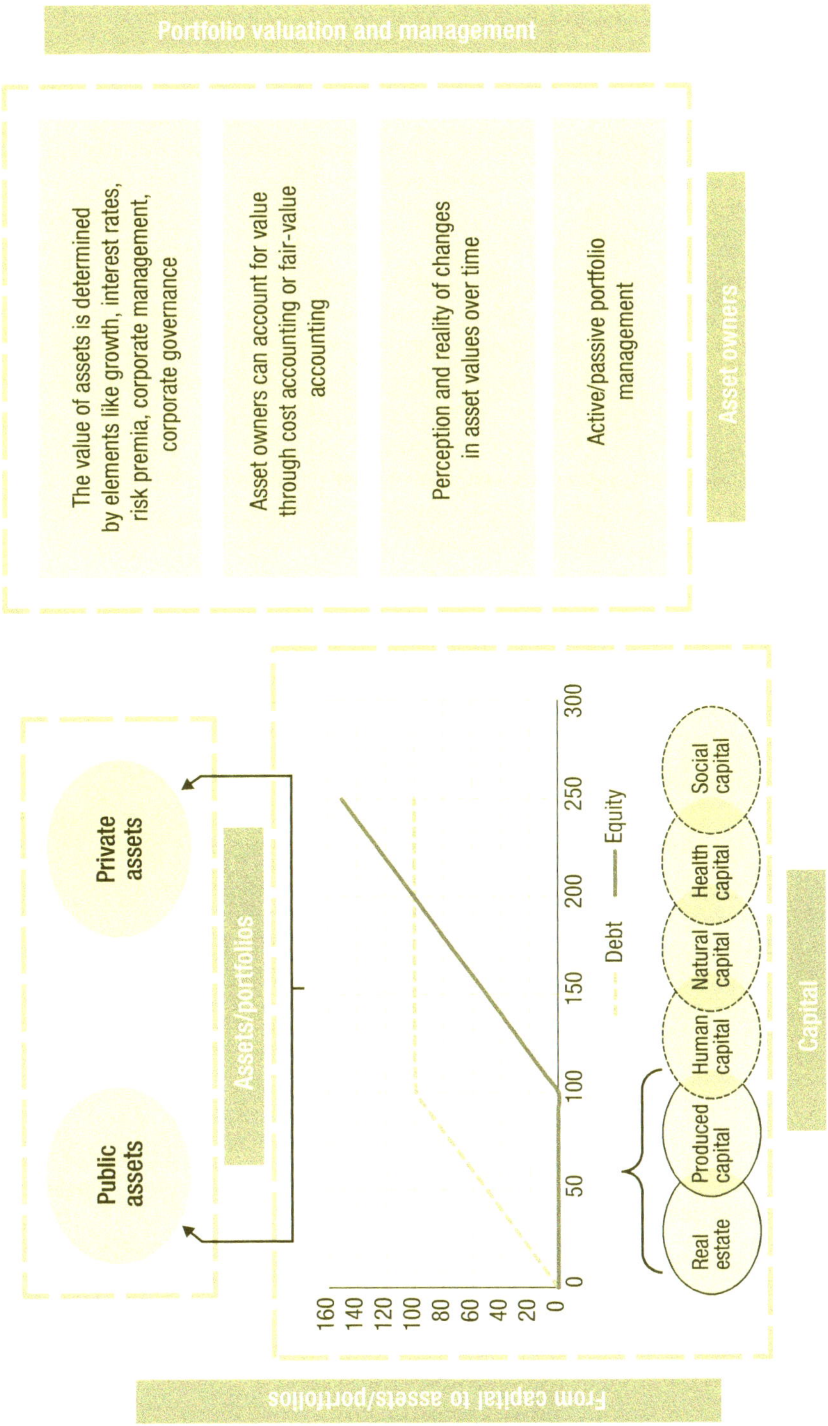

after utilitarian benefits (associated with expected return and risk); expressive benefits conveying values, tastes, and status; and emotional benefits, which are about personal feelings. Economics and finance have traditionally focused on utilitarian benefits (see Chapter 3). A behavioral finance approach developed from the 1980s and received a boost in the last three decades from empirical analyses documenting investors' "errors" or at least deviations from rationality. Behavioral finance may account for expressive and emotional benefits (Chapter 4). An important element in portfolio selection is the current situation: people who own a house where they live take the existence of their property as given and are unlikely to sell it to optimize the overall return/ risk trade-off. Entrepreneurs who own a non-diversified portion of wealth in a company are unlikely to sell it to exploit the opportunities provided by listed equity. In all of these cases, asset owners start from their current situation and decide on the investment of financial wealth taking their other assets as given.

A key element to judge financial performance (see the box above "asset owners" in Figure 1.2) is the rate of return earned on the various assets, which, over the life of the investment, may be known with certainty or just estimated, depending on whether assets are listed in public markets. Public assets are listed in markets and are characterized by a valuation that may change at each transaction. As a result, public asset owners know exactly the rate of return and the value of their wealth at any moment in time. Private assets, not listed in public markets, are often evaluated in a smooth way through so-called historical cost accounting, which maintains the value of assets at their purchasing cost, unless there is some very significant new information that may suggest the need for an impairment or a planned amortization. The importance of fair-value accounting versus historical cost accounting has been a subject of debate particularly during and after the Global Financial Crisis of 2008 (see Laux and Leuz, 2010). During a crisis, the stability of historical cost accounting may provide a benefit to investors, who may convince themselves that the fall in market prices observed in public markets does not apply to their own wealth. That is why Figure 1.2 refers to the perception and reality of changes in wealth. When returns are known from market prices it is possible to use data to estimate relevant parameters for selecting portfolios through the application of quantitative methods (Chapter 2, among others); when returns are estimated it is harder to decide investment and evaluate the performance of the asset supplier (Chapter 14).

Asset prices in public markets may deviate from their values. Prices are determined by demand and supply relations, whereas values are model-based reconstructions of present discounted future cash flows, accounting for the price of time (the interest rate) and the price of risk (the risk premium). There is a long debate about the correspondence between prices and values that will be explored in several chapters, mostly in the debate about the efficiency of financial markets in Chapter 13.

Prices and values are influenced by fundamentals (Chapter 12). The risk-free interest rate is a key one, as we have seen in 2022–2023, when central banks have gone through the fastest and largest ever increase in policy rates to contain inflation, which in Europe moved above 10% in October 2022. The risk-free rate is the price of time and is used to compare currency amounts today and in the future. Economic growth is another key parameter, regardless of the challenge that has been faced by researchers trying to spot an empirical relation between economic growth and stock prices. The underlying logic suggests that higher economic growth should increase future cash flows and be immediately incorporated in prices and values. Cash flows are risky (Chapter 2): their future realization may turn out to be higher or lower than the expected value, so asset owners run the risk that the price and value of their assets in the future will drop. As a result, they are willing to hold risky assets only if the expected return is larger than the risk-free rate. The risk premium is the compensation mechanism inducing independent agents to collectively hold the assets.

Assets (top left in Figure 1.2) are legally represented by contracts assigning property rights and rights to the payment of the cash flows that will be delivered by the assets. The most fundamental types of contracts are equity and debt, which are represented on the left of the figure through a diagram, introduced by Merton (1974), where the horizontal axis represents the value of assets of a company, going from 0 to 250 in the picture. On the vertical axis we have the corresponding value of two financial contracts: debt and equity. Debt-holders are entitled to the coupons paid by the asset, and the value of their bond is capped at the face value (equal to 100 in the picture). Things can go bad for debt-holders as the value of their credit may drop to zero if the assets of the company are below the face value of debt. The upside is reserved to equity-holders, who get all the value if assets are above the face value of their debt. The downside is that the value of their contracts can quickly drop to zero if the value of the company assets is below the face value of debt.

Other important links in the upper right of Figure 1.2 are corporate management and governance and active and passive management, included in the box on "Values." Corporate management and corporate governance are both tools to reassure asset owners that their investment in an enterprise is taken care of with the best possible skill and alignment of interest among management and owners. Corporate management includes all the skills and knowledge of people working for the company, aimed at creating value through the choice of a business model and operations guaranteeing a unique place in the market and the willingness of consumers to pay for the goods and services produced by the firm. Sometimes managers may not act in the unique interest of shareholders. Due to the impossibility of observing the effort put in by managers to generate the results, companies are run through a series of roles, responsibilities, and processes where the board of directors consults and monitors the management. Corporate governance is extremely important in providing the right monitoring and incentives for managers to produce the best results. We will return in Chapter 15 to the distinction between shareholders and stakeholders and to the debate about the social responsibility of corporations.

Active and passive management (see Figure 1.2) describe two different approaches that asset owners and/or their delegates, asset managers, may select. In the active case the manager selects a sub-universe of available assets that is particularly suitable from the point of view of the trade-off between expected return and risk; exposure to a subset of assets may change over time, also introducing an element of market timing over and above the selectivity. Passive management aims at replicating an index of the relevant market; it is made possible by the sophistication of financial markets and the contribution of index providers producing indices that aim at being representative of the different asset classes.

Passive management, whose intellectual foundations are provided by the Markowitz diversification model (Chapters 5–7), induces asset owners to replicate the structure of existing asset supply. This may or may not be desirable. Passive management may decrease costs of financial intermediation and leave more resources for other uses but delegates asset allocation decisions to index providers, which may be inconsistent with overall welfare. This issue is related to one of the big trends of our time: the relevance of sustainability (see Chapter 15). Directing capital towards firms that create environmental and social value requires special skills and judgment that is currently hard to replicate in stock and bond indices. This calls for an expanded role of asset managers, banks, and insurance companies. It is unlikely that substantial improvement towards sustainability may be activated through passive investing.

To discuss the bottom left of the figure it is worth noticing the variety of assets that are useful for production and/or direct utility generation. Real estate and productive capital are the two most visible assets in the context of economic activities. There are many others, however, including natural capital, human capital, social capital, and health capital. These assets are represented in dotted circles to stress that we seldom think of them as sources of economic value, even though we all enjoy living in a green environment allowing us to be healthy and happy, and we like to be social and meet people in a community. These nice characteristics improve productivity and not only happiness. Do asset owners recognize the value of such assets? The answer is unclear, but it is obvious that our national accounts do not (see Chapter 15). GDP is the global value added produced in an economy and only includes consumption and investment (the increase in productive capital). Some other sources of capital are currently ignored, both in national accounts and in company accounts. This is why we should think hard about the mission of the firm and the categories of stakeholders, beyond shareholders, that should be considered when making production and financing decisions.

1.3 Financial instruments

1.3.1 Bonds

A bond, either sovereign or corporate, is characterized by three main elements:

- face value: the amount of money the issuer of the bond will pay to the holder at maturity;
- maturity: the date the issuer of the bond promises to repay the face value;
- term to maturity: length of time between current date and maturity;
- coupon: the remuneration that is paid periodically (every six months or every year) by the issuer of the bond to the holder of the bond. The coupon is equal to the product of the coupon rate and the face value. The coupon rate is expressed as an annual value. Some bonds can pay the coupon on a semi-annual basis, in this

case by paying the annual coupon divided by two every six months. The coupon may be fixed in monetary value or may vary over time, for example depending on the development of short-term interest rates, as is the case when, for example, the coupon for a certain period is set from the level of the short-term interest rate of the previous year and therefore may vary from one period to another. Such a bond is called a "floater" as its coupon changes with the prevailing short-term interest rate. Securities that do not pay coupons are referred to as zero-coupon bonds.

For example, a bond with a face value of €1,000 issued in January 2024 maturing on December 31, 2028, with a coupon rate of 2% will pay the holder a coupon of €20 each year until the end of 2028 and on December 28, 2028, will repay €1,000 to the holder of the bond. If the face value of the same bond was indexed to the level of the consumer price index (CPI) and the CPI went up globally 10% between January 2024 and December 2028, then the holder would receive €1,100 on the expiration day. The value of the coupon would also change over time: if inflation had been equal to 4% during 2024, at the end of 2024 the monetary coupon would be equal to €20.8 (obtained from the product of 1,040 and 2%) due to the coupon rate being applied to a face value that increases over time with inflation Such a bond is called "linker" due to its link with inflation.

Among all types of bonds, we are often going to refer to risk-free ones, meaning they will have an initial price and pre-defined cash flows that will be paid for sure. Bonds close to this ideal picture are issued by a reputable state, with strong institutions and creditors' rights, and strong economic fundamentals including a relatively low public debt/GDP ratio. Examples of countries meeting these requirements are Germany, Norway, and the United States. Risk-free bonds are risk-free in nominal terms and do not help in the case of inflation shocks that reduce their real value. Moreover, risk-free bonds are truly risk-free only if held until maturity. The price of a long-term bond fluctuates in the short run and offers no certainty about the change in its value. The considerations about risky returns that will be offered in the different chapters also apply to risk-free bonds when their maturity is longer than the investor holding period.

1.3.2 Stocks

A stock is a contract assigning the holder an ownership stake in a company. Its main characteristics can be summarized as follows:

- it has a nominal value which is most of the time not relevant for the market price determination, contrary to what happens for a bond whose price fluctuates around the face value;
- it does not have an expiration date because it has an infinite life, and it is active as long as the company that issued it continues to operate;
- it offers periodic remuneration that is set in monetary terms, the dividend, which can also be null at the discretion of management.

Shareholders receive a residual cash flow, which materializes only after the rights of all other stakeholders of the company (suppliers, customers, workers, etc.) have been satisfied. This is incentive-compatible for all stakeholders: the category that takes the most risk in theory has the best incentives to carefully manage (or carefully monitor who runs) the company.[1]

Companies often adopt a dividend policy aimed at communicating a dividend stability objective over time. When earnings are stable this can be achieved by setting the dividend to a fixed percentage of earnings (payout). When earnings suddenly decrease because of a crisis, the management may decide to increase the payout to pay a stable monetary dividend. An alternative way of remunerating shareholders is to buy shares on the market (buyback). The buyback can be used by the company for various purposes, for example to signal to the market the undervaluation of the stock. Buybacks represent a shareholder remuneration when associated with the cancellation of the underlying shares, with the result of reducing the number of outstanding shares, which increases earnings per share and, all things being equal, the price of the securities that remain listed.[2]

Michaely and Moin (2022) document the existence of two different trends in the periods 1970-2000 and 2000-2018, defined respectively as "disappearing dividends" and "reappearing dividends" ad measured by the fraction of dividend-paying firms. The trends are driven by two factors: first, the tendency for a firm with a given set of operating and financial characteristics to pay dividends, and second, the changes over time in the characteristics of firms that can be associated with the decision to pay dividends. The paper finds that the disappearing dividends trend is driven on almost equal parts (53% and 47%) by time-changing characteristics and changes in the decision to pay dividends given the characteristics. But 82% of the reappearing dividend trend is explained by delisting of non-dividend paying firms and 18% to time-changing firm characteristics among which especially a lower earnings volatility. Buybacks become increasingly popular over the sample period and therefore cannot explain the time variability in the fraction of firms which pay dividends.

1.3.3 Asset classes

Both investors and individual/ institutions not owning stocks are interested in news about the index of the national stock market. Why is this so? And what is "the stock market?" The reason why investors in the stock market are interested in the daily value of a popular index, such as the S&P500 or the Eurostoxx, is obvious: they want to know the fluctuation of their wealth. The reason why individuals/ institutions not owning stocks are interested is less obvious but a popular interpretation is that they

---

[1] Consistently, the contractual framework that regulates the formation of a company provides that shareholders appoint the management.

[2] Buybacks in the US market in 2023 are estimated to be $795 billion according to S&P Global; see https://www.spglobal.com/spdji/en/corporate-news/article/sp-500-q4-2023-buybacks-increase-180-compared-to-q3/.

take it as a barometer of the strength of the economy. The public are particularly attracted by news on the stock market during crises, times at which even non-specialized newspapers and television reports refer to "stock market crashes."

The stock market is an example of an asset class. To understand more generally the meaning of the term "asset class," we need to refer to the characteristics of the securities included in the asset class. An asset class represents a set of financial instruments whose prices move over time due to factors that are common and partially different from the factors that underlie the movements of other asset classes. The concepts of correlation and diversification (see Chapter 7) allow us to better qualify this point.

The three main asset classes are represented by equities, bonds, and real estate. An important difference among them is that equities and real estate are examples of "outside assets," that is, assets representing ownership of real assets. A stock is part of the liability side of a balance sheet of the corporation issuing the stock but to its owner is part of wealth. When we sum up positions, we find that the positions of creditors and debtors offset each other, at least from the point of view of the nominal value of the contract, and what remains is the real asset sitting in the asset side of the balance sheet. The market price of the stock does not usually correspond to the accounting value of the asset, and the ratio is reflected in Tobin's Q. Sovereign bonds, like money printed by central banks, is an example of an "inside asset," that is, an asset that has a net zero sum due to every creditor being offset by a debtor. The sum of the value for the holder of the bond and the State is equal to zero at any moment in time.

An asset class is associated with a set of indices. The various indices that refer to the same asset class are correlated with each other and less correlated with indices representing other asset classes. In a sense, a relevant test of whether a certain asset may be part of a new asset class is the possibility of finding a high correlation with the other securities already included in that class and a low correlation with other assets. Often an asset class is divided into further segments, for example equity is segmented on the basis of geographic criteria (United States, Germany, Europe, Asia, etc.) and sector criteria (technology, banks, etc.), the bond market into segments that refer to issuers (corporate bonds, sovereign bonds, etc.), and real estate in the residential segment and the commercial segment (further divided into hotels, offices, etc.).

The identification of an asset class is linked to the presence of specific risk factors, different from the risk factors that influence the price dynamics of instruments belonging to another asset class. Ang (2014) argues that asset classes are only an intermediate concept and that investors should instead focus directly on the risk factors that cause asset valuations to change over time (factor investing will be discussed in Chapter 10). While there is no complete agreement on whether real estate can be considered as an asset class, Ang (2014) applies the multifactor logic (see Chapter 11) to transform exposure to real estate into equity and fixed income exposure, based on the observation that the risk factors relevant to real estate valuations are the same as those that cause stock and bond prices to fluctuate. Examples of risk factors relevant for the stock market and the bond market are interest rates, inflation, and economic growth. According to this logic, the investor should be interested not in the share of wealth invested in real estate but in the overall sensitivity of her portfolio cash flows to common factors. Based on his analysis, however, Ang (2014) himself believes that real estate can be configured as an asset class.

In some cases, an investment class can arise through informal coordination among investors, such as the "tulip mania" of Dutch investors at the beginning of the seventeenth century, still remembered today as the first example of a "speculative bubble" (see Chapter 12) that led in 1637 to an abnormal increase in bulb prices, which at the maximum peak reached a value equal to a year and a half of income for a bricklayer of the time. The tulip craze, which arose due to the custom of acquiring flowers when they were still in cultivation, was then followed by a wave of sales (so-called panic selling). Today, no one considers tulips an investment class. Finally, from an investor's point of view, as asset class may emerge when financial intermediaries create opportunities for investing. A recent and fascinating example is that of cryptocurrency, which started to generate interest in about 2009 with the introduction of Bitcoin and the early use of blockchain technology. Nowadays several other projects have extended the potential for investing in cryptocurrencies: platforms such as Ethereum allow developers to build and deploy applications and smart contracts; utility tokens provide access to specific services within a particular blockchain ecosystem and are often used to raise funds during initial coin offerings (ICOs); and security tokens represent ownership in a real-world asset such as stocks or bonds, tokenized on a blockchain for increased efficiency and transparency.

Finally, from an investor's point of view, an important element in defining an asset class is the need for specific skills that are necessary to spot opportunities and risks. Investors have no interest in devoting efforts to analyzing an investment possibility with a low investable value because the research cost may be larger than the benefit. Large asset managers may have no interest in spending resources to explore the value of cryptocurrencies unless they spot interest on the part of clients willing to provide an amount of assets under management that may create revenues larger than the cost.

1.3.4 Public and private assets

The book deals mainly with the allocation of wealth among various assets. The allocation process is an application of quantitative models that are best suited to liquid financial securities, though we will describe, especially in Chapter 14, the possibility of extending the models to non-listed, private assets. In what follows we will refer to two main types of asset classes, namely bonds and stocks, constituting the largest part of financial wealth owned by most institutions. Individuals usually have a heavy exposure to a third relevant asset class, real estate (which includes housing, land, and other assets related to real estate investment) due to ownership of their house. Whereas most financial contracts referring to bonds and stocks are listed and traded in financial markets, most real estate is a private asset as it is not traded.

We can invest in bonds, equities, and real estate by purchasing a contract representing ownership of the asset, which in turn can be listed or unlisted, or by purchasing shares in a diversified portfolio invested in the various assets. The latter happens through diversified portfolios supplied by asset managers.

When investment involves buying a contract that is not listed in a market, it can be difficult in the future to sell the contract to someone else. Buyers of apartments generally use the service of intermediaries or specialized operators who, upon payment of a commission, help the search process. The same happens when selling the apartment. When an individual lends money directly to a company, then she will typically have to wait until the dates set out in the contract for obtaining interest and capital reimbursement. Trading platforms are a way to create liquidity by facilitating buying and selling in decentralized markets.

At the same time, investment may involve the purchase of a financial security traded on financial markets. Such markets are not equally liquid. Some markets are very liquid because there are many investors interested in buying and selling, and this shortens the time and cost required to complete any transaction. Financial securities are generally the representation of ownership rights over real assets and the cash flows generated by them. With economic growth, the sophistication of financial markets increases, through the introduction of new financial contracts and new intermediaries that allow an increasingly efficient connection between units in financial surplus (typically households) and units in deficit (typically firms, which must find external resources to grow). However, during crises liquidity can evaporate quickly.[3]

The term "private assets" refers to that part of an asset class that is not publicly traded. No assets are completely public. Many companies are directly owned by an individual or a family, and the same is true of many buildings, so the three main asset classes—equity, bonds, and real estate—are both public and private. "Investable private assets" represents a situation where investors can purchase an unlisted asset through financial intermediaries such as private equity funds. Investable private asset investments are less liquid and require a longer-term investment horizon than public assets.

Technology is quickly changing the overall landscape for asset owners, extending the size of investable private markets and making public markets more efficient. Blockchain technology is increasingly used for a variety of assets such as art objects and real estate, allowing fragmentation of ownership of an asset through smart contracts. This improves risk management possibilities on the part of investors and may provide more financing and help economic growth. A new real estate project, for example, may proceed with financing obtained through smart contracts, enlarging the financial possibilities open to the developer. Deregulation may also help: securitization is a technique that may be used to repackage financial or real assets and to create new types of securities (defined tranches) with different risk/return characteristics that may be better suited to asset owners.

As a result of (a) increasing interest in investable private markets, (b) new technology, (c) smart legal contracts, and (d) deregulation, we are likely to observe in the future a continuous increase of assets that move from the private to the public space. This is one of the contributions of finance to economic growth and social welfare.

---

[3] Keynes (1936, p. 153) writes that through markets "investments which are 'fixed' for the community are made 'liquid' for the individual" but also that "of the maxims of orthodox finance none, surely, is more anti-social than the fetish of liquidity … there is no such thing as liquidity of investment for the community as a whole."

1.3.5 Corporate governance as an infrastructure for protecting financiers

Securities not only provide the right to future cash flows but also have other rights that contribute to make sure that cash flows are actually paid as promised. Potentially, managers could get financing from outsiders and walk away with the funds. This is part of the more general analysis of agency problems, an essential element of the contractual view of the firm, developed by Coase (1937) and Jensen and Meckling (1976). Agency problems arise because of the separation of management and finance, or of ownership and control. Monitoring is hard because owners and financiers do not perfectly observe the actions of the managers but only see the final result.

Corporate governance comes to the rescue of capital providers and is extremely important in those situations where managers can act in their own, rather than in financiers', interest. La Porta, Lopez-de-Silanes, Shleifer, and Vishny (2000, p. 4) provide a pragmatic definition of corporate governance: "corporate governance is, to a large extent, a set of mechanisms through which outside investors protect themselves against expropriation by the insiders defined as managers and controlling shareholders." Expropriation can take many forms, such as insiders selling the output or the assets of the firm they control to another entity they own at below market prices, installing possibly unqualified family members in managerial positions, or overpaying executives. For shareholders, legal rights include voting powers and ease of participation in corporate voting. For creditors, the rules are based on the respect for security of the loan, the ability to obtain assets in case of a loan default, and the inability of management to seek protection from creditors.

La Porta, Lopez-de-Silanes, Shleifer and Vishny (1998) empirically examine how laws protecting investors differ across forty-nine countries, how the quality of enforcement of these laws varies, and whether these variations matter for corporate ownership patterns around the world. They notice that commercial laws originate from two traditions: common law (English law) and civil law (Roman law), further distinguished in French, German, and Scandinavian variants. Commercial laws have spread around the world due to war, conquest, imperialism, and imitation. They find that civil laws (including their enforcement) give investors weaker legal rights than common laws do.

Large shareholders and large banks are institutions that are both in a good position to monitor managers and particularly important in situations where corporate governance is weak. Even though we will not frequently refer to corporate governance in the book, through an understanding of corporate governance we can interpret elements such as the structure and development of financial markets, the payment of dividends, the relative importance of intermediaries versus markets, and the market for corporate control implemented through corporate acquisitions.

There have been significant improvements in corporate governance around the world also due to investors recognizing its role for asset prices; however, this is not a straight road. For example, in best governance practices, all shares issued by a certain company have equal voting rights in corporate meetings. However, companies sometimes issue securities that are penalized from the point of view of the possibility of voting (dual-class structure) precisely to allow an owner, or a reference group of shareholders, to maintain control, but in a limited way and often in exchange for a privilege from an economic point of view. A typical dual-class structure allocates excess voting control to a particular group of shareholders, despite their claim to a smaller share of cash flow rights. Dual-class structures may entail substantial agency costs, as those shareholders with excess control rights bear only a small proportion of the financial consequences of their decisions but retain the ability to forestall takeovers and entrench themselves.

Feld and Lowry (2022) point out that the percentage of mature firms with dual-class structures has been decreasing in the last forty years for listed companies, but the opposite is true for IPO (initial public offering) firms, particularly in the period 2013–2023 (i.e., Google and Facebook). For example, almost 30% of IPOs in 2017–2019 had dual-class structures. The authors make the hypothesis that the prevalence of dual-class structures is the result of agency problems rather than an optimal governance solution, mainly due to the great availability of funding in the recent period. When founders have stronger bargaining power, they are better able to negotiate for greater control rights at the time of the IPO, and thus the firm is more likely to adopt a dual-class structure.

1.4 Financial markets

Financial markets allow the buying and selling of financial securities. In most cases, market exchanges are electronic and do not allow for personal knowledge of counterparties. Precisely for this reason, as we have already seen, a necessary infrastructure for developing financial markets lies in an efficient and functioning legal framework (understood as a set of rules and their application, corporate governance, and regulation) that allows the protection of the rights of those who hold securities.

1.4.1 Public firms

According to data from the World Federation of Exchanges, the number of listed companies was 58,200 as of the end of 2022. According to the World Bank (https://data.worldbank.org/indicator/CM.MKT.LDOM.NO), also declaring the use of the World Federation of Exchanges database, there were 47,926.[4] However, there has been a reduction in the number of listed companies worldwide over the past few years, as shown in Figure 1.3.

[4] The World Bank specifies that listed domestic companies, including foreign companies which are exclusively listed, are those which have shares listed on an exchange at the end of the year. Investment funds, unit trusts, and companies whose only business goal is to hold shares of other listed companies, such as holding companies and investment companies, regardless of their legal status, are excluded. A company with several classes of shares is counted once. Only companies admitted to listing on the exchange are included.

Figure 1.3 The number of listed companies around the world

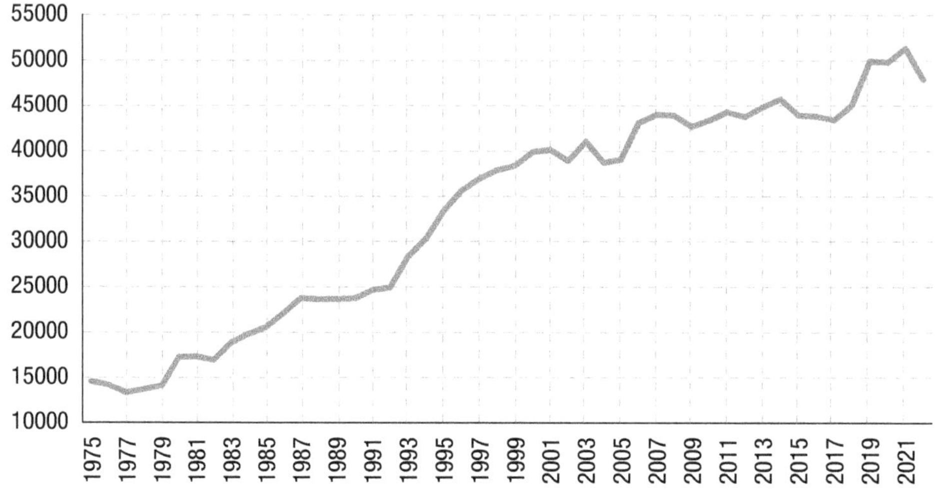

Source: Author's calculations based on World Bank data

The decline is more visible and more persistent in the United States, as shown by Figure 1.4, where the number of listed companies as of 2021 was less than 50% the number in the mid-1990s.

Figure 1.4 The number of listed companies in the United States

Source: Author's calculations based on FRED data

What are the reasons for the decline in the number of listed stocks around the world and particularly in the United States? The number of listed stocks increases with new listings in the primary market and decreases when listed companies fail or leave the market to become private.

1.4.2 Primary and secondary markets

Primary markets represent the place where a financial security is issued for the first time. This is when financial flows are passed on from investors to issuers. Finance experts are key in helping corporations to list stocks and bonds and governments to sell sovereign bonds, even though new technologies may somewhat change the competitive landscape. A good example is provided by direct listings in the equity market,[5] a mechanism based on an opening auction determining the initial share price and allocating shares by matching orders submitted from buyers and sellers. This regulatory innovation has the potential to negatively affect the business of underwriters (investment banks) that bundle services associated with underwriting and consulting, at the same time reducing the listing cost for corporations.

On secondary markets, securities are traded after the initial issuance. In this case, the cash flows are transmitted among investors and the issuer is not involved. Secondary markets are those that provide liquidity to securities and allow investors to mobilize their investments. The presence of a large secondary market also helps the development of the primary market, because investors are more interested in buying the securities if they know that it will be possible to sell them. Liquidity allows investors to reveal their true time horizons.

1.4.3 The cost and benefit of listing in stock markets

Theory suggests that a company decides to go public when the benefit of listing outweighs the cost of listing. The benefits of listing are first and foremost linked to the availability of financial capital that allows the company to make new investments and grow. Second, through listing, the original owners can liquidate a part of their investment and diversify their asset allocation. Third, listing represents a communication channel for the company, which uses the interest from analysts and investors to make its brand visible. Fourth, by opening up a new channel of financing through future secondary offerings of securities, listing may increase corporations' bargaining power with banks. Another advantage is related to the existence of a listing option for the private company, which can decide the best timing for the sale of securities on the market.

[5] On February 2, 2018, the Securities and Exchange Commission (SEC) approved a New York Stock Exchange (NYSE) proposal, "Selling Shareholder Direct Floor Listing," which allowed direct listing (DL) firms to list existing shares without underwriters but prohibited them from raising capital. On December 22, 2020, the SEC approved another NYSE proposal on "Primary Direct Floor Listing," which allowed DL firms to raise new capital.

The costs of listing are related to the direct costs, which must be paid to the trading venues hosting the exchanges, as well as the costs associated with the information requirements for communication with the market. Pagano, Panetta, and Zingales (1998) analyze the Italian case and find that (a) the probability of pursuing an IPO is positively linked to the market valuation of companies in the same sector, (b) the amount of capital raised is typically used to reduce leverage instead of financing new investments, and (c) the cost of bank credit is reduced.

International competition among stock exchanges to attract companies to listing is also played out on information requirements. All things being equal, companies prefer to list on exchanges that impose fewer requirements to save on transparency costs. But as is often the case in economics, the surrounding conditions are not stable: investors prefer to buy securities listed on stock exchanges that impose greater transparency requirements. The stock exchanges themselves therefore face the trade-off between costs and benefits when deciding on the levels of transparency to be imposed on companies.

Another important factor is the abundance of capital available to private equity and venture funds. The ease of raising capital is also demonstrated by the growing importance, in terms of number and value, of companies defined as "unicorns," that is, unlisted companies valued at more than a $1 billion (the term "decacorn" has been coined to describe companies worth at least $10 billion). The number of unicorns has increased almost exponentially in the last twenty years: the reference to the mythological animal that is so difficult to see is no longer correct from this point of view. In 2022 there were 399 unicorns with a combined value of $1.22 trillion according to CB Insights data. The main companies that were part of this group were Uber, Airbnb, SpaceX, Palantir Technologies, WeWork, as well as various Chinese companies such as Toutiao (Bytedance) and Didi Chuxing, the former active in intelligence applications, the latter in self-driving vehicles. As of March 2024 the total number was up to 1200.

Davydova, Fahlenbrach, Sanz and Stulz (2023) point out that the popularity of unicorns depends in part on the already discussed decrease in net benefit of being public for all firms. They claim there is a severe drop in net benefits of listing for firms that rely on intangible capital (research and development, and organizational capital) and network effects. Such firms may work more effectively without disclosing a lot of operational and organizational details to stock market investors.

1.5 Uses and misuses of markets

1.5.1 What are financial markets used for?

Financial markets have numerous functions. First, they help individuals take the desired risk in the investment of financial assets: every economic activity has elements of risk borne by the owners. Financial markets allow individuals to select the level of risk that best suits their characteristics. If there were no financial markets, the overall level of risk in the economy would be much lower (and presumably the same would happen to economic growth) because few individuals would have to take large risks on their own. As a result, few people would be willing to risk such a large part of their total assets. Thanks to markets, individuals who have business ideas and want to run a company can count on external investors who may bring in venture capital and increase the scale of operations.

Markets make it possible to manage the flow of consumption over time and across states of nature; for example, saving and investing for retirement is more efficient thanks to financial markets. Individuals can select the most suitable portfolio: an individual with a low appetite for risk and a long time horizon may decide to make investments with a higher degree of risk (and expected return) in order to have the desired degree of income to be transformed into consumption in the future.

Markets generate information, which is useful for monitoring the performance of companies and the actions of managers. Investors in the markets use any type of available information to predict the cash flows produced by each financial asset and to determine the price that reflects them. According to the theory of efficient markets, prices are an aggregator of all available information and therefore reflect the best valuation. By allowing the prices of listed securities to be correct and the expected returns of securities to be commensurate with risk, markets help investors direct financial capital to the best opportunities.

Markets allow for the separation of ownership and management: direct management of the business by owners can be sub-optimal, because in general, those who own it may not be the best managers. Over time, therefore, the separation between managers and shareholders has been achieved, which today represents the typical case for large companies. The presence of shares listed on the markets makes it possible to establish compensation mechanisms linked to results and to motivate managers to take care of management, reducing conflicts of interest by being remunerated in securities that can be easily sold on the markets.

1.5.2 Markets, business objectives, and investors

There has always been a wide debate, which has intensified in recent years, about the company's objectives. According to the title of a famous essay published in the *New York Times*, Nobel Prize winner Milton Friedman (1970, p. 17) asserted that "the social responsibility of business is to increase its profits." It is a simple and clear goal to pursue, and, in theory, everyone agrees on it: who would want to invest in a company that is not managed in a way that produces the greatest profits for the owners? However, this position is criticized by a growing number of people, who believe that the company has duties that go beyond the pure search for profit maximization to embrace the consequences for all stakeholders, including the people who work for the company, the customers who consume the goods and services produced, and, increasingly, the global community through its impact on the environment.

According to some, the presence of numerous negative externalities related to pollution and CO2 emissions, with their impacts on climate change, highlights that companies cannot limit themselves to maximizing profit but must take responsibility for solving global problems. Institutional investors, who professionally manage large amounts of assets, put pressure on companies. For example, the Church of England, on July 12, 2018, reiterated its intention to eliminate from its portfolio any company that emits CO2 in a significant way without having a decarbonization strategy consistent with the Paris Agreement. This is an example of "ESG investing" (Chapter 15), where ESG emphasizes the relevance of environmental, social, and governance aspects in the choice of securities to be included in the portfolio. ESG investing is understood differently across the world: for some investors, companies that produce weapons do not comply with ESG criteria, while for others, the companies to divest from are those related to genetic research because weapons used for self-defense are consistent with ethics. In many cases, the application of ESG criteria leads to portfolio exclusion policies (not investing in certain securities), and in some cases to positive action (overinvesting in certain securities).

There is a lot of debate about the effects of ESG investing. Some argue that there is no material impact because the value of a stock, as outlined in Chapter 11, is equal to the expected discounted value of future dividends, and for one investor who decides not to invest based on ESG criteria, there is another investor who ignores those criteria and therefore buys the security at a price corresponding to its value. Others believe that, in the presence of a demand curve for securities with a negative slope, the reduction in demand causes the equilibrium price to fall and can therefore harm the company, for example making it harder to raise new capital or when management is remunerated with incentive schemes that depend on the performance of the stock price.

A complementary approach from the point of view of many investors is one that considers engagement policies, that is, direct intervention in the shareholders' meetings of companies, in order to force management, and other shareholders, to respect the positions that emerge outside the company regarding the objectives to be pursued and the actions to be taken to achieve them. Pursuing engagement policies is costly for investors, who need to be informed about the company's strategies and need to know the company and the industry. There are therefore investment funds called activist funds, whose main objective is precisely to buy securities that they consider undervalued on the stock market due to mismanagement, to build a stake that forces management to change some relevant choices.

1.5.3 Critical issues in the use of markets

Any tool can be used in the right way or in the wrong way. A car can be driven recklessly and cause an accident, or it can be used to solve transportation problems. The same is true for financial markets. If, instead of rationally deciding their investments, investors bought and sold securities without looking at fundamentals (which will be identified in Chapter 12) or estimating the future value of such fundamentals in inappropriate ways, then market prices would be characterized by higher volatility than would be generated by investors who look only at fundamentals for their portfolio decisions. If managers use accounting tricks to artificially improve profits and set bonuses that are too high, investors might increase the price in the short run but eventually may lose confidence and divest.

Markets that are excessively volatile and characterized by companies that do not behave ethically do not perform the task for which they were created. Investors will tend to invest less in excessively volatile markets, and this can drive down asset prices and drive up their expected returns. Regulation is very important to avoid degeneration, but it can only prevent part of the problems. It also risks, by acting indiscriminately toward all operators, being punitive and making the operation of the system less efficient. The point was recognized by Keynes (1936, pp. 158–159):

> If I may be allowed to appropriate the term speculation for the activity of forecasting the psychology of the market, and the term enterprise for the activity of forecasting the prospective yield of assets over their whole life ... as the organisation of investment markets improves, the risk of the predominance of speculation does increase .... when he purchases an investment, the speculator is attaching his hopes, not so much to its prospective yield, as to a favourable change in the conventional basis of valuation ... The spectacle of modern investment markets has sometimes moved me towards the conclusion that to make the purchase of an investment permanent and indissoluble... might be a useful remedy for our contemporary evils....if individual purchases of investments were rendered illiquid, this might seriously impede new investment.

The secular debate about the economic impact of market trading is still unresolved. The market economy has been the only one to survive the test of time but, as usual, its efficiency depends on the users. Each investor produces externalities when trading. The positive side of the externality is the increased liquidity provided to fellow investors. The negative side of the externality lies in the extra volatility associated with the trading activity.

1.6 Collective investment vehicles

Collective investment vehicles allow for diversified investment as they allocate to the holder a share of a portfolio containing many financial securities. A small investor could not invest in a large portfolio of stocks on her own if she were forced to invest in each stock separately. Collective investment vehicles are managed through financial decisions that apply equally to small investments made by many individuals. The individual investor can enjoy many benefits, including primarily that of diversification.

1.6.1 Mutual funds/UCITS

Mutual funds/UCITS (undertakings for collective investment in transferable securities) are collective investment pools allowing investors to purchase diversified shares managed by a professional manager with a legal personality and capital distinct from those of the individual funds. In the United States, the Investment Company Act of 1940 regulates the organization of investment companies and the activities they engage in. The Investment Company Act of 1940 was passed in order to establish and integrate a more stable financial market regulatory framework following the stock market crash of 1929.[6] A family of funds (or fund family) includes all the separate funds managed by a single investment company. UCITS is the European Commission's regulatory framework for managing and selling mutual funds. UCITS funds can be registered and sold in any country in the European Union using unified regulatory and investor protection requirements.

A mutual fund has a board of directors and issues and invests in securities. Different mutual funds are characterized by different risk profiles and expected returns. The typical case is one in which the mutual fund is associated with a benchmark, that is, a model portfolio that includes certain proportions of various financial asset classes (e.g., 50% equity and 50% fixed income). There are also cases where the expected risk and return profile is characterized by a target return, for example a short-term rate of +3%, and cases where the fund is defined by both the risk and return profile and a time horizon (target date fund). Other relevant players are as follows:

- the distributor, bank, or securities brokerage company, which interacts with customers in the sales phase, in the after-sales phase, and also for reimbursement requests;
- the custodian bank, which holds the securities in the fund's portfolio and monetary resources and carries out control activities over the fund's operations;
- regulators, for example the Bank of Italy and Consob in Italy and the Securities Exchange Commission in the United States.

The net asset value (NAV) of a share issued by a mutual fund on a given day is equal to the market value of the assets on that day, net of any liabilities, divided by the number of outstanding shares. The fund must deliver a prospectus to those who want to subscribe to the fund. The prospectus contains three parts:

- information on the investment objective, the management strategy, the risks, the costs, and the benchmark;
- information on the fund's historical performance and how it compares to the benchmark;
- the subscription form.

[6] Galbraith (1954) is the best historical descriptive reconstruction of the great 1929 crash and the exuberance that predated it. Among the relevant financial innovations that affected investor behavior was the growth of investment trusts, institutions that sold securities to the public and used the proceeds to invest in stocks and bonds. There were two main types: management trusts where managers had discretion over the portfolio, and fixed trusts where the portfolio could not be changed. According to Carosso (1970), investment trusts grew from about forty in 1921 to over 750 in 1929.

Mutual funds can be "open-ended" or "closed" depending on their contractual life. The subscription of an open-ended fund typically takes place through the purchase from a distributor who also takes care of the return of capital in the event of disinvestment (in much less frequent cases, open-ended mutual funds can be subscribed directly on the stock exchange). The value of the open-ended mutual fund's share is known every day as the value of the fund's portfolio is revalued daily at the market prices of the assets.

The investor in an open-ended mutual fund has the option of liquidating his or her unit on a daily basis. This obligation imposes significant constraints on the manager in terms of the degree of liquidity of the assets that are part of the portfolio. In fact, the regulation restricts investment in illiquid assets on the part of open-ended mutual funds. Investing in illiquid assets is very often one of the causes of mutual fund management problems. In 2019, there were some examples of funds that were subject to sudden and significant redemption requests from subscribers precisely in correspondence with the spread of news relating to the lack of liquidity of a significant share of securities in the portfolio. Asset illiquidity becomes particularly dangerous when the market value of liquid assets falls, as illiquid assets are typically valued at cost and not market value, and their percentage relevance rises when market valuations of all portfolio components fall. If, for example, a fund holds liquid assets for 90% and illiquid assets for 10%, in the event of a drop in the value of the liquid portfolio from 90% to 70%, the share of illiquid assets rises to 12.5% (derived from 10/80) and may thus exceed the threshold imposed by regulators and force the manager to sell the illiquid assets, perhaps in a fire sale that is value punitive for shareholders.

The closed-end fund has a predefined duration, typically ten years, and can be bought and sold by trading with other investors on a secondary market, sometimes on the stock exchange. The number of participation fees is therefore fixed and the reimbursement of participants takes place only on predetermined dates. Thanks to the possibility of returning capital to investors at the end of a long time horizon, closed-end funds are used for investments in illiquid assets, including real estate or acquisitions of stakes in companies (private equity and venture capital funds). Since they are negotiated between investors and not directly with a distributor, the transaction can take place at prices that are also different from the net asset value.

The commissions directly received by intermediaries from clients who invest in mutual funds have various types, which can be summarized as follows:

- entry fee, which is charged to the investor, established as a percentage of the value of the initial investment;
- periodic management fees, which are charged to the fund's assets, set as a percentage of the value of the mutual fund;
- performance fees, which are charged to the fund's assets, set as a percentage and paid by the client to the manager only when the return of the mutual fund over a certain period (e.g., a calendar year) is above a certain reference value (the benchmark portfolio return or the target return).

UCITS VI is an EU Directive, which went into effect on January 1, 2023, requiring UCITS to provide a summary of the key elements in each fund, explaining the costs, risks, and potential for returns, all of which is summarized in the Key Information Document (KID).

1.6.2 Exchange traded funds

Wells Fargo bank introduced the first indexed fund at the beginning of the 1970s. The only purpose was to replicate the price dynamics of an index with a small cost for investors. A more popular way to replicate the price dynamics of an index is through the exchange traded fund (ETF), a particular type of investment fund, traded on the stock exchange like a share. In most cases, ETFs are associated with the idea of "passive management" as their sole investment objective is to replicate the index to which they refer (benchmark) through totally passive management. More recent examples can be described as "active ETFs," with management seeking to return above the benchmark. According to Ballentine (2021), active ETFs have a total asset value equal to 4% of total ETFs. Some active ETFs may publish portfolio composition information once a quarter instead of once a day, allowing the manager to adopt active strategies without running the risk of being immediately imitated by competitors.

An ETF combines the characteristics of a fund and a stock, allowing investors to easily gain exposure to the performance of an entire market in a diversified manner. The possibility of short selling also allows the instrument to be used for risk hedging purposes, for example for those who hold some shares in their portfolio and at certain stages consider it appropriate to reduce exposure without selling the securities themselves.

The cost of an ETF is tied to two components. The first component is the management fee, which is reduced as the manager does not have to spend resources in order to select financial instruments to allow subscribers to obtain a return higher than that of the benchmark. Ballentine (2021) reports an average management fee of 0.5% for passive ETFs and 0.71% for active ETFs. The second cost component, less visible but often more relevant from a quantitative point of view, is the differential between the purchase price and the selling price of the instrument, which penalizes investors who adopt an active portfolio management strategy with frequent trades.

Precisely because of its characteristic of a passive replication portfolio, the holder of the instrument obtains a return very close to that of the reference benchmark. The ETF has a market price that is constantly aligned with the value of the portfolio (NAV) due to the "creation/redemption in kind" process, which allows authorized participants to create and redeem units by exchanging ETFs for all the securities that make up the reference index, and vice versa. For example, when the price of the ETF is higher than the value of the securities in the portfolio, an authorized participant (a broker-dealer) buys the securities in the portfolio on the market and delivers them to the company that issued the ETF, which in turn issues additional securities (creation). Conversely, if the price of the ETF is lower than the value of the securities in the portfolio, the authorized participant buys an ETF security and exchanges it with the company that issued the ETF (redemption). Thanks to this arbitrage mechanism,[7] the price on the stock exchange is constantly aligned with the official value of the ETF.

The ETF benefits from periodic income obtained on the assets: the dividends and interest that the ETF collects against the securities held in its portfolio (as well as the proceeds from their reinvestment) can be distributed periodically to investors or capitalized permanently in the ETF's assets.

Listed ETFs are a particular type of mutual fund (UCITS), with separate assets from those of the companies that take care of their establishment, management, administration, and marketing activities. ETFs are therefore not exposed to the risk of insolvency even in the event of the bankruptcy of the companies mentioned above.

Since 2001, there have also been "synthetic ETFs" on the markets, especially in Europe, in which the ETF manager, instead of holding the basket of securities included in the index that serves as the product reference, signs a contract with an investment bank in which the latter pays the former the return of the basket that defines the benchmark and in return the former refunds the return on the asset actually held to the latter, which may have little to do with the benchmark basket. Regulators have highlighted the presence in these ETFs of an additional risk, often little known to investors, which can be defined as "counterparty risk" that could materialize if the counterparty is unable to honor the cash flows associated with the swap contract.

Pagano, Sánchez Serrano, and Zechner (2019) list a number of more general risk factors associated with the presence of ETFs. First, they allow investors to quickly trade the benchmark index, thereby increasing the correlation between all stocks in the index and exacerbating volatility. Second, any operating error in the creation/redemption in kind mechanism can cause the market price to deviate from the net asset value, particularly in times of crisis. These potential risks must be viewed, of course, relative to the contribution that ETFs make to the efficiency of investors' portfolios, especially retail portfolios.

Exchange traded commodities (ETCs) are financial instruments issued against a direct investment by the issuer in commodities or commodities derivative contracts. Exchange traded notes (ETNs) are financial instruments issued against a direct investment by the issuer in assets other than commodities. They are also passive investments in that they track the price of the underlying commodity but are different from ETFs because the latter must ensure a degree of diversification in compliance with UCITS VI.

[7] The arbitrage mechanism is explored in more detail in Chapter 10.

Summary

- An efficient financial system including financial markets and financial intermediaries is an essential tool to improve the rate of growth through, among other things, better connections between savers and investors, more data creation, and information processing.
- We can invest in bonds, equities, and real estate by purchasing a contract representing ownership of the asset, which in turn can be listed or unlisted, or by purchasing shares in a diversified portfolio invested in the various assets. The latter happens through diversified portfolios supplied by asset managers.
- The term "private assets" refers to that part of an available asset that is not publicly traded. No assets are completely public. Many companies are directly owned by an individual or a family, and the same is true of many buildings, so the three main asset classes—equity, bonds, and real estate—are both public and private. "Investable private assets" represents a situation where investors can purchase an unlisted asset through financial intermediaries such as private equity funds. Investable private asset investments are less liquid and require a longer-term investment horizon.
- A bond is issued by a government (sovereign bond) or by a company (corporate bond) and is characterized by three main elements: the maturity, that is, the date on which the issuer of the bond promises to repay the nominal value; the nominal value of the bond (also called face value), that is, the amount of money the issuer of the bond will pay to the holder at the time of maturity; and the coupon, that is, a remuneration that is paid periodically (every six months or every year) by the issuer of the bond to the holder of the bond. The coupon is equal to the product of the coupon rate and the face value. Securities that do not pay coupons are referred to as zero-coupon bonds.
- The main differences between a stock and a bond are represented by the absence of maturity, since the share has an infinite life as long as the company that issued it continues to operate, and by the potential temporal variability of the periodic remuneration, the dividend.
- Corporate governance is, to a large extent, a set of mechanisms through which outside investors protect themselves against expropriation by the insiders, defined as managers and controlling shareholders
- The number of listed companies is stable at the world level but has declined substantially in mature markets such as the United States and Europe, perhaps as a rection to an increase in the cost of listing and a decrease in benefits, particularly for innovative corporations.
- Financial markets have essential functions for economic growth: they allow you to invest your assets according to the desired risk profile, they allow you to invest your savings and thus to detach at least part of income streams from consumption flows, they allow you to incorporate the different information and opinions of investors into prices, and they foster the best allocation of capital between companies.
- An incorrect use of markets, linked to the wrong behavior of investors or unethical behavior on the part of companies, reduces their ability to contribute to economic growth.
- Asset management is about creating investment pools that allow investors to hold diversified portfolios even with small investments. Mutual funds are the best example of such pools. ETFs are becoming increasingly important in the markets. These are collective investment vehicles that can be bought and sold on the markets as if they were individual securities.

2 Asset returns

2.1 Introduction

The aim of the chapter is to discuss the statistical basis for describing asset returns as random variables. We introduce relevant definitions of returns, including the arithmetic and geometric average, and note that when we invest, we are not sure about the increase in the value of our investment and we need to account for different scenarios. In this chapter we describe scenarios and probabilities and focus on the normal probability distribution, which is completely described by only two parameters: the mean and the standard deviation (popularly known in financial jargon as volatility). Albeit very simple, the normal distribution is easy to use due to the possibility to compute probabilities of relevant return intervals based only on mean and volatility. This is the main reason why the normality assumption will be used throughout the book. We will review empirical indicators that may support or disprove the hypothesis of normality of stock returns. Probability distributions may be unconditional or conditional, depending on the information set that we use to define them. Unconditional and conditional probability distributions are both useful in practical applications, and we discuss both types of approaches in the estimation and use of unconditional and conditional expected return and return volatility. The chapter surveys long-run empirical evidence on the historical excess return characterizing stocks and bonds, an extremely important parameter for applying the methodology of portfolio optimization discussed in Chapters 7 and 8, and provides methodological insights for evaluating the empirical evidence in terms of statistical significance as well as index construction. A popular application of the conditional normal distribution has to do with the computation of Value at Risk based on the effort to compute the maximum possible loss (with a given probability) on a specific security or a portfolio of securities. We also introduce the possibility to use linear regression models to predict the conditional expected return, a topic that will be discussed again in Chapter 13 when considering empirical testing of market efficiency.

2.2 The rate of return

2.2.1 Arithmetic returns

The arithmetic return r of an asset is the ratio between the sum of its price change and the cash flow paid to the holder over a given interval of time and the initial price.

We denote with r_{t+1} the rate of return between time t and time $t+1$, to stress that the rate of return is known only at the end of the period, when the future price and the cash flow become known. We denote with P_t the price at time t, P_{t+1} the price at time $t+1$, and CF_{t+1} the cash flow paid at time $t+1$ (if there is no cash flow paid during this time interval then $FC_{t+1} = 0$) to get the following definition of return:

$$r_{t+1} = \frac{P_{t+1} - P_t}{P_t} + \frac{CF_{t+1}}{P_t}. \tag{1}$$

$\frac{P_{t+1} - P_t}{P_t}$ is the capital change, more specifically a capital gain in case it is positive and a capital loss when negative, whereas $\frac{CF_{t+1}}{P_t}$ is the yield. This definition applies generally to all assets; for stocks the cash flow is the dividend D_{t+1} and $\frac{D_{t+1}}{P_t}$ is the dividend yield, for bonds the (usually fixed) coupon C and $\frac{C}{P_t}$ is the coupon yield, and for real estate the rent net of operating costs RE_{t+1} and $\frac{RE_{t+1}}{P_t}$ is the rental yield.

Stock indices and stock prices are available from data providers in two versions: price index and total return index. The price index version assumes that dividends are paid out to shareholders and consumed or reinvested somewhere else. The total return index assumes that dividends are immediately reinvested in the stock or index. This means that the total return index initially coincides with the price, $TR_0 = P_0$, but diverges once dividends are paid; for example, when dividends are paid at time 1, then $TR_1 = P_1 + D_1$. There is no double counting in total return index because the price of the asset P_1 drops by the value of the dividend. The total return version reabsorbs the cash flow assuming it is immediately reinvested in the same asset. The rate of return for an asset when starting from the total return series is simply equal to $r_{t+1} = \frac{TR_{t+1} - TR_t}{TR_t}$.

The cash flow will generally be equal to zero for most assets if the time interval is short, for example if time is measured in days. If time is measured in years, most assets will pay a cash flow to the holder, be it in the form of a dividend for stocks, a coupon for bonds, or rents for an office or apartment. The difference between the return of an asset and the risk-free rate $r_{t+1} - r_{f,t}$ is the excess return. Note the timing convention that will be maintained throughout the book: the risk-free rate is denoted with $r_{f,t}$ to stress that its value is known at the beginning of the investment period. The average arithmetic return is computed from $\overline{r_A} = \frac{r_t + r_{t+1} + \ldots + r_T}{T-(t-1)}$.

Box 2.1 Is the dividend yield relevant for stocks?

Elena wants to understand the relevance of the dividend yield relative to the capital gain and downloads data on the S&P Composite Index from 1988 to 2023 in the price index version (which ignores dividends) and in the total return version (where dividends are reinvested). At the monthly level the average arithmetic return is equal to 0.87% with dividends and 0.69% without. At the yearly horizon the returns are respectively 10.4% and 8.5%. At the annual level about 20% of the return over the last thirty-five years has been due to the dividend yield. However, she also notices that Jorda, Knoll, Kuvshinov, Schularick, and Taylor (2019) and Ilmanen (2022) suggest that about 60% of the total return is due to dividends in the longer time period 1960–2020.

2.2.2 Logarithmic returns

Arithmetic returns are not additive over time. If in one period the arithmetic return is 10% and in the next period it is 20%, the cumulative return over the two periods is not equal to the sum, 30%. This is simply due to the value of the investment growing in the first period from 100 to 110, and in the second period from 110 to $110 \times 1.2 = 132$, with a cumulative return of 32%. Another example is even simpler: if the return is 50% in one period and –50% in the next period, the final value of the investment, starting from 100, is 150 after the first period and 75 after the second, with an overall loss equal to 25% regardless of the arithmetic mean being equal to zero.

To sum returns over time we need to use log returns, defined as $\ln\left(\frac{P_{t+1} + FC_{t+1}}{P_t}\right)$. In the previous example the log return for period one is $\ln\left(\frac{110}{100}\right) = 9.53\%$, and the log return for the second period is $\ln\left(\frac{132}{110}\right) = 18.23\%$. The sum of the two log returns is $9.53\% + 18.23\% = 27.76\%$, which corresponds exactly to $\ln\left(\frac{132}{100}\right)$. The multi-period log return is equal to the sum of the log returns in each individual period. Differently from arithmetic returns, log returns do not aggregate across assets: the log return of a portfolio is not the weighted average of the log returns of the individual assets.

The arithmetic average is different from the geometric average return defined as the rate r_G such that $\left(1 + \overline{r_G}\right)^{T-(t-1)} = \left(1 + r_t\right) \times \left(1 + r_{t+1}\right) \times \ldots \times \left(1 + r_T\right)$. The geometric average describes the experience of an investor who buys an asset and holds it over the horizon. Applying logarithms to both sides we get $(T - t + 1) \times ln\left(1 + \overline{r_G}\right) = ln\left(1 + r_t\right) + ln\left(1 + r_{t+1}\right) + \ldots + ln\left(1 + r_T\right)$, meaning that the log return over a time period is a simple average of individual log returns. In what follows, to simplify notation, we will not use the symbols $\overline{r_A}$ and $\overline{r_G}$ to distinguish between geometric and average returns and simply refer to $\bar{r}$.

2.3 Measuring risk in financial portfolios

2.3.1 The rate of return as a random variable

We have stressed in the definition that the rate of return is known at the end of the period. When purchasing an asset, only the initial price P_t is known with certainty. The selling price is not known unless the asset is risk-free. If an asset is purchased at a price equal to 100 at time t and sold at time $t+1$ for 102, after paying a dividend equal to 1, then the rate of return is $\frac{102-100}{100}+\frac{1}{100}=3\%$. The rate of return of a risky asset over the period can take on many values. In the previous example, if the selling price was 95 and the cash flow 0, the rate of return would be equal to $\frac{95-100}{100}=-5\%$, or if the price was 110 and the cash flow 5 then it would be $\frac{110-100}{100}+\frac{5}{100}=15\%$.

How do we consider such a variable at the time of buying? Statistics may help, with the definition of a random variable as a variable whose value is initially unknown. The simplest example is the toss of a coin. Before the coin is tossed there are two potential outcomes, head and tail, with equal probabilities. After the coin is tossed only one of the two outcomes is realized.

A random variable represents a quantity whose outcomes can be described ex ante in terms of many (potentially infinitely many) future realizations. In the previous return example, we described three possible outcomes for the rate of return: 3%, –5%, and 15%. If these were the only possible outcomes, then we would say this is a discrete random variable. The outcomes could be many more than three, and we could assume that the rate of return could have a realization among the infinite set of numbers included in the interval –50%, +50%. In this case we would define the return as a continuous random variable.

2.3.2 The probability function

An interesting question is: What is the probability that the rate of return turns out to be 3%, –5%, or 15% over the relevant period? We can answer this question using a probability function, specifying the probabilities of the possible outcomes of a random variable. Sometimes we may refer to the individual outcomes as "scenarios." For a discrete random variable, the probability function specifies the probability that a random variable takes on a specific value. For example, we could assume that, as shown in Table 2.1:

The first column defines the scenario, the second column the return in each scenario, the third column the probability of realization of the scenario, and the fourth column the probability of obtaining the scenario return or a lower return: the probability of obtaining –5% is equal to 30%, and the probability of obtain-

Table 2.1 **Example of a discrete probability distribution**

Scenario	Scenario return	Probability	Probability of return equal or below scenario return (cumulative probability)
Bad	−5%	30%	30%
Normal	3%	50%	80%
Good	15%	20%	100%

ing 3% or less than that is 80%, equal to the sum of the probabilities of obtaining –5% and obtaining 3%. Notice that the sum of the probabilities is equal to 1. The cumulative probability function gives the probability that a random variable is less than or equal to a particular value. For continuous random variables the probability function is called the probability density function, describing the probability that the random variable takes on a value in any interval (an interval can also be thought of as a scenario).

Among the various probability distributions, we will use the Gaussian (or "normal") distribution. Remarkably, the Gaussian distribution is completely characterized by only two parameters, the mean and the standard deviation, completely defining the location of the distribution. In financial jargon, we use the name volatility to describe the standard deviation of the rate of return of an asset, denoted with σ. The variance is the square of the standard deviation, σ^2. Figure 2.1 represents a Gaussian distribution of a rate of return, with average $Er = 10\%$ and volatility $\sigma = 20\%$:

Figure 2.1 **Gaussian probability distribution of a return with average 10% and volatility 20%**

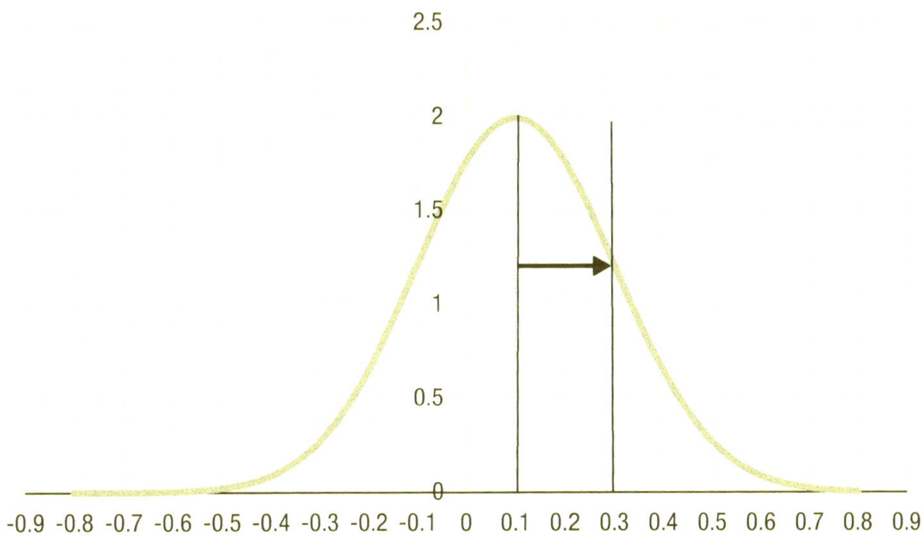

In Figure 2.1 the vertical line is drawn at 0.3, equal to the sum of the mean, 0.01, and the standard deviation, 0.2. The value 0.3 corresponds to the flexus, the point at which the function turns from concave to convex. This implies that volatility is graphically represented by the horizontal segment covering the distance from the mean to the flexus. In Figure 2.2 there are two different normal distributions, both having a mean Er = 10%. The dotted distribution has a 50% volatility and the continuous one a volatility of 25%.

Figure 2.2 Comparing normal distributions with different volatilities

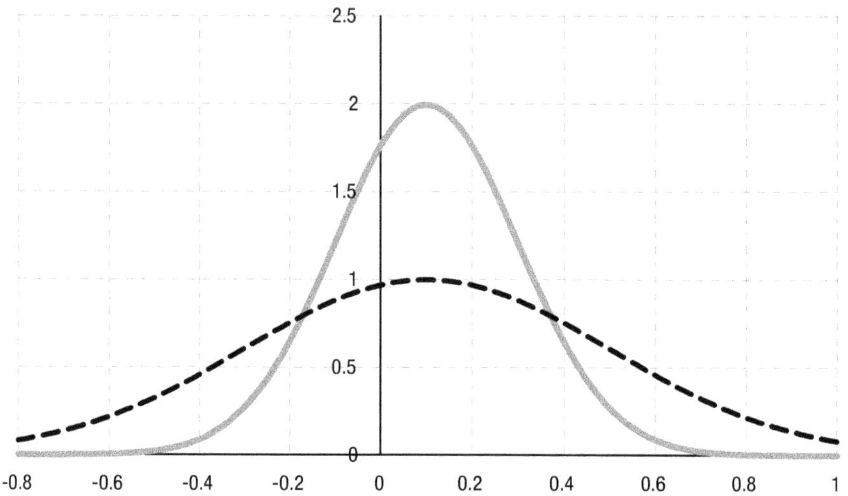

Figure 2.2 shows that a higher standard deviation increases the probability of having returns that are much above or below the mean. As we will see later, investors are particularly concerned with losses. A higher volatility, with the associated increase in the probability of very negative returns, is considered as an increase in risk.[1]

Figure 2.3 presents the same normal probability distribution both in the form of density function and in the cumulative probability version.

[1] The further interpretation of volatility as an indicator of risk seems to be difficult to understand in light of the observation that an increase in volatility in a Gaussian distribution also increases the chances of a strong gain. As we will see in Chapter 3, risk-averse individuals suffer (in terms of utility) from a loss more than they benefit from an equal gain in absolute value. Therefore, a distribution that is more dispersed because it is characterized by greater volatility symmetrically amplifies extreme gains and losses, which, however, are weighted asymmetrically by the investor, with the losses being more damaging than the benefits associated with the gains.

Figure 2.3 **Normal distribution represented as density and cumulative functions**

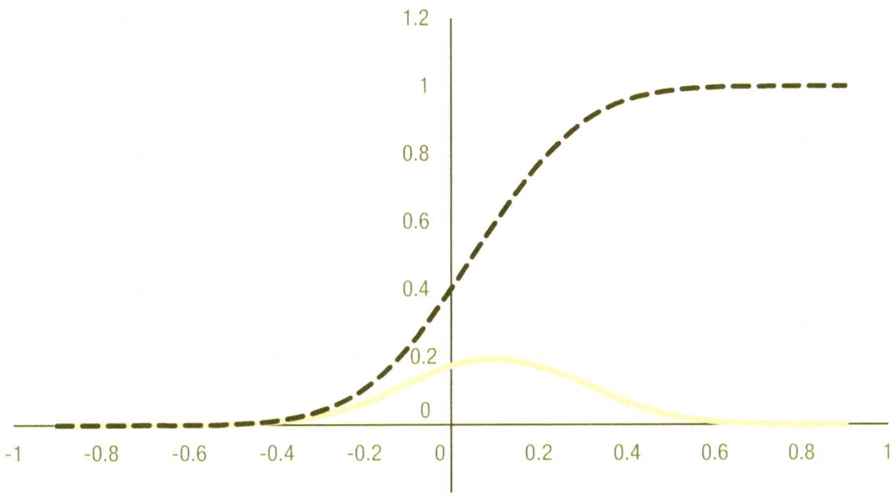

In Figure 2.3 the dotted curve, representing the cumulative description of the normal distribution, goes to one at about 50% return and remains there. This means that there is an almost 100% probability of obtaining a return less than or equal to 50%.

2.3.3 Relevant intervals in the normal distribution

There are a few intervals around the mean that are frequently considered by investors. Assuming a normal distribution, there are tables that are useful for computation of the probability that the rate of return has a realization inside such intervals. Table 2.2 reports the probabilities of three relevant intervals, that is, that the random variable takes on a value in the intervals defined respectively by the mean plus/minus the standard deviation, mean plus/minus two standard deviations, and mean plus/minus three standard deviations.

Table 2.2 **Probabilities of relevant intervals in the normal distribution**

Interval: mean ±	Probability that the return is included in the interval	Excel
$\pm\sigma$	68.26%	Norm.dist(mean+ σ; mean;σ;0)- Norm.dist(mean- σ; mean;σ;0)
$\pm 2\times\sigma$	95.44%	Norm.dist(mean+2 × σ;mean;σ;0)-Norm.dist(mean-2 × σ;mean;σ;0)
$\pm 3\times\sigma$	99.74%	Norm.dist(mean+3 × σ; mean;σ;0)- Norm.dist(mean-3 × σ; mean;σ;0)

Even such a simple representation may be very powerful to better understand investment implications. For example, a risky asset with an expected return equal to 5% and volatility equal to 25% has a 68.26% probability of being in the interval –20% (mean minus standard deviation) and +30% (mean plus standard deviation). For such an asset, a rate of return equal to –10% lies in the set of events happening with over two-thirds probability. Even if unpleasant for the asset holder, a 10% loss is one of those events that are included in the typical oscillation of the value of the asset. An owner fully understanding this result may interpret the return of her portfolio in a better way and avoid typical mistakes that will be described Chapter 4.

Box 2.2 Excel and the normal distribution

It is easy to use Excel to compute the probability that a random variable takes on a value less than or equal to any number. For example, in Figure 2.4, the vertical line is drawn at a rate of return equal to –25%. What is the probability that the rate of return is less than –25% when the mean is 5% and the volatility is 25%? From Excel, using the function norm.dist (–25%;5%;25%;1) we find a probability equal to 11.5%.

Figure 2.4 Probability distribution with mean 5% and volatility 25%

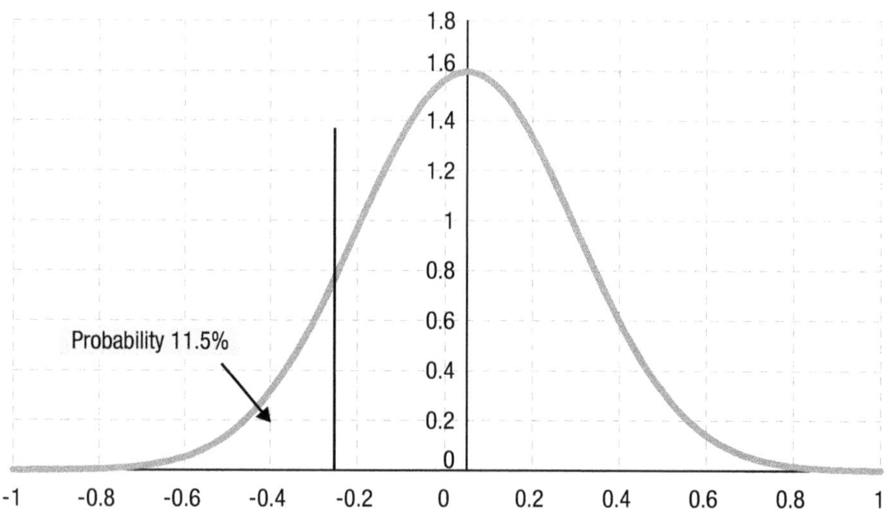

Similarly, from norm.dist(-20%;5%;25%;1), we find that the probability that the return is equal to or less than –20% (i.e., mean minus volatility) is equal to 15.87%. This is consistent with the probability of a realization in the interval going from mean plus volatility to mean minus volatility having a probability of 68.26%. The probability of having a return outside this interval is 100% – 68.26% = 31.74%. The probability of having a realization below the mean minus standard deviation is half that value, that is, 15.87%.

The normal distribution is therefore a simple tool to characterize asset returns as a random variable. In section 2.4.2 we will discuss the way to understand if historical data are consistent with such an assumption.

Box 2.3 When does something relevant happen in the markets?

Question: Sara has invested in the stock market and wants to have an indicator that highlights when something relevant is happening in the market and when the market has normal fluctuations. An advisor suggests that any return between mean and plus and minus standard deviation is an indicator that nothing particular is going on in the market. The consultant, who estimates the expected return at 5% and the volatility at 20%, turns to a statistician to calculate the probability that the return will be between the mean minus standard deviation and the mean plus standard deviation.

Answer: The range that according to the advisor indicates a situation of normal market fluctuation is bounded by the value –15% and +25%. Given the symmetry of the normal distribution, the answer is obtained by subtracting from 1 twice the probability that the return is less than –15%, that is, using Excel, 1-2X norm.dist(-15%;5%;20%;1) = 68.26%.

2.4 Unconditional probability distributions

2.4.1 The unconditional expected return and volatility

As we have seen, in the case of a normal distribution two parameters tell the whole story: knowing the mean and the standard deviation, we are able to compute all relevant probabilities. How do we estimate the mean and the standard deviation? When we assume that the rate of return belonging to a specific interval does not depend on past realized returns or other variables, we use the idea of unconditional probability distribution[2] and we may consider long-run information obtained from time series of observed rates of return to compute the sample mean and the sample standard deviation. The selection of the sample must be consistent with our time horizon. For example, if we want to decide how much wealth to invest in the stock market for a long horizon of time, then we may use empirical evidence available over the longest available sample period and regard the historical arithmetic mean as the best estimate of the expected return. The sample arithmetic mean $\bar{r}$ is an estimate of the unconditional expectation.

The simplest volatility estimator is the historical standard deviation of returns:

$$\bar{\sigma} = \sqrt{\frac{\sum_{t=1}^{T}\left(r_t - \bar{r}\right)^2}{T-1}}$$

where r_t is the return realized between moments $t-1$ and t. T is the length of the sample. This is an unconditional estimate of volatility because we refer to no specific recent information.

[2] Conditional probability distributions are presented in section 2.6.

2.4.2 Skewness and kurtosis

The simplest way to measure the consistency of a set of data with a normal distribution is to compute indicators of skewness and kurtosis, that is, respectively, indicators of whether the historical series of returns is symmetric around the mean and whether the tails of the distribution decline toward zero at the speed predicted by the normal distribution. Skewness measures the lack of symmetry of the distribution and can take on positive or negative values. To measure skewness, we compute:

$$SK = \sum_{t=1}^{T} \frac{(r_t - \bar{r})^3}{T \times \hat{\sigma}^3}$$

where $\hat{\sigma}^3$ is the estimated standard deviation raised to the power 3. Skewness can be positive or negative (the deviations from the mean are raised to a sign-preserving power) for a non-normal distribution and zero for a normal distribution. For example, in a distribution with a negative (positive) skew the left (right) tail is longer and the mass of the distribution is concentrated on the right (left) of the figure (see Figure 2.5).

Figure 2.5 A distribution with positive skew

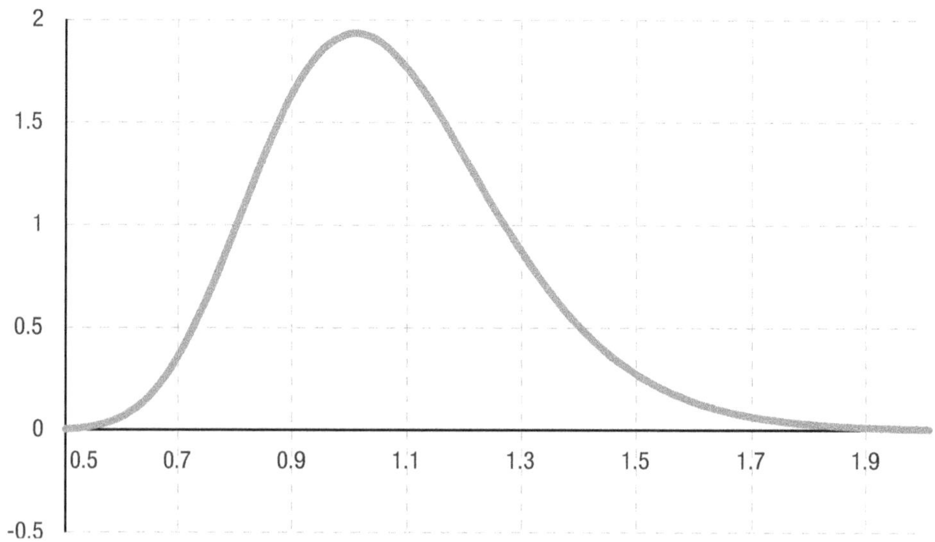

Kurtosis measures how thick the tails of the distribution are, that is, how much probability is left in the tails, where tails represent the probability values of events that are extremely high or low compared with the mean. It can be measured through:

$$KU = \sum_{t=1}^{T} \frac{(r_t - \bar{r})^4}{T \times \hat{\sigma}^4}.$$

For a normal distribution the kurtosis is equal to 3. We talk about excess kurtosis to denote cases when the coefficient is above 3. Distributions with high kurtosis (fat tails) are leptokurtic, see the dotted curve in Figure 2.6.

Figure 2.6 A distribution with positive kurtosis

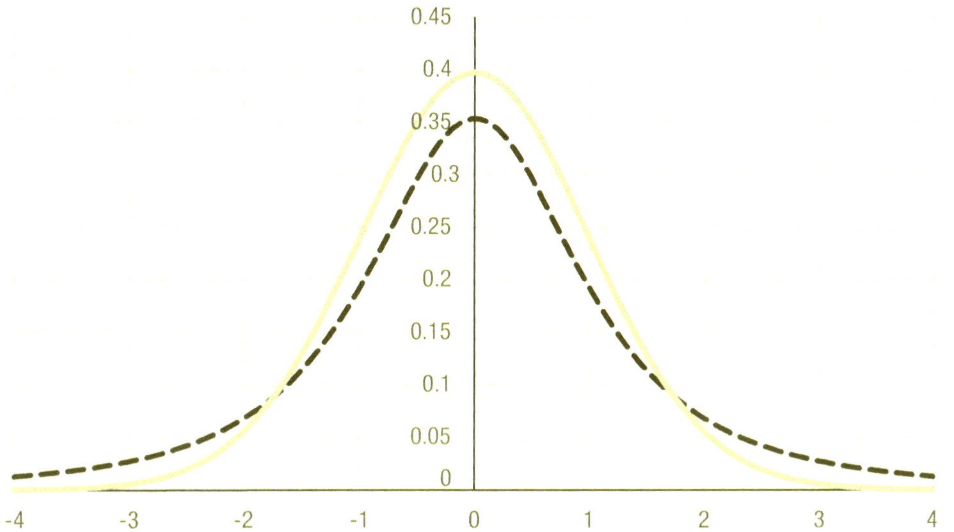

Box 2.4 Is the S&P normally distributed?

Question: Carola works in Risk Management and wants to understand whether the distribution of the S&P return can be characterized by normality. What does she need to do?

Answer: After downloading time series at daily, weekly, monthly, quarterly, and yearly horizons for the period January 5,1988–February 29, 2024, Carola computes the following table describing skewness and kurtosis coefficients for the various frequencies:

	Daily	Weekly	Monthly	Quarterly	Yearly
Mean	0.000	0.002	0.010	0.040	0.121
Volatility	0.011	0.024	0.045	0.055	0.168
Skewness	−0.220	−0.184	−0.351	−0.161	−0.720
Kurtosis	10.908	5.296	2.244	2.212	0.175

Carola notices that there are substantial deviations from normality in daily returns due to the very high kurtosis. At the daily level there are many more observations in the tails (particularly in the left tail as suggested by the negative skewness) than what a normal distribution would predict. The histogram describes the empirical distribution of daily data, reporting several bins on the horizontal axis and the number of observations that have been sampled in each bin, for example there have been 3,533 returns in the interval from 0 to 1%. At the daily level the worst day has been a return below –11%. Given a standard deviation equal to 1.1%, as estimated from daily data, a –11% return corresponds to a shock equal to ten times the volatility. The probability of such a shock for a normal distribution with that volatility is equal to 7,62 × 10^{-24} (a number obtained in Excel using the function norm.dist(-0,11;0;0,011;1)). There are twelve observations below –6.5% whereas there should be 0.000002 (see Figure 2.7)

Figure 2.7 **Empirical probability distribution of the S&P return**

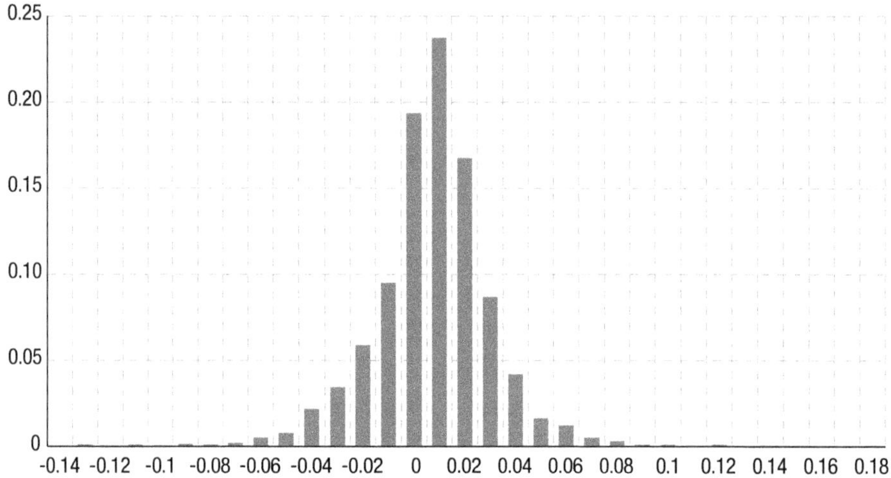

Evidence against normality is weaker at lower frequency returns. For example, monthly returns still show negative skewness but a modest amount of kurtosis. Carola understands that the normality assumption holds at lower frequencies such as the quarter or the year but not necessarily for short horizons.

2.4.3 The limits of normality

The Gaussian distribution is not necessarily suitable to describe the performance of all asset classes. For example, the return on corporate bonds is characterized by a long left tail, as shown in Figure 2.8, where the dotted histogram describes the cumulative probability distribution of a stock with 5% mean and 20% volatility, while the continuous line histogram describes the cumulative probability for a corporate bond return. The corporate bond return is capped at 10%, representing the best case scenario for the bondholder. There are small probabilities that the return of the bond becomes negative in case of default preventing the company from reimbursing the full value of the principal and the coupon. In most scenarios, there is no default and therefore the returns are positive, but every now and then there is a default that causes the total return to become heavily negative. See Chapter 6 for corporate bonds and credit risk.

Figure 2.8 **Cumulative probability distributions for equity and corporate bond market returns**

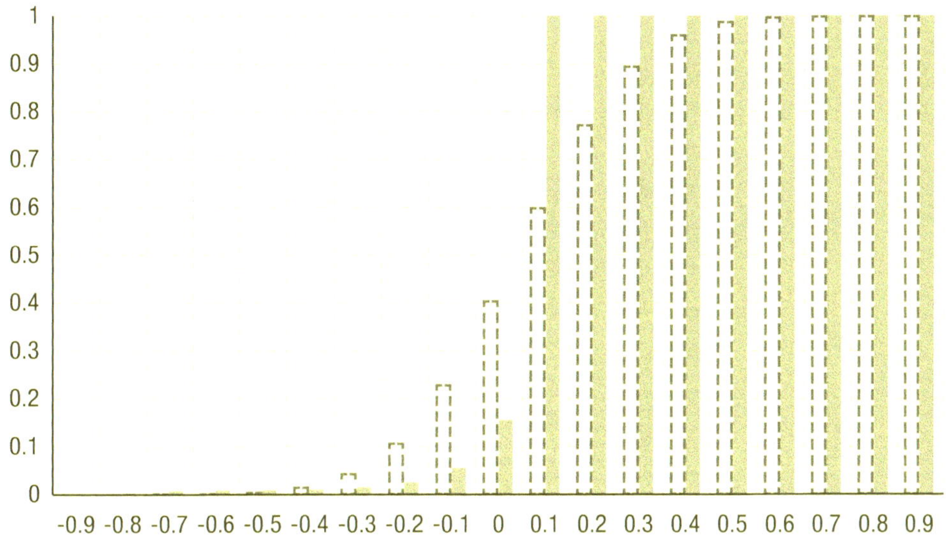

As far as the stock market is concerned, normality is a plausible assumption for time horizons that are longer than one month or one quarter. For shorter horizons, such as weekly or daily horizons, or when returns are measured at high-frequency observations, the Gaussian distribution is not a good approximation. Intuitively, at least at a monthly or quarterly horizon, negative and positive shocks, even if of significant absolute value, tend to cancel each other out and are not recorded in the historical series. If the rate of return in a week has been –10% and the following week +10%, the overall two-week arithmetic return is almost zero and the log return is –1%. A lot of repricing has happened over each week but not much appears to the analyst looking at the two-week period. The more frequently prices, and therefore returns, are detected, the more the distribution that describes the time series must also be able to consider events that are placed in the tails.

There are two ways to fit the distribution to time series that have a higher percentage of observations in the tails than expected by the normal distribution (so-called thick tail phenomenon). The first is to adopt a distribution with "fat tails," which are more relevant than the Gaussian (excess kurtosis phenomenon), for example the t-distribution of Student. The second, which does not exclude the first, is to use an estimate of volatility that changes over time, as we will discuss in measurement of Value at Risk in section 2.7.

2.5 Long-run average excess returns

2.5.1 Indices

To measure the performance of a financial market, we often think of a benchmark index, particularly in the case of the stock market. An index I_t for the overall value of a stock market at time t can be written as:

$$I_t = \left(\frac{\sum_{i=1}^{N} Q_{i,t-1} P_{i,t}}{\sum_{i=1}^{N} Q_{i,t-1} P_{i,t-1}} \right) \times I_{t-1}$$

where $Q_{i,t-1}$ is the number of shares issued by company i at time $t-1$ and $P_{i,t}$ is the price of the $i-th$ share at time t. The index can be rewritten as $I_t = \left(\frac{\sum_{i=1}^{N} Q_{i,t-1} P_{i,t-1} \frac{P_{i,t}}{P_{i,t-1}}}{\sum_{i=1}^{N} Q_{i,t-1} P_{i,t-1}} \right) \times I_{t-1}$, which can be interpreted as a weighted average of price ratios of a set of securities:

$$I_t = \sum_{i=1}^{N} w_{i,t} \frac{P_{i,t}}{P_{i,t-1}} \times I_{t-1}$$

where $w_{i,t}$ is the weight equal to the relative capitalization (the ratio between the total value of the $i-th$ company and the total value of all companies listed on the market).[3] The value of the index is set equal to a conventional value at the initial date, for example 100, and then varies with the changes in the prices of individual securities. In general, therefore, an index cannot be interpreted as the price of a security but provides information on the time change in the overall value of the securities. The index is used by investors to get a concise and immediate idea of how a specific market is moving when it is considered representative of the performance of that market, whether it is the entire market or a segment of it.

Among the main international indices we find, for example, the Dow Jones Industrial Average, including the thirty largest companies on the New York Stock Exchange, and the S&P 500, tracking the 500 largest US companies by capitalization. Another relevant one is the Morgan Stanley ACWI (All Country World Index), capturing large and mid-cap companies across twenty-three developed markets and twenty-four emerging markets.

Various indices are constructed to consider stocks with weights that reflect the actual free float available and not the overall supply. This reduces the index rele-

[3] In recent years, "smart indexing" has become popular, which describes a method of calculating an index where the weights are established on the basis of the information contained in relevant fundamental characteristics such as sales or book values. Smart indexing is closely related to the presence of anomaly-based portfolio formation strategies, described in Chapter 11.

vance of companies that have significant numbers of shares held by a limited number of long-term investors. In some cases, indices are calculated in such a way as to discriminate against stocks that are characterized by low liquidity. According to Dimson, Marsh, and Staunton (2019) these are among the reasons why emerging markets (e.g., China, South Korea, Taiwan, India) and frontier markets (e.g., Argentina, Vietnam, Morocco, Nigeria) contribute 55% of the world's gross domestic product and 68% of the world's population but only 12% of the total capitalization of the world's stock exchanges.

Among bond indices, the best known are the FTSE WGBI, representing the performance of global sovereign bonds (over twenty countries) in local currency, including various sub-indices that report the performance by specific segments (e.g., one to three year bonds, three to five years, and so on, by currency); J.P. Morgan's EMU Index, showing the value in euros of a basket of European sovereign bonds; and IHS Markit's iBoxx indices, representing a wide range of bond markets, including corporate and high-yield bonds.

2.5.2 Empirical evidence

Researchers have computed stock and bond market price indices over long periods of time. A very early and famous example is that of Shiller (1981), who reconstructed the performance of the American stock market since 1860.[4] Dimson, Marsh, and Staunton (2002) have carried out similar studies internationally, with data dating back to the 1900s.

The evidence from Dimson, Marsh, and Staunton shows that the US stock market is among the most profitable in the long run, with an average annual excess return of about 6%, similar to the average excess return offered by countries such as the United Kingdom, Canada, and Australia. The latest evidence currently available comes from Dimson, Marsh, and Staunton (2023), according to which in the United States from 1900 to 2022 the average annual nominal return of equities was 9.5%, compared with 4.7% for medium- and long-term sovereign bonds, 3.4% for short-term sovereign bonds, and 2.9% for inflation. Table 2.3 shows the long-term returns on equity investments over the period 1900–2022. Table 2.4 shows the long-term bond return over the period 1900–2022.

The average arithmetic real return on global equity investment was 6.5%, led by the United States (8.3%) and Japan (8.6%), with Europe at 6%. Volatility was more homogeneous, around 20% except in the Japanese case with a peak of over 29%. Figure 2.9, from the same source, shows specific data from various countries around the world, and shows the particularly negative performance of the Italian stock market, which in the long run gave an average real return of 2%, equal to less than a third of that offered by the US stock market and two-thirds of what is produced by the other major European economies.

[4] The data are available at http://www.econ.yale.edu/~shiller/data.htm.

Table 2.3 Returns (adjusted for inflation) on equities by country, 1900–2022

Country/ Asset class	Geometric average (%)	Arithmetic average (%)	Standard deviation (%)	Minimum return (%)	Year of minimum return	Maximum return (%)	Year of maximum return
Europe	4.1	5.9	19.7	–48.0	2008	75.2	1933
Japan	4.2	8.6	28.9	–85.5	1946	121.1	1952
United Kingdom	5.3	7.1	19.5	–56.6	1974	99.3	1975
United States	6.4	8.3	19.9	–38.6	1931	55.8	1933
World	5.0	6.5	17.4	–42.9	2008	67.6	1933

Table 2.4 Returns (adjusted for inflation) on bonds by country, 1900–2022

Country/ Asset class	Geometric average (%)	Arithmetic average (%)	Standard deviation (%)	Minimum return (%)	Year of minimum return	Maximum return (%)	Year of maximum return
Europe	1.2	2.4	15.8	–52.6	1919	72.2	1933
Japan	–0.8	1.7	19.4	–77.5	1945	69.8	1954
United Kingdom	1.8	2.7	13.5	–29.9	1974	59.4	1921
United States	1.9	2.4	10.3	–18.1	1917	35.2	1982
World	1.9	2.5	11	–31.6	1919	46	1933

Sources: Dimson, Marsh, and Staunton (2002) and (2023)

Figure 2.9 Real returns on equities, bonds and bills across countries, 1900-2022

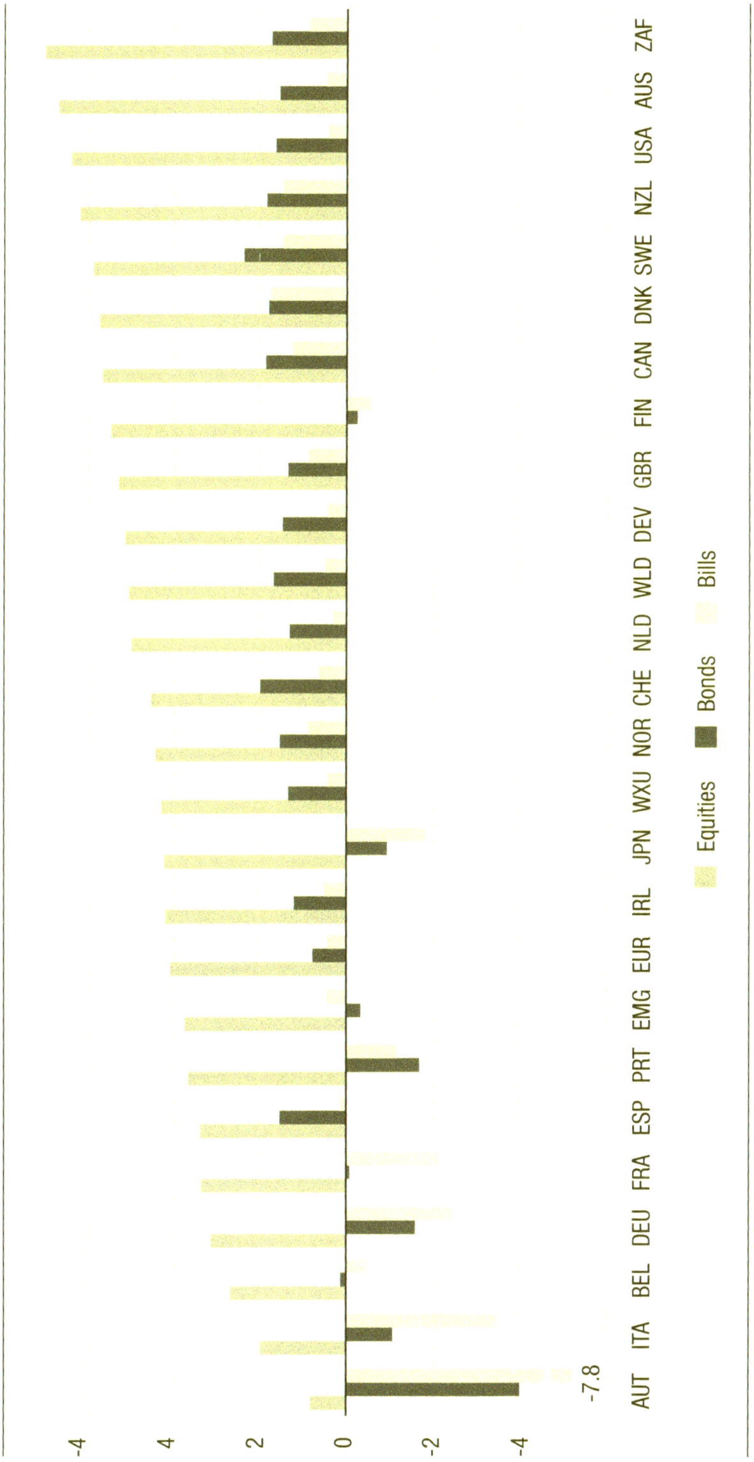

Various reasons may explain the divergences observed between countries, including:

- different long-term growth rates;
- different relevance of the stock market in Anglo-Saxon and European countries. In general, the Anglo-Saxon model is less based on intermediaries and more based on markets, and this may have favored investors;
- different legal regimes for shareholder protection;
- wars and conflicts that have particularly penalized Europe and Japan.

2.5.3 Compounded growth

If you invest your capital for a fixed compensation (interest) that is paid once per period and if you leave the interest in the same account, in the next period the new interest will be computed on a sum of money including the initial capital and the interest paid in the previous year. If you invest a unitary value and the per period interest is equal to i, then after one period you have $1 + i$ and after two periods $(1 + i) \times (1 + i) = (1 + i)^2$. After T periods the final capital will be $(1 + i)^T$. This mechanism is called compounding and gives rise to a value of capital characterized by geometric growth.

In order to understand the force of compounding and investing for the long term, notice that, using the average geometric average (second column of Table 2.3), we get $1.064^{122} = 1{,}936$. A dollar invested in the US stock market in the year 1900 has become $1,936 at the end of 2022.

2.5.4 Biases in stock indices

Research has highlighted the existence of a few biases in the construction of indices, which can give rise to results that do not correspond to the real experience of investors in those assets. The distortions that have been highlighted are as follows.[5]

- Survivorship bias: This appears when the time series for a set of units, such as a stock market index composed of individual stocks, or an index that describes the value of hedge funds (see Chapter 10), is constructed from the units present at the end of the sample period rather than at the beginning. Over time, some of the units that were initially present disappear due to various problems, for example

[5] The analysis of these biases is relevant to the construction of any database, for example to study the association between company profitability and the activity in acquisition of other companies. If the sample is built out of companies existing at the end of the sample period, then there may be a bias due to surviving companies being likely to be the most profitable. As a result we would not be able to understand the impact of profitability on acquisitions as we would not include information about low profitability companies that existed at the beginning of the sample but were more likely to disappear from the sample.

some publicly traded companies go bankrupt, and some hedge funds close. Investors who have selected these assets will have, by the end of the period, a return that is negatively affected by their performance. Calculating the index from the units at the end of the sample (the surviving units) means ignoring the performance information of the worst units and artificially inflating the average return. By definition, we observe the return of surviving companies and funds because they are alive and are probably the best. This bias is particularly important in hedge fund indices due to the high percentage of funds that disappear each year (attrition rate).

- Selection bias: This is present because returns are more likely to be observed when prices are high rather than low (see the various examples described by Ang, 2014). For example, real estate transactions take place in good market phases because in bad ones, owners prefer to avoid acknowledging losses through a sale at a price that is lower than the cost of purchase. In private equity and venture capital, portfolio companies, which are typically valued at cost, are more easily sold or taken to the stock market when prices are high. In all these cases, the index includes more success units because those that are not successful are not detected. An example of this type of bias is present in hedge fund indices since joining a database often involves the ability to communicate to investors the past history of returns, which is more likely to be made in the case of satisfactory returns rather than unsatisfactory returns (backfill bias).
- Reporting bias: In cases where reporting to the public is not mandatory, the decision to join a database managed by a vendor is up to the fund. Funds are more likely to report when the underlying returns are good, and to remain obscure when the return is not satisfactory.

Such biases are not present in main indices, whose returns largely represent the experience of the typical investor over the same period, but may be relevant to judge the historical performance of asset management products such as hedge funds and private equity funds, which are often built on a voluntary basis on the part of market players.

2.5.5 Interpretation of stock indices returns

How long does the observation period, and the averaging period, have to be in order to have a reliable estimate of average return and extrapolate it to an expected return? There is no single answer, but we can say that the choice of the time period must balance two considerations:

- statistical reliability, that is, the possibility of having an estimate that is as accurate as possible and reduces measurement error. If observations in the sample represent the true average with independent measurement errors, then statistical methodology suggests the selection of long time periods for the calculation of the average;

- structural changes, that is, the need to take account of economic and market changes that make the estimate based on old data unrepresentative of today's reality. Considerations of this kind lead to the selection of shorter and above all "similar" time periods to the current market situation. For example, the average stock return in a phase characterized by low growth and high inflation can be best estimated from historical return data obtained from similar historical periods.

The above two considerations lead to the selection of long periods when the objective is to have an estimate of average return that can be used for the next five to ten years, and sub-periods when the objective is to have an estimate applying to a certain well-identified phase of the market and the economy. For example, it is plausible to look primarily at empirical evidence from the 1970s and 1980s to estimate market returns at a time when inflation is expected to rise.

Even when the sample used is long, we should always keep in mind the need to perform statistical inference. To understand whether the average excess returns of two markets 1 and 2 are significantly different from each other, it is necessary to carry out a t-test, which, in the case of volatility common to the two markets, can be represented as follows:

$$\left(\overline{r_1 - r_{f,1}} - \overline{r_2 - r_{f,2}}\right) / \frac{\overline{\sigma}}{\sqrt{T}}$$

where $\overline{r_i - r_{f,i}}$ is the historical average excess return of the $i - th$ market, $\overline{\sigma}$ is the historical volatility obtained as the square root of the sum of the two variances, the degrees of freedom are $2T$–2, and T is the total number of observations. Given a volatility of 20%, two average return excesses of 5% and 3% observed over a secular period imply a t-test of $\frac{10 \times 0.02}{0.2} = 1$, which is not statistically significant at conventional 10% or 5% levels. It follows that even with one hundred years of data, two markets that have had two very different average excess returns (a euro invested at an average of 3% per year after a century produces 19.22 euros, while a euro invested at an average of 5% per year after a century amounts to 131.50 euros) are not statistically significantly different[6].

2.5.6 Asymmetry in the distribution of returns

Bessembinder (2018) argues that most of the excess return generated by the US equity market over the long run is related to the positive performance of a few stocks. In the universe of monthly returns of all stocks ever listed between 1926 and 2016, only 47.8% are higher than the risk-free rate of the same month. Only 42.6% of listed stocks produce a total return over their entire market life (the average life is seven and a half years!) higher than the risk-free rate over the same period. During the period,

---

[6] When volatilities and sample length are different in the two markets, the t-test is

$$\left(\overline{r_1 - r_{f,1}} - \overline{r_2 - r_{f,2}}\right) / \sqrt{\frac{\overline{\sigma_1^2}}{T_1} + \frac{\overline{\sigma_2^2}}{T_2}}.$$

25,300 companies issued equities, creating $35 trillion in excess of the value produced by the risk-free investment, of which 10% was created by just five companies and half created by ninety companies (0.3% of companies ever listed). One thousand ninety-two companies, 4% of the total, are responsible for 100% of the value created, while the remaining 96% of companies added no value compared with risk-free investment. The author provides a statistical explanation for the results, which depend on the asymmetry (positive skewness) present in the returns of individual stocks as well as the effect of compounding. The results are consistent with those of Fama and French (2004), which show that the US market has seen a sharp increase in new listings since the 1980s, particularly of companies with high asset growth rates and low profitability, many of which are destined not to survive for long. The high return of the market as a whole is therefore not due to a strength that applies equally to all securities but results from the exceptional performance of a minority of them.[7]

2.6 Conditional probability distributions

2.6.1 The conditional expectation

To understand the idea of a conditional expectation it is useful to start from a simple example. Suppose we have monthly data on the number of people who catch the flu in a city each month, collected by hospitals for every month of a twenty-year period (2000–2020). The unconditional expectation of rainfall for an unspecified day is the average of the rainfall amounts for those 7,300 days. The conditional expectation of the number of people newly sick with the flu in the month of January is likely higher than the unconditional expectation based on the average of all observations in the sample. The conditional expectation is computed from the number of people who are sick only in the month of January. The conditional expectation is the expected value of the random variable computed from the conditional probability distribution.

Similarly, when thinking about stock returns, we want to compute the expectation of the rate of return over a particular period that we know, or assume, is different from other periods. The difference may arise, as in our previous example, from a seasonality effect, something that is typically relevant in a specific period every year. In the case of the stock market, a relevant example of seasonality is provided by the average stock return in January, which in many empirical analyses is larger than the average return in the other months. Another example is the volatility of returns within a day: daily volatility has a typical pattern associated with a U curve, higher at the beginning and at the end of trading and lower during the day as traders react to news that was communicated before market opening and hurry to readjust their portfolios before closing in anticipation of news that may be released after trading stops.

Another example requiring conditional distributions is associated with using mac-

[7] We will describe stock picking in Chapter 10.

roeconomic variables such as the inflation rate, the interest rate, or the past return in the stock market to predict the future return. In the latter case, we may study past historical episodes and conclude that the average return in the stock market is lower after periods of large returns, and vice versa. A third and final example is provided by an exogenous shock such as the 2001 terrorist attack against the Twin Towers in New York. In the days of financial market closure following the attack, analysts studied the reactions of the stock market to past terrorist attacks believing that the market reaction to similar past shocks would be informative about the future. This is yet another example where we want to study the probability distribution conditional on specific events (a terrorist attack or the past return) and compute the empirical probability distribution looking at similar episodes.

2.6.2 The conditional expectation of the rate of return

The expectation computed using all available empirical evidence at time t relative to the event we are interested in, and therefore with specific reference to one or more variables known at time t, is denoted with the symbol E_t and is called conditional expectation. This expectation is called conditional to stress that we use all available information at time t. The expectation built based on long-run past information, without emphasizing recent data, is called unconditional expectation because the forecast is not made conditionally on recent information.[8] The conditional expectation of the future rate of return of a stock index is

$$E_t r_{t+1} = \frac{E_t P_{t+1} - P_t + E_t D_{t+1}}{P_t}$$

because the current stock price is known at the time the expectation is built. The conditional expectation may move over time. The expected one-year return on the European stock index as of January 2009 is likely to have been different from the expected one-year return on the same index as of March 2020. As an example of conditional and unconditional expectation, and as a way to discuss time variability in conditional expected return, let us assume we consider a regression model exploring the correlation between the rate of return in the stock market in one period and the value of a variable X_t known at the beginning of the period:

$$r_{t+1} = \alpha + \beta X_t + \varepsilon_{t+1}.$$

This is a forecasting regression, aimed at using current information on X_t to forecast the future return. X_t is the predictor. ε_{t+1} is a zero mean shock realized at time $t+1$. If the predictor is represented by the past rate of return, then we get:

$$r_{t+1} = \alpha + \beta r_t + \varepsilon_{t+1}. \tag{2}$$

[8] We will see next that we can also talk about the conditional expectation of the variance, $E_t \sigma^2_{t+1}$ to describe a probability distribution where the variance changes every period.

This is an auto-regressive model because the future value of a variable is explained by its most recent observed value. If we knew the parameters α and β, then, using equation (2), the expectation of the return for period t+1 conditional on knowing the rate of return in the last period, due to ε_{t+1} having a zero expected value, is:

$$E_t r_{t+1} = \alpha + \beta r_t. \qquad (3)$$

Notice that as we know the rate of return of the last period, we have $E_t r_t = r_t$. Equation (3) is the best forecast of the future return based on the recent value of the return.[9] The unconditional expectation is instead equal to:

$$E r_t = \alpha + \beta E r_{t-1} \rightarrow Er = \alpha/(1-\beta) \qquad (4)$$

due to the past return being unknown from the point of view of the unconditional expectation so that $E r_t = E r_{t-1}$. Equation (4) represents the long-run forecast of the average return with no particular place reserved to previous return. For example, if $\alpha = 5\%$ and $\beta = 0.1$ and $r_t = -20\%$, the conditional expectation is equal to 3% while the unconditional is equal to 5.5%. The intuition is simple: If there is persistence in returns, then a negative past return is a bad indicator for the next year's returns. The difference implies a 2.5% differential between conditional and unconditional expectations.

Technical Box 2.1 Multi-period forecasting with predictive regressions

Consider the regression model as an example:

$$r_{t+1} = \alpha + \beta X_t + \varepsilon_{t+1}$$

where X_t is a variable known at time t. This is a predictive regression, aimed at using the information available in X_t for forecasting future performance. If the forecast variable is the previous period's performance:

$$r_{t+1} = \alpha + \beta r_t + \varepsilon_{t+1}$$

the return of a certain period is explained by the performance of the previous period. This is a auto-regressive model because the current value of a variable is used to explain (and therefore predict) its future value. The expectation conditional on the information available at the time includes by definition the performance observed in that period, so that, given that the term $t\,\varepsilon_{t+1}$ has a zero expected value, we have:

$$E_t r_{t+1} = \alpha + \beta r_t$$

The equation can also be used to make predictions for even later periods. For the period $t + 2$, the equation becomes:

$$r_{t+2} = \alpha + \beta r_{t+1} + \varepsilon_{t+2},$$

---

[9] Technical Box 2.1 shows that the equation may be used to forecast more than one period in advance, for example $E_t r_{t+2} = \alpha(1+\beta) + \beta^2 r_t$ and, in general, $E_t r_{t+T} = \alpha \times \sum_{j=0}^{T} \beta^j + \beta^T r_t$.

and the expectation conditional on the information available at the time t must be applied to both the left and right sides of the equation to achieve:

$$E_t r_{t+2} = \alpha + \beta E_t r_{t+1}.$$

In summary, today's expectation, at time t, on the performance of the day after tomorrow, $t + 2$, depends on the expectation of tomorrow's return, time $t + 1$.
Using the two predictive equations together, that is, substituting $E_t r_{t+1} = \alpha + \beta r_t$ in $E_t r_{t+2} = \alpha + \beta E_t r_{t+1}$, we get the expectation of the return of $t + 2$ conditional on the information available at time t:

$$E_t r_{t+2} = \alpha + \beta E_t r_{t+1} = \alpha + \beta \times (\alpha + \beta r_t) = \alpha(1 + \beta) + \beta^2 r_t.$$

In general, if we continue to replace recursively, we get $E_t r_{t+T} = \alpha(1 + \beta + \ldots + \beta^T) + \beta^T r_t$. When the last horizon considered T tends to infinity, that is, if we consider a very distant moment in the future, we get the unconditioned expectation, that is, an expectation that ignores the information contained at the time t:

$$Er_t = \alpha + \beta Er_{t-1} \rightarrow Er = \alpha/(1 - \beta).$$

Unconditional expectation can also be obtained by applying the expectation operator E on both sides of the regression equation $r_{t+1} = \alpha + \beta X_t + \varepsilon_{t+1}$ since if it is not conditioned by information, it follows that $Er_t = Er_{t-1}$.

Box 2.5 Forecasting returns in the short and in the long run

Question: Sara wants to predict the rate of return of the stock market and uses available data to run a regression of current return on past return, yielding an estimated intercept $\alpha = 5\%$ and a slope $\beta = 0.1$. In 2018 the market return was –60%. What is the expected return for the long run? What about the years 2019 and 2020? What is the source of the different predictions?

Answer: As shown in the text, the long-run prediction is equal to the ratio between the intercept and $1 - \beta$, in this case $\frac{0.05}{0.9} = 0.055$. The 2019 forecast uses the recent empirical evidence on market return, that is, $0.05 + 0.1 \times (-0.6) = -1\%$. As a result, Sara predicts a negative return for 2019 and a positive return for the long run. The two forecasts are not inconsistent because the long-run one is not affected by the 2018 negative return while the prediction for 2019 accounts for the negative relation between returns across consecutive years as measured by the regression slope. The positive regression slope implies that a very negative return has a negative effect on the average return the following year. In the long run, Sara relies on positive shocks alternating with negative shocks in such a way to produce a positive average measured at 5.5%. Consistently, the 2020 forecast (see Technical Box 2.1) is equal to $0.055 + 0.01 \times (-0.6) = 4.9\%$, very close to the long-run value. The weak correlation in the data suggests to Sara that even a large negative shock equal to –60% is associated with a forecast for 2020 that is close to the long-run average. Figure 2.10 compares the forecasts over the years 2020–2022 and the long-run unconditional forecast.

Figure 2.10 **Short-run conditional forecast and long-run unconditional forecast**

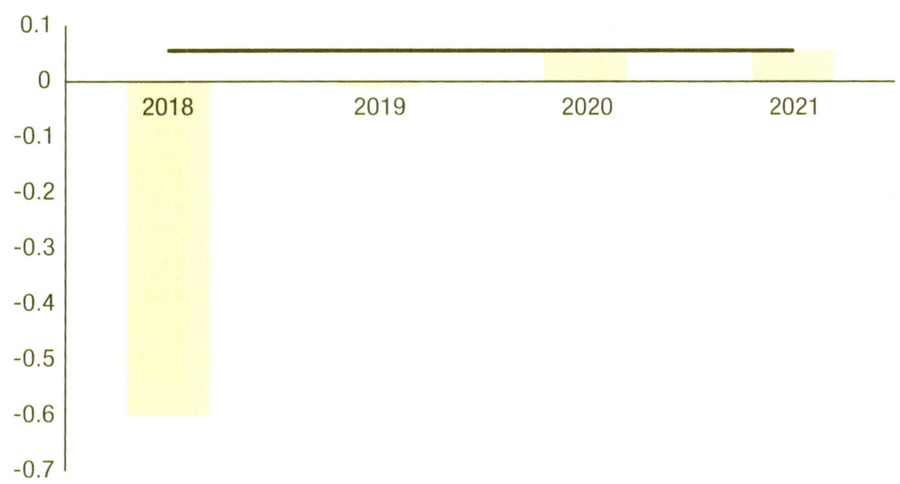

2.6.3 Computing the conditional mean: an example

As an application to the computation of a conditional mean let us consider the monthly time series of the rate of return of the MSCI Europe index over the period 2000–2017. The regression[10] of the monthly rate of return over the previous month rate of return[11] provides the following output:

Table 2.5 **Regression output**

R^2	0.0229			
Adj. R^2	0.0183			
Standard error	0.0424			
Number of observations	215			
	Coefficient	**Standard error**	**t Stat**	**P-value**
α	0.0039	0.0029	1.356	0.1765
β	0.1512	0.0676	2.235	0.0264

[10] Knowledge of linear regression and descriptive and inferential statistics is taken for granted in this volume.

[11] In Excel, in one column, copy the time series of the performance from February 2000 to December 2017 (dependent variable), and in the column next to it, the time series of the performance from January 2000 to November 2017 (independent variable), then select "Data," then "Data analysis," and

The regression explains 1.83% of the total variability of monthly returns as shown by the Adj. R^2. The intercept (α) is estimated at 0.0039, corresponding to a monthly 0.39% return, while the slope (β) is equal to 0.1512. Before using the estimated parameters to forecast the future return, we need to perform statistical inference. The coefficient α is not statistically different from zero (the t-test is equal to 1.356 with a p-value of 17.65%), while β is statistically different from zero at 5% (the p-value is 2.64%). The regression therefore is weak in terms of ability to predict the future return, because 98.17% of the variability is not explained by the past return. However, the slope is significant and shows that there is some correlation across months.

To compute a conditional expectation, using the most recent evidence about the rate of return of December 2017 equal to 0.81%, we get a forecast for January 2018 equal to 0.52% ($0.39\% + 0.1512 \times 0.81\%$). The conditional expectation would reduce to $0.13\% = 0.1512 \times 0.81\%$ in the case we ignore the intercept due to the estimated α not being significantly different from zero. The unconditional expectation, using equation (5), is equal to $\frac{0329\%}{1 - 0.1512} = 0.46\%$. The December 2017 return, larger than the long-run average, boosts expectations above the long-run unconditional average due to the empirical existence of momentum in returns with β>0.

2.6.4 Actual return, expected return, and shock

The realization of a random variable can always be decomposed into the sum of its expectation and the surprise. Consider a lottery where a coin is tossed and there is the following monetary payoff: heads you gain €1, tails you lose €1. The expected monetary value of the lottery is zero. After tossing the coin, the actual result is either +1 or –1. If the result was heads, then the realized value can be decomposed as +1 = 0 +1 because there was a positive shock equal to +1. If the result was tails, then we have –1 = 0 –1.

In what follows we will frequently refer to a decomposition of the actual ex post return into the expected return and a shock. If the expected return is unconditional then we have:

$$r_{t+1} = Er_{t+1} + \varepsilon_{t+1} \tag{6}$$

where ε_{t+1} is a zero-mean shock, the unexpected return. If the expected return is conditional, then we have:

$$r_{t+1} = E_t r_{t+1} + \varepsilon_{t+1} \tag{7}$$

where ε_{t+1} is again a zero-mean shock, a return that could not be expected based on all the information used to compute the conditional expectation. We will return to this decomposition in the following chapters. The unconditional variance of the con-

at the end of the list "Regression." Following the instructions will give you the regression output contained in the text.

ditional return can be decomposed into the components associated with conditional expected returns and shocks:

$$Vr_{t+1} = E(r_{t+1} - Er_{t+1})^2 = E(E_t r_{t+1} + \varepsilon_{t+1} - Er_{t+1})^2 = V(E_t r_{t+1}) + V\varepsilon_{t+1}.$$

The unconditional variance of the return is equal to the unconditional variance of the expected return plus the unconditional variance of the shock. An example of this decomposition is the predictive regression described in Table 2.5, where the adjusted R^2 is 1.8%, a statistic representing the share of total variability of returns explained by the variability of the predictor. The output shows that 98.2% of the total monthly variability is unexplained by the regression. Expectations based on the rate of return of the previous month do not move much regardless of the coefficient being statistically significant.

2.7 Value at Risk

2.7.1 What is the maximum potential loss?

Starting from the normal distribution we can estimate the maximum potential loss associated with one investment. It is clear that the maximum potential loss is equal to the total invested capital, that is, –100% in terms of the rate of return, assuming there is no leverage, that is, we invest in a risk asset by borrowing. If we invest €100 of which €50 represents our own capital and €50 represents borrowing, and if the value of the investment in the given horizon drops to zero, we still have to repay the initial debt, with a total loss of €100, equal to twice the initial investment of our own capital.

Abstracting from leverage, it may not be particularly useful in investment activities to keep measuring a maximum potential loss of –100% as a risk management tool. In the 1980s, J.P. Morgan analysts, together with Reuters (1996), developed the idea of Value at Risk (VaR). VaR is able to provide a more meaningful answer to the question "how much can we lose in a given time period" by computing the maximum loss with a given probability chosen by the user of the model. As we have seen in the description of probability distributions, we can arbitrarily select a value on the horizontal axis in the left tail of the normal distribution by selecting the probability describing the occurrence of a rate of return that is lower than the selected value.

VaR has several practical advantages for risk management in financial institutions, among which are a clear statement of the basic hypotheses, the possibility to involve different desks of the financial institutions in a set of rules that allow for control of the maximum loss, and, importantly, the possibility to compute a worst-case scenario in terms of amount of money rather than percentage points. The innovation of the VaR is not methodological: VaR was developed on the basis of an econometric methodology that drastically simplified the volatility models available as of the 1980s, that is, the

Generalized Auto Regressive Conditional Heteroskedasticity (GARCH) model invented by Nobel Prize winner Robert Engle (1982) to understand fluctuations in inflation. GARCH models are computationally intensive and hard to apply to large portfolios, whereas VaR computation (see section 2.7) is straightforward even for large portfolios. This is a great example of how business innovation in finance may be based on simplification rather than further sophistication and complication.

2.7.2 What is VaR?

VaR is the amount V (in monetary value, for example euros) defined in the statement: "given an initial investment of €I, we are certain with p% probability that we will lose no more than €V over the next T periods." VaR computation requires the combination of subjective elements, such as the choice of the probability p% and the reference time horizon, and objective elements such as the initial portfolio value. Figure 2.11 presents a graphical description of VaR under the assumption of normality of the distribution.

Figure 2.11 Graphical representation of VaR

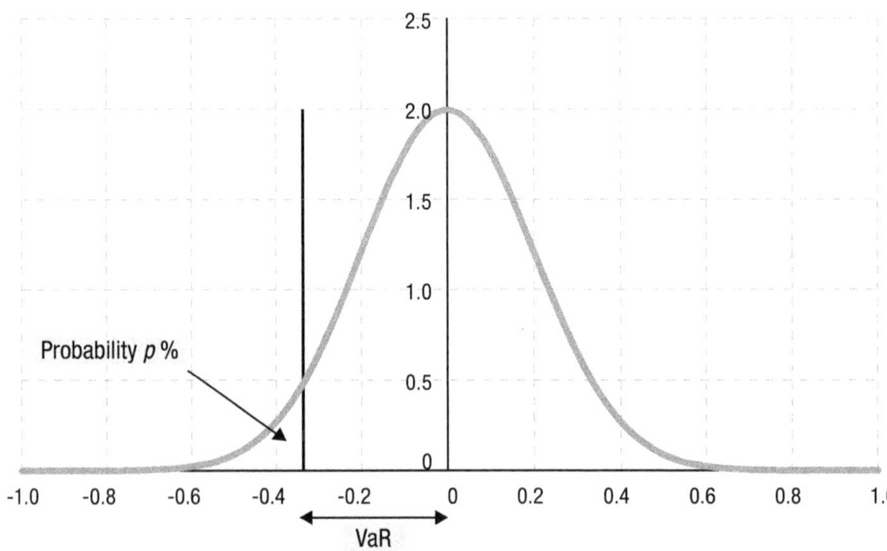

Let us consider a unitary investment ($I = 1$) in a risky asset with zero mean and 20% volatility over a one-year time horizon and identify the small probability with $p = 5\%$. From Excel (using norm.inv(0.05;0;0.2)) we find that the value of return leaving in the left tail the required 5% probability is –32.9%. The VaR is –32.9% that is we may lose more than €0.329 with a 5% probability.

Figure 2.12 **VaR with 5% probability**

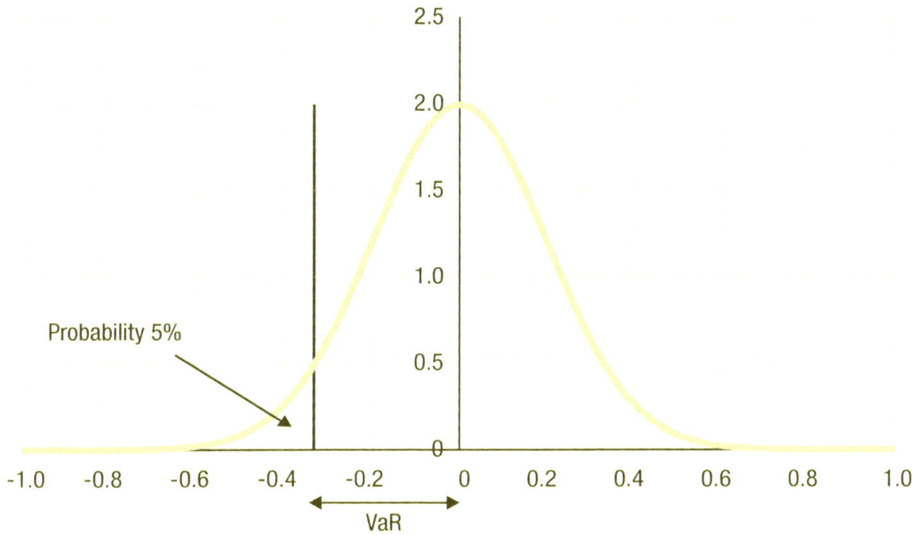

Notice that VaR does not provide an expected loss but only the maximum probabilistic loss. It is also possible to use the expected loss conditional to being in the tail, equal to the expected value of the return computed only including the returns that are below the VaR. Using Figure 2.12, the conditional expected loss would be the average of all returns below –32.9%. In Excel,[12] one could generate 10,000 realizations of a normal random variable with zero mean and 20% volatility and compute the average return across realizations below –32,9%, obtaining –42.1%. By definition, the conditional expected loss is always below the VaR, being an average of numbers below the VaR.

2.7.3 Computing VaR from volatility

The normality assumption allows us to compute the VaR from the volatility of returns. We can associate with each probability level, defining exactly what we mean by "left tail," a multiple of the standard deviation that leads us directly to the VaR. From the computation of the probabilities of the different intervals of realizations for a standard (zero mean, unitary standard deviation) normally distributed random variable, we learn that we have a 5% probability of observing a return lower than -1.645. If the volatility is equal to 20% and multiply -1.645 times 20%, we obtain –32,9%, a number leaving 95% of the distribution to the right and 5% to the left.

[12] From "data" then "data analysis" then "random number generation" then "normal."

Similarly, if we want to define the left tail in terms of a 1% probability, rather than 5%, the relevant multiplier is equal to 2.325. The VaR on a unitary investment with a 1% probability level is therefore 2.325 × 20% = 46.5%. As the left-tail probability goes down, the multiple goes up and the maximum probabilistic loss increases as well. A third reference probability level that is often used in practice is 2.5%, with an associated multiplier of 1.96.

Table 2.6 Relevant multipliers for VaR computation

Probability of maximum loss	Multiplier of the standard deviation
5%	1.645
2.5%	1.96
1%	2.325

2.7.4 The sensitivity of VaR to parameters

To move from the maximum potential loss on a unitary investment to the maximum potential loss on a general investment equal to €L, we just need to multiply the VaR previously computed by L. For example, if the initial investment is equal to €1,000 rather than €1, the VaR with 5% probability is equal to €329. The VaR with a 1% probability is €465.

Box 2.6 How much can Elena lose on a €15 million investment?

Question: Elena works as a risk manager and needs to compute the maximum loss of a €15 million investment, in order to understand whether the potential loss is more than compensated by the positive expected return. The portfolio has a volatility equal to 20%. She chooses a probability level equal to 2.5%.

Answer: The multiple associated with 2.5% is equal to 1.96. As a result the VaR is equal to 1.96 X 0.2 X €15,000,000 = € 5,880,000.</BOX>

Box 2.7 What is the probability that an initial capital of €5,000 will become €2,500 after a year?

Question: Carola has just invested €5,000 in the stock market, estimating the expected return at 5% and the volatility at 25%. She wants to know (a) what the expected value of her investment is after one year; (b) conservatively assuming a zero expected return, what the probability is that after one year the value of her investment will be less than €2,500; and (c) the probability that after one year the value of her investment will be less than €2,500 if she recognizes that the expected return is 5%.

Answer: (a) Carola expects to earn 5% on her investment and therefore expects to have €5,250; (b) if a zero expected return is assumed, the expected value of the investment at the end of the year is €5,000. Calculating the probability that the value is less than €2,500 is equivalent to evaluating the scenario where the return is less than –50%. To calculate the probability of the return being less than –50%, we need to calculate Pr(r<–50%). Dividing both sides of inequality by the standard deviation, the previous probability equals $\Pr\left(\frac{r}{25\%} < \frac{-50\%}{25\%}\right) = \Pr(z < -2)$. From Excel using =norm.dist(-2;0;1;1) we get 2.275%. The same result is obtained from norm.dist(-50%;0%;25%;1). Carola therefore has a 2.275% chance of seeing her investment reduced after one year to the value of €2,500 if she assumes a zero expected return; (c) if the expected return is 5%, the above calculation should be reformulated to take into account the following Pr(r<–50%) is equivalent to $\Pr\left(\frac{r-5\%}{25\%} < \frac{-50\% - 5\%}{25\%}\right) = \Pr(z < -2{,}2)$. From Excel using = norm.dist(-2,2;0;1;1) we get 1.39%. The probability of losing 50% of the initial investment is therefore reduced from 2.275% to 1.39% if the expected increase in the value of the investment itself is taken into account.

Another key parameter is the investment horizon. As the time horizon goes up, we have an increase of the maximum loss, as the volatility of the total return distribution is positively related with the time over which we measure the return. But the interesting question is whether there is a linear relation between time horizon and volatility. The "square root rule" is what we need to consider for such a computation, suggesting that the relation between horizon and relevant volatility is quadratic rather than linear: doubling the investment horizon less than double the volatility. This arises from a simple intuition. Consider the sum of two log returns over time and let us assume for simplicity that they both have zero mean and constant variance σ^2. If there is no correlation between them, the variance of the two-period log return is $V(r_1 + r_2) = V(r_1) + V(r_2) = 2 \times \sigma^2$. As a result, the standard deviation of the two-period return is the per period standard deviation times the square root of 2.

The square root rule implies that to move from the VaR computed from a time horizon corresponding to the definition of returns (for example, a yearly horizon for the volatility of annual returns) to another time horizon, we need to multiply by $\sqrt{N}$ where N is the ratio between the investor time horizon and the horizon initially considered to estimate the volatility parameter. For example, to compute the maximum loss on a two-year horizon when the volatility is computed from one-year returns, we need to multiply by $\sqrt{2}$. If we want to compute the maximum loss on a semester when the volatility is computed from one-year returns, we need to multiply by $\sqrt{1/2}$ because there are two semesters in a year. As another example, if the volatility of the annual return is equal to 20%, the relevant monthly volatility is equal to $20\% \times \sqrt{1/12} = 5.77\%$ and the volatility on a two-year horizon is $\sqrt{2} \times 20\% = 28.3\%$. Referring to the example in Box 2.5, how much can Elena lose on a €15 million investment over two years? The answer is $1.96 \times 0.2 \times €15{,}000{,}000 \times \sqrt{2} = 1.96 \times 0.2 \times €15{,}000{,}000 = €8{,}315{,}576$, larger than the previous maximum loss, computed at €5,880,000, due to the longer time horizon that can magnify losses. In general, the rule for VaR computation is:

$$VaR = \text{volatility multiple} \times \text{square root horizon} \times \text{volatility} \times \text{investment value}.$$

2.8 Estimating volatility

2.8.1 The VIX index

Dimson, Marsh, and Staunton (2020) show that in the period 1900–2019 the volatility of the excess return (difference between the return and the risk-free rate) of the stock market in the United States and in the United Kingdom has approximately been equal to 20% against values closer to 30% for Italy and Germany. In the same period, the volatility of excess return for long-term sovereign bonds has been 10% (US), 13% (UK), 14% (Italy), and 16% (Germany). Stock markets consistently show more volatility than bond markets, and different stock markets present different levels of volatility even in the long run. As an example, the larger volatility of continental European stock markets is associated with structural characteristics of the economic structure such as labor market flexibility, productivity, and monetary and fiscal policies, but also with historical episodes such as wars that have over the last century been more damaging for Europe than for the United States.

We have applied the ideas of conditional and unconditional probability distributions to estimation of the expected return, providing logical and empirical considerations supporting the interest in using specific subsets of information for forecasting. Does a similar argument hold for volatility? The answer is positive, and even more visible than for the case of the expected return, due to the existence of an index representing an observed and market-implied estimate of volatility at each point in time. Figure 2.12 describes the time series of the stock market volatility as estimated in the VIX index (obtained from the market prices of options) in 1990–2024. The average level of the VIX is 19.3% with spikes as large as 80% and a lower bound of about 10% in long periods of stability.

Figure 2.13 The VIX volatility index, 1990–2024

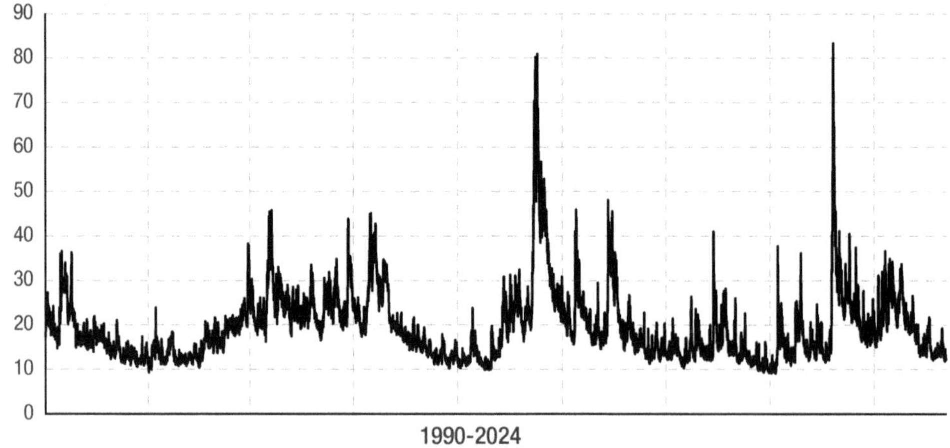

Sources: Datastream, Refinitiv

Figure 2.13 shows three important elements. First, volatility is not constant over time. The observed fluctuations in the VIX index, from 10% to above 80%, are too large to be explained by measurement error around a fixed value. This implies the need to adapt the normal distribution that we use to describe the return probability distribution through a timely and time-varying estimate of volatility. This topic will be discussed in the next section.

Second, volatility shoots up during economic/market/financial crises, for example the crisis of the Russian economy and the hedge fund Long Term Capital Management in 1998, the recessions and fall in value of Internet stocks in 2001–2002, the bankruptcy of Lehman Brothers in 2008, the peripheral crisis in 2011–2012 and Covid-19 in 2019. In such episodes, volatility spikes on the upside suddenly and unpredictably (unless one is able to predict the underlying source of the crisis).

Third, the time fluctuation of volatility is associated with a tendency to revert to a fixed mean. Every spike is quickly followed by prolonged periods of mean reversion.

The theory of efficient markets (Chapter 13) argues that the prices of risky assets are set at the level that takes into account all the information, and consequently that changes in the available information have an impact on prices. Moments of strong and persistent volatility should therefore be times when a lot of new information arrives in the market.[13]

2.8.2 Conditional variance computation

The temporal variability of volatility suggests that the estimate should be adjusted by paying more attention to the most recent observations. To do this, it is assumed that the variance depends on the square of past returns,[14] giving more weight to the most recent observations and less weight to the older ones (exponentially weighted moving average or EWMA), through weights that decrease exponentially for the oldest observations:

$$\sigma_t^2 = \sum_{i=0}^{\infty} (1 - \lambda) \times \lambda^i \times r_{t-1-i}^2 \tag{8}$$

where λ is the decay factor. J.P. Morgan/Reuters (technical document, 1996) suggests using a decay factor of 0.94 for daily data and 0.97 with weekly data. When using 0.94, it can be shown that the number of historical returns used for estimation in equation (8) is 75, because the weights of observations from 76 onwards are close to zero.[15] When using 0.97 the corresponding number is 150. Figure 2.14 describes the relationship between the weights and the distance of the observations from the current period, that is, the relationship between λ^i (y-axis) and i (x-axis) in the case of $\lambda = 0.97$.

[13] To test whether market volatility spikes correspond to crisis situations, Baker, Bloom and Davis (2016) calculate, using newspaper news, an index of uncertainty related to economic policy decisions (EPU) since the year 1900. Their analysis confirms the existence of a relationship between the phases of economic policy uncertainty and the moments of market volatility described.

[14] The squared return is used as in the calculation of sample variance, which is equal to the mean of the square of the deviations of the series from its mean. In this case, an average return value of zero is assumed, consistent with the use of daily or weekly data.

[15] For example $0.06 \times 0.94^{76} = 0.000544$.

Figure 2.14 The weights assigned to historical performance observations in the EMWA model

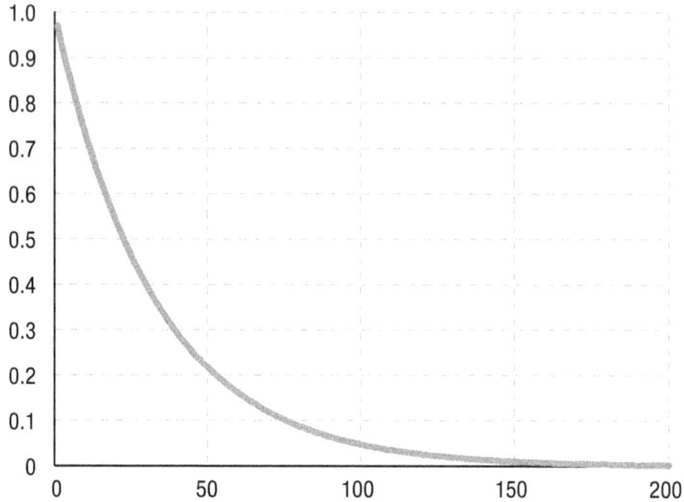

Box 2.8 How do you predict volatility from historical performance data?

Question: At the beginning of 2018, Elena manages a portfolio worth €5 million entirely invested in the US stock market and wants to have an estimate of the maximum loss over monthly, quarterly, and annual horizons with a probability of both 5% and 1%. She turns to Carola, who works in Risk Management, to get the results.

Answer: Based on the monthly returns of the S&P 500 Composite Index, Carola estimates a volatility for the month of January 2018 of 2.68%. With a multiple of 1.645, Carola estimates the following maximum loss on horizons of one month, one quarter, and one year, respectively: €220,430, €381,796, and €763,592. With a multiple of 2.325, she gets €311,550, €539,620, €1,079,241.</BOX>

2.8.3 The variance dynamics: an equivalent description

Equation (8) is equivalent to

$$\sigma_t^2 = \lambda \times \sigma_{t-1}^2 + (1 - \lambda) \times r_{t-1}^2 \tag{9}$$

which shows that the variance at time t is a weighted average of the previous period variance and the squared last period return.[16] Equation (9) has a simple interpre-

[16] The equation in the text is a special case of Engle model GARCH(1,1), which can be written as $\sigma_t^2 = \alpha_0 + \alpha_1 \sigma_{t-1}^2 + \alpha_2 r_{t-1}^2$. The EWMA model is achieved by imposing $\alpha_0 = 0$, $\alpha_1 + \alpha_2 = 1$. To obtain

tation: When variance increases, the future variance will also increase given other conditions, even though, due to $\lambda < 1$, the shock will gradually be absorbed over time. An increase in the variance is in turn associated with a large realization of the (absolute) value of past return, which also has a positive impact on current variance. For example, assuming $\lambda = 0.94$, a large rate of return equal to 10% on a given day has an impact equal to $0.94 \times 0.1^2 = 0.0094$ on the next day variance, equal to $0.94^2 \times 0.1^2 = 0.0088$ on the variance of the following day, and so on with a decreasing future impact. The same happens when the past return is equal to –10%. In contrast, a zero return on a given day has a negative effect on the future variance. Campbell and Hentschel (1992) notice that this mechanism implies that "no news is good news": We will see in Chapters 12 and 13 that prices move due to news, and as a result on days lacking new information it is more likely that the return is small in absolute value and that volatility drops, which is itself a positive development for risk-averse investors.

This hypothesis about the dynamics of variance has a drawback, though: When there is a large shock to the market, for example news of a big bank going bankrupt or news that an epidemic has suddenly started, the statistical model requires some time before estimated volatility increases. In contrast, the VIX index would immediately jump as a reaction due to traders immediately revising the prices of traded options from which the VIX is estimated.

Box 2.9 Forecasting volatility from data

Question: Elena must provide a statistical analysis for the calculation of volatility to support her VaR calculations for the portfolio of which she is a risk manager. She uses the following daily series of estimated five-day variance: 1%, 2%, 1.5%, 0.5%, 2% in order to:

(a) formulate the forecast for day six-volatility knowing that the return on day five was 2%;
(b) calculate the long-run volatility using the mean value of the variance observed in the sample;
(c) comment on the difference between expected volatility and long-term volatility.

Answer:

(a) The dynamics of the variance can be estimated using the model $\sigma_t^2 = \lambda \times \sigma_{t-1}^2 + (1-\lambda) r_t^2$. With daily data, the decay factor is 0.94. So the forecast is equal to 0.94 X 0.02 + 0.06X0.0004 = 0.0188. Volatility is the square root of the variance equal to 1.88% and therefore volatility is 13.72%.
(b) The long-run volatility is obtained from the mean of the square root of the variance:

$$\sqrt{\frac{0.01 + 0.02 + \ldots +0.02}{5}} = 11.83\%.$$

the equation that defines the variance conditioned by the latter equation, it is sufficient to consider the same equation for the moment $t-1$ $\sigma_{t-1}^2 = \lambda \times \sigma_{t-2}^2 + (1-\lambda) r_{t-2}^2$ and substitute in (2) to have: $\sigma_t^2 = (1-\lambda) r_{t-1}^2 + \lambda(1-\lambda) r_{t-2}^2 + \lambda^2 \sigma_{t-2}^2$. Continuing to replace backwards recursively, we obtain equation (1). From a mathematical point of view, we have solved backwards an equation with the differences of the first degree. In Chapter 12 we will see how, starting from the definition of return, we obtain an equation of the first degree differences in the price of an asset, which will be solved "forward."

(c) Given that the last observed volatility value is 14.14% (the square root of 2%), which is higher than the average of 11.83%, the model predicts the return of day six-volatility to the long-run value.

Covariances also change over time. Extending the equation describing the variance dynamics to covariance dynamics we get $\sigma_{ij,t} = \lambda \times \sigma_{ij,t-1} + \left(1 - \lambda\right) \times r_{i,t-1} \times r_{j,t-1}$.

2.8.4 Unconditional non-normality and conditional variance

We have discussed the validity of the normality assumption and pointed out that the higher the frequency of returns, the less likely it is that returns are normally distributed. At the same time, several institutional players (banks, insurance companies, asset managers) are interested in computing Value at Risk at daily or weekly horizons, exactly those frequencies for which normality is less likely to hold. The methodology we have highlighted in sections 2.7–2.8 maintains the normality assumption and combines it with a dynamic estimate of the variance obtained from the EWMA model. Are there any contradictions? The answer is negative. We can be consistent with the historical non-normality of daily and weekly returns through the repeated use of a conditionally normal distribution that changes over the same horizons by an updating of the volatility estimate. Using the definitions that have been introduced before, the conditional volatility estimator allows us to use a conditional normal distribution that is consistent with the evidence of non-normality of returns that cannot be explained based on an unconditionally normal distribution.

2.8.5 Evaluating the performance of a VaR model

A dynamic application of the model produces a time series of estimates of the maximum loss on the value of the portfolio. Comparing the time series of actual losses with the forecasts, it is possible to evaluate the ability of the VaR model to produce a dynamic risk estimate that is exceeded only a limited number of times. We do expect exceedances, as the very definition of VaR includes a maximum probabilistic loss. Even a fully functioning model would therefore fail $p\%$ of the time, that is, a 1% VaR over 300 days should be exceeded three times.

However, there are critical factors that may impair the effectiveness of the model. First, the VaR is a projection of estimated volatility, involving a measurement error like all estimated parameters. Any measurement error implying an underestimate of volatility will, by definition, be associated with a maximum loss projection that is not conservative enough and will produce a proportion of exceedance above $p\%$. Second, we assume that the daily return distribution is characterized by Gaussian, but this is only an approximation.

The comparison between the actual and expected loss (so-called unconditional accuracy) in each period is typically the metric by which to evaluate the functioning of VaR. If the maximum loss is calculated with a probability of 1%, it is expected that within 300 days there will be three episodes in which the actual loss exceeds the maximum loss. To develop a statistical test, one needs to know the distribution of the exceedances under the null hypothesis. The second relevant dimension is the timing of exceedances: in a well-specified model there should be no clustering of errors, that is, periods of time when errors are concentrated.

At the end of this chapter, we might feel there is a contradiction: On the one hand, we have shown that normality is not a good description for daily stock returns, but on the other hand, VaR is applied at the daily level under the assumption of conditional normality, using the conditional volatility estimate. How can the two things coexist? The intuition is: We can use normality to explain a times series of returns as long as the volatility parameter changes over time, so that tail returns are realized at times of high volatility.

If over 300 days we thought that volatility was stable at 1% we would predict a maximum loss (the 5% VaR) of 1.65% on a unitary investment. We would expect to lose more than 1.65% only fifteen times (5% of the total 300 observations). Suppose we had returns equal to –3% thirty times out of 300.[17] We would find thirty exceedances in the time series and we would reject the unconditional normality assumption. However, suppose that we knew that the volatility was equal to 5% on those thirty days when we had a return lower than –3%. The VaR on each of these days would be 8.25% and there would be no exceedance at all. We would not reject that the conditional distribution is normal, with volatility equal to 1% in 270 days and to 5% in the remaining thirty days.

Box 2.10 Does VaR work?

Question: Carola works in Risk Management and wants to evaluate how well her VaR model works, using a time series of monthly returns from the S&P 500 index from 2000 to 2017. What does she need to do to get an answer?

Answer: Carola needs to check whether the realized losses in the period exceed the month-over-month limit of the model, which is based on a decay parameter of 0.9 with an EWMA estimator using the last fifty monthly return data. Given the invested capital, which amounted to €5 million at the beginning of each month, Carola must estimate the monthly VaR corresponding to a probability of 1% and check how many times the actual losses exceed the expected ones. Her analysis shows that in three situations the loss was higher: in February 2001, when the index lost 9.1%, and then in January and June 2008, when the index lost 6% and 8.4% respectively. On a time series of 215 observations, the return should be less than the loss estimated by the model only two times (1% of 215 is 2.15). Carola concludes that the estimated model performs well because, despite a period marked by episodes of market downturns, including 2001 and 2008, the loss exceeds estimates a very limited number of times.

[17] The probability of observing a rate of return that is equal to -3% in a normal distribution with 1% volatility is equal to 0.13% (from norm.dist(-0.03;0;0.01;1)).

Summary

- The arithmetic return is equal to the percentage provided by the sum of the capital gain and the dividend relative to the initial price. Arithmetic returns do not add up over time, but log returns (equal to the log of one plus the percentage return) do. Arithmetic returns are used to estimate expected returns in a period; geometric returns are used to represent the actual dynamics of investment for a buy-and-hold investor.
- The rate of return is a random variable, that is, it is known at the end of the period and may take on many different outcomes (scenarios) that can be modeled through continuous or discrete probability functions.
- The normal distribution is the most widely used in finance because of its possibility to describe returns (especially at longer horizons) and because it is simple, being entirely characterized by only two parameters, the mean and the volatility. When the mean and the volatility are known (or estimated) it is possible to compute the probability of a realization of a random variable within any interval of time. Skewness and kurtosis are the two parameters that are most frequently used to detect deviations between the normal assumption and the data at hand.
- The probability distribution may be conditional or unconditional, depending on the subset of information used to define it. Depending on the distribution, we may use conditional or unconditional modeling.
- Indices are a weighted average of individual securities and are used by investors to get a concise and immediate idea of how a specific market or segment of it is moving.
- Indices allow us to think about financial asset classes. An asset class represents an investment in financial securities that move over time due to factors that are common to and partially different from the factors that underlie the movements of other asset classes.
- There is rich empirical evidence on average returns and return volatilities over time, across asset classes and across countries. Such evidence suggests the existence of a larger overperformance of the equity market relative to the bond market.
- Actual returns can be decomposed in the sum of the expected return and a shock.
- VaR is able to provide a more meaningful answer to the question "how much can we lose in a given time period" by computing the maximum loss with a given probability chosen by the user of the model.
- In general the rule for computing the VaR is VaR = volatility multiple × square root horizon × volatility × investment value and depends essentially on the estimated volatility.
- Volatility in the stock market is not constant over time, as can be seen by the VIX index. Volatility shows sudden and unpredictable shocks and is characterized by mean reversion, that is, a tendency to revert to a long-run average.
- The variance dynamics used in VaR computations relies on its persistence: Variance on a day is assumed to be equal to the weighted average of the variance the previous day and the squared return the previous day. This weighted average of two terms can be transformed into a weighted average of past squared returns by recursive substitution. This is the exponentially weighted moving average.
- VaR may be tested using unconditional accuracy and independence.

Problems

1. Calculate the probability that the return will be less than –50% when the average is 5% and the volatility is 25%.

2. Calculate the probability that the return will be above 30% when the average is 5% and the volatility is 25%.

3. Calculate the probability that the return will be above 30% when the average is 5% and the volatility is 20%.

4. Compute the probability that the return will be between +10% and –10% when the average is 5% and the volatility is 20%.

5. Calculate the probability that the return will be between +20% and –20% when the average is 5% and the volatility is 20%.

6. Calculate the probability that the return will be between the mean minus standard deviation and the mean plus standard deviation when the mean is 5% and the standard deviation is 20%.

7. Calculate the probability that the return will be between mean minus twice the standard deviation and mean plus twice the standard deviation when the mean is 5% and the standard deviation is 20%.

8. Calculate the probability that the return is between mean minus three times the standard deviation and mean plus three times the standard deviation when the mean is 5% and the standard deviation is 20%.

9. To make a prediction about stock market performance, the results of a stock index's linear regression to its past value are used, which implies a known term α equal to 10% and a slope β equal to –0.1. In 2018, the market return was –50%. What return forecast can be made for the long term? And what about 2019 and 2020? How do you intuitively explain the difference between the forecast for 2019 and the forecast for the long term?

10. (a) Calculate the interval around the mean for a normal with mean 5% and standard deviation 20% that contains 99% of the distribution. (b) What is the multiple of the standard deviation to which this interval corresponds?

11. For a portfolio with 20% annual volatility, what is the typical deviation of the return from the average at the daily interval, assuming there are 250 days in a year?

12. Calculate the daily Value at Risk (with probability 5%) of an investment of €15 million in a portfolio with zero expected return and annual volatility of 20%.

13. Calculate the weekly VaR (with probability 1%), assuming that there are fifty-two weeks in a year, of an investment of €25 million in a portfolio with expected return of 0% and annual volatility of 30%.

14 a. Calculate the annual VaR (with probability 1%) of an investment of €25 million in a portfolio with expected return of 0% and annual volatility of 20%.
b. Calculate the VaR over a two-year horizon with the same parameters.
c. How do the answers change if the value of the investment is € 35 million?

15 Use the daily return series for the last five days: –1%, 2%, –1.5%, –0.5%, 2% to make the forecast for day six volatility knowing that the variance on day five was 1%.

16 The average return of two equity markets in the last sixty-four years has been 2% and 6% respectively. The volatility is equal to 20% in both cases. Is the difference statistically significant?

17 A regression of log returns of a stock market on its lagged value gives

$$r_{t+1} = -\alpha \times r_t + \varepsilon_{t+1}$$

where the shock has variance equal to σ^2. Return volatility is 20%. What is the variance of a two-period average return?

Answers

1 From Excel, the norm.dist(-50%; 5%; 25%; 1) gives 1.39% as an answer.

2 The probability of the return being greater than 30%, that is, the sum of the expected return and volatility, is equal to the probability of the return being less than –20%, that is, the difference between the expected return and volatility. From Excel, the norm.dist(-20%; 5%; 25%; 1) provides 15.86% as a result.

3 The probability that the return is greater than 30%, that is, the sum of the expected return and 1.25 times the volatility, is equal to the probability that the return is less than –20%, that is, the difference between the expected return and 1.25 times the volatility. From Excel, the norm.dist(-20%; 5%; 20%; 1) gives 10.56%. Compared with the answer to the previous question, we see that, on average, the probability of having a return above 30% decreases if the volatility is lower, because it is less likely to move from the mean.

4 The probability of the return being less than –10%, that is, the difference between the expected return and 0.75 times the volatility, is obtained from norm.dist(-10%; 5%; 20%; 1), giving 22.66%. The probability that the return is greater than 10%, that is, the sum of the expected return and 0.25 times the volatility, is obtained from 1-norm.dist(10%; 5%; 20%; 1), giving 40.13%. The required probability is therefore equal to 1 – 0.2266 – 0.4013 = 37.21%.

5 From Excel, norm.dist(-20%; 5%; 20%; 1) gives 10.56%, and norm.dist(20%; 5%; 20%; 1) gives 77.34%, which means that the probability of the return being above 20% is equal to 22.66%. There is therefore a 100% – 10.56% – 22.66% = 66.78% probability that the return is outside the range provided.

6 From Excel, norm.dist(-15%; 5%; 20%; 1) provides 15.87%, while norm.dist(25%; 5%; 20%; 1) gives 84.13%. The probability of the required interval is therefore equal to the difference between the two probabilities, that is, 68.27%.

7 From Excel, norm.dist(-35%; 5%; 20%; 1) gives the result 2.27%, while norm.dist(45%; 5%; 20%; 1) is equal to 97.72%. The probability of the required interval is therefore equal to the difference between the two probabilities, that is, 95.45%.

8 From Excel, norm.dist(-55%; 5%; 20%; 1) gives the result 0.13%, while norm.dist(65%; 5%; 20%; 1) is equal to 99.87%. The probability of the required interval is therefore equal to the difference between the two probabilities, that is, 99.73%.

9 The reference model is $r_{t+1} = 0.1 - 0.1\, r_t + \varepsilon_{t+1}$. The long-term forecast is therefore equal to $\frac{0.1}{1.1} = 11.11\%$, while for 2019, taking into account the 2018, there is $0.1 - 0.1 \times (-50\%) = 15\%$. In 2020, using the forecast just made, we get $0.1 - 0.1 \times (15\%) = 8.5\%$. The result shows that the loss in 2018 has a positive impact on the 2019 forecast, while the forecast for 2020 is closer to the long-term forecast.

10 norm.inv(99.5%; 5%; 20%), which gives the value of the return that is exceeded in only 0.5% of cases, gives 56.52%. norm.inv(0.5%; 5%; 20%), which gives the value of the return that is exceeded only in 0.5% of cases, gives –46.52%. The desired range is therefore [-46.52%, 56.52%]. To answer the second question, consider the ratio of the lower value of the range minus the mean and divide by the standard deviation, that is, $\frac{51.52\%}{20\%} = 2.576$.

11 Applying the square root rule, we find $\frac{20\%}{\sqrt{250}} = 1.26\%$: a positive or negative fluctuation of 1.26% represents the typical deviation at the daily level.

12 Applying the rule, we find $15 \times 20\% \times \frac{1.645}{\sqrt{250}} = €312{,}117$.

13 Applying the rule, we find $25{,}000{,}000 \times 30\% \times \frac{2.325}{\sqrt{52}} = €2{,}418{,}146$.

14 a. Applying the rule, we find $€25{,}000{,}000 \times 20\% \times 2.325 = €11{,}625{,}000$.
b. On a two-year horizon and using the square root rule, we find $€25{,}000{,}000 \times 20\% \times 2.325 \times \sqrt{2} = €16{,}440{,}233$.
c. An initial value of €35,000,000 modifies the two responses to €16,275,000 and €23,016,326 respectively.

15 In this case, we need to use the formula $\sigma_6^2 = 0.94 \times \sigma_5^2 + 0.06\, r_5^2$. Using available data, $0.94 \times 0.01 + 0.06 \times 0.0004$. It is 0.94%, which in terms of volatility becomes equal to 9.71%.

16 The 4% differential must be divided by $\frac{20\%}{8}$ to get a t-test equal to 1.6, which is not statistically significant at conventional levels. We cannot reject the hypothesis that the two markets have the same return in the long run.

17 The average return for the two-year horizon is equal to $\frac{r_{t+1} + r_{t+2}}{2}$. The conditional expected value is $\frac{-\alpha \times r_t + \alpha^2 \times r_t}{2}$ and the shock is $\frac{(1-\alpha) \times \varepsilon_{t+1} + \varepsilon_{t+2}}{2}$. The variance equals $\frac{(1-\alpha)^2 \times \sigma^2 + \sigma^2}{4}$, which is less than the variance of the average two-year return $\frac{\sigma^2}{2}$.

3 Rational financial choices and the utility function

3.1 Introduction

We have described asset returns in terms of the normal probability distribution characterized by only two parameters: expected return and volatility. Most people would prefer assets with high expected returns and lower volatility but often have to compare an asset with another showing both higher expected return and higher volatility. This chapter is about the rational framework that we use to describe preferences in risky situations. We use the simplest possible assumption, albeit not well founded theoretically, which is that investors are only concerned with expected return and variance and use a relative weight of the two parameters depending on their degree of risk aversion.

This model is defined as mean/variance utility function. This chapter starts however from a more general and rigorous way to describe attitudes towards risk through a utility function, which is then simplified to the simpler expected return/ variance framework that will be used throughout the book. In this chapter we will not select securities to build a diversified portfolio, limiting ourselves to the simpler task of describing attitudes toward risk in the context of alternative assets, without any discussion about the possibility of combining them in portfolios, an exercise that will be conducted in Chapters 7 and 8. The description of individuals is totally based on the assumption of procedural rationality: we assume the investor is a mathematical model with a known objective function that is maximized by choosing from risky alternatives.

The next Chapter 4 will instead focus on a more plausible and intuitive, and to many people more fascinating, description of how individuals make financial choices (and errors) in real life. At the end of this Chapter we will have a short discussion about the ways we can try to measure the degree of risk aversion of investors, with hints, that we hope will pique the reader's curiosity about issues associated with regulation, psychology, and neuroscience. Estimating the risk aversion coefficient, be it in the context of the mean/variance utility function or in the context of a more expected utility model, is the main hurdle in the application of a rational framework for financial decision-making.

3.2 Risk and uncertainty

The situation we have described in Chapter 2, with a probability distribution of returns, is characterized as being risky. We do not exactly know what will happen in the future, but we describe it by assigning probabilities to different scenarios. When we are not able to assign probabilities to scenarios, we talk about uncertainty (see Knight, 1921).

An example of a risky situation is the classic tossing of a fair coin with equal probabilities for heads and tails. If the coin is associated with a bet where the player wins €50 in case of heads and loses €50 in case of tails, we have a fair game, where the expected value is equal to zero because $0.5 \times 50 + 0.5 \times (-50) = 0$. However, if we use a trick coin and the player does not know the true probabilities of the two events, it is not possible, before the first toss, to know its expected value. Only after a long series of tosses will it be possible to estimate the empirical probabilities of the two events and to compute the expected value, which, in the case of a trick coin, may be different from zero. In summary, whereas risk is about "known unknowns," uncertainty is about "unknown unknowns."

Are financial markets characterized by risk or uncertainty? Over the very long run it is hard to identify the possible events and the associated probabilities. What is the probability of humanity going to Mars to establish life there by the year 2050? What about the probability that the next pandemic will eliminate a large proportion of the world population? What is the probability that technology will be able to stop climate change and prevent the sea level rise? We have no empirical evidence for answering these questions. Meanwhile, in the short run, to be interpreted as the next few quarters, we may (or maybe we like to) believe that we are under conditions of risk that allow investors to rationally act based on a quantification of the upside associated with expected returns and the downside associated with the left tail of the distribution. This means ignoring the existence of unpredictable events that may completely change the scenario even in the short run: once a war starts between two European countries, will the historical business-as-usual distributions still be valid for the current scenario? Again, we have no answer to this, but we ignored the possibility of a European war until the end of 2021 and studied financial markets for the first quarter of 2022 based on risk considerations derived from standard data analysis especially after noting, a few weeks from the start of the war, that nothing "unusual" was taking place in European economies and financial markets.

Often a big shock that creates uncertainty is gradually reabsorbed by investors in a risk scenario as, over time, we update empirical probabilities. Covid-19 is a good example: Investors' view of the world suddenly changed when the virus was initially found in Codogno, Italy, and it was impossible to fully understand the economic implications of the pandemic. How large will the drop in GDP be? How many people will die? How long will it take before a vaccine is found? Will the network of hospitals be able to stand the pressure? We had no clue at the beginning. Then, over time, we had better information about the health problems and about how to slow down the transmission of the virus, and States all over the world intervened with monetary and fiscal tools to protect their economies. We observed market prices representing the evolving view of investors and were able to re-estimate relevant parameters. Gradually, uncertainty became risk. The appearance of uncertainty was very negative for equity prices.

The gradual transformation of uncertainty into risk was met with large increases in stock prices that suddenly recovered their pre-pandemic values. Our assumption does not imply that uncertainty is irrelevant for understanding asset prices: Ellsberg (1961) as well as Keynes (1921) have noticed that investors and firms may be averse to uncertainty. We skip the mathematical modeling of uncertainty due to its technical complexity.

3.3 The utility function

3.3.1 Expected utility

In the rationality framework, investors have well-defined and known preferences and make optimal choices to maximize the utility function. In the context where the consumer selects the quantities of two goods subject to the budget constraint, utility is defined over the quantity of the goods. In the case of financial choice, economic theory extends the framework by defining utility over total consumption (or total wealth) that depends on the financial investment.

If W denotes the random end-of-period wealth, W_0 denotes initial wealth, and r is the asset return, the relation among variables is $W = W_0 \times (1 + r)$. One possibility is to define utility directly on wealth, $u(W)$, or on the rate of return $u(r)$. Technically, this means defining utility over a random variable. Investors should evaluate assets in terms of the probability distribution of wealth generated by returns. As shown in Box 3.1, this calls for an understanding of the probability distribution of returns, from which the probability distribution of end-of-period wealth may be obtained. It is hard to compare probability distributions generated by different assets, so theory suggests we use the average utility as a way to select the best investment.

Box 3.1 Computing expected utility

Question: Based on her answers to a questionnaire, Sara believes that the utility of her sister Carola can be well defined by a log utility function defined on end-of-period wealth $u(W) = \ln(W)$. She asks her consultant, Elena, to understand if Carola would rather select the investment characterized by probabilities of the various returns shown in column 2 (probability for asset 1 $P(r_{s,1})$) or in column 3 (probability for asset 2 $P(r_{s,2})$) of the following table (the first column represents the rate of return of the asset in scenario s, r_s):

Table 3.1 **Returns and their probabilities over scenarios**

r_s	$P(r_{s,1})$	$P(r_{s,2})$
-0.6	0	0
-0.55	0.0002	0
-0.5	0.0002	0
-0.45	0	0
-0.4	0.0004	0
-0.35	0.003001	0
-0.3	0.007802	0
-0.25	0.011802	0
-0.2	0.025805	0.0006
-0.15	0.043009	0.0096
-0.1	0.064413	0.0504
-0.05	0.10122	0.1458
0	0.112623	0.2324
0.05	0.125225	0.2786
0.1	0.131226	0.189
0.15	0.116023	0.074
0.2	0.096419	0.017
0.25	0.068014	0.0022
0.3	0.046809	0.0004
0.35	0.026205	0
0.4	0.010802	0
0.45	0.004601	0
0.5	0.003001	0
0.55	0.0006	0
0.6	0.0006	0

Answer: Elena considers each outcome and first computes the end-of-period wealth for each return. Second, she multiplies such wealth by the probability of each scenario. All the computations are in the following table, where column 4 represents end-of-period wealth (initial wealth €10,000 multiplied by 1 plus the rate of return in column 1), column 5 is the outcome-by-outcome product of log wealth times the probability of asset 1, and column 6 performs the same computation for asset 2.

Average utility is the weighted average of final utility levels in the different scenarios computed from the elements in the different rows of the last two columns. The expected utility associated with asset 1 is 0.3566 (the sum of all the elements in column five) and the expected utility associated with asset 2 is 0.3554 (the sum of all the elements of column six). Carola would prefer to avoid the less risky asset and select instead asset 1 because expected utility is larger.

Table 3.2 **Returns, probabilities, and final wealth of two assets**

r_s	$P(r_{s,1})$	$P(r_{s,2})$	W_s	$u(W_s) \times P(r_{s,1})$	$u(W_s) \times P(r_{s,2})$
-0.6	0	0	4,000	0	0
-0.55	0.0002	0	4,500	0.001683	0
-0.5	0.0002	0	5,000	0.001704	0
-0.45	0	0	5,500	0	0
-0.4	0.0004	0	6,000	0.003481	0
-0.35	0.003001	0	6,500	0.026344	0
-0.3	0.007802	0	7,000	0.069072	0
-0.25	0.011802	0	7,500	0.105308	0
-0.2	0.025805	0.0006	8,000	0.231916	0.005392
-0.15	0.043009	0.0096	8,500	0.389134	0.086859
-0.1	0.064413	0.0504	9,000	0.586478	0.458891
-0.05	0.10122	0.1458	9,500	0.927081	1.335389
0	0.112623	0.2324	10,000	1.037292	2.140483
0.05	0.125225	0.2786	10,500	1.159475	2.579594
0.1	0.131226	0.189	11,000	1.221146	1.758768
0.15	0.116023	0.074	11,500	1.084829	0.691908
0.2	0.096419	0.017	12,000	0.905634	0.159675
0.25	0.068014	0.0022	12,500	0.641605	0.020754
0.3	0.046809	0.0004	13,000	0.443411	0.003789
0.35	0.026205	0	13,500	0.249224	0
0.4	0.010802	0	14,000	0.103126	0
0.45	0.004601	0	14,500	0.044086	0
0.5	0.003001	0	15,000	0.028853	0
0.55	0.0006	0	15,500	0.00579	0
0.6	0.0006	0	16,000	0.005809	0
0.65	0	0	16,500	0	0

Figure 3.1 describes the empirical probability distribution of the end-of-period wealth under the assumption of a logarithmic utility function, $u(W) = \ln(W)$, and two different assets: one with a normal rate of return with 5% expected return and 15% volatility, and the other with expected return 1% and volatility 7%. As shown in Box 3.1, the picture is obtained by defining several scenarios of returns and, starting from unitary initial wealth, computing final wealth and its logarithm. The distributions of end-of period wealth are clearly different: The one describing the riskier portfolio is more spread out over the horizontal line and is shifted to the right relative to the other.

Figure 3.1 **Utility function of end-of-period wealth**

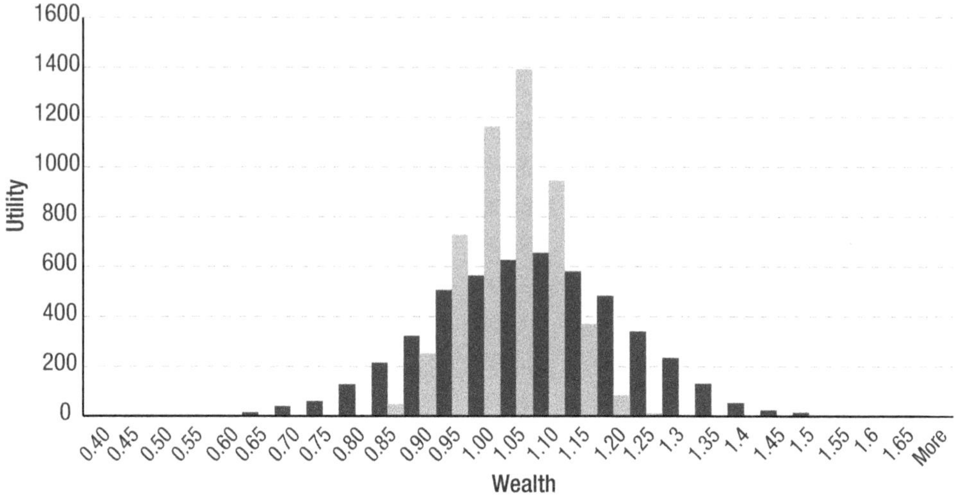

How does an investor compare the two distributions to choose the one providing the higher utility? Economic theory suggests the investor should choose the portfolio in such a way as to maximize expected utility. This approach is intuitive in terms of general principle but the final result of the comparison across assets is hard to predict due to the non-linearity of the utility function.

3.3.2 Utility functions and risk aversion

When the utility function is concave in consumption (or return or wealth) then one describes a risk-averse individual. When the utility function is linear, risk-neutral behavior is described. A convex utility function describes risk-seeking behavior.

In Figure 3.2, the utility corresponding to the 4% abscissa is 75, while the utility corresponding to 10% is 90. If we consider a situation in which the two events, 4% and 10%, are equally likely, the expected utility is the average of the two utility levels achieved in each of the two scenarios and corresponds to the average between 75 and 90, that is, 82.5. But from the graph it can be seen that if the individual could have 7% with certainty, the arithmetic average of 4% and 10%, the utility would be greater than 85. An investor with a concave utility function prefers to have the average value with certainty rather than maintain the risky situation with the associated expected utility.

The concave function is characterized by decreasing marginal utility. If you start from the 4% level in the graph and imagine an increase of 2% to 6%, you can see that there is a strong increase in utility, and that this increase is greater than the increase in utility as we move from 10% to 12%. A situation of low return (or low consump-

Figure 3.2 **Concavity and risk aversion**

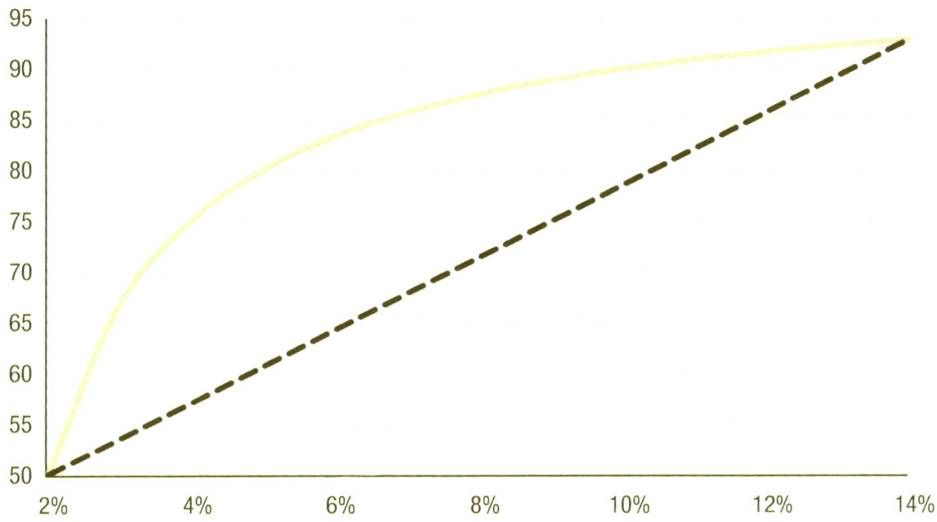

tion or low equity) is therefore characterized by high marginal utility because the increase in utility due to the increase in return is very strong, while a situation of high initial return implies low marginal utility.

3.3.3 The CRRA utility function

A utility function often used in academic research assumes constant relative risk aversion (CRRA) $u(W) = \frac{W^{1-\alpha}}{1-\alpha}$ with $\alpha > 0$ and $\alpha \neq 1$ becoming the log function $u(W) = \ln(W)$ when $\alpha = 1$. For this function, the relative risk aversion coefficient $-\frac{W \times u''(W)}{u'(W)}$ is equal to α, that is, it is independent of the level of wealth. With a CRRA function the choice between a risky and a risk-free security depends only on the risk aversion coefficient and is the same regardless of the level of wealth. The coefficient of relative risk aversion depends on the ratio between the second and the first derivative of the utility function. The first derivative measures the slope of the utility function defined at an initial level of wealth, whereas the second derivative measures the curvature of the utility function. The ratio between the two represents the degree of concavity of the utility function, consistent with the idea that the larger the concavity, the larger the aversion to risk.

Box 3.2 How much do you pay to take on the risk?

Question: Elena, Sara, and Carola have a CRRA utility function with risk aversion coefficients respectively equal to 0.5, 3, and 5. They have to evaluate a risky situation where they can earn €500 or €1,000 with equal odds. How much should they pay to participate in the game?

Answer: The result can be obtained by calculating the expected utility of the prizes and equating it to the utility of the ticket cost equal to C. If $\alpha \neq 1$ the computation is:

$$0.5 \times (1-\alpha)^{-1} 1{,}000^{(1-\alpha)} + 0.5 \times (1-\alpha)^{-1} 500^{(1-\alpha)} = (1-\alpha)^{-1} C^{(1-\alpha)}.$$

If $\alpha = 1$ instead:

$$0.5 \times \ln(1{,}000) + 0.5 \times \ln(500) = \ln(C).$$

By solving, we find the following values for the three women:

α	C
0.5	729
3	632
5	586

Elena is the least risk-averse and is willing to pay €729 for equal odds of winning €500 or €1,000. Elena would pay almost as much as a risk-neutral individual would pay, €750. Sara has an intermediate risk aversion and would pay €632, while Carola, the most risk-averse, would pay a maximum of €586.

Box 3.3 How risk-averse are you?

Question: Elena, Sara, and Carola have a risk aversion independent of the level of wealth, of the CRRA type. They want to estimate their risk aversion coefficient from information about how much they are willing to pay to buy a bet, in which they can earn €500 or €1,000 with equal odds (corresponding to the numbers found in Box 3.2). How can they estimate their risk aversion?

Answer: The result can be obtained by calculating the expected utility of the prizes and equating it to the utility of the ticket cost. In this case, however, the coefficient is the unknown and the amount paid to buy the bet is an input. Risk aversion can be calculated from the equation:

$$0.5 \times (1-\alpha)^{-1} 1{,}000^{(1-\alpha)} + 0.5 \times (1-\alpha)^{-1} 500^{(1-\alpha)} = (1-\alpha)^{-1} C^{(1-\alpha)}$$

where C is the price you're willing to pay. α can be found by solving the equation:

$$0.5 \times \left(\frac{1{,}000}{C}\right)^{(1-\alpha)} + 0.5 \times \left(\frac{500}{C}\right)^{(1-\alpha)} = 1$$

By solving, we find the following values for the three women, which of course correspond to the numbers in Box 3.2:

α	C
0.5	729
3	632
5	586

Ang (2014) presents a summary of the "plausible" values of the risk aversion coefficient, noting that most individuals would be willing to pay between €540 and €707 for the game described in Box 3.2 .

3.3 The mean/variance utility function

3.3.1 Preferences over mean and variance

For a generic utility function it is hard to understand the consequences of the characteristics of the return distribution on the utility level. To simplify the analyses, in this and the following chapters we use a much simpler assumption and define utility over the expectation and the variance of the distribution of returns. We call this the mean/variance utility function:

$$u(Er, \sigma^2) = Er - 0.5 \times A \times \sigma^2$$

where Er is the expected return, σ^2 is the variance of returns, and A is the coefficient of risk aversion (A is multiplied by 0.5 for the sake of simplicity in calculations that will be evident when maximizing utility and calculating its first derivative). The higher the value of A, the greater the total utility penalty due to a high level of variance for a given expected return level.[1]

Figure 3.3 depicts in a three-dimensional chart the utility (vertical axis) achieved for each combination of mean and volatility (horizontal axes) for an individual with a risk aversion coefficient of 3.

Figure 3.3 shows that with the same expected return, utility decreases with increasing volatility, while with the same volatility, utility increases with expected return. Thus, evaluating the investment in an asset using the MV utility function means, all other things being equal, preferring assets with higher expected returns and penalizing those with higher variance.

The utility function allows us to obtain a concise indicator of satisfaction on the value of an investment and to make comparisons between investments without the need to look at outcome-by-outcome realizations of the random variable and computation of the associated utility based on a non-linear utility function.

[1] The MV utility function does not necessarily require returns to be distributed according to the Gaussian distribution, but of course the utility calculation ignores all the parameters that are associated with the non-normality of returns.

Figure 3.3 The mean/ variance utility function in a three-dimensional space

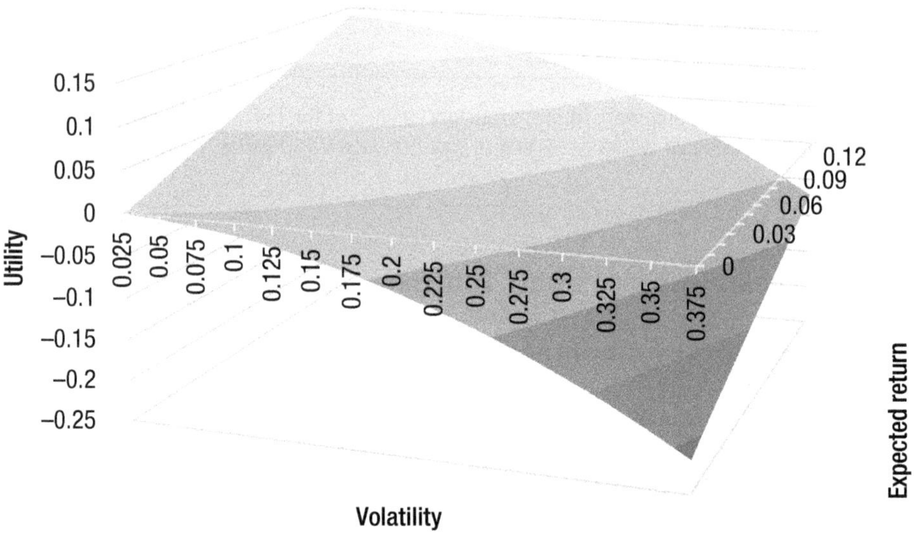

The two exercises described in Boxes 3.4 and 3.5 show how to apply the utility function first to the case of an investor who must select one investment and then to the case of what valuations various investors give to a single investment. The use of the utility function for financial choice implies the assumption of "rational behavior." Rational behavior understood in this way is simply the expression of the application of an automatic rule, which leads the investor to choose one possibility over the other in terms of which option is characterized by the highest utility. Rationality is therefore the application of a rule, in which there are no behavioral errors or emotions.

In the case of an investment in a risky security, the value of the utility function can be interpreted as the certain equivalent, that is, the value of the interest rate that would make the investor indifferent between buying the risky security and buying the risk-free one. For example, an investment with an expected return of 5% and a variance of 2% has a utility of 2% for an investor with a risk aversion coefficient of 3. This investor would therefore be indifferent between investing in the risky security just described and in the risk-free security with an interest rate of 2%. We may define the certainty equivalent as the level of the risk-free rate that would make the investor indifferent between a risky return and the risk-free investment. In the previous numerical example 2% is the certainty equivalent.

Box 3.4 How can an investor choose between investments with different expected returns and different risks?

Question: An advisor suggests four alternative investments to Sara, with varying levels of expected return and volatility. Sara is a rational individual whose preferences can be described by the utility function: $Er - 0.5 \times A \times \sigma^2$. What investment does Sara choose if A = 4? What if A = 0 (risk neutrality)?

Answer: Looking at the parameters of the four investments, Sara notices that the second one is the worst as it has a higher risk than the others and an expected return exceeded by investments #3 and #4. Investment #1 can also be discarded because it has higher volatility and lower expected return than investments #3 and #4. The choice between investments #3 and #4 is not obvious because #4 has higher risk but also higher expected return than #3 and the selection depends on the degree of risk aversion. Doing the calculations, we see, for example, that for investment #1 $0.12 - 0.5 \times 4 \times 0.3^2 = -0.06$. So, the utility of the following #4 alternative investments is:

Investment	*Er*	σ	*u*
1	0.12	0.30	-0.0600
2	0.15	0.50	-0.3500
3	0.21	0.16	0.1588
4	0.24	0.21	0.1518

Based on the calculations, we see that investment #3 is the best when A = 4. When Sara is risk-neutral, she simply selects investment #4 with the highest expected return, since volatility is not relevant.

Box 3.5 Which investment is best suited to which investor?

Question: Carola, Elena, and Sara have to evaluate a risky investment that has an expected return of 10% and a variance of 2%. Based on interviews with their advisors, they decide that their risk aversion levels are 4, 8, and 16, respectively. Which investment is best suited for each of the three?

Answer: We use the utility function to compare, from the perspective of three different levels of risk aversion, an investment in a risk-free security that pays a rate of 2% and a risky investment with an expected return of 10% and a return variance of 2%. The table below contains the utility level for each of the two choices and each of the three investors. The table shows that as risk aversion increases, investors prefer lower-risk investments with the same expected return. Note that the utility of the risk-free asset is equal to the value of the risk-free itself.

Risk aversion	**Utility associated with the risk-free asset**	**Utility associated with the risky asset**
4	0.02	0.06
8	0.02	0.02
16	0.02	-0.06

3.3.2 The indifference curve

The graphical representation of the utility function in Figure 3.3 is complex, requiring a three-dimensional graph. To simplify, we can describe preferences by taking a certain level of utility as given. The indifference curve comprises the pairs of expected return and variance that ensure a given level of utility. To find it, we need to determine a utility level and look for all the combinations of mean and variance that guarantee that utility. In mathematical terms, this means choosing a given utility level of, say, $\bar{u}$, and finding the pairs of expected return and variance such that:

$$\bar{u} = \text{Er} - 0{,}5 \times \text{A} \times \sigma^2.$$

For example, given different values of variance, the expected return levels that always leave the investor at the same level of utility $\bar{u}$ are:

$$\text{Er} = \bar{u} + 0{,}5 \times \text{A} \times \sigma^2$$

an equation that defines the indifference curve corresponding to a utility level equal to $\bar{u}$ and shows the different values of expected return that are necessary in the face of various values of variance to leave the overall utility unchanged.

Box 3.6 Which investments are equal from a utility perspective?

Question: Carola, with a risk aversion coefficient of 3, is very satisfied with an investment she made last year, which gave her a total utility of 5%. In order to evaluate other investment proposals, she wants to know which combinations of expected return and volatility will allow her to have the same level of utility.

Answer: To derive the indifference curve, we need to find the expected return and variance pairs that are compatible with the following equation $0.05 = Er - 0.5 \times 3 \times \sigma^2$. We can give some values to the standard deviation and derive the expected return value compatible with utility equal to 5%:

σ	σ^2	Er
0	0	0.05
0.05	0.0025	0.05375
0.1	0.01	0.065
0.15	0.0225	0.08375
0.2	0.04	0.11
0.25	0.0625	0.14375

From a graphical point of view, the indifference curve can be plotted in the two-dimensional chart described by volatility and expected return. In fact, the indifference curve is the intersection between the utility surface in the three-dimensional space described in Figure 3.3 and a plane parallel to the horizontal plane. In Figure 3.4 the indifference curve:

a) has a positive inclination, in that an increase in risk tends, with the same expected return, to lower the level of utility, and in order to maintain the same level of utility it is therefore necessary to compensate with an increase in the expected return;
b) is convex, as seen by the equation that describes a quadratic, non-linear relationship between expected return and volatility.

Figure 3.4 **Indifference curve as a function of risk**

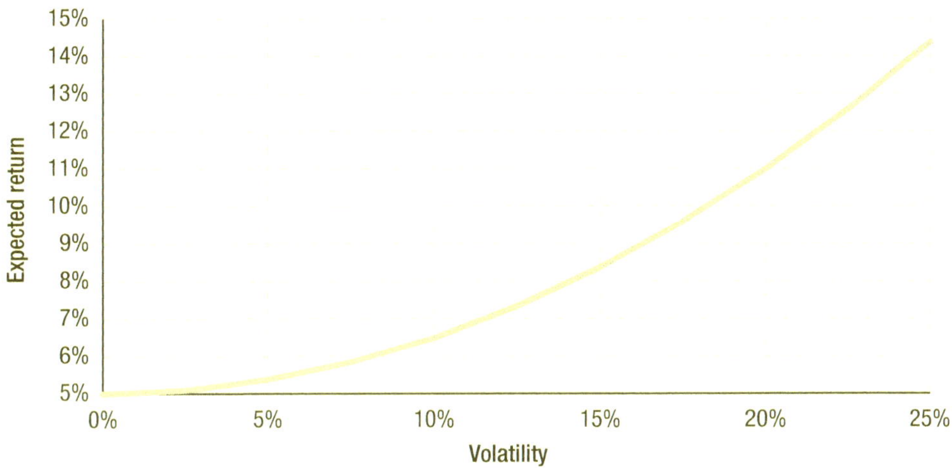

Box 3.7 **Which investments are equal from a utility perspective?**

Question: Elena and Sara have risk aversion coefficients of 0 and -3 respectively, and they want to know the combinations of expected return and risk that give the same level of utility of 5%.

Answer: As before, to derive the indifference curve, we need to find the pairs of expected return and variance compatible with the following equation $0.05 = Er - 0.5 \times A \times \sigma^2$. We can give some values to the standard deviation and derive the expected return value compatible with utility equal to 5%. When A = 0 (the case of risk neutrality that characterizes Elena) it is immediately seen that the indifference curve is flat at the level corresponding to that of the expected return. When, as in the case of Sara A = -3, that is, the individual is risk-lover because greater utility derives from both an increase in expected return and an increase in volatility, the indifference curve goes down because an increase in volatility per se increases utility and as compensation, in order to leave the same level of utility, the expected return must be brought down.

σ	σ^2	Er (A = 3)	Er (A = 0)	Er (A = -3)
0	0	0	0.05	0.05
0.05	0.0025	0.05375	0.05	0.04625
0.1	0.01	0.065	0.05	0.035
0.15	0.0225	0.08375	0.05	0.01625
0.2	0.04	0.11	0.05	-0.01
0.25	0.0625	0.14375	0.05	-0.0438

Figure 3.5 Indifference curves, varying degrees of risk aversion

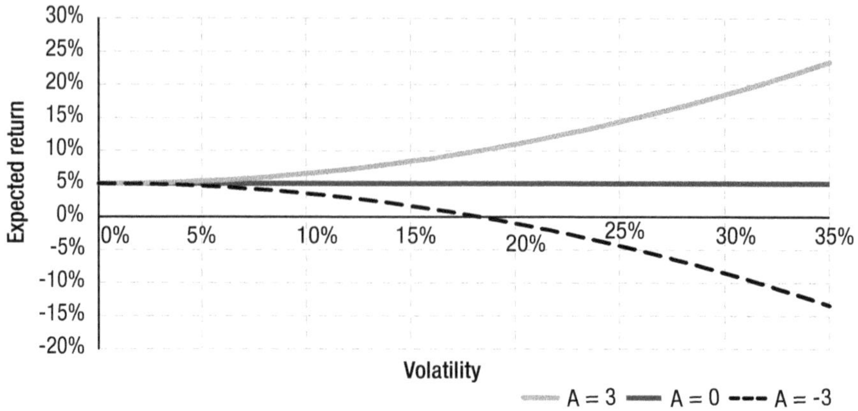

To understand how the indifference curve shifts in the graph as the total utility changes, let's imagine that the new total utility level is u'. The equation describing the new indifference curve is therefore equal to:

$$Er = u' + 0.5 \times A \times \sigma^2.$$

From a graphical point of view, there is a parallel shift of the indifference curve, upwards if $u' > \overline{u}$ (case described in Figure 3.6, where the total utility changes from the dashed curve to the continuous curve due to $\overline{u} = 5\%$ $u' = 8\%$) and downwards if $u' < \overline{u}$:

Figure 3.6 Parallel displacement of the indifference curve

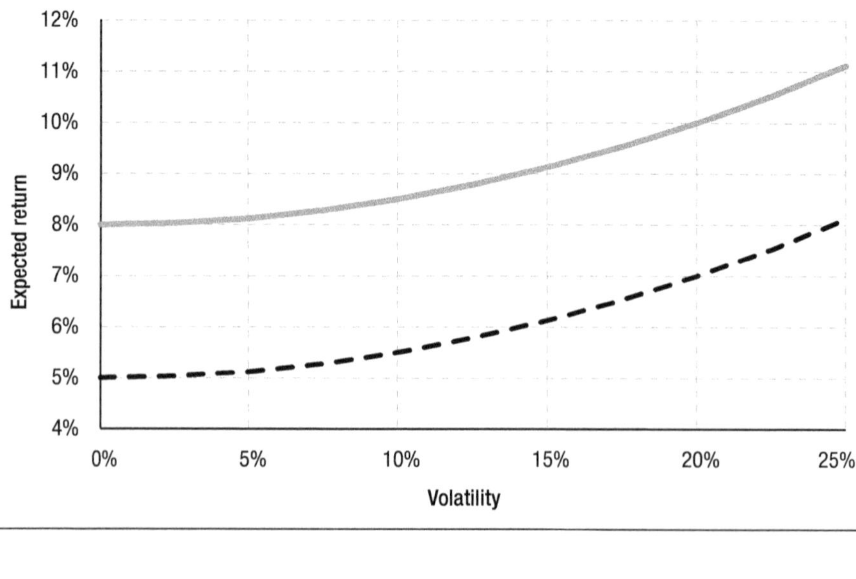

3.4 The risk premium

The utility function helps us understand and define the concept of risk premium, which is of paramount importance in finance. How much are you willing to pay to participate in a risky game, such as a game where you can lose €50 or gain €50 with equal probability? A risk-averse individual is not willing to pay anything. Paying a sum of money, for example €5, would mean participating in a game that has an expected gain, net of the cost of the ticket, equal to €45 if heads comes up and loss equal to €55 if tails is rolled, with an expected value of –€5.

A risk-averse individual voluntarily participates in risky play only if the expected value is positive. To voluntarily participate in a risky game when you are risk-averse requires a risk reward. In gambling, money is paid to take a position with negative expected return, but a risk-averse individual never chooses to participate in gambling.

Similarly, a risk-averse individual buys a risky asset only if its expected return is higher than the risk-free rate. The risk premium is the difference between the expected return on the asset and the risk-free rate. A risk-averse investor holds a risky security only if the certain equivalent is higher than the risk-free rate. In fact, one invests in a risky security if its utility is greater than that associated with investing in the risk-free security, and the utility associated with investing in the risk-free security is equal to the value of the risk-free security itself.

The risk premium is an ex ante concept, which can be defined as the expectation of excess return on the asset under consideration. Using notations introduced in previous chapters, the conditional risk premium required by an investor who uses all the information available at the moment is defined as:

$$rp_t = E_t\left(r_{t+1} - r_{ft}\right).$$

Risk-averse investors decide on the allocation of their assets based on risk premia and the amount of risk. Investors' expectations are not observable, so a market proxy must be used to measure the risk premium. The variable observed in the market that allows the risk premium to be measured ex post is the excess return, that is, the differential between the asset's return and the risk-free rate, observed on average over a certain period of time.

For example if the risk aversion coefficient is 3 for a volatility of 5%, the expected return of 5.375% gives a utility level of 5%. The spread between the expected return of the risky security and the 5% risk-free rate, that is, 0.375%, is the risk premium. Any expected return level below 5.375% would cause the investor to avoid the risky investment. If, meanwhile, the risk aversion coefficient was -3, the expected return compatible with indifference to the risk-free rate would be 4.625%, corresponding to a negative risk premium of -0.375%. Such an investor would pay to enter a risky situation.

3.5 Estimating risk aversion

The coefficient of risk aversion is a key driver of financial choice. We have seen that in the context of the selection of one of two assets and we will reinforce that message when discussing the weights of wealth invested in a risk-free asset and a risky portfolio. The implication is that both investors should be extremely careful in risk aversion estimation. Investors' consultants should be very interested too: an investor obtaining a wrong portfolio advice due to bad estimation of risk aversion is unlikely to be happy in the long run and more likely to switch to a different advisor. Unfortunately, the relevance of this parameter is inversely proportional to our ability to measure it for individual investors. In what follows we provide an idea about the challenges associated with risk aversion estimation through surveys and next we discuss recent frontiers of using psychology and neuroscience to make progress.

3.5.1 Estimating risk aversion from surveys

Regulators try to help investors by asking financial intermediaries and financial consultants in general to use structured methods for estimating the coefficient of risk aversion. In Europe, the MiFID (Markets in Financial Instruments Directive) questionnaire, established in 2007, consists of a series of questions that intermediaries who carry out personalized advisory activities must periodically administer to clients. The typical MiFID questionnaire involves topics such as:

- knowledge and experience: questions about past investment knowledge and experience, as well as educational qualification,
- financial situation and ability to sustain losses: the objective is to quantify the investor's assets, including possible future income/ expenses,
- financial goals,
- risk tolerance: psychological questions to assess risk appetite and possible reactions to future losses,
- investment time horizon,
- sustainability preference for investments (new, starting in 2022).

The goal of the questionnaire is to provide useful information to the financial consultant to estimate relevant parameters, including the coefficient of risk aversion. Below is a fictional example of a questionnaire:

1. What is your current age?
   a) 65 or older.
   b) 40 to 64.
   c) Under 40.
2. When do you expect to need to withdraw cash from your investment portfolio?
   a) In less than 1 year.
   b) Within 1 to 5 years.
   c) Not for at least 10 years.

3. Over the next few years, what do you expect will happen to your income?
   a) It will probably decrease.
   b) It will probably stay the same.
   c) It will probably increase.
4. What percentage of your gross annual income have you been able to save in recent years?
   a) None.
   b) 1% to 10%.
   c) More than 10%.
5. What are your return expectations for your portfolio?
   a) I don't care if my portfolio keeps pace with inflation; I just want to preserve my capital.
   b) My return should be slightly more than inflation, with only moderate volatility.
   c) My return should significantly exceed inflation, even if this could mean significant volatility.
6. Suppose you had €10,000 to invest and the choice of five different asset with a range of possible outcomes after a single year. Which of the following portfolios would you feel most comfortable investing in?
   a) A, which could have a balance ranging from €9,700 to €10,300 at the end of the year.
   b) Portfolio C, which could have a balance ranging from €9,000 to €11,000 at the end of the year.
   c) Portfolio E, which could have a balance ranging from €7,000 to €13,000 at the end of the year.
7. If the value of your investment portfolio dropped by 20% in one year, what would you do[2]?
   a) Move my money to more conservative investments immediately to reduce the potential for future losses.
   b) Monitor the situation, and if it looks like things could continue to deteriorate, move some of my money to more conservative investments.
   c) Consider investing more because prices are so low.
8. Do you know financial derivatives?
   a) No, I have never used them.
   b) Yes, I have theoretical knowledge of their pricing and uses.
   c) yes, I have used financial derivatives a few time in my investment life.

Scoring: give the following points for each answer: a = 1, b = 2, c = 3.

[2] In a live experiment, a similar question was asked to me and to ChatGPT to compare the answers. You can find the video (my answer can be found after one hour thirty-one minutes) at https://vimeo.com/951133880/a25984ac4d?share=copy.

The questionnaire aims at scoring a total number that is directly proportional to the risk that can be taken by the investor. However, what emerges from the questions is that there are several alternative dimensions that are surveyed, which may plausibly contribute to signaling an investor who may have more capacity to tolerate risk and wealth fluctuations but not necessarily have to do with risk aversion. The saving rate and income expectations may be key to understanding the time horizon of the investor and her capacity to absorb a negative financial shock (for example due to a stock market crash) but may not be directly related to risk aversion. The final result is unclear. Sometimes the risk aversion estimation error is not inconsistent with the desired outcome. For example, if the questionnaire identifies a low risk tolerance, then the result is consistent with high risk aversion and a prudential portfolio which may be optimal due to short-term liabilities. In other cases this may not happen. For example, past use of financial derivatives would raise the overall risk acceptance estimation and may induce the advisor to suggest larger exposure to risk when this is not warranted by short-term liabilities. Chapters 6 and 8 describe methods to hedge liabilities and their use may be very useful to investors, particularly those who are not sure about their real capacity to absorb risk.

3.5.2 Psychology, neuroscience and risk aversion

Psychology has important implications not only for the general description of individuals' behavior, but also for the estimation of the risk aversion coefficient. In fact, studies show that the adoption of risky behaviors depends on motivational factors, which in turn are influenced by personality, individual history, and social events, and is expressed differently in various contexts: the same person can make different decisions in the face of risky situations in the financial, health, and recreational fields. Psychology has developed several personality tests from which one can deduce information about risk aversion.

DOSPERT (domain-specific risk-taking; see Weber, Blais, and Betz, 2002) is a psychometric scale that assesses risk-taking orientation in five different dimensions: financial (divided into investments and gambling), health/safety, leisure, ethical/moral, and social. For each area, hypothetical situations are reported (there are a total of thirty questions) through which it is possible to detect the attitude to risk and the perception of the same. For example, the ethical/moral domain includes questions related to the willingness to make deductions that are not entirely clear in one's tax return or to appropriate the work actually done by others. The original version includes three measurements for each dimension: how likely it is that the individual is in the specific situation described (risk-taking), how much is perceived as risky (risk perceptions), and what the perceived benefits are (expected benefits). Blais and Weber (2006), using DOSPERT, show that the variation in risk appetite between domains for each participant is seven times the variability in mean risk appetite between individuals. Markiewicz and Weber (2013) focus on the financial dimension, differentiated between investment and gambling, and show the existence of a positive association between risk appetite in gambling and financial behavior measured on the basis of the number of transactions and the frequency of the same in the day.

In addition, personality tests are used, with the aim of drawing up a non-clinical character profile of the subjects analyzed. The attitude to risk is in fact considered a personality trait that must be evaluated and crossed with others, for example extroversion, anxiety, impulsivity, optimism, and so on. Durand, Newby, and Sanghani (2008) study the association between the investment decisions and portfolio performance of twenty-one investors and their psychological characteristics through two tests:

- the "Big Five" test, which analyzes five personality traits: extraversion, open-mindedness, agreeableness, emotional stability, and conscientiousness, on a scale of 1 to 5;
- the Jackson Personality Inventory, comprising five macro-areas (analytical skills, emotionality, extroversion, opportunism, reliability) in turn broken down into fifteen dimensions, including complexity, anxiety, innovation, and risk appetite, with a choice between true and false.

The results indicate that extroversion, innovation, and risk-taking are linked to various investment choices and modes. These findings were confirmed in a follow-up study by Durand, Newby, Peggs, and Siekierka (2013) using a sample of 115 subjects.

Neuropsychology, an emerging field in psychology, examines the relation between the brain and behavior relying on brain imaging techniques such as functional magnetic resonance imaging (fMRI), which is useful to monitor brain activity while performing some tasks.[3] Camerer, Cohen, Fehr, Glimcher and Laibson (2016, p. 153) define neuropsychology as "the study of the biological microfoundations of economic cognition and economic behavior. Biological microfoundations are neurochemical mechanisms and pathways, like brain regions, neurons, genes, and neurotransmitters. Economic cognition includes memory, preferences, emotions, mental representations, expectations, anticipation, learning, perception, information processing, inference, simulation, valuation, and the subjective experience of reward. In general, neuroeconomic research seeks to identify and test biologically microfounded models that link cognitive building blocks to economic behavior." Neuropsychologists are slowly finding patters of brain activity that are related to risky choices. Camerer, Cohen, Fehr, Glimcher and Laibson (2016, p. 177) note that "one clear finding is that risk and reward are reliably encoded in insula (risk) and striatum and medial OFC (reward). Since insula is activated by many felt emotions, this finding supports the hypothesis of risk as feelings". Barretto Garcia, de Hollander, Grueschow, Polania, Woodford and Ruff (2023, p. 1551) go a step further and ask why individuals are het-

[3] Damasio (2003, page 7) offers an early and interesting view on the use of fMRI for understanding human behavior: "[T]he investigation of how thoughts trigger emotions and of how bodily emotions become … feelings provides a privileged view into mind and body … explaining the biology of feelings and their closely related emotions is likely to contribute to the effective treatment of some major causes of human suffering, among them depression, pain, and drug addiction."

erogeneous in risk aversion. They claim that "noisy logarithmic coding of numerical magnitudes can lead individuals to underestimate the size of larger monetary payoffs, leading to apparent risk aversion even when subjective valuation increases linearly with the estimated amount … individual patterns of economic behavior may, at least partially, be determined by capacity limitations in perceptual processing rather than by processes that assign subjective values to monetary rewards …. this offers the intriguing possibility that from a neurocognitive perspective, individual differences in financial decision making may originate from biased perception originating in properties of parietal magnitude processing, rather than from subjective valuation processes instantiated in prefrontal and subcortical brain areas." Capacity-restricted internal representations of the risky choice and biases in the initial perception of the choice options may be responsible for what we call risk aversion and for financial choices, as already suggested in the "imprecise perception" literature see Woodford (2020). The idea that individuals are different in terms of brain activity suggests that financial behavior may be explained by exogenous brain features. See Dennison, Sazhin, and Smith (2022) for a more recent survey.

Summary

- Risk is different from uncertainty. The latter implies we do not know the probabilities of the various outcomes. A fair coin toss is an example of risk, while an unfair coin toss is an example of uncertainty. Financial markets are typically characterized by risk except when a large shock hits the economic system and the situation is characterized by uncertainty.
- The utility function may be used to define preferences over risky situations. A risk-averse individual voluntarily participates in a risky game with various outcomes described in various scenarios only if the expected value is positive. To voluntarily participate in a risky game when you are risk-averse requires a risk reward.
- Computations and examples are much easier when the utility function is simplified to the mean/variance utility function where $u = Er - 0.5 \times A \times \sigma^2$.
- The certain equivalent is the value of the interest rate that would make the investor indifferent between buying the risky security and buying the risk-free one. A risk-averse investor holds a risky security only if the certain equivalent is higher than the risk-free rate.
- The indifference curve comprises the pairs of expected return and volatility that ensure a given level of utility. To find it, you need to determine a utility level and look for all the combinations of mean and variance that guarantee that utility.
- The indifference curve is positively sloping (and convex) in the average volatility space when risk aversion is positive. It is flat when risk aversion is zero and is negatively sloped (and concave) when risk aversion is negative.
- The spread between the expected return of the risky security and the risk-free rate is the risk premium.
- The utility function can be defined on the performance of the security or portfolio, or on the level of consumption, that is, in general, $u(C)$. When the utility function is concave in consumption (or return) then the risk-averse behavior of an individual is described.

- Regulation requires financial intermediaries who help individual investors make portfolio choices to gather empirical evidence on risk aversion to select a portfolio consistent with the desired expected return/risk trade-off.
- Measuring attitudes toward risk is currently a very difficult enterprise. Psychologists have been discussing the possibility of measuring risk aversion in the context of personality tests. Recent advances in neuropsychology are investigating the physiological foundations of behavior in risky situations.

Problems

1 Consider four alternative investments characterized by:

Investment	Expected return	Variance
1	0.05	0.03
2	0.10	0.045
3	0.12	0.06
4	0.15	0.10

for an investor with a risk aversion coefficient of 4 and determine the preferred investment.

2 How does the previous choice change for investors with A = 2?

3 A stock has an expected return of 5% and a standard deviation of 18%. The risk-free rate is 2%. What is the maximum value of the risk aversion coefficient A such that the risky security is preferred to the risk-free security?

4 Determine the indifference curve when A = 3 for a utility level of 0.05.

5 Repeat the previous exercise for A = 4 and u = 4%.

6 Repeat the previous exercise for A = 0.

7 Repeat the previous exercise for A = –3.

8 An individual has a logarithmic utility function. What is the maximum price she would pay to acquire a bet that pays €100 or €300 with the same probability?

Answers

1 Using the utility function $Er - 0.5 \times A \times \sigma^2$ and substituting the values given in the table we find the following values respectively: –0.01, 0.01, 0.0, –0.05. The preferred investment is the second one.

2 Following the same methodology, we find in the case A = 2 respectively 0.02, 0.055, 0.06, 0.05, so the best investment is now the third one. A lower level of risk

aversion induces the investor to assign a lower weight to the variance and to prefer an alternative with larger expected return and risk.

3 The risky security is preferred to the risk-free one, for a generic value of risk aversion A, if $0.05 - 0.5 \times A \times 0.18^2 > 0.02$. This implies that the maximum value of the risk aversion coefficient is equal to 1.85.

4 You have to use the equation $Er = 0.05 + 0.5 \times 3 \times \sigma^2$ to find:

Volatility	0.05	0.075	0.1	0.125	0.15	0.175
Expected return	0.05375	0.058438	0.065	0.073438	0.08375	0.095938

5 You have to use the equation $Er = 0.04 + 0.5 \times 4 \times \sigma^2$ to find:

Volatility	0.05	0.075	0.1	0.125	0.15	0.175
Expected return	0.045	0.05125	0.06	0.07125	0.085	0.10125

6 In the case A = 0 the subject is risk-neutral and therefore is not harmed by an increase in volatility. The indifference curve is flat at the 4% level.

7 In this case, the individual appreciates the increase in volatility. In order to maintain it at the same level of total utility, it is now necessary to decrease the expected return:

Volatility	0.05	0.075	0.1	0.125	0.15	0.175
Expected return	0.03625	0.031563	0.025	0.016563	0.00625	-0.00594

8 The answer is found by setting the log of the price, measuring the utility cost of buying the ticket equal to the expected utility, in this case $\ln(P) = 0.5 \times \ln(100) + 0.5 \times \ln(300)$, which provides

$$\exp(0.5 \times \ln(100) + 0.5 \times \ln(300)) = €173.20,$$

less than the expected value of €200.

4 Behavioral finance

4.1 Introduction

Neoclassical economics assumes that decisions are always rational. A rational rule describes the best decision to make given a certain set of inputs. With the same input, the decision is always the same. Do you agree with such an assumption? Or do you think that individuals make decisions that can be influenced by other elements that are not perfectly rational?

Behavioral finance describes the behavior of individuals who can make mistakes, attributable to misuse of available data and/or real behavioral distortions. Behavioral finance encompasses both theoretical analyses, which illustrate alternative models to those based on pure rationality and include, for example, the description of heuristics (simplified models that can be used to deal with complex situations) and the mix of "slow and fast thinking", and empirical analyses illustrating the portfolios and investment styles used by individual investors. These empirical analyses illustrate typical mistakes in financial asset management, such as too much trading, using the wrong information, and not enough diversification, and document the sometimes large wealth losses for investors who suffer from cognitive and/or emotional biases.

Can something be done to help investors use financial investment in a way that may produce better risk-adjusted returns? There are many potential solutions, ranging from regulation to nudging. Regulation prevents retail investors from pursuing some very risky investments, albeit without a clear and coherent framework: Retail investors cannot invest in hedge funds but can overinvest in meme stocks. Moreover, regulation monitors corporations and financial intermediaries and helps diffuse symmetric information conditions among market participants. Nudging is more respectful of individual choice, which, according to some thinkers, should involve the freedom to make mistakes. Nudging experts help policymakers design policies and affect behavior in such a way to produce socially efficient outcomes. Financial education is a key tool in the effort to help people use financial markets in the best way. Financial education is the ultimate tool to democratize finance.

4.2 Behavioral finance

Behavioral finance is a development of behavioral economics. It is hard to find a universal definition of behavioral economics but a very useful one has been provided by Thaler (2016, p. 1577), referring to a "psychologically realistic depiction of the representative agent" that does not substitute the neoclassical rationality paradigm, which should be augmented "with additional descriptive theories that are derived from data rather than axioms." In one of the founding papers of behavioral economics, Simon (1955, p. 99) suggested that to make economic models more useful "the task is to replace the global rationality of economic man with a kind of rational behavior that is compatible with the access to information and the computational capacities that are actually possessed by organisms, including man, in the kind of environments in which such organisms exist." Thaler (2016, p. 1577) echoes that "the behavioral approach offers the opportunity to develop better models of economic behavior by incorporating insights from other social science disciplines." Interestingly, Wundt (1832–1920) established psychology as an experimental science that was separate from philosophy, but it took almost a century (see Watson, 1919) to define psychology as the objective study of behavior and the stimuli that produce such behavior (see Martin, Carlson, and Buskist, 2013).

Box 4.1 Does the expected utility model work?

Question: Which experiment do you choose?

Experiment 1: Do you prefer: (A) a 61% chance of winning €520,000, (B) a 63% chance of winning €500,000?

Experiment 2: Do you prefer: (A) a 98% chance of winning €520,000, (B) a 100% chance of winning €500,000?

Answer: Evidence against the expected utility model goes back to the 1950s. Interestingly, the same theorists who created the expected utility paradigm showed preferences that were inconsistent with their model. Experiments 1 and 2 are associated with the "Allais paradox" (see Kahneman, 2011), named after the French economist who in 1952 submitted in a congress to various theorists (and future Nobel Prize winners for Economics) the choice between possibilities (A) and (B) in the two experiments. In most cases those present chose (A) in experiment 1 and (B) in 2, even if this choice violates the principle of expected utility. If (A) is preferred to (B) in experiment 1, the same choice should be made in experiment 2. In Experiment 1 alternative (A) should be preferred if $0.61 \times u(520{,}000) > 0.63 \times u(500{,}000)$. Now add the same quantity to both sides to get $0.61 \times u(520{,}000) + 0.37 \times u(500{,}000) > 0.63 \times u(500{,}000) + 0.37 \times u(500{,}000)$. The quantity on the right-hand side of the last inequality is $u(500{,}000)$ corresponding to payoff (B) in experiment 2. On the other hand, payoff (A) in experiment 2 is preferred to $0.61 \times u(520{,}000) + 0.37 \times u(500{,}000)$ because payoff (A) is $0.61 \times u(520{,}000) + 0.37 \times u(520{,}000)$. Therefore consistency would suggest that $0.98 \times u(520{,}000) > 0.61 \times u(520{,}000) + 0.37 \times u(500{,}000) > u(500{,}000)$. So if (A) is preferred to (B) in experiment 1 the same should happen in experiment 2, contrary to observations. The interpretation is that people overweight outcomes that are certain, giving rise to a "certainty effect." If the monetary sums in the previous experiments were negative rather than positive (for example, losing €500,000 rather than gaining €500,000), preferences would switch and loss aversion would prevail.

In the 1980s, some economists began to ponder how to overcome the classical paradigm of economics and finance in which decisions are made by rational, emotionless agents who maximize utility or profit functions subject to resource constraints. Kahneman (2011, p. 411), one of the fathers of behavioral finance, stresses the specific meaning of the word "rational," as opposed to "reasonable," in economics and finance: "[T]he only test of rationality is not whether a person's beliefs and preferences are reasonable, but whether they are internally consistent."

The methodology of science suggests that a model should be judged based on its predictions rather than its assumptions. The assumption of rational agents is potentially extremely helpful in interpreting economic agents' decisions as drivers of actions that are made in the personal self-interest, without recurring to a patchwork of ad hoc explanations. Potentially, even though nobody believes that people choose financial portfolios on the basis of utility maximization, the model may be very useful to interpret the empirical evidence about portfolio choice. Unfortunately, empirical results regarding both individual portfolio choices and market prices are hard to interpret using the full rationality model.

Robert Shiller and Richard Thaler, Nobel Prize winners in 2013 and 2017, were among the architects of "behavioral finance," which borrowed many concepts from psychology, also thanks to scholars such as Kahneman who worked on the border of the two disciplines.

Kahneman (2011, p. 411) argues that the rational model is so hard to implement, requiring full information and full understanding of the consequences of all possible choices, that "reasonable people cannot be rational by that definition." Barberis (2018) argues that behavioral finance has sought to improve the realism of the description of behavior from a psychological point of view, considering (a) belief-forming processes based on investors' limited ability to calculate probabilities, (b) preferences that deviate from the paradigm of expected utility, for example because gains and losses are weighed asymmetrically, and (c) cognitive limitations.

Economists who have worked in the field of behavioral finance have dealt with theoretical and empirical analyses. The theoretical analyses that are closer to the typical models used by economists try to interpret, by means of mathematical models, empirical aspects such as the predictability of sectors/equity portfolios, interpreting predictability as the result of "overreaction" or "underreaction" to certain news, or the determination of stock prices and returns. Theoretical analyses produced by psychologists deviate more fundamentally from the typical economists' approach and start from a model of the way the human mind works.

Empirical analyses have studied investors' behaviors and financial results, highlighting various situations of sub-optimal use of financial markets, for example in terms of inefficient portfolios, and, consequently, have measured the opportunity cost of utility maximization deviation in terms of lower expected return and/or greater risk compared with the case in which investors behave in a way that avoids major mistakes.

One of the criticisms initially leveled at behavioral finance (see, e.g., Fama, 1998) concerned the excessive freedom open to economists to describe individual behavior, as one can deviate from rationality (understood as expected utility maximization) in many different forms. This is the point we made earlier on: The utility model provides discipline in our interpretation of the data that otherwise can be interpreted ad hoc in a variety of unrelated frameworks. Of course, what is the right framework and what is the meaning of the word "discipline" is partially subjective: Twenty years after Fama, Barberis (2018) claims that behavioral models have maintained a discipline that has been characterized by a focus on elements such as extrapolation,[1] overconfidence, and the asymmetry of the utility of financial losses and gains.

4.3 Examples of behavioral finance theories

In this section we describe some theoretical elements on which various models of behavioral finance are built. The field is very broad, and we limit ourselves to three topics. The first is a general hypothesis related to the functioning of the human mind according to which there are two systems interacting in our brain, requiring different amounts of mental resources. We use a combination of the two systems for making judgments and decisions and this may create judgmental errors. The two-system model may also be used to better understand rules of thumb (heuristics) that we use in our everyday life, which is our second focus. In the third focus we present one of the very early examples of the use of behavioral finance to understand relevant financial issues, in this case the tendency of investors to hold losing stocks too long in their portfolios.

4.3.1 Thinking, fast and slow

Kahneman (2011) proposes a description of individuals' decisions as the result of the interaction between two systems, the fast system (System 1), operating quickly and automatically, and the slow system (System 2), allocating mental resources to the tasks to be done at a certain time and requiring attention and concentration. System 1 is thought to operate constantly, while System 2 is assumed to only intervene when necessary, for example in very complex situations and in cases where the potential cost of error is very high. System 2 is tiring to use (ego depletion) and must be used sparingly. Economics teaches that when resources are scarce, they must be allocated where the benefit outweighs the cost.

System 1 is very often based on the association of memories and images, activates automatic systems, and prefers simple and reassuring explanations, even obtained on the basis of a few data or a few impressions. This leads individuals to dwell on the first impression and believe that the available evidence is sufficient to deal with a certain situation. Typically, the two systems work together, and System 2 is only activated when System 1 cannot handle a situation. One of System 2's functions

[1] It is ironic that in 2018 some scholars claimed that new models of finance should use extrapolative mechanisms to better understand individuals' choices. Fifty-seven years earlier, Muth (1961) had initiated the revolution of rational expectations precisely by criticizing the prevailing models at the time, which often used the assumption that individuals used extrapolative mechanisms to make predictions.

is to monitor what System 1 suggests and interfere when it thinks actions are wrong, but this only happens if the stakes are high enough. Sometimes System 1 deceives System 2 by creating illusions. System 1 performance can improve based on a long experience of situations, which make someone become an "expert" in a field who is able to decide quickly, typically in the right way, on a new case.

An important implication in the field of financial choice concerns the interpretation of phenomena: System 1 often uses the causality hypothesis, sometimes in a hasty and incorrect way. If there was adequate statistical knowledge, System 2 could intervene to correct the interpretations given by System 1, even though there may be cases where System 2 is too lazy and/or the cost of error is low. Kahneman and Tversky refer to heuristics to discuss reasoning schemes used by individuals. The use of heuristics is due to the activation of System 1, and a more intensive use of System 2 could prevent the use of heuristics from leading us astray.

4.3.2 Heuristics (rules of thumb)

Martin, Carlson and Buskist (2013, page 428) define heuristics as "cognitive shortcuts or inferential rules" and note that "when there are no algorithms to follow, we must follow a heuristic to guide our search for a path to the solution." Heuristics are a reasoning scheme that is based on association: If a problem is too difficult to solve, a simpler one is solved by trying to find an answer that also applies to the first one. Therefore, heuristics is a rule of thumb used by individuals for making decisions in a complex and uncertain environment, especially when time is limited. To some extent, heuristics are used when System 1 finds a specific problem too hard to solve. Psychology has illustrated the existence of many heuristics. Tversky and Kahneman (1974) emphasize "representativeness," "availability," and "anchoring," but there are relevant others such as mental accounting.

1. Representativeness: the tendency to calculate the probability of an event based on its superficial similarity to a phenomenon rather than on objective probabilities. If, for example, one must guess the profession of an individual who is described as shy and quiet and with a predisposition to help others, it is more likely that, in the absence of any other information, the inference is that the individual works in a library rather than as a lawyer. There is a tendency to use information about the character of the individual, ignoring the evidence that there are many more lawyers than library clerks in the United States. This heuristic describes the effort to match characteristics that we observe with schemas of different situations or groups of people. According to Barberis (2018), the use of such heuristics can explain the frequency of extrapolative expectation formation, for example when the expected return of an asset is considered high only because it has had historically high returns, ignoring the possibility that historical returns result only from a series of positive shocks that do not equate to a high expected return. This heuristic may explain why people sometimes substitute probability with plausibility:

In some cases, the probability of an event is evaluated based not on probabilistic rules but on the plausibility of a scenario resembling the one under examination; see as an example Box 4.2.

Box 4.2 Plausibility and probability

Question: Which event do you think is most likely next year:
(A) a flood in North America that will kill more than 1,000 people,
(B) an earthquake in California that will cause a flood in which more than 1,000 people will die.

Answer: Most responses consider scenario B to be more likely than scenario A, although a probabilistic analysis suggests that scenario A is the most likely, since the probability of a flood in the United States is, by definition, higher than the probability of a flood triggered by an earthquake in California.

2. Availability: the tendency to calculate the probability of an event based on the ease with which examples of that event can be remembered; for example, the probability of a heart attack in a middle-aged person is estimated based on examples that have occurred among one's acquaintances. Tversky and Kahneman ask people to say whether English words starting with "k" are more common than English words having "k" in the third position. Most people wrongly responded in a positive way. The reason is that thinking of words that start with a particular letter is easier than thinking of words that contain the letter in another position. People who tend to be guided by their System 1 are more likely to be affected by availability.

Box 4.3 Visual judgments

Question: Are the images in Figure 4.1 the same height?

Figure 4.1 **The height of the figures**

Are the images in Figure 4.2 the same size?

Figure 4.2 **The size of the tables**

Answer: The three figures are the same, although they appear different if no measurement tool is used, and the same is true for the tables. The experiments described in Box 4.3 are examples of availability heuristic-induced errors: The immediate perception is that the figures are different because the lines induce the use of reasoning schemes that refer to images in three dimensions, while the images are drawn in two dimensions. By measuring, you will be able to verify that they are the same.

3. Anchoring: the tendency to calculate the probability of an event from a prior event that acts as a reference anchor, without using available information to update the probability in a rational way. The prior event that serves as a reference point may or may not be objectively relevant to the evaluation.[2] An anchor is a number or an idea, perhaps objectively irrelevant, that affects the estimate of a quantity of interest to a person. Kahneman and Tversky showed the existence of this effect by rigging a wheel of fortune that was supposed to mark from 0 to 100, so that it would only stop at either 10 or 65. After spinning the wheel, they asked students their best guess about the percentage of African nations also being part of the United Nations. The average estimates of those who saw 10 from the wheel was 25, and the average estimate of those who saw 65 was 45. The number from the wheel was an (irrelevant) anchor for the answer. An experiment conducted by Bargh (2017) at Yale University showed that individuals are influenced in their behavior simply by hearing certain words. In the experiment, groups of young people were timed as they walked through a hallway after hearing words reminiscent of youth or old age. The results show that it takes longer to walk down the hallway if you have been exposed to words that remind you of old age. In other experiments, people who read money-related words are more independent and persistent than others, exert more effort to solve a problem, and are more selfish. One interpretation of the anchoring proposed by Kahneman (2011) relies on the

[2] The implications of such bias are extremely important for marketing and negotiation techniques when one of the two parties has the opportunity to "make a first offer" to initiate a bargain.

influence of System 1 in a situation where System 2 does not intervene due to the absence of a cost related to the choice of action. The potentially irrelevant signal is a priming effect evoking compatible evidence: System 1 believes the initial signal and actively selects compatible thoughts to create associative coherence, while System 2 elaborates examples that are easy to retrieve.

4. Mental accounting is another example of a heuristic, referring to the tendency to think in "silos," for example managing one's equity portfolio ignoring that in most cases this constitutes a small part of wealth that also includes many non-traded assets. People may use such heuristics to break complex financial decision-making into smaller, more manageable parts. Outcomes within an account are evaluated jointly, whereas outcomes in different accounts are evaluated separately. A classic example, mentioned by Thaler and Sunstein (2008), is when gamblers accumulate (or decumulate) money in a casino and separate the money, putting the amount that was brought from home in one pocket and the money that was won (called "house money") in the other, in such a way that they increase the probability that the worst case scenario at the end of the evening is to go home with the same amount of money. The house money effect seems to be at work during phases of huge stock market gains such as the 1920s in the United States, when more and more people took very risky bets using wealth they had just accumulated. Another example of mental accounting is when each stock in a portfolio is analyzed in a way that is disconnected from the overall performance of the portfolio and from the other stocks. The same can be extrapolated for wealth management in general: For most individuals, their own apartment makes up the largest portion of their total wealth, followed by bond investment, and many invest limited amounts in equity assets. Many of these individuals actively manage their stock portfolio as if it represented 100% of their assets, forgetting about their other assets. Mental accounting can be bad for financial decisions: For example, in market downturns such as that in 2020, many investors overreact to falling prices, trying to "protect" their assets and forgetting that due to the increase in the value of bonds and houses held in their portfolios, the total value of assets may have gone up instead of down at that stage.

4.3.3 Loss avoidance

4.3.3.1 *Prospect theory*

According to the expected utility theory, the level of utility associated with the wealth invested in a financial asset is an increasing function of the value of the asset. Tversky and Kahneman (1974) propose a variation of the expected utility model, using a value function that is concave or convex depending on whether the value of the financial asset has risen or fallen, as evident from Figure 4.4. The reference point (the origin of the axes) for the utility function is the status quo. Experimental evidence is consistent with the idea that people use reference points (see, e.g., Box 4.4). Kahneman (2011) interprets prospect theory as being the manifestation of System 1.

Box 4.4 Reference points

Question: Which experiment do you choose?

Experiment 1: In addition to what you own, you are given €1,000. Now you are asked to choose between one of the two: (A) Get €500 for sure, (B) 50% chance of winning €1,000.

Experiment 2: In addition to what you own, you are given €2,000. Now you are asked to choose between one of the two: (A) Lose €500 for sure, (B) 50% chance of losing €1,000

Answer: Most people in experiment 1 prefer to get €500 for sure, and in experiment 2 prefer to gamble.

Notice that in terms of final wealth the two experiments in Box 4.4 are the same, involving a choice between €1,500 for sure or a 50% probability of winning €2,000. However, if the initial gifts of €1,000 and €2,000 are the reference points, then in both cases you are averse to losing the initial gift.

The value function in Figure 4.4 is steeper for losses than for gains: To the right you gain, and to the left you lose. Such a value function is consistent with loss aversion, whereby losing something makes you more miserable than gaining the same makes you happy.

Figure 4.3 Kahneman and Tversky's value function

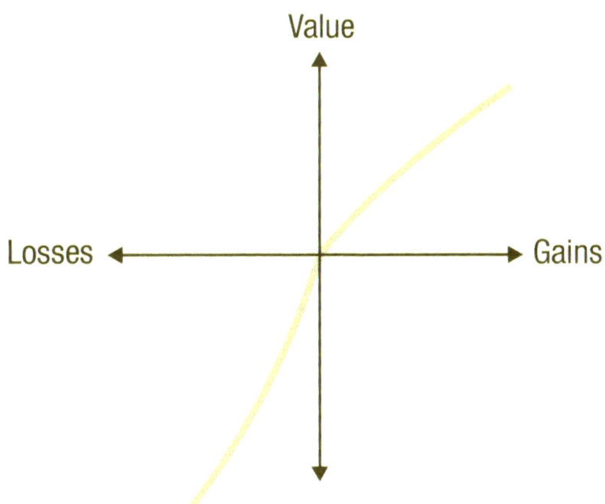

To better understand the theory, consider the experiments described in Box 4.5.

Box 4.5 Evaluating losses

Question: Which experiment do you choose?

Experiment 1: A disease is expected to kill 600 people. There are two alternative programs to cope with this: (A) Program A saves 200 people, (B) Program B has a 1/3 chance of saving 600 people and a 2/3 chance of saving no one. Which program is preferred?

Experiment 2: A disease is expected to kill 600 people. There are two alternative programs to deal with this: (A) Program A is associated with the death of 400 people, (B) Program B is associated with a 1/3 chance of saving everyone and a 2/3 chance of having 600 deaths. Which program is preferred?

Answer: Experiments 1 and 2 have the same consequences in the two alternatives, but most individuals choose (A) in experiment 1, preferring certainty over risk, and (B) in 2, preferring risk over certainty. Kahneman (2011) interprets this result in light of the theory just presented: Individuals are risk-averse when alternatives are presented in terms of gains, and they are risk-lovers when alternatives are presented in terms of losses.

Box 4.6 **The possibilities of investing with two stocks and leverage**

Question: Carola and Sara buy a stock market index at the beginning of 2023. Their utility function as of the beginning of 2024 is equal to:

$$u = Er - \frac{A}{2}Vr \text{ if } r(-1) \geq 0$$

$$u = Er + \frac{A}{2}Vr \text{ if } r(-1) \leq 0$$

where r(-1) is the rate of return of the stock market in 2023 and $A = 4$. Both women suffer from mental accounting, that is, they evaluate their stock portfolio independently of their wealth in their bank account with a remuneration equal to zero. They both agree that $Er = 5\%$, $Vr = 4\%$. If the decision at the beginning of 2024 is whether to maintain their investment in the stock market or put all their wealth in the bank account:

a. What are they going to do if the stock return in 2023 was equal to 10%?
b. What if the stock return in 2023 was equal to -10%?
c. How do you explain the different solutions?

Answer: If the 2023 return was positive they are risk-averse and, given their expected return and variance, they prefer to hold the risk-free asset, that is, they will sell the risky portfolio. The opposite happens if the 2023 return was negative. The different solutions are explained by the existence of mental accounting and their resistance to recognizing losses.

4.3.3.2 *The disposition effect*

Prospect theory may be useful to explain the disposition effect,[3] characterizing the tendency of investors to hold loss-making stocks in their portfolios for too long. Obviously, the difference between the purchase price and the market price is not an element that should be used to evaluate the composition of one's portfolio. Barber and Odean (2013) document that the probability of selling stocks up between 18% and 22% since purchased is 2.65 (1.77) times greater than the probability of selling stocks

[3] Shefrin and Statman (1985) also discuss the relevance of other behavioral biases to justify the disposition effect, in particular mental accounting, regret avoidance, and self-control, which will be discussed in the following sections.

that have experienced returns between -2% and 2% (-18%, -22%). Odean (1999) finds that investors realize their gains at about a 50% higher rate than their losses.

Shefrin and Statman (1985) note that a combination of mental accounting and prospect theory is consistent with such observations. Mental accounting implies that each stock is assigned to a different place and the investor does not evaluate the overall portfolio but separately looks at each component. In case a losing stock is considered, investors want to avoid the regret associated with recognizing a financial loss and avoid selling. In terms of risk aversion, we can say that when the value of the security rises, it is in the concave zone (risk aversion), and when it falls, it is in the convex zone (risk appetite). For an investor to the right of origin, there must be a risk premium for holding a risky security, a higher premium than the one that originally led to the purchase. If the expected return of the stock has not changed over time, it is easier for the investor to sell the stock. An investor who is on the left (who likes risky situations) holds the risky stock even if the expected return is negative. It is therefore more likely that the expected return that led the investor to buy it will be more than enough to continue to hold the stock in the portfolio even if its performance has been negative. The behavior is therefore consistent with "loss aversion," that is, the loss is avoided.

4.3.3.3 *The endowment effect and the status quo bias*

Prospect theory may explain other observed behaviors. Kahneman, Knetsch, and Thaler (1991) clarify this with a simple example: A person purchased some nice Bordeaux wines years ago at $10 a bottle, considerably less than the current price of $200. This person drinks some of the wine occasionally but would not be willing to either sell the wine at the market price or to buy an additional bottle at that price. Thaler (1980) called this pattern—the fact that people often demand much more to give up an object than they would be willing to pay to acquire it—the endowment effect. The endowment effect describes a circumstance in which an individual places a higher value on an object that they already own than the value they would place on that same object if they did not own it. This feeling is entirely consistent with the asymmetric value function as described in prospect theory.

Samuelson and Zeckhauser (1988) consider a preference for the current state that biases the person against both buying and selling her wine. The status quo bias is a tendency for people to stick with the current situation, either because they find comfort in what they have done and which has not caused any problems, or because they lack sufficient attention due to the stakes not being high enough to require activation of System 2.

An important implication for financial choices is that any "default option" will attract a lot of selection. The status quo bias has been documented in several situations, such as selecting a pension plan, portfolio holdings of households, stock picking, and mutual funds. In an experimental study, Samuelson and Zeckhauser (1988) find that the extent to which individuals are subject to a status quo bias positively depends on the number of alternatives they have to choose from.

Box 4.7 The possibilities of investing with two stocks and leverage

Question: Two sisters, Carola and Sara, have identical risk aversion coefficient A=2.5 and they originally hold two identical portfolios, each worth €100,000, characterized by volatility equal to 10% and an expected return equal to 2.5%. The risk-free rate is zero. We assume that their total utility is equal to their wealth multiplied by the mean/variance function, that is, $u(W) = W \times \left(1 + Er - \frac{A}{2}Vr\right)$. Their parents have an equally balanced portfolio of stocks and bonds. After their deaths, they leave Carola the bond portion of their portfolio and Sara the equity portion. Each portion is worth €100,000. The testament forces both daughters to maintain the new overall portfolios for five years. As a result, the Carola's new portfolio has 5% volatility and a 1.25% expected return, while Sara's has 15% volatility and 3.75% expected return.

a) What would Sara and Carola do without any constraints about portfolio reallocation?
b) What would behavioral finance suggest Sara and Carola will do at the end of the five years if they suffer from an extreme form of endowment effect/status quo?

Answer:

a. The bequest displaces both from the initial allocation and decreases their utility: We know that because otherwise they would have chosen a different portfolio than the one originally selected. If they had no constraints, they would change the asset allocation to return to the initial expected return and volatility. Their total utility was originally equal to $100{,}000 \times \left(1 + 0.025 - \frac{2.5}{2} \times 0.1^2\right) = 100{,}000 \times (1.0125) = 101{,}250$. The new total utility enjoyed by Carola is equal to $200{,}000 \times \left(1 + 0.0125 - \frac{2.5}{2} \times 0.05^2\right) = 200{,}000 \times 1.009375 = 201{,}875$ and the new total utility enjoyed by Sara is $200{,}000 \times \left(1 + 0.0375 - \frac{2.5}{2} \times 0.15^2\right) = 200{,}000 \times 1.009375 = 201{,}875$. Their new total utility is higher due to the larger amount of wealth, but lower than the same amount of wealth invested with the original asset allocation, equal to $200{,}000 \times 1{,}0125 = 202{,}500$
b. After five years the two sisters could get used to the new status quo and be subject to an endowment effect. They could decide to maintain the new allocation. Carola could potentially be unwilling to give up the low volatility situation, and Sara could potentially be unwilling to give up the high expected return associated with the new allocation. As a result, their total utility would remain higher because of the extra wealth, but lower than the total utility they would get with the original asset allocation.

4.4 Human behavior and undesirable outcomes

The endowment bias is an example of behavior where psychological factors induce the person to hold onto an asset rather than sell it for a high price, but at the same time she would not buy it for the same price. This is an example of inconsistency: The self when owning the bottle is different from the self when owning cash. *De gustibus non est disputandum*. The status quo bias, explained by the same self-inconsistency, is an example of a potential error if the individual selects a sub-optimal portfolio in order to maintain an inefficient status quo. This introduces the possibility that people do not act in their own interest. Why can people behave sub-optimally? The possible reasons are the following:

a) People do not think hard enough (cognitive bias). Kahneman (2011) has shown that the use of System 1 and System 2 may induce behavior leading to sub-optimal outcomes, which can probably be improved with the right incentives and knowledge (which would allow System 1 to be activated in the best way).
b) People are affected by elements different from money (emotional biases). An individual may trade frequently in the stock market because she is overconfident and believes she has superior stock picking abilities.

Attributing biases to the cognitive or the emotional sphere is somewhat arbitrary: Is overconfidence the result of an individual attribute or instead the result of one's inability to collect data on the results of one's actions and learn? Particularly in financial investments, where the monetary consequences of mistakes are often large, we would assume that people have enough incentives to look at all available evidence and avoid all errors except those that are intrinsically related to behavioral traits. Recent advances in neuropsychology, discussed at the end of Chapter 3, make this question more fascinating than ever.

4.4.1 Behavioral biases

4.4.1.1 *Misusing statistics*

Psychologists argue that our minds do not use statistics in a natural way and instead prefer simple deterministic reasoning of cause and effect. Kahneman (2011) explores reasons why it is difficult for us to think statistically. For example, the law of small numbers describes our inability to make statistical inferences and our belief that few data can signal patterns of general validity. This is the false assumption that the law of large numbers extends to small samples, induced by our tendency to exaggerate the coherence of what we see. The search for causal explanations typical of human beings becomes dangerous under these conditions because they try to justify by intuitive reasoning facts that are not really expressions of a precise model. An example reported by Kahneman (2011) concerns the performance of schools in national rankings, where smaller schools often end up in both first and last place. Small schools, however, are not necessarily the best, but they are more likely to end up at the extreme points of the ranking for random reasons. Barberis (2018) believes that the tendency to use extrapolative expectations is the result of applying a heuristic according to which one looks to history to predict the future. Such extrapolation may arise out of the belief that the law of small numbers applies to the most recent sample of data, so that it is possible to understand the parameters of the data-generation model using a sample size that is too small for statistical analysis.

Another example of misuse of statistics is the misunderstanding of mean reversion (see Box 4.8).[4]

Box 4.8 Understanding mean reversion

Kahneman (2011): Consider the sales (in millions of euros) of the following four stores of a supermarket in 2018, similar in size and breadth of the offer, and make the forecast for 2019 knowing the total:

Retail outlet	2018	2019
1	11	
2	23	
3	18	
4	29	
Total	81	89.1

Many individuals fill in the table applying the same percentage increase (10%) to all stores. In this way, they ignore the role of random factors in determining the data available to us. Sales in 2018 were driven by factors not covered in the table, such as location, and other factors that are beyond our understanding or are not predictable or measurable, for example changes in the tastes of consumers who come to each store. Statistics therefore suggest that the forecasts of the four stores must take into account the role played by unknown elements ("luck" and "bad luck") and that it is rational to hypothesize a phenomenon of "return to the average," predicting sales that grow less (more) for those units that had the best (worst) performance in 2018.

System 1 may be responsible for the law of small numbers: It eliminates doubt by suppressing ambiguity and automatically constructing coherent stories that help us to explain our observations. As a result, System 1 is prone to jumping to conclusions and constructing a vision of reality that is coherent and believable. Humans are pattern seekers and look for meaning in their observations. People do not expect to observe regular patterns from a random process and when they do see a potential correlation, they are too quick to reject the assumption that the process is entirely random. Overall, Kahneman believes people are prone to exaggerating the consistency and meaning of what they see. A tendency toward causal thinking also leads people to sometimes see a relationship when there is not one.

[4] The idea of mean reversion is also associated with the general idea of linear regression that may be unintuitive to the human brain. Kahneman (2011) notes that linear regression, presented for the first time on February 9, 1877, by Francis Galton, was discovered two hundred years after the theory of gravity and differential calculus. Some of the topics discussed in the following chapters, for example the future returns of stocks or the possibility of predicting the trend of the entire market, can be associated with the existence of a return to the mean.

4.4.1.2 *Learning what we don't know or confirming what we think we know?*

When forming impressions and accumulating information for making decisions, are we trying to objectively learn and use a methodology that is reminiscent of the scientific approach, which is trying to show that hypotheses are wrong if data are inconsistent with them, or are we going the other way round and trying to find data consistent with our hypotheses? The confirmation bias and the halo effect are consistent with the latter rather than the former.

The confirmation bias is a tendency to pay more attention to information that is consistent with our initial assumptions and to ignore inconsistent evidence. This is often associated with the use of System 1 and with exaggerating the probability of rare events. Instead of objectively finding positive and negative information, we prioritize the information that we believe is the most correct. A behavior consistent with this bias is defined by Sharot (2017) as "Google is always on my side": When we search for information on Google we do not get objective results, for several reasons: first, companies buy the spaces that can give them more visibility, second, the algorithm is adaptive to our past search and behavior, and third we ourselves try to eliminate the information that is not consistent with our prior beliefs.

Human beings are not made to react rationally to information. Information can make us less sensitive to data because we have become accustomed to finding support for whatever we want to believe. Our desires shape our beliefs. Sharot (2017) makes the hypothesis that those with stronger analytical skills are likely to use their intelligence not to draw more precise conclusions but to find more flaws in the data that don't satisfy them; for example, they give more weight to information that supports their previous investments and less to information that casts doubt on them. Several other biases may be interpreted as the result of not using available data in the best way. For example, Kahneman (2011, page 82) defines the halo effect as "the tendency to like (or dislike) everything about a person—including things you have not observed … it is one of the ways the representation of the world that System 1 generates is simpler and more coherent than the real thing." The halo effect leads us to be influenced by the first impression received, for example on the qualities of a certain individual. Good looks help to make a good impression on others, who are often inclined to give more consideration to what is said by a beautiful person regardless of the substance of his considerations. The halo bias has an explanation linked to the confirmation bias: In both cases a very simplified, and reassuring, description of reality is used, not giving due weight to new elements.

4.4.1.3 *Changing our mind to fit the data*

Our tendency to not use available data in the best way can go the other way round: Another way our mind can make sense of the world is by adjusting memories to fit new data. This effort is facilitated by our imperfect ability to reconstruct past states of knowledge. This produces the hindsight bias, that is, the tendency to think (ex post) that we have foreseen what has happened. For example, in 2009 we could convince ourselves that back in 2007 we "knew" that there would be a crisis in 2008. This can lead to thinking that we are able to make choices sooner and better than others and thinking that we are better able to predict the future, even when there is no such ability. This bias, which is extremely dangerous if it leads to the adoption of careless behavior, is explained by Kahneman (2011) using System 1's attempt to interpret the world in a simple and causal way, assigning ex post explanations even in the presence of a small number of elements that can support the beliefs that are formed.

4.4.2 Emotional biases

4.4.2.1 *Optimism and overconfidence*

Many people have a particular predisposition to optimism. According to Sharot (2011), this tendency to see "the glass half full" has a utilitarian explanation: The optimistic inclination protects us from accurately perceiving the pain and difficulties that the future holds for us and can defend us from seeing that the options in our lives are limited. As a result, stress and anxiety are reduced, health improves, and motivation to act is strengthened. The brain is organized in a way that allows optimistic beliefs to change the way we see and interact with the world, making optimism a self-fulfilling prophecy.

The brain is good at seeing what it wants, to the point that any misalignments from what you think are more easily identified when new information is positive, but when new information is unpleasant, the brain does not react as accurately. Experiments show that there is a correlation between moderate optimism and sensible decisions, while extreme optimism correlates with seemingly irrational decisions.

Overconfidence is the false belief that we are better than average at doing something. For example, everyone thinks they drive their car better than average, and active traders think they can manage their portfolio better than average. A certain amount of overconfidence can be helpful in facing the challenges that arise with optimism and determination, but an excessive level of confidence can be detrimental. Where does overconfidence come from? Kahneman (2011) hypothesizes that overconfidence is the result of the predominance of System 1 and the tendency to stop at WYSIATI (what you see is all there is). Overconfidence in one's own abilities can be due to errors in estimating probabilities, perhaps due to lack of a time series of data. After years of driving, we are not likely to objectively consider our track record of accidents and compare it to that of our peers (people of similar age and driving experience). If we looked at the data, we might find that we have had more accidents than the average driver. This is even more likely in the case of trading. Most investors do not really know their track record or they do not have enough knowledge to apply performance evaluation model (see Chapter 11) to their own historical returns. They could therefore remain with the impression of being better than average and reinforce the overconfidence that led them to start an active trading career.

4.4.2.2 *Self-control*

Self-control problems often arise in choices involving costs and benefits at two different points in time. One way to define self-control is the ability of our current self to control our future selves. Very often self-control problems are associated with dynamically inconsistent behavior, for example associated with engaging in physical exercise. Today we make a plan that we will start going to the gym the following week, but when the moment comes, the decision is procrastinated to the following week. Shefrin and Thaler (1988) propose the behavioral life-cycle (BLC) hypothesis, according to which people act as a result of a conflict between a "planner" who thinks about the long run and a "doer" who is more concerned about the current situation, a mechanism closely resembling the relevance of System 1 and System 2. The ability to self-control is potentially very relevant for our financial behavior, for example when it comes to savings.

According to some hypotheses, our ability to self-control is either inherited or developed very early in life: In Mischel, Shoda, and Rodriguez (1989), preschool children were presented with the simple marshmallow test, in which they could either eat a small snack right away or wait fifteen minutes and get a larger snack. Around 67% of the children in the original study failed to resist temptation and ate the small snack, indicating a lower level of self-control. The researchers followed the children in the original sample for more than five decades, tracking how the ability to exercise self-control at an early age was correlated with various life outcomes as the children grew into adults. The results were striking. Children who were successful in resisting temptation and delaying gratification were more successful in almost every outcome measured. They had higher SAT scores, educational attainment, sense of self-worth, and ability to cope with stress. Additionally, they were less likely to be addicted to drugs and had lower body mass index.

4.4.2.3 *Regret aversion bias*

According to the Cambridge Dictionary, regret is "a feeling of sadness about something sad or wrong or about a mistake that you have made, and a wish that it could have been different and better." Regret is a negative emotion, and when making choices we often balance the benefit of doing something with the cost of regretting that action in the future if things turn out to be bad.

Box 4.9 Being robbed by hitchhikers

Consider the following scenarios, from Kahneman (2011):

A. Mr. Brown almost never picks up hitchhikers. Yesterday he gave a man a ride and was robbed.
B. Mr. Smith frequently picks up hitchhikers. Yesterday he gave a man a ride and was robbed.

Question 1: Who of the two will experience the greater regret over the episode?
Question 2: Who will be criticized most severely by others?

Answer 1: 88% of respondents mention Mr. Brown.
Answer 2: 77% of respondents mention Mr. Smith.

The answers to the two questions in Box 4.9 illustrate the role of what we and society regard as "normality." Kahneman (2011, p. 347) notes that "regret and blame are both evoked by a comparison to a norm, but the relevant norms are different. The emotions experienced by Mr. Brown and Mr. Smith are dominated by what they usually do about hitchhikers. Taking a hitchhiker is an abnormal event for Mr. Brown, and most people therefore expect him to experience more intense regret. A judgmental observer, however, will compare both men to conventional norms of reasonable behavior and is likely to blame Mr. Smith for habitually taking unreasonable risks." Regret avoidance is a tendency to reduce remorse and therefore to make conventional choices, since experiments show that people feel more remorse when mistakes are the result of more original choices. Keynes (1936, page 158) himself suggested that "worldly wisdom teaches us that it is better for reputation to fail conventionally than to succeed unconventionally." His statement is consistent with the asymmetric value function in prospect theory: A negative payoff when a failure follows conventional inaction, and a smaller positive payoff when a success follows unconventional action, may push people to stick to the status quo.

Box 4.10 Explaining regret

Question 1 From Kahneman (2011): consider the following situations:

Situation 1: Paul owns shares in company A. During the past year he considered switching to stock in company B, but he decided against it. He now learns that he would have been better off by €1,200 if he had switched to B.

Situation 2: George owned shares in company B. During the past year he switched to company A. He now learns that he would have been better off by €1,200 if he had kept his stock in company B.

Who feels greater regret? How do you explain this answer?

Answer: Eight percent of respondents say Paul, 92% say George. The portfolios of Paul and George are identical. The only difference is George acted whereas Paul failed to act. This exercise shows that regret is magnified by past actions: When the same situation is associated with inaction, regret is likely to be less.

4.4.2.4 *Framing bias*

Kahneman (2011) describes framing as an unjustified influence of problem formulation on beliefs and preferences, using as an example the gambles in Box 4.11. The framing bias arises when individuals make decisions based on how an issue is presented rather than on the facts presented. The increasing attention that our society gives to presenting materials, for example, through well-crafted PowerPoint presentations magnifies the relevance of such bias.

Box 4.11 Comparing gambles

Question: Consider the following gambles, from Kahneman (2011):

A. Would you accept a gamble that offers a 10% chance to win $95 and a 90% chance to lose $5?
B. Would you pay $5 to participate in a lottery that offers a 10% chance to win $100 and a 90% chance to win nothing?

Answer: A little thinking reveals the two gambles are the same in terms of wealth: The expected value of (A) is 9.5 -4.5 = 5, and the expected value of (B) is -5 + 10 = 5. In both cases you have a 10% probability of being richer by $95 and a 90% chance of losing $5. However, subjects are more likely to prefer (B) rather than (A). The explanation has to do with framing. In (A) attention is captured by the loss, whereas in (B) the bad outcome is framed in terms of the cost of a lottery. Losses evoke stronger negative feelings than costs.

A non-financial example is the reaction to a doctor's judgment that you need heart surgery. Most people feel better when being told that the probability of survival is 90% than when they are told that the probability of death is 10%: The result is the same, but the frame differs, and the patient's decision may potentially be affected by the presentation. While in the case of surgery people have all incentives to use System 2 and go beyond the framing effect, in other cases that may not be true. For example, an investor may decide to buy a risky portfolio when the seller's emphasis is on gains and to buy a risk-free asset when the presentation emphasizes possible losses associated with risky investing.

4.5 Typical mistakes in financial choice

4.5.1 Underinvesting in stocks

Haliassos and Bertaut (1995) find that most households do not invest in risky assets, which is puzzling based on the result of utility maximization showing a proportionality between investment and the risk premium of any risky portfolio characterized by a positive risk premium (see Chapter 13). Kaustia, Conlin, and Luotonen (2023) document heterogeneity of stock market participation in several European countries using data from 100,000 individuals from nineteen European countries, interviewed between 2004 and 2013. Total participation is on average much larger in countries such as Sweden and Denmark (from 60% to 70%) and much lower in Italy and Spain (on average 20% and 10% respectively). Moreover, total stock market participation increased from 2004 to 2013 in Austria, Belgium, Denmark, and Italy but declined in Sweden and remained flat in Switzerland and Spain. Heterogeneity is explained by country factors, "traditional" individual variables such as gender, age, education, income, wealth, and risk aversion, which jointly explain 49% of the variability, and "new" individual variables such as sociability, trust, cognitive skills (and its subcomponents), health, religiosity, political orientation, hard life experiences, optimism, bequest motive, body mass index, and height, which jointly explain 19% of the variability.

Surveying the academic literature, Guiso and Sodini (2013) find that theorists have been trying to explain the participation puzzle with a few elements such as fixed costs (for example the cost of opening a trading account, the cost of information, and the cost of learning about financial products), the predominance of behavioral factors relative to a standard rationality model, the perception that financial markets are characterized by risk rather than uncertainty coupled with uncertainty aversion, and lack of complete trust.

4.5.2 Excessive trading

Odean (1999) analyzes the trading records of 10,000 investors at a large discount broker over the period 1987–1993 and finds that the stocks bought by individuals underperform the stocks sold by twenty-three basis points per month in the twelve months after the transaction. Individual investors in stocks pay a large opportunity cost by pursuing active trading. Barber and Odean (2000) find that in a sample of 66,465 households with accounts at a discount broker,observed between 1991 and 1996, the 20% who trade the most earn an average net-of-cost return of 11.4% each year, compared with a market return of 17.9% also similar to the net return of the 20% of investors who trade the least, see Figure 4.4, reporting the annualized index return, the actual annualized portfolio returns (dotted histogram), and the monthly portfolio turnover (dashed histogram). The average household earns an average of 16.4% and prefers to hold high-beta securities, issued by small companies, with a low market price relative to book value, and has a portfolio turnover of 75% per annum. The opportunity cost of high trading is therefore substantial, amounting to almost 30% of the returns obtained.

Figure 4.4 The relationship between trading intensity and returns

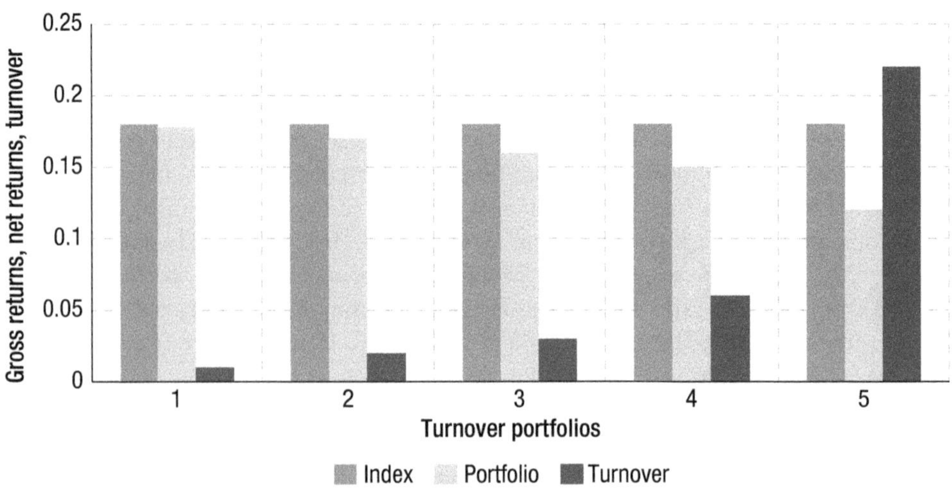

Results for Taiwan confirm that retail investors have an annual opportunity cost of 3.8% due to their excess trading, equivalent to 2.2% of GDP (see Barber, Lee, Liu and Odean, 2009).

What are the possible reasons for this systematic inability to select stocks? Particularly in buying decisions, investors are influenced by the media attention paid to a certain stock, and this attention often coincides with moments of temporary overvaluation of the stock itself. Barber and Odean (2008) confirm the hypothesis that individual investors are buyers of attention-grabbing stocks, that is, those that are newsworthy, have high trading volume, and exhibit extreme daily returns. This is a rational response to the multiplicity of securities that can be purchased.

One explanation for these empirical results lies with the presence of overconfidence and sensation-seeking on the part of traders. Shiller (2000) refers to word of mouth as a key channel for spreading opinions, even more relevant than news, quoting evidence from a survey that he sent out on October 19, 1987, during the occurrence of a stock market crash. The survey revealed that investors had acted in the market on the same day even before reading printed information the next day. Active traders suggested, when answering the survey, that oral communication with other people was widespread during that day.

Day traders represent an interesting category of investors due to their activity requiring closing the trading book every day. What do we learn from them? Analysis by Barber, Lee, Liu, Odean and Zhang (2020) covers the survival time of individual day traders in Taiwan between 1992 and 2006, showing that about half of them leave the market within a year, with only 5% lasting at least ten years, providing strong evidence of persistent ability for a relatively small group of day traders. Stocks bought by successful traders outperform those they sell by sixty-two basis points per day.

Why do unsuccessful day traders keep doing what they do? The easy explanation is that they like to trade, a proposal originally made by Black (1986). Economists prefer avoiding as much as possible explanations that directly involve the utility function because it is possible to explain most observations by assuming actions are due to preferences. Another possibility is that they try to learn their trading ability. This is consistent with the idea that most day traders quit relatively quickly. The timing of the process may be slowed down by a mix of overconfidence and other behavioral biases (see Barber, Lee, Liu, Odean and Zhang, 2020).

The existence and performance of day traders must be evaluated relative to changes in the trading venues, especially in light of the zero-commission model, by which brokers do not charge commission fees to investors. The model was introduced by the company Robinhood in the mid-2010s and spread to other major brokers including Charles Schwab and TD Ameritrade in 2019. The explosion in trading following the abolition of commissions might have been, based on available empirical analyses, negative for retail investors.

4.5.3 Insufficient diversification

Investors do not diversify enough from the point of view of the number of stocks held in their portfolio: Barber and Odean (2000) find that, on average, investors hold only four stocks. Moreover, investors do not diversify enough internationally and suffer from home bias: French (2008) documents that the fraction of the aggregate US investor portfolio allocated to foreign stocks grew from 2% in 1980 to 8.5% in 1990 and 27.2% in 2007. Despite these trends, the home bias remains a strong phenomenon around the globe (Solnik and Zuo, 2010; for a more recent survey, see Gaar, Scherer, and Schiereck, 2022). Differently from the past, there are many financial products that are available to investors today and allow international diversification.

Lack of international diversification may be interpreted in light of a familiarity belief, that is, the belief that one has better information on local investments. Familiarity beliefs also matter in other dimensions: Massa and Simonov (2006) analyze portfolio holdings of Swedish investors and document that they tilt their portfolio toward stocks that are most closely related to them, either professionally (e.g., a financial professional investing in a finance stock) or geographically (e.g., a Seattle investor investing in a Seattle stock). Similarly, Ivkovic and Weisbenner (2005) find that people living in New York mainly buy stocks issued by financial institutions because they think they have more information about the financial sector, while in California there is more investment in technology stocks.

4.6 Solutions

4.6.1 Policy solutions

Realizing that humans behave in ways that are individually sub-optimal is no consolation to economists, especially when individual errors have aggregate implications for society. Thaler and Sunstein (2008) describe such aggregate implications of sub-optimal behavior and discuss the role of the state in trying to improve welfare, proposing an approach that they call "libertarian paternalism" in the middle between pure paternalism (state intervention to influence people's choices) and pure libertarian (people should be free to do what they like) philosophies. In the libertarian paternalism approach, so-called choice architects attempt to move (nudge) people in directions that will make their lives better.

The nudging approach to public action very often uses some of the biases that have been previously described and a default option that is regarded the best choice of citizens. The nudging approach is by no means limited to public intervention; private companies can also adopt it for the purpose of having a positive impact. A great example is the financial investment scheme devised by Benartzi and Thaler (2013) known as "Save More Tomorrow" (SMT), where participants to a pension plan are invited to commit to a series of contribution increases associated with future salary raises in such a way that participants never see their take-home amounts go down. Of course, the SMT scheme needs first to be supported by participation to the pension plan, and this can be achieved more successfully by making participation the default option rather than the active choice. The power of the default option comes mainly from the status quo bias, according to which people stick with an initial outcome because they do not want to use mental resources to evaluate other alternatives. Default options are key nudges.

The previous discussion neglects the basic individual option that is open to everyone: force oneself to avoid bad decisions (see Thaler and Sunstein, 2008, for several examples). An easy non-financial example is to use smaller dishes and smaller glasses to eat and drink less. More complex strategies need to be used when facing more complicated problems, one example being Ulysses, who wanted to hear the song of the sirens but did not want to die afterwards. So, the captain ordered his crew to lash him to the ship's mast under strict orders not to untie him, after which they blocked their ears until they were safely out of range of the sirens. Elster (1979) interprets this myth using modern concepts of time inconsistency on the part of the self: Ulysses understands that going to the sirens is a sub-optimal choice but also knows that if he were free to choose when getting close to the song, his future self would predominate over his current self. He therefore manages a way to make sure that today's self predominates over the future self. There are many examples of actions about which we procrastinate, and we need some external commitment (or nudging) to make sure that we get over our time inconsistency and select the best choice.

4.6.2 Financial education

4.6.2.1 *What is financial education?*

The OECD (2005, p. 118) defines financial education as "the process by which investors improve their understanding of financial products, concepts and risks, and, through information, education and/or advice, develop the skills and confidence to become more aware of financial risks and opportunities, in order to make informed choices, know where to go for help and take action to improve their financial situation." It is therefore a process that, to have choices as an outlet, cannot stop at basic concepts but must necessarily understand what it is necessary to know in order to consciously manage one's assets (either directly or through the help of consultants).

Lusardi and Mitchell (2008, 2011a, 2011b) developed three questions to measure financial education according to the criteria of simplicity, relevance in daily decisions, synthesis, and ability to discriminate subjects. In the original application to people over fifty years of age in the United States, the correct answers to the three questions were 67%, 75%, and 52%, respectively. Only one in three people answer all three questions correctly.

Box 4.12 Financial education questionnaire

Let's say you have $100 in a savings account, with an interest rate of 2% per year. After five years, how much do you think you have in the account?

A) more than $102;
B) exactly $102;
C) less than $102;
D) I don't know; I refuse to answer.

Imagine that the interest rate on your savings account is 1% per year and inflation, on the other hand, is 2% per year. After a year, with the money in the account you are able to buy:

A) more than before
B) exactly the same as before
C) less than before
D) I don't know; I refuse to answer.

The following statement: "Buying a single share of a company usually offers a safer return than a mutual fund" is:

A) True
B) False
C) I don't know; I refuse to answer.

Lusardi and Mitchell (2014) recall that numerous other tests have been developed, also from the point of view of measuring financial sophistication, revealing, for example, that only 21% know the inverse relationship between interest rates and bond prices. Moreover, the application of the three original questions to an international context shows that the results of the United States also extend to other countries, for example in Italy the correct percentages of answers to the three questions are 40%, 59%, and 52% respectively, and only 25% answer correctly to all three questions. The OECD has added financial education to the tests contained in the Programme for International Student Assessment (PISA). Klapper, Lusardi, and van Oudheusden (2015) use the results of the Standard & Poor's Ratings Services Global Financial Literacy Survey to show that only 52% of Europeans correctly understand basic financial concepts

4.6.2.2 *Financial education and choices*

There is not much empirical evidence regarding the relationship between financial education and portfolio choice, mainly due to the lack of datasets containing individual information on both aspects. Existing evidence seems to show that higher levels of financial education are associated with more dynamic and risk-exposed portfolios, for example through a higher share of investment in equities (see, e.g., Bianchi, 2018; van Rooij, Lusardi, and Alessie , 2012; Yoong, 2011). Despite laudable methodological efforts, in cases such as these it is hard to reject the possibility that the results are driven by the presence of reverse causality, according to which those with portfolios more exposed to risky securities are more interested in elements related to financial education. From the beginning, the academic literature has focused on the so-called endogeneity of financial education, even in the theoretical field (see the review by

Lusardi and Mitchell, 2014). Jappelli and Padula (2013) consider investing in financial education as an individual optimal choice that is pursued when the benefit of financial education is larger than its cost and show that higher levels of financial education cause higher levels of wealth and savings.

Clark, Lusardi, and Mitchell (2015) shows that those with better financial education achieve higher risk-adjusted returns than others (1.3% on average per year) but at the same time hold portfolios associated with higher levels of idiosyncratic risk, while Von Gaudecker (2015) and Bianchi (2018) find a positive relationship with the degree of financial education at average risk-adjusted returns. Bianchi (2018) notes that financially literate individuals on average hold riskier portfolios when expected returns are higher, tend to manage portfolios more actively, and adopt a contrarian investment style by increasing purchases of assets where returns have been negative.

A study by Kaiser, Lusardi, Menkhoff and Urban (2022) starts from the results published in academic journals and uses the results in the context of an econometric model (this is an example of a meta-study) to show that financial education programs have, on average, across seventy-six randomized experiments with a total sample of 160,000 individuals, positive causal treatment effects on financial knowledge and downstream financial behaviors. Treatment effects are economically meaningful in size, similar to those realized by educational interventions in other domains (e.g., health, energy conservation), and robust to accounting for publication bias in the literature.

Summary

- Behavioral finance aims to overcome the classical paradigm of economics and finance in which decisions are made by rational, emotionless agents who maximize utility or profit functions.
- Examples of theoretical analyses that have inspired behavioral finance models are slow and fast thinking, according to which the individual uses two different modes of reasoning, the first predominantly intuitive and the second predominantly structured, and heuristics, in which complex problems are simplified in an attempt to find general answers.
- A combination of System 1/System 2 and heuristics can explain the disposition effect, according to which investors hold too long in their portfolios assets whose market price is below the purchasing price. Investors tend to sell winners and hold losers, perhaps in an effort to avoid recognizing financial losses and judgmental errors.
- Experiments in psychology have shown the existence of various behavioral errors, which have been used to explain empirical evidence related to investor behavior: overconfidence, self-serving bias, hindsight bias, confirmation bias, narrative fallacy, representativeness heuristic, framing bias, anchoring bias, herding, law of small numbers, mental accounting, and regret avoidance.
- Empirical analyses of behavioral finance have highlighted the presence of typical errors in the management of financial assets, such as too much trading, using wrong information, not diversifying the portfolio sufficiently, and holding stocks at a loss for too long.
- In the context of investor behavior analysis, an extremely relevant problem, also from the point of view of public policies and regulation, is the level of financial education, and the relationship between knowledge and behavior patterns in terms of portfolio choices and risk.

---

5 Sovereign bonds

5.1 Introduction

A sovereign bond is an interesting security to study. When investors do not attach any probability to the possibility of the issuer not repaying coupons and/or principal, the only risk factor is the interest rate and this will simplify the derivation of our first deterministic, albeit non-linear, pricing equation. The same pricing equation highlights that the short-run dynamics of the price of a long-maturity bond are risky and allows us to compute an average return, known as yield to maturity, obtained if the bond is held until maturity. The tools that we have discussed in Chapters 2–4 are relevant to understand the expected return and risk of holding bonds over a horizon shorter than their time to maturity. Bonds are also directly related to the price of time that is the value of a monetary payoff now and in the future. We introduce spot interest rates as the remuneration for holding bonds paying no coupons and show that the spot rate is the price of time. Recognizing the existence of a multiplicity of interest rates, the so-called term structure of interest rates, marginally complicates theoretical pricing but at the same time requires some thinking about empirical measurement of the relation between interest rates and bond maturity, with the goal of using prices of all traded bonds to estimate the term structure. The term structure of interest rates is a rich source of information about macroeconomic variables such as economic growth and inflation, and theories of the term structure shed light on expectations about future interest rates that we can derive from current market prices. We will use the definition of forward rates to highlight theories of bond price determination that stress both the role of expected future interest rates as well as investors' concerns that may create segmentation in the market.

5.2 Bond price in secondary markets

5.2.1 Compound interest and present value

The present value today of €1 T periods from now is equal to $\left(1 + r_f\right)^{-T}$. If there is a cash flow C paid one year from now, the current value is less than C. An investor would prefer €C today to €C tomorrow. If she borrowed an amount of money that would correspond to €C one year from now, she would have to pay an interest to compensate the lender for the loan. The amount of money that she would get today would be $\frac{C}{(1+r_f)}$. If she had to pay a cost of debt equal to i she would have to repay the capital borrowed, $\frac{C}{(1+r_f)}$, plus she would have to pay an interest equal to $\frac{C}{(1+r_f)} \times r_f$. The total to be repaid after one year would be $\frac{C}{(1+r_f)} + \frac{C}{(1+r_f)} \times r_f = C$. It follows that the present value of €C one year from now is equal to €$\frac{C}{(1+r_f)}$.

Compounding can be done at various intervals. If the interest rate refers to one year and compounding is carried out m times during the year, we will have $\left(1+\frac{r_f}{m}\right)^{m\times T}$. If compounding happens infinitely frequently during the year, that is, $m \rightarrow \infty$, we get $\lim_{m\rightarrow\infty}\left(1+r_f/m\right)^m = e^{icc}$ where we define the continuously compounded rate as icc and refer to continuous compounding, describing exponential growth. With continuous compounding, the final capital at time T will be $e^{icc\times T}$ and the present value is equal to $e^{-icc\times T}$.

5.2.2 Invoice price and flat price

A bond is initially issued on the primary market and can then be traded on the secondary market. The price on the secondary market fluctuates with each trade and is typically different from the face value of the bond. The price observed on the secondary market (flat price) does not represent the amount of money actually paid by the buyer, since the seller must also be remunerated for the value corresponding to the current coupon at least for the period she held the bond before the next coupon day. We define accrued interest as the share of the coupon that must be recognized to the seller and define the invoice price as the sum of the flat price and the accrued interest.

For example, assume a bond with face value equal to 100, maturing on December 31, 2030, was sold on March 31, 2024, for a flat price equal to 98. The buyer of the bond on March 31, in case she holds it to maturity, receives the full coupon paid on December 31, even if she did not hold it in the first quarter of the year. The exchange is then carried out in such a way that the buyer pays to the seller in advance the portion of the coupon corresponding to the remuneration of the first quarter. It is assumed by convention that the coupon, say equal to €2, matures proportionally over time, and therefore that at the end of March a value of €0.5 (equal to the portion of the total value of €2 attributed to the first quarter) is paid to those who hold the bond at that time (accrual). The buyer of the bond at the end of March must therefore pay an invoice price of €98 + €0.5 = €98.5.

5.2.3 Price determination

We start by assuming there is only one interest rate in the market, denoted with r_f. We initially assume the interest rate does not change over time. To determine the secondary market price of a bond at time t, we apply the definition of the present value of cash flows. A bond pays a stream of cash flows called a coupon for T years and pays the face value FV. The price of the bond is the present discounted value of future cash flows:

$$P_{0,T} = \sum_{t=1}^{T} \frac{C}{\left(1 + r_f\right)^t} + \frac{FV}{\left(1 + r_f\right)^T} \tag{1}$$

where $P_{0,T}$ is the time 0 price of a bond with T years to maturity, C the coupon, FV the face value, and r_f the interest rate. $c = C/FV$ is the coupon rate.

Some bonds can pay the coupon semi-annually. In this case, the evaluation is made considering half the coupon at the numerator and half the interest rate at the denominator, of course doubling the total number of terms to $2 \times T$, that is, $P_{0,T} = \sum_{t=1}^{2\times T} \frac{C}{\left(1 + r_f/2\right)^t} + \frac{FV}{\left(1 + r_f/2\right)^T}$.

The pricing equation (1) can also be retrieved from a backward induction argument where we start from the price of the bond on the expiration day: After the last coupon is paid, the flat price must be equal to the face value FV, so that $P_{T,0} = FV$. One period before expiration, the price is the present discounted value of the coupon and the price at expiration:

$$P_{T-1,1} = \frac{C + FV}{1 + r_f}. \tag{2}$$

Notice that the sum of the two terms in the subscript is always equal to T. At time $T - 2$, the holder of the bond at time knows that next period she will earn the coupon and the future price (remember we are assuming no risk at this point) and the relation must be:

$$P_{T-2,2} = \frac{C + P_{T-1,1}}{1 + r_f} \tag{3}$$

because the holder knows for sure that the price she is paying at time $T - 2$ will entitle her to receive a coupon and the price at time $T - 1$. The same logic keeps applying, so in general $P_{t,T-t} = \frac{C + P_{t+1,T-t-1}}{1 + r_f}$. If we substitute equation (3) into equation (2) we get $P_{T-2,2} = \frac{C}{1 + r_f} + \frac{C + FV}{\left(1 + r_f\right)^2}$ and, in general, we obtain equation (1).

A consol is a bond with infinite maturity. The pricing equation becomes:

$$P_{t,\infty} = \frac{C}{1 + r_f} + \frac{C}{\left(1 + r_f\right)^2} + \ldots = \frac{C}{r_f}.$$

$C = 0$ describes a zero-coupon bond. Such securities are of particular interest to institutional investors who are not looking for periodic payments for consumer financing, and for whom such payments are a flow that must be reinvested in the portfolio, incurring transaction costs. The market price of a zero-coupon bond only depends on its (discounted) face value:

$$P_{t,T-t} = \frac{FV}{\left(1 + r_f\right)^{T-t}}.$$

It can be shown through the application of simple financial mathematics rules that the price described in equation (1) can be rewritten as:

$$P_{t,T-t} = C \times \frac{1}{r_f}\left[1 - \frac{1}{\left(1 + r_f\right)^{T-t}}\right] + FV \times \frac{1}{\left(1 + r_f\right)^{T-t}} \qquad (2)$$

which decomposes the total price into the annuity factor, the first term on the right-hand side, representing the present value of a constant flow C paid for $-t$ periods discounted at rate i, and the face value factor, the present value of the cash flow paid at maturity.

Box 5.1 **What happens to the price if the interest rate is negative?**

Question: Elena wants to invest €10,000 in a ten-year German bond, and she talks to her advisor about what rate she will get and what price she will have to pay.

Answer: The consultant warns Elena that the interest rate on German ten-year bonds is negative, -0.2%. As a result, the price she will have to pay to buy a bond with a coupon rate of 0.1% is equal to $\frac{1{,}000 \times 0.1\%}{(-0.2\%)}\left[1 - \frac{1}{(1 - 0.2\%)^{10}}\right] + 1{,}000 \times \frac{1}{(1 - 0.2\%)^{10}} = 1{,}030.33$. Elena should therefore lose money for the decade in order to be able to lend her money to the German state in case she intends to buy the bond to keep it in her portfolio until its natural maturity: She would pay €10,303.30 now to obtain €10,000 after ten years and in the meantime obtain only €10 each year. Elena is better off holding her money in a bank deposit if the bank does not charge any cost for the deposit.

5.2.4 The relationship between price and interest rate

Equation (1) shows that there is an inverse relationship between the interest rate and the price. Increasing the market interest rate at which coupons are discounted causes the secondary market price of the bond to fall. Equation (2) can be rewritten as follows (let us ignore the subscript for the sake of simplicity):

$$P = c \times FV \times \frac{1}{r_f}\left[1 - \frac{1}{\left(1 + r_f\right)^{T}}\right] + FV \times \frac{1}{\left(1 + r_f\right)^{T}} =$$

$$= FV\left\{c \times \frac{1}{r_f}\left[1 - \frac{1}{\left(1 + r_f\right)^{T}}\right] + \frac{1}{\left(1 + r_f\right)^{T}}\right\}$$

showing that if $c = r_f$ the bond price is equal to the face value (at par). When $c > r_f$

then $P > FV$, the price is above the face value (above par), and when $c < r_f$ then $P < FV$, the price is below the face value (below par). Bonds issued on primary markets have a price close to the face value because issuers propose coupon rates that are close to prevailing market rates.

Why does the secondary market price move inversely to the interest rate? For a simple economic behavior, if a bond is issued at par for the first time and the interest rate subsequently rises (falls), investors pay less (more) to buy the previously issued bond, offering a lower (high) coupon rate, preferring, other things being equal, to buy the new bonds issued for a higher coupon rate. Figure 5.1 shows that the function that links the price to the interest rate is convex. It follows that an increase in the rate implies a reduction in the price in absolute value that is less than the increase in price resulting from an equal reduction in the interest rate, that is, there is an asymmetry between the consequences on the price of an equal increase or decrease in the interest rate:

Figure 5.1 **The price–rate relation**

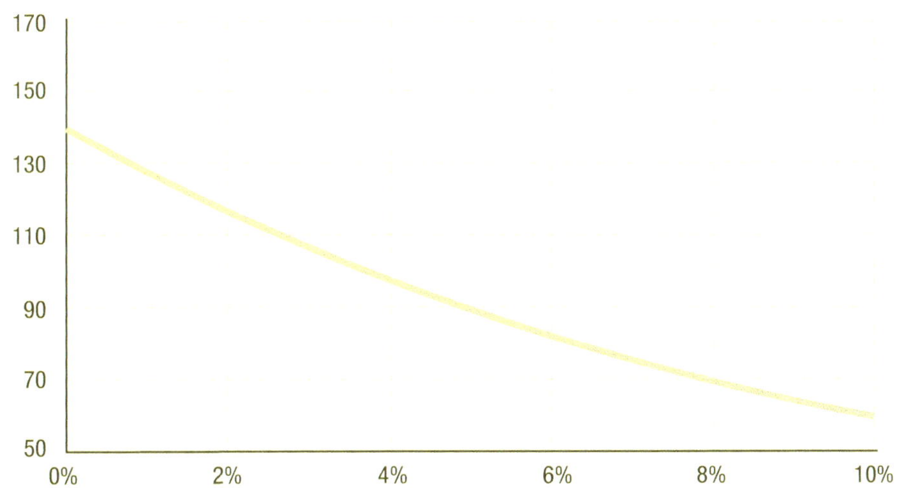

Interest rate risk is the only relevant risk factor for a bondholder, at least when it is assumed that there is no risk about actual payment of coupons and face value. We will return to interest rate risk analysis for bonds after we introduce the concepts of duration and credit risk in Chapter 6.

5.2.5 The holding period return

Given the prevailing interest rate at a given time, investors are willing to pay a purchase price described by equation (1). From one day to the next, conditions in the market will change and therefore the interest rate will change, resulting in a change in the price of bonds on the secondary market.

When the bond is held for a period less than its maturity, for example holding a ten-year bond for one month, it becomes important to describe the periodic return, including the coupon paid (more precisely, the accrual acquired over the period) and the percentage change in the price of the security. We indicate with $h(t, t+1, T)$ the holding period return for a purchase at time t and a sale at time $t+1$ of a bond with maturity T. By definition:

$$h(t, t+1, T) = \frac{C + P_{t+1,T-t-1} - P_{t,T-t}}{P_{t,T-t}}.$$

From the buyer's point of view, at time t the holding period return is a random variable that depends on the future price of the security, which, as we have seen, fluctuates according to the future levels of interest rates.

The holding period return can have elements of predictability related to the differential between the market price and the nominal value. On the maturity day, the price of the bond must be equal to the face value. It follows that, if the current price is different from the market value, the price converges over time to the face value (price drift). Figure 5.2 describes the two cases of a bond "above par" (market price initially above face value) and a bond "below par" (market price initially below face value).

Figure 5.2 The price drift

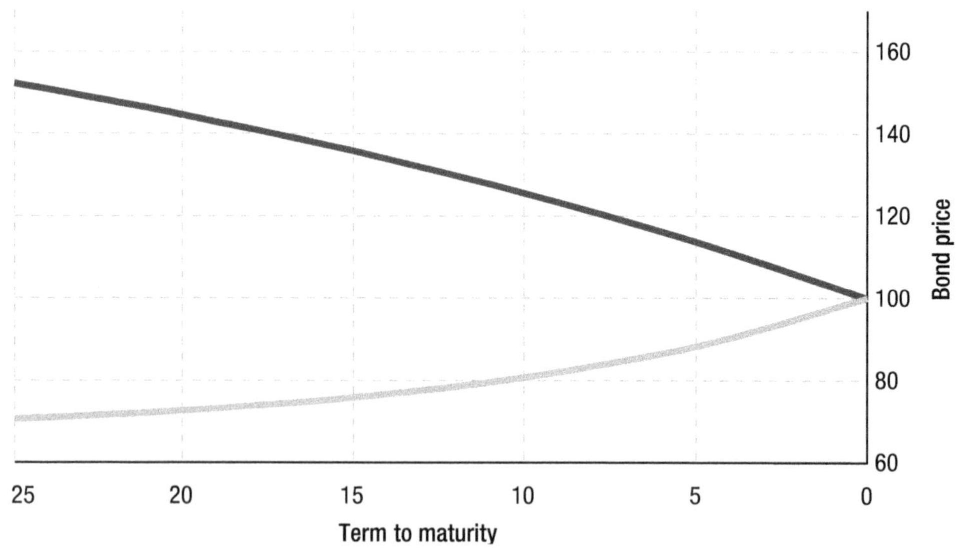

Over time, and all things being equal, both bonds tend to converge towards the nominal value because the bond on the day of maturity will have a value exactly equal to its face value. Figure 5.2 assumes the interest rate does not change over the time horizon. If there were changes in interest rates then we know from the pricing equation that bond prices would also change, but this volatility would not affect the conclusion that on the last day of trading the market price must equal the face value, as shown in Figure 5.3.

Figure 5.3 **The price drift with changing interest rates**

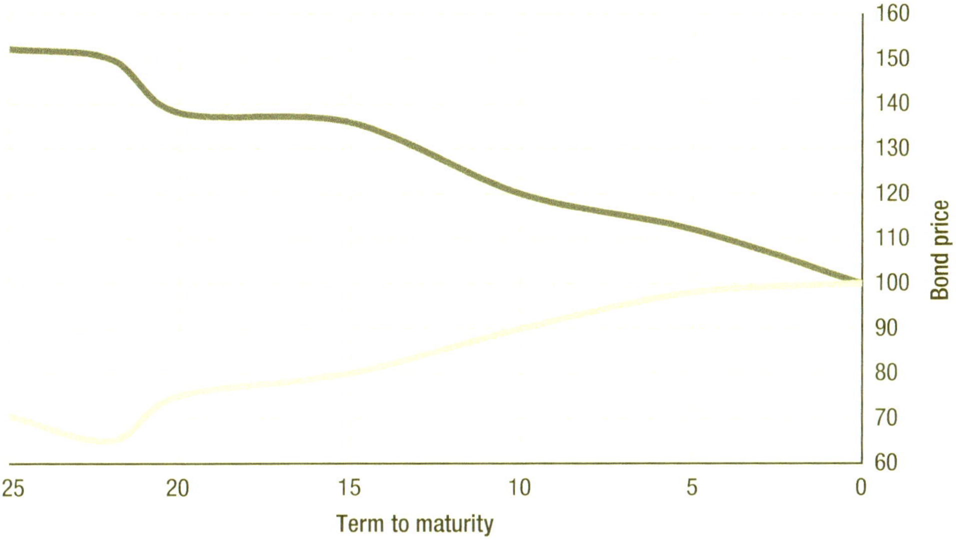

Price drift is therefore a predictable component of periodic returns which does not cause any particular reaction from investors: Holders of high-coupon bonds know they will suffer from a capital loss but they are happy holders because they are compensated by a high coupon yield.

Box 5.2 **Do we necessarily lose when we buy a bond with a negative rate?**

Question: Elena invested €10,000 in a ten-year German bond with a coupon rate of 0.1% and a rate of -0.2% but one hour after the purchase she looks at her custody account and discovers that the market value of the bond has gone up instead of falling. Pleasantly surprised, she calls her consultant to get an explanation.

Answer: The advisor warns Elena that the interest rate on German ten-year bonds fell again after her purchase. Initially she paid a price equal to 1,030.33 (see Box 5.1) but, after the rate has fallen to -0.6%, the price has become equal to $\frac{1{,}000 \times 0.1\%}{(-0.6\%)}\left[1 - \frac{1}{(1-0.6\%)^{10}}\right] + 1{,}000 \times \frac{1}{(1-0.6\%)^{10}} = 1{,}072.37$. In one hour, she has therefore gained 4.08% on an investment characterized by a negative interest rate.

For bonds whose residual maturity is longer than the investor's time horizon, the holding period return is a random variable whose value is determined above all by the future trend of interest rates, the main driver of the market price.

5.2.6 The yield to maturity

Let's assume that we know the price by observing it in the market, and that we look for a synthetic indicator of the "average profitability" of the bond if held to maturity. Yield to maturity (YTM) is the rate used for discounting future cash flows that makes the present value of coupons and face value equal to the price of the bond.[1] To calculate the YTM, we must solve the following equation for the unknown y:[2]

$$P = \sum_{t=1}^{T} \frac{C}{(1+y)^t} + \frac{FV}{(1+y)^T}.$$

The YTM is the compounded average annual growth rate of an initial investment equal to the price of the bond, such that the finale value corresponds with the face of the bond including the reinvestment of all intermediate flows:

$$P \times (1+y)^T = \sum_{t=1}^{T} C \times (1+y)^{(T-t)} + FV.$$

The assumption implicit in the calculation is that all coupons obtained during the life of the bond are reinvested to the same YTM. We can define the realized yield to maturity y^{post} as the actual ex post average return that one gets by reinvesting all the intermediate cash flows at the same rate r_f' where r_f' is potentially different from the risk-free rate prevailing at the time the YTM was computed:

$$P \times (1+y^{post})^T = \sum_{t=1}^{T} C \times (1+r_f')^{(T-t)} + FV.$$

If the actual reinvestment takes place at rates lower than the YTM, the realized YTM would be different from the YTM calculated ex ante. Consider, for example, a two-year bond with a coupon rate of 5%. If the reinvestment rate is 5%, the coupon 5 is reinvested for one year to provide a total amount of 110.05. The operation consisting of investing 100 to have 110.05 after two years corresponds to an internal rate of return, that is, a realized yield to maturity, of exactly 5%. However, if the reinvestment rate falls to 0%, the final amount is equal to 110 and the realized YTM becomes equal to 4.88%.

---

[1] The YTM is different from the current yield, which is the ratio of the coupon to the market price. The result of this equation is also known as the internal rate of return (IRR), a concept we will use in discussing performance of private asset funds.

[2] In Excel, use the "yield" function and specify the following parameters: settlement date, maturity date, coupon rate, price, face value.

5.3 The term structure of interest rates

5.3.1 The spot rate: definition

There is no single interest rate in the market, but an interest rate for each time maturity. The spot rate (or zero rate) for a maturity T is the interest rate associated with the price of a zero-coupon bond with the same maturity, with symbol $r_{f,t,T}$ for the spot rate prevailing at time t for maturity T with term to maturity $T-t$. To be more specific, let us arbitrarily define the "short-term rate" as the prevailing rate on bonds with a maturity of one year, $r_{f,t,t+1}$, and the "long-term rate" as the prevailing rate on ten-year bonds, $r_{f,t,t+10}$.

5.3.2 The term structure and bond pricing

We can observe spot rates though the prices of zero-coupon bonds. We denote with $P_{t,T}$ the price at time t of a zero-coupon bond with T periods to maturity, maturing at $t+T$. We know that $P_{t,T} = \frac{FV}{\left(1 + r_{f,t,T}\right)^{T-t}}$. The price of a zero-coupon is therefore equal to the present value of its face value. Inverting the formula, the value of the spot rate can be obtained from the price of the zero-coupon bond from $r_{f,t,T} = \left(\frac{FV}{P_{t,T}}\right)^{\frac{1}{t-T}} - 1$.

The spot rate is the price of time for a specific maturity. Coupon bonds cannot provide information on the price of time for a specific future period, due to their involving cash flows defined over several future periods. To see this point, let us first notice that a coupon bond can be interpreted as a portfolio of zero-coupon bonds. For example, a two-year bond with coupons C and face value FV can be seen as a portfolio consisting of a zero-coupon bond with a one-year face value C and a two-year zero-coupon bond with face value $(C + FV)$.[3] Lacking arbitrage opportunities in financial markets, that is, a possibility to create a portfolio with a positive cash flow today and no value in the future,[4] the price of the two-period coupon bond must be equal to the sum of the prices of the two zero-coupon bonds.

If the two-year coupon bond paid a coupon of 5 next year and a total sum of 105 (face value plus coupon) in two years, and if, say, the price today of a one-year zero-coupon bond with a face value equal to 5 was 4.8, and the price today of a two-year zero coupon bond with a face value of 105 was 103, then we could conclude the price today of the two-year coupon bond must be 107.8. If the price was 109 instead of 107.8, the arbitrage possibility would consist of buying the portfolio of the two zero-coupon bonds, spending 107.8, and selling the two-year coupon bond, obtaining

---

[3] Or, if we consider zero-coupon bonds with a unitary face value, consisting of C one-year zero-coupon bonds and $C + FV$ two-year zero-coupon bonds.

[4] We will consider arbitrage for the pricing of stocks in Chapter 11.

109. Today the net cash flow would be 1.2. Next year the arbitrageur would obtain 5 from the expiration of the one-year zero-coupon bond and would have to pay 5 to the holder of the two-year coupon bond. Two years from now the arbitrageur would get 105 from expiration of the two-year zero-coupon bond and spend 105 to the holder of the coupon bond. At the end, there is a positive immediate cash flow equal to 1.2 and no other future cash flow. Any opportunity arising from misalignment of prices would therefore imply buying the one-year zero-coupon bonds and selling the two-year coupon bonds. As a result of excess demand, prices would readjust until they do not create any more arbitrage opportunities.

We have shown that:

$$P_{0,2}^{C} = \frac{C}{\left(1 + r_{f,0,1}\right)} + \frac{C + FV}{\left(1 + r_{f,0,2}\right)^{2}}$$

where $P_{0,2}^{C}$ is the price at time 0 of a coupon bond maturing at 2. For example, the value of a bond with a coupon rate of 10% and a nominal value of 1,000, using the one-year spot rate structure: 5% at one year, 6% at two years, and 7% at three years, is equal to:

$$P_{0,3}^{C} = \frac{100}{1.05} + \frac{100}{(1.06)^{2}} + \frac{1{,}100}{(1.07)^{3}} = 1{,}082.17.$$

To see the difference between the spot rate and the YTM in this example, we can compute the YTM y of the bond using:

$$1{,}082.17 = \frac{100}{(1 + y)} + \frac{100}{(1 + y)^{2}} + \frac{1{,}100}{(1 + y)^{3}}$$

to get $y = 6.88\%$. Note that the YTM is different from the spot interest rate used for the third-year cash flow discount, precisely because of the existence of intermediate cash flows associated with coupon payments. The YTM is affected by the value of the coupons paid over the life of the bond, whereas the spot rate for the third period is the pure price of time for that interval.

Through a procedure called "bootstrapping" it is possible to use information on zero coupon bonds and coupon bonds simultaneously. Let's imagine that the one-year spot rate is 5% and the two-year rate is 6%, and that we observe a price of a three-year bond with a 10% coupon rate of 1,082.17 on the market. The pricing equation can be rewritten as:

$$1{,}082.17 = \frac{100}{1.05} + \frac{100}{(1.06)^{2}} + \frac{1{,}100}{\left(1 + r_{f,0,3}\right)^{3}} = 1{,}082.17$$

which, resolved, provides a three-year spot rate of 7%.

5.3.3 The term structure of interest rates

The term structure of interest rates is the whole set of rates prevailing on the various maturities. In Figure 5.4 we see a representation of the typical term structure.

Figure 5.4 **The term structure of interest rates**

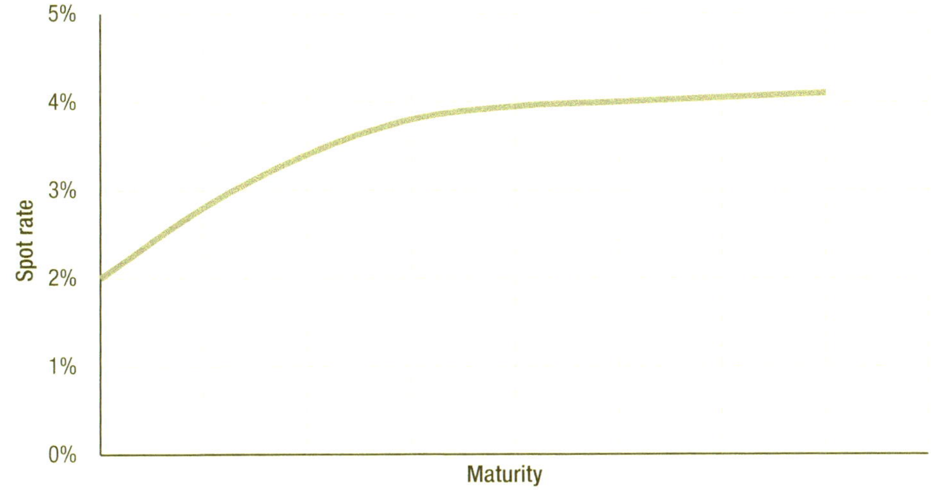

Source: Refinitiv

The term structure shown in Figure 5.4 is consistent with the historical average in most countries, as it has higher long-term rates than short-term rates. However, the curve can also have very different shapes; for example, Figure 5.5 describes the term structure for German debt on August 2, 2019.

Figure 5.5 **The German term structure on August 2, 2019**

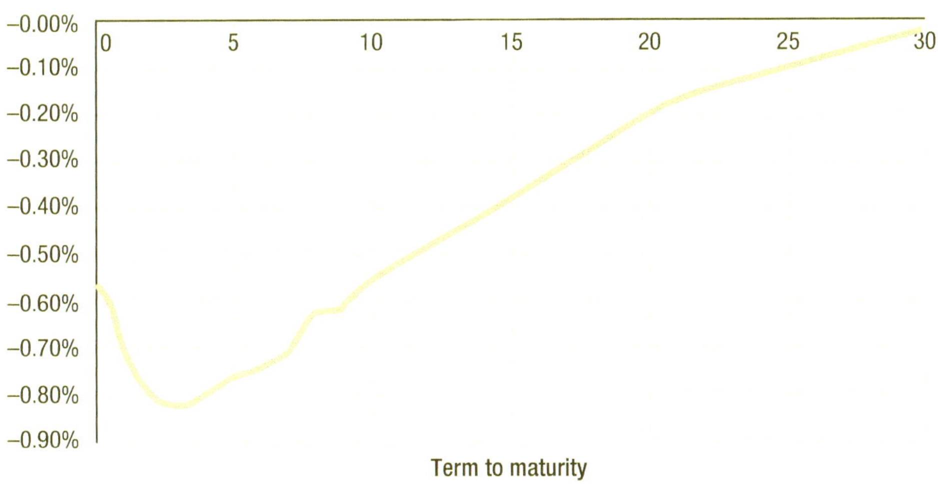

Source: Refinitiv

The curve is completely negative![5] Investors were willing to lend money to the German State without receiving any remuneration over a thirty-year horizon, in order to benefit from Germany's reliability. The curve is even downward sloping for maturities between one month and three years, with the rate at -0.8%. The ten-year benchmark is -0.6%.

Box 5.3 How can the curve be completely negative?

Question: Carola would like to invest in German bonds but notes that the rates are all negative, even for very long maturities. She asks Sara, who works at an asset management firm, to explain to her what's happening in the markets. How is it possible that we prefer to lose 0.6% a year for ten years rather than "keep the money without investing it?"

Answer: Sara replies that Carola sees things from the point of view of a retail investor, who in effect may decide to keep the money in a bank account or at home in banknotes. However, large institutions, which manage hundreds of millions of euros, cannot do the same and must therefore buy bonds. In addition, keeping money in a bank account exposes the depositor to the risk of bank failure, with personal consequences because bank deposits are only insured by the state up to a certain threshold. Institutions therefore cannot avoid losing money on the cash held; they can only decide how to limit the loss by choosing the most attractive maturity. The choice of maturity is influenced by the elements present in both the theory of expectations and the theory of segmentation (see later). Expectations about future short-term rates are significant, as is the existence of preferred maturities, and also the presence of liquidity premiums. Finally, expectations and demand are also influenced by empirical evidence that Germany's debt-to-GDP ratio is continuously declining, reaching 60%, less than half of Italy's, in 2019. As a result, some investors fear a "scarcity" effect in the future. Similar fears existed for US Treasuries at the end of Bill Clinton's administration, but successive administrations have increased the government deficit and thus the bond supply, allaying investors' concerns. In the coming decades, it is likely that major trends, including in particular the aging of the population, will make government intervention necessary, with the consequent repercussions on the supply of German government bonds.

A negative interest rate does not cause arbitrage in the bond market. Single investors of course would not buy a sovereign bond with a negative interest rate: They would rather hold cash in their pockets or leave money in their bank accounts if these paid a non-negative rate. However, institutional investors with large sums of money would have no alternative to hold their cash: An alternative would be to buy a storage deposit and fill it with money, but there would be costs associated with storage and transportation that would make the negative interest rate on the sovereign bond a better alternative.

[5] The total number of bonds trading on the markets at negative rates is estimated at $15 trillion as of August 2019, accounting for about 25% of the total supply of sovereign and corporate bonds.

5.3.4 The forward rate

The forward rate is a mathematical definition representing a reward to be obtained in the future. For example, we define the forward rate $f_{0,T-1}$, as the one-period return, known at time 0, on an investment in a one-year bond over the period from $T-1$ to T:

$$f_{0,T-1} = \frac{\left(1 + r_{f,0,T}\right)^{T}}{\left(1 + r_{f,0,T-1}\right)^{T-1}} - 1. \tag{3}$$

To economically interpret the meaning of the forward rate, it is useful to rewrite equation (3) as:

$$\left(1 + r_{f,0,T-1}\right)^{T-1} \times \left(1 + f_{0,T-1}\right) = \left(1 + r_{f,0,T}\right)^{T}.$$

The forward rate can therefore be interpreted as the prevailing remuneration known at the initial time 0, in a future period $T-1$ with the following property: investing a sum of money for $T-1$ periods at rate $r_{f,0,T-1}$ and for one period at rate $f_{0,T-1}$ (active strategy) produces a final value identical to that produced by an investment for T periods at rate $r_{f,0,T}$ (buy-and-hold strategy).[6] The forward rate is the same as the spot rate in case the curve is flat and the spot rates are the same for all maturities.

We have so far defined the forward rate as the implicit rate on a one-year bond issued in the future. From the current term structure, we can also compute forward rates for bonds of maturities longer than one year. We define with $f_{0,v,t}$ the forward rate computed at time 0 for an investment starting at time v and ending at time t. For example, $f_{0,1,3}$ is the rate that should be paid by a two-year bond issued next year:

$$\left(1 + r_{f,0,1}\right) \times \left(1 + f_{0,1,3}\right)^{2} = \left(1 + r_{f,0,3}\right)^{3}.$$

The variable $\left(1 + f_{0,1,3}\right)^{2}$ can be interpreted as the interest rate on a two-year bond issued next year that makes the investor indifferent between a three-year bond buy-and-hold strategy $\left(1 + r_{f,0,3}\right)^{3}$ and a rollover strategy starting from investing now in a one-year bond and investing next year in a two-year bond $\left(1 + r_{f,0,1}\right) \times \left(1 + f_{0,1,3}\right)^{2}$.

[6] With continuous compounding, the equality between the amounts of the two investment strategies, the active and the buy-and-hold, is $e^{fcc(0,T)\times T} \times e^{icc_{0,T-1}\times(T-1)} = e^{icc_{0,T}\times T}$ where fcc denotes the forward rate under continuous compounding. Applying the logarithm to both sides and simplifying, we find the relationship between forward rate and spot rates $fcc(0,T) = \left(icc_{0,T} + \left(icc_{0,T} - icc_{0,T-1}\right) \times \left(T-1\right)\right)/T$ which shows how the forward rate for a future period that starts at $T-1$ and ends at T is equal to a weighted average between the spot rate for the period from now until the end of the future period T and the future spot rate change.

5.4 Why does the term structure move over time?

5.4.1 The expectations theory of interest rates

Expectation theory argues that the forward rate is equal to the expectation of the spot rate that will prevail in the future, that is, $f_{0,T-1} = E_0(r_{f,T-1,T})$ where E_0 is the expectation at time 0. This is due to investors being risk-neutral and being willing to hold bonds of any maturity, with a switch in the composition of their bond portfolios toward assets offering a higher expected return. This has a double implication, one for strategies holding bonds with different maturities and one for the possibility to use the observed term structure to infer market-based expectations of future rates.

The implication for strategies may be understood by noting that if $E_t h(t, t+1, T) > E_t h(t, t+1, T-t')$, that is, if the expected holding period return between time t and time $t+1$ differed between bonds maturing at dates T and $T-t'$, then investors would demand the bond maturing at T and sell bonds maturing at $T-t'$, pushing up and down prices to the point where expected returns are equal. In general, risk-neutral investors would hold bonds in their portfolios only if the expected holding period return would be the same across maturities.

One implication of the theory is that investors should be indifferent between buying long-term or short-term bonds. For example, the return obtained by investing at time 1 in a two-year bond or in a series of two one-year bonds would make the two strategies completely indifferent from the point of view of the expectation of the final amount because:

$$\left(1 + r_{f,0,2}\right)^2 = \left(1 + r_{f,0,1}\right)\left(1 + E_0 r_{f,1,1}\right).$$

The result shows why the information provided by the term structure may help predict future rates: one can start from the term structure observed today to compute all forward rates and estimate market expectations regarding the future evolution of future rates. According to the expectations theory, the spot rate on a two-year bond is the geometric average between the current rate on a one-year bond and the expected rate that will prevail in the future. If we assume that central banks determine the short-term rate, then this means that markets set interest rates on all the other maturities to levels that account for current and future decisions of central banks.

The period 2023–2024 is a great example. After the quick and strong increase of interest rates decided by central banks in 2021–2022 due to an inflationary shock, with inflation rising above 10% (as a consequence of the Russian invasion of Ukraine the associated increase in the price of gas, and as a result of the large demand shock due to post-Covid-19 fiscal policies around the world), investors started to expect a future reduction of interest rates as a consequence of inflation quickly returning to the 2% threshold pursued by central banks. Long-term bond rates decreased first, with a negatively sloped term structure, as predicted by the expectations theory. However, over the period 2023–2024 there was sometimes contradictory news about the inflation rate that cast doubt on the time it would take for it to decrease to 2%, with consequent changes in expectations of short-term future interest rates and immediate revisions in the level of long-term interest rates.

5.4.2 Segmentation theory

The segmentation (or preferred habitat) hypothesis argues that investors have a preference for investing at certain maturities, often due to the presence of liabilities. If an institution needs to pay an amount of money L at a future time period many years from now, then it may want to invest in a long-term bond that will pay exactly that amount of money at that specific time period. In the case instead of a preference for short-term bonds (this assumption is known as the liquidity preference theory), investors would need a premium for holding long-term bonds, because all things being equal, they would prefer short-term bonds. This preference may, for example, be due to the higher risk of long-term bonds in relation to interest rate volatility. The premium on long-term securities is acquired in the form of a higher interest rate than there would be based on pure expectations of future interest rates, and therefore:

$$\left(1 + r_{f.0,2}\right)^2 > \left(1 + r_{f.0,1}\right)\left(1 + E_0 r_{f.1,2}\right).$$

This implies that the term structure should be positively sloped unless a sharp decline in the short-term rate is expected in the future. Conversely, if most investors preferred to invest in long-dated bonds, such as two-year bonds, a premium would be required to induce them to buy short-term bonds, such as bonds with a one-year maturity. In this case:

$$\left(1 + r_{f.0,2}\right)^2 < \left(1 + r_{f.0,1}\right)\left(1 + E_0 r_{f.1,2}\right)$$

and the maturity structure on a like-for-like basis will be sloped downwards to convince investors to hold shorter-maturity bonds. Such a rate configuration may be due to the prevalence of investors facing long-term liabilities.

In the case of segmentation, the above inequalities indicate that the yield curve tends to be sloping, either positively or negatively as the case may be. Inequalities can be interpreted as reflections of maturity premia, that is, excess required returns providing compensation for preferences and needs. In the case of a liquidity preference, we are talking about a positive liquidity premium that must compensate those who hold long-term securities:

$$\left(1 + r_{f.0,2}\right)^2 = \left(1 + r_{f.0,1}\right)\left(1 + E_0 r_{f.1,2} + LP_2\right). \tag{4}$$

The forward rate is no longer equal to the expected rate but also includes a premium. For example, an expected rate of 3% and a premium of 1% give rise to a forward rate of 4%. We cannot, therefore, use forward rates to infer expected short-term rates. In the case of preferences for longer maturities, equation (4) always applies, but with a negative liquidity premium, for example, a forward rate of 4% is compatible with an expected rate of 5% and a premium of -1% because investors are willing to give up a portion of the yield to hold long-term securities. In this case, the long-term rate is lower than the short-term rate, and the forward rate is lower than the expected short-term rate for the future.

Box 5.4 Why can strategists' expectations diverge?

Question: Elena looks at the following spot rate curve on one- to three-year maturities: 1%, 2%, and 3%. She asks Sara and Carola, strategists at the company, to tell her what rates the market expects for the next two years. Carola responds that in her opinion the market expects a rate of 6.03% for the third year as a consequence of strong economic growth, while Sara believes that the expected rate is 4.03% because the market expects a recession.

Answer: Sara and Carola easily calculate forward rates and find 3.01% for the forward rate for the second year and 5.03% for the third year. However, Carola believes that there is a liquidity premium of -1% for three-year bonds in the market, while Sara believes that the market prefers short-term securities and therefore that there is a risk premium of 1% for holding long-term securities. As a result, according to Carola, the expected rate is 5.03%, since the 1% premium must be deducted from the forward rate of 6.03% to determine the expected rate. In contrast, Sara believes that investors prefer one-year bonds and therefore that a 1% premium should be added to the expected rate of 4.03% to induce investors to hold long-term bonds.

Following the 2008–2009 Global Financial Crisis, central banks introduced so-called non-conventional monetary policy, consisting of direct purchasing of long-term bonds (quantitative easing, or QE). The goal was to affect long-term rates over and beyond the effects of expectations of future declining interest rates, based on the idea that long-term rates are more relevant than short-term rates to affect aggregate demand due to corporations and households typically borrowing long to finance their investments. This may be seen as a form of segmentation, with central banks directly intervening on specific portions of the bond market that became segmented from other segments (see Bhattarai and Neely, 2022, for an evaluation of the quantitative impact of QE).

5.4.3 The predictive power of the term structure

The slope of the interest rate curve is often used to infer market expectations about economic growth. The slope can be measured alternatively as the differential between the ten-year bond rate and the three-month bond rate, or by the differential between the ten-year bond rate and the two-year bond rate.

The "inversion" of the yield curve, that is, the existence of a negative spread, often signals a subsequent recession. Every single recession since 1965 has been preceded by a flattening of the US yield curve, with the spread between long-term and short-term rates reaching as low as zero or sometimes negative, as in the mid-1970s and early 1980s. The economic reason why a flat curve can be a warning sign of recession is related to the theory of expectations, according to which long-term rates lower than short-term rates can be explained by an expectation of lower future short-term rates, caused by a monetary policy aimed at restarting aggregate demand to counter the economic slowdown. The mechanism therefore relies on the association between economic growth, inflation, and monetary policy with central bank reduction of interest rates to avoid recessions and increase of interest rates to contain inflation. In the last ten to fifteen years the relation between the term structure and future growth has somewhat weakened for a number of reasons. The first is the presence of financial crises (the global credit crisis in 2008 and the peripheral European crisis in 2012) that have induced central banks to introduce a non-conventional monetary policy based on direct purchasing of bonds of long-term maturities in the market. This has reduced the slope of the term structure and successfully prevented economic recessions. The second is the inflationary shock of 2022–2023 that has induced central banks to raise interest rates with no subsequent recession (at least, at the time of writing). Whether the term structure is a good predictor of future economic growth needs further research incorporating more recent data.

Summary

- The main contractual features of a bond are its maturity, the coupon rate, and the face value.
- On the secondary market we distinguish between the flat price (ignoring coupon) and the invoice price that is actually paid by the buyer.
- The price is determined by discounting future cash flows at the prevailing market rate. Depending on the relation between the coupon rate and the interest rate, the bond can be priced at par, above par, or below par. The price drift is the predictable trend in the price of the bond until maturity that offsets any advantage/disadvantage associated with the current differential between the coupon rate and the interest rate.
- On the contrary, given the price, it is possible to calculate the yield to maturity as a synthetic indicator of average profitability. The yield to maturity holds ex post only if the coupons are reinvested at the same rate over the life of the bond.
- The price is inversely linked to the interest rate in order to maintain a profitability of the bonds in line with that of the new securities issued on the market.
- The holding period return is the rate of return obtained from the coupon yield and the capital gain. When the period over which the return is measured coincides with the maturity of the bond, the holding period return is known in advance.
- The spot rate (or zero rate) for a maturity T is the interest rate associated with the price of a security at a discount to that maturity, with symbol $.i_{t,T}$.
- The "term structure of interest rates" refers to the whole set of rates prevailing over the various maturities at a given point in time. The term structure can also use prices of traded coupon bonds through the bootstrap procedure.
- To account for the rate structure, the price of a coupon bond can be calculated as a basket of the prices of individual zero coupon bonds that represent future cash flows.
- The forward rate can be calculated from the current structure of spot rates and can be interpreted as future remuneration which makes the investor indifferent between two investment horizons.
- The main theory to explain the shape and dynamics of the interest rate structure is that of expectations, according to which the current shape of the rate curve is determined on the basis of expectations of the future dynamics of spot rates.
- The segmentation theory argues that investors have a preferred time habitat, and that they buy securities that mature in a time period outside their habitat only if there is an additional premium. So if all investors prefer short-term securities, they will only be willing to buy long-term ones if there is further compensation.

Problems

1 Fill in the following table with the missing information for the various zero-coupon bonds with a face value of 1,000:

Price	Maturity (years)	Spot rates
400	20	
500	20	
500	10	
	10	10%
	10	8%
400		8%

2 A bond with a nominal value of 1,000 and a three-year maturity pays a coupon of 50 every six months. The semi-annual rate is 4% and is known to be constant also in the future.

a. What is the current price?
b. What will the price be in six months?
c. What is the holding period return?
d. What would its price be if the coupon of 50 was paid annually in two installments?

3 A twenty-year bond with a face value of 100 and a coupon rate of 5% has a YTM of 8%, corresponding with the interest rate. After a year, the interest rate falls to 7%. What is the holding period return?

4 A two-year bond is quoted at par, and its coupon rate is 10%. Calculate the realized YTM at the end of the period for short-term future rate values of alternatively 8%, 10%, and 12%.

5 Compute forward rates based on the following data, and interpret the results in light of the expectations hypothesis of the term structure:

Maturity	Price	Spot rates
1	943.40	6.00%
2	898.47	5.50%
3	847.62	5.67%
4	792.16	6.00%

6 Bond A has a maturity of three years, a coupon rate of 10%, and a face value of 100, and its market price is 98.40. Bond B has a maturity of two years, a coupon rate of 6%, and a face value of 100, and its market price is 97.02. Which of the two is better to buy if the spot rates for the three relevant maturities are 5%, 8%, and 11% respectively?

7 The term structure for rates of one-, two-, and three-year maturities is 10%, 11%, and 12% respectively.

a. What are the forward rates?
b. Assuming the validity of the assumption of expectations, what will be the curve next year?
c. What is the expected holding period return from holding a two-year and a three-year bond, both with a nominal value of 1,000?
d. What is the current price of a three-year bond with a coupon rate of 12%? What is its expected holding period return?

8 The spot rate on one-year bonds is 6%. The rate on two-year bonds is 7%. An issuer wants to sell a two-year bond with a coupon rate of 8% and a face value of 1,000.

a. What is the price of the coupon bond?
b. What is the yield-to-maturity?
c. What is the expected price next year if the expectations theory is true?
d. What is the expected price if there is a liquidity premium equal to 10%?

Answers

1 The spot rate is found, for example, from $400\left(1 + r_f\right)^{20} = 1{,}000$ to get 4.69%. The price can be found from, for example, $P(1 + 0.1)^{10} = 1{,}000$, which produces 385.44. The maturity can be found from $400(1.08)^T = 1{,}000$, producing T = 11.9.

2 The annuity factor is $C \times \frac{1}{r_f}\left[1 - \frac{1}{\left(1 + r_f\right)^T}\right]$, therefore $50 \times \frac{1}{0.04}\left[1 - \frac{1}{(1.04)^6}\right]$ = 262.11. The face value factor is $FV \times \frac{1}{\left(1 + r_f\right)^T} = 790.31$.

The total value is 1,052.42.

If the rate remains at 4% after six months, the same method is used to obtain 1,044.52.

The holding period return is 4%, obtained from $\frac{50 + (1{,}044.52 - 1{,}052.42)}{1{,}052.42}$. The semester holding period return corresponds with the interest rate on the six-month bond paying 4%: Under conditions of certainty about the future rate, there would be no reason for a discrepancy in the returns obtained by different bonds over the same period of time.

Now the equation is $25 \times \frac{1}{0.02}\left[1 - \frac{1}{(1.02)^{12}}\right] = 264.38$.

3 The starting price is $5 \times \frac{1}{0.08}\left[1 - \frac{1}{(1.08)^{20}}\right] + 100 \times \frac{1}{(1.08)^{20}} = 70.546$.

After one year, given the new interest rate, we have

$$5 \times \frac{1}{0.07}\left[1 - \frac{1}{(1.07)^{19}}\right] + 100 \times \frac{1}{(1.07)^{19}} = 79.392.$$

The holding period return is $\frac{50 + 79.329 - 70.546}{70.546} = 19.54\%$. The holding period return is magnified by the decrease in the interest rate, which has a big impact on the price due to the long maturity of the bond.

4 If the coupon of the first year is reinvested at the rate $x\%$, the final amount will be $10 \times (1 + x) + 110$. The realized YTM can be thought of as the constant rate on a zero-coupon bond that makes the future value of the initial investment equal to the actual value of the final investment $10 \times (1 + x) + 110 = 100 \times (1 + y^{post})^2$. Therefore:

Short rate	Final value	y^{post}
8%	120.8	$\sqrt{1.208}-1 = 0.0991 = 9.91\%$
10%	121	10.00%
12%	121.2	10.09%

5 The term structure in this example is:

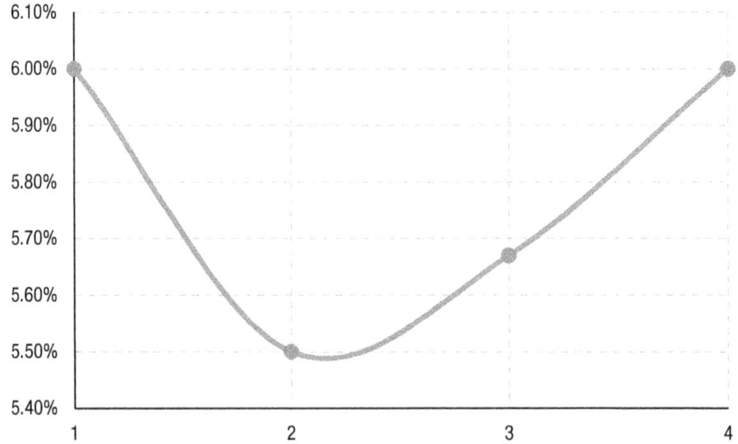

The computation of the forward rates follows from:

Maturity	Price	Spot rates	One-period forward rate
1	943.40	6.00%	
2	898.47	5.50%	$(1.055^2/1.06) - 1 = 5.0\%$
3	847.62	5.67%	$(1.0567^2/1.055^2) - 1 = 6.0\%$
4	792.16	6.00%	$(1.060^4/1.0567^3) - 1 = 7.0\%$

Under the expectations hypothesis, the forward rate is the expectation of the future spot rate. The one-year spot rate is expected in this example to decline for the second period, from 6% to 5%, and then to recover to 6% and end up higher at 7%. For example, the market may expect a temporary recession for year 2, requiring a decrease in interest rates on the part of the central bank, which, after the stabilization, may raise rates to the current level and then perhaps raise them even further in expectation of an inflationary period. Such expectations are immediately recorded by the term structure, as is clear, for example, by the rate on the two-year bond, which is lower than the rate on the one-year bond. Investors immediately buy the two-year bond anticipating a decline in the remuneration on future one-year bonds, and this raises the price and decreases the rate of two-year bonds. The increase in the price of two-year bonds is necessary to make purchasing of two-year bonds indifferent to a rollover strategy of purchasing one-year bonds for two years in a row. Buying a two-year bond at time 1 for a price of 898.47 and reselling it when it is a one-year bond for a price equal to 952.381 (obtained from $\frac{1{,}000}{1{,}05}$) produces a holding period return equal to 6%, identical to the spot rate that can be earned in the first year on one-year bonds. Notice that what we have done is mathematically not correct: the expected price of a bond is $E\frac{FV}{1+r_f} \neq \frac{FV}{1+Er_f}$. Strictly speaking the expectation of a non-linear function (face value divided by one plus rate) is different from the linear function evaluated at the expectation (one divided by one plus expected rate).

6 The theoretical value of A is $\frac{10}{1.05}+\frac{10}{1.08^2}+\frac{10}{1.11^3}=98.53$. In the case of B, $\frac{6}{1.05}+\frac{106}{1.08^2}=96.59$. Bond A is undervalued, while bond B is overvalued. The investor should buy the undervalued bond, which could in principle be separated in two zero-coupon bonds, offering more value to the holder.

7 a. The forward rates are computed from:

Maturity	Spot rate	Forward rate	Price
1	10%		1,000/1.10 = 909.09
2	11%	(1.11/1.10) − 1 = 12%	$1{,}000/1.11^2 = 811.62$
3	12%	$(1.12^3/1.11^2) - 1 = 14\%$	$1{,}000/1.12^3 = 711.78$

The expected spot rates for year 2 and 3 are therefore 12% and 14%.

b. The expected interest rate on a two-year bond next year is obtained from solving $1.12^3 = \left(1+f_{0,1,3}\right)^2 \times 1.1$, giving $f_{0,1,3} = 13\%$. The same result can be obtained by $\sqrt{1{,}12 \times 1{,}14} - 1$. The curve next year is expected to have a one-year rate equal to 12% and a two-year rate equal to 13%.

c. We can find next year's prices and spot rates by discounting the face value using forward rates:

Maturity	Price
1	1,000/1.12 = 892.78
2	$1{,}000/1.13^2 = 782.93$

Note that this year's positively sloping curve implies an upward shift of the entire curve for next year.

Next year, the two-year zero coupon bond (ZCB) will be a one-year ZCB and will be priced at 1,000/1.12 = 892.78. Similarly, the three-year ZCB will become a two-year ZCB and will be priced at 782.93. The expected returns are therefore:

$$\text{2-year ZCB: } \frac{892.78}{811.62} - 1 = 10\%$$

$$\text{3-year ZCB: } \frac{782.93}{711.78} - 1 = 10\%$$

d. The value of the coupon security is the value of the basket of zero-coupon bonds. Price = (120 × 0.90909) + (120 × 0.81162) + (1,120 × 0.71178) = 109.0908 + 97.3944 + 797.1936 = 1,003.68.

Similarly, the expected prices of zero-coupon bonds in a year's time can be used to calculate the expected price in one year's time: expected price in one year = (120 × 0.89278) + (1,120 ×0.78293) = 107.1336 + 876.8816 = 984.02. The expected holding period return is $\frac{120 + 984.02 - 1{,}003.68}{1{,}003.68} = 10\%$. Expected returns on all investment strategies are equal to the one-year spot rate.

8 a. $P = \frac{80}{1.06} + \frac{1{,}080}{1.07^2} = 1{,}018.8$

b. The yield-to-maturity is the solution to: $\frac{80}{1+y} + \frac{1{,}080}{(1+y)^2} = 1{,}018.8$

from which y = 6.961%.

c. The forward is f_2 in: $f_2 = \frac{1.07^2}{1.06} - 1 = 8\%$.

Therefore the expected rate is 8% and the expected price is:

$$P = \frac{1{,}080}{1.08} = 1{,}000.$$

d. If LP = 1% the expected rate is lower than the forward rate due to a preference for short-term bonds requiring a higher rate on the two-year bond, in turn causing a forward rate reflecting such liquidity premium. If we take out the liquidity premium from the forward rate then we have:

$$Er_2 = f_2 - LP = 8.01\% - 1\% = 7.01\%.$$

The expected price is: $\frac{108}{1.0701} = 1{,}009.6$.

6 Risk and management of bond portfolios

6.1 Introduction

The chapter introduces elements useful for the analysis of the main risk factors of the bond portfolio, namely interest rate risk and credit risk. The first part deals with interest rate risk, that is, the risk of short-term fluctuations in bond prices caused by changes in market rates. Given the complexity and non-linearity of pricing formulas, the definition of duration is introduced to have a linear approximation that simply describes the impact of the change in the rate on the market price of the bond. Using the definition of convexity, we can provide a better quadratic approximation to the bond pricing equation. From the definition of duration, it is then easy to determine the expectation and the volatility of the holding period return of a bond based on the expectation and the volatility of the change in interest rates. Duration can be interpreted as the point in time when the reduction in the price of a bond caused by an increase in the market rate is offset by the advantage associated with the possibility to reinvest the coupons at a higher rate. This intuition is useful to hedge against interest rate risk: we can match durations of assets and liabilities to make the value of a portfolio as close as possible to the value constituted by liabilities (asset-liability management problem). As a result, duration leads to the concept of immunization. In the final part, the chapter briefly discusses the relevance of credit risk for bond pricing and introduces the definitions of probability of default and loss given default, which make it possible to measure the risk associated with fluctuations in the issuer's creditworthiness as a result of changes in the value of the assets as compared with the value of the liabilities. Several tools associated with credit risk can be used to study loan pricing, which must account for expected credit loss as well as a risk premium to provide the lender with a remuneration which is compatible with its use of capital.

6.2 Duration

6.2.1 Definition

The idea of maturity is ambiguous for coupon bonds because it does not provide a true picture of how long it will take to repay the investment. The higher the coupon, the faster the repayment of invested money, so two bonds can have different maturities but can repay the invested capital at different speeds. Moreover, everything else being equal, bonds with long maturities have steeper price-yield curves than bonds with short maturities, so interest rate sensitivity is different. How can we measure these concepts?

We use the idea of duration (the Fisher-Weil duration), equal to the ratio of the sum of the product between the times t when payments are made and the present value of cash flows FC, divided by the sum of the present value of the cash flows, that is, the price of the bond:

$$D = \frac{\sum_{t=1}^{T} t \times FC_t \times \left(1 + r_{f,0,t}\right)^{-t}}{\sum_{t=1}^{T} FC_t \times \left(1 + r_{f,0,t}\right)^{-t}} = \sum_{t=1}^{T} t \times w_t \,.$$

Macaulay specializes such a definition when there is a unique spot rate (flat term structure) corresponding to the YTM y. In such a case it is possible to obtain duration from the first derivative of the price relative to the yield:

$$\frac{dP}{dy} = -\sum_{t=1}^{T} t \times FC_t \times \left(1 + y\right)^{-t-1} = \frac{-\sum_{t=1}^{T} t \times FC_t \times \left(1 + y\right)^{-t}}{(1 + y)} \,.$$

Dividing both sides by P, we get:

$$\frac{1}{P} \times \frac{dP}{dy} = \frac{-\sum_{t=1}^{T} t \times FC_t \times \left(1 + y\right)^{-t}}{P \times (1 + y)} = -\frac{D}{1 + y} \tag{1}$$

We define modified duration as $D_M = \frac{D}{1 + y}$. Whereas duration is measured in years, modified duration is measured as the percent change in the price per one percentage point in yield. Equation (1) shows that modified duration is a synthetic measure associated with the sensitivity of bond returns to changes in rates.

6.2.2 Duration and maturity

As can be seen from Figure 6.1, duration is shorter than maturity for all bonds except ZCBs, but the same for ZCBs due to the absence of payment flows other than the return of the face value. It can be shown that the duration of a perpetuity is $(1 + y)/y$.

Keeping the residual maturity constant, the duration of the bond increases as the coupon rate decreases (in Figure 6.1, see the comparison between the function with $c = 4\%$ and those with $c = 2\%$ and $c = 0\%$). If the coupon rate is constant, duration typically increases with the remaining maturity. Taking into account the other factors, the duration of a coupon bond increases as the yield to maturity decreases (as can be seen from the comparison of the result with yields of 4% and 2%, all other factors being equal).

Figure 6.1 **The relation between duration and maturity**

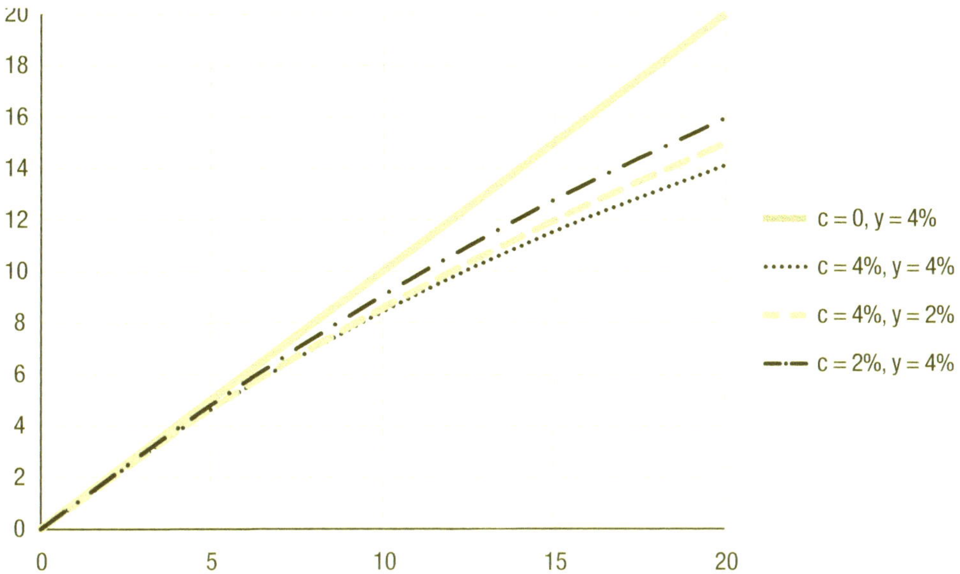

6.2.3 Duration and rate risk

Duration can be used to approximate the percentage change in the price of a bond. To see this let us use equation (1) and consider a linear approximation to a discrete change in the yield:

$$\frac{\Delta P}{P} \approx -D_M \times \Delta y\,.$$

The crucial element in managing a bond portfolio is the expected return and risk associated with interest rate fluctuations, and according to this insight, duration is a measure of the sensitivity of bond returns to changes in yields. Modified duration may be used as a proxy for discrete price changes.

The formula is useful to compute the expected return and volatility of bond returns:

$$E\frac{\Delta P}{P} \approx -D_M \times E\Delta y$$

$$\sigma_{\frac{\Delta P}{P}} = D_M \times \sigma_{\Delta y} \qquad (2)$$

confirming the relevance of changes in YTM, and therefore interest rates, as the crucial element for the expected return on bonds.

Empirically, there is debate as to whether bond yield volatility can be better explained by a slight change in equation (2). Multiplying and dividing the right-hand side of equation (1) by the initial level of the YTM gives an alternative formulation that $\sigma_{\frac{\Delta P}{P}} = D_M \times y \times \sigma_{\frac{\Delta y}{y}}$, which suggests measuring the volatility of the return through the volatility of the percentage change in the YTM (instead of just the absolute change) and multiplying by the product of modified duration and interest rate. Ben Dor et al. (2007) present empirical evidence on the increased temporal stability of $\sigma_{\frac{\Delta y}{y}}$ relative to $\sigma_{\Delta y}$ for bonds whose volatility depends primarily on the credit spread. An important risk measurement tool when the term structure is not flat is key rate duration, computed as:

$$D_{kr,t} = \frac{P^-_{0,t} - P^+_{0,t}}{2 \times \Delta r_{f,0,t}}$$

where $P^-_{0,t}$ is the bond price if the key interest rate increases by a small amount $\Delta r_{f,0,t}$, and $P^+_{0,t}$ is the bond price if the key interest rate decreases by a small amount $\Delta r_{f0,t}$. The key rate duration for maturity t is useful to understand which bonds are more sensitive to a change in the spot rate for a particular maturity. For example, the two-year key rate duration measures a bond's sensitivity to changes in the two-year interest rate along the yield curve. If a bond has a two-year key rate duration of 2, it means that the bond's price will change by 2% for every 1% change in the two-year interest rate. The overall key rate duration measures a bond's sensitivity to changes in interest rates across the entire yield curve.

6.2.4 Convexity

Duration is a first-degree approximation to the relationship between price and rate. To get a better approximation, we can use the quadratic function. Approximating the non-linear relation between price and YTM with the quadratic function, and using $\frac{dP}{dy}(y_0)$ to denote the first derivative of the price relative to the yield (evaluated at the initial yield y_0) and $\frac{d^2P}{dy^2}(y_0)$ to denote the second derivative of the price relative to the interest rate (always evaluated at the initial rate y_0), we get:

$$P(y) = P(y_0) + (y - y_0)\frac{dP}{dy}(y_0) + 0.5\,(y - y_0)^2\frac{d^2P}{dy^2}(y_0)$$

where the derivatives are evaluated at the initial yield y_0. Dividing by the initial price and defining $\Delta P = P(y) - P(y_0)$:

$$\frac{\Delta P}{P(y_0)} \approx \Delta y \times \frac{1}{P(y_0)} \times \frac{dP}{dy}(y_0) + 0.5 \times \Delta y^2 \times C$$

where C is convexity, defined as $C = \frac{\frac{d^2P}{dy^2}(y_0)}{P(y_0)}$. The above formula takes advantage of the introduction of the quadratic term to obtain a better approximation to the actual price change.

Convexity is desirable for bondholders: It is multiplied by the square of the change in rates in the formula, so any movement has a positive impact on returns. The market price of a security therefore, other things being equal, has a level that rises with convexity.

> **Box 6.1 How important is hedging risk in asset allocation?**
>
> **Question**: Elena purchased thirty-year bonds, with a modified duration of 11.26 years and convexity of 212.4, at a coupon rate of 8%, quoted at par. The day after the purchase, the rate on these bonds rose from 8% to 10%. How much did Elena lose if the return is approximated?
>
> **Answer**: If the yield rises from 8% to 10%, the price of the bond falls to 811.46, that is, -18.85%. Using duration gives a linear approximation of $-11.26 \times 0.02 = -22.52\%$. Using convexity, it is $-11.26 \times 0.02 + 0.5 \times 212.4 \times 0.02^2 = -18.27\%$.

6.3 Immunization

6.3.1 Duration, reinvestment risk, and price risk

An investor holding a bond is subject to two sources of risk. The first is "price risk," consisting of the variability of the market price of the bond. The second is "reinvestment risk," consisting of the risk associated with reinvesting the coupons of the bond at unknown future spot rates. For a short-horizon price risk is the dominant force, while the opposite is true for a long horizon. The only relevant risk when the horizon corresponds with the maturity of the bond is reinvestment risk because the price cannot change on the maturity date being equal to the face value.

Consider, for example, a three-year bond with a coupon of 10% and a yield to maturity of 10%. At the end of the second year, if there has been no change in the interest rate, the value is given by the amount of the first coupon, equal to $10 \times 1.1 = 11$, plus the value of the second coupon, equal to 10 plus the present value of future cash flows equal to $\frac{110}{1.1} = 100$, for a total value equal to 121. If, immediately after the initial purchase, the market rate rises to 12%, the first coupon has a final value of $10 \times 1.12 = 11.2$ (larger than initially expected) and the present value is $\frac{110}{1.12} = 98.214$ (lower than initially expected) for a total value of 119.414 also considering the intermediate coupon equal to 10. The value after two years is lower than initially expected if there is an increase in interest rate from 10% to 12%: Price risk dominates reinvestment risk. Similarly, if the rate fell to 8%, the first coupon would have a final value of $10 \times 1.08 = 10.8$ and the present value would be $\frac{110}{1.08} = 101.851$ for a total value of 122.652, greater than the previous one. The value of the bond and reinvested coupon after two years moves with the price.

For the two-year horizon, therefore, the price factor dominates the reinvestment factor since the total future value of the investment moves inversely with the interest rate. For a longer horizon, the reinvestment factor would predominate. In the previous example the total final value at the end of year 3 is given by $10 \times 1.1^2 + 10 \times 1.1 + 110 = 133.1$. The final value is equal to 133.74 when the yield goes up to 12% ($10 \times 1.12^2 + 10 \times 1.12 + 110 = 133.74$) and 132.46 when the yield goes down to 8%. This is intuitive: When the horizon is equal to the maturity of the bond the holder gains (loses) from an increase (decrease) in interest rates allowing for better (worse) reinvestment opportunities.

Duration corresponds to the time when price risk and reinvestment risk offset each other and the future value of the investment is not affected by small changes in interest rates. In the previous example, the Macaulay duration is equal to 2.73 years. The final value at that time as a function of the reinvestment rate y is equal to $10 \times (1+y)^{1.73} + 10 \times (1+y)^{0.73} + \dfrac{110}{(1+y)^{0.27}}$. When $y = 10\%$ the final value is 129.79, when $y = 9\%$ the final value is 129.83, and when $y = 11\%$ the final value is 129.74, with a very small 0.04% change.

Of course, the value of the duration is a function of the level of the yield: After the yield changes following a change in interest rates, the duration of the security also changes and with it the horizon of compensation for price risk and reinvestment risk.

6.3.2 Immunization

Immunization describes the goal of keeping the future value of the portfolio close to the value of a predetermined future sum. The future sum, which can be interpreted as a liability, can be thought of as the value of a ZCB security, which is to be covered by a bond portfolio. Immunizing the portfolio means structuring it so that its value is close to the value of the liability even in the presence of changes in interest rates.

The easiest, and most effective, way to immunize a liability is to form a portfolio of ZCBs that provide exactly the cash flows needed in the future. If, for example, there is a need to have a sum of 100 in three years' time and 100 in five years' time, it will be sufficient to buy a three-year ZCB and a five-year ZCB at the prices prevailing on the market today.

However, this technique, referred to as cash flow matching, is not always feasible due to the lack of risk-free bonds maturing on the scheduled dates. In the example above, there may not be a ZCB that expires in exactly five years, but a ZCB that expires in five years and three months. In this case, at the relevant date, you would have a bond that has a residual maturity of three months and therefore does not necessarily ensure the value necessary to meet the liability. Or there could be a ZCB that matures in exactly five years but was issued by a company (corporate bond) or is denominated in a currency other than the one in which the liability is denominated. Both of these cases would carry other elements of risk, namely default risk and currency risk.

An alternative is to use the guidance provided by duration. We have seen that duration must be understood as the date on which the change in the future values of reinvested coupons and the change in the present value of future coupons and face value exactly offset each other, leaving the value of the asset unchanged. This result can be used for immunization: if the duration of the asset matches the duration of the liability, a one-off change in interest rates will change the future value of the asset and liabilities in the same way, ensuring that the risk of a change in the interest rate is fully covered.

To better describe this solution to the problem of immunization, let us assume the need for a sum of money equal to 107.99 in 3.8839 years. Let us also assume that it is only possible to buy a four-year bond with a coupon rate of 2%, face value and price equal to 100 (due to the interest rate initially being equal to the coupon rate), and a duration of 3.8839 years. Table 6.1 shows that small changes in the interest rate (from 2% to 1% or from 2% to 3%) have little impact on the final value because the coupon effect offsets the price effect.

Table 6.1 Financial immunization

	Rate 2%	Rate 1%	Rate 3%
Final value coupons after 3.8839 years	6.23	6.11	6.35
Bond present value	101.766	101.882	101.66
Total	107.996	107.992	108.01

In fact, it can be seen in the first column (2% rate) that in the initial conditions the debt of 107.99 is fully repaid by the coupons reinvested at the rate of 2% (6.23) and the present value of the bond (101.766). In the second column (1% rate) we can see that, when the rate falls to 1%, the value of coupons decreases (from 6.23 to 6.11) but the present value of the bond rises to 101.88 at the new rate of 1%. In column 3 (3% rate) the opposite happens, but the total is always the same as the predetermined value (apart from a small approximation error). In general, therefore, to immunize a liability, it is necessary to buy a bond, or form a portfolio of bonds, with a duration equal to the duration of the liabilities (in the example above, the duration of the liability coincides with its maturity because it is a single flow of debt). Box 6.2 and Problem 5 at the end of the chapter show how to deal with the case of creating a portfolio of bonds of varying time durations by making the duration of the bond portfolio equal to the duration of the liabilities.

Immunization only applies to one change in interest rates. Of course, given a time horizon, there is no guarantee that there will be a single change in interest rates. After a variation, all the parameters of the problem have changed; it is therefore necessary to change the structure of the portfolio to get protection from new future changes. Such immunization strategy is therefore a dynamic portfolio choice that can result in high transaction costs.

Box 6.2 How to form a portfolio that immunizes a flow of liabilities

Question: Carola must form a portfolio that allows an investor to hedge a liability consisting of an outflow of 100 for five years, using a one-year bond with a 6% coupon rate and a four-year bond with an 8% coupon rate. The current rate is 10%. What does she need to do?

Answer: Carola must first calculate the duration of the liability, using the analysis in the table below, reporting the year in column 1, cash flows (CF) in column 2, discount factors (DF) in column 3, present value of cash flows (PVCF) in column 4, and the product of present values and cash flows in the last column.

Liability

Year	CF	DF	PVCF	PVCF ×Year
1	100	0.9091	90.91	90.91
2	100	0.8264	82.64	165.29
3	100	0.7513	75.13	225.39
4	100	0.6830	68.30	273.21
5	100	0.6209	62.09	310.46

The present value of the liabilities obtained from the sum of the present value of the flows is equal to 379.07. The sum of the product between the payment dates and the present value of the disbursements, which must be entered in the numerator of the duration indicator, is equal to the sum of the numbers contained in the last column and is equal to 1065.26. Duration is the ratio of 1065.26 to 379.07, that is, 2.81 years.
Carola now has to calculate the duration of the bonds. The duration of the first bond is evidently equal to one year because it has a single flow of coupon and face value payments. The duration of the four-year bond is calculated in a manner similar to that used for the duration of liabilities.

Year	CF	DF	PVCF	PVCF ×Year
1	8	0.9091	7.27	7.27
2	8	0.8264	6.61	13.22
3	8	0.7513	6.01	18.03
4	108	0.6830	73.77	295.58

The duration is therefore equal to 335.58 divided by 93.66, which gives 3.56 years.
The investment portions in the two bonds that make the duration of the asset equal to that of the liabilities solve the equation $w + (1 - w) \times 3.56 = 2.81$, which provides 0.293 and 0.707. Given that the present value of liabilities is 379.07, Carola needs to invest 111.21 in the one-year bond and 267.86 in the four-year bond.

Box 6.3 How to manage a portfolio that immunizes a liability

Question: Sara has to form a portfolio to meet an expense of 10 million in a year and 4 million in five years. The term structure is flat at 2%. Which bond should she choose and how should she manage her portfolio to meet her debts?

Answer: Sara must first calculate the duration of the liability, using the analysis in the table below.

Liabilities

Year	CF	PVCF	PVCF × Year
1	10	9.80	9.80
5	4	3.62	18.10

The present value of liabilities obtained from the sum of the present value of flows is equal to 13.42. The sum of the product between the payment dates and the present value of the disbursements, which must be entered in the numerator of the duration indicator, is equal to the sum of the numbers contained in the last column and is equal to 27.90. Duration is the ratio of 27.92 to 13.42, that is, 2.08 years.

Sara must therefore invest €13.42 million in a 2.08-year-old ZCB. After one year, the value of the bond is 13.69. Carola withdraws €10 million to pay off the first flow of debt. The remaining value of €3.69 million remains invested in the bond and rises to 4 in period 5, allowing the full payment of the debt in the fifth year.

6.4 Corporate bonds

6.4.1 General features

Corporate bonds are issued by companies. The description of a corporate bond includes more features than those described above and typically sufficient to describe sovereign bonds. The details of the issuance are described in a contract (indenture) also describing covenants that include collateral, restrictions on the dividend policy, and on any further future financing. To protect their position, bondholders may require that the issuance of any new debt be subordinated to the previous debt, that is, in case of default current bondholders are paid before the other creditors. They can also constrain the dividend policy so that shareholders do not decide to use cash to remunerate shareholders, making the company's overall position weaker due to the reduction in the equity base.

The value of corporate debt, be it in the form of bonds or loans, is depicted in Figure 6.2 as a relation to the value of assets, an idea originally introduced by Merton (1974). The nominal value of debt is assumed to be equal to 100, and for levels of assets above the nominal value, the market value of debt is equal to the face value, as shown in the dotted line. Shareholders, whose value is described in the continuous line, get all the surplus above the face value of debt. At the same time, whenever the value of assets is below the face value of debt, then the value of equity is equal to zero, and the value of debt is equal to the value of assets. If the company closed down when the value of assets was below the face value, then all the value would be appropriated by bondholders. When the value of assets is equal to 160, the value of debt remains equal to 100 and the value of equity is 60.

Figure 6.2 The relation between the value of debt and the value of assets

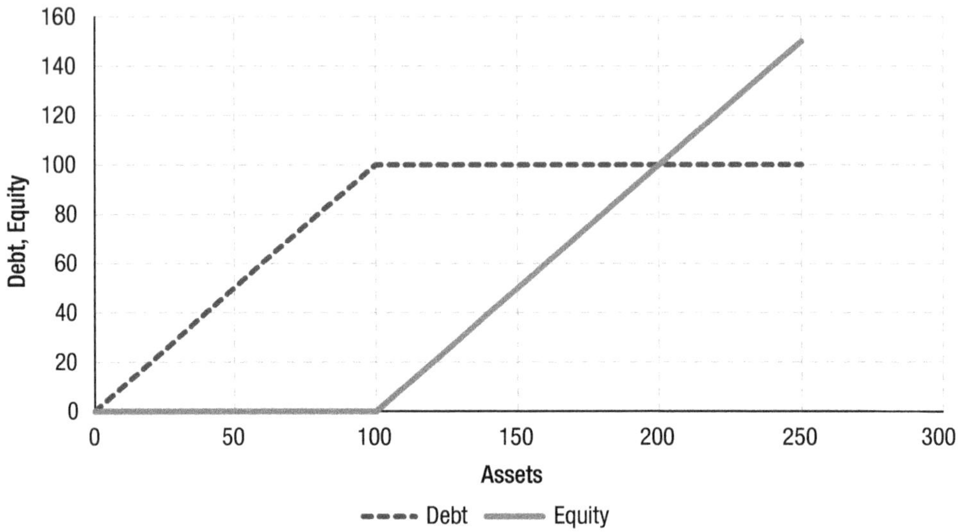

The possibility that the value of assets goes below the face value of debt is considered by lenders and buyers of corporate bonds at the time of issuance. It is an element of risk that needs to be measured ex ante and compensated through an appropriate remuneration. Credit ratings are a tool for ex ante measurement of risk, and the corporate spread is the risk premium inducing lenders and bondholders to provide credit to corporations.[1]

This is the main distinction between risk-free sovereign bonds and corporate bonds: The short-run dynamics of both depends on the dynamics of interest rates, but corporate bond prices (and loan market value) also reflect the short-run dynamics of credit and the associated risk premium. This distinction is artificial of course: Even sovereign bonds are priced by accounting for the risk that the state may not be able to pay the coupons and/or the face value during the life of the bond.

[1] This observation has been developed in an extensive academic literature starting from the structural model of Merton (1974), which adopts the arbitrage models used to determine the price of derivative instruments by decomposing credit into a risk-free component and a short position on a put option on the value of the company's assets.

6.4.2 Credit ratings

Corporate bonds are rated by one or more of the three major agencies, Standard & Poor's, Moody's, and Fitch. The rating is assigned considering the financial health of the issuer and therefore the probability of repayment of interest and principal. The scale with which the rating is expressed varies from one agency to another; for example, Moody's uses a scale with nine levels from Aaa up to C.

Depending on the rating received, corporate bonds can be considered "investment grade" or "non-investment grade" (or high yield or speculative). For example, in the case of Moody's, high-yield bonds are those placed in the Ba to C tiers. Investment-grade bonds typically have less risk (but Lehman Brothers had issued investment-grade bonds) and therefore pay less interest. Non-investment-grade bonds are considered "speculative investments" and pay higher coupons to compensate for the higher risk. A change in the issuer's health over time may result in a change in the rating.

Ratings are important not only for corporate issuers, but also for states. A rating deterioration, a downgrade, is typically associated with an increase in the cost of debt to the state. The consequences of a downgrade reverberate on the domestic corporate sector in general, as typically corporate companies and even financial institutions in a certain country can issue bonds at a cost equal to that paid by the government plus a spread that reflects the specific riskiness of the issuer.

6.4.3 Probability of default and loss given default

The market rate and price of the bond are determined by investors based on various elements, including, as we saw in Chapter 5, maturity. Among the elements that are particularly relevant for corporate bonds[2] is investors' perception of risk in relation to the issuer's ability to pay coupons and principal.[3] A default is a legal procedure reserved to a debtor who is unable to service his debts. In a default all creditors, depending on the contractual characteristics and the degree of priority assigned, obtain only a share of their credit, which depends on the value of the company's assets at the time of default, the price obtained at the time of sale of these assets, and the priority of the creditors in relation to the others'.

Investors then estimate how likely it is that default will occur (probability of default, PD) and what the loss (in terms of the present value of the coupons that have yet to be paid and the payment of the par value) could be in the event of default (loss given default, LGD). The LGD parameter is highly sensitive to the position of the considered liability class in the priority scale.

The product of PD and LGD is called the expected loss because it represents the

---

[2] Sovereign bonds are also not necessarily considered risk-free, particularly after some episodes of outright default (Argentina) or debt restructuring (Greece).

[3] It is often assumed that only corporate bonds are subject to the risk of default. In fact, investors also value PD and LGD for sovereign bonds.

portion of the loan that is not expected to be repaid. The higher the PD and LGD values, the lower the price investors are willing to pay to buy the bond and therefore the higher the interest rate. In the case of a bank or fund providing a loan (private debt funds; see Chapter 14) and in the case of an investor buying a corporate bond, a higher level of PD and LGD is associated with a higher interest rate to compensate investors for the risk incurred. On a unit loan or bond, the expected value of the contract $1+x$ at the end of the period is equal to:

$$1 + x = (1 + i) \times (1 - PD) + (1 + i) \times (1 - LGD) \times PD$$

where i is the contractual rate. According to the formula, if the company does not go bankrupt, which happens with probability $1 - PD$, then the creditor receives the agreed interest. Meanwhile, if the company goes bankrupt, probability PD, then the creditor receives the amount of money $(1 + i) \times (1 - LGD)$.

The expected remuneration x must compensate for the cost of time and the cost of risky lending or investing and therefore must include a risk premium that we may think of as a spread s over the remuneration of the risk-free asset r_f, so that $x = r_f + s$. Among the factors relevant to the explanation of the credit spread over and above risk factors, we need to consider liquidity and the presence of contractual options.

The contractual break-even rate for the creditor is therefore:

$$i = \frac{r_f + s + PD \times LGD}{1 - PD \times LGD}.$$

The ability on the part of the investor to obtain the contractual break-even rate depends on the price of corporate bonds. When the equation is applied to describe the cost of lending by a bank or a private debt fund then there are crucial considerations about competition in the lending market. If there is high competition on the part of several lenders, then the actual cost of debt may be below the break-even rate. Some lenders may decide to opt out from such a contract if the cost of capital is larger than such rate, but other lenders may decide to fund a corporation at a rate below the contractual rate if they need to deploy capital (for example a private debt fund has committed to invest investors' money within a fixed time horizon) and/or if they want to exploit so-called cross-selling benefits consisting of the lenders obtaining profits from other services that are provided in conjunction with the loan.

Box 6.4 What coupon rate to pay for a new issue?

Question: Sara is an advisor to a corporation that is considering the possibility of issuing a new bond with a nominal value of €10 million with a maturity of five years. Sara must estimate the coupon rate that will have to be provided in this bond to make it of interest to the market.

Answer: Sara must first estimate the parameters of PD and LGD. The estimation of these parameters requires a large database which is difficult to obtain, because it would have to include histories of many companies, with an indication of their main characteristics over the years, including companies that have gone bankrupt and that can give valuable information about what can go wrong in companies that are currently active. Sara then buys the information from a specialized data provider that indicates a PD of 1.4% and an LGD of 50%. Second, Sara needs to know what rate of return the investor requires to purchase the bond, assuming that the bond is held to maturity. Looking at market prices, she estimates that investors want a 3.5% return from such an investment. Sara calculates the contractual rate using $\frac{3.5\% + (1.4\%) \times 50\%}{1 - 1.4\% \times 50\%}$, which equals 4.23%.

6.4.4 Corporate bond returns

The interest rate received by investors must compensate for the risk elements highlighted above. The credit spread, the interest differential on corporate bonds and sovereign bonds, should compensate for both the average losses incurred by holding the securities and the risks of loss.

Ang (2014), for the period 1987–2011, reports an excess return of 0.32% for AAAs, 0.43% for As, and 0.86% for CAAs,[4] and a spread level of 0.93%, 1.45%, and 10.19% respectively. The average losses realized across the three rating classes were 0%, 0.02%, and 13.34% respectively. There is therefore a significant gap between the average level of the credit spread, also adjusted for realized losses, and the average returns actually obtained, in light of the observation that the expected loss, the product of PD and LGD, should, over long periods, coincide with the average realized losses.

Such a gap is not well explained by theoretical models: When we use realized losses to calibrate the models, they return a lower spread between the risky lending rate and the risk-free rate than the one observed, resulting in the "credit spread puzzle" phenomenon, which is particularly relevant for investment-grade corporate bonds, as noted for example by Huang and Huang (2012).

Giesecke et al. (2011) construct a database dating back to 1866 and find that in the period up to 2008 the average LGD was 50% and the PD was 1.5%, which gives a rough estimate of annual losses of 75 basis points. Over the same period, the average credit spread was 153 basis points, about double the expected losses, at a premium of 0.8%. Econometric analyses find little correlation between credit spreads and default rates and between changes in spreads over time and macroeconomic variables, consistent with the results of Collin-Dufresne, Goldstein, and Martin (2001).[5]

DeJong and Driessen (2012) consider not only average liquidity but also the liquidity

---

[4] DeJong and Driessen (2012) present information on the premiums received by investors, which in the United States for the period 1993–2002 were 0.52% for AAA-rated bonds and 2.56% for CCC-rated bonds.

[5] Ang (2014) highlights the similarity between the equity premium puzzle and the credit spread puzzle and highlights the sharp increase in credit losses seen in recessions, which causes risk-averse investors to demand a high level of compensation because losses on corporate bonds, especially speculative bonds, occur at the riskiest times of the cycle and, in the logic of the Capital Asset Pricing Model (CAPM) and Consumption Capital Asset Pricing Model (CCAPM), they have a high beta. This observation will make sense to the reader after the corresponding chapters discussing the equity premium puzzle, the CAPM, and the CCAPM.

shock risk premium, which they estimate to be responsible for an excess yield of 0.6% for long-term investment-grade bonds and 1.5% for high-yield bonds. Results highlighting the relevance of the liquidity premium are also presented by Longstaff, Mithal, and Neis (2005). Bongaerts, De Jong, and Driessen (2017) find a material impact on the level of liquidity and exposure to liquidity shocks in the equity market, but not those in the corporate bond market, explaining the result by the lack of trading existing in the corporate bond market. According to the authors, liquidity-sensitive investors typically act in the stock market and avoid the corporate bond market because it is not very liquid under normal conditions and completely illiquid during crises. Bongaerts, De Jong, and Driessen (2017) also argue that their empirical model may offer an explanation for the credit spread puzzle, due to the typical level of liquidity of corporate bonds. Asvanunt and Richardson (2017) extend the available data backward in time and find a credit premium on investment-grade corporate bonds between 1936 and 2014 equal to 1.5%. Ilmanen (2022) looks at more recent evidence and finds an average excess return of 0.75% for investment-grade bonds and 2.8% for high-yield bonds.

6.4.5 Corporate bond risk measurement

Credit risk is caused by an unexpected deterioration in the borrower's ability to pay. Default is only the extreme case. A deterioration in credit merit associated, for example, with a downgrade from A to BBB is an example of realization of credit risk. We have already defined the *PD* (probability of default) and the *LGD* (loss given default). We now introduce the exposure at default (*EAD*) and find that in general the expected loss (*EL*) is equal to:

$$EL = PD \times LGD \times EAD.$$

Unexpected loss is the difference between the actual loss and the expected loss. If the lender must hold equity capital, for example in the case of a bank, then it follows that the expected loss must be offset by the cost of lending while the unexpected loss must be covered by equity capital. The actual loss depends on the riskiness of the loan portfolio and it is therefore partially under the control of the bank.

Models for measurement of credit risk of a portfolio of loans or bonds are complex, especially due to the need to estimate the correlation across defaults of various issuers. Fortunately, companies' defaults are not so frequent and even long time series do not allow significant estimate of relevant parameters. The reader is invited to refer to Risk Metrics Group (2007) for a description of one such portfolio methodology. Methodologies for measuring credit risk have been developed based on probabilities of joint changes in the ratings of the corporate bonds in the portfolio which represent realizations of risk. The main empirical challenge lies in measuring the correlations of such rating changes. Risk Metrics Group (2007) describes the estimation of transition matrices, measuring the probabilities of migration of a bond currently part of a specific rating into another rating class, and the use of information obtained from the equity market to estimate correlation of rating changes on the basis of the Merton (1974) asset value model described above.

Summary

- Duration is an indicator of the average length of time associated with coupon payments and the nominal value of debt.
- Thanks to duration, it is possible to link the percentage change in the price of a coupon bond to the change in its yield to maturity in a simple but approximate way. The approximation applies to small changes in yield.
- Duration also allows us to calculate the volatility of the bond's yield due to the volatility of the change in yield to maturity.
- A better approximation of the holding period return of the bond as the yield changes is obtained with the quadratic approximation, which also introduces an element of convexity.
- In terms of hedging the risk of interest rate changes, duration can be interpreted as the date on which the price risk is exactly offset by the risk of redeployment.
- Immunizing a position means buying a bond or portfolio of bonds in such a way that the value of the bond or portfolio at a fixed future date is constant and independent of any changes in interest rates.
- The easiest and most effective way to immunize is to follow the cash flow matching technique, which is based on a portfolio that pays the necessary cash flows at exact future times.
- When cash flow matching is not possible, duration can be used: one needs to buy a bond or portfolio whose duration is equivalent to the duration of the liability that represents the spending target. Ownership only applies to a change in the interest rate, after which the portfolio needs to be rebalanced.
- In the event that the target is not a single expense stream but a series of expense streams, the duration of the liability must be calculated and a portfolio with a duration similar to that of the liability must be formed.
- A general approach to immunization is asset/liability management, where the surplus (the difference between assets and liabilities) is calculated and the portfolio is managed in a way that maximizes the expected value of the surplus and minimizes its variance.
- Corporate bonds are characterized by an element of risk in addition to interest rate risk, namely credit risk. The important parameters for describing credit risk are the probability of default and the loss given default. The product of the two is called an expected loss. The rate initially set by the bond buyer takes into account the expected loss and the existence of a risk premium.
- Empirical analyses of corporate bond pricing show the presence of a credit risk premium, as well as premium components related to the bond's typical illiquidity and illiquidity risk. Structural models, which make assumptions about the economic and financial equilibrium of the firm in order to estimate the expected loss, produce theoretical spreads for credit risk that are significantly lower than the observed spreads.
- Bank loans have a credit spread comparable to that of corporate bonds, but they offer greater protection against losses related to borrowers' repayment difficulties.

Problems

1 What is the percentage change in price for a nine-year bond with a 10% YTM and a duration of 7.194 years if the YTM changes by 0.5%?

2 Find the duration of a bond with a coupon rate of 6% that makes annual payments if it has a residual maturity of three years and a YTM of 6%. What is the duration if the YTM is 10%?

3 An insurance company has to pay a customer €10 million in a year and €4 million in five years. The yield curve is fixed at 10%. If you want to immunize and fully finance your debt with a single purchase of a ZCB, what maturity should you choose? What should be the face value and market value of the ZCB?

4 You have to pay €10,000 per year for the next two years. Interest rates on bonds are 8%.

a. What is the present value and duration of debt?
b. Which ZCB do you need to buy to immunize debt?
c. What happens to the debt and ZCB if the bond rate rises to 9% immediately after purchase?
d. What happens if the rate drops to 7%?

5 The manager of a €1 million portfolio has a target duration of ten years and can invest in two bonds, a ZCB with a maturity of five years and a perpetual bond, both with a 5% interest rate. How much do you hold of each bond in your portfolio?

Answers

1 $\frac{-D}{1+y} \times \Delta y = \frac{-7.194}{1.1} \times 0.005 = -3.27\%.$

2 When the YTM is 6%

(1) Payment dates (years)	(2) Cash flow	(3) PDV of CF at 6%	(4) Weight	(5) Col. (1) × Col. (4)
1	60.00	56.60	0.0566	0.0566
2	60.00	53.40	0.0534	0.1068
3	1.060.00	890.00	0.8900	2.6700
		1,000.00	1.0000	2.8334

Duration = 2.833 years. If the YTM is 10%:

(1) Payment dates (years)	(2) Cash flow	(3) PDV of CF at 10%	(4) Weight	(5) Col. (1) × Col. (4)
1	60.00	54.55	0.0606	0.0606
2	60.00	49.59	0.0551	0.1102
3	1,060.00	796.39	0.844	2.6532
		900.53	1.0000	2.8240

Duration is 2.824 years.

3

(1) Payment date (years)	(2) Cash flow	(3) PDV of CF at 10%	(4) Weight	(5) Col. (1) × Col. (4)
1	10,000,000	9,090,000	0.7857	0.7857
5	4,000,000	2,480,000	0.2143	1.0715
		11,570,000	1.0000	1.8572

D = 1.8572 years, corresponding to the maturity of the ZCB. The market value of the ZCB must be €11.57 million, such as the present value of liabilities. The face value must be €11.57 × $1.1^{1.8572}$ = €13.81 million.

4 a.

(1) Payment date (years)	(2) Cash flow	(3) Cash flow present value (discounted at 8%)	(4) Weight	(5) Col.(1) × Col.(4)
1	10,000.00	9,259,259	0.51923	0.51923
2	10,000.00	8,573,388	0.48077	0.96154
		17,832,647	1.00000	1.48077

Duration = 1.4808 years.

b. To immunize the debt, you need to choose a ZCB that matures in 1.4808 years. Since the current value of the bond must be 17,832.65, the face value must be:

$$€17{,}832.65 \times 1.08^{1.4808} = €19{,}985.26$$

c. If the rate rises to 9%, the value of the ZCB falls to: $€\frac{19{,}985.26}{1.09^{1.4808}} = €17{,}590.92$, and the present value of the debt falls to €17,591.11. The total net position decreases by 0.19.

d. If the rate falls to 7%, the value of the ZCB rises to $€\frac{19{,}985.26}{1.07^{1.4808}} = €18{,}079.99$, and the present value of the debt rises to €18,080.18. The net position falls by 0.19.

5 The duration of the perpetual bond is 1.05/0.05 = twenty-one years. Let w be the weight of the ZCB. It must be:

$$w \times 5 + (1 - w) \times 21 = 10$$

from which $w = 0.6875$. The portfolio weights will be 11/16 invested in ZCB and 5/16 in the perpetual bond. Next year, the ZCB will have a duration of four years and a perpetuity of twenty-one years. To have the target duration of nine years, we solve for w:

$$w \times 4 + (1 - w) \times 21 = 9$$

from which $w = 0.7059$; as a result, the weight invested in the ZCB rises to 12/17 and that in the perpetuity decreases to 5/17.

7 The expected return/risk trade-off and the benefits of diversification

7.1 Introduction

The main use of the utility function in Chapter 3 was to select the best possible investment, with a view to choosing a security or another security in an alternative way. Investing does not typically involve choosing just one asset but is about the best combination of individual securities in portfolios. In Chapter 3 we identified expected return and variance, or volatility, as the indicators for making choices aimed at increasing utility. The same approach will be used for portfolio selection: The analysis concerns the definition of expected return and risk of portfolios starting from the analogous parameters relating to individual securities. This chapter starts from the simple case of a risk-free and a risky asset and derives the capital allocation line (CAL) as a key tool for understanding the expected return/risk properties of portfolios combining two such assets.

We next understand how to create a portfolio of risky securities, choosing their weights and starting with the case of two risky stocks. Some relevant questions are the following: How do we describe the relationship between expected return and risk among the infinite portfolios that can be composed based on two risky securities? What are the benefits of diversification? The mathematical aspect is more complex than that described in the case of the combination of a risk-free security and a risky security because in general the standard deviation of the return of a portfolio composed of two risky securities is not the weighted average of the standard deviation of the return of the individual securities. The combinations of expected return and volatility in the general case are represented by a curve that lies within a triangle defined by the two extreme cases of correlation of +1 and -1. For any value of the correlation coefficient below 1, the benefits of diversification are obtained: Given a target expected return, the lower the correlation coefficient, the lower the volatility of the portfolio, precisely because the volatility of the portfolio is lower than the weighted average of the volatilities of the individual securities.

Finally, to combine the risk-free rate and the portfolios composed of the two risky securities, it is possible to find the tangency portfolio, which maximizes the ratio of expected return to volatility, and the minimum variance portfolio. The CAL, as before, describes the infinite portfolios that can be obtained by combining the risk-free security and the tangency portfolio.

7.2 From individual assets to the portfolio

7.2.1 Portfolio return

Portfolio returns, known with certainty only ex post at the end of the investment period, can be characterized by indicators that can be estimated ex ante (at the beginning of the investment period). This is crucial to manage the expected return/risk trade-off in selecting a portfolio. The simplified case we are dealing with is that of a portfolio "*c*" consisting of a risky security (or portfolio) *p* and a risk-free asset with return r_f (a short-term risk-free rate), the value of which is, by definition, known at the beginning of the investment period:

$$r_c = w \times r_p + (1 - w) \times r_f. \quad (1)$$

For example, if $N = 2$, then the total value of the portfolio is 100, the value of security 1 is 20, and the value of security 2 is 80; we have $r_p = 0.2 \times r_p + 0.8 \times r_f$. If $r_p = 10\%$ and $r_f = 5\%$, we have $r_p = 0.2 \times 10\% + 0.8 \times 5\% = 6\%$. Equation (1) describes the return of the portfolio at the end of the investment period. For an investor who needs to select the weight *w*, the portfolio return is a random variable due to the risk associated with investing in the risky security: the risk associated with r_p is transmitted to the return of the overall portfolio r_c. Based on the summary statistics we have described in Chapter 2, a portfolio with a high percentage of stocks will have higher expected return and volatility than a portfolio largely invested in risk-free assets. Therefore, the rate of return on a portfolio is an endogenous random variable depending on its composition. It is endogenous because the investor chooses the weights of the assets and may therefore decide to hold a safe and low-expected-return portfolio or a risky and high-expected-return one. A very risk-averse person will be inclined to have a portfolio composition with a greater presence of the risk-free asset. If an individual is not very risk-averse, she will choose a portfolio composition with a higher presence of risky securities. Choosing *w*, the investor influences the properties of the overall portfolio in terms of both expected return and variance/volatility.

7.2.2 Expected return and volatility with a risky and a risk-free asset

We can easily find the expected return and volatility of the return of a portfolio consisting of a risky portfolio and the risk-free stock. In equation (1) both the weight *w* and the risk-free rate r_f are known. The expected return of the composite portfolio is therefore:

$$Er_c = E\left(w \times r_p + (1 - w) \times r_f\right) = w \times E\,r_p + \left((1 - w) \times r_f\right) \quad (2)$$

Equation (2) can also be rewritten as:

$$Er_c = r_f + w \times \left(Er_p - r_f\right) \tag{3}$$

showing how the expected return of the overall portfolio can be interpreted as the sum of the expected return of two portfolios: the first with an investment of 100% in the risk-free rate, the second obtained from a "long" investment in the risky security financed by debt at the risk-free rate, that is, a leveraged investment. The economic logic is simple: Investing initial wealth equal to 100 as 40 in risk-free and 60 in a risky portfolio is equivalent to investing 100 in risk-free, borrowing 60, and investing 60 in the risky portfolio. This is a purely illustrative interpretation: In reality, it makes no sense to borrow to invest in a risk-free security because the cost of debt is higher than that of investing in a risk-free asset. However, here we are ignoring the difference between the cost of debt and the risk-free rate.

The variance of the return of the composite portfolio is found by applying the definition of variance as the mean of the square of the deviation of the variable from its mean:

$$\sigma_c^2 = w^2 \sigma_p^2 \tag{4}$$

The standard deviation is the square root of the variance and therefore:

$$\sigma_c = w \times \sigma_p \tag{5}$$

Equations (3) and (5) describe how the expected return and volatility of the composite portfolio can be controlled by the investor by selecting the portion invested in the risky portfolio.

Box 7.1 Which portfolio provides the desired expected return?

Question: The expected return on the risky portfolio is 5%, the risk-free is 1%, and the volatility is 20%. Sara has an expected target return of at least 3% and wants to know if a portfolio invested 70% in the risky portfolio and 30% in the risk-free bond allows her to reach the target. If the risk portfolio consists of three stocks, A, B, and C, in proportions of 25%, 35%, and 40%, what is the share of assets invested in the risk-free and in the individual securities that make up the risk portfolio?

Answer: The expected return is $0.7 \times 5\% + 0.3 \times 1\% = 3.8\%$. The standard deviation is $0.7 \times 20\% = 14\%$. Sara therefore far exceeds her target. The share of assets invested in the individual securities is obtained by multiplying the portion invested in the risky portfolio (70%) by the shares invested in the three securities. The share of security A is $70\% \times 25\% = 17.5\%$, that of security B $70\% \times 35\% = 24.5\%$, and that for security C $70\% \times 40\% = 28\%$.

7.3 The capital allocation line

7.3.1 The relationship between expected return and risk

We now set ourselves the goal of combining the equation describing the expected return and the one describing volatility into a single equation explaining expected return directly as a function of risk. This can be done by solving for the portfolio share in one equation and then substituting in the other. If we use equation (5) and solve for the portion invested in the risky security, we find $w = \frac{\sigma_c}{\sigma_p}$. Substituting in equation (2):

$$Er_c = r_f + \sigma_c \times \frac{\left(Er_p - r_f\right)}{\sigma_p} \tag{6}$$

describing a linear relationship between expected return and standard deviation of the portfolio "c." The equation is the capital allocation line (CAL), showing the relationship between expected return and volatility. Figure 7.1 is plotted for risk-free equal to 2%, expected return 5%, and volatility 20%. The figure highlights four alternative portfolios (the points on the line) with a share invested in the risky portfolio ranging from 0 to 1.5.

Figure 7.1 **The capital allocation line**

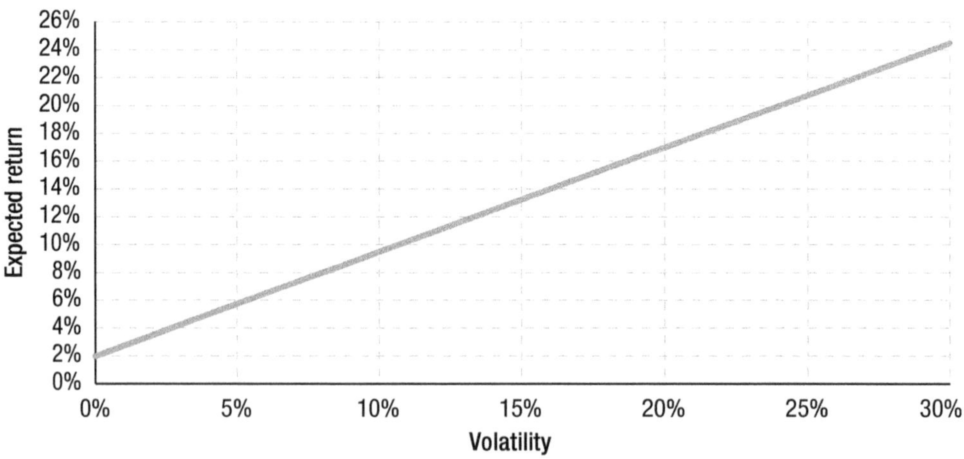

There is no volatility if the share invested in the risky security is zero, and the chart confirms that in this case the expected return corresponds to the risk-free rate (2%).

The slope of the line, $\frac{\left(Er_p - r_f\right)}{\sigma_p}$, known as the Sharpe ratio, is the risk premium per unit of volatility of the risky portfolio. We assume the Sharpe ratio is positive due to:

1. long-term empirical evidence (see Chapter 2) showing that there is an average equity market excess return, supporting investors using the historical average return to form their own long-run expectation;
2. the market risk aversion hypothesis, which implies that investors are willing to buy a risky portfolio only if its expected return is higher than the value of the risk-free rate.

The line describes the maximum expected return that can be achieved for each level of volatility, or the volatility that must be endured to achieve a certain expected return as a target. Figure 7.1 highlights a very important result that will be mentioned very often in the following pages: Every point on the CAL represents a different portfolio composition. The CAL is the set of infinitely many portfolios that can be formed based on a risk-free and a risky asset.

Box 7.2 Investment possibilities with two assets

Question: Elena's portfolio is 60% risky and 40% risk-free. The risk-free is 6%, the risk premium is 10%, and the volatility of the risky stock is 14%. Elena wants to know what the expected return and volatility of her portfolio are, and what the Sharpe ratio is.

Answer: The expected return of the risky security is equal to the sum of the risk-free rate and the risk premium: 6% + 10% = 16%. The expected return from the portfolio is therefore the weighted average of the expected return of the two assets $0.6 \times 0.16 + 0.4 \times 0.06 = 12\%$. The standard deviation of the portfolio is equal to the share invested in the risk asset times the standard deviation of the latter, $0.6 \times 0.14 = 8.4\%$. The Sharpe ratio is the ratio between the risk premium and the standard deviation of the risky security (not affected by the composition of the portfolio held by Elena) equal to $\frac{10}{14} = 0.71$.

Box 7.3 How is the CAL calculated?

Question: Sara is an advisor to Carola and tells her that the two main investment options are the risk-free rate (2%) and a risky portfolio *p* with an expected return of 5% and volatility of 20%. However, Carola wants to have a complete overview of the investment possibilities, because she believes that the risk-free rate is very low, but that putting up with a volatility of 20% to have an expected return of 5% does not correspond to her risk aversion. What should Sara do?

Answer: Sara must represent to Carola the whole set of investment possibilities through the capital allocation line, whose intercept corresponds to the risk-free rate of 2%, with a slope equal to $\frac{5-2}{20}$. The CAL obviously passes through the portfolio *p*, and its graphical representation is depicted in Figure 7.1.

Box 7.4 CAL sensitivity analysis

Question: Elena is the head of investment of an institutional investor that has traditionally invested 50% of her assets in the S&P 500 index, with an average return of 5% and volatility of 20%, and 50% in a risk-free stock. She asks Sara if the average return achieved historically, of 3.5%, with a volatility of 10%, can be maintained even in the current market configuration where risk-free interest rates are at -1%.

Answer: Sara calculates the CAL using market parameters and estimating a fixed risk premium of 3%. In fact, historically, Elena's portfolio has been invested 50% in an asset with an average return of 5% and one with a return of 2%, giving rise to the return achieved. Historical data are therefore consistent with a risk premium of 3%. If rates are now -1%, then the expected return on the portfolio has fallen to 2%, with volatility of 10% if the risk premium has risen to 6%. Sara represents the old and new situation on the CAL in Figure 7.2, in which she also draws a "theoretical" line, which includes the current interest rate but also the assumption that the expected return of the market is associated with the stability of the risk premium over time. If the risk premium remains at 3%, as in the old situation, if the interest rate falls to -1%, the expected return becomes 2%. The "theoretical" CAL therefore represents a net deterioration compared with the old situation because it is characterized by a lower risk-free rate, equal volatility, and a lower expected return of the risky portfolio. Investors must therefore choose: In order to maintain an expected return similar to the past one, it is necessary to assume a greater risk of volatility by shifting the portfolio toward risky assets (to maintain an expected return of 3.5% in the new situation, even assuming that the expected return of the risky asset is fixed at 5%, it would be necessary to invest 75% of the assets at risk). Alternatively, if you maintain the same target volatility, you need to reduce the expected return from your allocation.

Figure 7.2 **CAL and sensitivity to parameters**

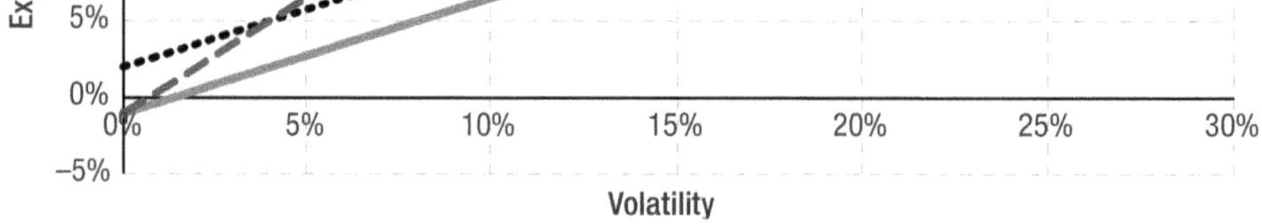

7.3.2 Leverage

Each point of the CAL represents a different portfolio, with a different combination of expected return and volatility. The point $w = 0.5$ in Figure 7.1 represents an equally balanced investment of 50% in each asset. $w = 1$ describes a 100% investment of wealth in the risky portfolio p. All the points on the line to the right of $w = 1$ represent leveraged investments where debt is used to invest in the risky portfolio an amount of money larger than initially available wealth. Borrowing at the risk-free rate and investing in the risky security with an expected return higher than the risk-free rate increases both the expected return and the risk.

Box 7.5 The possibilities of investing with two stocks and leverage

Question: Sara has a starting net worth of €100. The expected return of the risky portfolio is 7%, the volatility is 20%, and the risk-free is 2%. However, Sara wants to have an expected target return of 8% and is considering borrowing 20% to reach her goal. Elena is her advisor. She wants to highlight the risk, as well as the expected return, resulting from borrowing.

Answer: Elena notes that if Sara borrows €20, the total investment in the risky portfolio is €120. It follows that the expected return of the portfolio corresponds to Sara's objective. The volatility of the portfolio is 24%. She warns Sara that borrowing leads to an increase in the expected return but reminds her that ex post the return may be very different from the expected one, and that the realization of a shock equal to the volatility would cause her to lose more than 24% of her initial investment because 1.2 × (–0.2) – 0.2 × 0.02 = 0.244.

If the rate at which one borrows is higher than risk-free, $r_B > r_f$, the CAL has a break. The first part, valid in the case of investing in both risky and risk-free stocks, is the one already seen and described by equation (6). The second part, describing the case in which one borrows, becomes:

$$Er_c = r_B + \frac{\left(Er_p - r_B\right)}{\sigma_p} \times \sigma_c$$

Notice that both the intercept and the slope are affected by the cost of debt. Overall, the CAL is described in Figure 7.3.

Figure 7.3 **The CAL when the cost of debt is higher than risk-free**

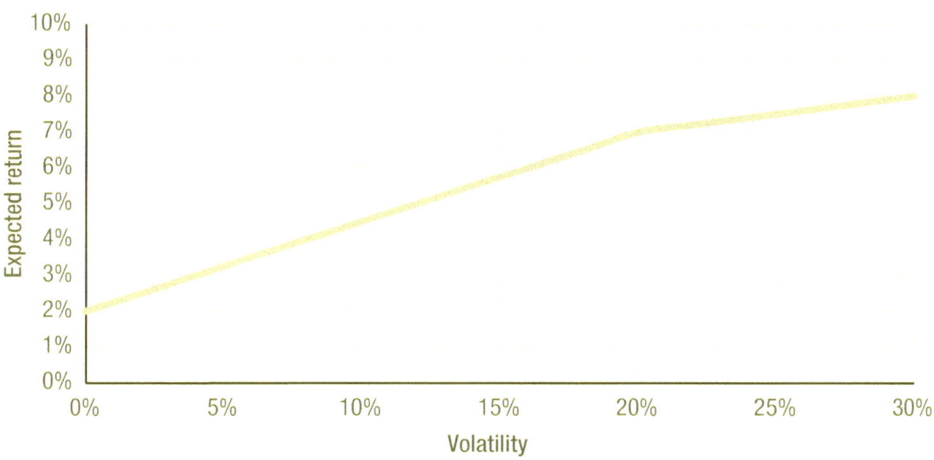

> **Box 7.6 How much worse are the investment possibilities if the cost of borrowing is high?**
>
> **Question**: Elena wants to have a complete overview of the possibilities of combining an investment in the risk-free rate of 2% and a risky portfolio with an expected return of 5% and volatility of 20%. Since Elena has a low risk aversion, she does not rule out the possibility of borrowing even if the cost of debt is 4%.
>
> **Answer**: Elena must compute the capital allocation line, which is described by a broken line.
>
> The first part of the graph is described by $Er_c = 0.02 + \sigma_c \times \frac{(0.05 - 0.02)}{0.2}$. The second part, valid only for volatility levels above 20%, is described by $Er_c = 0{,}04 + \sigma_c \times \frac{(0.05 - 0.04)}{0.2}$.

When leverage is impossible, the CAL starts at risk-free and ends at the point that describes the properties of the risky portfolio. It is not possible to have expected return levels that are higher than the expected return of the risky portfolio.

7.4 The benefits of diversification

Before discussing the optimal portfolio choice between a risky asset and a risk-free asset, we keep studying the portfolio problem with the goal of describing the combinations of expected return and volatility that can be obtained by mixing the available assets and introduce the case with two risky assets. The discussion in the remaining part of the chapter will not use, as we have done so far, any information about the coefficient of risk aversion of the investor.

7.4.1 Two risky assets

We continue to consider the case of $N = 2$ securities, but with both being risky. Portfolio return is the weighted average of the returns of the securities:

$$r_p = w \times r_A + (1 - w) \times r_B$$

Applying the expectation operator, we find the expected return:[1]

$$Er_p = w \times Er_A + (1 - w) \times Er_B$$

[1] To get the result, simply apply the expectation operator to the portfolio return and then develop to find $Er_p = E(w \times r_A + (1 - w) \times r_B) = w \times Er_A + (1 - w) \times Er_B$.

The variance of the portfolio return is found by applying the definition of variance as the mean of the square of the deviation of the variable from its mean:[2]

$$\sigma_p^2 = w^2\sigma_A^2 + \left(1 - w\right)^2\sigma_B^2 + 2w(1 - w)\sigma_{AB}$$

where σ_{AB} represents the covariance between the returns of the two securities.[3] The covariance is equal to the product of the correlation coefficient and the standard deviation $\sigma_{AB} = \rho_{AB} \times \sigma_A \times \sigma_B$. The reason why analyses are typically carried out by reference to the correlation coefficient instead of covariance is that the former is bounded by the interval [-1,+1] and is therefore easily interpretable. Both covariance and correlation are indices of linear association.

Box 7.7 How strong is the impact of correlation on portfolio volatility?

Question: Carola wants to know what the risk is of a portfolio described by the following parameters $\sigma_A = 20\%$, $\sigma_B = 5\%$, $\rho_{AB} = 0.5$, $w_A = 30\%$, $w_B = 70\%$. Since she is unsure of the real correlation between A and B securities, she wants to repeat the analysis for cases $\rho_{AB} = 0$ and $\rho_{AB} = 1$.

Answer: Applying the definition:

$$\sigma_p = \sqrt{w^2 \times \sigma_A^2 + (1 - w)^2 \times \sigma_B^2 + 2 \times w \times (1 - w) \times \sigma_A \times \sigma_B \times \rho_{AB}},$$

Carola finds volatility equal to:

$$\sqrt{0.3^2 \times 0.2^2 + 0.7^2 \times 0.05^2 + 2 \times 0.3 \times 0.7 \times 0.2 \times 0.05 \times 0.5} = 8.3\%.$$

Repeating the analysis for the zero correlation, she finds

$$\sigma_p = \sqrt{0.3^2 \times 0.2^2 + 0.7^2 \times 0.05^2 + 2 \times 0.3 \times 0.7 \times 0.2 \times 0.05 \times 0} = 6.9\%.$$

Finally, in the case of unit correlation,

$$\sigma_p = \sqrt{0.3^2 \times 0.2^2 + 0.7^2 \times 0.05^2 + 2 \times 0.3 \times 0.7 \times 0.2 \times 0.05 \times 1} = 9.5\%.$$

It can therefore be seen that the reduction of the correlation coefficient decreases the volatility of the portfolio.

---

[2] Using:

$$\sigma_p^2 = E\left(r_p - Er_p\right)^2 = E\left\{w \times r_A + (1 - w) \times r_B - E\left[w \times r_A + (1 - w) \times r_B\right]\right\}^2 =$$
$$= E\left[w \times (r_A - Er_A) + (1 - w) \times (r_B - Er_B)\right]^2 = \left[w^2 \times E(r_A - Er_A)^2 + (1 - w)^2 \times\right.$$
$$\left.\times E(r_B - Er_B)^2 + 2w(1 - w)E(r_A - Er_A)(r_B - Er_B)\right] = w^2\sigma_A^2 + \left(1 - w\right)^2\sigma_B^2 + 2w(1 - w)\sigma_{AB}.$$

[3] The standard deviation is the square root of the variance $\sigma_p = \sqrt{w^2\sigma_A^2 + (1 - w)^2\sigma_B^2 + 2w(1 - w)\sigma_{AB}}$

7.4.2 The risk/reward trade-off for extreme values of the correlation coefficient

In the presence of two risky securities, it is not easy to substitute for the expected return and volatility equations to identify a direct relationship between the two parameters.

However, we can proceed if the correlation coefficient assumes its maximum value of 1 or its minimum value of -1. When the correlation is unitary:

$$\sigma_p = \sqrt{w^2 \times \sigma_A^2 + (1-w)^2 \times \sigma_B^2 + 2 \times w \times (1-w) \times \sigma_A \times \sigma_B} =$$

$$= \sqrt{(w \times \sigma_A + (1-w) \times \sigma_B)^2} = w \times \sigma_A + (1-w) \times \sigma_B$$

The volatility of the portfolio is equal to the weighted average of the volatilities of the two stocks.

In the exercise in Box 7.7, when the correlation is unitary, the portfolio volatility is 9.5%, exactly corresponding to the weighted average, with weights 30% and 70%, of the two volatilities, equal to 20% and 5%. Any value of the correlation coefficient below 1 provides a portfolio volatility that is below the weighted average volatility and ensures the benefits of diversification.

In the case of unitary correlation, solving for w, the equation that describes volatility, we find $w = \frac{\sigma_p - \sigma_B}{\sigma_A - \sigma_B}$. Substituting this result in the equation defining the expected return gives us a straight line in the expected return/portfolio volatility space:

$$Er_p = Er_B + \frac{Er_A - Er_B}{\sigma_A - \sigma_B} \times (\sigma_p - \sigma_B)$$

generalizing the equation that had been found in the case of a risk-free asset. The slope is the ratio of the difference in expected returns to the difference between the volatilities of the two assets. Graphically, we have again a straight line in the expected return/volatility space, plotted for the values of the shares invested in the two assets between 0 and 1 (see Figure 7.4).

As in the CAL, each point of the line represents a different portfolio.

Figure 7.4 **Expected return and risk with two risky, perfectly correlated assets**

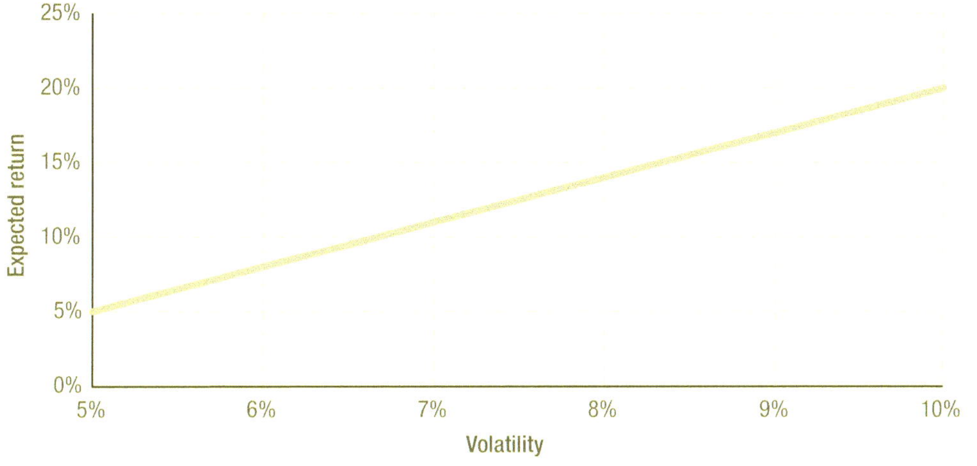

Box 7.8 **Calculating investment possibilities**

Question: Sara can invest in two risky securities characterized by the following parameters: Stock S has expected return 16% and standard deviation 30%; stock B has expected return 12% and standard deviation 15%. Correlation between the two stocks is 1. Sara asks her consultant Elena to plot the expected return and risk combinations of various portfolios composed of S and B in a table, assuming that the share of S ranges from 0% to 140% in 20% increments.

Answer: Elena's analysis is easy since when the correlation is 1 both the expected return and the volatility are weighted averages of the parameters of the individual assets. She therefore fills in the following table that allows Sara to understand expected returns and risk levels of the various portfolios, including those that are leveraged:

Share in S	Share in B	Expected return	Risk
0	1	0.12	0.15
0.2	0.8	0.128	0.18
0.4	0.6	0.136	0.21
0.6	0.4	0.144	0.24
0.8	0.2	0.152	0.27
1	0	0.16	0.3
1.2	-0.2	0.168	0.33
1.4	-0.4	0.176	0.36

If the correlation is -1, then the relationship is a two-line set (see Figure 7.5)[4] described by $w = \pm\frac{\sigma_B}{\sigma_A + \sigma_B}$, highlighting that it is possible to build a zero-risk portfolio with two risky securities.

Figure 7.5 **Expected return and risk when correlation = -1**

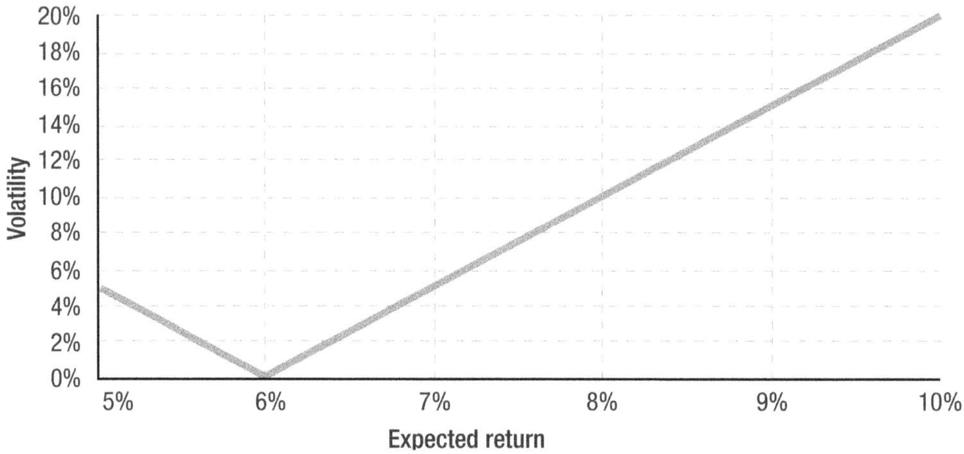

7.4.3 The general case for a two-risky-asset portfolio

The graphs describing the extreme situations of correlation coefficient equal to +1 and -1 identify a triangle delimiting curve describing combinations of expected return and risk for general values of the correlation coefficient.

In Figure 7.6 the horizontal axis represents the expected return and the vertical axis the volatility. It contains three curves, each of which describes the combinations of expected return and risk for a different correlation coefficient (1, -0.5, and -1). The chart shows that when the correlation is equal to 1 there are no diversification benefits since an increase in risk is associated with a proportional increase in expected return. Any correlation below 1 creates benefits of diversification, as each level of risk is associated with a higher level of expected return than in the case of a unit correlation. Figure 7.6 also shows that the benefit of diversification can be interpreted as lower volatility for a given level of expected return (a horizontal line intersects the three functions for lower levels of volatility, the lower the correlation coefficient), or as a higher expected return for a given level of volatility (a vertical line intersects the three functions for higher levels of expected return, the lower the coefficient correlation).

[4] In this case $\sigma_p^2 = \left(w \times \sigma_A - (1-w) \times \sigma_B\right)^2$ from which $\sigma_p = \left|w \times \sigma_A - (1-w) \times \sigma_B\right|$. The equation shows that it is possible to choose the weights in such a way as to eliminate volatility, solving $\left|w \times \sigma_A - (1-w) \times \sigma_B\right| = 0$ from which $w = \pm\frac{\sigma_B}{\sigma_A + \sigma_B}$.

Figure 7.6 **Expected return and risk in the general case**

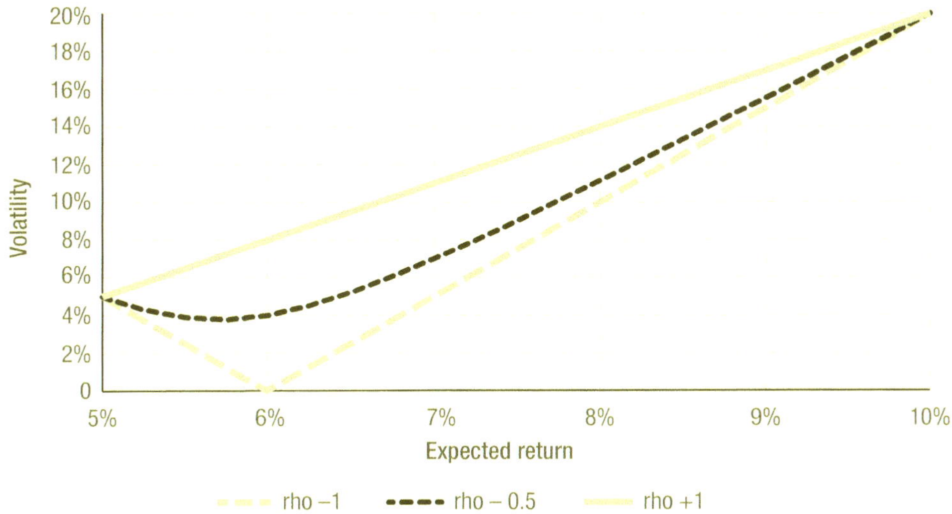

> Box 7.9 **How much does the risk increase if the correlation increases?**
>
> **Question**: Carola formed a portfolio of two funds, one equity S and one bond B, with the following characteristics: Stock S has an expected return of 5% and standard deviation 15%; stock B has an expected return of 1% and standard deviation of 5%. At the time of the portfolio's formation, the correlation between the two stocks was 0.1 because in a phase of economic growth, changes in interest rates were not strongly linked to share prices. Today, however, growth is weakening and the correlation between the two markets is estimated to have risen to 0.5. The portfolio is currently 50% invested in each of the two funds, and the risk-free rate is zero. How much has the risk of Carola's portfolio increased?
>
> **Answer**: The expected return of the portfolio remained equal to the average of the two expected returns, that is, at 3%. The risk, however, has changed. It was initially equal to:
>
> $$\sigma_p = \sqrt{0.5^2 \times 0.15^2 + 0.5^2 \times 0.05^2 + 2 \times 0.5 \times 0.5 \times 0.15 \times 0.05 \times 0.1} = 8.1\%$$
>
> and has now become equal to:
>
> $$\sigma_p = \sqrt{0.5^2 \times 0.15^2 + 0.5^2 \times 0.05^2 + 2 \times 0.5 \times 0.5 \times 0.15 \times 0.05 \times 0.5} = 9\%.$$
>
> The increase in market correlation has significantly worsened the ratio of expected return to risk.

Figure 7.6 depicts only the portion of the curve describing the expected return and the risk of portfolios that invest a non-negative share in the two assets. This means that the curve describes the combinations of expected return and volatility that are obtained from different portfolios that are found based on a linear combination of non-negative weights of the two assets, as empirically shown in Box 7.10.

Box 7.10 Computing the expected return/risk relation

Question: Elena considers two mutual funds. Fund S has 6% expected return and 15% volatility, while B fund has 2% expected return and 5% volatility. In addition, $\rho_{SB} = 0.1$. To understand the opportunities offered by several portfolios, she plots the investment opportunity set in a table, using investment proportions in fund S from 0% to 50% with an increment of 10%.

Answer: First of all, it is necessary to represent the expected risk and return of the portfolios composed of the two risky securities, which can be calculated in Excel using the definitions of volatility and expected return of the portfolio to find:

Share	Volatility	Expected return
0	5.00%	2.00%
10.00%	4.88%	2.40%
20.00%	5.23%	2.80%
30.00%	5.97%	3.20%
40.00%	6.97%	3.60%
50.00%	8.14%	4.00%

However, it is theoretically possible to short-sell one of the two assets to invest in the other an amount of wealth larger than the initial availability. Short-selling refers to the practice of borrowing the asset, selling it at the prevailing market price, and then buying it in the future before the expiration of the lending contract. Figure 7.7 describes what happens with short-selling, for a correlation coefficient equal to -0.5, expected returns equal to 5% and 10%, and volatilities equal to 5% and 20%.

Figure 7.7 Expected return and risk in the general case with short-selling

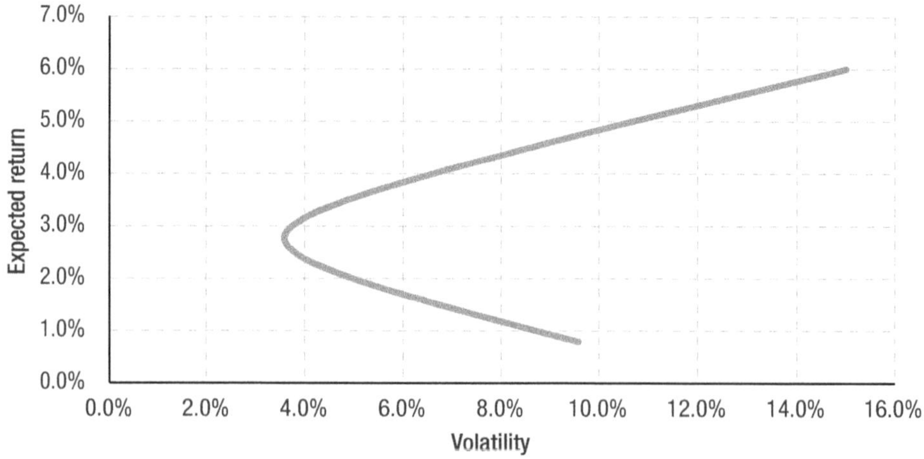

7.4.4 Currency risk

The correlation coefficient is relevant to determine the total quantity of risk even in the case the rate of return of an asset is affected by a multiplicity of sources of risk. For example, investing in a foreign currency introduces an element of risk due to the need to convert the foreign currency into the domestic currency at the end of the investment horizon: a European investor who wants to buy a US stock will first have to exchange euros for dollars at the prevailing rate, then use the dollars to buy the security, and at the end of the investment period sell the dollars to get the euros back. This last step will be settled at an exchange rate established on the international market that is unknown at the time of purchase of the share. An example may be useful to clarify the dynamics.

A European investor wants to buy 1,000 Microsoft shares at a price of $200 each. To complete the purchase, she will first need to convert euros into dollars. Since the value of the investment is $200,000, she will have to spend the euros needed to buy $200,000. If the exchange rate is 1.2, then she will have to spend 200,000/1.2 = €166,667. If, after two months, the Microsoft stock is sold at a market price of $210, the value of the investment in dollars will have grown to $210,000. If the euro had appreciated by 10%, the $210,000 would be exchanged at a rate of 1.32 to get €159,050. Overall, the return was negative because the increase in the dollar price of the stock is more than offset by the weakening of the dollar against the euro.

Exchange rate risk is precisely related to the impact of temporal changes on the exchange rate. Formally, the return in euros of a foreign currency investment is:

$$\frac{\left(P_{t+1} + D_{t+1}\right) \times S_{t+1} - P_t \times S_t}{P_t \times S_t}$$

where S_t is the exchange rate at time t. Obviously, the presence of the exchange rate for the t+1 period, unknown at the time the investment begins, confers additional risk. If no dividends are paid, or if a total return index is used, the log return $\log\left(\frac{P_{t+1} \times S_{t+1}}{P_t \times S_t}\right)$ is equal to:

$$\Delta p_{t+1} + \Delta s_{t+1}$$

where p_{t+1}, s_{t+1} indicate the logarithm of the price and the exchange rate, respectively. The expected value and volatility of the investment are respectively:

$$E\left(\Delta p_{t+1} + \Delta s_{t+1}\right)$$

$$\sqrt{\sigma^2_{\Delta p} + \sigma^2_{\Delta s} + 2\rho_{\Delta s \Delta p}\sigma_{\Delta s}\sigma_{\Delta p}}$$

The definition of volatility highlights the role played by the correlation between price and exchange rate in determining the return for the international investor: The volatility of the foreign currency return is less than the sum of the volatility of the two return components if the correlation is less than one. Empirical research has shown that the correlation between stock indices and domestic currency is often low, so that international investment is riskier than domestic investment, but the increased risk is mitigated by a low level of correlation.

Of course, the relevance of currency risk to overall risk varies for each investment: Equity investing is by its nature already very volatile, and therefore the possible addition of currency risk does not change the overall picture much. In the case of investing in bonds, meanwhile, volatility is limited, and therefore currency risk can lead to a sharp increase in overall volatility.

Currency risk can be hedged by using the "forward exchange rate," that is, an exchange rate determined today for currency exchange in the future. If the forward rate is defined with the symbol F_t, then the return on investment becomes equal to:

$$\frac{\left(P_{t+1}+D_{t+1}\right)\times F_t - P_t \times S_t}{P_t \times S_t}$$

from which the exchange rate risk has disappeared. In logs, the expected value and volatility of the investment become respectively $E\left(\Delta p_{t+1}+f_t-s_t\right)$ and $\sigma_{\Delta p}$, where f_t is the logarithm of the forward exchange rate. As can be seen, in the case of currency risk hedging, the expected return on the investment is modified due to the differential between the forward rate and the spot rate which, according to the theory of "hedged interest rate parity," corresponds to the differential between the national interest rate and the prevailing rate in the reference currency.

7.5 The risk-free asset and two risky securities

How can we combine the risk-free asset and a portfolio of risky stocks? We saw initially that the portfolios obtained by combining risk-free with any risky portfolio are located on a straight line. This property remains valid regardless of the number of risky securities considered and therefore can be applied to describe what happens when we combine the risk-free rate with any risky portfolio that is itself composed of multiple risky securities. In Figure 7.8, the line represents the expected return/risk combinations that are obtained by combining the risk-free with a randomly selected portfolio p on the minimum variance frontier:

But why choose portfolio p? Can the choice be improved from the point of view of the trade-off between expected return and risk? The best combination of the two risky securities is the one that maximizes the overall ratio of expected return to risk. In Figure 7.9, we define a portfolio, called a "tangency portfolio," which can be combined with the risk-free security to maximize the ratio of expected return to risk.

The best combination of the two risky stocks was identified solely based on efficiency considerations. Given the expected return and risk parameters that are taken as given by the investor, risk aversion plays no role in determining the tangency portfolio and the latter shows how to combine the risk-free security with a portfolio formed by the two risky securities in the market. The line that is obtained from the

Figure 7.8 **Expected return and risk with a risk-free asset**

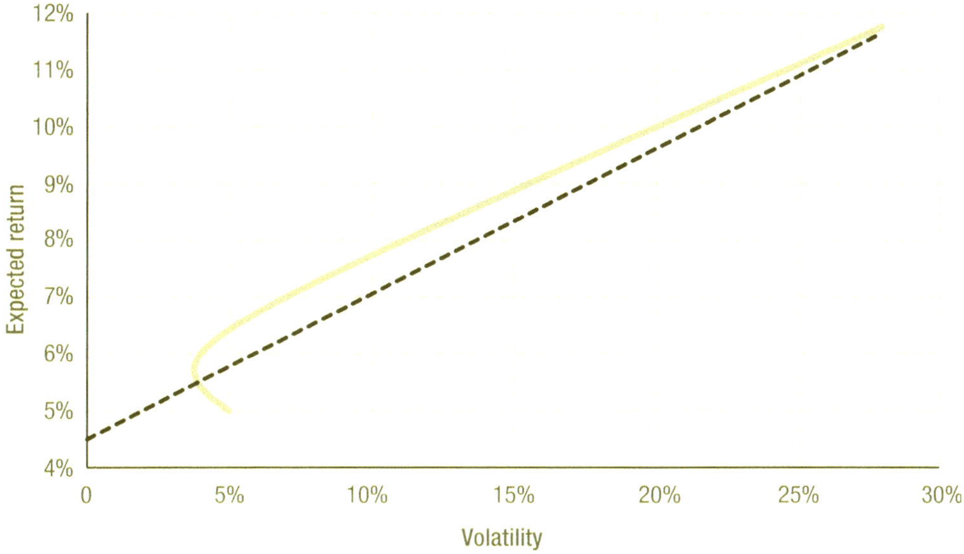

Figure 7.9 **The CAL in the general case**

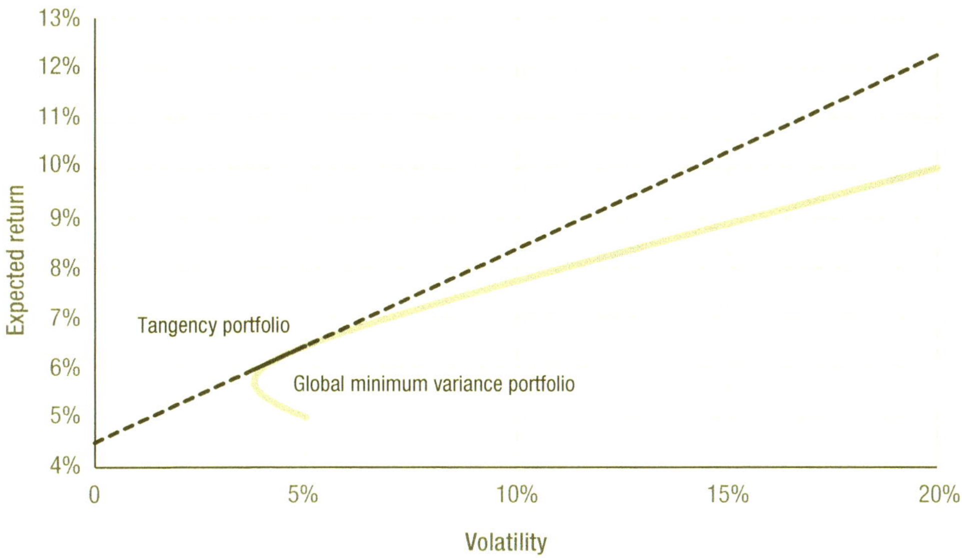

combination of the risk-free security and the tangency portfolio describes infinite portfolios with different levels of expected return and risk, from which a risk-averse investor will choose.

From a mathematical point of view, the tangency portfolio is the answer to the specific problem of Sharpe ratio maximization $max_w \frac{Er_p - r_f}{\sigma_p}$. If, instead, securities shares are chosen to minimize the overall variance of the portfolio, $min_w \sigma_p^2$, we find the "minimum variance portfolio," that is, the combination of the two risky securities that minimizes risk:

$$w_{GMV,B} = \frac{\sigma_A^2 - Cov(r_A, r_B)}{\sigma_A^2 + \sigma_B^2 - 2Cov(r_A, r_B)}$$

where $w_{GMV,B}$ is the share of the security B in the portfolio with minimum variance. It can be seen from the formula that the minimum variance portfolio is not affected by the expected return parameters, consistent with the objective of pure risk reduction.

Box 7.11 Should I choose only the investment with the lowest volatility to reduce risk?

Question: Two risky securities are characterized by the following parameters: stock S expected return 16% and standard deviation 30%, bond B expected return 12% and standard deviation 15%. Correlation between the two stocks is 0.1. There is no risk-free rate. Calculate the composition of the minimum variance portfolio, its expected return, and risk.

Answer: The minimum variance portfolio is found by using:

$$w_B = \frac{0.3^2 - 0.3 \times 0.15 \times 0.1}{0.3^2 + 0.15^2 - 2 \times 0.3 \times 0.15 \times 0.1} = 83\%$$

$$w_S = 1 - w_B = 17\%$$

Its expected return is 12.52% and its variance 1.94%. The exercise shows that the minimum variance portfolio has a high share invested in the asset with lower volatility. The general implication is that to reduce volatility one may not necessarily only invest in the least risky asset. A riskier asset, but with a low correlation, can make a useful contribution to reducing the overall volatility of the portfolio.

The CAL is again a straight line that passes through the risk-free and the tangency portfolio. By using leverage, one can borrow to increase the expected return (and risk) of the overall portfolio. When leverage is not allowed, as in Figure 7.10 , the set of investment opportunities is described for the first part by the straight line and for the second part by the curve joining the risky securities A and B.

Figure 7.10 **The unleveraged CAL**

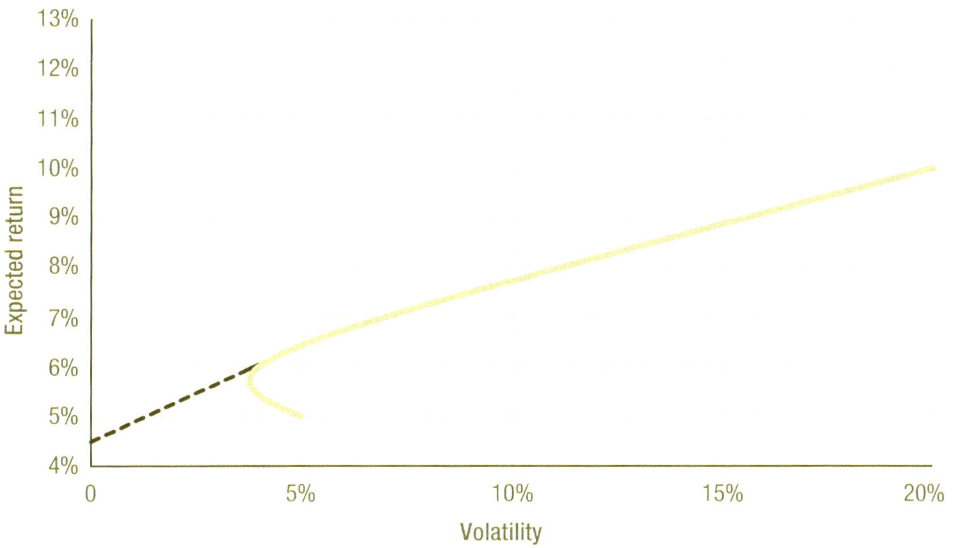

> Box 7.12 **Stock/bond diversification**
>
> **Question:** Carola has traditionally invested all her wealth in bonds, with historical return and volatility respectively equal to 4% and 6%. She asks her financial consultant Sara if her historical choice has been a good one or whether there are other possible solutions. The goal is risk minimization.
>
> **Answer**: Sara agrees that 4% and 6% are the right parameters to describe the expected return and volatility of the bond market. However, she claims that investing a portion of wealth in the stock market can also be useful for the purpose of risk minimization, depending on the correlation between the two assets. Historically she has read papers, for example Shiller and Beltratti (1992), measuring such correlation at -0.5, which would offer a great benefit in terms of risk reduction. The minimum variance portfolio invests approximately 14% in stocks and 86% in bonds, with a volatility equal to 3.8%, lower than the volatility of a pure investment in bonds estimated at 4%. Sara alerts Carola that things may change quickly and that the correlation coefficient between stock and bond returns may change. An example of such volatility has been provided during the great inflation shock of 2022–2023 associated with the Ukraine war, where the two markets first decreased together and then increased together, bringing the correlation coefficient to 0.8. A 0.8 correlation coefficient eliminates all the diversification potential of stocks, to the point that the minimum variance portfolio is now shorting stocks for almost 21% to invest in bonds 121%.

Summary

- The return of a portfolio is the weighted average of the returns of individual assets.
- For a portfolio consisting of an investment in a risky security and a risk-free security, the expected return is equal to the weighted average of the risk-free and the expected return of the risky security, while the volatility is equal to the product of the portion invested in the risky security times the volatility of the risky security.
- The infinite portfolios that can be obtained by varying the shares invested in the risk-free security and in the risky security are described by a straight line in the expected return/volatility graph, with an intercept equal to the risk-free security and an inclination equal to the Sharpe ratio. This line is known as the capital allocation line (CAL).
- The CAL provides for the use of leverage in cases where you invest more than the initial assets in the risky security.
- When the rate at which you borrow is higher than the rate you get when you invest in a risk-free security, the CAL is made up of a broken line and not a straight line.
- An analysis of a portfolio with two risky securities shows that in the general case it is mathematically difficult to describe with a single equation the combinations of securities that allow for various combinations of expected return and risk.
- The crucial coefficient within the portfolio with two risky stocks is the correlation ratio. When this ratio is taken on a unit value, the portfolios of the two risky securities achieve combinations of expected return and risk that lie along a straight line, as in the case of a risky security and a risk-free security.
- The lower the correlation coefficient, the better the trade-offs between expected return and risk: A given level of volatility allows for a higher expected return if the correlation is lower, and a given target expected return can be achieved with less risk if the correlation is lower.
- We talk about the benefits of diversification whenever the correlation coefficient is less than 1.
- Given the correlation coefficient, it is possible to introduce the risk-free security in a simple way by noting that, as already seen in the previous chapter, portfolios that combine risk-free with any risky portfolio are described by combinations of expected return and volatility that are localized on a straight line.
- The risk-averse investor is interested in the best possible trade-off between expected return and volatility, the one that maximizes the Sharpe ratio. Maximizing the Sharpe ratio makes it possible to identify the tangency portfolio, the one that lies at the tangency between the line that emanates from the risk-free and the curve that joins the two risky securities.
- Another portfolio of considerable interest is the one that describes the minimal variance.
- The line that has an intercept equal to the risk-free rate and a slope equal to the Sharpe ratio, and which touches the curve at the point that describes the tangency portfolio, is known as the CAL.
- All points of the CAL that have an expected return higher than the expected return of the tangency portfolio involve the use of leverage, that is, debt. When debt is not possible, the investor is forced to choose portfolios that are initially on the straight line and then, for target expected return levels higher than that of the tangency portfolio, on the curve that combines expected return and risk of the two risky securities.

Problems

1. The risk-free rate is 0%, the risk premium is 5%, and volatility of the risky portfolio is 20%.

   a. What is the expected return and volatility of a portfolio invested 60% in risky and 40% in risk-free assets?
   b. What is the Sharpe ratio?

2. The expected return of the risky index is 5%, the risk free is -1%, and the volatility is 10%.

   a. What is the expected return and volatility of a portfolio invested 70% in the risky portfolio and 30% in the risk-free stock?
   b. If the risky portfolio consists of three stocks, A, B, and C, in proportions of 25%, 32%, and 43%, what is the investment in risk-free and in the individual securities that make up the risky portfolio?

3. Use the data from the previous question but also consider the existence of a mutual fund with an expected return of 6% and volatility of 9%. Compute the Sharpe ratio of an investor who buys the index and one who invests in the mutual fund.

4. With the parameters of previous questions, calculate the portfolio chosen by an investor who intends to have an expected return of 4%, and calculate the volatility of the portfolio. Compare the result with what you would have if you could not invest in the mutual fund, but only in the risky index.

5. Correlation coefficients ρ between pairs of stocks are $\rho_{AB} = 0.85$, $\rho_{AC} = 0.60$, and $\rho_{AD} = 0.45$. Each stock has an expected return of 8% and a standard deviation of 20%.

   a. If the initial portfolio is entirely invested in A, and if you were to add another stock, which security would you add, B, C, or D?
   b. What is the composition of the minimum variance portfolio?
   c. How does the answer to (a) change if investors are not risk-averse?

6. The expected return of the stock market is 8%, with standard deviation of 22%; the expected return of gold is 4%, with standard deviation of 25%.

   a. Does it make sense to invest in gold?
   b. Would the answer change if the correlation between the two assets was 100%?
   c. Produce an Excel table describing the portfolios and their expected returns and volatilities as the correlation coefficient moves from -1 to +1 with a step equal to 0.1.

7. The expected return of the tangency portfolio is 6% and its volatility is 10%. The minimum variance portfolio is characterized by an expected return of 3% and volatility of 6%. The two portfolios have a correlation of 50%. The risk-free rate is zero. Which portfolio is selected by an investor who has an expected return target of 8% in case leverage can be used? What is its volatility? How does the answer change if leverage cannot be used?

8 The market has an expected return of 6% and volatility of 20%. Risk-free is zero. An active fund that is perfectly correlated with the market has an expected return of 5% and volatility of 25%. Find the CAL and graph it. What happens to the expected return and volatility of the portfolio of an investor who initially invests 70% of his assets in the active fund and then switches to the index instead?

9 A stock market index has an expected return of 13% and volatility of 25%. An active fund, perfectly correlated with the index, has a volatility of 15% and an expected return of 11%. The risk-free rate is 0.

a. Would an investor with a risk aversion coefficient A = 3 prefer the index or the fund? What about an almost risk-neutral investor with A = 0.2?
b. What is the CAL?
c. What would the CAL be if the risk-free rate was 12%?
d. Compare and comment on the different results in a and b.
e. What is the maximum fixed management fee that can be set by the mutual fund in the presence of a risk-free rate of 5%?
f. How would your previous answer change if the management fee also involved a performance fee equal to $1 - \delta$ times the gross rate of return?

Answers

1 a. The portfolio's return is 3% and its volatility is 12%.
b. The Sharpe ratio of the portfolio is equal to 3/12, that is, 25%, which naturally corresponds to the Sharpe ratio of the risky security equal to 5/20.

2 a. The expected return of the portfolio is 3.2% and its volatility is 7%.
b. The portfolio is invested for 17.5% in A, 22.4% in B, 30.1% in C, and 30% in the risk-free. The percentages for the risky assets can be obtained by multiplying the composition of the risky portfolio by 0.7, the share of wealth invested in the risky portfolio.

3 The index Sharpe ratio is 6/10 = 60%, the fund 7/9 = 77.8%. The best choice is therefore to compute the CAL on the basis of the risk-free and the fund.

4 To have an expected return of 4%, the investor invests 71.43% of the assets in the mutual fund and 28.57% in the risk-free. The volatility of the portfolio is 6.43%. If the investor were forced to select the index, we would have a portfolio with shares (83.33%, 16.64%) and volatility would be 8.33%, up sharply from the previous value of 6.43%. The need to achieve a certain level of target expected return by investing in a more volatile asset with a lower expected return penalizes the investor both from the point of view of the need to invest more in the risky index and from the point of view of volatility per investment unit.

5 a. The stock with the lowest possible correlation would be added to decrease volatility with the same expected return.

b. The portfolio with minimum variance is equally invested in security A and in D. To see this consider the equation for the variance:

$$\sigma_p^2 = w^2\sigma_A^2 + (1-w)^2\sigma_D^2 + 2w(1-w)\sigma_{AD}$$

The first derivative relative to the weight w is:

$$\frac{d\sigma_p^2}{dw} = 2w\sigma_A^2 - 2(1-w)\sigma_D^2 + 2\sigma_{AD} - 4w\sigma_{AD}$$

By setting the derivative equal to 0 and solving for w one gets:

$$w = \frac{2(\sigma_D^2 - \sigma_{AD})}{2(\sigma_A^2 + \sigma_D^2 - 2\sigma_{AD})}$$

Using the information provided in the exercise $\sigma_A^2 = \sigma_D^2 = \sigma^2$:

$$w = \frac{2(\sigma^2 - \rho_{AB} \times \sigma^2)}{2(2\sigma^2 - 2\rho_{AB} \times \sigma^2)} = 0.5$$

independently of the correlation coefficient.

c. If investors are risk-averse, they prefer to increase volatility and therefore combine stock A with stock B.

6 a. Gold is apparently an investment to be discarded because the Sharpe ratio associated with it is lower than the Sharpe ratio of the stock market. However, a sufficiently low level of correlation can change the outcome because the frontier that unites the risk assets can allow for a tangency portfolio that encompasses both assets. For example, if the correlation between the two assets is zero and the risk-free is zero, we find from the equation describing the tangency portfolio that the weight of gold is 28%.

b. When the correlation is unitary, the two risk assets are linked by a straight line and the CAL includes only the stock market.

c. The required table is:

Correlation	Gold	Equity	Er	σ
-1	42.86%	57.14%	7.86%	0
-0.8	40.40%	59.60%	7.98%	0.0029
-0.6	37.38%	62.62%	8.13%	0.0059
-0.4	33.57%	66.43%	8.32%	0.0090
-0.2	28.63%	71.37%	8.57%	0.0123
0	21.95%	78.05%	8.90%	0.0156
0.2	12.43%	87.57%	9.38%	0.0192
0.4	-2.26%	102.26%	10.11%	0.0230
0.6	-27.84%	127.84%	11.39%	0.0271
0.8	-83.61%	183.61%	14.18%	0.0301
1	-300.00%	400.00%	25.00%	0

Notice that there are two extreme portfolios, for the correlation coefficient being equal to +1 and -1, when there is no volatility. This is consistent with the existence of two solutions for weights that produce zero risk when the correlation is -1.

7 To achieve an expected return of 8%, 133% of your assets must be invested in the tangency portfolio and 33% must be borrowed, as the weight must be such that $w \times 6\% = 8\%$. The volatility of the selected portfolio is 13.3%. If it is not possible to use leverage, you should borrow by short-selling the minimum variance portfolio, investing 167% in the tangency portfolio since $w \times 6\% + (1 - w) \times 3\% = 8\%$. The associated volatility is equal to 15.1%, much higher than the previous one: Borrowing in a risky asset such as the minimum variance portfolio, with an expected return closer to that of the tangency portfolio, represents a major deterioration in the investment opportunity set.

8 The CAL is the line that joins the origin (since the risk-free is zero) to the asset with the best Sharpe ratio. Given that the market's Sharpe ratio is higher than that of the fund and the two are perfectly correlated, investors will prefer to select portfolios that comprise the index. The expected return when investing in the fund is 3.5% and the volatility is 17.5%. When we move on to the index, the results are 5.3% and 14%, respectively.

9 a. The utility-based comparison would involve $0.13 - 1.5 \times 0.25^2 = 3.625\%$ and $0.11 - 1.5 \times 0.15^2 = 7.265\%$ and would privilege the active fund. However, if A = 0.2 we would have $0.13 - 0.1 \times 0.25^2 = 10.5\%$ and $0.11 - 0.1 \times 0.15^2 = 9.5\%$ and the index would be the preferred choice.

b. The CAL links the risk-free rate with the asset with the highest Sharpe ratio. The mutual fund's Sharpe ratio is 6/15 = 40%, while the index's Sharpe ratio is 8/25 = 32%. The CAL is therefore $Er_C = 0.4 \times \sigma_C$.

c. Such a huge increase in the risk-free rate would change the CAL. Now the market would become the support for the risk-free rate and the CAL would be $Er_C = 0.12 + 0.32 \times \sigma_C$ with a large improvement in the intercept and a gentler slope. Very risk-averse investors would benefit the most from such a change in the investment opportunity set.

d. The CAL is based on the index fund regardless of risk aversion, purely on the basis of investment efficiency. An almost risk-neutral investor could obtain the same volatility of the market, 25%, by investing 166% in the fund, borrowing 66%, with an expected return equal to 18.33% and a total utility equal to $0.1833 - 0.1 \times 0.25^2 = 17.71\%$, much higher than the utility of the index.

e. The imposition of a management fee reduces the expected return and also the Sharpe ratio, which becomes equal to $\left(Er - r_f - fee\right)/\sigma$, and it is only sustainable if the Sharpe ratio is higher than that of the index. This happens if the fee is less than 3.2%.

f. Now the overall after-fee return would be equal to $r \times \delta - fee$. The expected return would be $Er \times \delta - fee$ but now the volatility would also change to $\delta \times 0.15$. The Sharpe ratio would be $\frac{\delta \times Er - fee}{\delta \times 0.15}$ and the indifference between the Sharpe ratios would take place at $\frac{\delta \times 0.11 - fee}{\delta \times 0.15} = \frac{0.13}{0.25}$, that is, $fee = \delta \times 0{,}032$.

8 The efficient frontier and the optimal portfolio

8.1 Introduction

The chapter deals with the case of a general number of risky securities. Initially, we will not consider the problem of optimization, that is, the formation of a portfolio that minimizes risk for each target return level, but instead study a large and equally balanced portfolio, to show that its variance tends to mean covariance between securities as the number of securities increases. This first part is useful to illustrate the benefits of diversification simply associated with building a large and balanced portfolio, an activity that does not require any mathematical analysis.

By choosing the portfolio to minimize variance for each target expected return level, we can find a formula that describes the minimum variance frontier, the upper part of which represents the efficient frontier (Markowitz model). The advantage of optimization relative to an equally balanced portfolio has to do with exploitation of all the individual relevant parameters for risk and correlation. We find again, in a more general formulation with many risky securities, some objects that had been described in the case of only two risky securities, namely the tangency portfolio, the minimum variance portfolio, and, from the combination with the risk-free rate, the capital allocation line. The striking implication of the Markowitz model is the two-fund separation theorem: The investor can select a portfolio mixing the risk-free asset and the tangency portfolio. The optimal portfolio for a low-risk aversion investor is identical to the optimal portfolio for a high-risk aversion investor as far as the share of wealth invested in risky assets is concerned. The two investors differ in the weight invested in the risk-free asset.

The final part of the chapter discusses issues associated with practical applications of the model, including challenges in estimating the relevant parameters, using the model to hedge liabilities, non-negativity constraints, and indicators for the risk contribution of individual assets.

8.2 Equally balanced portfolio

We consider the general case of portfolios composed of N risky securities. As usual, the portfolio return is a weighted average of the return of individual stocks, with weights equal to the relative importance of each security within the portfolio:

$$r_p = \sum_{i=1}^{N} w_i r_i$$

where w_i is the weight of the $i - th$ asset. The sum of the weights of the various securities is 100%, that is, $\sum_{i=1}^{N} w_i = 1$. We know that the variance for a portfolio of two stocks is equal to $\sigma_p^2 = w^2 \times \sigma_A^2 + (1 - w)^2 \times \sigma_B^2 + 2 \times w^2 \times (1 - w^2) \times \rho_{AB} \times \sigma_A \times \sigma_B$. It can be shown that the general variance formula for a portfolio of N stocks is:

$$\sigma_p^2 = \sum_{i=1}^{N} \sum_{j=1}^{N} w_i w_j Cov(r_i, r_j)$$

Before addressing issues related to portfolio optimization, that is, the choice of selected weights to maximize the expected return and minimize risk by taking into account volatilities and correlations among securities, we analyze the case of an equally weighted portfolio, where the weight of each security is 1/ N. Such a portfolio is interesting because its properties can be extrapolated to the case of large portfolios, albeit not equally balanced. In the case of an equally balanced portfolio, the formula can be rewritten:

$$\sigma_p^2 = \frac{1}{N}\sigma_M^2 + \frac{N-1}{N} Cov_M \tag{1}$$

Equation (1) shows that the variance of an equally balanced portfolio is equal to the weighted average of the mean variance σ_M^2 and the mean covariance Cov_M. As the number of securities in the portfolio increases, the variance tends to cancel out if the mean covariance is zero, otherwise the portfolio variance tends to mean covariance. Contrary to popular belief, in a portfolio of many stocks, variance is primarily determined by average covariance.

We distinguish between "unique risk" (or idiosyncratic risk, or diversifiable risk) and "market risk" (or non-diversifiable risk). Idiosyncratic risk disappears in a diversified portfolio, while non-diversifiable risk remains even in a large and diversified portfolio. If the correlation between pairs of securities is zero, it follows that the risk of an equally weighted portfolio is zero. As the "law of large numbers" suggests, a portfolio composed of a large number of uncorrelated securities does not have a systematic risk because positive idiosyncratic shocks are outweighed by negative idiosyncratic ones. At the same time, if the average correlation is positive, the shocks are more likely to be predominantly positive, and this creates volatility for the portfolio as a whole.

Figure 8.1 shows the number of stocks in the portfolio on the horizontal axis and the volatility on the vertical axis if the average correlation between the stocks is non-zero:

Figure 8.1 **The relationship between risk and the number of securities in the case of a non-zero mean correlation**

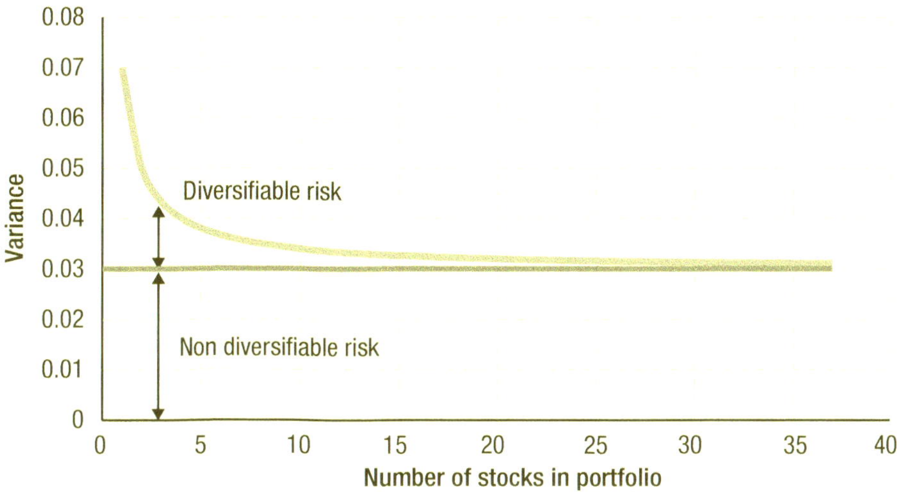

Figure 8.1 shows that in the case of a non-zero average correlation, the risk does not cancel out even in the case of infinite securities, so there is a risk that cannot be diversified. Figure 8.2 considers the case where the average correlation is zero.

Figure 8.2 **Risk and number of securities in the case of zero mean correlation**

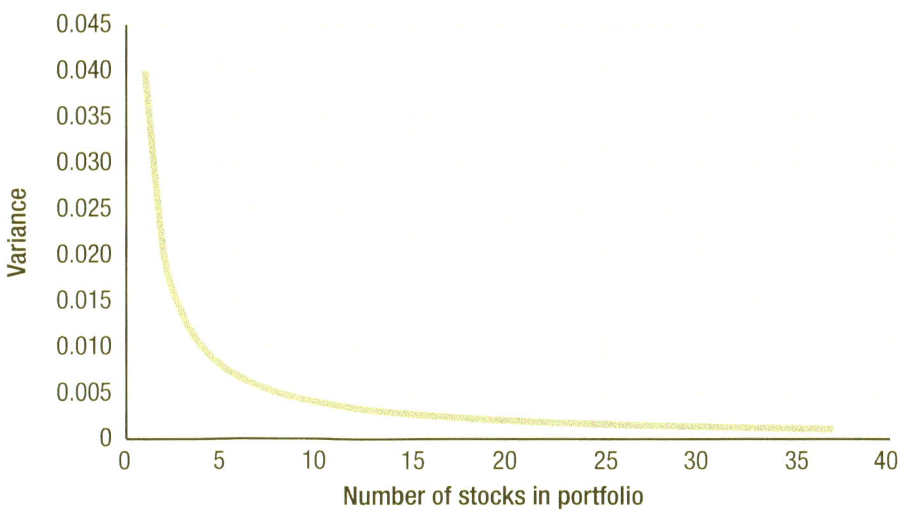

Figure 8.2 shows that in the case of zero correlation, portfolio risk decreases as the number of securities increases, and there is no non-diversifiable risk.

This discussion highlights that the first rule which must be followed by an investor is to hold a (balanced) portfolio composed of many securities, to avoid that a portfolio composed of few securities is characterized by a level of risk that can easily be eliminated with adequate diversification. In the example described in Figure 8.1, a portfolio with few stocks has variance of 0.05 (volatility of 22.4%), while a portfolio containing many stocks has variance of 0.03 (volatility of 17.3%): It is possible to reduce volatility by 5 percentage points simply by holding a large and balanced portfolio. Is it possible to further reduce the risk and at the same time control the expected return? This is the topic addressed in the context of portfolio optimization.

8.3 The Markowitz model

8.3.1 Portfolio optimization

As we saw in Chapter 7, when there are only two risky assets, we can form portfolios that combine them in various proportions and describe the expected return and volatility of each portfolio in a picture, using a curve determined by the correlation coefficient. There is no need for complex mathematical computations: We just need to compute, by brute force, the variance of each portfolio combination.

But what happens when there are more than two risky assets? When there are three risky assets, there are three correlation coefficients (between assets 1 and 2, between assets 2 and 3, and between assets 1 and 3). When the risky assets are N, the number of correlation coefficients is equal to $N \times (N - 1)/2$. With twenty assets, we have 190 correlation coefficients!

How can we find portfolios that best combine assets with so many expected returns, volatilities, and correlation coefficients? Nobel Prize laureate Harry Markowitz (1952) created a mathematical model to find the portfolios that minimize the variance for each level of target expected return.

8.3.2 Notation

To derive the efficient frontier in the general case, we need to use matrix algebra. We use a vector of size $(N,1)$ to describe the weights of the N shares $w = (w_1\ w_2 \ldots w_N)'$, another $(N,1)$ vector for expected returns $Er = (Er_1\ Er_2 \ldots Er_N)'$, and an $(N,1)$ vector $i = (1\ 1 \ldots 1)'$ where all elements are equal to 1. This unitary vector is useful to sum elements in other vectors; for example, $i'w = w'i = 1$ show that the sum of the weights is equal to 1. We use an (N, N) matrix to describe variances and covariances. If $N =$ 3, for example:

$$V = \begin{bmatrix} \sigma_1^2 & \sigma_{12} & \sigma_{13} \\ \sigma_{21} & \sigma_2^2 & \sigma_{23} \\ \sigma_{31} & \sigma_{32} & \sigma_3^2 \end{bmatrix}$$

With such notation, the variance of a portfolio can be described as:

$$\sigma_p^2 = w'Vw \tag{2}$$

while the expected return is $w'Er$.

8.3.3 Efficiency without a risk-free asset

Markowitz's (1952) model (without a risk-free asset) solves the problem of finding the portfolio minimizing variance for a given target expected return level r_{TAR} and the constraint that the sum of the weights is equal to 1, namely:

$$min_w 0.5 \times w'Vw$$

subject to:

$$w'Er = r_{TAR}$$

$$w'i = 1$$

Technical Box 8.1 The Markowitz solution without a risk-free asset

Markowitz (1952) solves the problem:

$$min_w 0.5 \times w'Vw$$

subject to $w'\ Er = r_{TAR}$

$$w'i = 1.$$

by writing the Lagrange function $min_w\ L = 0.5 \times w'Vw + m_1 \times (r_{TAR} - w'Er) + m_2 \times (1 - w'i)$ and next calculating the N first derivatives with respect to the w, using the rules of matrix derivation $\partial w'Vw/\partial w = 2Vw$ and $\partial w'Er/\partial w = Er$, and the two derivatives relative to the scalars m_1 and m_2 and equating them to 0, to find:

$$Vw - m_1 \times Er - m_2 \times i = 0$$

$$r_{TAR} - w'Er = 0$$

$$1 - w'i = 0$$

We first rewrite the first N equations as $w = m_1 \times V^{-1} \times Er + m_2 \times V^{-1} \times i$. Next, we pre-multiply this set of N equations by i' and use the second constraint to find $1 = m_1 \times a + m_2 \times c$ where $a \equiv Er \times V^{-1} \times i$, $c \equiv i'V^{-1} \times i$. If we pre-multiply the same set of equations by $(Er)'$ and use the first constraint, we obtain $r_{TAR} = m_1 \times b + m_2 \times a$ where $b = Er \times V^{-1} \times Er$. Solving the two equations for the scalars m_1 and m_2, we find:

$$w = \frac{(c \times r_{TAR} - a)}{(b \times c - a^2)} V^{-1} \times Er + \frac{(a \times r_{TAR} - b)}{(a^2 - b \times c)} \times V^{-1} \times i$$

Moreover, from $Vw - m_1 \times Er - m_2 \times i = 0$ we can write, by pre-multiplying by the inverse of the variance and covariance matrix, $w = m_1 \times V^{-1} \times Er + m_2 \times V^{-1} \times i$, which can be rewritten as $w = V^{-1} \times \begin{pmatrix} Er\ i \end{pmatrix} \begin{pmatrix} m_1 \\ m_2 \end{pmatrix}$ where $(Er\ i)$ is an $(N,2)$ matrix with first column the vector of expected returns and the second column the unitary vector. Pre-multiplying the latter equation by the matrix $(Er\ i)'$, we find $\begin{pmatrix} Er\ i \end{pmatrix}'w = \begin{pmatrix} Er\ i \end{pmatrix}'V^{-1} \times \begin{pmatrix} Er\ i \end{pmatrix} \begin{pmatrix} m_1 \\ m_2 \end{pmatrix}$. The term on the left is a (2,1) vector $\begin{pmatrix} Er_p \\ 1 \end{pmatrix}$ where Er_p is the expected return of any portfolio p whose structure is described by the solution of the Markowitz model. Solving the latter equation for $\begin{pmatrix} m_1 \\ m_2 \end{pmatrix}$, we find $\begin{pmatrix} m_1 \\ m_2 \end{pmatrix} = \frac{1}{(Er\ i)'V^{-1}(Er\ i)} \begin{pmatrix} Er_p \\ 1 \end{pmatrix}$, an equation that can be substituted into $w = V^{-1} \times \begin{pmatrix} Er\ i \end{pmatrix} \begin{pmatrix} m_1 \\ m_2 \end{pmatrix}$ to find $w_p = \frac{V^{-1} \times (Er\ i)}{(Er\ i)'V^{-1}(Er\ i)} \begin{pmatrix} Er_p \\ 1 \end{pmatrix}$, according to which the composition of an efficient portfolio (now written as w_p to stress that this is the efficient portfolio whose expected return is Er_p) depends on its expected return.

One of the main results of the optimization model is the minimum variance frontier. The minimum variance frontier is the set of expected returns/variance pairs obtained from portfolios described in Technical Box 8.1. A relevant portfolio on this frontier is the "global minimum variance portfolio" (see Figure 8.3) describing the combination of risky assets producing the lowest possible risk.

Figure 8.3 Minimum variance frontier in the general case

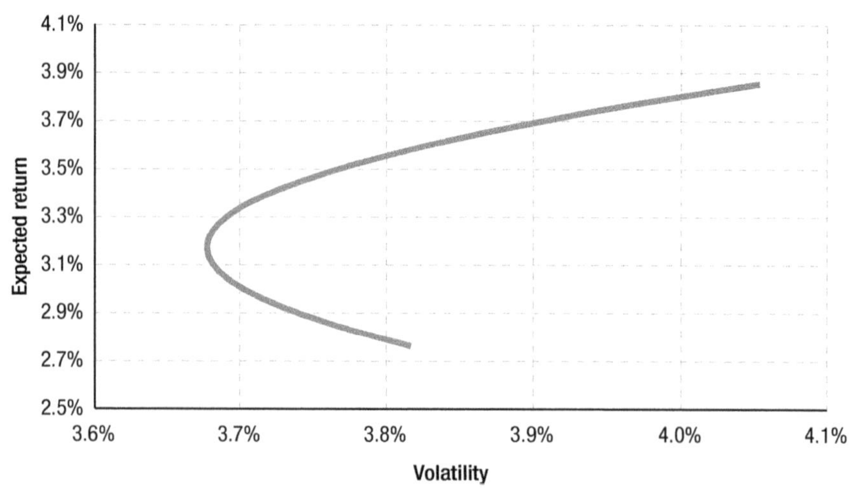

The curve depicted in Figure 8.3 is only apparently similar to the one seen in the two-asset case. The difference is that in the two-asset case there was no need for complex mathematical computations. Once the correlation coefficient is known it is possible to plot the curve describing the expected return and variance (or volatility) of the portfolios simply trying out all the possible combinations of the two assets. However, if there are at least three assets we cannot just compute all the possible combinations because many portfolios will be useless: We are only interested in portfolios that have the lowest possible variance for each level of target expected return. To systematically find those portfolios, we need to write the optimization model where we find the portfolio minimizing the variance for each level of target expected return.

The upper part (starting from the global minimum variance portfolio) of the minimum variance frontier, known as the "efficient frontier," describes the subset of portfolios whose investment may be of interest to a risk-averse investor who wants to maximize the expected return for each risk level. In Figure 8.4, the efficient frontier therefore includes only those portfolios that, for each level of variance, offer the highest possible expected return, neglecting the lower part of the curve.

Figure 8.4 The efficient frontier

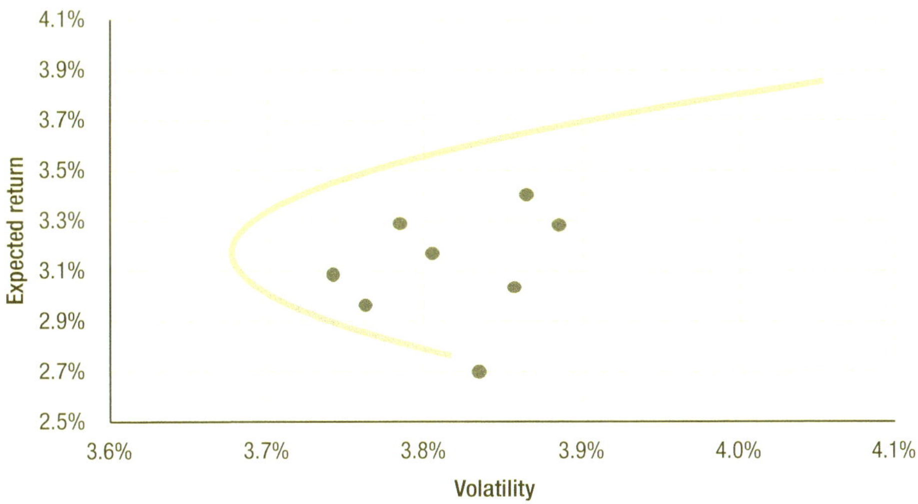

Importantly, the weight of any portfolio on the efficient frontier can be obtained from a weighted average of the weights of two other efficient portfolios. For example, the composition of any portfolio on the minimum variance frontier can be written as a linear combination of the composition of two portfolios that belong to the same frontier,[1] $w_p = \alpha w_{GMV} + \left(1 - \alpha\right) w_T$.

[1] When solving the Markowitz problem without a risk-free asset we have found that for an efficient

8.3.4 Efficiency with a risk-free asset

When there is a risk-free asset, and the sum of the weights need not to sum to 1 because the rest can be invested in (or borrowed from) the risk-free asset, the expected return of the portfolio becomes:

$$Er_p = w'Er + (1 - i'w)\, r_f = r_f + w'\left(Er - i\, r_f\right)$$

a formula that resembles the one already seen in the case involving a risk-free and a risky security. As illustrated in the second equality on the right, the expected return of the overall portfolio can be thought of as the return that is obtained by investing all the initial assets in risk-free and then borrowing, at the same rate, a share of assets corresponding to that invested in the risky securities.

Technical Box 8.2 The Markowitz solution with a risk-free asset

Markowitz (1952) solves the problem of forming a portfolio that minimizes variance for a given target expected return level, namely:

$$min_w 0.5 \times w'Vw$$
$$\text{subject to } w'Er + (1 - i'w)\, r_f = r_{TAR}$$

due to the expected return of the portfolio with a risk-free asset being written as:

$$Er_p = w'Er + \left(1 - i'w\right) r_f$$

There is no constraint that the sum of the weights is equal to 1: the difference can be invested into the risk-free asset or obtained by borrowing in the risk-free asset. Again, the problem is solved by the Lagrange function:

$$min_w\, L = 0.5 \times w'Vw + m \times \left(r_{TAR} - r_f - (Er - r_f i)'w\right)$$

Calculating the N first derivatives with respect to the vector w and the derivative with respect to m and putting them equal to 0, we find:

---

portfolio p the solution is represented by $w_p = \frac{V^{-1} \times (Er\ i)}{(Er\ i)'V^{-1}(Er\ i)}\begin{pmatrix} Er_p \\ 1 \end{pmatrix}$ (see Technical Box 8.1). Suppose we apply this representation to the tangency portfolio $w_T = \frac{V^{-1} \times (Er\ i)}{(Er\ i)'V^{-1}(Er\ i)}\begin{pmatrix} Er_T \\ 1 \end{pmatrix}$ and the global minimum variance portfolio $w_{GMV} = \frac{V^{-1} \times (Er\ i)}{(Er\ i)'V^{-1}(Er\ i)}\begin{pmatrix} Er_{GMV} \\ 1 \end{pmatrix}$, and we define the expected return of any portfolio as a linear combination of the expected returns of the tangency and the global minimum variance portfolios, $Er_p = \alpha w_{GMV} + \left(1 - \alpha\right) w_T$. It then follows that $w_p = \alpha w_{GMV} + \left(1 - \alpha\right) w_T$.

$$Vw - mEr + m \times i \times r_f = 0$$
$$\left(r_{TAR} - r_f - (Er - r_f i)'w\right) = 0$$

With a series of algebraic manipulations,[2] we find:

$$w = H^{-1}\left(r_{TAR} - r_f\right) \times V^{-1} \times \left(Er - r_f i\right)$$

a solution showing that the portfolio minimizing variance for the expected return target simultaneously depends on all expected return parameters and all variances and covariances. Using this solution, we will now find: (a) the composition of the tangency portfolio, (b) the composition of the global minimum variance portfolio, and (c) the general equation for the Capital Allocation Line.

The composition of the tangency portfolio: as we have already seen in the case $N = 2$, the tangency portfolio is the part of the curve describing the allocation to risky assets and is characterized by having the sum of the shares invested in risky securities equal to 1. By imposing this constraint, we find the composition of the tangency portfolio:[3]

$$w_T = \frac{V^{-1} \times \left(Er - r_f i\right)}{i'V^{-1} \times \left(Er - r_f i\right)}$$

The composition of the global minimum variance portfolio: this is obtained by means of the Lagrange function written to take into account only the constraint that the sum of the invested shares is equal to 1:

$$min_w\, 0.5 \times w'Vw + m \times \left(1 - i'w\right)$$

By calculating derivatives with respect to w and to m and placing them equal to 0, and by manipulating the results,[4] we find the composition of the global minimum variance portfolio:

$$w_{GMV} = \frac{V^{-1}i}{i'V^{-1}i}$$

The Capital Allocation Line: by using the equation $w = H^{-1}(r_{TAR} - r_f) \times V^{-1} \times \left(Er - r_f i\right)$, and using the definition of the portfolio excess return $\left(Er - r_f 1\right)'w = r_{TAR} - r_f$, we see that the variance of the

---

[2] Rewriting the first equation as $w = m \times V^{-1}\left(Er - r_f i\right)$ and pre-multiplying both sides by $(Er\text{-}r_f i)'$ and using the second equation gives $m = \dfrac{r_{TAR} - r_f}{c \times r_f^2 - 2 \times a \times r_f + b}$ using the definitions of coefficients a, b, c given in Technical Box 8.1. Defining $H = c \times r_f^2 - 2 \times a \times r_f + b$ we get the equation in the text.

[3] The tangency portfolio can be obtained by requiring that the sum of the shares invested in risky securities be equal to 1, that is, $i'w = H^{-1}\left(r_{TAR} - r_f\right) \times i' \times V^{-1} \times \left(Er - r_f i\right) = 1$, from which $H^{-1}(r_{TAR} - r_f) = 1/i' \times V^{-1} \times \left(Er - r_f i\right)$. Substituting in $w = H^{-1}(r_{TAR} - r_f) \times V^{-1} \times \left(Er - r_f i\right)$ the general solution is the composition of the tangency portfolio given in the text.

[4] By calculating the first derivatives and setting them equal to 0, we find:

$$Vw - mi = 0$$
$$1 - i'w = 0$$

Pre-multiplying the first equation by V^{-1} we find $w = mV^{-1}i$. Pre-multiplying the latter equation by i' we find $i'w = mi'V^{-1}i$ from which $m = 1/i'V^{-1}i$. Substituting back in the first equation we find the solution for the global minimum variance portfolio $w = \dfrac{V^{-1}i}{i'V^{-1}i}$.

portfolio associated with the target return r_{TAR} can be written as $\sigma^2_{TAR} = w'Vw = H^{-1}(r_{TAR} - r_f)^2$. The relationship between expected return and variance is then described by the parabola $(r_{TAR} - r_f)^2 = H \times \sigma^2_{TAR}$, and in the expected return/ volatility graph, the relationship is $r_{TAR} = r_f \pm \sqrt{H} \times \sigma_{TAR}$. The positive slope $r_{TAR} = r_f + \sqrt{H} \times \sigma_{TAR}$ represents the general relation between expected return and risk of any efficient portfolio.

Technical Box 8.2 shows that the solution for the efficient portfolio weights is a vector:

$$w = H^{-1}\left(r_{TAR} - r_f\right) \times V^{-1} \times \left(Er - r_f i\right) \tag{3}$$

where $H = \left(Er - r_f i\right)' \times V^{-1} \times \left(Er - r_f i\right)$. The solution demonstrates that the portfolio that minimizes variance for the expected return target simultaneously depends on all expected return parameters and all variances and covariances. Note that if the investor sets herself the goal of having a target expected return equal to the risk-free rate, she invests the assets completely in the latter: Why take an unnecessary risk when the risk-free asset can allow the achievement of the goal without any volatility? What is remarkable is that the demand for an asset depends on all the parameters describing the properties of all existing assets.

Equation (3) provides the portfolio composition of the $N + 1$ assets (the risk-free investment is in fact equal to 1 minus the sum of the units invested in risky assets) from which the capital allocation line is derived. As shown in Technical Box 8.2, the Capital Allocation Line in the general case is (using the same notation used in Chapter 7 to denote composite portfolios):

$$Er_C = r_f + \sqrt{H} \times \sigma_C$$

In the multivariate case, it is useful to analyze the tangency and the minimum variance portfolios, already studied for the case of two risky assets. It can be shown (see Technical Box 8.2) that the tangency portfolio is composed as follows:

$$w_T = \frac{V^{-1} \times \left(Er - r_f i\right)}{i' \times V^{-1} \times \left(Er - r_f i\right)}$$

The tangency portfolio is obtained by multiplying the inverse of the variance matrix by the vector of risk premia, normalized by a scalar representing the sum of the components of the vector itself. At the same time, the composition of the global minimum variance portfolio is:

$$w_{GMV} = \frac{V^{-1} i}{i' V^{-1} i}$$

The global minimum variance portfolio is obtained by multiplying the inverse of the variance matrix by the vector containing the constant 1, normalized by a scalar representing the sum of the components of the vector itself.

Box 8.1 Tangency and global minimum variance portfolios

Question: Sara wants to calculate the tangency portfolio and the global minimum variance portfolio when there are three stocks A, B, and C with expected returns of 6%, 5%, and 4% and standard deviation of 25%, 20%, and 15% respectively, $\rho_{AB} = 20\%$, $\rho_{AC} = 40\%$, $\rho_{BC} = 10\%$, risk-free equal to 1%.

Answer: Sara must first calculate the variance–covariance matrix of size (3,3) using the definition of covariance equal to the product of standard deviation and correlation coefficient:

$$\begin{pmatrix} 0.25^2 & 0.25 \times 0.2 \times 0.2 & 0.25 \times 0.15 \times 0.4 \\ 0.25 \times 0.2 \times 0.2 & 0.2^2 & 0.2 \times 0.15 \times 0.1 \\ 0.25 \times 0.15 \times 0.4 & 0.2 \times 0.15 \times 0.1 & 0.15^2 \end{pmatrix} = \begin{pmatrix} 6.25\% & 1\% & 1.5\% \\ 1\% & 4\% & 0.3\% \\ 1.5\% & 0.3\% & 2.25\% \end{pmatrix}$$

Inverting the V matrix using Excel's MINVERSE function gives:

$$\begin{pmatrix} 19.653 & -3.970 & -12.572 \\ -3.970 & 26.055 & -0.827 \\ -12.572 & -0.827 & 52.936 \end{pmatrix}$$

The H-scalar is obtained from:

$$\begin{pmatrix} 6\% - 1\% \\ 5\% - 1\% \\ 4\% - 1\% \end{pmatrix}' \times \begin{pmatrix} 19.653 & -3.970 & -12.572 \\ -3.970 & 26.055 & -0.827 \\ -12.572 & -0.827 & 52.936 \end{pmatrix} \times \begin{pmatrix} 6\% - 1\% \\ 5\% - 1\% \\ 4\% - 1\% \end{pmatrix} = H = 0.0829$$

The tangency portfolio is $w_T = \dfrac{V^{-1} \times (Er - r_f i)}{i' \times V^{-1} \times (Er - r_f i)}$ is:

$$\begin{pmatrix} 19.653 & -3.970 & -12.572 \\ -3.970 & 26.055 & -0.827 \\ -12.572 & -0.827 & 52.936 \end{pmatrix} \times \begin{pmatrix} 6\% - 1\% \\ 5\% - 1\% \\ 4\% - 1\% \end{pmatrix} / 2.192 = \begin{bmatrix} 0.204 \\ 0.373 \\ 0.423 \end{bmatrix}$$

The global minimum variance portfolio is:

$$w_{GMV} = \frac{V^{-1} i}{i' V^{-1} i} = \begin{pmatrix} 19.653 & -3.970 & -12.572 \\ -3.970 & 26.055 & -0.827 \\ -12.572 & -0.827 & 52.936 \end{pmatrix} \times \begin{pmatrix} 1 \\ 1 \\ 1 \end{pmatrix} / 63.904 = \begin{bmatrix} 0.049 \\ 0.333 \\ 0.619 \end{bmatrix}$$

The computations show that the tangency portfolio, located at the top of the efficient frontier, is more invested in the higher expected return than the minimum variance portfolio.

Substituting the composition of the tangency portfolio into equation (3):

$$w = H^{-1}\left(r_{TAR} - r_f\right) \times i'V^{-1} \times \left(Er - r_f i\right) \times w_T$$

we see that the weights of risky securities describing efficient portfolios are proportional to the tangency portfolio structure. The differential between target and risk-free expected return represents a scale factor that requires different overall solutions, all of which, however, respect the logic of investing in a single risky portfolio whose expected return and volatility are placed, as already in the case with two risky assets, at the point of tangency between the CAL and the minimum variance frontier.

Box 8.2 Portfolio optimization

Question: Sara wants to calculate the efficient portfolio that allows her to have a target expected return of 4.5% with the same three stocks considered in Box 8.1. She also wants to know whether the equally balanced portfolio in the three stocks is efficient.

Answer: Building on previous results, Sara computes the optimal vector as:

$$w = 0.0829^{-1}(4.5\% - 1\%) \times \begin{pmatrix} 19.653 & -3.970 & -12.572 \\ -3.970 & 26.055 & -0.827 \\ -12.572 & -0.827 & 52.936 \end{pmatrix} \times \begin{pmatrix} 6\% - 1\% \\ 5\% - 1\% \\ 4\% - 1\% \end{pmatrix} = \begin{pmatrix} 0.189 \\ 0.346 \\ 0.391 \end{pmatrix}$$

The portion that remains from the sum of the three, 0.074, is invested in the risk-free asset. In order to know whether the equally balanced portfolio is efficient, it is necessary to check whether it can be expressed as a weighted average of the two efficient portfolios previously found, that is, whether there is a weight α such that $\alpha \begin{bmatrix} 0.049 \\ 0.333 \\ 0.619 \end{bmatrix} + (1 - \alpha) \begin{bmatrix} 0.204 \\ 0.373 \\ 0.423 \end{bmatrix} = \begin{bmatrix} 0.333 \\ 0.333 \\ 0.333 \end{bmatrix}$.

Using Excel's "Solver," Sara realizes that there is no suitable weight, and therefore that the equally balanced portfolio is not efficient.

Box 8.3 The cost of inefficiency

Question: Carola wants a target expected return of 4.5% when there are three stocks A, B, and C with expected returns of 6%, 5%, and 4% and standard deviation of 25%, 20%, and 15% respectively, $\rho_{AB} = 20\%$, $\rho_{AC} = 40\%$, $\rho_{BC} = 10\%$, risk-free of 1%. Given the coincidence between the expected return and the target return, considers purchasing a portfolio that invests equal shares in B and C securities. She turns to her consultant Sara to find out if it's a good idea. What does Sara suggest?

Answer: Sara replies that it is a mistake. The portfolio consisting only of securities B and C has a risk of 13.1%. But the portfolio optimization technique allows for the formation of a set of the three stocks that allows achievement of the target return at lower volatility. Using the calculations made above, Sara knows that the tangency portfolio is defined by 20.4%, 37.3%, and 42.3%, while the minimum variance portfolio is made up of 4.9%, 33.3%, and 61.9%. The former has an expected return of 4.78%, the latter of 4.4%. An investment of 20% in the tangency portfolio and 80% in the global minimum variance portfolio yields an expected return of 5%. The portfolio equates to an investment of 8% in stock A, 34% in B, and 58% in C and has an overall volatility of 12.53%, a sharp reduction from the simple portfolio combining B and C.

Box 8.4 The risk-free rate and the tangency portfolio

Question: Elena is a financial advisor and she is faced with the problem of examining the impact of the reduction in the risk-free rate on the asset allocation suggested to her clients. In particular, Elena wants to calculate the efficient portfolio that allows to have a target expected return of 4.5% when there are three stocks A, B, and C with expected returns that remain equal to 6%, 5%, and 4%, standard deviation respectively equal to 25%, 20%, and 15%, correlations between A and B equal to 20%, between A and C equal to 40%, between B and C equal to 10%, and the risk-free rate is zero.

Answer: Elena's assumptions are associated with an increase in the risk premium, which for the three available securities becomes equal to the expected return. Applying the mathematics of efficient frontiers, she finds that the composition of the tangency portfolio now becomes 17%, 36%, and 47% compared with the weight of 20%, 37%, and 42% previously calculated when the rate was at 1%. At the same time, if the risk premiums were constant, the reduction in the risk-free rate would be associated with a reduction in expected returns, with a parallel downward shift in the CAL that would leave the composition of the tangency portfolio unchanged.

Box 8.5 Sensitivity to parameters

Question: Carola wants to form the tangency portfolio starting from A, B, and C securities with expected returns of 6%, 5%, and 4%, standard deviation of 25%, 20%, and 15% respectively, $\rho_{AB} = 20\%$, $\rho_{AC} = 40\%$, $\rho_{BC} = 10\%$, risk-free of 1%. Looking back, she worries that it may be more prudent to assume an expected return of 3.5% on C and asks Sara if assuming 4% or 3.5% could have a major impact on the composition of the tangency portfolio.

Answer: Sara replies that when the expected return on stock C is 3.5%, the composition of the tangency portfolio is 26%, 41%, and 33%, compared with 20%, 37%, and 42% when the expected return on C is 4%. In presenting the results, she notes that a small spread of 0.5% has significantly changed the share invested in all assets: Stock C has a share that grows with its expected return, while shares in A and B both fall. Sara suggests to Carola that this is a general problem of the Markowitz model, which predicts results that are extremely sensitive to the value of the parameters, especially the expected return.

Box 8.6 How to efficiently increase risk

Question: Carola wants to have a target expected return of 6% on her assets of €2 million. Knowing that there are three stocks A, B, and C with expected returns of 6%, 5%, and 4%, standard deviation of 25%, 20%, and 15% respectively, $\rho_{AB} = 20\%$, $\rho_{AC} = 40\%$, $\rho_{BC} = 10\%$, risk-free equal to 1%, she believes it is sufficient to buy stock A to achieve her objective. She turns to her consultant Elena to find out if this is a good idea.

Answer: Elena performs a portfolio optimization analysis and discovers that the tangency portfolio has an expected return of 4.78%. Its risk is 15%. The capital allocation line therefore suggests that the best way to have a target expected return of 6% is to use leverage. In this case, it is necessary to invest 132.5% in the tangency portfolio and to borrow 32.5%. She therefore suggests that Carola borrows €650,000 and invests €2,650,000 in the tangency portfolio, with a risk of 19.87%. That risk is much lower than the 25% risk associated with only investing in A.

8.4 The Markowitz model and investors' portfolios

8.4.1 The capital allocation line and the two-fund separation theorem

We have seen that the portfolio combining the risk-free asset with the risky portfolio generates combinations of expected return and risk that are on a straight line. The tangency portfolio is precisely the one that supports the capital allocation line with the highest level of Sharpe ratio (see Figure 8.5).

Figure 8.5 The efficient frontier and the CAL in the general case

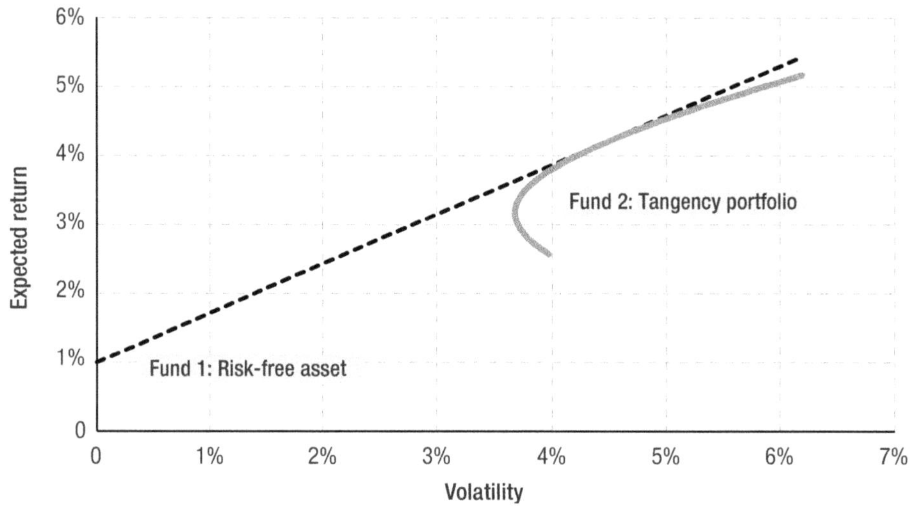

The "separation theorem" in two funds states that to invest efficiently, it is sufficient to combine the investment in the risk-free security (Fund 1) and the investment in the tangency portfolio (Fund 2).

To intuitively understand why the straight line is the most efficient set of portfolios, consider Figure 8.5, for example, to see that for any level of volatility, the expected return obtained by choosing the portfolio on the straight line is higher than the expected return obtained by choosing the corresponding portfolio on the curve.

We are back to the simplest two-asset case we started from in Chapter 7: The investor simply needs to select the best combination of risk-free asset and risky portfolio. The Markowitz model is useful to find the composition of the tangency portfolio. The risky portfolio supporting the CAL is not randomly chosen from the set of N risky assets. It has a well-specified composition obtained by a methodology delivering the largest expected return for any level of volatility, accounting for all the correlations across assets.

8.4.2 Qualitative investment implications

Given N risky securities and a risk-free asset, the investor can simply choose combinations of the tangency portfolio and the risk-free security. To have portfolios at various levels of expected return and risk, it is not necessary to change the composition of the risky portfolio. It is sufficient to vary the investment mix in the risk-free and tangency portfolio.[5] According to this theory, investors do not differ in terms of the composition of the portfolio invested in risky securities, which maintains the same structure regardless of the risk aversion coefficient. The underlying assumption is that all investors estimate the same set of optimization inputs: expected returns, volatilities, and correlations.

To better understand how this happens, let's assume that the tangency portfolio consists of three stocks A, B, and C with weights of 25%, 25%, and 50% respectively. Investor 1 invests 20% of his assets in the tangency portfolio; 80% of his assets are therefore invested in risk-free, 5% (20% of 25%) in risky security A, 5% in risky security B, and 10% in risky security C. Investor 2 invests 40% of his assets in the tangency portfolio; 60% of its assets are invested in risk-free, 10% (40% of 25%) in risky security A, 10% in risky security B, and 20% in risky security C.

The two portfolios are different, but in both cases, A and B account for 25% of the value of assets invested in risky securities, and C accounts for 50% of the value of assets invested in risky securities. What distinguishes one investor from another is the share invested in the risk-free stock, not the composition of the risky portfolio.

Box 8.7 How heterogeneous can portfolios be?

Question: Elena, a financial consultant, is evaluating the portfolios of two investors. One, Paul Young, is thirty years old; the other, Jeff Old, is seventy years old. They both invest in three sectors: utility (low volatility), consumer goods (medium volatility), and technology (high volatility). Young's portfolio is characterized by the following allocation across the three sectors: 10%, 30%, 60%. Old's portfolio is 60%, 30%, 10%. Young and Old ask Elena to evaluate their portfolios and suggest potential improvements.

Answer: Elena applies the Markowitz portfolio optimization model and finds a tangency portfolio with the following structure: utility 30%, consumer goods 40%, technology 30%. She suggests that both investors modify the structure of their risky portfolios to improve the return/risk trade-off.

Box 8.8 An asset allocation puzzle

Question: Carola is puzzled by different suggestions coming from different professionals. Private banker A suggesting that she holds 5% in cash, 70% in equity, and 25% in bonds, while

[5] As already pointed out, the result does not apply if leverage cannot be used and the target expected return is higher than the expected return of the tangency portfolio.

private banker B suggests a composition of 25% in cash, 25% in equity, and 50% in bonds. She asks her sister Sara what she should do.

Answer: Sara talks to both A and B and concludes that they hold the same expected returns, volatility, and correlations assumptions. She prefers to follow Markowitz and recommends that Carola hold the tangency portfolio. She tells Carola that she should not be surprised: Canner, Mankiw, and Weil (1997) systematically compare recommendations from financial advisors about the distribution of wealth between cash, bonds, and equities and find that in general advisors recommend that clients hold a higher ratio of stocks to bonds when risk aversion is low. The authors refer to the inconsistency between advisors' suggestions and the implications of the theory as an asset allocation puzzle.

8.4.3 Choosing the optimal portfolio: graphical solution

How does an investor select "the" best portfolio among the infinitely many available? The weights invested in the risk-free asset and the tangency portfolio can be determined using the indifference curve. We have seen that the indifference curve is a convex and upward-sloping quadratic function in the expected return/volatility space. The investor has an interest in selecting the indifference curve with the largest intercept.

At the same time, the capital allocation line (CAL) describes infinite efficient portfolios representing investment opportunities: This is the investment opportunity set, meaning the best an investor can do in terms of the expected return per unit of volatility. An investor who wishes to attain the highest indifference curve must select a solution that touches the CAL. We can achieve a level of utility associated with the indifference that is tangential to the CAL to find the truly optimal portfolio, that is, the one that maximizes mean/variance utility subject to the constraint imposed by the investment opportunity set.

Figure 8.6 The optimal portfolio and the CAL

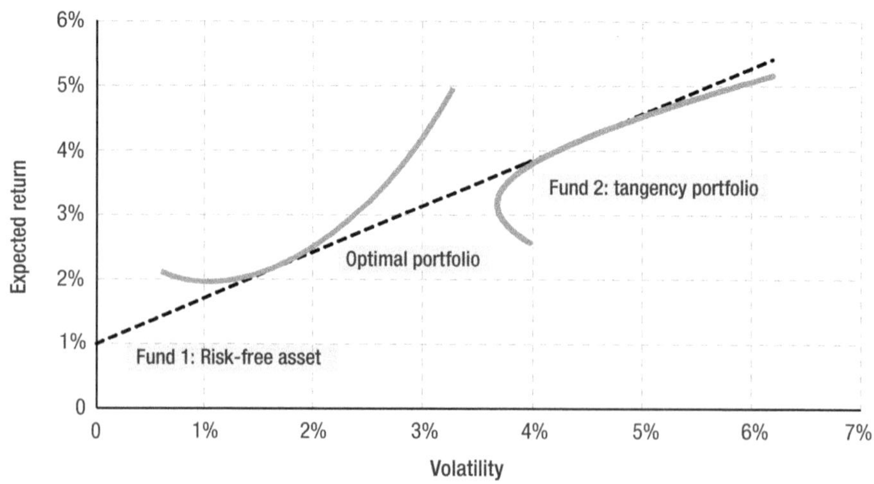

8.4.4 Choosing the optimal portfolio: analytical solution

The weights invested in the risk-free asset and the tangency portfolio can be determined analytically through the maximization of the utility function. Formally, using the relation between the portfolio return and the weight, $r_C = w \times r_T + (1 - w) r_f$, to compute the expectation and the variance of return and substituting in the utility function, the objective function becomes:

$$\max_w u\left(Er_T, \sigma_T^2\right) = w \times Er_T + (1 - w) r_f - 0.5 \times A \times \sigma_T^2$$

where Er_T indicates the expected return and σ_T^2 indicates the variance of the tangency portfolio return. It can be demonstrated that if you choose the portion invested in the tangency portfolio to maximize the utility function,[6] you get the following result:

$$w = \frac{Er_T - r_f}{A \times \sigma_T^2} \tag{4}$$

Box 8.9 The optimal portfolio

Question: Carola believes that the stock market is described by the parameters $Er_p = 5\%$, $\sigma_p^2 = 2\%$, $r_f = 1\%$. Her financial advisor has estimated her risk aversion ratio at $A = 4$ and suggests that she invests 30% in the equity market. On a purely rational basis, would you share the consultant's advice? How would you describe the sensitivity of the optimal solution relative to small changes in the risk aversion coefficient?

Answer: We can compare the advice Carola received with the implication of the model previously used, according to which the portion invested in the risky portfolio should be:

$$w_1 = \frac{5\% - 1\%}{4 \times 2\%} = 50\%$$

A small change in the risk aversion coefficient has an immediate consequence for the optimal choice of portfolio. Its impact can be quantified by using equation (4) to calculate the first derivative of the optimal portfolio with respect to the risk aversion coefficient of $\frac{-(Er_T - r_f)}{A^2 \times \sigma_T^2}$, which always has a negative value.

The weight invested in the tangency portfolio (using the data in Box 8.9):

- goes up when the risk premium (the differential between the expected return of the risky portfolio and the risk-free) increases; for example, if the risk premium is 6% instead of 4%, the share invested in the risky portfolio is 75%;

[6] To obtain (4) the following procedure is applied: The equations describing the expected return and the risk are substituted in the objective function, that is, $\max_{w_1} u = w_1 \times Er_T + \left(1 - w_1\right) \times r_f - 0.5 \times A \times w_1^2 \sigma_T^2$. By calculating the derivative before the portion invested in the risky portfolio and setting it equal to zero, we find the necessary condition for identifying the optimal portfolio $Er_T - r_f - A \times w_1 \times \sigma_T^2 = 0$, which is solved by the portion invested in the risky portfolio described in (4).

- goes down when risk aversion rises; for example, if A is equal to 8 instead of 4, the share invested in the risky portfolio is equal to 25%;
- goes down when the variance in the return of the risky portfolio increases; for example, if the variance rises from 2% to 4%, the share invested in the risky portfolio is 25%.

8.4.5 Reverse engineering the optimal portfolio solution

We have seen in Chapter 3 how difficult it is to accurately estimate an investor's risk aversion coefficient. However, if we have an equation that links the choice of the optimal portfolio to the risk aversion coefficient, we can reverse engineer and start from the historical portfolio choice to deduce the value of the risk aversion implicit in the choices observed. For example, if an investor chose a 50% weight in the tangency portfolio at a time when the variance was equal to 2% and the risk premium was 4%, we can infer that $50\% = \frac{5\% - 1\%}{A \times 2\%}$, from which we find $A = 4$. The implicit estimation of risk aversion can be useful to understand how to react to a change in the relevant parameters: Given an estimate of $A = 4$, an increase in variance from 2% to 4% suggests halving the share invested in the risky portfolio from 50% to 25%.

The investment implications are very substantial: The investor does not change the composition of her risky portfolio but simply increases the share invested in the risk-free asset without changing the composition of the risky securities portfolio in any way.

8.4.6 The Markowitz model and the democratization of finance

The Markowitz model implies that even in the presence of a very large number of risky securities, what matters to the investor is only the tangency portfolio, because it represents the most efficient structure, the one capable of obtaining the highest expected return for each level of volatility. This is a significant step in the process of democratizing finance, meaning the possibility for all investors to profit as much as possible from the existence of financial markets.

Decades ago, life was difficult for investors. They did not have empirical regularities that could be studied based on long samples of data and as a result found themselves under conditions of uncertainty. To some extent we can say that investors one hundred years ago opened the way for markets as we know them today by investing their own money and experimenting with the volatility of returns, crashes, and average returns. Moreover, financial engineering had not created tools for diversified investment. Without mutual funds and exchange traded funds it was hard to select a large portfolio of assets also due to constraints on the minimum amount of wealth that could be invested in each trade. Investors had to select individual stocks and bonds and the resulting portfolio was largely under-diversified and affected by idiosyncratic risk. It was no surprise that investors had large allocations to cash, which was the best way to control for overall portfolio risk.

Before Markowitz opened our eyes, it was hard to understand and implement diversified investment in a scientific way. The minimum variance frontier, accounting for all sources of risk, was not available at the time. This is another reason why investors had to sustain extra risk relative to what is necessary today. The combination of investor knowledge and financial products decreases the overall level of risk that must be faced by investors. If investors choose on the basis of the maximum level of risk they want to take, then more knowledge and better products may drive investors toward more risk-taking in terms of asset classes: If, in the 1920s, investing in equities meant taking a 40% volatility and today it means taking a 20% volatility, it is possible to double the equity position with no increase in total risk.

Finally, investors before Markowitz had to deal with much complexity. They had to select portfolios among thousands of securities and it was difficult for them to understand what to buy. The existence of a tangency portfolio dramatically simplifies the picture: An investor can nowadays select a portfolio choosing the weights in the risk-free asset and in the tangency portfolio. A one-thousand-asset investment problem is simplified to a two-asset problem. As we saw in Chapter 4 on behavioral finance, not all investors want to exploit this possibility. Some investors want to actively trade and others want to pick only the stocks they believe will be more valuable in the future. There is nothing wrong with so many investment styles coexisting around the world: Some people may fall in love with investing and find it an intellectually challenging and rewarding experience, an experience that becomes even more interesting if it may contribute to increasing one's wealth. Understanding geopolitical risks with the interested eyes of an investor is a different experience than reading news that does not have any direct implications for her life. Other people may enjoy movies, music, and sport more than investment and may deeply appreciate the possibility to simply invest for the long run by selecting proportions in two assets. This is a clear example of finance democratization: opening possibilities to better manage wealth.

From the industry point of view, the Markowitz model lies at the origin of the separation between asset management and wealth management: although the distinction is somewhat blurred in many cases, the former is mainly about forming efficient portfolios, and the latter is about helping investors to select optimal portfolios considering their targets and constraints. Section 8.5 is devoted to the study of a few important elements associated with wealth management. Section 8.6 discusses some relevant challenges, and their solutions, for asset management.

8.5 Wealth management: liabilities, time diversification, and non-traded assets

8.5.1 A general approach to hedging liabilities

In Chapter 6 we looked at cash flow matching and portfolio immunization as techniques to hedge the risk of interest rate changes. Using cash flow matching, an investor can identify her goals, and the timing and amount of expenditures that are necessary to pursue them, with the purpose of investing the present value in risk-free bonds. This solution, while highly efficient to allow investors to reach their goals with minimum cost and risk, does not affect the structure of the portfolio of assets: The tangency portfolio would still be the efficient solution for the risky portfolio and the only change would be the amount of wealth invested in it.

However, using the Markowitz model, we can think more generally about a hedging liability problem as the goal of investing wealth not for the purpose of maximizing its expected value and minimizing its volatility but for the purpose of making the asset portfolio return as close as possible to the return of an asset highly correlated with a liability. The typical example is that of a pension fund managing a stream of future liabilities associated with paying pensions to its subscribers. Such pensions can be identified with bonds of several maturities. In such a case risk for a pension fund would not be associated with volatility of assets return per se but rather with the volatility of the difference between assets and liabilities returns.

Sharpe and Tint (1990) set up the problem in terms of surplus, *S*, defined as the difference between assets *ASS* and liabilities *L*, multiplied by a coefficient *k* which describes the importance that the decision-maker wants to assign to liabilities. For example, if $k = 0.5$, liabilities contribute only partially to the surplus. The ratio of surplus at the end of the period to the initial surplus can be written as:[7]

$$r_{AS} - k\frac{L_0}{AS_0}r_L$$

where r_{AS} is assets return and r_L is the liability return. Defining $z \equiv \left(r_{AS} - k\frac{L_0}{AS_0}r_L\right)$, we can write the mean/variance optimization problem as maximizing $Ez - \frac{A}{2}Vz$ where as usual *A* is the degree of risk aversion. Maximization of the variance-corrected expected return is an innovative way to consider risk as an issue of mismatch.

Regarding Ez , we can drop the expected return on liabilities due to being a parameter that does not depend on the choice of asset allocation and simply consider the maximization of Er_{AS}. As to Vz, we have :

$$Vz = Vr_{AS} + \left(k\frac{L_0}{AS_0}\right)^2 Vr_L - 2 \times k \times \frac{L_0}{AS_0}C(r_{AS}, r_L)$$

[7] In fact, $\frac{AS_1 - kL_1}{AS_0} = \frac{AS_1}{AS_0} - k\frac{L_0}{AS_0} \times \frac{L_1}{L_0} = \left(1 - k\frac{L_0}{AS_0}\right) + \left(r_A - k\frac{L_0}{AS_0}r_L\right).$

where we identify the existence of a term linked to the covariance between the return on assets and liabilities. After dropping terms that do not depend on portfolio choice, and highlighting the choice variables represented by the weights invested in the assets w_i, the function to be maximized under the mean/variance utility assumption can be written as follows:

$$\sum_{i=1}^{N} w_i \left(Er_i + A \times k \frac{L_0}{ASS_0} \times \sigma_{iL} \right) - \frac{A}{2} \sigma_{ASS}^2$$

where σ_{iL} indicates the covariance between the i-th asset and the liability. As can be seen, for each asset the expected return is increased by the presence of a positive covariance with liability, which makes the asset valuable also from the point of view of hedging liability risk.

Box 8.10 How important is hedging risk in asset allocation?

Question: Elena is an advisor to an institutional investor who needs to establish the strategic asset allocation for a portfolio of European equities and ten-year German bonds. The investor believes that the expected return on equities is 6%, and that of bonds is -0.5%. The risk-free rate is zero. The total value of the investor's assets is equal to the value of the liabilities and $k = 1$. The coefficient of risk aversion is equal to 4. The variance of bond returns is estimated at 0.25% (given the volatility of 5%) while for stock returns it is estimated at 4% (given the volatility of 20%). The investor's liability is perfectly correlated with the bond return. Which asset allocation should be chosen by the investor? And what asset allocation would she have chosen if $k = 0$?

Answer: Elena must first estimate the correlation parameter between stocks and bonds. Based on a qualitative analysis, she believes that the correlation is zero and this implies that the excess return (over and above the expected return of 6%) assigned to equities is zero, while that assigned to bonds is equal to four times the variance of the bond return (since the covariance between bonds and liabilities in this case is equal to the variance of the bonds that is $A \times k \frac{L_0}{ASS_0} \times \sigma_{iL}$ equals $4 \times 1 \times \sigma_L^2$). Therefore, bond expected return is +0.5% since the expected return of -0.5% is offset by a liability hedging premium equal to 1%. So, the investor allocates 0.06/(4 × 0.04) = 37.5% to equity and 0.005/(4 × 0.0025) = 50% to long-term bonds. The remaining 12.5% is invested in the risk-free asset. The presence of a liability perfectly correlated with ten-year bonds induces the investor to invest half her wealth in an asset with an expected return of -0.5%. If the investor had ignored liability, that is, if $k = 0$, bond investment would have been $\frac{-0.5\%}{4 \times 0.0025} = -50\%$.

Box 8.11 What is the allocation to the Italian stock market?

Question: Elena has turned to the consulting firm A.F.I. for guidance on the weights to invest in the various asset classes. To understand what share is appropriate to invest in the Italian stock market, she has asked A.F.I. for the Italian stock market expected return, obtaining 3%

as an answer. Elena now asks the consultant to verify the composition of a portfolio invested in Italian equities and German bonds using as expected return 3% for the Italian market and -0.5% for bonds, confirming that her future liabilities are perfectly correlated with German government bonds. All other parameters correspond with those in Box 8.10.

Answer: Assuming that the correlation between the return of the Italian equity and the German bond is zero, and using the assumptions presented in Box 8.10, Elena assigns to the bonds a liability-driven excess return equal to four times the variance of the bond return (since the covariance between bonds and liabilities in this case of unitary correlation is equal to the variance of bonds). The variance is estimated at 0.25% (given the volatility of 5%). Therefore, the expected return parameter to be entered for bonds is +0.5% since the expected return of -0.5% is offset by +1%, which is obtained by multiplying the variance by four. The investor would allocate $0.03/(4 \times 0.04) = 18.75\%$ to Italian equity and $0.005/(4 \times 0.0025) = 50\%$ to long-term bonds. The remaining 31.25% would be invested in the risk-free asset. The presence of a liability induces Elena to invest half in an asset that has an expected return equal to -0.5%. If she had considered the existence of an inverse correlation, let us say of -0.5, between the return of Italian equities and the bond, Italian equity would have had an expected excess return of four times -0.005, obtained from the product of the risk aversion coefficient and the estimated covariance between Italian stocks and German bonds. In this case, the problem would be solved by maximizing $w_S(Er_S + A \times \sigma_{SL}) + w_B(Er_B + A \times \sigma_{BL}) - (A/2)\left(w_S^2\sigma_S^2 + w_B^2\sigma_B^2 + 2 \times w_S \times w_B \times \sigma_{SB}\right)$. With the assumed parameters the function becomes $w_S(0.03 + 4 \times 0.05 \times 0.2 \times (-0.5)) + w_B(-0.005 + 4 \times 0.0025) - 2 \times \left(w_S^2 \times 0.04 + w_B^2 \times 0.0025 + 2 \times w_S \times w_B \times 0.05 \times 0.2 \times (-0.5)\right)$. Taking first derivatives and solving we get that the amount invested in Italian shares would be 16.7% and in German bonds 83.3%. The share of bonds further increases because a negative correlation between stocks and bonds also means a negative correlation between stocks and the liability which makes stock investment less attractive. If Elena's advisor had added some qualitative considerations about the correlation between the return of the Italian stock market and her labor income, then it would have been rational to further reduce the share of financial assets invested in Italy to decrease the correlation between capital income and labor income for reasons discussed in section 8.5.3.

8.5.2 Time diversification

The Markowitz model is purely static, that is, it assumes that decisions take place at the beginning of a certain period, and the results are evaluated at the end of the period. This period can be long, so let's imagine it stretches over a multi-year horizon, assuming the portfolio is chosen at the beginning of the period without any future changes. Should the investor consider the length of the period when choosing the initial portfolio allocation? The answer seems to be positive when considering the average return. In fact, with logarithmic returns, as seen in Chapter 2, the return over a T-period horizon is the sum of the returns of each period, and therefore the average return obtained over the entire period is:

$$\overline{r_{t,t+T-1}} \equiv \frac{r_{t,t+T-1}}{T} = \frac{r_t + r_{t+1} + \ldots + r_{t+T-1}}{T}$$

If expected return is constant, then the expected average return is equal to the average single period return, $E(\overline{r_{t,t+T-1}}) = m$ where $Er_t = m$. At the same time, if the returns of each period are not correlated with each other, the variance of the multi-period return is equal to the sum of the variances of each return since there are no covariance terms:

$$V(\overline{r_{t,t+T-1}}) \equiv \frac{V(r_{t,t+T-1})}{T^2} = \frac{V(r_t)}{T}$$

Moreover, notice that volatility of the multi-period horizon decreases with the square toot of time $\sigma_{\overline{r_{t+1,t+T-1}}} = \frac{\sigma}{\sqrt{T}}$. The assumption of non-correlation of returns and constant variance therefore implies a constant reduction in the variance of the average return as the time horizon increases. If there was mean reversion, for example if it were true that $r^c_{t+1} = \beta r^c_t + \varepsilon_{t+1}$, con $\beta < 0$, as suggested by Fama and French (1988), the result would be even stronger. Of course, the variance of the total return increases with the time horizon $V(r_{t+1} + r_{t+2} + \ldots + r_{t+T-1}) = T \times \sigma^2$.

Box 8.12 What is the risk in the event of mean reversion?

Question: Carola wonders whether investing for a two-period horizon is less risky than investing for a one-period horizon, especially considering the result of the following regression $r^c_{t+1} = -0.1 \times r^c_t + \varepsilon_{t+1}$. The volatility of the one-period return is 20%.

Answer: The two-period return variance is equal to the sum of the variance for two periods plus twice the covariance, which in this case can be calculated as $COV(r^c_{t+1}, r^c_t) = -0.1 \times 0.04 = -0.004$ since the beta coefficient of regression is by definition equal to the ratio of the covariance between the returns of two consecutive periods and the variance in the return. The variance of the total return is 0.04 + 0.04 - 0.008 = 0.072, the volatility is the square root of 7.2% equal to 26.8%. The variance of the average two-period return is 0.013 (since the variance for the average of two terms is equal to the variance of the total return divided by four), whose square root is 11.4%. Carola therefore concludes that the risk of the average return over two periods is significantly lower than the risk of the one-period return.

The inverse relationship between the asset's holding time horizon and average return variance is known as time diversification, a terminology reminiscent of the diversification across assets in a single period, see Chapter 7 where we have shown that the risk of a portfolio's return is less than the weighted average of individual risks if the correlation is less than 1. Similarly, the risk of a security held for multiple periods is less than the sum of the risks when the correlation between the returns of the various periods is less than 1. This would seem to suggest that a long-term investor should have a high proportion of the portfolio invested in risky assets, as risk, as measured by variance or volatility, decreases as the holding period increases.

Empirical evidence partially supports this theory. Estrada (2013) examines the long-run data from Dimson, Marsh, and Staunton (2019) and shows that the volatility of the average return of the world stock index falls monotonically from 17% over the annual horizon to 1.7% over the thirty-year horizon. Moreover, Estrada (2013) shows that the volatility of the cumulative return rises with the horizon, as does the spread between the highest and lowest returns. However, it also highlights how the minimum total return achieved over various horizons reaches a minimum of -48.8% over the ten-year horizon and then increases to +87.3% over the thirty-year horizon. The increase in volatility and the spread between the best and worst cumulative returns takes place in the context of a worst-case scenario that still includes an increase in the value of invested assets in real terms. The reduction in the volatility of average returns is also associated with a reduced tail risk: If volatility of annual return is 15%, expected return is 5%, and volatility of a ten-year return, using $\sigma_{\overline{r_{t+1,t+T}}} = \frac{\sigma}{\sqrt{T}}$, is 4.7% then the probability of a negative return drops from 36.9% to 14.4%.[8] Recent research offers new perspectives about the downside: Anarkulova, Cederburg and O'Doherty (2022) use a broad cross section of 39 developed countries over the period 1841-2019 and, through simulations, estimate a 12% chance that a diversified investor with a 30-year investment horizon will lose relative to inflation. Pástor and Stambaugh (2012) on the contrary claim that the variance of the annual return over a long-run horizon is higher than that of the return over an annual horizon, due to the imperfect knowledge of the model that generates the returns. In their estimates, the variance of the annual return over a thirty-year horizon is 30% higher than that of the annual variance.

Regardless of statistical estimates, standard models of expected utility maximization imply that the investment time horizon is irrelevant to the share to be invested in equity. Over a long horizon, the small probability of a negative return is offset by a very high financial loss associated with keeping the asset in the portfolio for decades. Japanese and Italian investors who have invested in the stock market in recent decades are unfortunate examples of what happens to assets when the average return is zero or negative:[9] a small negative average return multiplied by twenty or thirty years has a very high impact on the final value of the investment.

8.5.3 Non-traded assets: the case of human capital

Real non-traded assets, for example human capital, may affect portfolio choice. Suppose an investor wants to invest a 50% share of her wealth in equity, and that wealth includes a financial part and a part related to human capital (the discounted present value of wages). Suppose that at the age of thirty both the financial assets and the human capital are equal to 100 and that w = 50%. The value of the equity investment should be 100, equivalent to 100% of the financial assets. After ten years, let's assume that financial assets are 150 and human capital is 50. Suppose that w is always 50%. The equity investment should be 100 and the share of financial assets invested in equity should fall by around two-thirds. It follows that the time horizon is appar-

---

[8] Using the Excel function norm.dist(0;0.05;0.15;1).

[9] The Nikkei index in 2024 reached the maximum of 1989. The FTSE Mib in 1989 was higher than the level at the time of writing this book in 2024. Both numbers ignore dividends.

ently important for the determination of non-financial assets and therefore for the investment choice of financial assets.

However, human capital and time horizon are also important in determining the optimal share *w*. The nature of the income generated by human capital is crucial from the point of view of co-movement with the stock market: A positive correlation should decrease the share optimally invested in equity, while a low/negative correlation improves its role in reducing the overall risk. It follows that employees with a fixed wage those with an income from employment should invest proportionately more in the stock market than those who are self-employed. On the other hand, investors with a long time horizon may invest more in equities due to the option of working harder and further increasing their labor income after a stock market crash.

Box 8.13 Does the portfolio depend on the profession?

Question: Carola is a medical doctor, and her income is linked to the health status of the population. Carola has financial assets of €1 million and values her human capital at €3 million (her future income is discounted at the risk-free rate). Sara works in the financial industry and her income, especially her variable component, is strongly correlated with the performance of the stock market. Sara has financial assets of €0.5 and values her human capital at €4.5 million (her future income is discounted at a rate including a risk premium). They ask Elena, a financial advisor, for guidelines for structuring the risky component of their stock portfolios.

Answer: Elena suggests that they invest 75% of their total assets in stocks, due to the long investment horizon and other factors. This means that Carola would have to invest €3 million in equity. In the absence of a desire for debt reported by the client, Elena suggests investing the entire €1 million in the stock market. Elena speculates that there is no covariance between Carola's income and the stock market, as she is not aware of any studies on the covariance between market performance and average health (covariance that could be negative if phases of volatility and market falls create anxiety and depression among investors). She therefore believes that she can make a diversified investment across the entire stock market. Things are different for Sara. In her case, the investment in equity securities should be €3.75 million assuming that the risk is equal to the market risk. However, Sara's income is equivalent to an investment in financial securities with a beta of 1.5 relatively to the market, so to have an overall risk similar to that of the market she would have to invest only €2,5 million in equity. Sara's current position therefore already includes too high a risk, and Elena suggests that Sara invest her financial assets in a diversified portfolio of fixed income securities.

8.6 Asset management and the practice of portfolio optimization

8.6.1 Asset allocation terminology and benchmarks

The Markowitz model can be used, for example, to choose asset allocation from a top-down perspective, that is, by selecting the weights to invest in various asset classes (e.g., US equity, European equity, European sovereign bonds, corporate bonds). "Strategic allocation" is the top-down choice of the fraction of assets to be invested in financial assets over the long term (at least two to three years). The parameters used to choose the allocation can be estimated based on long time series and refer to the average conditions prevailing in the future period. "Tactical allocation" is the top-down choice of the fraction of assets to be invested in financial assets in the short term (one to three months). The parameters used to choose the allocation can be estimated on the basis of short time series and refer to the average conditions prevailing in the short term. Investment policy may constrain tactical and strategic portfolio deviations to avoid excessive portfolio movements.

In asset management, it is often necessary to identify a so-called benchmark portfolio, which describes the long-term average choice of the various asset classes. The composition of the benchmark is selected on the basis of a strategic asset allocation analysis, for example, 60% equity, 30% fixed income, and 10% cash. Investment policy may suggest that portfolio weights include a range of 10 percentage points around the benchmark, for example, equity 50–70%, fixed income 20–40%, and cash 0–20%. Tactical allocation may suggest that for the current quarter the allocation should be 55% equity, 30% fixed income, and 15% cash. The investment policy must also specify the maximum time needed for actual choices, for example, three business days. The results suggest that about 80% of returns are determined by strategic asset allocation.

Benchmarks are sometimes dynamic portfolios themselves. Some financial advisors suggest that clients shift the share of their assets from stocks to bonds over time, for example, keeping a percentage invested in bonds no higher than their age. Life-cycle products, also known as target date fund, have benchmarks that in some way resemble this solution: Used for retirement investment with a view to long-term accumulation, they have a time horizon of at least twenty years and include the advance determination of the portion invested in the various asset classes at any point in time, for example 100% equity initially, 80% equity and 20% fixed income after five years and so on. Parker, Schoar, and Sun (2023) find that target date funds implement a contrarian strategy that is for example they sell stocks after the stock market has gone up and buy bonds after the bond market has gone down. The importance of such funds (in the United States they account for about one third of the assets under management of all mutual funds) amplifies their impact on market prices, that, due to the macrocontrarian strategy just described, become less volatile.

Other funds are characterized by a target return, for example, equal to short-term rate + 5%, and have a very dynamic investment strategy, selected through quantitative models that aim to minimize the probability of not achieving the target return.

8.6.2 Parameter estimation

We have seen that the optimal portfolio depends on all the relevant parameters, that is, those of expected returns, variances, and covariances, in a highly non-linear fashion. Best and Grauer (1991) have shown that a mean/variance efficient portfolio's weights are extremely sensitive to changes in asset expected returns. This is a real challenge to users of the Markowitz model who, unfortunately, do not know the relevant parameters but need to estimate them. The optimizer arrives at the optimal solution conditional on the inputs received. If inputs are incorrectly estimated, optimized portfolios will also suffer from these weaknesses (GIGO: garbage in, garbage out).

As far as parameter estimation is concerned, there are various possibilities, which depend mainly on the time horizon of use of the model. Tactical asset allocation is based on parameters describing the short-run distribution of the assets and must consider market conditions in a way that is not relevant for strategic optimization.

As far as the variance and covariance matrix is concerned, the models described in Chapter 2 can be used to estimate the parameters more directly associated with risk. The exponentially weighted moving average methodology is good to project existing risk environments to the future when there are no major shocks due to its intrinsic assumption per persistence and slowly moving variances and covariances. The methodology fails when there are shocks, for example Covid-19 or Lehman Brothers, that disrupt prevailing valuations and induce investors to collectively start searching for a new set of prices. This search process is typically associated with market losses, high correlations, and high volatilities.

The estimation of expected returns is even more complex for a short-run horizon due to the need to use a model yielding a conditional estimate rather than an unconditional estimate. In this case, model risk is added to estimation risk.

Strategic asset allocation, meanwhile, is based on metrics based on longer-term observations, often using historical estimates of means, variances, and covariances. A purely historical estimate of the variance and covariance matrix may be considered plausible for a long-term analysis, and similarly the use of long-term average return values is well founded when the investor wishes to have an indication for a portfolio to be considered stable.

In an international equity market portfolio allocation, Jorion (1985) suggests shrinking the estimate of the mean return of an equity market toward the "grand mean" represented by the general average return across the market with a weight α to be determined empirically to find $Er_i = \alpha\overline{r}_i + (1-\alpha)\overline{r}$ where $\overline{r}$ is the historical cross-country average return and $\overline{r}_i$ is the historical average return of market i. Ledoit and Wolf (2003) apply the technique of shrinkage estimation of the estimated variance and covariance matrix to the variance and covariance matrix obtained from the application of the index model (see Chapter 9). The resulting matrix is a weighted average of the sample matrix and the one obtained from the application of the index model. In the application of Ledoit and Wolf to US stocks (data from 1972 to 1995) the weight is about 80%, so the variance and covariance matrix used is equal to $0.8 \times V + 0.2 \times V_I$. A similar shrinkage technique is associated with Elton and Gruber (1973) estimating a single correlation coefficient applicable to all stocks to avoid estimating all pairs of correlation coefficients.

8.6.3 Non-negativity constraints

The Markowitz model presented so far does not include any non-negativity constraints, so the percentages invested in the various assets can be negative. A negative weight on an asset prescribes short-selling. In the case of a security, this generally involves borrowing the security itself for a period, selling it, and then buying it back when the loan must be repaid, paying a shorting fee.[10] In the case of asset class indices, short positions use futures contracts and can be implemented at minimal cost given the liquidity that exists in the futures market.

However, many institutional investors are unwilling or unable to take short positions due to internal rules and/or psychological reasons. The career implications of losing money, say €1 million, after shorting an asset can be worse than not gaining the same amount of money due to not investing in an asset.

To provide results that can guide these investors in their actual portfolio choices, the model can be extended to include non-negativity constraints and other constraints on groups of assets:

$$min_w 0.5 \times w'Vw$$

subject to:

$$Er_p = r_{TAR}$$
$$w'i = 1$$
$$w \geq 0$$
$$w_j \leq U$$

where all the weights should be non-negative and the weight of asset j is bounded above by the limit U. Upper bounds can be due to internal or external rules or simply the wish to limit exposure to one or more asset classes. In this case, the problem of minimizing risk must be solved numerically rather than analytically, so we do not have nice solutions describing the compositions of relevant portfolios like the global minimum variance and the tangency portfolios and, through their linear combinations, all the other efficient portfolios.

The presence of non-negativity constraints is also useful for reducing excess sensitivity to parameters associated with measurement error. Jagannathan and Ma (2003) show that portfolios optimized with non-negativity constraints are equivalent to portfolios obtained without such constraints if the historical estimates of variances and covariances are modified to decrease the parameters that appear to be higher in absolute value.

The intuition that non-negativity constraints may decrease the sensitivity of optimal portfolios to relevant parameters is associated with the further constraints imposed on the solution of the optimizer. Say we strongly believe that market i will perform very well and input an expected return equal to 15%, which by itself would

[10] The size of the shorting fee changes over time and between securities, and generally depends on supply and demand conditions in the securities lending market. The demand for short-selling securities depends on the expectations of the most active investors regarding the future of the company. The offer comes from institutional investors who have securities in their portfolios that they hold for the long term, without any desire to sell them. They are therefore interested in lending the securities on the market for a limited period in order to increase the average return of the overall portfolio, paying attention to the counterparty risk associated with the lending of the securities.

drive up investment in such an asset. At the same time, we wish to avoid investing more than 5% of our wealth in asset *i*, maybe due to internal constraints or maybe because of the extreme risk of the asset. The two conflicting signals provided by the expected return input and the non-negativity constraints partially offset each other to leave the portfolio with a share invested in the asset that is limited upward regardless of the investor optimism.

Summary

- The equally balanced portfolio is a useful benchmark to understand the relevance of diversification and the difference between systematic and idiosyncratic risk.
- The general portfolio problem can be studied and solved based on a matrix notation approach.
- The Markowitz solution to optimal asset allocation consists of a mathematical solution to the problem of variance minimization given constraints about target expected return and portfolio weights.
- The Markowitz solution gives rise to the minimum variance frontier and to the efficient frontier. The former is the set of risky portfolios that minimize variance for each level of target expected return, while the latter is the subset of minimum variance portfolios that are of interest to a risk-averse investor.
- According to the two-fund separation theorem, to invest efficiently, it is sufficient to combine the investment in the risk-free security (Fund 1) and the investment in the tangency portfolio (Fund 2).
- According to this theory, investors never change the composition of the portfolio invested in risky securities, which maintains the same structure regardless of the risk aversion coefficient. What distinguishes one investor from another is the amount invested in the risk-free asset.
- Combining the mean/variance utility function with the mathematics of efficient risky portfolios, we can find the optimal portfolio defined as the share of wealth optimally invested in the two relevant funds. Mathematically, the proportion of the portfolio invested in risky securities is the ratio of the tangency portfolio risk premium to the product of variance and the coefficient of risk aversion.
- We can reverse engineer and start from the historical portfolio choice to deduce the value of the risk aversion implicit in the choices observed.
- The Markowitz model may be used in the context of an asset/liability problem to understand how an optimal portfolio needs to be changed in the presence of a liability.
- In asset management, tactical asset allocation refers to the top-down choice of asset classes on the part of an investor with a short horizon, while strategic asset allocation is used by a long-term investor. The two types of asset allocation differ in terms of the input parameters that need to be chosen with different horizons in mind.
- The Markowitz solution is extremely sensitive to the parameter inputs, particularly expected returns. The possibility to add non-negativity constraints to the problem is a way to decrease the sensitivity of the mathematical solution to the estimated parameters.
- We can define and measure in the portfolio context the contribution to overall risk of each security in the portfolio. Sometimes this may lead to portfolios that are not optimal in the Markowitz sense but may balance the risk arising from each individual security (risk parity portfolios).

Problems

1 Calculate the optimal portfolio for an investor with A = 4 when the parameters are $Er_p - r_f = 5\%$, $\sigma_p = 20\%$. Repeat in the event that $Er_p - r_f = 4\%$, $\sigma_p = 10\%$ and compare the solutions found.

2 Determine the range of values of A for an investor who invests 100% of his assets in the risky security when the expected return of the risky portfolio is 5%, the rate r_f that you obtain from buying the risk-free asset is 1%, the one that you pay when you borrow is 4%, and the volatility of the risky portfolio is 20%.

3 A manager can invest in two mutual funds, S and B, and the risk-free is 1%. The expected return of the S fund is 5% and its volatility is 20%. The expected return of the B fund is 2% and its volatility is 5%. The correlation between S and B is 10%.

a. What are the weights of the two funds in the minimum variance portfolio (MVP)?
b. What are the expected return and standard deviation of the MVP?
c. What are the weights of the two funds in the tangency portfolio?
d. What is the expected return and standard deviation of the tangency portfolio?
e. What is the CAL equation?
f. If the investor's target return is 3%, what is the associated volatility?
g. Which portfolio provides a target expected return of 3%?
h. Assuming there is no risk-free asset, what portfolio of risky securities provides the expected target return?

4 There are three stocks A, B, and C with expected returns of 6%, 5%, and 4%, standard deviation of 25%, 20%, and 15% respectively, $\rho_{AB} = 20\%$, $\rho_{AC} = 40\%$, $\rho_{BC} = 10\%$, risk-free of 1%. Which portfolio is selected by an investor with an expected return target of 5%? Which one is selected in the case where the expected target return is 7% in the presence of leverage? And what if the expected target return is 5% but it is not possible to borrow at the risk-free rate?

Answers

1 According to the theory presented, the optimal investment in the risk asset is $\frac{Er_p - r_f}{A \times \sigma_p^2}$. The initial solution is therefore equal to $\frac{0.05}{4 \times 0.04} = 31.25\%$. The reduction in premium and volatility have an overall positive impact on the desire to invest in the risky asset because you now have $\frac{0.04}{4 \times 0.01} = 100\%$.

2 The investor decides to use leverage if $\frac{Er_p - r_f}{A \times \sigma_p^2} > 1$ and to invest in the risk-free stock if $\frac{Er_p - r_f}{A \times \sigma_p^2} < 1$. With the parameters given by the problem $\frac{5\% - 4\%}{A \times 0.04} > 1$,

that is, $A < 0.25$ and $\frac{5\% - 1\%}{A \times 0.04} < 1$, that is, $A > 1$. For risk aversion ratios between 0.25 and 1, the investor invests 100% of his assets in the risky security. Unlike when the lending and borrowing rates coincide, the different slopes of the two segments of the CAL at the point where 100% of the portfolio is invested in risky securities means that small changes in the risk aversion coefficient are not immediately associated with changes in the optimal portfolio structure.

3 a. The formula in matrix notation suggests that $w_{GMV} = \frac{V^{-1}i}{i'V^{-1}i}$. The variance and covariance matrix in this case is equal to

$$V = \begin{bmatrix} 0.2^2 & 0.1 \times 0.2 \times 0.05 \\ 0.1 \times 0.2 \times 0.05 & 0.05^2 \end{bmatrix}.$$

The inverse matrix is $V^{-1} = \begin{bmatrix} 25.25 & -10.10 \\ -10.10 & 404.40 \end{bmatrix}$, the product $V^{-1}i$ is $\begin{bmatrix} 15.15 \\ 393.94 \end{bmatrix}$, and therefore $w_{GMV} = \begin{bmatrix} 4\% \\ 96\% \end{bmatrix}$. The second fund, with lower volatility, has a very important share in the portfolio with minimum variance.

b. The expected return is 2.11% and the standard deviation is 4.94%.

c. We know that $w_T = \frac{V^{-1} \times (Er - r_f i)}{i'V^{-1} \times (Er - r_f i)}$. Using the vector of premia $\begin{bmatrix} 4\% \\ 1\% \end{bmatrix}$ and we get $w_T = \begin{bmatrix} 20\% \\ 80\% \end{bmatrix}$.

d. The expected return and tangency portfolio volatility are 2.6% and 5.93%, respectively.

e. Using the expected return and volatility of the tangency portfolio, the CAL equation is $Er = 0.01 + \frac{0.016}{0.0593}\sigma$.

f. Substituting the target expected return 3% into the CAL, we find $\sigma = 0.02 \times \frac{0.0593}{0.016} = 7.41\%$.

g. To get a target expected return of 3%, you need to solve the equation $0.03 = \alpha \times 0.026 + (1 - \alpha) \times 0.01$, from which you can see the portfolio must be invested 125% in the tangency portfolio and -25% in the risk-free, and therefore 25% in S and 100% in B.

h. In this case, we limit ourselves to using the minimum variance portfolio and the tangency portfolio to have 33% in S and 67% in B, which is obtained by solving $0.03 = \alpha \times 0.026 + (1 - \alpha) \times 0.021$ providing $\alpha = 1.8$, so that $1.8 \times \begin{bmatrix} 0.2 \\ 0.8 \end{bmatrix} - 0.8 \times \begin{bmatrix} 0.04 \\ 0.96 \end{bmatrix} = \begin{bmatrix} 0.33 \\ 0.67 \end{bmatrix}$. The same result for the investment in the two funds can be obtained directly by solving $0.03 = \alpha \times 0.05 + (1 - \alpha) \times 0.02$. The interpretation of the result is as follows: The expected returns of the minimum variance portfolio and the tangency portfolios are close to each other and as a result the target expected return requires a large overinvestment in the tangency portfolio and shorting the global minimum variance portfolio.

4 We know from the definition of the tangency and global minimum variance portfolios that $w_T = \begin{bmatrix} 0{,}204 \\ 0{,}373 \\ 0{,}423 \end{bmatrix}$ and $w_{GMVP} = \begin{bmatrix} 0{,}049 \\ 0{,}333 \\ 0{,}619 \end{bmatrix}$. The two expected return levels are 4.78% and 4.43%, respectively. To have an expected return of 5%, it is therefore necessary to invest 106% in the tangency portfolio by borrowing 6%. If the target expected return is 7%, the portfolio is 159% and -59%. If there is no risk-free asset, you can invest 734% in the tangency portfolio while shorting 634% in the minimum variance portfolio.

9 The capital asset pricing model

9.1 Introduction

As we broaden the horizon of analysis from the investor to the market, questions arise about the determination of the expected return and the price. How do we take into account the existence of risk when determining the risk premium on individual securities and portfolios? How do we determine the amount of risk of a single stock? Is it volatility, as is the case with portfolios, or are conceptual changes needed? Has a stock that has historically returned 10% satisfied its holders?

The chapter examines the consequences of the portfolio optimization model for determining the risk premia required by investors on individual securities. It starts with the observation that the risk premium must be proportional to the amount of risk contained in a single security. In the logic of portfolio diversification seen in the previous chapters, the investor is interested in determining the amount of risk inherent in a given security in terms of its contribution to the overall portfolio risk. It follows that the amount of risk in the security depends on the portfolio in which it is placed.

Moreover, the optimization model described in the previous chapter requires that all investors hold the market portfolio and therefore all agree on the amount of risk contained in each security. The amount of risk is measured, according to the Capital Asset Pricing Model (CAPM), by the beta coefficient, equal to the ratio of the co-variance between the return of the security and the return of the market, divided by the variance of the market. The CAPM thus argues that the risk premium for a security is equal to the product of beta and the market risk premium. The CAPM is still one of the most widely used models in finance for determining the expected return, measuring performance, and calculating the cost of equity capital, albeit empirical tests based on regression models, have given less and less favorable results to its explanatory capacity.

9.2 An asset marginal contribution to portfolio risk

We have learned that rational and risk-averse investors exploit the benefits of diversification and select a large portfolio, including all existing stocks. How should such investors evaluate the risk of a single stock in the portfolio? In previous chapters we have referred to volatility as the risk indicator to compare portfolios. Does the same hold true for a single component of a portfolio? Does a rational investor worry about the volatility of one of the many stocks in her portfolio? The answer we are developing in this chapter changes the perspective of risk measurement at the level of the single stock, starting from the idea of measuring its contribution to the overall portfolio volatility rather than the single stock volatility per se.

To appreciate the relevance of this new perspective, a useful starting point has to do with a better understanding of the risk of a single stock in the context of a portfolio. We have discussed at length the role of correlation coefficients in determining the overall risk of a portfolio. In the case of two risky assets we have shown that the correlation coefficient is the key determinant of the expected return/risk trade-off associated with the infinite portfolios including the two stocks. Figure 9.1 describes the risk of a two-stock portfolio as a function of the weights of the two stocks.

Figure 9.1 Portfolio risk and weights

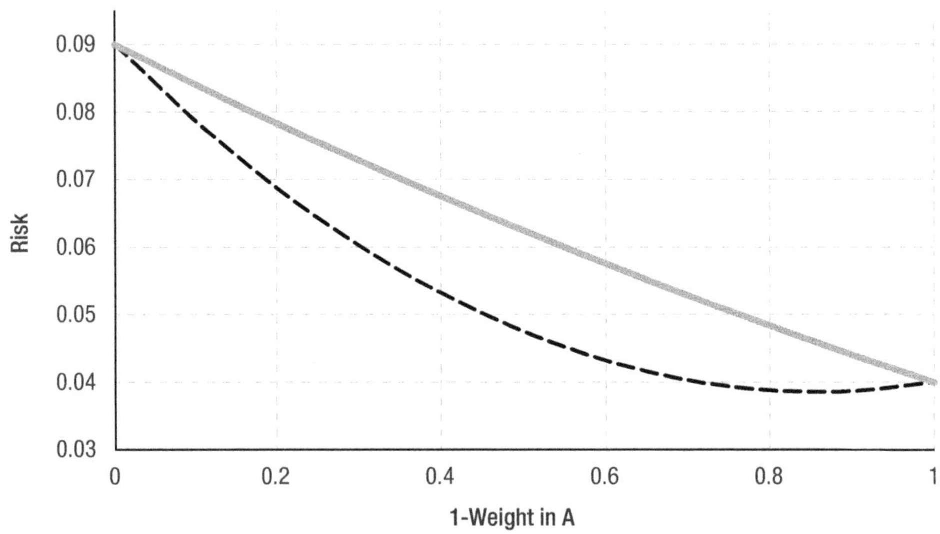

For both curves we start from a portfolio totally invested in a stock A with 9% volatility. For the continuous line we start to diversify into a stock B with unitary correlation with A and volatility equal to 4%. For the dotted curve we start to diversify into a stock C with 0.5 correlation with A and volatility equal to 4%. The vertical distance between the curve and the line represents the volatility advantage of diversifying into a stock with lower correlation. Therefore, a risk-averse investor will view the risk of stock B and of stock C differently even though they have the same 4% volatility. Different correlation coefficients have a different impact on the overall portfolio risk.

Box 9.1 What is the risk of technology stocks?

Question: Carola and Elena don't seem to agree on whether to put a tech stock in their portfolios, and they turn to Sara to find out who's right.

Answer: Sara replies that they are both right because Carola has an overall portfolio that includes investment in many technology stocks, while Sara has invested mainly in financial stocks. Putting a technology stock in a portfolio of technology stocks will increase portfolio risk a lot given the high correlation between the stock and others, while putting the technology stock in a portfolio of financial stocks will not increase the portfolio risk due to the low correlation between the technology stock and financials. As an example, use the following data:

	Expected return	Volatility	Correlations		
A	6%	25%	1	0.2	0.8
B	5%	20%		1	0.1
C	4%	15%			1

and consider the following portfolios:

Portfolio	Share A	Share B	Share C	Expected return	Volatility
1	0%	100%	0%	0.04	0.2
2	0%	0%	100%	0.0225	0.15
3	50%	50%	0%	0.030625	0.17
4	50%	0%	50%	0.03625	0.19

Sara points out that if you put stock A with a 50% weight in a portfolio entirely composed of B (portfolio 1) to get an equally balanced portfolio (portfolio 3), volatility drops from 20% to 17%, even though stock A has a higher volatility than stock B, due to the low correlation between the two. At the same time, inserting stock A into a portfolio entirely composed of C (portfolio 2) to obtain a balanced portfolio (number 4) increases volatility from 15% to 19% both because the volatility of A is much higher than that of C and because the correlation between the two stocks is high.

In general, it can be shown that the marginal contribution to risk is proportional to the covariance between the return of the security (the i-th security) and the return of the portfolio p held by the investor, $Cov(r_i, r_p)$. For example, for a portfolio of two stocks, volatility can be written as a weighted average of the portfolio's covariances with each of the two stocks:[1]

$$\sigma_p = w_A \frac{COV(r_A, w_A r_A + w_B r_B)}{\sigma_p} + w_B \frac{COV(r_B, w_A r_A + w_B r_B)}{\sigma_p}$$

[1] The equation can be proved by starting with the definition of volatility $\sigma_p = \sqrt{w_A^2\sigma_A^2 + w_B^2\sigma_B^2 + 2w_A w_B \sigma_{AB}}$ and calculating the first derivatives with respect to weights from which $\frac{\partial \sigma_p}{\partial w_A} = \frac{w_A \sigma_A^2 + w_B \sigma_{AB}}{\sigma_p}$ and

In Markowitz's portfolio model, all investors allocate their assets by investing in the risk-free asset and the tangency portfolio, and therefore all investors have the same portfolio of risky securities. In this model, the marginal contribution to risk by a single security is homogeneous across investors, since everyone diversifies as much as possible and therefore holds the tangency portfolio. We define the total contribution to risk of a single stock as $TRC_i = w_i \frac{COV(r_i, r_p)}{\sigma_p}$, in such a way that $\sigma_p = \sum_{i=1}^{2} TRC_i$, which is useful to decompose the total risk into the contribution of each stock. If we define the marginal risk contribution of a single stock as $MRC_i = \frac{COV(r_i, r_p)}{\sigma_p}$, then $\sigma_p = \sum_{i=1}^{2} w_i \times MRC_i$. Such relations obviously generalize to the case with N risky securities.

Box 9.2 Risk parity

Question: Elena considers a portfolio of the three securities A, B, and C described above in proportions 30%, 40%, and 30%, whose volatility is 13.97%. Elena wonders if the three stocks contribute to the overall risk in proportion to their weights.

Answer: Using the data from the previous box, we can calculate that the covariances are $\sigma_{AM} = 0.03175$, $\sigma_{BM} = 0.0199$, $\sigma_{CM} = 0.01695$. For example, $\sigma_{AM} = cov(r_A, 0.3 \times r_A + 0.4 \times r_B + 0.3 \times r_C) = 0.3 \times \sigma_A^2 + 0.4 \times \rho_{AB} \times \sigma_A \times \sigma_B + 0.3 \times \rho_{AC} \times \sigma_A \times \sigma_C = 0.03175$. It follows that $MRC_A = 21.13\%$, $MRC_B = 13.25\%$, $MRC_C = 11.28\%$ and $TRC_A = 6.34\%$, $TRC_B = 5.30\%$, $TRC_C = 3{,}38\%$. The first asset has weight 30% but its risk contribution is 42% of the overall risk, the second has a weight equal to 40% and percentage risk contribution 35%, and the third respectively 30% and 23%. To avoid an asset having such a large contribution to overall portfolio risk, we can choose the portfolio composition in such a way that each asset has the same marginal contribution. Using the Excel Solver and choosing the portfolio weights to minimize the standard deviation across marginal risk contributions, we find that for the portfolio 22.7%, 37.1%, and 40.1%, each asset contributes a third of the overall risk of 14.29%. Clearly this is an inefficient portfolio as the same expected return could be obtained by a portfolio with lower risk.

$\frac{\partial \sigma_p}{\partial w_B} = \frac{w_B \sigma_B^2 + w_A \sigma_{AB}}{\sigma_p}$ so by definition $\sigma_p = w_A \frac{\partial \sigma_p}{\partial w_A} + w_B \frac{\partial \sigma_p}{\partial w_B}$. But since $\frac{w_A \sigma_A^2 + w_B \sigma_{AB}}{\sigma_p} = \frac{COV(r_A, w_A r_A + w_B r_B)}{\sigma_p}$ and $\frac{w_B \sigma_B^2 + w_A \sigma_{AB}}{\sigma_p} = \frac{COV(r_B, w_A r_A + w_B r_B)}{\sigma_p}$ you get precisely $\sigma_p = w_A \frac{COV(r_A, w_A r_A + w_B r_B)}{\sigma_p} + w_B \frac{COV(r_B, w_A r_A + w_B r_B)}{\sigma_p}$.

Alternatively, the proof can be obtained by rewriting the volatility as $\sigma_p = \sqrt{w_A^2 \sigma_A^2 + w_B^2 \sigma_B^2 + 2 w_A w_B \sigma_{AB}}$

$\sigma_p = w_A \frac{w_A \sigma_A^2 + w_B \sigma_{AB}}{\sigma_p} + w_B \frac{w_B \sigma_B^2 + w_A \sigma_{AB}}{\sigma_p}$. But since $\frac{w_A \sigma_A^2 + w_B \sigma_{AB}}{\sigma_p} = \frac{COV(r_A, w_A r_A + w_B r_B)}{\sigma_p}$ it follows that $\sigma_p = w_A \frac{COV(r_A, w_A r_A + w_B r_B)}{\sigma_p} + w_B \frac{COV(r_B, w_A r_A + w_B r_B)}{\sigma_p}$.

Box 9.3 Risk parity for three uncorrelated assets with the same Sharpe ratio

Question: Elena considers a portfolio of stocks, bonds, and commodities assuming they have the same Sharpe ratio and zero correlations. She wants to build a portfolio where each asset contributes equally to the overall risk. What is the Sharpe ratio of the optimal risk parity portfolio relative to the Sharpe ratio of each security?

Answer: The portfolio variance is $w_S^2 \times \sigma_S^2 + w_B^2 \times \sigma_B^2 + w_C^2 \times \sigma_C^2$. If each asset must contribute one-third to the overall variance, then for each i, $i = S, B, C$ it must be that $w_i^2 \times \sigma_i^2 = \sigma_p^2/3$, from which $w_i = \frac{\sigma_p}{\sigma_i \times \sqrt{3}}$ with a unitary volatility. The portfolio Sharpe ratio is $\sum_{i=S,B,C} \frac{rp_i}{\sigma_i \times \sqrt{3}} = \sum_{i=S,B,C} \frac{SR_i}{\sqrt{3}} = \sqrt{3} \times SR$, where we have used the assumption that the Sharpe ratio is unique. The portfolio Sharpe ratio is therefore equal to $\sqrt{3}$ the individual asset Sharpe ratio. If stocks, bonds, and commodities have respectively 15%, 5%, and 30% volatility and the Sharpe ratio is equal to 0.3, then the risk parity portfolio invests in stocks in the proportion 22%, in bonds 66%, and in commodities 11%. Bonds have more weight in the risk parity portfolio because their volatility is the lowest. The overall portfolio Sharpe ratio is equal to 52%, which is substantially more efficient than any individual asset.

9.3 The CAPM

9.3.1 Introduction: the Markowitz relation between risk and expected return

Roll (1977) shows that the mathematics of the efficient frontier implies a proportional relation between the risk premia on stocks and any efficient portfolio p risk premium,[2] described as:

$$\left(Er - r_f i\right) = \frac{V \times w_p}{\sigma_p^2} \times \left(Er_p - r_f\right)$$

This shows how, simply using the algebra of the efficient frontier, we find that the excess of the expected returns of the various securities is equal to the ratio of the covariance of each with the efficient portfolio, measured by $(N, 1)$ vector $V \times w_p$, divided by the variance of the same portfolio and multiplied by the risk premium on the selected efficient portfolio. Note that we have not assumed any market equilibrium condition. Simply by inverting the equation describing the efficient portfolio chosen for a level of target expected return, we have found an explanation for the risk premia on all the stocks included in the portfolio. We will elaborate on this result after obtaining the same through an equilibrium condition.

[2] Using the results from Chapter 8, we notice that $V \times w$ is a (N,1) vector representing the covariances of the various returns with any portfolio. We know from Chapter 8 that for an efficient portfolio p, $V \times w_p = H^{-1}\left(r_{TAR} - r_f\right) \times \left(Er - r_f i\right)$, which can be rewritten as $\left(Er - r_f i\right) = H \times V \times w_p / \left(r_{TAR} - r_f\right)$. Using the result of Chapter 8 (see Technical Box 8.2) according to which $\left(r_{TAR} - r_f\right)^2 = H \times \sigma_{TAR}^2$ we then have $\left(Er - r_f i\right) = \frac{V \times w_p}{\sigma_p^2} \times \left(Er_p - r_f\right)$.

9.3.2 The equilibrium interpretation of the Markowitz relation between risk and expected return

Sharpe (1964) noticed the investment implications of the Markowitz model, according to which investors select the optimal position allocating wealth across two funds, observing that in equilibrium there must be a balance between the demand for securities described by Markowitz's model and the supply constituted by the existing quantity of securities listed on the market. He added a key assumption: homogeneity of market views, that is, the assumption that all investors agree on the key parameters of expected returns, variances, and covariances. In this case, they all perceive the same investment opportunity set and therefore they all choose the same tangency portfolio. Under these conditions we know the structure of demand for the N risky securities, which corresponds to the tangency portfolio. We also know the total wealth invested in the securities because each investor decides a different allocation to the risk-free asset and the tangency portfolio.

What is the market equilibrium under this hypothesis? We describe the existing supply through the definition of the market portfolio, a list with the proportions of all the securities that are traded in the market with the capitalizations (resulting from the multiplication of the number of shares and the market price) of each security.

The assumption that investors follow the Markowitz model coupled with homogeneity of market views implies that the tangency portfolio selected homogeneously by all investors must match the market portfolio. If this was not the case, then there would be no equilibrium.

To see this, assume we start from a situation where, say, the weight of stock A in the tangency portfolio is equal to 5% while the same stock weighs 10% in the market index. Assume there are only two investors. Sara invests €1 million in the tangency portfolio and Elena invests €5 million. Sara invests €50,000 in stock A, and Elena invests €250,000. Total demand is €300,000. The total market capitalization is equal to €6 million, corresponding to the sum of wealth invested by Elena and Sara. It is not possible to have stock A with a weight equal to €600,000 (10% of total market capitalization) in the market portfolio, as it would not match the demand. The conclusion is that stock A must have a weight of 5% in the market portfolio. Demand drives supply because we assume a very short-run analysis where the supply is fixed and investigate under what price conditions investors are happy to hold in their portfolios the number of shares that companies have sold at the time of their IPO. In equilibrium, the tangency portfolio must match the market portfolio.

Formally, if W_i denotes the wealth invested by the i-th investor, w_i the portfolio invested in risky assets, and w_T is the structure of the tangency portfolio, then total demand in monetary terms for the N risky stocks is $\sum_{i=1}^{N} W_i \times w_i = w_T \times \sum_{i=1}^{N} W_i = w_T \times W$. In equilibrium, monetary demand must correspond to the market portfolio, defined as the value of the stocks that are listed in the market and that must find their place in investors' portfolios: If no investors wanted to invest any money in a specific stock, its price would go to zero and the stock would drop out of the market. It follows that in equilibrium:

$$w_T \times \sum_{i=1}^{N} W_i = w_M \times \sum_{i=1}^{N} W_i$$

where w_M is the market portfolio, defined as the proportions of the risky stocks in terms of relative capitalization, that is, the ratio between the market capitalization of each stock and the global market capitalization. Through this equilibrium interpretation, we can identify the tangency portfolio with the market portfolio: In an equilibrium where all investors hold the same structure of risky asset, such structure must correspond with the market portfolio. The capital allocation line going through the tangency portfolio becomes the capital market line going through the market portfolio.

Figure 9.2 **The capital market line**

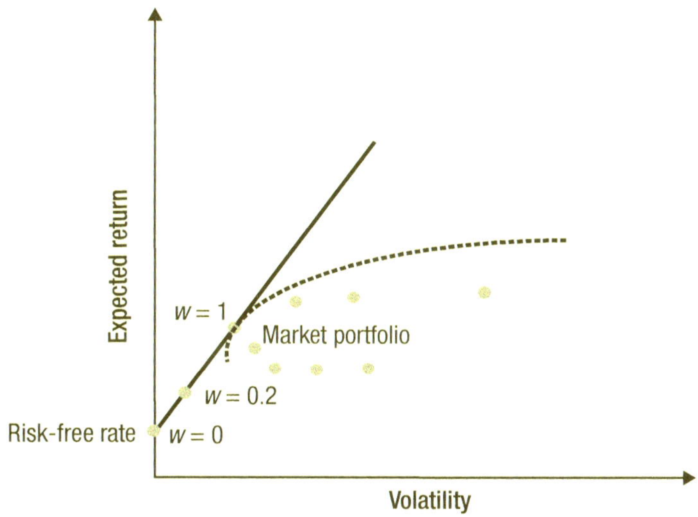

The capital market line links the risk-free rate to the expected return/risk combination of the market portfolio w_M. Investors can simply select a portfolio consisting of a risk-free security and a market index, favoring one or the other based on their risk aversion. We obtain the expected return/risk relation highlighted in section 9.3.1 by using the market portfolio as the reference portfolio:

$$\left(Er - r_f i\right) = \frac{V w_M}{\sigma_M^2} \times \left(Er_M - r_f\right) \qquad (1)$$

according to which the excess of expected returns of the various securities is equal to the ratio of the covariance of each with the market portfolio divided by the variance of the same portfolio. The equation is a vector representation of the risk premia required by the market to hold the various stocks in their portfolios, in such a way that demand is equal to supply.[3]

9.3.3 The CAPM pricing equation

The Capital Asset Pricing Model is used to determine the expected return of individual stocks. The CAPM argues that the expected return of a stock is equal to the sum of the risk-free rate and the product between the stock's beta and the equity market risk premium (EMRP). Introducing the term $\beta_i = \frac{C(r_i, r_M)}{V(r_M)}$ [4] and defining with Er_i the expected return of the i-th stock, and Er_M the expected return of the market portfolio, we write explicitly the i-th row of equation (1) as:

$$Er_i = r_f + \beta_i (Er_M - r_f) \tag{2}$$

according to which the expected return from the i-th security is equal to the sum of the risk-free and the product between beta and equity market risk premium. The CAPM equation can be represented by the security market line (SML), which describes the relationship between expected return and beta of a single stock (see Figure 9.3).

Figure 9.3 Expected return and the security market line

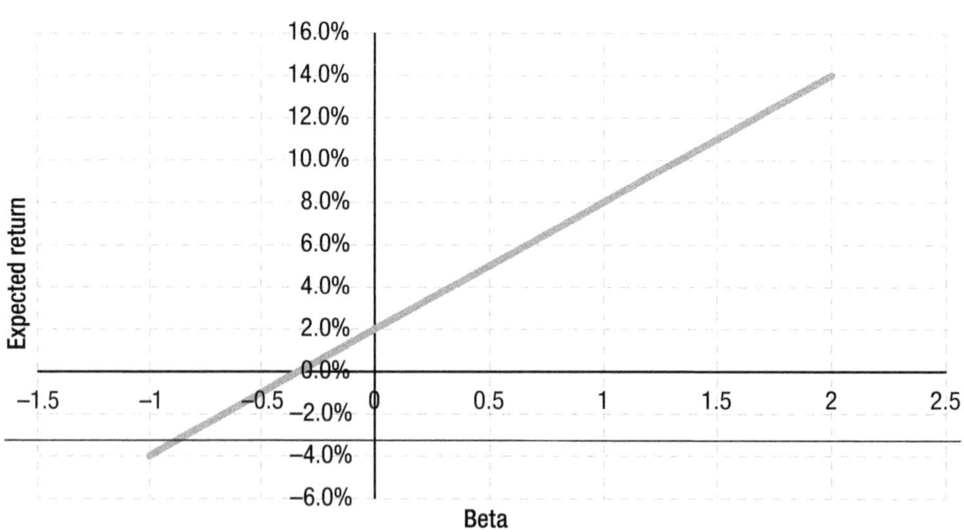

[3] Notice that Vw_M represents the product of a (N, N) matrix and a $(N, 1)$ vector representing a vector of covariances of each asset with the market portfolio.

[4] This corresponds to the i-th element of the vector Vw_M.

It is also possible use the excess return on the vertical axis, $Er_i - r_f = \beta_i(Er_M - r_f)$, to represent the risk premium and get a line going through the origin:

Figure 9.4 Risk premium and the security market line

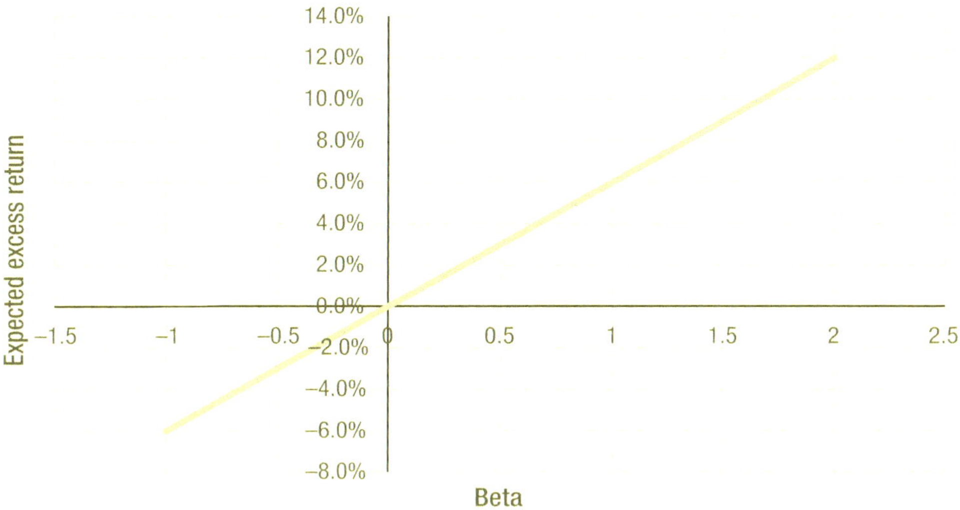

The CAPM explains the expected rate of return on a stock from the point of view of the final investor holding a diversified portfolio. What investors consider an expected return is taken by the company as a constraint: The expected return highlighted by a pricing model also measures the average return that must be paid to investors, through a combination of dividend yield and capital gains, to meet their expectations. In corporate finance this idea is defined as the cost of capital. It is therefore of fundamental importance to measure the expected return by means of a model, which becomes the cost of equity capital for the company.

9.4 The index model

9.4.1 The index model and alpha

The CAPM is written in terms of expected returns. Our data, however, refer to observed returns, and we need a way to understand the link between a theoretical model written in expected returns and data expressed in terms of actual returns. This can be done by looking at a regression line relating a security's excess return to market excess return:

$$r_i - r_f = \alpha_i + \beta_i \times (r_M - r_f) + \varepsilon_i \quad (3)$$

The regression model is known as the index model and was proposed by Sharpe (1964). Considering the expectations of both sides of the equation and noting that the expected value of the shock in a regression model is zero, we find:

$$E(r_i - r_f) = \alpha_i + \beta_i \times E(r_M - r_f) \tag{5}$$

The CAPM is a constrained version of the regression model, as it assumes that:

$$\alpha_i = E r_i - r_f - \beta_i \times EMRP = 0$$

where $EMRP \equiv E(r_M - r_f)$. The term alpha is used in asset management to refer to deviations from the CAPM. $\alpha_i > 0$ indicates the presence of a positive average excess return over and above the component that is warranted by the sensitivity to the market portfolio, that is, an average return component that is not explained by the risk associated with beta. We do not discuss here the reason why alpha exists: One possibility, as we will observe in Chapter 12, is that alpha is due to mispricing arising from investors not being able to fully recognize expected cash flows. The other possibility is that alpha is a proxy for risk factors that are unknown to the analyst, a possibility we will return to in Chapters 10 and 11.

9.4.2 The index model and risk

The index model also allows for a more general way to distinguish between market risk and idiosyncratic risk. Subtracting equation (4) from equation (3), we see that the unexpected return at time t is:

$$r_{i,t} - Er_{i,t} = \beta_i(r_{M,t} - E r_{M,t}) + \varepsilon_{it}$$

This implies that the return shock has two sources, which have already been discussed in a previous chapter: one related to the market return shock and one related to company-specific shocks. A market return shock is a source of systematic or non-diversifiable risk because all securities are affected by it, albeit to a heterogeneous extent. Computing the variance of both sides of the last equation we get:

$$V r_{it} = E\left(r_{it} - E r_{it} \right)^2 = E\left(\beta_i(r_{mt} - E r_{mt}) + \varepsilon_{it} \right)^2 = \beta_i^2 V r_{mt} + V \varepsilon_i$$

The total variance of the return therefore contains a systematic component that depends on market sensitivity and an idiosyncratic component. The same model can also be used to find covariance:

$$\begin{aligned} Cov\left(r_{it}, r_{jt} \right) &= E\left(r_{it} - E r_{it} \right)\left(r_{jt} - E r_{jt} \right) = \\ &= E\left(\beta_i(r_{mt} - E r_{mt}) + \varepsilon_{it} \right)\left(\beta_j(r_{mt} - E r_{mt}) + \varepsilon_{jt} \right) \\ &= \beta_i \beta_j V r_{mt} \end{aligned}$$

If the matrix V collects variances and covariances, then the index model suggests that:

$$V = \begin{bmatrix} \beta_1^2 & \beta_1\beta_2 & \beta_1\beta_N \\ \beta_1\beta_2 & \beta_2^2 & \\ & & \cdots \\ \beta_1\beta_N & & \beta_N^2 \end{bmatrix} V r_{mt} + \begin{bmatrix} V\varepsilon_1 & 0 & 0 \\ 0 & V\varepsilon_2 & \\ & & \cdots \\ 0 & & V\varepsilon_N \end{bmatrix}$$

We have seen that the Markowitz model requires the estimation of N parameters of expected return and $\frac{N \times (N-1)}{2}$ variance and covariance parameters. Using the index model, it is sufficient to estimate N idiosyncratic variances, N betas, and the variance of the market portfolio, totaling $2 \times N + 1$ parameters if idiosyncratic variances are ignored and $3 \times N + 1$ otherwise. With $N = 10$ we move from forty-five parameters to thirty-one.

Box 9.4 The index model for Microsoft, Amazon, and Apple

Question: Elena wants to estimate the index model for some technology stocks to analyze their metrics and distinguish between overall risk and systematic risk. She uses the S&P 500 as a market index, which is probably less influenced by the performance of technology stocks and therefore allows for more reliable estimates, and the three-month Treasury Bill as a risk-free rate.

Answer: Elena considers the time series of stocks and the index from 2000 to August 2019. Regressions give the following results:

Microsoft				
R^2	0.38			
Standard error	0.07			
Observations	236			
	Coefficients	**Standard error**	**t Stat**	**P-value**
Alfa	0.0047	0.0044	1.0628	0.2890
Beta	1.2007	0.1008	11.9152	0.0000

Apple				
R^2	0.26			
Standard error	0.10			
Observations	236			
	Coefficients	**Standard error**	**t Stat**	**P-value**
Alfa	0.0205	0.0066	3.1037	0.0021
Beta	1.3898	0.1513	9.1831	0.0000

Amazon				
R^2	0.24			
Standard error	0.12			
Observations	236			
	Coefficients	**Standard error**	**t Stat**	**P-value**
Alfa	0.0176	0.0081	2.1890	0.0296
Beta	1.5831	0.1847	8.5706	0.0000

The regressions explain a limited part of the variability in the returns of the three stocks. The alpha coefficient is positive for all three, but not statistically significant for Microsoft. These are economically significant values because they are obtained from monthly returns. The beta coefficients are all greater than unity.
The decomposition of historical variance into the systematic and idiosyncratic parts, taking into account the market variance over the period, equal to monthly 0.19%, yields:

	Microsoft	**Apple**	**Amazon**
Total variance	0.00726	0.01387	0.01996
Systematic variance	0.00274	0.00367	0.00477
Residual variance	0.00452	0.01020	0.01519
% Systematic variance	38%	26%	24%
% Residual variance	62%	74%	76%

In all three cases, more than 60% of the variance is explained by idiosyncratic forces, which confirms the ability of each of the three stocks to diversify from the market index. The comparison between historical covariance and systematic covariance, taking into account beta coefficients, is shown in the table below.

	Historical covariance	**Systematic covariance**	**%**
Microsoft/Apple	0.0047	0.0032	68%
Microsoft/Amazon	0.0047	0.0036	77%
Apple/Amazon	0.0055	0.0042	77%

As a final note, remember that we have analyzed a decomposition of portfolio risk in terms of the marginal contribution of each single asset, where we defined $MRC_i = \frac{COV(r_i, r_p)}{\sigma_p}$. Notice that, using the definition $\beta_i = \frac{COV(r_i, r_p)}{\sigma_p^2}$, the marginal contribution to risk can be written in terms of the beta relative to portfolio p, $MRC_i = \beta_i \times \sigma_p$.

9.5 Econometric testing of the CAPM

9.5.1 The index model and CAPM testing

The analyses described in Box 9.4 consider three individual stocks. The results show that the estimated alpha is significantly different from zero at standard confidence levels for Apple and Amazon, whereas Microsoft does not have an alpha that is statistically different from zero. The evidence is therefore inconsistent with the CAPM for two stocks out of three. Notice the CAPM implications, for example, for the risk premium of Apple: a beta equal to 1.39 implies a premium due to systematic risk equal to $1.39 \times 0.06 = 0.0834$ (assuming the equity market risk premium is equal to 6%). The index model would also add the alpha to get overall $0.0205 + 0.0834 = 0.1039$. There is almost a 25% difference between the data-driven index model and the theory-driven CAPM. It is therefore relevant to understand whether the CAPM is a good description of the return of most stocks.

To get a general answer, we cannot stop at testing three stocks; we must find a way to consider many stocks or portfolios. To see how, let us review the main implications of the CAPM: stocks and portfolios with high beta should have a high premium; stocks and portfolios with zero beta should have no risk premium.

The two variables characterizing the SML are unfortunately unobserved. We do not observe the true beta but estimate it from the time series of returns, whereas we do not estimate the risk premium but observe the historical realization of the excess return. We observe both variables with measurement error.

The academic literature has devoted much attention to the empirical verification of CAPM. The methodology invented by Fama and MacBeth (1973) involves the use of two phases.

- The first phase proceeds to the estimation of the beta coefficient for each stock with a regression that uses time series regression data, and it uses the estimated betas to compute the betas of portfolios representing the testing assets.
- The second phase analyzes the relationship between the average returns of various portfolios (taken as an approximation of the expected returns) and the betas estimated in the first phase, with a regression using cross-section data (multiple stocks observed in the same period).

9.5.2 CAPM testing: graphical analysis

CAPM testing involves measurement errors because neither expected returns nor betas are known. Even if the model held exactly, as hypothesized in Figure 9.5 in which the line (the SML) indicates the relation between expected return and beta predicted by the CAPM, the average and beta return pairs observed on individual stocks would not exactly be on the line but would be placed outside the line:

Figure 9.5 Beta and average return around SML

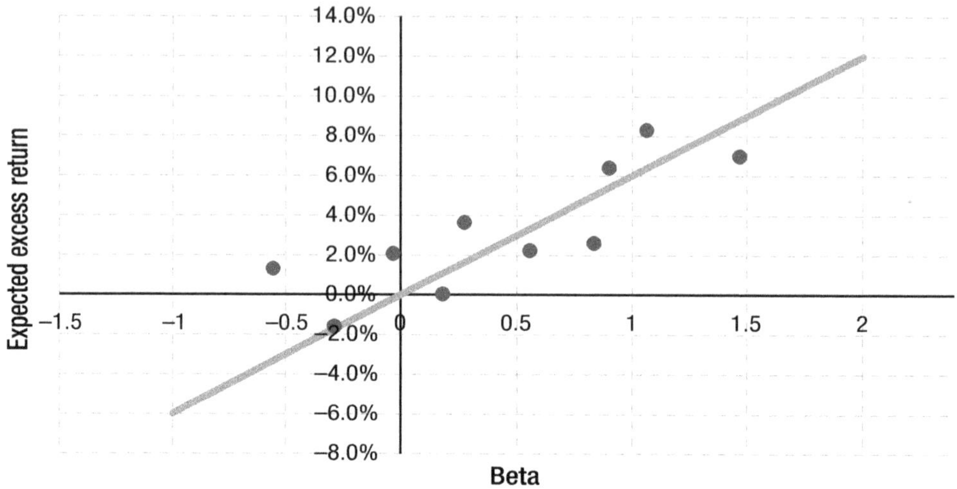

The aim of the empirical analysis is to start from the observed pairs to verify whether there is a linear relationship between them as predicted by the theory, that is, whether the average excess returns are linearly explained by the betas with a line passing through the origin. As in Figure 9.6, the researcher looks at average and beta returns of a set of securities but does not know for sure which line describes the "true" model.

Figure 9.6 Observations about beta and average return

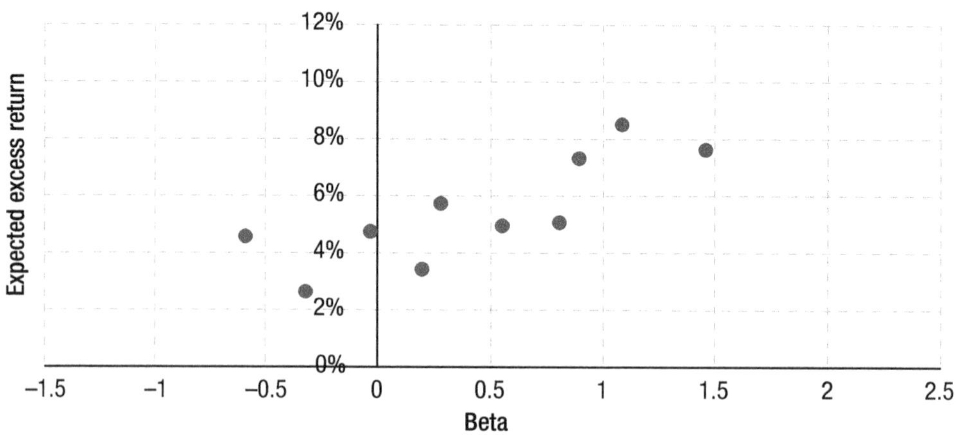

Figure 9.7 describes the output of the researcher's statistical analysis, which used the available observations to estimate a regression line known as the empirical SML. Notice that such a regression is obtained from a regression of individual assets' aver-

age returns on individual assets' betas. This is known as a cross-sectional regression rather than a time series regression.

In general, the line does not pass exactly from the origin, even if the CAPM describes the data. A statistical test must be carried out to verify the hypothesis that the estimated intercept is zero.

Figure 9.7 **Beta, mean return, and the empirical SML**

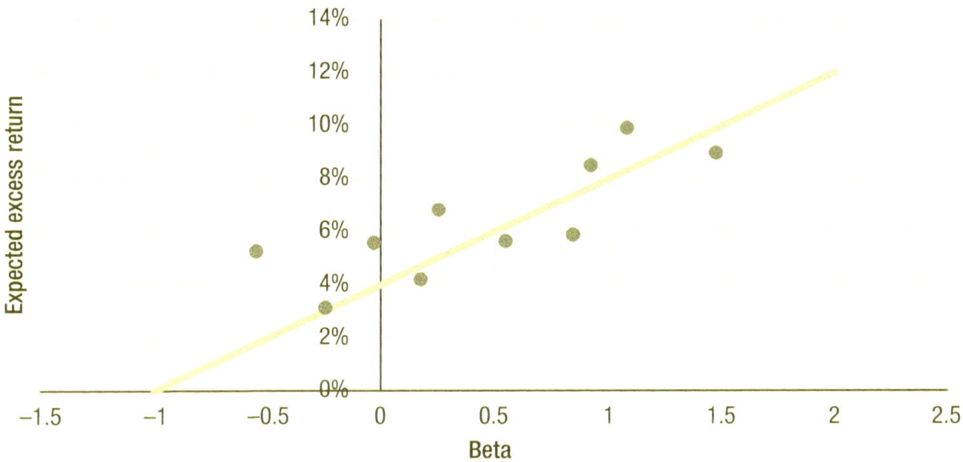

One way to reduce the existence of measurement error is to test the CAPM equation on portfolios rather than on individual securities. The beta of a portfolio is in fact a weighted average of the betas of the individual stocks that compose it, and the estimate of the average is more stable and less prone to measurement error than the estimate of individual betas.

9.5.3 CAPM testing: econometric analysis

In general, we use a two-step procedure to test for the validity of the CAPM.

1. The first step is to estimate the beta coefficient for each asset involved in the analysis by time series regressions for a subset of available observations.
2. In the second step, the average returns are regressed on the estimated betas.

The econometric methodology can be implemented once, using all the available observations, or alternatively in a dynamic fashion that is represented in Figure 9.8,[5]

[5] See Cochrane (2005) for an in-depth treatment and a comparison with cross-sectional and panel methods.

depicting a situation where betas are re-estimated each month on the basis of the previous sixty observations and the cross-section uses such betas to explain the excess returns for the following month.

Figure 9.8 The Fama–MacBeth methodology

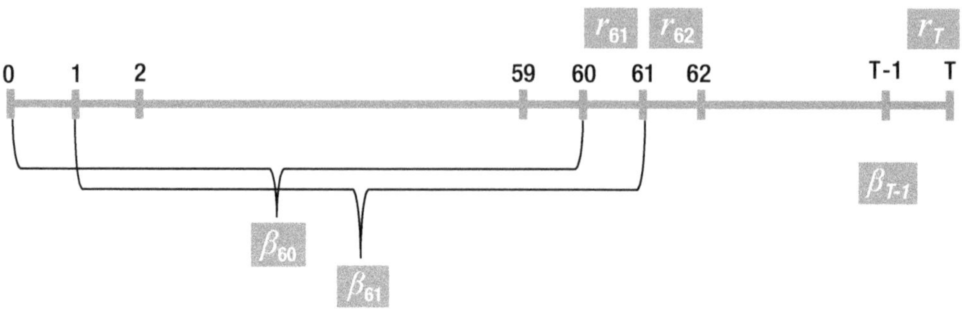

More precisely, following Fama and MacBeth, the typical choice is to select blocks of sixty observations with monthly data. The first step is obtained from:

$$r_{i,t} - r_{f,t} = \alpha_i + \beta_i(r_{M,t} - r_{f,t}) + \varepsilon_{i,t},\ t = 1\ldots60$$

A way to make the methodology more robust in the face of measurement error in the betas is to select as dependent variables the rate of return of portfolios rather than of individual securities. The motivation is that the covariance of the rate of return of a single stock may have peculiarities in a short sample that may bias the estimated betas upward or downward: Stocks that have been estimated with a large (small) beta are more likely to have been affected by a positive (negative) measurement error. By estimating the beta of a portfolio rather than of a single stock, $r_{p,t} - r_{f,t} = \alpha_p + \beta_p (r_{M,t} - r_{f,t}) + \varepsilon_{p,t}$, the resulting beta, $\beta_p = \sum_{i=1}^{N} \beta_i$, is a weighted average of individual betas, and it is reasonable to expect that stocks that have had a positive beta shock in the sample period will be offset by other stocks with a negative beta shock, with a stabilization effect on the portfolio beta.

The second step involves a cross-section analysis for month 61, with the estimation of the coefficients, denoted as gamma to distinguish them from the estimated parameters of the index model estimated in step 1, namely:

$$\overline{r_{i,61} - r_{f,61}} = \gamma_{0,61} + \gamma_{1,61}\beta_{i,60} + \varepsilon_{i,61}$$

Notice that in this cross-sectional regression there is a lag between the average return and the estimated beta. The former refers to month 61 while the latter is estimated using data from the sample period $t = 2\ldots60$. The two variables do not overlap to minimize the risk of creating an artificial relation between beta and return when the two variables are measured from the same data. The sample is then moved forward one observation. The second time series regression is then estimated for the sample $t = 2 \ldots 61$, and the second cross-section regression is:

$$\overline{r_{i,62} - r_{f,62}} = \gamma_{0,62} + \gamma_{1,62}\beta_{i,61} + \varepsilon_{i,62}$$

Finally, after running the last cross-section with the data for the last available period T, statistical inference is made on the time series of the estimated gamma parameters. We first compute the mean:

$$\overline{\gamma_j} = \sum_{t=61}^{T} \gamma_{j,t} / (T - 60)$$

and then compute a t-test with a standard deviation obtained from the sample variability of estimated coefficients:

$$\frac{\overline{\gamma_j}}{\sqrt{\sum_{t=61}^{T} \left(\gamma_{j,t} - \overline{\gamma_j}\right)^2 / (T - 60)^2}}$$

If the CAPM were true, the constant should be zero and the estimate of the slope should be positive because it should correspond to the estimate of the risk premium. In other words, if the model were true, the data would have to be generated from equation (1) and the cross-section regression would have to return statistically significant values only for the coefficient that multiplies the betas, since other variables would not have to be relevant to explain the cross-sectional heterogeneity of realized risk premia. Moreover, the estimated $\varepsilon_{i,t}$ can be interpreted as pricing errors, which should be zero on average. See Cochrane (2005) for a statistical test using information from the average pricing errors.

9.5.4 Increasing the power of the test

The test as described so far may not be very powerful: Everything revolves around the statistical significance of the estimated intercept. In a case where the CAPM is rejected, the source of the rejection is not clear.

To make the test more powerful, we can add more variables on the right-hand side of the equation and test for their relevance. The list of potential variables is long, as only beta should matter under the null hypothesis. The candidates that we may want to add on the right-hand side of the regression should be good proxies for alternative pricing models.

Fama and MacBeth (1973) add beta square and the volatility of the return, which according to the CAPM should be irrelevant to the determination of the expected return:

$$\overline{r_i - r_f} = \gamma_0 + \gamma_1\beta_i + \gamma_2\beta_i^2 + \gamma_3\sigma_i + \varepsilon_i$$

Volatility is a very interesting alternative: The popular pricing model before the development of the CAPM suggested that expected return should be related to risk, which in turn would be proxied by volatility. The square of beta is a test for the validity of a linear rather than non-linear relation.

Fama and MacBeth (1973) do not obtain evidence against the CAPM, which is instead seriously questioned for the first time by Banz (1981), who shows that the average return of securities is negatively linked to their capitalization in the regression $\overline{r_i - r_f} = \gamma_0 + \gamma_1\beta_i + \gamma_2 S_i + \varepsilon_i$ where S_i is the market capitalization of company i. Notice an important point: Having returns being negatively related to market capitalization would, by itself, be consistent with the CAPM if betas were in turn negatively related to market capitalization.

However, if market capitalization is significant in the previous regression, then the explanation cannot rely on market cap being a proxy for beta, as beta is explicitly considered in the regression. γ_2 may be interpreted as a risk premium for a portfolio correlated with size, and a negative γ_2 means that size affects returns even after accounting for betas. In other words, size explains beta-adjusted returns, $\overline{r_i - r_f} - \gamma_1\beta_i = \gamma_0 + \gamma_2 S_i + \varepsilon_i$, meaning beta is not the only driver of return heterogeneity, which can instead be explained by a combination of beta and size. This is not what the CAPM would imply.

Initially, the relevance of size in the cross-sectional regression was regarded an "anomaly": no variables other than beta should predict the cross-section of average returns according to the CAPM, so any evidence to the contrary in anomalous given the theory.

Moreover, the relevance of size in the cross-section may inspire portfolio strategies: a portfolio tilted towards small stocks should provide larger average returns than a portfolio replicating the market. Any significant variable in the regression would have the same implications. It is not surprising that, since the beginning of the 1980s, the search for such variables has attracted a lot of attention among academics and practitioners.

A long series of subsequent research has highlighted the existence of many other variables that are linked to the cross-sectional dispersion of stock returns. Chapter 10 presents an extensive review of these "anomalies" from the point of view of the equity strategies that can be implemented starting from the econometric analyses.

Box 9.5 Testing the CAPM

Question: Elena wants to understand whether the CAPM explains the average returns of twenty securities, observed over sixty months, using data on the excess return of the various securities and the market. What does she need to do?

Answer: First, Elena realizes the possibility of being able to perform only one cross-section regression given the scarcity of data. On the same sample, she then estimates the betas of each stock and the average return. She obtains respectively:

Stock	Beta	Expected return
1	0.54	4.18%
2	0.26	3.86%
3	0.56	3.69%
4	0.76	4.77%
5	-0.57	7.60%
6	0.82	6.73%
7	0.81	3.79%
8	1.21	0.76%
9	1.11	9.07%
10	0.56	1.01%
11	0.89	0.68%
12	0.87	9.08%
13	1.39	12.49%
14	1.05	9.80%
15	1.17	8.50%
16	1.08	7.01%
17	1.56	19.21%
18	1.26	0.89%
19	1.39	3.61%
20	1.11	16.48%

Although there are deviations from a perfectly proportional relationship (e.g., stock 18 has an average return of 0.89% compared with an estimated beta of 1.26), the relationship appears to be positive. She then performs a cross-section regression of average returns on betas to get:

Regression output				
R^2	0.209			
Adjusted-R^2	0.165			
Standard error	0.0466			
Observations	20			
	Coefficients	**Standard error**	**t -Stat**	**P-value**
Constant	0.0021	0.0314	0.0669	0.9474
Slope	0.0679	0.0312	2.1802	0.0428

The results are interpreted in favor of CAPM: The constant is not significantly different from zero (the t-test is equal to 0.06693), while the slope is estimated to be 6.79%, a plausible estimate of the risk premium.

Summary

- Each asset risk in a portfolio can be determined based on its marginal contribution, that is, its contribution to overall portfolio volatility.
- In the Markowitz model the marginal contribution to risk of each security is identical across investors due to the two-fund separation theorem.
- The Capital Asset Pricing Model (CAPM) shows that the quantity of risk in a given stock is measured by the beta coefficient, which can also be interpreted as the risk contribution of the stock to overall portfolio volatility.
- The CAPM suggests that the marginal contribution to risk of a given stock is given by its beta, equal to the ratio between the covariance between stock excess return and market excess return, and the market variance.
- The CAPM predicts that the expected return on a stock is equal to the sum of the risk-free rate and the product between its beta and the equity market risk premium (EMRP).
- The CAPM equation can be represented in a graph known as the security market line (SML), describing the linear relation between betas and expected returns.
- A stock with low beta helps to stabilize the portfolio volatility, and investors are happy to include it in their portfolios for an expected return lower than that of a high beta stock.
- The index model $r_i - r_f = \alpha_i + \beta_i(r_M - r_f) + \varepsilon_i$ is the application of a linear regression to the relation between the time series of excess returns on a stock or portfolio and the market excess returns.
- The CAPM is a constrained version of the index model, based on the hypothesis that $\alpha_i = E\, r_i - r_f - \beta_i \times EMRP = 0$, implying that the risk premium is completely driven by its beta.
- The index model may be used to decompose the total return variance Vr_{it} into a systematic component $\beta_i^2\, Vr_{mt}$ and an idiosyncratic component $V\varepsilon_{it}$.
- CAPM testing must deal with several challenges associated with the existence of measurement error in expected returns and betas. The most common methodology, by Fama and MacBeth, uses a two-step regression where a time series analysis delivers the betas for each testing asset while the cross-section estimates the risk premia and the alphas, which should be zero if the model is supported by the data.

Problems

1 An analyst's expected return on a stock is 11%, risk-free is 2%, its beta is 1.2, and the market's expected return is 7%.

a. Does the analyst use CAPM to estimate the expected return of the stock?
b. What is the alpha of the title?

2 The beta of a stock is 1.2, the risk-free is 2%, and the expected return from the market portfolio is 7%. The current share price is 50 and the expected dividend for the end of the year is 6. What is the expected price of the stock at the end of the year?

3 A perpetual stream of 1,000 generated by a security whose beta is estimated to be 0.6 should be evaluated. The risk-free is 2% and the expected market return is 7%. What price are you willing to pay to buy perpetual flow? How much would you pay if the beta was estimated to be 1?

4 Are the following statements true or false?

a. Securities with zero beta offer a zero expected return.
b. According to the CAPM, investors require a high return to hold the most volatile securities.
c. You can build a portfolio with beta = 0.75 by investing 75% of your portfolio in risk-free and 25% in the market.

5 Are the following parameters compatible with the CAPM given the same market portfolio?

Portfolio	Expected returns	Beta
A	2	1.4
B	3	1.3

6 Are the following parameters compatible with CAPM?

Portfolio	Expected return	Standard deviation
A	3	35
B	4	25

7 Are the following parameters compatible with CAPM?

Portfolio	Expected return	Standard deviation
Risk-free	7	0
Market	16	30
A	14	15

8 A mutual fund with a beta = 0.8 has an expected return of 14%.

a. If the risk-free is 5% and the expected return from the market portfolio is 15%, should I invest in the fund?
b. What is its alpha?
c. Which passive portfolio composed of the market and risk-free has the same beta as the fund?
d. How do you interpret the difference between the expected return of the fund and the expected return of the passive portfolio?

9 Two mutual funds have the following returns and betas: $r_1 = 19\%$; $r_2 = 16\%$; $\beta_1 = 1.5$; $\beta_2 = 1$, the risk-free is 6% and the expected market return is 14%. Which of the two managers showed better stock picking skill?

Answers

1 a. CAPM implies an expected return of $0.02 + 1.2 \times (0.07 - 0.02) = 8\%$.
b. The analyst then implicitly estimates an alpha equal to 3%.

2 Using CAPM, the expected return on the stock is $0.02 + 1.2 \times (0.07 - 0.02) = 8\%$. The expected price must therefore guarantee an expected return of 8%, that is, $50 \times (1.08) - 6 = 48$.

3 According to the CAPM, the expected return is 5% and the value of an infinite flow, equal to the ratio of the value of the flow to the expected return, is 20,000. If the beta was equal to 1, the expected return would be 7% and the value would be 14,286.

4 a. False. If the beta is zero, the expected return is equal to risk-free.
b. False. According to the CAPM, what matters is the beta and not the volatility.
c. False. It is necessary to invert the odds described in the problem to have a beta of 0.75.

5 No, a higher beta must correspond to a higher expected return.

6 Potentially yes, since you can have simultaneously $3\% = r_f + \frac{\rho_A \times 0.35}{\sigma_M} \times \left(Er_m - r_f\right)$ and $4\% = r_f + \frac{\rho_B \times 0.25}{\sigma_M} \times \left(Er_m - r_f\right)$.

7 According to the CAPM, the expected return of A should be equal to $0.07 + \frac{\rho_A \times 0.15}{0.3} \times 0.09$. Therefore, the expected return indicated in the table is compatible with the expected return of the model only if the correlation is greater than 1, which cannot happen.

8 a. A portfolio with a beta of 0.8 should have an expected return of 13% according to the CAPM.
b. An expected return of 14% therefore implies an alpha of 1%, which makes the fund attractive to the investor.
c. The passive portfolio that tracks the fund consists of an investment of 80% in the market index and 20% in the risk-free which has an expected return of 13%.
d. The difference between the expected return of the fund and the replica portfolio can be explained based on the manager's ability to select securities.

9 According to the CAPM, the first fund should have an expected return of 18% and the second of 14%. Both managers have shown stock-picking skills because their alphas are respectively equal to 1% and 2%, with a preference for the second manager which is characterized by higher alpha.

10 Picking stocks and investing with style

10.1 Introduction

The Markowitz solution is associated with passive investing. Investors should diversify as much as possible and hold all listed stocks in the proportions characterizing the market portfolio. The equilibrium implication is the Capital Asset Pricing Model (CAPM), which, however, is not a good representation of historical returns. How do we exploit deviations from CAPM, that is, cases where stocks present an average return inconsistent with the idea that the risk premium is given by the product of the equity market risk premium and the beta sensitivity? The answer to this question is also a motivation for active investing, a strategy where the investor does not hold the market portfolio but only subsets of the available stocks.

Active investing can be extreme: An investor may decide to hold only, say, twenty stocks out of the 7,000 available, presumably those characterized by the largest alphas. This strategy may increase expected return but definitely increases risk. The first part of this chapter is about building numerically small, long-short portfolios. The Treynor–Black model is a way to rationally form the active portfolio and combine it with passive investing accounting for the trade-off between alpha and idiosyncratic risk. Alternatively, an investor may decide to hold a long-short portfolio with many stocks both in the long and in the short leg to control for idiosyncratic risk. This investment style is between passive and active, and we may call it semi-active; nowadays it is known as factor investing. The driver of factor investing is the variables that are responsible for deviations from the CAPM, mainly size, value, and momentum. The most relevant factor investing styles will be considered in this chapter.

The final part of the chapter is about reflections on the drivers of extra returns in factor investing, a crucial consideration for investors who need to answer the following question: By including such a strategy in a diversified portfolio, are we enjoying a free lunch or are we perhaps adding unknown and poorly understood sources of risk? The answer depends on our ability to understand the reasons for the average extra returns. The literature has alternatively highlighted the risk premium hypothesis (the extra return is a compensation for a source of risk that is collectively known by investors but unknown to academics) and the error hypothesis (the extra return exists because of behavioral errors and/or agency problems).

10.2 Alpha and small portfolios

10.2.1 Alphas

The index model is atheoretical and contemplates the existence of alpha. The CAPM predicts there should be no alpha. The immediate implication of the CAPM rejection is that heterogeneity in average excess returns is not explained entirely by heterogeneity in betas. We call alpha the part of average excess returns that is not explained by exposure to systematic risk factors. If the risk factors are the market and size, then alpha is the component of average return that is not explained by sensitivities to the market and size. If there are other risk factors, then alpha is the component of average return not explained by these other factors. This chapter will describe the growth in the number of factors discovered in the empirical finance literature over the last forty years and Chapter 11 will show how the evidence has been considered in pricing models extending the Capital Asset Pricing Model.

Alpha has pricing implications. Remember that, given expected future cash flows, there is an inverse relation between expected return and price. A positive alpha implies the existence of an expected excess return that is larger than implied by a reference model like for example the CAPM. In terms of the return/price relation, a positive alpha is therefore consistent with a price lower than the level consistent with the determination of the risk premium according to a model. Very often market practice suggests searching for alpha in terms of the relation between the market price and the fundamental-based value, which will be explored in Chapter 12. If the market price of the stock is equal to 100 and the value is estimated at 130, then there is a 30% upside. A convergence period of five years would amount approximately to an alpha of 6% per year.

10.2.2 Undiversified alpha portfolios

Let us consider two stocks with a non-zero alpha. In terms of the index model:

$$r_A - r_f = \alpha_A + \beta_A\left(r_M - r_f\right) + \varepsilon_A$$

$$r_B - r_f = \alpha_B + \beta_B\left(r_M - r_f\right) + \varepsilon_B$$

with $\alpha_A > 0$ and $\alpha_B < 0$. By investing \$1 in stock A and \$-1 in stock B (short-selling), with a zero net investment, the long-short portfolio return is equal to:

$$r_A - r_B = \alpha_A - \alpha_B + \left(\beta_A - \beta_B\right)\left(r_M - r_f\right) + \varepsilon_A - \varepsilon_B$$

where $\alpha_A - \alpha_B > 0$ by assumption. We denote the rate of return of the long-short portfolio as $r_{LS} = r_A - r_B$.The portfolio expected return is:

$$Er_{LS} = \alpha_A - \alpha_B + \left(\beta_A - \beta_B\right)\left(Er_M - r_f\right).$$

It can therefore be seen that deviations from the CAPM have an implication in terms of the expected return of the long-short portfolio. In Figure 10.1, assuming $\beta_A - \beta_B = 0.5$, if the CAPM was valid the expected value of the return differential between the two portfolios would be exactly on the security market line (SML), the point indicated by the arrow. The presence of alpha terms, meanwhile, implies an expected return from the long-short portfolio that is higher than that of the SML.

Figure 10.1 **The Security Market Line**

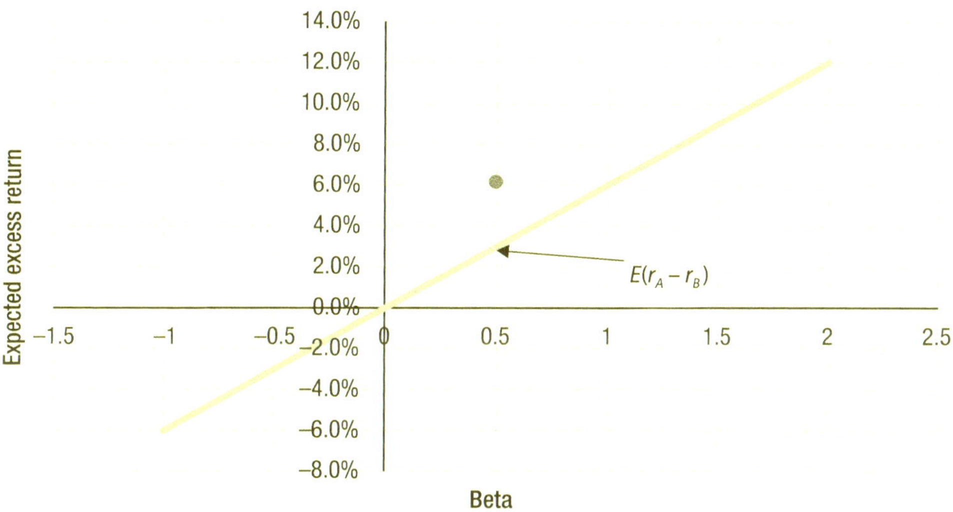

A long-short portfolio is generally subject to risk, that is, $r_{LS} = Er_{LS} + \varepsilon_A - \varepsilon_B$, its actual return is equal to the expected return plus an unpredictable shock. Risk is linked not only to market portfolio shocks but also to idiosyncratic risk, given that as usual the variance can be found by computing the expected value of the square difference between the return and its expectation:[1]

$$Vr_{LS} = (\beta_A - \beta_B)^2 Vr_M + V\varepsilon_A + V\varepsilon_B$$

The long-short portfolio is defined as "active" because it consists of only two securities and is therefore very different from a "passive" portfolio that tracks the market index. Under what conditions is an investor interested in holding such a portfolio? The active portfolio has the potential to take advantage of excess return due to alpha, but it generates diversifiable risk. It is therefore up to the investor to decide whether the excess return due to the presence of alpha is sufficient to remunerate the excess risk due to the presence of idiosyncratic shocks. Treynor and Black's model,

[1] There is no covariance between α_A and α_B given that these describe shocks specific to the individual stock..

described in the next section, shows how to formally treat the choice of the combination of an active portfolio that is not necessarily diversified and a passive portfolio that is a reference.

Box 10.1 What are the properties of that active portfolio?

Question: Elena wants to form an active, long-short portfolio using two stocks, A and B, whose market price is in both cases equal to 5. What expected return and risk are associated with the portfolio if the market volatility is 20%, the risk-free is zero and the market expected return is 5%? Does it make sense for her to form the portfolio if her utility function is mean/variance with a risk aversion coefficient of 4?

Answer: Elena proceeds to estimate the index model for two stocks, obtaining the following results:

Stock	Alfa	Beta	Idiosyncratic volatility
A	1%	1.05	5%
B	-2%	0.95	10%

She then decides to buy one unit of Stock A and short-sell one unit of B. The resulting portfolio has an alpha of +3%, a beta of 0.1, an expected return of 3% + 0.1 x 5% = 3.5%, a variance of $0.1^2 \times 0.04 + 0.0025 + 0.01 = 0.0129$ and therefore a volatility of 11.4%. To find out if it is worth acquiring the portfolio, Elena can calculate the utility level of $0.035 - \frac{4}{2} \times 0.0129$. The utility is positive and so Elena proceeds to form the portfolio.

10.3 Optimal selection of an active portfolio: the model by Treynor and Black

We have built an example of an alpha portfolio, but we have discussed neither the possibility that there is an optimal way to decide the weights of the securities nor the combination of such active portfolio with a passive portfolio fully replicating an index. Treynor and Black's (1973) model shows how to choose the weights invested in the securities that make up an active portfolio and how to combine it with a passive portfolio that fully replicates the performance of a benchmark index.[2] We start from an initial position in the two stocks that equals the ratio between alpha and individual idiosyncratic variance:

$$w_A^0 = \frac{\alpha_A}{V\varepsilon_A},\ w_B^0 = \frac{\alpha_B}{V\varepsilon_B}$$

[2] Technically, they solve a mean/variance minimization problem, assuming the investment in the market portfolio is the $n + 1$ asset and lack of correlation across idiosyncratic shocks of the individual securities.

The initial choice is intuitively simple: The weight must be proportional to the alpha and inversely proportional to the idiosyncratic risk. However, $w_A^0 + w_B^0$ do not necessarily sum up to one and as a result the initial choice is not a portfolio. We get the shares invested in the stocks in the active portfolio by normalizing each initial assumption by the sum of the two positions:

$$w_A^{ACT} = \frac{\frac{\alpha_A}{V\varepsilon_A}}{\frac{\alpha_A}{V\varepsilon_A} + \frac{\alpha_B}{V\varepsilon_B}}, \; w_B^{ACT} = \frac{\frac{\alpha_B}{V\varepsilon_B}}{\frac{\alpha_A}{V\varepsilon_A} + \frac{\alpha_B}{V\varepsilon_B}}$$

w_A^{ACT} and w_B^{ACT} are the weights of the active portfolio, with a beta equal to:

$$\beta^{ACT} = w_A^{ACT} \times \beta_A + w_B^{ACT} \times \beta_B$$

idiosyncratic variance (given the absence of correlation between idiosyncratic shocks):

$$V\varepsilon_{ACT} = \left(w_A^{ACT}\right)^2 \times V\varepsilon_A + \left(w_B^{ACT}\right)^2 \times V\varepsilon_B$$

and alpha equal to:[3]

$$\alpha^{ACT} = w_A^{ACT} \times \alpha_A + w_B^{ACT} \times \alpha_B$$

In what percentage of initial wealth do we want to combine the active portfolio with the market portfolio? It can be shown that this weight is equal to:

$$w_{ACT} = \frac{w_{ACT}^0}{1 + \left(1 - \beta^{ACT}\right) w_{ACT}^0}$$

where:

$$w_{ACT}^0 = \frac{\frac{\alpha^{ACT}}{V\varepsilon_{ACT}}}{\frac{Er_M - r_f}{\sigma_M^2}} \; .$$

The equation shows a positive relation between the beta of the active portfolio at the denominator β^{ACT}(due to its minus sign) and the share of the active portfolio in the overall investment. The intuition is the following: The higher the beta, the more similar the two portfolios are from the point of view of systematic risk, which makes the active portfolio more attractive because of its alpha.

For example, consider the case $\alpha_A = 0.5\%$, $\alpha_B = -0.25\%$, $\beta_A = 0{,}5$, $\beta_B = 1.5$, $V\varepsilon_A = 0.25\%$, $V\varepsilon_B = 1\%$, $Er_M = 5\%$, $\sigma_M = 20\%$. With these numbers, we have $w_{ACT} = 66\%$ that is, the investor invests 66% of her assets in the active portfolio and

[3] The ratio between the portfolio alpha and the portfolio idiosyncratic volatility is known as the information ratio.

34% in the index. The active portfolio consists of 114% invested in Stock A and -14% in Stock B and therefore the overall portfolio is invested for 75% in Stock A, -9% in B, and 34% in the market index.

The comments made when discussing the application of the Markowitz portfolio optimization model can be repeated here: The investment value is created by the parameters that are the inputs to the model rather than from the mathematical equation. Estimating the parameter simply based on history may not be a good strategy as it may induce the investor to form the best historical backward-looking portfolio rather than the optimal forward-looking one.

Box 10.2 What weight should you give to your favorite stock?

Question: Sara is a consultant for Carola, who is committed to social issues and thinks that the electric car can be an answer to environmental challenges. Carola wants to overweight Tesla stock and asks Sara to tell her what percentage of the portfolio to invest in that stock.

Answer: Sara starts from the historical series of daily prices of Tesla and Nasdaq for the period June 29, 2010–September 14, 2021. After calculating the percentage returns, she obtains the following results from an application of the index model (the t-test in parentheses):

Stock	Alpha	Beta	Idiosyncratic volatility
Tesla	0.13% (2.32)	1.35	3.08%

Sara concludes that the stock has had a high ability to produce a higher return than the Nasdaq throughout the period (0.13% refers to the daily return!). To answer Carola's question, she first calculates an "adjusted beta" equal to a weighted average (weight 1/2) between the estimated beta and 1, which returns 1.18. Tesla's ratio of alpha to idiosyncratic variances is 1.37. The assumed risk premium for the Nasdaq is 6% per annum and the variance is taken from the time series at 0.00014. The expected return-to-risk ratio for the Nasdaq is therefore $\frac{0.06}{250 \times 0.00014} = 1.71$. The ratio between the two ratios is $\frac{1.4}{1.71} = 0.8$ and the subsequent correction for the estimated beta produces a suggested investment in Tesla equal to 0.93. Investing 93% in a single stock and only 7% in the market portfolio is an extreme choice that can be explained based on the very large alpha obtained from the regression. A daily 0.13% alpha amounts to an annualized value of about 32.5%. The Treynor–Black model produces a large active investment due to this extraordinary number. A prudent investor would be skeptical of such a large estimate and might shrink the estimated alpha toward zero, which would produce a more balanced portfolio. This reminds us of the discussion associated with the practical application of the Markowitz optimization model: The mathematical model elaborates the estimated inputs. Mathematics per se adds no value. Value is added by a reasonable choice of the inputs.

10.4 Long-short diversified portfolios

10.4.1 Searching for alpha

The construction of active portfolios based on non-zero alpha stocks described in the previous section involves small portfolios characterized by sizable idiosyncratic variance. We know from Chapter 9 that idiosyncratic variance decreases as the number of stocks included in the portfolio goes up. If we found many stocks with non-zero alphas, then we could combine them in large positive alpha portfolios and decrease idiosyncratic risk.

How do we search for alpha? Academics and practitioners have been inspired by empirical results that reject the CAPM. We have seen in Chapter 9 that Banz (1981) has shown the existence of a negative relation between the size of a company (as measured by its market capitalization) and the average stock return: Small stocks pay higher average returns than large stocks. It should then be possible to form a long-short portfolio (long small stocks and short large stocks) with a positive average return. If both the long and the short legs of the portfolio are well diversified, this would have the benefit of strongly reducing idiosyncratic variance while at the same time maintaining the alpha for the long-short portfolio.

Empirical research has shown the existence of many similar strategies associated with rejections of the CAPM in the contest of the Fama–MacBeth methodology and the possibility to build well-diversified long-short portfolios with positive average returns and small correlation with the market return. The term "anomaly" was introduced to describe situations in which portfolios formed based on observable characteristics produce average returns that are significantly positive and cannot be explained on the basis of beta coefficients, that is, situations in which market sensitivity cannot fully explain the average risk premium.

10.4.2 Building long-short portfolios

How do we build a long-short portfolio to exploit the size anomaly? Answering this question will provide a method for turning econometric results about significant cross-sectional variables into portfolio strategies. Remarkably, the methodology we are going to describe will provide indications on how to form and modify over time a portfolio aimed at capturing the relevance of a specific characteristic, purely based on information available at the time of portfolio formation and update.

If we want to build a portfolio strategy aimed at exploiting the econometric result that the size coefficient is statistically significant in the regression, following Fama and French (1992), a list of companies is compiled in June of each year based on capitalization. For example, if there are 500 companies in the market, to avoid the definition of arbitrary thresholds where stocks with a market cap above value X are defined as "big" and stocks with a market cap below Y are defined as "small" we can proceed based on relevant percentages of the distribution. For example, we could decide to divide the universe of stocks into five buckets that are identical in terms of the number of stocks and place the 100 largest companies in a "big" portfolio and the 100 smallest in the "small" one. The 100 companies in each of the two portfolios can be equally balanced or weighted by capitalization.

Of course, the relative prices of the various stocks move over time, so in general it will not be true that the 100 smallest (largest) companies in June of the year of portfolio formation will still be the smallest (largest) after a few months. If the portfolio of small (large) companies is to contain smaller-cap (larger-cap) companies, periodic rebalancing should be done. In the original application of Fama and French, you hold the portfolio for one year and in June of the following year you rebalance. Over time, there is a time series of return of the long-short portfolio whose returns must be due to the different size of the long and the short leg of the portfolio.

There is no optimal frequency of rebalancing. The less frequently you rebalance, the greater the risk that the composition of the portfolio will not reflect the desired characteristic. But frequent rebalancing implies higher transaction costs.

By consistently applying this process in the sample, the compositions of the "big" and "small" portfolios are known on each day and consequently the return can be calculated each period. If the CAPM were valid, the average return of a portfolio that is long in small stocks and short in big stocks would be equal to the beta differential of the two portfolios. If the CAPM does not apply in that we have an average positive return with no beta differential, then we have identified an anomaly describing an excess return for the investor.

10.5 The most relevant anomalies/portfolio strategies

The literature has systematically applied the research methodology described above, identifying hundreds of characteristics that seem to be able to suggest the formation of portfolios whose average return is not fully explained by beta. In this section, we look at the strategies that are best known among investors. This method of investing is also known as "style investing."

10.5.1 The size premium

The size premium is the difference in average return between a portfolio of small-cap stocks (equally invested in 10% of smaller-cap stocks) and one composed of large-cap stocks (equally invested in 10% of larger-cap stocks). In the United States, this premium averaged 5.16% per annum for the period 1926–2023, as shown in Figure 10.2, which depicts the average (nominal) return of ten portfolios that divide the market universe by capitalization.

Such a large average return can be consistent with the CAPM: If small-cap stocks had a higher beta than large-cap stocks, then potentially beta heterogeneity could be the driver. If we compute the betas of the ten decile portfolios with the market over the period 1926–2023, we get Figure 10.3, where average return is on the horizontal axis and beta is on the vertical axis.

Figure 10.2 **The size premium: average return of portfolios formed by capitalization, 1926–2023**

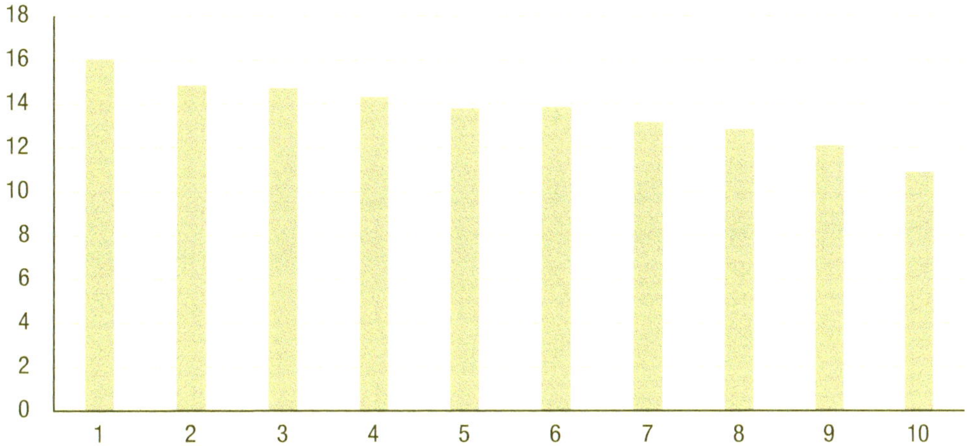

Source: Ken French website

Figure 10.3 **The beta/return relation for size portfolios**

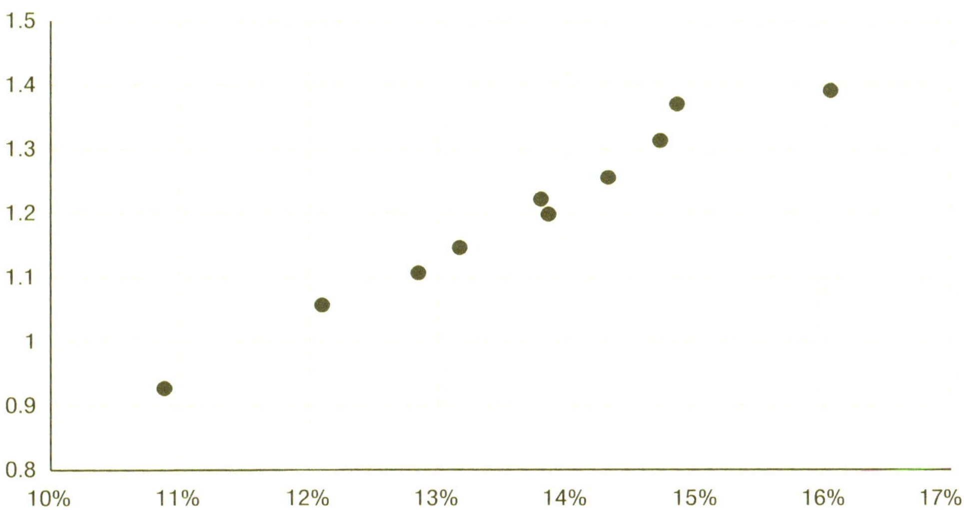

There is a positive relation, which, however, does not fully justify the return heterogeneity. The small-cap portfolio has a beta equal to 1.39 while the large-cap portfolio has a beta equal to 0.93. If the beta difference of 0.46 is multiplied by a 6% equity premium, we get a warranted return differential equal to 2.77%, about half the average excess return over the sample period. This is consistent with the results of applying the Fama–MacBeth methodology, where size is significant even after accounting for beta. We will return to a more complete discussion of potential reasons for these results after a description of other empirically important anomalies.

10.5.2 The value premium

The "value premium" is the difference in average return between a portfolio composed of securities with a high book-to-market (BTM) (a portfolio equally invested in the top 10% of the highest BTM securities) and one composed of low BTM securities (a portfolio equally invested in the bottom 10% of the lowest BTM securities). In the United States, this premium is 3.79% on average per year for the period 1926–2023. Figure 10.4 depicts the average returns of BTM deciles.

Figure 10.4 The value premium: average return of book-to-market portfolios, 1926–2023

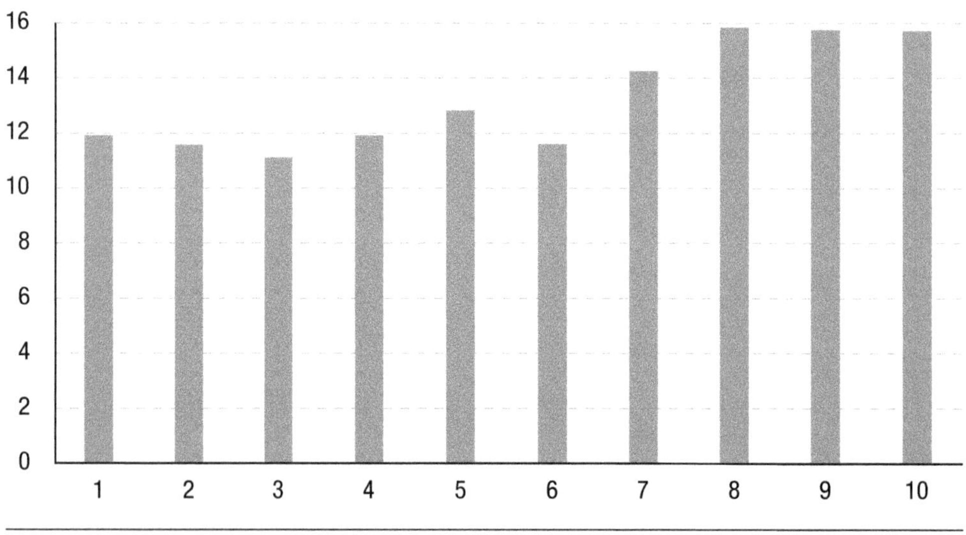

Source: Kenneth French website

One of the first examples of "style investing" is "value investing" (Graham and Dodd, 1934), which consists of the systematic purchase of securities that seem to be undervalued by the market, securities that can be identified for example based on the relationship between book value and market value (book-to-price). It is possible to make the definition of value stocks even more precise by simultaneously also using variables such as earnings/price, cash flow/price, and sales on price (see Lakonishok, Shleifer, and Vishny, 1994).

10.5.3 The momentum premium

A price momentum strategy takes advantage of divergences in relative returns and consists of buying stocks whose prices have risen (winners) in the last six to twelve months and selling securities whose prices have fallen (losers) in the last six to twelve months.

The key reference is Jegadeesh and Titman (1993), who propose a strategy based on a k-month formation period and a h-month holding period. Each month the winner and loser portfolios are selected based on past returns in the last k months, and the portfolios are held for h future months. When h is larger than 1 there are overlapping portfolios.

Suppose, for example, that $h = 2$ and the strategy starts in April based on returns of March and February with the goal of holding the portfolio for April and May. In May the portfolio formed in April is still held in the strategy, and a new winner/loser portfolio is formed based on returns in April and March.

The strategy therefore involves two portfolios that are held by the investor. In June there is liquidation of the portfolio built in April, the portfolio built in May is still held, and there is a new portfolio formed in June.

Figure 10.5 depicts the average return achieved based on momentum portfolios (portfolios are formed excluding the last month to avoid reversals). Portfolio number 1 is made up of the "losers," that is, stocks that have had the lowest return in the last twelve months, while portfolio number 10 is made up of the "winners," that is, stocks that have had the highest return in the last twelve months:

Figure 10.5 The momentum premium: average return of momentum portfolios, 1926–2023

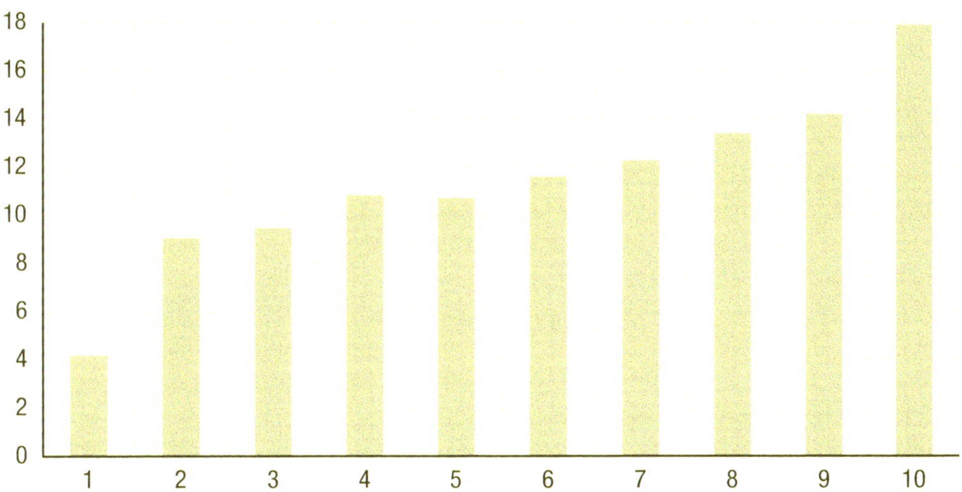

Source: Kenneth French website

Figure 10.5 shows that the ten portfolios perform very differently from each other. A strategy that systematically buys the stocks that have been winners and shorts those that have been losers has produced an average double-digit return over the period under consideration (13.7%).

The momentum strategy can be extended along two dimensions: applying it to other asset classes and exploiting both cross-sectional and time series momentum. Momentum is not limited to the stock market: Ilmanen (2011), Moskowitz, Ooi, and Pedersen (2012), and Asness, Moskowitz, and Pedersen (2013) present results of its application to commodities, bonds, currencies, and stocks in a variety of international markets. Moreover, such papers also explore time series momentum and not only cross-sectional momentum. Whereas cross-sectional momentum builds portfolios across individual securities, time series momentum looks at past returns of each individual asset. The simplest example for an equity index is a going long the index if the previous month return was positive and going short if the previous month return was negative. Again, like in Jegadeesh and Titman (1993), it is possible to explore combinations of formation periods and holding periods. Asness, Moskowitz, and Pedersen (2014) show that both momentum strategies and value strategies are positively correlated between markets but negatively correlated with each other within a certain financial asset class. In other words, if momentum works in the United States, then it is also likely to work in Europe, but if momentum works in the United States, then value in the United States is likely to do poorly.

Barroso and Santa-Clara (2015) highlight an interesting risk element associated with this strategy, that is the tendency to crash when the market recovers from previous important declines: in 1932 the strategy lost 91% in two months and in 2009 the negative return was 74% in three months. By using momentum in the context of a dynamic strategy that scales invested capital up and down relatively to predicted volatility, the Sharpe ratio doubles (relatively to unmanaged momentum) from 0.53 to 0.97, the excess kurtosis falls from 18.24 to 2.68 and asymmetry moves from -0.47 to -0.42.

10.5.4 The carry premium

The carry premium is a strategy that originally originated in the currency market, consisting of buying currencies with a high interest rate and selling currencies with a low interest rate. The strategy exploits deviations from the "uncovered interest rate parity" (UIP) according to which $r_f = r_f^* + E\Delta s$, where s is the logarithm of the spot rate and r_f^* is the risk-free rate prevailing in the foreign market. The UIP therefore argues that the domestic risk-free rate is the same as the international rate plus expectations of currency depreciation. If the uncovered parity of rates were valid, investors would be indifferent between buying currencies with high or low interest rates: a risk-neutral investor would be indifferent between investing in the foreign currency with a rate of 10% but prospects of depreciation of 5% or in the domestic currency with a 5% rate.

However, various empirical analyses have shown that the UIP does not explain the performance of most currency markets because the currency of the country with high interest rates typically tends to depreciate less than the theory predicts. A trade that invests in the high-interest currency and sells the low-interest currency therefore tends to be profitable on average because the depreciation of the purchased currency does not completely erode the interest rate differential advantage.

Ilmanen (2011) considers the following strategy as an example: At the beginning of each week (from 1983 to 2009) the currencies of the G10 countries are sorted according to the level of interest rates, and a long portfolio is formed in the currencies of the three countries with higher rates and a short portfolio in the currencies of the three countries with lower rates, in both cases with weights 50%, 30%, and 20%. The strategy's average annualized return is 6.1% with a Sharpe ratio of 0.61. The currency portfolio with high carry (high interest rates) at any given time produces a higher average return than that offered by the portfolio with low carry. The strategy was extrapolated to the bond market (using the yield curve), the commodity market (using futures contracts), and the stock market (using the dividend yield).

10.5.5 The low-risk premium

Econometric tests of the CAPM suggest that the empirical SML is too flat. It could be therefore that a strategy of shorting high-beta stocks and buying low-beta stocks could produce excess returns, a point explored by Frazzini and Pedersen (2014). If low risk is enjoyed by investors, then perhaps low idiosyncratic volatility stocks could present higher excess returns than high idiosyncratic volatility stocks, a point explored by Ang, Hodrick, Xing, and Zhang (2006). Figures 10.6 and 10.7 are based on deciles of stocks in the United States from 1963 to 2023.

Figure 10.6 Average returns of beta-sorted portfolio, 1963–2023

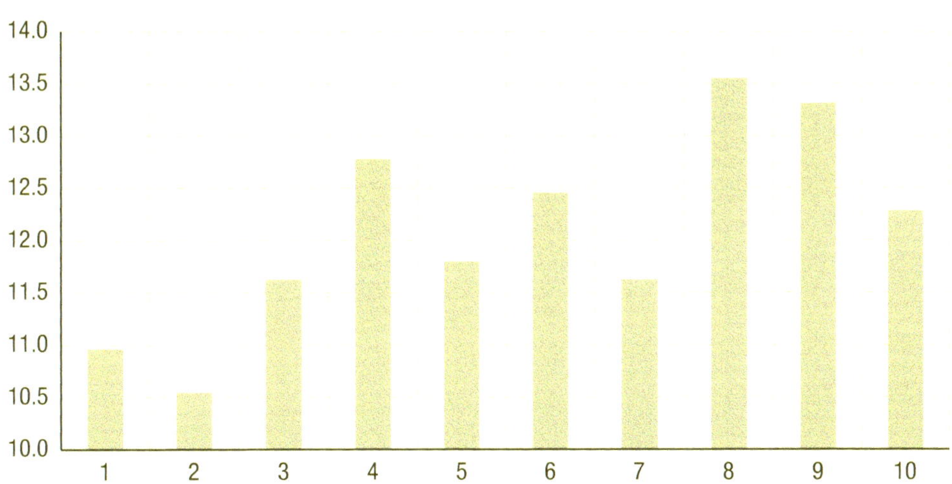

Source: Kenneth French website

Figure 10.7 Average returns of volatility-sorted portfolios, 1963–2023

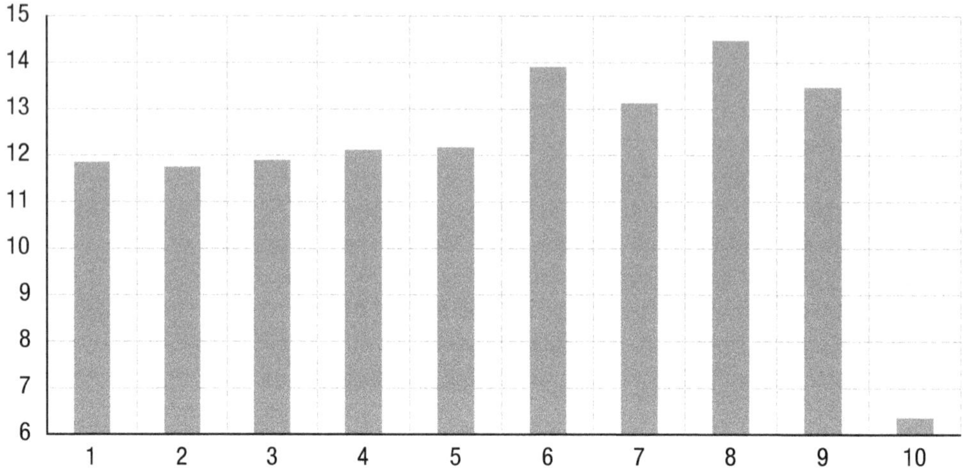

Source: Kenneth French website

Figures 10.6 and 10.7 show that the returns of this strategy are not as uniform as those of the other strategies. As far as the beta strategy is concerned, the relation is far from monotonic. In the case of volatility, the result is entirely driven by portfolio 10, whereas the others show a increasing return/volatility relation.

10.5.6 The quality premium

Previous strategies have been built on one characteristic at a time. Asness, Frazzini, and Pedersen (2019) present an innovation to this literature by forming portfolios based on a set of characteristics and constructing a "quality factor" for the US stock market in 1957–2016 and twenty-four other markets in 1989–2016 based on three characteristics: profitability (high profits), growth (growing profits), safety(low risk), and payout. In turn, each characteristic is measured based on several indicators; for example, profitability depends on "gross profits on assets," "return on equity," "return on assets," "cash flow on assets," "gross margin," and "share of profits represented by cash flow." To combine the various indicators, each month they normalize each observation for each indicator by subtracting the cross-sectional mean and dividing by the cross-sectional standard deviation $z(x_i) = \frac{x_i - m_x}{s_x}$ and then they average. For example, the profitability characteristic is

$$Profitability = (z_{GPOA} + z_{ROE} + z_{ROA} + z_{CFOA} + z_{GMAR} + z_{ACC})/6$$

and the final indicator is

$$Quality = (Profitability + Growth + Safety + Payout)/4.$$

The authors find that high-quality stocks have higher average returns than junk stocks even though they have less exposure to factors such as market, size, value, and momentum.

10.5.7 Other anomalies

Volume: Chordia and Swaminathan (2000) form portfolios by cross-referencing information contained in firm size and transaction volume and show that daily and weekly returns of portfolios consisting of securities with high transaction volume anticipate the returns of portfolios consisting of securities with low transaction volume, explaining the result on the basis of the delayed reaction of the prices of securities with low trading volume. Gervais, Kaniel, and Mingelgrin (2001) find that high trading contains useful information for predicting the future performance of securities: Stocks with an abnormally high (low) trading level on a day or week tend to rise (fall) over the next month. In this case, the explanation is related to the increased visibility associated with trading, which in turn further increases demand and prices. Han, Huang, Huang, and Zhou (2022) elaborate on the joint relationship between volume of trading, mispricing and expected returns, and find that trading volume amplifies mispricing: a positive shock to trading volume is associated with higher (lower) expected returns for underpriced (overpriced) stocks, which due to the negative relation between price and expected return become even more underpriced (overpriced). If trading volume is interpreted as a proxy for investor disagreement, then the results are consistent with the theory of Atmaz and Basak (2018).

Post-earnings announcement drift (PEAD): Stock prices react to earnings "surprises" in a correct but delayed manner, that is, they continue to rise (fall) for several quarters after announcing earnings that are higher (lower) than analysts' expectations. According to Bernard and Thomas (1990), the long-short strategy of buying stocks with positive surprises and selling those with negative surprises achieves an annual return of 18%, although the most recent estimates according to Fink's literature survey (2021) are considerably lower and highlight the existence of significant returns, especially in the quarter following the announcement.

Sentiment: Baker and Wurgler (2006) define sentiment based on a "propensity to speculate" and ask whether it can predict the cross-section of stock returns. The results show that situations where sentiment is low at the beginning of a given month tend to be associated with particularly positive returns in those stocks that are difficult to value and characterized by strong arbitrage constraints, that is, securities (a) issued by small companies, (b) issued by young companies, (c) characterized by high volatility, (d) with operating losses, (e) not paying dividends, or (f) in situations of financial stress. The monthly sentiment index is extracted using the main components methodology from the following variables: the discount (percentage difference between market price and net asset value, or NAV) on closed-end investment funds, the turnover of securities on the stock market, the number of initial public offerings (IP-

Os) and the average return of IPOs on the first day of trading, the ratio between the value of newly issued shares on the market and the total market value, and the percentage ratio of the market-to-book ratio of companies that pay dividends to those that don't.

The most recent analyses define sentiment in an applied way, using the news flows available from the media. Tetlock (2007) uses an algorithm to transform *Wall Street Journal* articles into numerical values by first assigning the words contained in the article to various categories and then counting the relevance of the various categories. The factor generated in this way is interpreted as a daily indicator of pessimism, and the regressions indicate that the indicator has predictive power for the performance of the stock market (Dow Jones index) of the following day: A deviation of the indicator equal to a standard deviation predicts a negative return of 0.08%, which is then almost entirely reabsorbed over the following days. To highlight the economic significance of the forecast, it is enough to note that the average daily return over the period was equal to 0.06%: A shock to the pessimism index therefore has a value approximately equal to the average market return. Tracy Ke, Kelly, and Xiu (2019) use machine learning techniques to make sentiment identification even more general: Instead of assigning words a positive or negative meaning based on a vocabulary, they let the model determine whether the content of a document is interpreted positively or negatively by the market based on the performance of the headline to which the news refers. In an out-of-the-sample learning application, a strategy that buys the fifty stocks with positive news every day and sells the fifty stocks with negative news gets an annualized Sharpe ratio of 4.29.

10.6 Why are there anomalies?

There are various hypotheses about the causes of the anomalies, including:

a) rational premiums for systematic and non-diversifiable risk factors
b) behavioral errors by investors
c) institutional characteristics due to the typical functioning of the financial intermediation sector
d) information gaps among investors
e) statistical errors related to inappropriate methodologies
f) failure to take into account transaction costs
g) leverage.

10.6.1 Rational risk premia

One possibility is that excess returns are rational premia for the systematic risk associated with holding a certain portfolio. According to this explanation, if a portfolio compensates holders with a particularly high return over the long term, it must be a particularly risky portfolio. For the premium size, it can be thought that small companies are (a) particularly exposed to the economic cycle, (b) more indebted and therefore sensitive to interest rate shocks, and (c) poorly diversified from the point of view of products/outlet markets.

For the value premium, it can be thought that companies with low market prices compared with the book value are often perceived as distressed companies and therefore particularly risky. Companies under stress suffer particularly during crises. In addition, they may have a lot of fixed capital that is difficult to use flexibly to manage the phases of business transformation. Petkova and Zhang (2005) hypothesize that a relevant dimension of value risk, though insufficient to explain the entire premium, is that their beta moves over time along with the equity market risk premium, that is, the market sensitivity of value portfolios rises precisely in the riskiest phases.

In other cases, it is hard to find intuitive explanations: Why would winners be riskier than losers in the momentum strategy? Why would high-quality stocks be riskier than junk stocks?

10.6.2 Behavioral errors

According to some scholars, the anomalies are the result of factors related to behavioral finance, in particular the presence of errors in the treatment of available information and errors in the use of data analysis results. According to this explanation, a portfolio can compensate holders with a particularly high return, which does not disappear even in the long run, because investors do not understand that the expected return-to-risk ratio of such portfolios is particularly high.

In the case of value stocks, La Porta (1996) argues that the price can be irrationally low because investors extrapolate low or negative earnings over an extended period of time, overlooking the evidence that it is difficult to predict long-run earnings growth, as shown by Chan, Karceski, and Lakonishok (2003). La Porta (1996) shows that value stocks are more likely to have positive surprises than growth stocks on earnings announcements and therefore are more likely to surprise the market on the upside on those days. This is consistent with the empirical evidence suggesting that earnings are hard to forecast and with the hypothesis that value stocks are undervalued rather than the result of risk premia.

From a behavioral finance perspective, momentum can be the result of a delayed reaction to news: In the presence of good (bad) news about a certain security, the market does not change the price to the new equilibrium level but only partially adjusts it, leaving room for future price growth (decline) toward that level.

10.6.3 Agency issues

Agency problems refer to the impossibility on the part of a principal to observe the effort of the agent. In asset management, the investor is the principal and the asset manager is the agent. Investors do not observe the effort of managers but only see the final results, especially the rate of return and periodic information about portfolio composition. Lakonishok, Shleifer, and Vishny (1994) claim that agency problems may be a reason for the unwillingness on the part of professional asset managers to hold value stocks, and this would create the existence of a value premium.

During a financial crisis, the asset manager may prefer to avoid stocks that are particularly hit, for example banks during the 2008 Global Financial Crisis, because investors may infer that bad returns may be due to a misunderstanding of the causes of the crisis. The asset manager may be convinced that buying stocks that have suffered during the crisis are the best opportunity for the investor but may hesitate to do so due to the risk of losing the money under management. Alternatively, the asset manager may believe that the time horizon of clients is not long enough and thus would not give enough time for the strategy, for example the value strategy, to pay off.

10.6.4 Lack of information

If the results of the strategies were at least partly due to information deficiencies, one would expect them to be absorbed over time. In such a scenario, a strategy is initially discovered by an investor, then its use spreads because other investors realize its validity. The combined effect of the buying and selling of an increasing number of investors begins to affect the relative prices of the securities that create the excess return. The prices of the securities in the long (short) portfolio tend to rise (fall) relative to the others, and this makes the strategy less attractive from a return perspective. McLean and Pontiff (2016) estimate a drop in the average return of such strategies of 33–38% after the results of the research are published in academic journals. Jacobs and Muller (2020) extend the analysis to an international context (listing as many as 231 anomalies) and show that the reduction in average returns observed in the United States does not extend to the international context.

10.6.5 Inappropriate statistical methodologies

Some researchers express doubt that the high number of anomalies highlighted in the academic literature (over 300!) is the result of inappropriate methodologies. The wide availability of data in finance can sometimes be a problem that, if not methodologically managed, can fool even academic journals for years. Harvey, Liu, and Zhu (2016) suggest using a statistical t-value greater than 3 as an informal rule to account for the multiplicity of strategies that can be examined. Harvey (2017) suggests that a stricter rule may even exacerbate the problem, given the strong incentive of research paper authors and journal editors to publish papers that report statistically significant results.

10.6.6 Transaction costs neglect

One reason why excess returns in strategies persist may be related to the presence of transaction costs that prevent investors from forming the portfolios needed to replicate returns. An extreme form of transaction costs is related to the prohibition of short-selling, externally imposed by regulators or imposed by self-chosen policies. For example, most institutional investors cannot or decide not to sell short. This prevents the pursuit of strategies to replicate the risk factors identified above.

Sometimes, investors who can and want to pursue long-short strategies may not do so due to market characteristics. First, on many securities, especially the very small ones, there is no market that allows short-selling. Second, sometimes the cost of short-selling, the so-called shorting fee, is so high that it discourages any trade.

However, various studies have tried to replicate the returns of anomalies on the basis of strategies that take into account the transaction costs actually incurred by intermediaries in certain case studies (see, e.g., Engle, Ferstenberg, and Russell, 2012) or estimating them on the basis of existing microstructure data (see, e.g., Novy-Marx and Velikov, 2016). The latter paper reports low average transaction costs (bid–ask spreads) for size and value factors (about 0.05% per month) and higher for the momentum factor (about 0.48% per month), also highlighting that the transaction cost is higher for small and highly volatile securities.

Generally, the literature shows that returns net of transaction costs are nil unless strategies are modified to mitigate the amount of transactions on higher-cost securities. Patton and Weller (2020) estimate the average returns associated with risk factors by comparing the theoretical results obtained by theoretical portfolios of individual stocks and the operating results obtained by portfolios managed by mutual funds, finding, for example, that the return of momentum strategies cancels out completely while that of value strategies decreases substantially.

10.6.7 Leverage

The explanation given by Frazzini and Pedersen (2014) for the low average return of high-beta securities, which precisely suggests a financial strategy in which low-beta securities are bought and high-beta securities are sold, is linked to the impossibility of leverage. Figure 7.11 in Chapter 7 illustrates the set of investment opportunities when leverage is not possible. Let us assume that the tangency portfolio has an expected return of 6% and a volatility of 12%. All investors who wish to pursue a target expected return of more than 6% can only purchase a portfolio composed exclusively of risky securities and different from the tangency portfolio. Such a portfolio is likely to consist of a large proportion of stocks with high beta and high volatility. The consequence of excess demand from investors seeking to achieve a high expected return is a higher price of stocks with high beta and volatility. As we know from the previous chapters, with the same expected value of future cash flows, a high-priced security has a lower expected return.

10.7 Investment implications

10.7.1 Using anomalies

The investment implications depend on the investor's belief that the average return of a given portfolio is explained by the existence of a rational reward for risk (consistent, as we will see in Chapter 13, with the market efficiency hypothesis) or by the existence of behavioral errors. In the first case, there is no particular interest in investing in portfolios that are capable of producing anomalies, because the higher average return is a reward for the greater risk. In the second case (behavioral errors on the part of other investors) the ratio between expected return and risk is particularly favorable and one may be led to invest particularly intensively in these strategies.

There is an evolution in the market's interest in investing in strategies that can be considered as anomalies. Initially, only professional managers, especially hedge funds, knew about these anomalies and used them to manage their stock portfolios. Over time, diversified products have been created as active funds for retail investors that are based on exactly these anomalies. For a few years now there have been exchange traded funds (ETFs), often known as "smart beta" ETFs, that allow you to invest in such anomalies. The previously mentioned findings of McLean and Pontiff (2016) are consistent with increasing excess demand for the securities that underlie the anomalies, resulting in higher prices and lower average returns.

Factor investing can be used in the context of mean/variance optimization to exploit their diversification properties. Ilmanen (2022) reports a -61% correlation between momentum and value, a -8% correlation between value and defensive, and a 16% correlation between momentum and defensive. This suggests that the Markowitz model may exploit the diversification potential created when combining different equity strategies. Moreover, starting from the definition of active portfolio provided in section 10.3, it is also possible to consider an active factor portfolio including factor strategies and add it, through the Treynor–Black model, to a passive index investing strategy. Using monthly data from Professor French library, a momentum strategy defined as long in the highest momentum decile and short the market has average return equal to annualized 9.81%, with a 11.92% volatility. A value strategy, defined as long the highest value decile portfolio and short the market, has an average return equal to 7.65% and volatility of 18.65%. When running regressions against the market portfolio, the momentum strategy has (monthly) alpha equal to 0.81% and beta to 0.017, the latter showing the almost zero correlation with the market, and the value strategy has respectively 0.34% and 0.44. If these two factor strategies are considered as stocks in an active portfolio, using the Treynor–Black model we get an active portfolio investing 82% in momentum and 18% in value. When such a portfolio is combined with the market portfolio, the weight of the active portfolio is 84%, with only 16% left for passive investing. The active weight drops to 68% if the two estimated alphas are divided by 2.

10.7.2 Hedge funds

The first hedge fund, and the name of the financial product, is attributed to Alfred Winslow Jones, who in 1949 claimed his fund was hedged against market risk. The hedge fund industry has grown over time, and as of the end of 2023 hedge funds are estimated to manage more than $5 trillion (see Figure 10.8).

Figure 10.8 **Assets under management by hedge funds worldwide, 1997–2023**

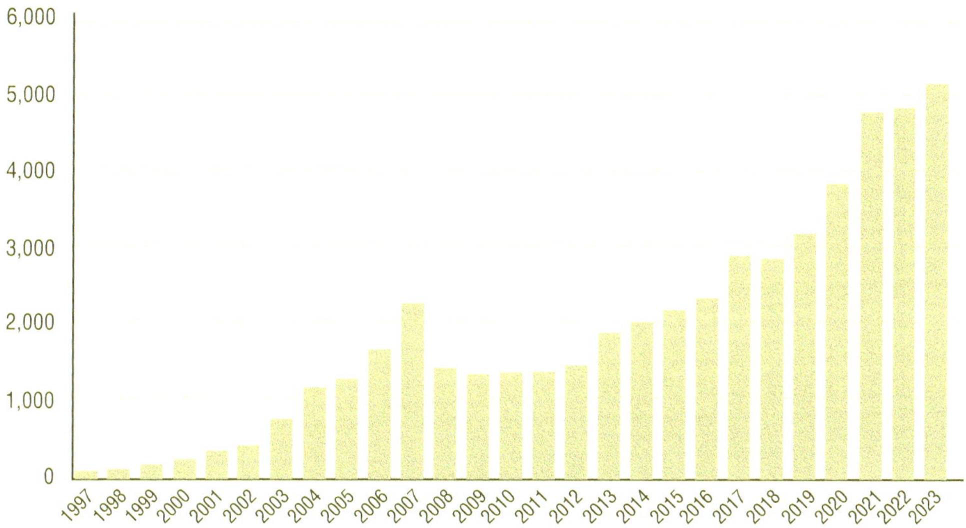

Source: Statista

The peculiarities of hedge funds, relatively to mutual funds, include the following:

- Management fees: The predominant structure involves a management fee of 2% and an incentive fee of 20% on overperformance relative to a hurdle rate. Suppose, for example, the hurdle rate is 4% and the rate of return of the hedge fund is 10% before fees. The after-fixed fee return becomes 8%. The performance fee will be equal to $(8\% - 4\%) \times 0.2 = 0.8\%$ and the total fee is 2.8%. In theory, this structure allows for the reimbursement of heavy costs due to the need to provide in-house research for active strategies and, above all, aligns the interests of investors and managers, since the latter are also interested in increasing the value of the investment. Such a cost structure has not changed since the inception of the industry regardless of increasing competition due to new hedge funds opening every year and may therefore be justified by the commercial strength of hedge funds vis-à-vis investors. Fees are often subject to a high-water mark, meaning that in case of losses the hedge fund can charge performance fees only after recovering the losses.

- Limited number of investors and limited disclosure requirements: Regulation allows a maximum number of investors and consequently hedge funds require a minimum significant investment that still allows them to reach a sufficiently large asset level. In exchange for limited transparency hedge funds are prevented from soliciting money from investors in general so that only accredited investors can invest in them.
- Transparency: The absence of regulation requiring hedge funds to publish portfolio value data means that there is no daily NAV. However, commercial considerations lead many hedge funds to publish the value of their portfolio at weekly or monthly intervals for their investors, even though they have no duty to report to public databases. This lack of transparency is the main reason why academics have applied at length performance evaluation techniques to mutual funds that have heavy reporting requirements.
- Management flexibility: The manager is free to use short-selling, derivative contracts, and leverage, the use of which is limited in mutual funds. In addition, there is no benchmark (except in some cases an indication of a performance target).
- Liquidity: There are lock-up periods, that is, periods during which it is not possible to sell the units back to the company that manages the hedge fund, and redemption notices, that is, the need to notify the manager weeks or months in advance of the intention to sell the units. During the 2008–2009 financial crisis, various hedge funds imposed "exit gates" on investors with the aim of preventing divestment decisions from forcing them to sell their assets at "fire sale" prices.

Some hedge funds, contrary to the name that refers to a strategy of risk protection (hedging), have very volatile returns due to their very dynamic investment policy. The term hedge fund is nowadays consistent with using derivatives and short-selling to reduce risk, or to increase risk with the goal of increasing expected return. A similar ambiguity also exists from the point of view of the investor, who can invest in a hedge fund for speculative purposes to increase the expected return of the portfolio or try to allocate a part of the assets to an asset that moves in a way that has little correlation with the rest of the portfolio, thus contributing above all to containing the periodic volatility of the market value of the same.

According to various academic papers, the average annual mortality rate of hedge funds is 10–15%, with much higher peaks in crisis phases such as 2008–2009. There is a lot of debate about the ability of hedge funds to create value, that is, to provide positive returns to investors once they have adjusted for risk and management costs. Getmanski, Lee, and Lo (2015) present a review of various aspects of the hedge fund industry. Pedersen (2015) presents an application of relevant financial modeling to the hedge fund industry.

Summary

- The term "anomaly" was introduced to describe situations in which (long-short) portfolios formed based on observable characteristics produce average returns that are significantly positive or negative and cannot be explained on the basis of beta coefficients.
- If the portfolios are small, they also include diversifiable risk and the investor must decide whether it is worthwhile to buy them, perhaps to combine them with a passive portfolio following the methodology of Treynor and Black.
- The main strategies followed in the sector concern the formation of large and diversified portfolios, based on one or more observable characteristics, capable of producing excess returns without assuming any idiosyncratic risk. In academic studies, such strategies involve the creation of long-short portfolios, comprising short-selling on various securities and give rise to factor investing.
- The main anomalies are related to size, the relationship between price and book value, and momentum, but there are now hundreds of anomalies that have been described in academic papers.
- There is a lot of debate about the factors that create anomalies, the two main possibilities being rational premiums for systematic risk associated with holding a certain portfolio or errors in the processing of available information and errors in the use of data analysis results.
- Hedge funds have traditionally been the only suppliers of long-short portfolio strategies to investors, but financial engineering has provided opportunities to bring factor investing also to retail investors through Exchange Traded Funds.

11 Theory and practice of multifactor models

11.1 Introduction

The CAPM can be interpreted as a model in which risk-averse investors demand a premium that rewards them for each stock's exposure to market index fluctuations, as measured by the beta coefficient. The Arbitrage Pricing Theory (APT) model is an extension of the CAPM that takes into account the existence of a generic number of risk factors. Instead of relying on Markowitz's demand model, the APT starts with a hypothesis about the mechanism that determines stock returns and then applies the consequences of the no-arbitrage assumption to derive a "pricing equation" that allows the expected return to be determined. Since arbitrage requires the cancellation of idiosyncratic risk, APT applies to the pricing of diversified portfolios and not to the pricing of individual securities.

In the most general case, in the presence of a generic number K of non-diversifiable risk factors, the pricing equation argues that the expected return on the security is equal to the sum of the product terms between the sensitivity to the individual risk factor and the risk premium that can be obtained on a portfolio that is perfectly (and exclusively) sensitive to that risk factor. The chapter presents a series of applications of APT, including research on the identity of relevant factors, the definition of portfolios that replicate these factors (factor tracking portfolios), the use of factors in empirical models for determining the expected returns of equities, the best known of which is that attributed to Fama and French, the use of the model for performance evaluation, and in the context of analysis of global portfolios.

11.2 The multifactor model and arbitrage

In the CAPM, and even in the index model, systematic risk is represented by market volatility. Risk-averse investors want a premium for investing in the market and therefore also a premium for buying individual securities. If individual portfolios are fully diversified, the premium should only compensate for the exposure to systematic risk. Unsystematic risk does not need to be compensated for because it disappears within the portfolio. The market is the risk factor, and individual stocks receive a premium that depends on their co-movement with the market as measured by beta. Steve Ross's (1976) APT is based on two pillars:

a) a multifactor model describing returns;
b) a pricing equation derived under the assumption of no arbitrage.

11.2.1 The multifactor model

The multifactor model describes return as the sum of expected and unexpected components. Unexpected components are shocks to sources of macroeconomic risk and sources of specific risk:

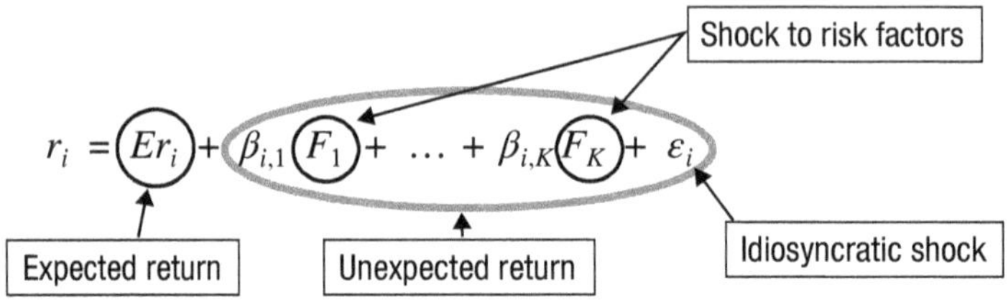

$$r_i = Er_i + \beta_{i,1} F_1 + \ldots + \beta_{i,K} F_K + \varepsilon_i \tag{1}$$

In equation (1), F_k is a zero-mean random variable, $EF_k = 0$, describing the surprise to the macroeconomic risk factor. Equation (1) argues that realized returns are different from expected returns when factors have unexpected realizations and/or when there are idiosyncratic shocks. The multifactor model (1) has no economic significance. It is simply a statistical description of performance, reminiscent of a regression equation. Equation (1) makes sense when observed from the point of view of typical stock market movements. For example, a very important piece of information is provided by the data on new employment in the United States announced on the Friday of the first week of each month. According to equation (1), if the employment report provides valuable information, then we should see a reaction of stock prices to surprises. How do we assess a surprise? By comparing the consensus forecast with the actual number. Say the expected number of new jobs is equal to 200,000 people and the actual number is 220,000, a 10% positive surprise. Let us also say that the surprise is positive for stock prices, meaning that an employment report that is stronger than expected signals an economy that is stronger than expected and this is conducive to better expectations for business activity, earnings, and dividends on the part of listed corporations (we will discuss this channel at length in the next chapter). Stock prices should increase after the publication of the job report, consistent with the idea of a positive return driven by new information.

11.2.2 Arbitrage and the pricing equation

Is a reaction on the part of the stock market to a specific piece of new information systematic, that is, does the reaction take place most of the time when there is bad or good news? If that is the case, we would also expect that stock prices account for the expectation of the values of the relevant factors. From the previous example, we would guess that the level of stock market prices the second before the new announcement is consistent with the consensus forecast. Again, this link between expectations and price levels will be the subject of the next chapter, but it is crucial to mention it here to better understand the meaning of the return models we are discussing.

The pricing equation aims to determine the expected return required by risk-averse investors acting in a market where there are no arbitrage possibilities. In fact, risk-averse investors only invest if they are compensated for exposure to systematic risk factors, given that the specific risk factors are diversified across portfolios.

To understand how the pricing equation is obtained, it is first necessary to define arbitrage as the possibility of creating a portfolio without any monetary investment but capable of offering a probability of positive return in the future, without any possibility of loss (conversely, we would have an arbitrage opportunity also in case it is possible to enter a zero-sum contract today with a non-negative payoff in the future). It is the financial equivalent of a "free lunch." The presence of risk defined as a small probability of a loss does not allow the opportunity to be identified as arbitrage. For example, investing \$1 million with a 90% probability of gaining 10% and a 10% probability of losing \$10 is not an arbitrage opportunity.

Suppose two banks borrow and lend money at two different rates, one at 5% and one at 10%. The investor would go to the bank that lends money at 5% to get a loan of C. She would then go to the bank that pays 10% to leave the money as deposits. The investor would not have invested any money initially, but after one year she would have a net gain of 5% of the capital C initially borrowed. Can an arbitrage opportunity persist? In our example, customers would keep visiting the 5% bank first and then the 10% bank. The two banks would realize the imbalance that is created in the market: One bank would have many loan applications and the other would have many deposits. These actions on the part of the customers would be the financial choices made to exploit the arbitrage opportunity. Each bank would react by varying its interest rate. If both banks lent and accepted deposits at 9%, all activity would cease. The same would apply to a rate of 6%, or any other rate.

In summary, the presence of arbitrage opportunities triggers capital flows that then have an impact on prices and returns, until the moment when the opportunity ceases to be profitable without any risk.

11.2.3 Arbitrage with equal betas

The arbitrage methodology has been used since the 1970s for option pricing. Researchers would form a portfolio including the option and the underlying to form a risk-less portfolio that should earn the risk-free rate. From the resulting condition it would be possible to price the option out of the price of the underlying and the risk-free rate regardless of the market degree of risk aversion. This is a very attractive methodology as it promises to price risky securities without any assumption on risk aversion. Is it possible to apply such methodology to the stock market? This is the contribution of Ross (1976).

To see how things work in the stock market, let us reconsider the multifactor equation (1), noting that the same equation also describes the return for any portfolio p:

$$r_p = Er_p + \beta_{p,1} F_1 + \ldots + \beta_{p,K} F_K + \varepsilon_p$$

If the portfolio includes many securities and is well balanced (diversified portfolio), then the analysis performed in the context of the index model suggests that the specific risk tends toward zero due to the lack of correlation between specific shocks. Therefore, for such a diversified portfolio:[1]

$$r_p = Er_p + \beta_{p,1}F_1 + \ldots + \beta_{p,K}F_K$$

Let us now assume, without loss of generality but in order to carry out a simpler analysis from a formal point of view, that we have two large and diversified portfolios, A and B, with the same beta coefficient, $\beta_{A,1} = \beta_{B,1} = \beta_1$, relative to the unique common risk factor, that is, $K = 1$:

$$r_A = Er_A + \beta_1 F_1$$

$$r_B = Er_B + \beta_1 F_1$$

Suppose that the expected return of A is higher than that of B. We form a portfolio "long" A and "short" B (long-short portfolio). "Being long" A means investing an amount of money, say €1, to buy the portfolio. "Being short" B means selling (without owning it) portfolio B in order to get €1 and finance the purchase of A. The resulting long-short portfolio is described by the following return:

$$r_{LS} = r_A - r_B = Er_A - Er_B + \beta_1 F_1 - \beta_1 F_1$$

Given the beta equality hypothesis:

$$r_{LS} = r_A - r_B = Er_A - Er_B$$

The return of the portfolio, which, it should be remembered, does not imply any net capital investment because the short part finances the long part, has two important characteristics:

a) it is positive given the initial assumption of expected returns;
b) it is risk-free: there is no specific risk because these are two well-diversified portfolios, and there is no systematic risk given the assumption of equality of beta coefficients.

We have therefore created an arbitrage: It is possible to invest zero euros in a long-short portfolio that at the end of the period will offer a certain positive return equal to the differential of expected returns. Interpreting our result in general terms, we can say that an expected return differential across two diversified portfolio is inconsistent with lack of arbitrage where there is one (and only one) systematic risk factor. As economists, we study markets where we assume there are no arbitrage opportunities: If there was one, it would mean professional traders are slow to intervene and are reluctant to make money with no risk, that is, they have no appetite for a free lunch. It fol-

[1] For this reason, in general, the logic of arbitrage does not apply to the pricing of individual stocks, for which idiosyncratic risk is relevant.

lows that, absent arbitrage, the price of large and diversified portfolios should be such as to make expected return equal in a one-factor model. In the absence of arbitrage, therefore, $\beta_A = \beta_B \rightarrow Er_A = Er_B$ and the return of the long-short portfolio is zero.

11.2.4 Arbitrage with different betas

What happens when the betas of the two portfolios are different from each other? Existing securities must be combined to create a new portfolio with a beta equal to that of the combination of the two original portfolios we are studying. Let's create a portfolio C that invests w cents in portfolio A and $1 - w$ cents in the risk-free stock:

$$r_C = \mathrm{w} \times r_A + \left(1 - \mathrm{w}\right) \times r_f$$

and create a long-short portfolio buying portfolio B and selling portfolio C, whose return is:

$$\mathrm{r}_{LS} = r_C - r_B = w \times (Er_A + \beta_A \times F_1) + (1 - w) \times r_f - Er_B - \beta_B \times F_1$$

If the weights are chosen so that $w \times \beta_A = \beta_B$, then:

$$r_{LS} = r_C - r_B = w \times Er_A + (1 - w) \times r_f - Er_B$$

which must be equal to zero to prevent arbitrage, so that $w \times \left(Er_A - r_f\right) = \left(Er_B - r_f\right)$.

Using $w = \dfrac{\beta_B}{\beta_A}$ we get:

$$\frac{Er_A - r_f}{\beta_A} = \frac{Er_B - r_f}{\beta_B}$$

according to which the ratio of risk premium to beta must be the same for both assets in the absence of arbitrage. This is Ross's pricing equation of the APT.

Box 11.1 How do you exploit arbitrage when betas are different?

Question: Assume there are two diversified portfolios, A and B, with $\beta_A = 1.5, \beta_B = 0.75$. A's risk premium is 8%, B's risk premium is 5%, and the risk-free rate is zero. Is there an arbitrage opportunity? What should the expected return be from A to prevent arbitrage?

Answer: Let's create a portfolio C that invests 50 cents in portfolio A and 50 cents in the risk-free asset, with a return $r_C = 0.5 \times r_A + 0.5 \times r_f$. The multifactor equation describing the return of portfolio C is $r_C = 0.5 \times (Er_A + \beta_A F_1) + 0.5 \times r_f$. The return of the long-short portfolio that invests in C and shorts B is therefore equal to $r_{LS} = r_C - r_B = 0.5 \times (Er_A + 1.5 \times F_1) + 0.5 \times r_f - Er_B - 0.75 \times F_1 = 0.5 \times Er_A + 0.75 \times F_1 + 0.5 \times r_f - Er_B - 0.75 \times F_1 = 0.5 \times 0.08 - 0.05 = -0.01$. There is therefore the possibility of arbitrage consisting of selling Portfolio C and buying Portfolio B. To prevent arbitrage, it is necessary that $Er_A = \dfrac{0.05 \times 1.5}{0.75} = 10\%$.

Box 11.2 Does idiosyncratic volatility really make arbitrage impossible?

Question: Assume there are two diversified portfolios, A and B, with $\beta_A = 1.5, \beta_B = 0.75$. A's risk premium is 8%, B's risk premium is 2%, and the risk-free rate is zero. The stock is characterized by an idiosyncratic shock that can be +3% with probability 0.5 and -3% with probability 0.5. Is there an arbitrage opportunity? What should the expected return be from A to prevent arbitrage?

Answer: Let's create a portfolio C that invests 50 cents in portfolio A and 50 cents in the risk-free stock. The multifactor equation that describes the return of portfolio C is $r_C = 0.5 \times (Er_A + \beta_A F_1 + \varepsilon_A) + 0.5 \times r_f$. The return of the long-short portfolio that invests in C and shorts B is therefore equal to $r_{LS} = r_C - r_B = 0.5 \times (Er_A + 1.5 \times F_1 + \varepsilon_A) + 0.5 \times r_f - Er_B - 0.75 \times F_1 = 0.5 \times Er_A + 0.75 \times F_1 + 0.5 \times r_f + 0.5 \times \varepsilon_A - Er_B - 0.75 \times F_1$. The expected return is $0.5 \times 0.08 - 0.02 + 0.5 \times \varepsilon_A$. The positive expected return is not certain in this case because it is necessary to account for the realization of a negative idiosyncratic shock on A that would subtract 1.5% from the actual return. Even in the worst-case scenario, the total return is still positive at 0.5%, so arbitrage can be carried out. But if the absolute value of the idiosyncratic shock had been -5% instead of -3% in the negative scenario, the portfolio return would have been -0.5%, eliminating the possibility of arbitrage and simply leaving the possibility of assessing the interest in investing in a long-short portfolio with an expected return of 2% and an actual return in the two scenarios of -0.5% and 4.5%. Such risky arbitrage (see Chapter 13 for more information) may or may not be attractive depending on the risk aversion coefficient.

11.2.5 The APT pricing equation

Ross's model shows that to prevent arbitrage in equity markets where there is a single risk factor, the ratio of risk premium to beta must be the same for all securities. If this ratio denotes the equity market risk premium (EMRP), it follows that:

$$Er_i - r_f = \beta_i \times EMRP.$$

This results in a pricing equation generalizing the CAPM, because it does not use assumptions about investors' preferences. To prevent the existence of arbitrage possibilities, investors simply need to be characterized by a utility function positively related to wealth.

In general, the pricing equation with K risk factors is:

$$Er_i - r_f = \sum_{k=1}^{K} \beta_{i,k} rp^{(k)} \tag{2}$$

where $rp^{(k)}$ is the risk premium on a portfolio that is perfectly correlated with the K -th risk factor and has no correlation with the other risk factors (defined as a factor tracking portfolio). Equation (2), known as the pricing equation of the APT, generalizes the CAPM, which is a special case when the only factor presenting a non-diversifiable risk is the market. In the general case, equation (2) assigns to each diversified portfolio, through its betas, the premia for the exposure of the portfolio to the risk of all the non-diversifiable common risk factors.

Equation (2) represents a logic of linear decomposition of the risk premium: The K non-diversifiable factors each require a premium for incorporating in a portfolio a factor-tracking portfolio with perfect sensitivity to only one factor. A diversified portfolio with sensitivities $\beta_{i,1}, \beta_{i,2}, \ldots \beta_{i,K}$ warrants a premium equal to the product of each sensitivity times the risk premium on each factor.

For example, if, with risk premia on the two factors equal respectively to $rp^{(1)} = 8\%$ and $rp^{(1)} = 2\%$, a portfolio with a beta of respectively 1.5 and 0.5 will have a premium of 13% while a portfolio with a beta of -0.5 and 2 respectively will have a premium equal to 0. The second portfolio is less risky than the first portfolio due to a negative sensitivity to the riskier factor characterized by an 8% premium. A sensitivity of -0.5 relative to such a risky factor makes this portfolio a great hedge against bad realizations of such a risky common factor. The second portfolio does not have a risk premium as it is very sensitive to a factor that investors consider to be low risk and even negatively correlated with the riskier factor: In aggregate, the second stock is highly priced due to its portfolio stabilizing properties.

Substituting equation (2) into equation (1) gives an equation that considers both factor shocks and risk premia:

$$r_i = r_f + \sum\nolimits_{k=1}^{K} \beta_{i,k}\left(rp^{(k)} + F_{\mathrm{k}} \right) + \varepsilon_i$$

The return of the security therefore has an expected component given by the sum of the risk-free and the sum of the products of the beta sensitivities and the products, and an unexpected component given by the idiosyncratic shock and the sum of the products of the beta sensitivities and the shocks to non-diversifiable risk factors.

11.2.6 Pricing individual stocks

Technically speaking, the pricing equation only applies to diversified portfolios. We cannot use the argument to price two securities with idiosyncratic risk. To demonstrate this point, let us reconsider the two-asset case assuming we are discussing individual stocks rather than diversified portfolios and that these stocks have the same beta:

$$r_A = Er_A + \beta_1 F_1 + \varepsilon_A$$

$$r_B = Er_B + \beta_1 F_1 + \varepsilon_B$$

When we form the long-short portfolio we have:

$$r_{LS} = r_A - r_B = Er_A - Er_B + \beta_1 F_1 - \beta_1 F_1 + \varepsilon_A - \varepsilon_B$$

Differently from before, the rate of return of the long-short portfolio is not risk-free due to the presence of the idiosyncratic shocks. Building a long-short portfolio of two individual stocks (or portfolios that are not fully diversified) with different expected returns does not create an arbitrage opportunity even when the two sensitivities to the common factor are identical. Suppose, for example, $Er_A = 6\%$ and $Er_B = 5\%$, which would create an arbitrage opportunity without idiosyncratic shocks. Suppose, however, that in one specific scenario ε_A has a realization equal to -3% and ε_B takes a value of 1%. Overall, in such a scenario the right-hand side of the equation would be equal to 6% - 5% - 3% - 1% with a total equal to -3%. There would be no arbitrage, even in the case that this was the only scenario with a negative return.

The APT applies to large, diversified portfolios and is at best an approximation for individual stocks and small, undiversified portfolios. The arbitrage methodology works lacking idiosyncratic risk in the assets we are trying to price.

11.3 Factor identification

Application of the multifactor model requires making several empirical hypotheses about which the model is silent. Considering equations (1) and (2), we realize that we need to (a) make assumptions about the number of factors K, (b) estimate the factor shocks in order to apply (1), and (c) compute the factor premia to obtain the expected return. There are two ways to achieve these goals. The first is to start from an identification of the factors from plausible macroeconomic variables, and the second is to start from the results of the anomalies literature.

11.3.1 Macroeconomic factors

Initially (see Chen, Roll, and Ross, 1986) the identity of the factors was sought in the context of macroeconomic variables such as economic growth, inflation, consumption growth, interest rates, and oil prices. It makes sense to assume that such macroeconomic factors represent undiversifiable sources of risk to which stock markets should react. Informal evidence is consistent with this idea: when new, unexpected information about a macroeconomic variable hits the market (we have been talking about the example of the employment report) then prices react. If the intuition is extended to several macroeconomic variables, then we might hope to explain risk premia based on portfolios sensitivities to macroeconomic risk factors.

Chen, Roll, and Ross (1986) started from plausible macroeconomic variables, estimated the monthly shock through econometric models (nowadays the same result could be obtained more simply starting from time series of consensus expectations obtained from market surveys), and, in an application of the Fama–MacBeth methodology, estimated the betas from time series regressions and the premia from cross-sectional regressions. In the cross-section, the betas are the regressors and the coefficient multiplying the betas can be interpreted as risk premia, as was already pointed out in the discussion of the Fama–MacBeth methodology.

Unfortunately, the results were generally not satisfactory: Macroeconomic variables have a limited ability to explain risk premia in the stock market, see, for reference research in this field, Flannery and Protopapadakis (2002) finding some more convincing evidence but failing to find any impact of industrial production and gross national product.

Failing to provide a stable basis for the APT is not the same as saying that macroeconomic variables do not affect market prices. Boyd, Hu, and Jagannathan (2005), find that, on average, an announcement of rising unemployment is good news for stocks during economic expansions and bad news during economic contractions, depending on the relative importance of the relevance of the news on future interest rates and economic growth. During expansions, when central banks are trying to cool down the economy, a surprising increase in unemployment is good for stock prices as a signal of more relaxed future monetary policy.

Ai and Bansal (2018) document that macroeconomic variables announcements matter: Stock returns realized around pre-scheduled macroeconomic announcements, such as the employment report and the Federal Open Market Committee statements, account for 55% of the market equity premium. The average return on days with macroeconomic announcements is 11.2 basis points (BPS), which is significantly higher than the 1.27 BPS average return on non-announcement days. High-frequency-data-based evidence shows that much of this premium is realized within hourly windows around announcements, or within a few trading hours prior to the announcements.

11.3.2 Factor replicating portfolios

"Factor replicating portfolios," or "tracking portfolios," are portfolios that can be estimated to find a "financial equivalent" of a variable whose fluctuations presumably affect the assets purchased in the markets. In the spirit of the APT, if shocks to a factor are relevant determinants of returns, then a regression of the factor on asset returns should provide coefficients that can be interpreted as portfolio weights that can replicate the factor.

Suppose we consider a one-factor APT for portfolio p: $r_{p,t} = Er_p + \beta_1 F_{1,t} + \varepsilon_{p,t}$ and suppose we observe the time series of factor realizations $F_{1,t}$. We can then regress the time series of factor realizations on the time series of assets that are correlated with the factor $F_{1,t} = \alpha + \sum_{i=1}^{I} \beta_i r_{i,t} + \varepsilon_{i,t}$ where the β_i are the regression coefficients and I denotes the assets included in the regression. The product of the (rescaled) estimated coefficients and the asset returns $\sum_{i=1}^{I} \beta_i r_{i,t}$ can be interpreted as the time t return of a portfolio that has maximum correlation with the factor.

Lamont (2001) extends this methodology to track factors that have realizations several periods into the future, for example the level of a variable y_{t+k} realized in a future period $t + k$, also allowing for the possibility that there are predictability components in future factor realizations, see Technical Box 11.1.

Technical Box 11.1 Economic tracking portfolios

As usual, we can write the realization of a random variable as the sum of its expected value and the surprise, but this time we write the expectation for period $t+k$ as the sum of the expectation at the beginning of the month plus the change in expectations between t and $t+1$, namely $y_{t+k} = E_t y_{t+k} + \Delta E_{t+1} y_{t+k} + v_{t+k}$ where $\Delta E_{t+1} y_{t+k}$ indicates the change in the expectation of the future variable (to be known at time $t+k$) between t and $t+1$. Intuitively, the value of the variable at time $t+k$ can be thought of as the sum of an initial expectation, a revision in expectation, and a shock. If a predictive variable X_t may help predict the future value of the variable of interest, $y_{t+k} = f \times X_t + e_{t+k}$ and therefore $E_t y_{t+k} = f \times X_t$, it follows that $y_{t+k} = f \times X_t + \Delta E_{t+1} y_{t+k} + v_{t+k}$. Finally, if the change in expectations between t and $t+1$ is associated with asset returns, that is, $\Delta E_{t+1} y_{t+k} = a \times r_{t+1} + \eta_t$, then $y_{t+k} = f \times X_t + a \times r_{t+1} + \varepsilon_{t+k}$. The estimated coefficients a can be interpreted as portfolio weights and the product as a portfolio return $a \times r_{t+1}$ that is maximally correlated with news about the variable of interest. That is why these are called economic tracking portfolios.

11.3.3 The Fama–French model

From the early 1980s, researchers started to explore the possibility that the equity strategies described in Chapter 10 could be considered as proxies for risk factors. If the stock market is efficient, any portfolio that pays an average excess return over the long run must be characterized by a higher level of risk. If the risk is not associated with market risk, then the portfolio must be a proxy for risk factors other than market risk.

In this stream of literature, factors are identified with portfolio strategies giving rise to anomalies, such as portfolios sensitive to size and book-to-market. The identification of factors with portfolios opens the way to a much simpler application of the model: The average return of the portfolio is interpreted as the risk premium, and the demeaned time series of returns as monthly realizations of the shocks to the factors.

After careful review of the literature and considerable effort to eliminate redundant factors, Fama and French (1992, 1993) proposed the following three-factor model, which is entirely consistent with equation (2):

$$Er_i - r_f = \beta_{iM}(Er_M - r_f) + \beta_{iS} Er_{SMB} + \beta_{iV} Er_{HML}$$

where the risk premium of the individual security depends not only on the market premium (as in the CAPM) but also on its sensitivity β_{iS} to the size premium Er_{SMB} where SMB (small minus big) represents the return differential between the portfolio of smaller-cap securities and the portfolio of larger-cap stocks, and its sensitivity β_{iV} to the value premium Er_{HML} where HML (high minus low) is the differential between the portfolio of high book-to-market securities and the portfolio of low book-to-market securities (the latter are sometimes referred to as growth stocks).[2]

This model offers a new measurement of alpha: by regressing the return of a portfolio strategy on market, size, and value returns, one can measure alpha along with beta coefficients that measure risk for the strategy's sensitivity to systematic sources of risk. If one does not agree with the market efficiency hypothesis, then one can interpret Fama and French's model as a synthetic way to account for the most important anomalies in an atheoretical way. Of course, under the assumption of market efficiency, the model should capture the sources of systematic risk, and the risk premia of the various securities and portfolios should be explained without the presence of any alpha.

Box 11.3 The implications of Fama and French's model for the cost of capital

Question: Elena was tasked with calculating the cost of capital for LB bank using the market model (under the assumption that the risk-free rate is 1.5%) but also providing a robustness analysis with the Fama-French model.

Answer: Elena calculates two regressions that produce the following results (variables expressed as excess return):

$$r_i = 0.01 + 1.5 \times r_M + \varepsilon_i$$

$$r_i = 0.005 + 0.9 \times r_M - 0.5 \times r_{SMB} + 0.8 \times r_{HML} + \varepsilon_i .$$

She estimates the equity market risk premium at 5%, the size premium at 2%, and the value premium at 4%. She concludes that if you use the simple CAPM, the cost of capital is 10% (given by the sum of 8.5% and the risk-free rate), and if you use the Fama and French model you get 8,7% (given by the sum of 7.2% and the risk-free rate). The explanation for the lower cost of capital with the three-factor model is the lower estimation of alpha and market beta in the regression and the negative beta relative to the size factor.

The number of anomalies discovered by academic studies is very high. In addition to those already discussed, the most relevant are the following:

- profitability (the tendency of the most profitable companies to produce higher equity returns);
- asset growth (companies with higher asset growth have higher returns).

Fama and French (2004) present an analysis of the characteristics of IPOs in the United States that shows that since the 1980s (a) the number of companies that have turned to the stock market has greatly increased compared with the previous period, and (b) newly listed companies have a high rate of asset growth and low profita-

---

[2] The data necessary for the estimation of the model, together with many other data, including international data, on factor replication portfolios, are available at http://mba.tuck.dartmouth.edu/pages/faculty/ ken.french/data_library.html.

bility.[3] The pricing equation (five-factor Fama and French model) that takes into account these two additional elements is:[4]

$$Er_i = r_f + \beta_{i,M}(Er_m - r_f) + \beta_{i,SMB}E(r_{SMB}) + \beta_{i,HML}E(r_{HML}) + \beta_{i,RMW}E(r_{RMW}) + \beta_{i,CMA}E\left(r_{CMA}\right)$$

that is, it includes the RMW (robust minus weak operating profitability) and CMA (conservative minus aggressive investment) portfolio. For a portfolio formed in June of year t, profitability is measured by revenues minus operating costs, interest expense, and overhead, all divided by book value at the end of the prior year. Investment is the growth of total assets divided by assets at the end of the previous year.

11.4 Application of the Fama–French model

11.4.1 Liquidity risk

Fama and French's model has become the new benchmark for measuring the alpha generated by strategies. A great example can be found in liquidity risk analysis. In the traditional setting, the liquidity premium referred to the excess return associated with relatively low liquidity securities according to a range of dimensions such as the spread between bid and ask prices, number of transactions, and the like (see Amihud and Mendelson, 1986). Given that securities are characterized by a certain typical level of liquidity that is relatively stable over time, the theory and applications were not attributable to risk.

Pástor and Stambaugh (2003) broaden the scope to measure the premium payable for liquidity risk, a different concept from that of liquidity. From a risk perspective, liquidity is a random variable with some variance, and the investor who wants to buy or sell a security at a certain time may find herself in a situation where liquidity is higher or lower than expected. Typically stocks with a low average level of liquidity can be expected to be those with high liquidity risk, but in general, average liquidity and liquidity risk may not be perfectly correlated. It is plausible that risk-averse investors will therefore pay a lower price and seek a higher expected return for securities that have not only less liquidity but also higher liquidity risk.

Once you consider the presence of liquidity risk, you are faced with the question of how to measure it. Pástor and Stambaugh (2003) consider liquidity as an aggregate risk factor. For a given $i-th$ stock, the liquidity beta for the month is measured by the coefficient γ_{it} in a regression that uses daily data within the month:

---

[3] The evidence is therefore consistent with that presented in Chapter 1, which illustrates the reduction in the total number of listed companies in the United States, a country where the stock market plays a central role in the financing of new ventures, which are born and die to a much greater extent than in Europe. The investor in the American market therefore bears a high level of risk simply because of the characteristics of the companies that go on the list, characterized by high mortality.

[4] To intuitively explain why profitability and asset growth may be relevant, Fama and French (2015) refer to the stock value model illustrated in Chapter 12 (see section 12.5.2).

$$er_{i,d+1,t} = \theta_{it} + \phi_{it} er_{i,d,t} + \gamma_{it} sign(er_{i,d,t}) \times v_{i,d,t} + \varepsilon_{i,d+1,t}$$

where $er_{i,d+1,t} = r_i - r_f$ is the excess return of the day within the month, $d+1\ t$, $sign(er_{i,d,t})$ is the sign, positive or negative, of the previous day's excess return, and $v_{i,d,t}$ is the monetary value of transactions on the security. The intuition is as follows: If liquidity on the stock is low, you expect the return on a certain day to be offset the next day, especially if the previous day the return was driven by many transactions. The coefficient γ_{it}, representing the correlation between the previous day's volume of trading and the next day's return is therefore inversely linked to liquidity. If the variable considered in the regression was simply $v_{i,d,t}$ we would get confusing signals: A large volume of trading with an increasing price would be followed by a negative return, while a large volume of trading with a declining price would be followed by a positive return. As a result the estimated coefficient would be zero. That is why the model considers $sign(er_{i,d,t}) \times v_{i,d,t}$: When trading volume is large on a negative return day, the combined variable becomes negative and the observation contributes to measuring a negative γ_{it}.

Pástor and Stambaugh (2003) uses the liquidity estimate obtained for each security to calculate the average between securities in each month, γ_{it}, and then estimate the market liquidity shock each month by means of the regression residue $\Delta\gamma_t = a + b\Delta\gamma_{t-1} + L_t$. The sensitivity of the return of the individual security to aggregate liquidity shocks is obtained from the estimation of the coefficient β_{iL} in:[5]

$$Er_i - r_f = \alpha_i + \beta_{iL} L + \beta_{iM}(Er_M - r_f) + \beta_{iS} Er_{SML} + \beta_{iV} Er_{HML}$$

In the previous regression, L is a risk factor obtained from an econometric estimate and not from market prices. It is therefore a "non-traded factor." The traded factor equivalent to the non-traded factor can be calculated as above by forming portfolios of securities based on estimated liquidity betas and then measuring their return over each period. Estimates of the reward for liquidity risk based on this methodology are around 4% (see also Pástor and Stambaugh, 2019; Li, Novy-Marx, and Velikov, 2019).

Subsequent analyses have shown that liquidity risk is also relevant in other asset classes such as hedge funds (Sadka, 2010), private equity (Franzoni, Nowak, and Phalippou, 2012), emerging markets (Bekaert, Harvey, and Lundblad, 2007), and corporate bonds (Bongaerts, de Jong, and Driessen, 2017).

11.4.2 Pricing in international markets

In moving from the capital allocation line to the capital market line, that is, in identifying the tangency portfolio with the market portfolio, we simply referred to the stock market index of the market as a whole, without asking ourselves questions

[5] The equation is an application of the Fama French model where we control for the three risk factors and verificy whether liquidity is relevant.

about the geographical extent of the reference market. However, the correct identification of the relevant market portfolio is of utmost importance, especially in markets that are becoming increasingly global. If investors think globally, they have an incentive to hold all the stocks offered in the market around the world, as any exclusion would only increase diversifiable risk. So what is the correct pricing model for a stock in a global market? The simplest answer is to consider a global market index, such as the MSCI All Country Index, as a benchmark for regression.

The presence of additional risk factors that cannot be diversified suggests that Fama and French factors calculated on a local market should also be included in the regression. Fama and French (2012) present such an international model and conclude that the best ability to explain returns in international markets is obtained from an intermediate model that incorporates locally defined risk factors (that is, for areas such as North America, Europe, Japan, and Asia) rather than global ones. Fama and French (2017) also confirm the results in the context of the five-factor model.

Box 11.4 The Italian stock market during Covid-19

Question: A pension fund asks Elena to understand whether the equity performance of the Italian market during the market downturn caused by Covid-19 was excessive and whether the subsequent recovery was also too large.

Answer: Elena starts from the data and observes that in the worst phase of the fall of international markets, from February 20 to March 23, 2020, the Italian market lost an average of 1.96% per day. To assess whether the loss was excessive compared with the typical market trend, she calculates a regression (with daily data for the year 2019) of the excess return of the Italian equity market on the excess return of the MSCI All Country Index, finding a slope of 1.02 and an alpha of −0.026%. Using the fall of the world market in the period considered, equal to 1.69% per day, she finds an anomalous return of $-1.96\% + 0.026\% - 1.02 \times (-1.69\%) = -0.21\%$. She concludes that the stock market's performance was worse than that associated with the normal relationship with the performance of international markets. She also estimates a three-factor Fama and French model using global factor return estimates on Professor Kenneth French's website and finds $\beta_{i,M} = 0.153$, $\beta_{i,SMB} = 0.399$, $\beta_{i,HML} = 0.113$, with an alpha equal to 0.038%. Using these estimates and the performance of the three factors over the period considered (-1.576%, -0.171%, and -0.433% respectively), she finds an anomalous return of -1.644%, even worse than the previous one. The average daily return in the period from March 24 to December 31, 2020, equal to 0.251%, becomes equal to -0.002% and 0.156% when calculated in terms of anomalous return compared with the global index model and the global model of Fama and French. On the day the discovery of the vaccine was announced, November 9, 2020, the Italian stock index jumped 4.97%. The calculation of the anomalous returns with the international index model and the global model of Fama and French leads to 3.664% and 5%, respectively.

11.5 Performance evaluation

Some introductory remarks are useful to introduce performance evaluation and to understand the relevance of the Fama–French model for the applications.

11.5.1 Introduction to performance evaluation

Performance evaluation is very important in finance. The problem, implicit in different sections of the book, is to evaluate the average return offered by an asset manager in the context of an agency problem: The asset owner in general does not know the asset manager caring for her money and, observing only a little bit of information such as the periodic return, needs to understand whether the after-cost return is large enough to compensate for the risk associated with the investment style.

The simplest indicator of performance evaluation is the Sharpe ratio, which was introduced in Chapter 7 as the slope of the capital allocation line, that is, the ratio between the excess return and total volatility. The Sharpe ratio is very simple but has two drawbacks. First, it is not theoretically appropriate when volatility is not the right measure for risk. We know that the right quantity of risk for an asset or a portfolio is provided by the beta and not by the volatility, which is a better measure for the risk of a whole asset class or for the risk of overall wealth of an investor. Second, it is hard to carry out statistical inference on the Sharpe ratio, being the ratio of two random variables that in general is not normally distributed.

11.5.2 The index model and the CAPM

Jensen (1968) showed how to interpret the index model for the purpose of performance evaluation.[6] We have already seen how the index model can be used to analyze the ability of CAPM to explain the average return of individual stocks and portfolios. When the model is applied to the explanation of a portfolio's return, the well-known term regression can be used as an indicator of the manager's excess/lack of performance relative to the market:

$$r_{i,t} - r_{f,t} = \alpha_i + \beta_{i,M}(r_{m,t} - r_{f,t}) + \varepsilon_{i,t}$$

In the performance evaluation, the intercept is referred to as "Jensen's alpha." The manager who produces positive (and statistically significant) alpha ensures that their investors receive an average return that is higher than what would be needed to compensate for market risk.

How can a manager produce a positive alpha? There are two basic sources of alpha: stock picking and market timing. Stock picking means building a portfolio de-

[6] Elton and Gruber (2020) offer a recent review from the point of view of the use of the models discussed here in an applied capacity.

viating from the composition of the market. Market timing means varying over time the exposure of the portfolio to the market.

The performance evaluation literature has further generalized the model to estimate the manager's ability to anticipate market trends (market timing) separately from the ability to select stocks with positive alpha (stock picking). Pure stock picking can be measured by Jensen's alpha, but market timing poses a challenge. Any decrease in the exposure of the portfolio to the market means a lower beta, and the contrary happens when exposure increases. As a result, active market timing amounts to time-varying betas, a scenario that is not consistent with the standard regression model.

The ability to modify market exposure before the rise and fall phases can be captured by including a quadratic term in the market return:[7]

$$r_p - r_f = \alpha_i + \beta_{pM}(r_M - r_f) + \gamma\left(r_M - r_f\right)^2 + \varepsilon_p$$

The significance of the coefficient $\gamma > 0$ indicates the ability to carry out market timing, that is, to increase exposure to the market in phases of positive return and reduce it in phases of negative return. In this context, the intercept can be interpreted purely as an indicator of stock picking.

11.5.3 Performance evaluation and the Fama–French model

The presence of anomalies could not fail to influence the methodology for evaluating performance: A manager using the "size" effect, for example, could be able to produce an excess return simply by holding a portfolio that is more exposed than the market portfolio to small-cap stocks. The interpretation of this excess return depends on the assumption about the efficiency of the market: If the "size" factor is thought to be an expression of a systematic risk factor, then the manager's performance should not be rewarded since the increase in return is associated with the increase in systematic risk. If, however, the "size" factor represents a management strategy capable of producing high average returns without particular risk, then the manager's performance has nevertheless achieved a return in excess of the systematic risk incurred. This observation also explains how alpha may simply reflect the failure to include one or more risk factors in the regression. For example, let's say that the model that describes the manager's performance is:

$$Er_p - r_f = \beta_{pM}\left(Er_M - r_f\right) + \beta_{pS}Er_{SMB}$$

but that the performance analysis is carried out based on the simple index model. In this case the measured alpha is interpretable as $\alpha_p = \beta_{pS}Er_{SMB}$. In other words, what

[7] A similar result can be obtained by inserting a term reminiscent of a call option, that is, where the last regressor is zero, or equal to the market return if the latter is positive $r_p - r_f = \alpha_i + \beta_{pM}(r_M - r_f) + \gamma\max\left(0, r_M - r_f\right) + \varepsilon_p$. The two approaches are based on Treynor and Mazuy (1966) and Henriksson (1984).

appears to be overperformance from the point of view of the index model is simply exposure to the risk factor.

The Fama–French model is therefore useful for assessing the performance of asset managers to identify which asset manager is able to produce an average return above the market risk associated with it, that is, which manager is able to produce alpha. The application of the three-factor Fama–French model to evaluate the risk-adjusted performance of a portfolio relies on the standard time series regression model:

$$r_{i,t} - r_{f,t} = \alpha_i + \beta_{i,M}(r_{m,t} - r_{f,t}) + \beta_{i,SMB} r_{SMB,t} + \beta_{i,HML} r_{HML,t} + \varepsilon_{i,t}$$

which may be used to jointly estimate the sensitivities to the risk factors and the α_i.

When applying performance evaluation models, it is therefore necessary to interpret the results in light of one's own convictions about the efficiency of the market and, above all, in light of one's knowledge of the management strategy and the objectives that one sets for oneself by including the manager in one's portfolio. From the latter point of view, one of the advantages of Jensen's alpha is precisely that it takes into account the beta with respect to the market index, or the reference portfolio, an element that is completely ignored when performance is evaluated using the Sharpe ratio, which neglects the structure of the rest of the investor's portfolio. The additional advantage of Jensen's alpha over the Sharpe ratio is the ease of making statistical inferences, which can be obtained by calculating the t-test for regression interception.

Box 11.5 Skill or systematic risk?

Question: A pension fund asks Sara to evaluate the performance of an equity fund that has had an excess return of 6% over the past year, compared with a market excess return of 4%.

Answer: Sara estimates the beta of the fund and finds a value of 1.2. The CAPM would therefore suggest that a fair reward for the risk taken would be 4.8%. The fund's alpha therefore appears to be 1.2%. To subject the results to robustness analysis, Sara also estimates a regression of the fund's excess return on the market excess return and size factor, finding $\beta_M = 1$ and $\beta_{SMB} = 0.5$. Knowing that the SMB portfolio delivered a 5% performance over the reporting period, she estimates an alpha from the two-factor model of $6\% - 1 \times 4\% - 0.5 \times 5\% = -0.5\%$ concluding that the alpha produced by the manager in the context of the market portfolio actually hides exposure to small companies, which has not been sufficiently rewarded.

11.5.4 Evidence

The literature on mutual fund performance is very extensive and impossible to summarize comprehensively in a few pages. It shows that funds on average have a gross alpha generation capacity, but not net of costs. For example, Gruber (1996) finds that on average funds achieved lower returns than market indices by 0.65% per year in 1985–1994, and Carhart (1997) shows that net returns are inversely correlated with costs and alpha is inversely related to turnover. Wermers (2002) uses fund portfolio data and shows that on average funds hold securities with an alpha of 1.35% per year, but the alpha after costs is -2.3% due to management and trading costs (1.6%).

Alpha is difficult to find not only when the comparison is made with market indices, but also when the comparison is with other managed portfolios. Elton, Gruber, and de Souza (2019) study the differential between mutual fund and ETF returns, using a dynamic model in which each year the fund's return is compared with the return of the ETF portfolio that best approximates the fund's past history, and find that ETF portfolios perform better than fund portfolios 77% of the time if you ignore the costs and 90% of the time if you deduct the costs.

The result applies to the average and not to all managers. Fama and French (2010) analyze the cross-section of managers' alphas using simulations to distinguish the skills and luck of managers with higher returns and argue that only a small minority of managers produce value through talent. Kacperczyk, Nieuwerburgh, and Veldkamp (2014) find more favorable results for the ability of funds to create alpha (25% of the managers in the sample) by analyzing the expansion and recession phases separately, showing that stock picking is prevalent in expansionary phases and market timing in recessionary phases, but that, by exploiting data on portfolio composition, it is possible to identify the best managers, which have both market timing and stock picking capabilities.

Alpha is hard to come by in the long run, but some favorable evidence exists in the short run. Typically, we are looking for alpha persistence, that is, the possibility that the alpha of a certain period predicts the alpha of the next period. Carhart (1997) shows that there is temporal persistence in returns but not in alpha when this is calculated using a multifactor model that includes momentum. Bollen and Busse (2004) highlight the presence of persistence in alpha at the quarterly level: Funds belonging to the group of the top 10% of managers in a given quarter have an abnormal return of 25–39 basis points in the following quarter.

To produce alpha, active management must be carried out as a necessary condition. Cremers and Petajisto (2009) introduce the active share (AS), which is the sum of the absolute values of the differences between the shares invested in the various securities in the portfolio and the shares of the same securities in the reference benchmark. The paper shows that AS predicts alpha before and after management costs and to identify persistence in performance. The worst funds are characterized by low AS and low tracking error (volatility of the differential between the fund's return and the benchmark's return). If they present themselves to investors as active funds, they are referred to as "false assets" or "closet indexers." Amihud and Goyenco (2013) instead use the coefficient R^2 obtained from the regression of the return on multifactor models as a predictive variable and show that a long-short portfolio of mutual funds classified on the basis of the indicator R^2 produces an annualized alpha of 3.8%.

The evidence that they can deliver performance when they are needed most, that is, in recessions, is more supportive of asset managers. Moskowitz (2000) shows that the returns of active funds in 1975–1994 in recessions are higher by an average of 6%, a figure similar to that reported by Kosowski (2011) (3–5% annually in 1962–2005). Kacperczyk, van Nieuwerburgh, and Veldkamp (2014) find higher alphas in recessions of 1.6–4.6% annually in 1980–2005. In contrast, Pástor and Vorsatz (2020) find that funds produced below-market returns during the Covid-19 crisis, even though this is a peculiar episode from the point of view of market intensity and reaction.

Berk and Green (2004) provide a rationalization of several results highlighted by the performance evaluation literature based on assuming competitive markets, rational investors, and decreasing returns to assets under management. In the model investors observe past performance and use it rationally to infer the existence of superior management ability. New money flows to the fund to the point at which expected excess returns going forward are competitive. Asset management skill is rewarded through higher fees, and the associated increase in assets under management for the best funds is the cause of reduction in future performance.

Summary

- CAPM can be interpreted as a factor model with a single risk factor, namely the market. Steve Ross's Arbitrage Pricing Theory (APT) is based on two pillars: (a) a multifactorial model (an equation that describes return generation) and (b) the assumption that there is no arbitrage in the markets (a pricing equation).
- In the multifactorial equation, the unexpected components are the sum of shocks to sources of macroeconomic risk and sources of specific risk, where the terms F are the surprises to macroeconomic risk factors.
- The pricing equation aims to determine the expected return required by risk-averse investors acting in a market where there are no arbitrage possibilities.
- Arbitrage is the ability to create a portfolio without any monetary investment but capable of offering a probability of positive return in the future.
- The presence of arbitrage opportunities triggers capital flows that then impact prices and returns, until the opportunity ceases to be an opportunity.
- Fama and French's three-factor model and five-factor model use strategies to define portfolios that are interpreted as non-diversifiable risk factors that contribute to the measurement of risk premia for individual securities.
- Fama and French's model has many applications, including establishing an empirical basis for researching new risk factors, such as liquidity, the relevance of local and global factors to pricing in global markets, and performance evaluation.

Problems

1 Consider a one-factor return model $r_i - r_f = \beta_i(r_m - r_f) + \varepsilon_i$. Three stocks are described by:

Stock	β_i	$Er_i - r_f$	σ_{ei}
A	0.8	6%	25%
B	1	9%	10%
C	1.2	10%	20%

a. Compute the variance of the returns of the three stocks knowing that market volatility is equal to 20%.
b. What is the variance of a portfolio composed of a large number of uncorrelated stocks with the same parameters as stock A?
c. Are there any arbitrage opportunities?

2 Consider the following data for diversified portfolios in a one-factor (market) model when the risk-free is 6%:

Portfolio	Er	β
A	12%	1.2
E	8%	0.6

Is there an arbitrage opportunity?

3 How does the answer to the previous question change if A is a stock (rather than a portfolio) characterized by the presence of an idiosyncratic shock that may take on values +4% and -4% with equal probabilities?

4 Consider the following data:

Portfolio	β_1	β_2	Expected returns
A	1.5	2.0	15%
B	2.2	-0.2	6%

The risk-free rate is 6%. What is the pricing equation?

5 A portfolio is characterized by the following data:

Factor	Beta	Risk premium	Expected value	Realization
Inflation	1.2	6%	4%	5%
Production	0.5	8%	6%	3%
Oil	0.3	3%	0%	2%

What is the expected return of the portfolio if the risk-free is equal to 1%? What is the ex post return?

Answers

1 a. The variance of A is $0.8^2 \times 0.04 + 0.25^2$; a similar computation applies for B and C.
b. A portfolio with many uncorrelated stocks all equal to A has a variance equal to $0.8^2 \times 0.04$. Idiosyncratic risk disappears in such a large portfolio.
c. There is an arbitrage opportunity because a portfolio equally invested in stocks A and C has an 8% expected return, lower than B, but the same beta coefficient. The arbitrage consists of short-selling the equally weighted portfolio and buying B.

2 An equally balanced portfolio of A and the risk-free has an expected return of 9% and beta equal to 0.6. It is possible to short-sell portfolio E to buy the equally weighted portfolio.

3 The arbitrage portfolio in the previous answer sells E and buys the equally weighted portfolio. Now, if A is a single stock rather than a diversified portfolio, even assuming the pricing relation applies without error to the stock, we need to consider whether the arbitrage portfolio return is non-negative in the two scenarios defined by the realization of the idiosyncratic shock. When the idiosyncratic shock is equal to +4%, the ex post return of the arbitrage portfolio is equal to 1% (the return differential between the equally weighted portfolio and E) plus 2% (considering that stock A is given weight 50% in the arbitrage portfolio). However, when the idiosyncratic shock takes on the value -4%, then the total return is 1% – 2% = -1. This is not an arbitrage portfolio anymore: We have found one scenario where the arbitrage portfolio has a negative return. If the idiosyncratic shocks had realization +2% and -2% in the two scenarios, then the returns of the arbitrage portfolio would be 1.5% and 0% and this would again be an arbitrage portfolio. The presence of idiosyncratic risk per se does not affect the identification of an arbitrage portfolio as we have first to verify the existence of non-negative returns in each scenario.

4 The two stocks are characterized by $15\% = 6\% + 1.5 \times pr_1 + 2 \times pr_2$ and $6\% = 6\% + 2.2 \times pr_1 - 0.2 \times pr_2$, two equations that provide the risk premia equal to $pr_1 = 0.4\%$ and $pr_2 = 4.2\%$. The pricing equation for any diversified portfolio is therefore $Er_p = 0.06 + \beta_{p1} \times 0.004 + \beta_{p2} \times 0.042$.

5 The expected return is $0.01 + 1.2 \times 0.06 + 0.5 \times 0.08 + 0.3 \times 0.03 = 0.131$. The actual return differs from 13.1% due to the surprises to the factors, which have the following impact on the portfolio: $1.2 \times (0.05 - 0.04) + 0.5 \times (0.03 - 0.06) + 0.3 \times 0.02 = 1.1\%$. The actual return is 13.4%.

12 Prices and values

12.1 Introduction

This chapter introduces fundamentals-based stock valuation models. However, it is important to state that the general valuation scheme described here applies to all assets, since valuation always involves the present value of fundamentals. In what follows, we will refer to "value" to indicate the amount of money that is appropriate to pay for the purchase of a stock based on fundamental estimates, without any reference to the potential existence of synergies for the buyer. The difference between price and value, albeit potentially confusing, is useful to discuss situations when prices may deviate from values, an issue that will be considered in Chapter 13 on market efficiency.

The discussion starts from the definition of a stock's return as the sum of dividend yield and capital gain and identifies the fundamentals in dividends, risk-free interest rates, and risk premia. In the most general version, the fundamental valuation horizon is equal to the entire future life of the company. To make the model more applicable, one can assume that the variables grow forever at a constant rate or are fixed, which produces Gordon's model, or identify periods of differentiated growth. In the case of companies that are not in a situation of equilibrium, either because they are able to produce strong earnings growth rates, because they are start-ups and do not yet have a well-defined structure, or because on the contrary they are going through a restructuring phase, it is not possible to assume a constant dividend growth rate. In these cases, a multi-phase model is used, where each phase allows different assumptions about the dynamics of cash flow growth, considering that the long-term growth rate can be determined by the choices regarding the use of profits for reinvestment and dividend payments. An application to Microsoft is used to have a practical view of the application of the various possible approaches.

In the final part, we focus on the relationship between market price and theoretical value, discussing the presence of a speculative bubble as an example of divergence between price and value. We also show how the model can be applied to the analysis of the relationship between price and earnings, even at an aggregate level, to have an indicator of potential over/undervaluation. Finally, it should be noted that the fundamentals-based model is also useful for understanding the determination of unexpected returns, which are explained by the new information received on fundamentals.

12.2 Valuation and infinite horizon

12.2.1 Value with a one-period horizon

In Chapter 2, when introducing unconditional expectations, we noticed that we can think of the price of a stock as the expectation of future prices and cash flows, discounted at a rate incorporating the risk-free rate and the expected return. We have discussed risk aversion and the willingness on the part of risk-averse investors to buy a risky asset only if the expected returns provide a compensation for risk. We introduced the idea of a risk premium $rp_t = E_t\left(r_{t+1} - r_{ft}\right)$ exactly to describe the extra return that an investor may expect to gain by buying the asset. The risk premium can also be defined in unconditional terms as $rp = E\left(r_{t+1} - r_{ft}\right)$. By solving the last equation for the expected return and substituting into the equation for the price, and using the notation V_t to stress the focus on value rather than price, we get:

$$V_t = \frac{\left(E_t V_{t+1} + E_t D_{t+1}\right)}{1 + rp + r_f}$$

If the risk premium is provided by the CAPM we get:

$$V_t = \frac{\left(E_t V_{t+1} + E_t D_{t+1}\right)}{1 + \beta_i\left(Er_M - r_f\right) + r_f}$$

We observe that any assumption about the risk premium has an impact, given expectations about cash flows and future values, on current value, and vice versa. The CAPM is an example of a "pricing model" because it helps determine the price of the asset through the hypothesis about the risk premium.

Box 12.1 How much to pay for a stock

Question: Carola and Sara predict that the Belcasael stock will pay a dividend of €6 next year, and they both predict that the price of the stock will be €100 in a year's time. The risk-free rate is zero. However, they do not agree with today's valuation of the stock. Carola wants to include the stock in a small amount in her portfolio, currently invested in the market, while Sara intends to invest in that stock with the purpose of achieving a target Sharpe ratio of 0.5. Carola estimates the beta of the stock at 1.2 and assesses the equity market risk premium at 5%. Sara estimates the stock's volatility at 40%. What price are they willing to pay?

Answer: the divergence is motivated by the expected return of the stock, which in turn is linked to the different risk calculation models. Carola calculates an expected return of 6% and is therefore willing to pay $\frac{106}{1{,}06} = 100$. Sara wants a return of $0.4 \times 0.5 = 20\%$ and is therefore willing to pay $\frac{106}{1.2} = 88.3$.

12.2.2 Value with an infinite horizon

The relationship in section 12.2.1 appears to be "circular," since today's value is explained based on the expectation of tomorrow's value. But what determines the expectation of value at time t+1? For consistency's sake, we can think that it will depend on the expectations of value and dividends at time t+2, namely:

$$V_{t+1} = \frac{E_{t+1}\left(V_{t+2} + D_{t+2}\right)}{1 + r_{t+1}}$$

It can be seen from the comparison of the two formulas that today's value depends on the expectation of tomorrow's value and dividend, and that tomorrow's value depends on the expectations of the next period's value and dividend, in an endless chain that links today's value to the expected dividends for the future. Continuing to reason in this way, we arrive at a formula that explains the value at time t as the present discounted value of all future dividends up to the period $t + T$:

$$V_t = E_t\left[D_{t+1} \times R_{t,t} + D_{t+2} \times R_{t,t+1} + \ldots + \left(D_{t+T} + V_{t+T}\right) \times R_{t,T}\right]$$

where $R_{t,T} = \frac{1}{\left(1 + r_t\right)\left(1 + r_{t+1}\right)\ldots\left(1 + r_{t+T}\right)}$ is the dividend discount factor applying at each time period and where we have used a statistical result (the law of iterated expectations) according to which for a random variable X_{t+2}, $E_t E_{t+1} X_{t+2} = E_t X_{t+2}$, that is, today's conditional expectation of tomorrow's conditional expectation is equal to today's expectation. As the conditional expectation is computed based on the information set at each point in time, it is intuitive that today we form our expectation of tomorrow's expectation using today's information set. Continuing to substitute forward recursively, one can arrive at the formula with an infinite horizon:

$$V_t = E_t\left[D_{t+1} \times R_{t,t} + D_{t+2} \times R_{t,t+1} + D_{t+3} \times R_{t,t+2} + \ldots\right] \quad (1)$$

where we have used the transversality condition $lim_{T\to\infty} E_t V_{t+T} \times R_{t,T} = 0$, stating that the present discounted value of the asset's expected price at an infinitely distant moment in time is zero: Any expected long-term growth in value must be weaker than the discount factor.

According to equation (1),[1] the value is high if dividend expectations are high and if discount rates are low, that is, if the risk-free rate and risk premium are low. A higher risk is associated with a lower price level because the shareholder intends to have a higher remuneration as a reward for holding the asset. The formula does not imply that future capital gains will not have an impact on today's value. On the contrary, future capital gains are themselves a function of dividends.

---

[1] For readers with mathematical interests, the methodology used to find the value-determining formula is equivalent to the forward solution of a first-order difference equation.

12.3 Gordon's model

12.3.1 Simplifying assumptions

Equation (1) seems hard to apply in practice. If the discount rate is constant over time, (1) becomes:

$$V_t = E_t\left[\frac{D_{t+1}}{(1+r)} + \frac{D_{t+2}}{(1+r)^2} + \frac{D_{t+3}}{(1+r)^3} + \dots\right]$$

If we add another assumption, this time related to the expected growth rate of dividends equal to g, the formula is further simplified (the term in parentheses is a geometric progression that grows at the rate of $\frac{(1+g)}{(1+r)}$) to get Gordon's equation:[2]

$$V_t = \left[\frac{(1+g)D_t}{(1+r)} + \frac{(1+g)^2 D_t}{(1+r)^2} + \frac{(1+g)^3 D_t}{(1+r)^3} + \dots\right] = \frac{(1+g)D_t}{r-g}$$

Gordon's equation shows that the value is equal to the expected future dividend divided by the differential between the required return on the stock and the growth rate. The equation implies that small changes in dividend expectations have a major impact on value estimation, given that if $r = 6\%$ and $g = 4\%$ and the expected dividend is equal to 1, you get a value of 50. However,

- an expected dividend increase to 1.05 implies an increase in value to 55;
- an increase in the expected return to 6.5% implies a reduction in value to 40.

The model is very simple, but it cannot be applied in some cases, for example in the case of companies with a high growth rate that will fall in the long run.

Box 12.2 How do you apply Gordon's model?

Question: Elena is an analyst, and a fund manager asks her to determine, with the simplest possible assumptions, the value of a stock whose last dividend paid was equal to 5, when the long-term growth rate is 2%, the risk-free is 4%, the beta is equal to 1.5, and the market risk premium is 4%.

Answer: Elena uses the CAPM to estimate the expected return and then uses the Gordon formula to find a value $V_t = \frac{(1+0.02)\times 5}{0.04+0.06-0.02} = 63.75$.

[2] Notice that the expectation operator disappears because we use the geometric growth assumption for dividends to compute the conditional expectation $E_t D_{t+i} = (1+g)^i \times D_t$.

Box 12.3 Do analysts use Gordon's model to estimate the consensus price forecast?

Question: Analysts expect Microsoft Corporation's stock price to be \$142.31 a year from now. The current price stands at \$129.77 and there is an expectation of a one-year dividend payout of \$1.819 per share. Given the following information: beta (calculated with monthly data over a five-year horizon) 1.23, risk-free rate 2.7%, expected return from the market index 8.3% (EMRP equal to 5.6%), what is the value of the stock to date (V_0)?

Answer: The CAPM expected return is $2.7\% + 1.23 \times 5.6\% = 9.6\%$. Using the consensus forecast of the future price, we find the current value at time 0 from $V_0 = E_0\left(\frac{P_1 + D_1}{1 + r_t}\right) = \frac{142.3 + 1.819}{1 + 9.6\%} = 131.51$. Alternatively, assuming that the dividend growth rate is 6%, we get $V_0 = E_t\left(\frac{D_1}{r_t - g}\right) = \frac{1.819}{9.6\% - 6\%} = 50.5$. The two models give different results. The expected price in a year's time implicit in Gordon's model is $(1 + r_{t+1})\, V_t - E_t D_{t+1} = 1.096 \times 50.5 - 1.81$ $9 = 53.529$. Moreover, in the case of a stock with a high and constant growth rate, it may be restrictive to assume that the growth rate is lower than the historically observed rate. Under these conditions, the discrepancy between the price and value derived from Gordon's model is consistent with the low applicability of the model to the case at hand.

12.3.2 Growth and earnings reinvestment

Gordon's model illustrates the positive relationship between dividend growth and value. But is it always true that by increasing the dividend a company can also increase the value of its stock? In the long run, how can the company grow dividends? Presumably, based on elements related to the company's ability to increase its assets and use them to produce profits. One way to increase assets is to reinvest profits instead of paying them in the form of dividends: The dividend growth rate can be broken down into the product of the return on equity (ROE) and the rate of reinvestment of earnings, the so-called plowback ratio b equal to one minus the dividend payout ratio, that is, the share of profits paid as remuneration to shareholders in the form of dividends:[3]

$$g = ROE \times b \tag{2}$$

Equation (2) highlights that the company can increase future dividend growth with greater reinvestment of earnings, thus paying fewer dividends today. Is it possible to reduce today's dividends and simultaneously increase the stock price? Yes, and that

[3] The proof starts from the observation that if the ROE is fixed (as in the assumptions of Gordon's model) then all variables, including dividends D, earnings U, and the book value B of the company, grow at the same rate. Therefore, $g = \frac{U - D}{B} = \frac{U - D}{U} \times \frac{U}{B} = b \times \text{ROE}$.

happens when the ROE is higher than the cost of capital. In this case, the company can reinvest profits instead of distributing them as dividends, thus serving the interest of shareholders, who are happy to know that a company with a high ROE decides to reinvest profits instead of distributing them.

Box 12.4 Can the company pay lower dividends and increase value?

Question: A company has a ROE of 15% and has produced earnings per share of €5. During the conference call following the shareholder meeting to take place next week, the CEO wants to offer the market a high level of dividend because she wants to increase the value of the shares, whose price has long been around €45, with a generous remuneration to shareholders. She then consults with Sara, the Chief Financial Officer, about the dividend proposal to be made to the Board of Directors that will then have to be communicated to the market and asks her if a dividend per share of €5 could be well received by the market. What will Sara say?

Answer: Sara believes that the expected rate of return required by the market for holding the company's shares is 12.5%. She estimates that the fair value of the stock should be equal to the sum of the dividend to be paid next week, equal to €5, and the present discounted value of dividends paid from next year on. She uses Gordon's model and estimates that a dividend per share of €5, corresponding to a payout ratio of 100%, can be associated with a share price equal to €$\left(5 + \frac{5}{0.125 - 0}\right)$ = €45, consistent with the recent performance of the stock. Sara suggests to the CEO that it is instead appropriate to signal to the market that the company's ROE is high and will remain high in the future, higher than the cost of capital. She therefore assumes a payout ratio of 40%, corresponding to a dividend of €2 instead of €5, and a long-term growth of $g = ROE \times b = 0.15 \times 0.6 = 9\%$. Applying Gordon's model again, she estimates that the stock price could rise to $2 + \frac{2 \times 1.09}{0.125 - 0.09} = 59.14$. Had ROE been equal to 5% then the 40% payout ratio would produce $g = ROE \times b = 0.05 \times 0.6 = 3\%$ and the Gordon model implied price would be $2 + \frac{2 \times 1.03}{0.125 - 0.03} = 23.68$ much lower than the current price due to the decision to invest in a business characterized by a low ROE.

Box 12.5 Can the level of the dividend be irrelevant to the share price?

Question: A company has a ROE of 12.5% and expects to have earnings per share of €5. The CEO wants to offer the market a high level of dividend because she wants to increase the value of the shares, whose price has long been around €45, with a generous remuneration to shareholders. She then consults with Sara, the Chief Financial Officer, about the dividend proposal to be made to the Board of Directors that will then have to be communicated to the market and asks her if a dividend per share of €5 could be well received by the market. What will Sara say?

Answer: Sara believes that the expected rate of return required by the market for holding the company's shares is 12.5%. She uses Gordon's model and estimates that a dividend per share of €5, corresponding to a payout ratio of 100%, can be associated with a share price of €$\left(5 + \frac{5}{0.125 - 0}\right)$ = €45, therefore consistent with the recent performance of the stock. Sara suggests to the CEO that under these conditions, the announcement of the dividend and payout policy is not able to change the valuation of the company by the market. In fact, even if it were decided to immediately distribute €2 and announce that in the future the dividend will be equal to only 40% of the profit, the growth rate would be equal to $g = ROE \times b = 0.125 \times 0.6 = 7.5\%$. Applying Gordon's model again, she estimates that the stock price would be $€\left(2 + \frac{2 \times 1.075}{0{,}125 - 0{,}075}\right) = €45$ without any price increase.

12.3.3 How much are growth opportunities worth?

We have seen that a company whose profitability is above the cost of capital can reinvest profits instead of distributing them as dividends, thus serving the best interests of shareholders.

What portion of value depends on growth opportunities? Value in the absence of growth ($g = 0$ is associated with a policy of total distribution of profits to shareholders) is equal to the ratio between profits (which are equivalent to dividends in these conditions) and the expected return. The difference between the total value of the company and the value in the absence of growth is referred to as the present value of growth opportunities (PVGO):

$$V_t = \frac{E(U_{t+1})}{r} + PVGO \tag{3}$$

where U_{t+1} is next period earnings. This allows you to better interpret the market's reactions to announcements of a change in dividend policy: A dividend cut can be associated with an increase in the share price if investors are convinced that it will help future dividend growth. A company that has missed out on growth opportunities is worth less in the market.

12.4 The multi-phase model

As we have seen, to simplify equation (1) we can assume that the growth rate is constant. However, the plausibility of this hypothesis is low, both in the case where the company is new and successful and therefore has a high earnings growth rate that is not necessarily sustainable in the long term, and in the case where the company is going through a restructuring phase, which could improve prospects for earnings growth once the difficult phase is over.

To account for the possibility that the rate of dividend growth will be variable over the future horizon, a "two-phase" or "three-phase" model can be used. In the two-phase case, the first phase refers to the first T years (for example $T = 5$), the second from period $T + 1$ to infinity. The first phase considers expected dividends for the next T years, while the second includes the terminal value at time $t + T$:

$$V_t = E_t\left[\frac{D_{t+1}}{(1+r)} + \frac{D_{t+2}}{(1+r)^2} + \ldots + \frac{D_{t+T} + V_{t+T}}{(1+r)^T}\right]. \tag{4}$$

In this way, it is not necessary to assume that the growth rate of dividends is constant forever, but it is instead possible to estimate dividends for some future years, factoring in a growth rate that gradually tends to the long-term value (for example, that of the reference sector).

The number of phases that must be considered is functional to the difference between the current value and the steady state value of the relevant parameters. If the earnings growth rate is currently 30% and the steady state growth rate is 10%, it may be appropriate to think that in the second phase the growth rate gradually decreases from 30% to 20%, in the third phase from 20% to 10%, and then stabilizes at steady state value. In the last phase, we tend to use Gordon's model as an evaluation element because we can assume that we have reached a period in which the company grows at stable parameters in the long term.

Box 12.6 How much is Microsoft stock worth?

Question: At the beginning of May 2019, Refinitiv's Eikon platform shows that analysts' expectation for Microsoft Corporation's one-year share price is \$142.31, with a current price equal to \$129.77 and an expectation of a one-year dividend equal to \$1.819 per share. In addition, beta (using monthly return data over the last five years) is estimated at 1.23, risk-free rate equal to 2.7%, and expected return on the stock market 8.3% (EMRP of 5.6%). Earnings per share is equal to \$4.590, the plowback ratio $b = 0.604$, and ROE is 9.42%. The manager of an equity fund asks analyst Elena to provide a valuation of the stock and estimate the PVGO.

Answer: Elena uses the CAPM to estimate the expected return, obtaining $2.7\% + 1.23 \times 5.6\% = 9.6\%$. The valuation linked to the market consensus is therefore $E_0\left(\$\frac{P_1 + D_1}{1 + r_t}\right) = \$\frac{142.3 + 1.819}{1 + 9.6\%} = \$131.51$, very close to the market price. To consider alternative models, Elena estimates the long-term dividend growth rate using the company's ROE and payout ratio. For Microsoft, the following data is collected: $ROE = 40\%$ and $b = 0.604$, therefore $g = ROE \times b = 0.4 \times 0.60 = 24\%$, too high to fit into Gordon's model requiring the growth rate to be less than the expected return. If, however, $ROE = 9.42\%$ and $b = 0.604$, we get $g = ROE \times b = 9.42\% \times 0.604 = 5.69\%$. Applying Gordon's model in the simplest version, that is, starting from analysts' dividend expectations, we get $\$\frac{1.819}{9.6\% - 5.69\%} = \$46.52$, significantly lower than the previous one. As a further analysis, noting that the expected dividends are equal to the expected earnings multiplied by the payout ratio, Elena applies Gordon's model to estimate the price-to-earnings ratio $\frac{P_t}{U_t} = \frac{(1+g) \times (1-b)}{r - ROE \times b}$. Using the available data, she finds $\frac{P_t}{U_t} = \frac{(1 + 0.0569) \times (1 - 0.604)}{9.6\% - 9.42\% \times 0.604} = 10.7$. Given the earnings for period 1, the estimated initial value based on the multiple is \$49.22. As far as PVGO is concerned, using equation (3) we have $\$(129.77 - 4.6/0.096) = \$(129.77 - 47.82) = \$81.9$.

However, she also wants to provide a stock valuation using a three-step model, which is shown in Table 12.1. The "EPS" row shows the expected earnings per share over the fifteen-year horizon considered, which grows from the historical value of 3.88 to 13.29. The compounded annual growth rate over the next five years (F5Y CAGR, that is, the average compounded annual rate over the five-year period) of 10.7% (first phase) and 7.5% (F10Y CAGR) in the second phase. The "expected payout ratio" line contains forecasts for the share of earnings per share that is paid in the form of a dividend, with an increase over the period from 40% to 50%. From the product of the payout ratio and the profit, the dividend per share is obtained. The last predicted value in the period, 6.64, is used to estimate the terminal value using Gordon's model, with an expected return parameter of 9.3% and a constant growth rate of 6%, corresponding to the rate at which it converges at the end of the fifteen-year period. Adding the terminal value to the present value of the expected dividends (discounted at 9.3%) gives $244.09.

Table 12.1 **Example of a three-stage model applied to Microsoft stock**

Pase	Histor-ical	1					2										3
Year		1	2	3	4	5	6	7	8	9	10	11	12	13	14	15	Terminal value (Gordon)
EPS	3.88	4.6	4.95	5.41	5.91	6.46	7.04	7.65	8.28	8.95	9.63	10.33	11.05	11.79	12.54	13.29	
Growth (%)	17.20	18.40	7.80	9.30	9.30	9.30	9.00	8.60	8.30	8.00	7.60	7.30	7.00%	6.70%	6.30	6.00	
	F5Y CAGR: 10.7 %						F10Y CAGR: 7.5 %										
Payout ratio (%)		40.00	42.40	43.70	44.40	44.60	45.20	45.70	46.20	46.80	47.30	47.90	48.40	48.90	49.50	50.00	
Dividend per share		1.84	2.1	2.36	2.62	2.89	3.18	3.5	3.83	4.18	4.56	4.94	5.35	5.77	6.2	6.64	
Terminal value (Gordon)																	213.28
(Discount rate 9.3 %)		1.84	1.92	1.97	2.01	2.02	2.04	2.05	2.05	2.05	2.05	2.03	2.01	1.98	1.95	1.91	

In summary, for Microsoft stock, the current price of the stock is difficult to justify based on fundamental valuation models because the analyst consensus provides a value of $131.51, but Gordon's model using expected dividends provides a value of $46.52, the price-earnings (PE) multiple yields a value of $49.14, the three-phase model predicts $244.09.

12.5 Applications

12.5.1 The price–earnings ratio

Investors continuously search for any signal of stock market over/undervaluation because they do not believe that market prices are equal to value, at least not all the time. We shall see at the end of Chapter 13 that economic theory supports the possibility that there are systematic, perhaps short-term, discrepancies between values and prices. One way to understand the existence of valuation errors is to compare the observed price with some measures of fundamentals, albeit in a very simple and rough form.

One possibility is to compare the price to the dividend, even though more often analysts and investors compare a stock's price to earnings instead of dividends. This does not negate the fact that the value of the stock is determined by dividends. Simply, they adopt an evaluation benchmark linked to a variable closer to the company's operations, not influenced by decisions relating to the short-term remuneration of shareholders. According to Gordon's model, the price-to-earnings ratio should be[4]:

$$\frac{P_t}{U_t} = \frac{(1 + ROE \times b) \times (1 - b)}{r - ROE \times b}.$$

In terms of price-to-expected earnings ratio:

$$\frac{P_t}{E_t U_{t+1}} = \frac{(1 - b)}{r - ROE \times b}$$

obtained from the previous equation by dividing both sides by one plus the rate of growth. Empirical evidence suggests that earnings forecasts are not easy, at least statistically. Chan, Karceski, and Lakonishok (2003) point out that it is difficult to predict corporate earnings over the long term, noting that few companies manage to maintain a high earnings growth rate, contrary to what many analysts predict: Only 10% of companies grow at a rate above 18% for at least ten years, and only 3% of companies manage to produce a profit growth rate above the median value for at least five consecutive years. The inability to forecast earnings leaves a mark on prices, which do not react correctly and immediately to profit announcements: Bernard and Thomas (1990) point out that the price reaction to the announcement of a certain quarter is partially predictable based on the announcements made in the previous two quarters.

One problem with the use of the price-to-earnings ratio is the temporal variability of the earnings themselves, which, especially for individual companies, can be negative by eliminating the economic significance of the ratio. Campbell and Shiller (1987) use the cyclically adjusted price–earnings ratio (CAPE), using a ten-year moving average of historical earnings to avoid being overly affected by short-term earnings volatility (especially when earnings are negative, in which case the indicator has no meaning). As can be seen from Figure 12.1, which shows the performance of the indicator and the long-term interest rate over a century of US stock market history, at the beginning of 2019 the value of CAPE was only lower than the value reached in 2000, at the peak of the market. In addition, Figure 12.1 shows that the CAPE in 2019 was similar to the value reached by the indicator in 1929 and that the Covid-19 crisis had a limited impact on the market's valuation relative to average earnings.

---

[4] To understand this definition, notice that dividend is equal to the profit multiplied by one minus the plowback ratio *b*, and the growth rate is the product of the reinvestment rate and profitability. In other words, the denominator uses g = ROE × b, and the numerator writes expected dividends of the Gordon model as current dividend (itself equal to current earnings times 1 minus the plowback ratio) multiplied by (1 + *g*) or (1 + ROE × b).

Figure 12.1 **Long-term rates and CAPE for the US stock market, 1871–2024**

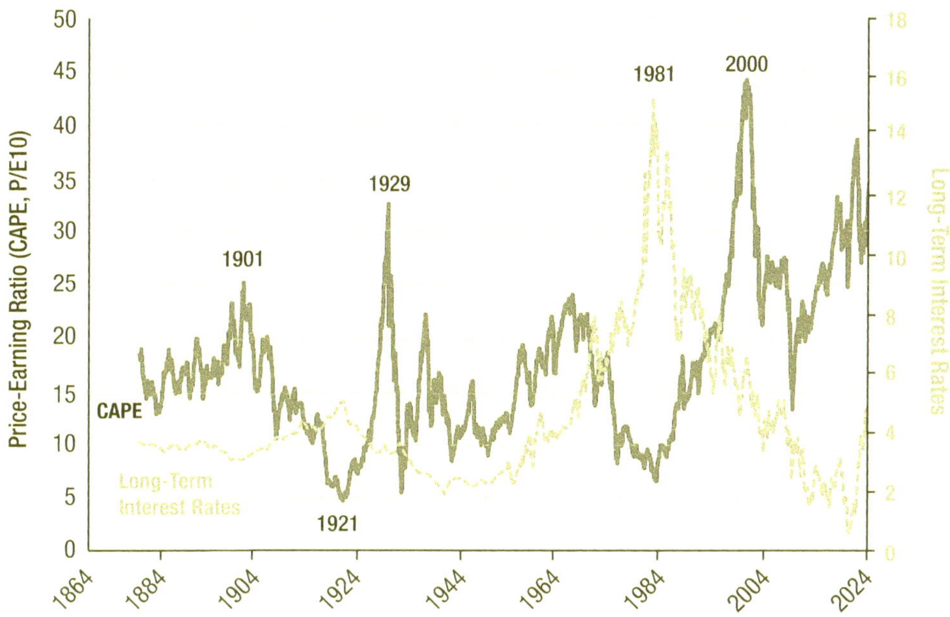

Source: Robert Shiller webpage

CAPE is often cited as an indicator that suggests that the market is overvalued or undervalued, despite concerns raised by some analysts about the possibility of earnings manipulation that can distort the meaning of the price-to-earnings ratio.

Beyond the technical interpretations of the indicators, it is important to avoid being misled by the analysis of a chart such as the one shown in Figure 12.1, which seems to suggest "obvious" margins of action. A good example is 2000, when CAPE reached 45, or March 2009, when the S&P 500 index reached 680. Watching events in real time is different from watching them ex post. In March 2009, the price-to-earnings ratio of the S&P 500 index was above 100 due to the collapse in corporate earnings. Who could rule out a further fall in the index despite the massive economic policy measures put in place to combat the crisis? The investor horizon becomes crucial to understand the reaction to events.

12.5.2 The book-to-price ratio

The equation that explains the price as the expected discounted value of dividends can be rewritten by substituting dividends with the difference between earnings U and the growth of the book value ΔB. This substitution is motivated by the accounting identity according to which the profit not paid to shareholders in the form of dividends is reinvested in the company and increases its book value. Dividing both sides of the fundamental valuation equation by the book value gives a theory for determining the relationship between price and book value:

$$\frac{V_t}{B_t} = \frac{E_t \sum_{i=0}^{\infty} \left(U_{t+i} - \Delta B_{t+i}\right) / \left(1 + r\right)^i}{B_t} \tag{5}$$

The equation is useful to understand the five-factor model proposed by Fama and French (2015), described at the end of Chapter 9. Assuming the market price P_t is equal to value V_t, the equation shows that there is a positive relation between the book-to-market, V/B, and required return r (the larger the required return, the lower the numerator on the right-hand side), profitability U/B, and a negative relation with the rate of growth of book value growth, $\Delta B/B$ (to be interpreted as a low level of investment). This is a "theoretical" justification for the inclusion of these variables in the range of risk factors considered by the five-factor model.

The fundamental value model can also be rewritten to highlight the relevance of the company's book value in pricing, such as:[5]

$$V_t = B_t + E_t\left[\frac{\left(ROE_{t+1} - r\right) B_t}{(1 + r)} + \frac{\left(ROE_{t+2} - r\right) B_{t+1}}{(1 + r)^2} + \frac{\left(ROE_{t+3} - r\right) B_{t+2}}{(1 + r)^3} + \ldots\right]$$

according to which the market value is equal to the book value plus the expected discounted difference between the return on equity and the cost of equity. This equation highlights how the company may create value by producing an accounting return that exceeds the cost of capital using "residual income," equal to the difference between earnings and the equity charge defined as the product of the cost of equity and the book value. Situations where the market value is less than the book value are likely to be cases where investors estimate that the company is not able to produce profitability to an extent compatible with the cost of equity. These are the same situations previously described as cases where the company may have an interest in returning capital to shareholders through a generous dividend policy.

12.5.3 Market value and expected return

Are there other ways to estimate the long-run expected return on an asset apart from simply assuming it is equal to its sample mean, as was done in Chapter 2? From its very definition, the average return of a stock depends on the expectation of dividend yield and the expectation of capital gain:

$$Er = E\frac{D_{t+1}}{P_t} + E\frac{\Delta P_{t+1}}{P_t}$$

[5] Multiply both sides of equation (5) by B_t, then add and substitute B_t on the right hand side and develop a few terms to see the equivalence.

Equation (4) determines the value from the expected return and cash flow expectations but can be used as a tool for estimating the expected return of a security based on the observation of the market price (so-called implied cost of capital). Chava and Purnanandam (2010) consider a specification where analysts' expected earnings and plowback ratio assumptions generate free cash flow expectations for the next two years. For the remaining thirteen years of the time horizon, earnings growth is assumed to converge toward the long-run average growth rate of the economy to estimate the cash flows to be included in equation (4). The terminal value is estimated by applying Gordon's equation. By placing the value equal to the market price, we can see that the expected return is the only unknown. Chava and Purnanandam (2010) show that the cross-section of expected returns on equities is positively linked to default risk, contrary to other analyses that use the returns actually observed over a historical period instead of the implied cost of capital.

12.5.4 The price-to-earnings ratio and expected return

Ilmanen (2022) uses results by Avdis and Wachter (2017) as a remedy to estimate expected return on the stock market by running a regression of monthly returns on a valuation ratio. We use Shiller's long-run data and the inverse of the CAPE as a regressor to run, with monthly data (in real terms after subtracting inflation), $r_t = \alpha + \beta \times \Delta \frac{1}{CAPE_t} + \varepsilon_t$. The regressor is the change in the earnings yield. Over the long sample period 1872–2023 the earnings yield has gone down, on average, an annualized 0.02%. Potentially this could be a proxy for an increasing valuation of stock prices relative to earnings that might disappear in the future. The estimated regression is $r_t = 0.006 \pm 10.647 \times \Delta \frac{1}{CAPE_t} + e_t$. The intercept of the regression represents the estimate of the long-run real return correcting for the in-sample valuation increase. The estimated intercept, when annualized, is equal to 7.22%, marginally below the sample mean over the same period equal to 7.77%. The earnings yield as of the last observation at the time of writing, equal to 2.91%, is way below the long-run average 6.81%. If the earnings yield were to go back over ten years to its long-run average, the resulting 3.90% increase would imply an average stock return equal to $r_t = 12 \times 0.006 - 10.647 \times \frac{3.9\%}{10} = 3.06\%$. If the end of the sample was affected by a market overvaluation to disappear in ten years (assuming the earnings yield would stop at its long-run mean), then the average real stock return would fall from 7.22% to 3.06%.

12.6 Speculative bubbles

The idea of a "speculative bubble" is used to justify a prolonged period of deviation between price and value. Bubbles may be irrational or rational. Irrational bubbles have no specific theoretical foundations and are associated with price increases causing investors to extrapolate more price increases in the future, even though there are no specific restrictions to such price increases provided by theoretical models. Shiller (1993) notes that irrational speculative bubbles involve investors reacting both to price increases and to communications among themselves taking the form of fads and fashions. Shiller (2013b, p. 460) defines a speculative bubble "as a situation in which news of price increases spurs investor enthusiasm, which spreads by psychological contagion from person to person, in the process amplifying stories that might justify the price increases and bringing in a larger and larger class of investors, who, despite doubts about the real value of an investment, are drawn to it partly through envy of others' successes and partly through a gambler's excitement."

When the condition of transversality does not hold, the price is different from the value due to the presence of a rational speculative bubble SB_t:[6]

$$P_t = V_t + SB_t$$

where the speculative bubble, like value, moves over time with an expected dynamic:

$$SB_t = E_t\left(\frac{SB_{t+1}}{1 + r_{f,t} + pr_t}\right)$$

The above equation states that the bubble today is the expected discounted value of tomorrow's bubble. Reading the equation backwards, that is, $E_t(SB_{t+1}) = \left(1 + r_{f,t} + pr_t\right)SB_t$, we can see that the expectation is for a bubble that grows at the same rate of return expected by the asset. Of course, this is only an expectation, but it explains that an investor may be rationally willing to pay a price higher than the value if he is convinced that tomorrow someone will pay an even higher price. When the bubble bursts, the last investor who bought the stock at too high a price realizes that he has lost, at least in the short term.

Empirical tests to demonstrate the presence of speculative bubbles have always met with a strong limitation: Since the only variable observed is the price, any estimate of the speculative bubble depends on the estimate of the value, and therefore any error in the estimate of the value automatically translates into the estimate of the bubble. Giglio, Maggiori, and Stroebel (2016), however, find an ingenious way to verify the presence of a speculative bubble by comparing the market price of real estate assets in the United Kingdom and Singapore by exploiting the presence of contracts that may concern ownership or the concession of use of very long duration: 99 or 999 years in Singapore, and 99, 125, 150, 250, and 999 years in the United Kingdom. If it is assumed that the price of the concession does not incorporate the speculative bubble, due to the contract finite horizon, then it is necessary to verify whether, all

[6] Very often commentators refer to sentiment rather than speculative bubbles. Intuitively, while the idea of a speculative bubble is used to describe episodes of strong and concentrated price increases followed by ruinous falls, the idea of sentiment is used to describe situations in which price changes do not seem to be clearly associated with changes in fundamentals. Sentiment is then informally considered to justify price changes likely caused by investor moods. Blanchard and Watson (1982) introduce the idea of a speculative bubble in a simple way.

things being equal, there are significant differences in the price of the property compared with that of the concession. Using data from between 1995 and 2015, a period that other studies have said was characterized by the presence of speculative bubbles, the paper is unable to confirm the presence of bubbles.

Greenwood, Shleifer and You (2018) consider all cases in which the prices of a certain sector in the American market grew more than 100% in two years between 1928 and 2017 and find forty episodes, and they define a crash as a 40% drop in prices in the following two years. According to statistics, when the average price increase in the previous two years rises from 50% to 100%, the probability of a crash rises from 20% to 53%, and an increase of 150% is associated with an 80% probability of a crash.

Box 12.7 Is it worth buying if there is a bubble?

Question: Elena reads that all investors are interested in the tech stock FaceRecord, which has a market price of $150. She turns to her trusted advisor, Carola, to find out what her estimate of the value of the stock is and whether it is appropriate to proceed with the purchase.

Answer: Carola performs a fundamental analysis and estimates that the value of the stock is $120. She tells Elena that the expected return on the stock is 20% per year. If the overvaluation is due to the presence of a speculative bubble such as the one studied in academic papers, the price of the stock is expected to be $180 in a year's time. However, there is a possibility that the bubble will burst and that the price of the stock in a year's time will be equal to its fundamental value, estimated at $144. The purchase at $150 therefore exposes Elena to the risk of a moderate loss next year, which could, however, be reabsorbed as early as the following year if the growth dynamics of the stock's value remain at 20%.

12.7 Fundamentals and unexpected returns

Several times in previous chapters we have talked about decomposing observed returns into expected and unexpected components. The valuation model helps us to better understand the unexpected component. If the price depends on expectations about fundamentals, then the capital gain component of return depends on changes in such expectations. Applying equation (1) to two periods t and t' (ideally, let us think of this as a short period so that $t' < t + 1$), we see that:

$$V_{t'} - V_t = E_{t'}\left[V_t^*\right] - E_t\left[V_t^*\right]$$

where V_t^* is the perfect foresight value, that is the (unobserved) value associated with knowing the path of future fundamentals. The unexpected component of a security's return therefore depends on the change in expectations of cash flows and risk premiums over the long term. For short time horizons (say, a day or a week), the expected return component is quantitatively small, so that actual returns are dominated by the unexpected return component, while the opposite happens for long-run horizons.

We can further decompose the unexpected return into a component associated with revisions of cash flows and revisions of risk premia:

$$r_i = Er_i + \eta_{i,CF} - \eta_{i,DR}$$

where $\eta_{i,CF}$ is the component of change in expectations about future cash flows, while $\eta_{i,DR}$ is the component of change in expectations about discount rates. A positive shock to expected cash flows is a positive surprise for prices, driving returns up, while a positive shock to discount rates is a negative surprise for prices, driving returns down. The relevance of the decomposition arises from the different properties of the two components.

Cash flow shocks are reversible only on the basis of opposite shocks and can therefore be considered as permanent, that is, the reduction in the value of a security affected by a downward revision of cash flow expectations can only be counterbalanced by a subsequent increase in the case of a positive shock. On the contrary, the value impact of shocks to discount rates has a positive implication for prices: An increase in the present value of risk premia must be associated with an average upward trend in future prices, which, barring further shocks, allows for the effective realization of excess returns that compensate holders for risk.

Campbell and Vuolteenaho (2004) use the previous definition to decompose beta. By definition $\beta_i = \dfrac{Cov(r_i - Er_i, r_M - Er_M)}{Var(r_M - Er_M)}$. If the return shock depends on shocks to expectations of cash flows and risk premia, we can write:

$$\beta_i = \frac{Cov(r_i - Er_i, r_M - Er_M)}{Var(r_M - Er_M)} = \frac{Cov(r_i - Er_i, \eta_{M,CF})}{Var(r_M - Er_M)} + \frac{Cov(r_i - Er_i, -\eta_{M,DR})}{Var(r_M - Er_M)} = \beta_i^{CF} + \beta_i^{DR}$$

Like cholesterol, beta can be thought of as the sum of "good" and "bad" components: "Bad" beta is related to covariance with cash flow shocks, while "good" beta is related to covariance with discount rate shocks. β_i^{DR} is the "good" beta in that the investor prefers to hold a stock that co-moves with the market in terms of risk premia, which have a mean reversion component that mitigates the long-term impact. In contrast, securities whose cash flow shocks have high covariance with market cash flow shocks are particularly risky if shocks are permanent. Campbell and Vuolteenaho (2004) show that value stocks (analyzed in the previous chapter together with those of the various anomalies) are characterized by a higher β^{CF} than growth stocks, an observation that helps explain the premium on Fama and French's HML portfolio.

Interpreting unexpected returns as being the result of the contribution of shocks to expectations of cash flows and risk premia allows for a new interpretation of the results of the anomalies presented in the previous chapter: The high return of a portfolio strategy may be due to unexpected return components linked to positive surprises to the ability to generate dividends and the amount of risk. Investors can be repeatedly surprised by continuous improvements in a group of stocks on items that have become more relevant over time, explaining large in-sample returns.

Summary

- The value of a stock is the sum of expected dividends discounted to the present at a rate summing the risk-free rate and the risk premium. If all future dividends are included in the computation, then there is no expected future price that is relevant.
- The transversality condition states that in expectation the discounted future value is equal to zero and does not affect current value, which is only based on dividends.
- To avoid duplications, value considers expected dividends and not expected earnings, as the latter may be reinvested in the business and contribute to today's value through future expected capital gains.
- Gordon's model assumes that the discount rate is constant and dividends grow forever at a constant rate. Gordon's model predicts that value is proportional to the last dividend paid to shareholders but is very sensitive to small changes in parameters.
- Long-run dividend growth is endogenous and may be thought of as the product between the return on equity and the plowback ratio, the percentage of earnings that is reinvested in the company.
- The present value of growth opportunities may be estimated by the difference between value and the perpetuity associated with short-run expected earning that would remain constant without any investment on the part of the firm.
- The version of the fundamental value model typically used by analysts divides the life of the company into two or three "phases" characterized by different projections of the dividends.
- Stock market investors use the price-to-earnings ratio as an indicator of value in the stock market as a whole. The CAPE modifies the standard PE ratio by substituting the most recent earnings with a ten-year moving average of earnings.
- The book-to-price ratio can be interpreted in light of expected earnings and reinvestment within the firm but also in terms of the present discounted value of the difference between the return on equity and the cost of capital.
- The term speculative bubble denotes a deviation between price and value. It may be due to irrationality or to a rational expectation of a future increase in the bubble component of the price that justifies purchasing a stock even when a bubble is present. Empirical analyses of bubbles are hard, and researchers more often study episodes of over/underpricing of the market or of single stocks by studying sentiment.
- The present discounted value model is useful to understand the origin of asset unexpected returns, which, according to the model, may be explained in terms of new information about future cash flows and/or discount rates. This decomposition may be used to explain the beta of a stock as the sum of a cash flow beta and a discount rate beta.

Problems

1 Determine the value of a stock whose last earnings was 5, with a plowback ratio of 40%, when the long-run growth rate is 2%, the risk-free is 4%, and the risk premium is 6%. Determine PVGO and ROE. Based on the result obtained, what change to the shareholder remuneration policy would you suggest to the company?

2 The risk-free is 5%. The expected market return is 12%. The current price of a stock is 40, the expected price after one year is 41, and the expected dividend is 1. The beta of the stock is -0.5. Is the stock properly priced?

3 A security has an expected return of 10%, and the risk-free is 2%. The stock has a unitary beta and the market risk premium is 8%. The stock price is 50 and the dividend is expected to have no future growth. What impact does a doubling of the stock's correlation coefficient with the market have on the price?

4 A company has a ROE of 16% and a plowback ratio of 50%. Earnings for the following year are expected at 2 per share.

a. What is the market price of the stock if its expected return is 10%?
b. What is the expected stock price in three years?

5 The consensus on a company's ROE is 9%, and the plowback ratio is 2/3. Earnings are €3 per share. The expected return from the market is 14% and the risk-free is 6%.

a. What is the value?
b. What is the ratio of the value to earnings?
c. What is the PVGO (present value of growth opportunities)?
d. What would be the value of the stock if the plowback ratio fell to 1/3?

Answers

1 The last dividend is equal to the profit multiplied by 1 minus the plowback, that is, 3. The expected return is equal to the sum of the risk-free and the risk premium, 10%. The value is therefore equal to $\frac{3 \times 1.02}{0.1 - 0.02} = 38.25$. We know that ROE may be found from the ratio between the growth rate 0.02 and the plowback ratio 0.4, therefore 5%. The PVGO is equal to the difference between the value of the stock and the value that would be obtained by paying all the profit in the form of a dividend, that is, the difference between 38.25 and 5/0.1=50. There is a negative PVGO because ROE is much lower than expected return. Under these conditions it is a good idea to increase the distribution of earnings to the shareholders.

2 According to the CAPM, the expected return should be 1.5%. The expected return from market prices is 42/40 – 1 = 5%. The CAPM suggests the stock is undervalued.

3 Doubling the correlation coefficient with the market will double the beta. The new expected return from the CAPM is 14%. The value of the stock initially implied an expected dividend (and profit) of 4. With this dividend, the increase in the expected return implies a new value equal to 4/0.14 = 28.57.

4 a. The value is 1/(0.1 – 0.08) = 50.
b. The price growth corresponds to the growth of profit and dividend. Using the product between ROE and the plowback, growth is 8%. The expected price at the end of the three-year period is therefore $50 \times (1.08)^3 = 63$.

5 a. The value is $\frac{1 \times 1.06}{0.14 - 0.06} = 13.25$.
b. The price/historical earnings ratio is $\frac{13.25}{3} = 4.42$ the price/forward earning ratio is $\frac{13.25}{3 \times 1.06} = 4.17$.
c. The PVGO is 13.25 minus the ratio between expected earnings and required return. The PVGO here is negative because ROE is lower than the cost of capital.
d. If the plowback ratio decreased to 1/3, the value would be $\frac{2 \times 1.03}{0.14 - 0.03} = 18.73$; the value would go up because the company would reinvest less in a low profitability business.

13 Market efficiency

13.1 Introduction

The efficiency of financial markets is a central issue for understanding the role of finance in contributing to economic growth. According to Fama (1970), market efficiency is based on quick and correct incorporation of information on market prices. As there is no doubt about the ability of markets to incorporate information at maximum speed, we focus in this chapter on valuation efficiency, which boils down to the question: Are prices equal to values? We discuss three methodologies: excess volatility tests, return predictability tests, and event studies. These three methodologies look at three different elements of efficiency: (a) Do prices move in line with expected fundamentals? (b) Is it possible to predict stock returns based on available information at various horizons? (c) Do prices react to news? We present relevant evidence and conclude that (a) prices move too much to be justified by fundamentals (at least for the market as a whole, albeit there is more single-company micro-efficiency); (b) there is very little predictability at short horizons but relevant predictability at multi-period horizons, which seems, however, to indicate the incorporation of information explaining a time-varying risk premium; and (c) company prices react to news even though for the market as a whole it is often hard to find ex post justification for very large price movements.

Deviations from efficiency can be explained in the strict economic sense in an equilibrium situation where financial intermediaries need some noise in prices to justify the accumulation of costly information that is constantly driving prices toward value. There is also a discussion about the use of behavioral finance models to explain excess volatility, particularly in the form of information contagion. Finally, we discuss the interplay between smart traders and ordinary investors: Why might smart traders fail to pursue risky arbitrage and not eliminate inefficiencies? The literature on the limits of arbitrage provides suggestions about the possible answers.

13.2 The definition of an efficient market

13.2.1 Characteristics of market efficiency

Market efficiency is simultaneously about:

a) the reaction of stock prices to relevant news, that should be immediate and complete,
b) the incorporation of all available information in the current price level, and
c) the inclusion of expected fundamentals into the current price level.

Point 1 above involves both a technological element that we may define as "information efficiency" and a valuation element that we define as "valuation efficiency." Points 2 and 3 have mainly to do with valuation efficiency. The general definition of efficient markets (see Fama, 1970) includes both information efficiency and valuation efficiency, suggesting that market efficiency implies that prices fully and quickly incorporate all available information in the way predicted by the fundamental valuation model discussed in Chapter 12. Fama (1965, p. 76) writes that "in an efficient market, competition among the many intelligent participants leads to a situation where, at any point in time, actual prices of individual securities already reflect the effects of information based both on events that have already occurred and on events which, as of now, the market expects to take place in the future. In other words, in an efficient market at any point in time the actual price of a security will be a good estimate of its intrinsic value."

13.2.2 Why efficiency is important

The efficiency of the financial market is extremely important for the functioning of the economy. To realize this, it is enough to think that if the market is not efficient, companies with overvalued securities can obtain capital from investors at too low a cost, while companies with undervalued securities, characterized by an excessive cost of capital, can be forced to give up investment opportunities that are profitable and useful for economic growth.[1] An efficient market is therefore better than a central planner: The planner should have very detailed information about consumer needs and the capabilities of firms to determine who produces what and to whom goods and services go. The efficient market carries out all these analyses only based on decentralized information when each agent pursues his or her own well-being. This is the view proposed by Adam Smith, one of the fathers of economics, proposing an explanation of the "invisible hand" as the mechanism for efficient allocation of capital (Chapter 15 will discuss such vision in the presence of externalities).

[1] Keynes (1936, p. 159) wrote that "when the capital development of a country becomes a by-product of the activities of a casino, the job is likely to be ill-done."

But how can the market achieve such a formidable goal? Models explain some of the mechanisms by which agents with heterogeneous information demand assets and influence prices, but we need to better understand how these mechanisms can achieve an overall coordination goal, resulting in prices that reflect expectations about future cash flows. It is reassuring to rely on the "wisdom of the crowd" (Surowiecki, 2004), but the example used to describe the concept, the ability of a thousand people gathered in a square in 1907 to guess the average weight of an ox, overlaps in a limited way with the effort to make market prices coincide with the values of the securities. In 1907 people did not coordinate to guess the weight of an ox, and the law of large numbers would make the mean a good point estimate of the true number. In modern times, the correlation among investors' opinions can be relevant and prevent the law of large numbers from helping the average of individual attempts to match value.

13.2.3 Brief remarks on information efficiency

Information efficiency is the ability of the market to incorporate new information in the shortest possible time. There is no doubt that technological improvements in data analytics have resulted in continuous improvement in this type of efficiency. According to the reconstruction of Ferguson (2017), in 1815 the Rothschilds family sent observers to the hills of Waterloo to obtain relevant information about the performance of the French army under Napoleon. The private couriers carried the news to London in twenty-four hours (at the time letters from Paris to Frankfurt took two days but mail from London could take up to a week to reach Frankfurt), which encouraged the buying of British sovereign bonds listed in the London market. Two centuries ago, it took several hours to deliver relevant news that could then be incorporated in asset prices.

Compare this with the current situation, where algo traders can get an advantage if they are able to complete trading micro-seconds before the rest of the market. There is no doubt that continuous progress in information technology has shortened the time lag between news and price reaction, but also increased the amount of news that becomes value-relevant. The availability of new machine learning techniques that are able to interpret text has made it possible to create sentiment indicators that try to predict the short-run dynamics of asset prices.

In what follows we do not discuss further information efficiency, as everybody agrees that markets are totally efficient from this point of view. The incentive provided to traders to adopt the most recent and quick type of information technology (both infrastructure and human capital for coding and treating big data) is particularly relevant for a business model relying on intensive trading platforms, but in general all investors and financial intermediaries gain in using the newest technologies, especially if assets under management are large and allow for the application of quantitative models in large-scale trading. That is why finance is at the forefront of adopting and investing in new technologies.

If other sectors, for example the public sector, had similar incentives to invest in technologies and data-gathering, we would probably have more reliable datasets on elements associated with social and environmental issues, for example the number of homeless people, immigrants, number of trees, and forestry areas. Lower marginal value of information acquisition may explain lower incentives to accumulate and use data.

13.3 Efficiency tests

There are three methodologies for verifying market efficiency. Each methodology considers a different implication of efficiency as defined by Fama (1985). The first method is to test whether the price level of an asset is determined based on expectations of fundamentals, which in the case of a stock are dividends and discount factors. The second method aims to test whether current prices incorporate all available information, otherwise there is room for predictability of equity returns by means of a regression analysis. The third method investigates whether prices react correctly to unexpected news through event studies. We will see that stock prices are not efficient in incorporating expected fundamentals with the lowest possible volatility; that return prediction is more an analysis of risk premia variability than market efficiency; and that there is evidence that the stock market is macro-inefficient but micro-efficient, that is, the market as a whole has large swings that are hard to explain based on macroeconomic news but individual stocks seem to react promptly and broadly correctly to news about corporate actions.

13.4 Valuation efficiency and return variance

13.4.1 Excess volatility

Valuation efficiency implies the ability of the market to incorporate new information into prices in the "correct" way. We saw in Chapter 12 that value is the expectation of discounted future cash flows. Efficient markets should set prices equal to value. Shiller (1981) showed that the market index is characterized by "excess volatility," that is, the stock market index moves more than would be justified by fundamentals. His methodology is based on the "perfect foresight" price P_t^*:

$$P_t^* = \left[D_{t+1} \times R_{t,t} + D_{t+2} \times R_{t,t+1} + \ldots + \left(P_{t+T}^* + D_{t+T}\right) \times R_{t,T}\right]$$

Equation (1) in Chapter 12 states that value is equal to the expectation of the perfect foresight price. Efficient markets would require that prices are equal to value and therefore equal to the expectation of the perfect foresight price. Let us use once again the decomposition of the realization of a random variable into expectation and shock, in this case suggesting that the perfect foresight price should be equal to the market price (which under the null hypothesis of efficiency corresponds to the expectation) plus a forecast error:

$$P_t^* = P_t + e_t$$

In the absence of correlation between the expectation error e and the market price P, a hypothesis associated with the rationality of expectations in that we assume that errors have no correlation with any information contained in the price,[2] the following inequality must therefore hold:

$$VP_t^* > VP_t$$

where V is the variance operator. We have described in various chapters the volatility of the stock market, noting its time variability. However, lacking a theory, we could never study whether volatility was "too" large relative to a benchmark. When Shiller (1981) estimated the perfect foresight price he found that the variance of the actual price is greater than the variance of the perfectly predicted price. Campbell and Shiller (1988) generalize the result using more advanced econometric methodologies that allow us to better characterize the long-term trend of the market.

The result can be interpreted as an overreaction of investors to the performance of the economy. Investors are too optimistic in good times and too pessimistic in bad times, extrapolating the current situation far into the future and forgetting about the tendency of the economy to stabilize in the medium term. Markets seem to extrapolate from recent events, ignoring the ability of the economic system to recover from bad shocks and neglecting, in good times, the possibility that crises may occur. Consequently, prices move too much compared with the fluctuation that would be justified by the actual variability of cash flows and discount rates. The stock market sems to be inefficient, at least if judged by its ability to reflect expected fundamentals with the lowest level of volatility. Bordalo, Gennaioli, La Porta and Shleifer (2024) argue that stock price volatility is explained by belief overreaction to good news as measured by analysts' consensus earnings expectations. The paper builds an index of short-term and long-term expected earnings growth for S&P500 firms which predicts returns in the aggregate market and in the cross section of stock returns. Moreover, high aggregate optimism predicts stronger earnings forecast disappointment for firms with a high expected earnings growth than for firms with low expected earnings growth.

Vuolteenaho (2002) and Cohen, Polk, and Vuolteenaho (2003) apply the methodology to the study of the variability of prices of individual stocks and find that cash flow expectations play a greater role (about two-thirds) in explaining price variability than expected return variability (about one-third). Jung and Shiller (2005) frame the greater importance of cash flow expectations at the level of individual stocks rather than at the market level by referring to what Samuelson wrote in a letter: "Modern

---

[2] A positive correlation, for example, would suggest that investors make on average larger mistakes when the market price is larger. Rational investors would understand that and revise their evaluation upwards when the price is high, thereby eliminating any residual correlation between prices and expectational errors.

markets show considerable micro efficiency (for the reason that the minority who spot aberrations from micro efficiency can make money from those occurrences and, in doing so, they tend to wipe out any persistent inefficiencies). In no contradiction to the previous sentence, I had hypothesized considerable macro inefficiency, in the sense of long waves in the time series of aggregate indexes of security prices below and above various definitions of fundamental value" (a hypothesis known as Samuelson's dictum). Keloharju, Linnainmaa, and Nyberg (2021) present results in line with previous ones, illustrating the trend toward the temporal convergence of expected returns on various equities; that is, expected returns may be different in the short term but tend to converge in the long term.

Micro-efficiency does not seem to harm the possibility of active management. Black (1986) suggested that micro-efficiency is to be interpreted as suggesting that individual company stock prices are between half true value and twice true value at least 90% of the time.

13.4.2 Asset pricing and consumption

The Shiller (1981) approach looks at the relation between prices, dividends and expected returns but does not link the stock market to general economic conditions. We now jointly consider consumption and the stock market to provide a new description of asset prices and returns. We now assume that a representative investor evaluates the trade-off between buying an asset at time t and selling it at time $t + 1$ in terms of the following equation:

$$u'(C_t) \times P_t = E_t\left[\delta\left(P_{t+1} + D_{t+1}\right) \times u'(C_{t+1})\right]$$

where C_t is consumption at time t, $u'(C_t)$ is the marginal utility[3] of consumption at time t, δ is a discount factor (less than one) representing the rate of preference for the present relatively to the future consumption, P_t and D_t have the usual interpretation of price and dividend. Importantly, we assume that C_t and C_{t+1} are not exogenously given but are optimally selected by the investor/consumer along an optimal path accounting for current and future labor income and capital income. In other words, there is a complicated long-horizon consumption/ investment problem that provides a joint solution for the optimal consumption path and the equilibrium value of the asset. The equation points out that, along such an optimal path, the utility cost of buying the asset (the left-hand side), must be equal to the expected present discounted value of cash flows obtained at time $t + 1$ when selling the asset, also evaluated in terms of utility (the right-hand side).

Why do we interpret the equation in terms of utility? The intuition is simple: If the price of consumption is equal to one, then buying an asset at the market price P_t requires giving up P_t units of consumption that decrease utility by the amount $u'(C_t)$. The left-hand side is therefore the utility sacrifice associated with buying an asset

[3] The marginal utility represents the change in utility associated with a change in consumption.

rather than consuming. When the asset is sold at time $t + 1$, the owner obtains a monetary benefit associated with the future cash flow and the future price, $P_{t+1} + D_{t+1}$, which, in turn, increase consumption by C_{t+1} units with an increase in future utility measured by the marginal utility of future consumption $u'(C_{t+1})$. The expected value of the product is discounted back to the current period to make it comparable with the left-hand side, by multiplying by a discount factor representing preference for current rather than future consumption.

13.5 Valuation efficiency and predictability of returns

13.5.1 Predictive regressions

The alternative way to test for efficiency is to analyze the expected return, namely:

$$E_t r_{t+1} = r_{ft} + rp_t$$

which can be rewritten in terms of actual returns as:

$$r_{t+1} - r_{ft} = rp_t + \varepsilon_{t+1} \quad (1)$$

with, as usual, $E\varepsilon_{t+1} = 0$.[4] Before the 1980s, predominant economic theory suggested that the risk premium for the market and for individual securities was stable over time[5], implying that equation (1) becomes:

$$r_{t+1} - r_{ft} = rp + \varepsilon_{t+1} \quad (2)$$

that is, excess return of time $t + 1$ is equal to a constant plus an unpredictable error. According to equation (2), it should be impossible to predict the oscillations of future excess returns around the risk premium. How do we test for such an extreme implication? Early empirical analyses sought to verify whether it is possible to predict excess returns on stocks or equity indices based on variables observed at the beginning of the period, that is, with regressions such as:

$$r_{t+1} - r_{ft} = \alpha + \beta X_t + \varepsilon_{t+1} \quad (3)$$

where the null hypothesis, jointly representing market efficiency and a time constant risk premium, is that the slope of the regression is equal to zero.

Any predictive variable can be considered on the right-hand side, for example past performance (a regression where the future excess return is regressed on the past excess return), dividend yield (the ratio between dividend and price), earnings yield (the ratio between profit and price), term spread (the difference between the rate on long-term sovereign securities and the rate on short-term sovereign securities, that is,

[4] Taking the expectation of both sides of equation (1) provides exactly $E_t r_{t+1} = r_{ft} + pr_t$.

[5] Looking back at equation (1) in Chapter 12, this implies that all price changes are due to either the change in interest rates or the change in cash flow expectations.

the slope of the curve by interest rate maturity), and the default spread (the difference between the rate on low-rated corporate securities and the rate on high-rated corporate securities).[6] The results initially showed that excess return is not predictable over short horizons such as day, week, or month, even when combining all these variables in multi-variate regressions.

13.5.2 Predictive regressions and market efficiency with a constant risk premium

These results were considered consistent with the joint hypothesis of market efficiency and a constant risk premium. To understand why lack of predictability is consistent with market efficiency, consider a mental experiment where a variable X_t predicts the future excess return, with, say, $\beta = 0.5$ and the last observed value of $X_t = 10\%$. Then the conditional prediction of the excess return based on the most recent observations of X_t would be equal to 15% if the intercept of the regression was equal to 10%. Suppose that only one investor knows this regression and she uses it to predict stock returns at 15%. She would buy the stock at the beginning of the period and expect to gain 15% due to her superior predictive ability.[7] Now suppose instead all investors know about this econometric result: They all immediately buy the market index and push the price up 5%, leaving the remaining 10% as the normal compensation associated with the risk premium. The future gain has materialized right away and no extra return is left for the future. Only dumb investors, populating an inefficient market, would not exploit this predictability. However, if predictability is exploited, then predictive ability disappears once information is impounded in prices.

13.5.3 The random walk

The unpredictability results had a strong implication for the description of the dynamics of stock prices that were associated with a "random walk."[8] If p_t denotes the logarithm of the price, unpredictability implies (for simplicity, let us assume the risk-free rate is zero and there is no constant in the regression) that $r_{t+1} = \varepsilon_{t+1}$. If the rate

---

[6] Fama (1970) refers to the different tests as checks of weak efficiency when the regression includes only past performance, semi-strong efficiency when it includes any publicly available information, and strong efficiency when it also includes private information.

[7] The other investors would obtain a lower average return associated with the normal long run return. To see this, consider the forecasting equation described in Chapter 2, $r_{t+1} = \alpha + \beta X_t + \varepsilon_{t+1}$, and notice that $Er_{t+1} = \alpha + \beta EX$. Assume that $EX = 0$ and $\alpha = 10\%$ as assumed in the example. Then the long run return would be 10%.

[8] If you ask a drunk to walk through a room, you do not know exactly what path he will take, because his state will lead him to wander and take every step randomly to the right or left. But there is no ex-ante reason to think that the drunk will continue to move consistently to the right or left and therefore the best prediction as to his position when he crosses the room is that he will move in a straight line.

of return is defined in logs (see Chapter 2), then $r_{t+1} = p_t - p_{t-1}$ and we get the random walk model of stock prices:

$$p_t = p_{t-1} + \varepsilon_t$$

Prices move over time as a sequence of unpredictable shocks. The price level is the sum of all past shocks, as can be seen by substituting backwards (for example $p_{t-1} = p_{t-2} + \varepsilon_{t-1}$, and so forth) to obtain $p_t = \varepsilon_t + \varepsilon_{t-1} + \varepsilon_{t-2} + \ldots + p_0$.[9] Intuitively, the unpredictability of price changes means that the best predictor of the future price level is the current price:

$$E_{t-1} p_t = p_{t-1}$$

which holds for any future period:

$$E_{t-1} p_{t+i} = p_{t-1}.$$

The current price is the best forecast of the future price of an asset whose price follows a random walk. The exchange rate is a remarkable example where the random walk hypothesis is hard to reject.

13.5.4 Predictability, efficiency, and time-varying risk premium

Subsequent analyses have shown the existence of temporal predictability when the reference horizon is at least greater than one year. Fama and French (1988) present results of multi-period return regressions, where the multi-year future return (from one to ten years) is explained by past return, and show the existence of mean reversion, that is, a forecastable component of return that tends to revert to a long-run mean. Such transitory component is particularly relevant for the three- to five-year horizon and small firms. For example, the returns of the past three to five years are negatively correlated with those of the future three to five years, a phenomenon known as mean reversion, and are predictable based on the macroeconomic and financial variables described earlier. These results undermine the possibility of describing price dynamics in terms of random walks.

How can we explain the predictability of price changes over time? Should predictability necessarily be interpreted as inefficiency? Given equations (1) and (3), the statistical significance of the variable X can be explained, in the context of the efficient market, in terms of the temporal variability of the risk premium, since the regression equation can be reconciled with (1) if $pr_t = \alpha + \beta X_t$. The valuation efficiency of the equity market can therefore be justified by the assumption of temporal variability of risk premia, which could create elements of predictability in excess returns.

Such predictability does not create any possibility of risky arbitrage, as investors

[9] Contrary to what happens in the EWMA volatility model seen in equation (8) of Chapter 2 to describe the variance, for the price level there is no $\lambda < 1$ coefficient implying a decay of far-away shocks on the current price.

would only be able to predict future equity returns at times of higher risk than usual. Expecting a high price increase during a crisis, when prices have fallen due to the presence of a very high level of risk, is not inconsistent with efficiency. Of course, the possibility of interpreting the results on predictability in terms of market inefficiency also remains open: In the latter case, predictability certainly suggests the use of the variable X in the context of dynamic portfolio choice strategies, which can allow a higher average return without a corresponding increase in risk. Which variables X can plausibly be associated with long-run predictive ability? The list includes mainly variables that may be correlated with the risk premium such as past returns, the default spread, and volatility.

The possibility to interpret return predictability regressions in terms of a time-varying risk premium reduces the relevance of this literature to test for market efficiency. Any predictability result can be justified by the regressor being a proxy for a risk premium. We have no accepted theoretical model for a risk premium and as a result it is hard to test for market efficiency based on an undefined null hypothesis.

13.5.5 Prediction and alternative data

The variables that have been mentioned so far have been widely analyzed by investors and analysts. Much attention is focused on finding fresh pieces of information that may not be fully incorporated into prices. What are the candidate variables for the predictability of stock prices? A variable might be predictor of stock prices if it is economically relevant, difficult to measure, and subject to attention by a limited number of operators. If variables were easy to obtain and widely known, investors would react immediately to the announcement of a new realization of variables that have historically shown predictive ability, but in doing so they would immediately contribute to the change in the current price, to the point where prediction is lost. If the inefficiency is temporary, predictability will disappear when investors use the information for current pricing.

In recent years, increased technological capabilities have significantly increased the amount of information available to investors. For example, "alternative data" obtained from satellite imagery make it possible to measure in continuous time the transport of goods (e.g., from the position of ships in the water), the level of activity in production facilities (from photographs of incoming and outgoing goods), consumer demand (from the number of cars parked near department stores), and social interactions and opinions (from the analysis of tweets). Alternative data is expensive today. Is it a good idea to buy them? It depends on the amount of assets under management and the management style. These data are available to a minority of professionals and as such have a potentially high impact in terms of predictability, but the choice depends on the subjective characteristics of the forecaster.

13.6 Valuation efficiency and price reactions

13.6.1 News and prices

The efficient market theory has very simple implications with regard to (a) the price level, (b) the expected return, and (c) the ex post return: The price should incorporate the expected values of the fundamentals, the expected return should include a risk premium linked to the risk of non-diversifiable factors affecting the fundamentals, and the ex post return should differ from the expected return due to elements that lead to the revision of fundamentals' expectations.

Empirically verifying this mechanism is not easy when the volatility attributed to shocks is very high. Various studies (see, e.g., Cutler, Poterba, and Summers, 1989) have started from apparently important news to verify whether they had an impact on the market index, while other studies have started from the different point of view of considering days of strong price fluctuations to understand whether there had been relevant news on those days to justify such fluctuations. In general, these studies have struggled to find a systematic relationship between news and price changes.

13.6.2 Event studies

An event study aims to understand whether and how there is a systematic reaction of stocks to certain easily determinable categories of news, such as price reactions after the announcement of an acquisition, or after a quarterly earnings announcement. To achieve this, you must first use theory to determine how to measure the reaction of the stock price. A stock that rises on a certain day along with the rest of the market is not easily linked to the existence of potentially relevant news for that stock. For example, a stock that rises 1% when the market rises 5% is not necessarily reacting correctly to positive news for the stock.

To account for the overall market trend, the simplest methodology is to assume that on a certain day the price of the stock should follow the market, possibly correcting for its beta. Abnormal return is then defined as $AR_{i,t} = r_{i,t} - \alpha_i - r_{M,t}$ or, if its beta coefficient is taken into account, as $AR_{i,t} = r_{i,t} - \alpha_i - \beta_i \times r_{M,t}$.

To obtain general results that are not limited to a single stock, the average of the anomalous return on the sample of N observations $AR_t = \sum_{i=1}^{N} AR_{i,t}$ is taken. The cumulative abnormal return (CAR), defined as $CAR_t = CAR_{t-1} + AR_t$, is examined from a graphical and statistical point of view.[10]

A well-known example is the reaction of stock prices to announcements of corporate acquisitions. To understand the average reaction of stock prices to such an event, you can look at the price movement in the ten days before and ten days after the announcement of an acquisition. Looking at a sample of stocks, day 0 is the day

---

[10] Campbell, Lo, and MacKinlay (1997) present in detail the event study methodology also from the point of view of stati5stical tests.

of the announcement, which of course represents a different day for each stock. The average abnormal return will then be the average across companies in the announcement day. In an efficient market three things should happen: (a) there should be no cumulative abnormal returns before time 0, (b) the market should react immediately, and (c) nothing more should happen in the following days.

Box 13.1 Is the reaction to mergers and acquisitions announcements correct?

Question: Elena runs an equity fund that specializes in pharmaceutical stocks and given the high mergers and acquisitions activity in the sector, she wants to know whether the average return of the acquired companies is positive and whether the market reacts appropriately to the acquisition announcement. She calculates the average percentage returns of a group of acquired pharmaceutical companies for ten days before the announcement and ten days after the announcement, finding the following data:

Day	Pharma	Market	Abnormal return	Cumulative Abnormal Return
-10	-0.5%	-1%	0.5%	0.5%
-9	0.1%	1%	-0.4%	0.1%
-8	0.2%	0.5%	-0.3%	-0.2%
-7	0.3%	0.4%	-0.1%	-0.3%
-6	0%	-0.2%	0.2%	-0.1%
-5	0.1%	-0.5%	0.6%	0.5%
-4	-0.1%	0%	-0.1%	0.4%
-3	0.2%	0.5%	-0.3%	0.1%
-2	0.3%	-0.3%	0.6%	0.7%
-1	1%	1%	0%	0.7%
0	4%	0.5%	3.5%	4.2%
1	1%	1.1%	-0.4%	3.8%
2	-0.5%	-0.7%	0.2%	4.0%
3	0.3%	0.3%	0%	4.0%
4	0.5%	0.5%	0%	4.0%
5	0.2%	-0.2%	0.4%	4.4%
6	0.1%	0%	0.1%	4.5%
7	-0.2%	0.1%	-0.3%	4.2%
8	-2%	-1.9%	-0.1%	4.1%
9	-1%	-0.5%	-0.5%	3.6%
10	2%	2.5%	-0.5%	3.1%

Elena turns to Sara to find out if, based on this data, she can conclude that the announcement of an acquisition really creates value for the shareholders of the target companies as apparently shown by the 4% average return on the day of the announcement.

Answer: Sara replies that to answer this question, you first need to know what the average return of the stock market is on the same days. Once the calculations are done, you can compute the abnormal returns (assuming a beta equal to one) and the cumulative abnormal returns also represented in Figure 13.1:

Figure 13.1 **Cumulative Abnormal Returns**

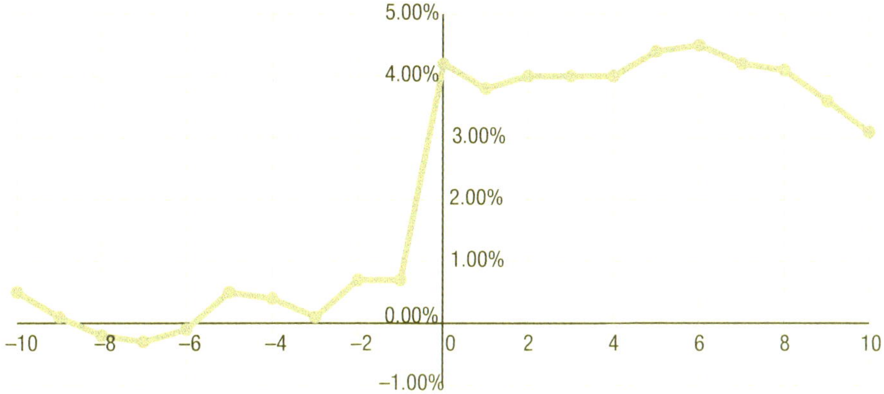

The result seems to show a consistent reaction with an efficient market because the anomalous returns are concentrated on the day of the announcement.

13.7 The equity premium

The equity premium was defined in Chapter 2 as the ex-ante expected excess return inducing a risk-averse investor to hold a risky asset rather than a risk-free asset. In Chapter 2 we saw long-run data on average excess returns in the stock market. If this historical average return is taken by investors as a proxy for the equity premium, we can then use the historical evidence to better understand the drivers of the equity premium.

13.7.1 The equity premium and the mean/variance utility function

What determines the equity market risk premium? Using equation (4) of Chapter 8 and noting that in equilibrium all the capital stock listed in the market must be held by investors, so $w = 1$, one gets, for the market:

$$E r_M - r_f = A \times \sigma_M^2$$

according to which the premium is equal to the product of the risk aversion coefficient and the variance. If the premium is 6% and the variance is 4%, a risk aversion coefficient of 1.5 is compatible with long-run data. A volatility of 15%, corresponding to a variance of 2.25%, is consistent with a coefficient $A = 2.7$. According to this theory, therefore, empirical data on equity premium and variance are consistent with entirely plausible average levels of risk aversion.

13.7.2 The equity premium and covariance with consumption

When asset pricing is studied in an equilibrium situation where the investor is also a consumer who rationally uses financial markets to smooth her consumption over time (trying to minimize the volatility of future consumption), then we can find an equilibrium explanation for values and returns based on the covariance with consumption growth. The generalization of the CAPM is intuitive: In the CAPM investors assign a large risk premium to stocks that covary with the market return, which represents the variable that they would like to smooth. If the benchmark for smoothing is consumption, then risk should be measured by the covariance between asset returns and consumption growth.

The representation of this model uses the pricing equation described in section 13.4.2 and the stochastic discount factor (SDF) approach, where the SDF is defined as $M_{t+1} = \delta \times u'(C_{t+1})/u'(C_t)$. The SDF is a ratio of marginal utility of consumption across two consecutive periods: If each marginal utility function is inversely related to the level of consumption, then the SDF is inversely related to consumption growth. If consumption growth is large, then the SDF is low. Based on the definition of the SDF, we may rewrite the pricing equation as:

$$V_t = E_t\left[\left(V_{t+1} + D_{t+1}\right) \times M_{t+1}\right] \tag{4}$$

Solving forward, the fundamental value then becomes $V_t = E_t \sum_{j=1}^{\infty} M_{t+j} \times D_{t+j}$. Developing the product of the expectations in equation (4), we get:

$$V_t = E_t\left[\left(V_{t+1} + D_{t+1}\right)\right] \times E_t[M_{t+1}] + COV_t[(V_{t+1} + D_{t+1}), M_{t+1}]$$

A positive covariance implies that future cash flows are high when consumption growth is low, which is beneficial from the point of view of hedging. Such hedging ability is recognized by investors in a high asset price. Technical Box 13.1 shows that the risk premium resulting from the model is:

$$E_t r_{t+1} = r_f + \frac{COV_t[r_{t+1}, M_{t+1}]}{V_t[M_{t+1}]} \times \left(-\frac{V_t[M_{t+1}]}{E_t[M_{t+1}]}\right) \tag{4}$$

The stochastic discount factor approach corresponds with the risk premium approach: in both cases expected cash flows are discounted at a rate including the risk-free rate and a risk premium. The contribution of this approach is to explain the risk premium based on the covariance between the rate of return and the SDF, that is, between the rate of return and consumption growth.

The model then generalizes the CAPM: The amount of risk is not given by the covariance between the return of the security and the return of the market, but by the covariance between the return of the security and the growth of the marginal utility of consumption. Technical Box 13.1 shows that when utility is logarithmic, then $M_{t+1} = C_t/C_{t+1}$. A security is particularly risky (positive covariance) when on average it generates low returns in periods of declining consumption, that is, when C_t/C_{t+1} is small. When consumption declines, you would want to hold a high-return stock (thanks to high dividends and/or a high market price) and sell it to stabilize overall consumption.

Given the relevance of aggregate consumption in stock pricing, the model, originally proposed by Lucas (1978), has been called the Consumption Capital Asset Pricing Model (CCAPM). The expected return on a given security can be expressed in this model as follows:

$$Er_i = r_f + \beta_i^C\left(Er_C - r_f\right)$$

where r_C is the return on a portfolio of stocks that is perfectly correlated with the SDF (consumption tracking portfolio) and β_i^C the beta of the asset relative to the consumption tracking portfolio.[11] According to the CAPM, the amount of risk is due to the covariance between the return of the asset and the return of the market portfolio; according to the CCAPM, with a view to general equilibrium and analysis of the contribution of each financial asset to the dynamic planning of consumption flows, what matters is the ability of the asset to have a high payoff in situations where aggregate consumption is decreasing.

Technical Box 13.1 **Deriving the CCAPM**

The equation $V_t = E_t\left[\left(V_{t+1} + D_{t+1}\right) \times M_{t+1}\right]$ may be used to price a risky asset and a risk-free asset, respectively obtaining:

$$1 = E_t\left[\left(1 + r_{t+1}\right) \times M_{t+1}\right]$$

$$1 = \left(1 + r_{f,t}\right)E_t\left[M_{t+1}\right]$$

The second equation shows that the observed risk-free rate is equal to the inverse of the expected stochastic discount factor. Using $\frac{1}{\left[E_t M_{t+1}\right]} = \left(1 + r_{f,t}\right)$ in the equation for the risky asset we get $1 = \frac{E_t\left(1 + r_{t+1}\right)}{\left(1 + r_{f,t}\right)} + COV_t\left[\left(1 + r_{t+1}\right), M_{t+1}\right]$, from which $E_t r_{t+1} = r_{f,t} - \frac{COV_t\left[r_{t+1}, M_{t+1}\right]}{E_t M_{t+1}}$, which can

[11] Use equation (4) for the rate of return of the consumption tracking portfolio, $r_{C,t+1}$ and notice that $COV_t\left[r_{C,t+1}, M_{t+1}\right] = V_t\left[M_{t+1}\right]$ so that $\frac{COV_t\left[r_{t+1}, M_{t+1}\right]}{V_t\left[M_{t+1}\right]} = 1$ so that $E_t r_{C,t+1} - r_f = -\frac{V_t\left[M_{t+1}\right]}{E_t\left[M_{t+1}\right]}$. Define $\beta_i^C = \frac{COV_t\left[r_{t+1}, r_{C,t+1}\right]}{V_t\left[r_{C,t+1}\right]}$ and use $E_t r_{C,t+1} - r_f = -\frac{V_t\left[M_{t+1}\right]}{E_t\left[M_{t+1}\right]}$ to get the equation in the text.

be rewritten to include a "consumption beta" as $E_t r_{t+1} = r_f + \frac{COV_t[r_{t+1}, M_{t+1}]}{V_t[M_{t+1}]} \times \left(-\frac{V_t[M_{t+1}]}{E_t[M_{t+1}]}\right)$.

It follows that $V_t = \frac{E_t(V_{t+1} + D_{t+1})}{1 + r_{f,t} - \frac{COV_t[r_{t+1}, M_{t+1}]}{E_t M_{t+1}}}$. The model then generalizes the CAPM. In the case of logarithmic utility, $u(C_t) = \ln(C_t)$, the marginal utility of consumption is $u'(C_t) = 1/C_t$, and the ratio becomes $u'(C_{t+1})/u'(C_t) = C_t/C_{t+1}$. With log utility, therefore, $COV_t[r_{t+1}, M_{t+1}] = COV_t\left[r_{t+1}, \frac{C_t}{C_{t+1}}\right]$. A security is particularly risky (positive covariance) when on average it generates low returns in periods of declining consumption, that is, when C_t/C_{t+1} is small. When consumption declines, you would want to hold a high-return stock (thanks to high dividends and/or a high market price) and sell it to stabilize overall consumption.

Box 13.2 Using the consumption beta

Question: Two assets A and B have covariances of 0.024 and -0.012, respectively, with the return of the consumption-tracking portfolio, which in turn has an expected return of 5% and variance of 4%. The risk-free rate is 1%. What should be the expected return on the two assets in theory?

Answer: The consumption beta of A is $\frac{0.024}{0.04} = 0.6$ and the beta of B is -0.3. The expected return pf A is equal to $0.03 + 0.6 \times 0.04 = 0.054$ whereas for B we have $0.03 - 0.3 \times 0.04 = 0.018$.

13.7.3 The equity premium puzzle

Mehra and Prescott (1985) study whether the consumption-based model explains the size of the equity premium observed in the stock market in the United States, using a calibration approach, which requires matching the observed long run average excess return with the expected excess return obtained from a theoretical model where the representative investor follows the logic of the CCAPM.

Some parameters in the model, for example dividend and consumption volatility, are calibrated to historical data. The risk aversion coefficient (in a constant relative risk aversion (CRRA) utility function), lacking a reliable point estimate, is assumed to stay in a range compatible with the experimental evidence on behavior in risky situations. For plausible values of the risk aversion coefficient, the model generates an equity premium of 0.6%, about a tenth of the historical realized average excess return. Mehra and Prescott therefore coined the term "equity premium puzzle" to describe the discrepancy between the data and the theoretical implications.

Among the many possible explanations of the puzzle, we focus on the following:

a) unpredictable shocks
b) survivorship bias
c) behavioral finance
d) tail events and long-term risk.

According to the first three explanations, the equity premium puzzle is linked to an incorrect use of statistics, whereas according to the others it depends on deficiencies in the models.

13.7.3.1 *Unpredictable shocks*

Over a certain period, the ex post return of an asset can be very high either because the average return (expected ex ante) is high or because there has been an unexpected and positive shock, linked for example to positive news about the asset's price level. The estimation of the expected return on the basis of the historical return assumes that the shocks were relatively small and of zero global impact, so that over a long time sample the estimate coincides with the average. However, it is not correct to extrapolate to the future the average return of an asset that in a certain sample period had a very high return due to the unexpected realization of factors that were positive, but which could turn out to be negative in the future. This is the explanation for the equity premium according to Fama and French (2002), who noted that the average excess return recorded in the United States over the previous 120 years had two different levels depending on the period before and after World War II. In fact, the data show that the risk premium was lower in the first part and higher in the second part of the sample, while the growth rate of the economy was stable over time.

Fama and French argue that the high return in the second sub-period was the result of positive shocks that increased the equilibrium price of the stock market in a completely unpredictable way, including:

- the stabilization of the economic cycle linked to institutions' improved ability to use monetary and fiscal policy; and
- the introduction of financial instruments such as mutual funds that allow investment in the stock market in a diversified manner and therefore with less risk, with the consequent increase in demand and the associated increase in the equilibrium price and the reduction of the risk premium.

Such unexpected positive shocks should be ignored for an estimation of the long-term risk premia, because they are linked to a particularly high ex post return that will not necessarily be able to occur ex ante. Shiller (1999) lists a number of factors that could represent negative shocks to market returns over the course of the 21st century.[12] Fama and French propose to estimate the average percentage change in stock prices with the average percentage change in earnings and dividends, a methodology consistent with the idea that in the long run the value of the stock market index must be proportional to the level of earnings and dividends, that is, $P_t \approx D_t \approx U_t \approx GDP_t$, from which $\frac{\Delta P_t}{P_t} \approx \frac{\Delta D_t}{D_t} \approx \frac{\Delta U_t}{U_t} \approx \frac{\Delta GDP_t}{GDP_t}$.

Based on this assumption, the equity return, equal to the sum of the capital gain and the dividend yield, can be calculated as the sum of the growth rate of the economy and the dividend yield. This method produces a more conservative estimate of the risk premium of around 4% in real terms.

Box 13.3 What is the long run expected return from the stock market?

Question: The stock market dividend yield is 3%. Historically, the average market return (including dividends) has been 8%, and the earnings growth rate has been 3%. The average risk-free rate was 1%. What equity risk premium estimates can be made based on this data?

Answer: On a purely historical basis, the average realized excess return was 7%. However, the data show that the capital gain component was 5% (the difference between historical return and the dividend yield). Fama and French suggest that an alternative estimate of the equity premium can be obtained from the sum of the average dividend yield and the growth rate of earnings. This approach provides an estimate of 5% by adding historical dividend yield (3%) to earnings growth (3%) minus risk-free (1%).

13.7.3.2 *Survivorship bias*

If you take a population made up of multiple markets, in the end one of them will be, by definition, the best or among the best from a performance standpoint. However, it would not be prudent to use this market to estimate the average return that can be expected from all markets in the future.

This is an example of survivorship bias, a statistical error that occurs when the properties of a population are evaluated solely on the basis of the properties of a few elements of the population. Jorion and Goetzmann (1999) studied a sample of thirty-nine markets between 1921 and 1996 and noted that the average return of the US market in their sample was about five times the average return of those of other countries, in part due to prolonged periods of closure of other markets, typically due

[12] The title is linked to a phrase uttered by Alan Greenspan when he was Fed Chairman on December 7, 1996, at Shiller's suggestion. Greenspan's full sentence (see New York Times, December 7, 1996, Section 1, p. 37) is "Clearly, sustained low inflation implies less uncertainty about the future, and lower risk premiums imply higher prices of stocks and other earning assets. We can see that in the inverse relationship exhibited by price/earnings ratios and the rate of inflation in the past. But how do we know when irrational exuberance has unduly escalated asset values, which then become subject to unexpected and prolonged contractions as they have in Japan over the past decade? And how do we factor that assessment into monetary policy?"

to wars and revolutions. In the case of the United States, the survival bias can be very important due to the dynamism of the market, highlighted by the data of Fama and French (2004): From the 1980s onwards the number of new listed companies was very high, and these were companies with high asset growth and low profitability, and therefore at high risk of bankruptcy. Under these conditions, the investor, while diversifying, holds a portfolio of securities with a higher risk and therefore demands a corresponding premium.

13.7.3.3 *Behavioral finance*

The high average return of the stock market could be the explanation for elements of investor irrationality. Barberis, Huang, and Santos (2001) argue that the equity premium is related to the presence of narrow framing and loss aversion, already examined in Chapter 3. Narrow framing implies that investors evaluate the performance of the stock market independently of the performance of the other assets, financial or real, held in the portfolio. Loss aversion implies that investors want to hedge against the risk of equity market losses by providing a high long-term average return, a premium that would not be justified if the stock market were valued in the context of all assets.

The presence of arbitrage limits could prevent professionals from intervening massively enough to remove the traces of irrationality from prices and returns.

13.7.3.4 *Tail events and long-term risks*

Rietz (1988) argues that the equity premium is due to the risk of "tail" events, defined as catastrophic situations from the point of view of consumption, and shows how the same model of Mehra and Prescott (1985) can justify the observed premium when it is extended to introduce an economic state, which may occur with low probability, of a sharp decline in consumption. Barro (2009) examines international data and highlights the existence of situations in which the consumption of an entire economy has fallen significantly. This has typically happened in conjunction with wars and revolutions (see, e.g., the cases of Russia, Germany, Japan, and Italy). Investors in the stock market may not rule out similar eventualities for the future and may determine expected prices and returns taking into account the possibility of catastrophes, even in markets where such destructive events have never historically occurred.

A situation that is less catastrophic than those described above, but which has long-term negative consequences for the investor-consumer, concerns the risk of a low growth rate of consumption in the long run. Bansal and Yaron (2004) show how to model this situation, which in fact seems to be empirically relevant to what has happened to economies such as Japan and Italy. In the latter, output growth from 2000 to 2019 had been about 0.3% on average per year even before the Covid-19 pandemic.

Box 14.1 What is the expected return of the Italian stock market?

Question: Carola turns to the consulting firm A.F.I. for guidance on the shares to invest in the various asset classes. In particular, she asks what the expected return on the Italian stock market is.

Answer: A.F.I. observes that the Italian stock market in the long run has provided an average real return of 2%, equal to less than one-third of that offered by the stock market in the United States and two-thirds of what is produced by the other major European economies. However, the consulting company also considers factors such as the high degree of uncertainty in any estimate of average returns and the existence of random shocks that must be considered to avoid falling into the error of simply extrapolating the past trend. A.F.I. revises the expected return for Italy considering the 6.5% average return on world equity markets. Using an average that puts one third of the weight to the world return, it obtains an estimate of 3.5%. Finally, A.F.I. considers Fama and French's (2002) suggestion to estimate future expected return as the sum of the dividend yield and the growth rate of the economy. From this point of view, however, the results do not substantially change the historical estimate of average return, given that in the previous twenty years the Italian economy had grown by an average of 0.3% per year. A.F.I. concludes that the estimated expected return on Italian equities is close to 3%.

13.8 Psychological drivers of market prices

Keynes (1936, p. 154) anticipated by almost a century an approach to understanding the stock market that relies on psychology. In Chapter 12 of *The General Theory of Employment, Interest and Money* (about "the state of long-term expectations") he writes that "in abnormal times in particular, when the hypothesis of an indefinite continuation of the existing state of affairs is less plausible than usual even though there are no express grounds to anticipate a definite change, the market will be subject to waves of optimistic and pessimistic sentiment, which are unreasoning and yet in a sense legitimate where no solid basis exists for a reasonable calculation."

In modern times, Shiller (2000, p. 136) has written extensively about the possibility that stock prices are partially driven by psychological factors. As Shiller puts it, "investors are striving to do the right thing, but they have limited abilities and certain natural modes of behavior that decide their own actions when an unambiguous prescription for action is lacking." According to this hypothesis, the market is anchored by quantitative factors such as the current or past level of stock market indices, or qualitative anchors associated with storytelling and narratives. We saw in Chapter 4 that people may select financial assets based on rules of thumb that may affect demand and therefore market prices. However, a prolonged period of aggregate prices moving up or down requires some sort of informal coordination among investors. What may give rise to such coordination?

Recent history provides an example of explicit coordination among a group of investors. In 2021 attention was focused on the extraordinary volatility of meme stocks propelled by posts on the Reddit group r/Wallstreetbets,[13] where people shared trading ideas on a group of stocks that were disliked by professional investors such as hedge funds. Actually, news reported by the international press suggests that the coordination among investors was so effective that it created a "short squeeze" for hedge funds: Retail investors pushed up the prices of meme stocks to the point where hedge funds had to close their short positions to avoid excessive losses but could not easily find the shares in the market due to their low liquidity and large demand.[14]

Economists have also studied what we learn from psychology, especially social psychology. Shiller (2000) uses the well-known results of psychologists Asch (1952) and Deutsch and Gerard (1955) to understand the relevance of social influence. In experiments, a relevant proportion of subjects gave wrong answers to simple questions with clear and correct solutions based on knowing that a reference group had given the same wrong answer, probably reacting to the information that a large group of people had reached a different judgment from theirs. Informational cascades can arise when people react to evidence about reference group behavior. An isolated investor who thinks the stock market is overvalued may change her mind and start buying after evidence of continued price increase.[15]

---

[13] A meme is an idea or some element of popular culture that spreads and multiplies. Memes gained increasing prevalence and relevance as the internet and social media grew. They allow people to rapidly spread humorous, interesting, or sarcastic videos, images, or posts to others around the world (see https://www.investopedia.com/meme-stock-5206762). According to Britannica (https://www.britannica.com/topic/meme), a meme is a unit of cultural information spread by imitation. The term meme (from the Greek mimema, meaning "imitated") was introduced in 1976 by British evolutionary biologist Richard Dawkins in his work The Selfish Gene. Dawkins conceived of memes as the cultural parallel to biological genes and considered them, in a manner similar to "selfish" genes, as being in control of their own reproduction and thus serving their own ends. Understood in those terms, memes carry information, are replicated, and are transmitted from one person to another, and they have the ability to evolve, mutating at random and undergoing natural selection, with or without impacts on human fitness (reproduction and survival). Shiller (2019) views memes as tools to spread narratives and mentions literature going back to the 1840s about efforts to understand and describe the spread of narratives.

[14] According to Aggarwal, Choi, and Lee (2023, p. 1401), "GameStop had been losing money and was facing a liquidity crisis. The market had been predicting (as evidenced by the low stock price) that the company would likely file for bankruptcy and possibly be liquidated in the near future. A number of hedge funds—most prominently Melvin Capital—had taken a large short position against its stock, betting that the price would drop even further. In January 2021, retail investors engaged in an active "buy" campaign to dramatically push up the GameStop stock price to the stratospheric level of over $483 per share from less than $4 per share. Retail investors' influx seems to have been driven in part to create a "short squeeze" against the hedge funds. The end result was a large loss—and ultimate retreat—by the hedge funds. Market analysts observed that meme traders used Reddit to decide on target firms that typically had few outstanding shares. Incidentally, the price of the most famous meme stock, GameStop, is above $13 as of March 22, 2024. At least judged with a three-year horizons, retail investors were better than hedge funds at valuing the stock. An example of "wisdom of the crowd?"

[15] The SIR (susceptible/infective/recorded) model of the spread of contagion that we learned about during the 2020–2021 Covid-19 pandemic is a mathematical description that may be used to describe the deterministic diffusion of opinions about investing (see Shiller, 2019).

13.9 Risky arbitrage

It is now possible to summarize the implications of previous chapters to reflect on market dynamics. In doing so, we will take up the concepts seen when talking about behavioral finance (Chapter 4), anomalies (Chapter 10), multifactor model of risk and return (Chapter 11), and evaluation (Chapter 12). Following the literature, we will use the term "smart trader" to refer to the existence of a group of professional traders (typically, portfolio managers working in asset management firms) who operate with knowledge, information, and analytical tools that are superior to those used by individual investors (who may be referred to as retail investors).

We have seen that:

a) anomalies persist, although various methodological doubts about their existence;
b) it is not clear whether or not the returns of the anomalies are justified by the presence of risk elements related to the non-diversifiable factors described by the arbitrage pricing theory model;
c) retail investors make systematic errors in asset management, which have a significant impact on the ratio between average return achieved and risk incurred; and
d) there is excess volatility at the level of market indices, whereby equity prices move more than would be justified on the basis of rational responses to fundamentals.

Why do smart traders fail at eliminating that part of the anomaly returns that is not justified by the reward for systematic risk factors? Why do not they take advantage of the discrepancy between price and value and help reduce market volatility? To answer these questions, it should first be noted that to react to anomalies and the discrepancy between price and value, smart traders must implement "risky arbitrage" strategies. Such arbitrage involves buying the security when the market price is below fair value, and vice versa, and forming portfolios that can take advantage of anomalies. However, there are margins of risk in all these operations, referred to as "arbitrage limits," which prevent smart traders from taking full advantage of the opportunities created by irrational behavior. The main limitations are due to:

- model risk: The difference between market price and fair value can be estimated but is never known with certainty. Smart traders will therefore always take into account the possibility of making a mistake in the calculation of the "fair value" due to a wrong model;
- non-diversification risk: In order to take advantage of the difference between price and value, it is necessary to form portfolios that are not very diversified because the relevant differences appear in a limited number of securities, and as we saw in Chapter 10, this creates diversifiable risk that must be adequately compensated by the ability to select securities;
- risk of market irrationality: The presence of overvaluation or undervaluation of market prices can continue for unforeseeable periods (Keynes said that "markets can remain irrational longer than you can remain solvent"); and

- transaction costs: Financial transactions have direct costs and also indirect costs related to the acquisition and study of information.

Finally, it is worth mentioning the existence of the "information paradox" identified by Grossman and Stiglitz (1980), according to which prices can never correspond exactly to values because if this were the case, smart traders would have no incentive to incur the costs of acquiring and processing information. In fact, investors bear the costs of data collection and analysis precisely in order to obtain rewards for active management. Such premiums would never materialize if prices were always equal to values, since it would be irrational to spend resources on having information that is already embedded in prices. The evidence that market participants incur costs to acquire information is therefore consistent with a situation in which, at least at the level of individual securities, prices are not always equal to values.

Summary

- Market efficiency can be considered from the point of view of the speed of incorporating the available information ("information efficiency") and from the point of view of correctly assessing the implications of a news item for the price ("valuation efficiency"). The general definition of an efficient market encompasses both information efficiency and valuation efficiency, and the efficiency of the financial market is extremely important for the functioning of the economy as a whole.
- Some tests aim to understand whether the value of a stock or stock index is determined by discounting future dividends for an appropriate discount rate. Such tests generally find the presence of excess volatility.
- Regression analyses typically do not find room for temporal predictability of returns over short horizons such as day, week, month, and even year. Predictability emerges strongly when analyzing multi-period returns, for example two, three, or five years.
- For short-term horizons, prices are well described by the random walk hypothesis, which implies a future price expectation equal to the last observed price.
- It is possible to empirically identify portfolios that replicate the return of factors (factor tracking portfolios) of particular interest, also taking into account the existence of predictability.
- Predictability of returns can be made compatible with market efficiency if the share of predictable returns is associated with a risk premium that varies over time.
- The event study methodology aims to analyze the reactions of securities subjected to a certain news category to measure their differential returns to the market and understand whether the reactions are compatible with the theory of efficient markets.
- The theory of risky arbitrage highlights a number of elements that prevent professional investors from taking advantage of price-to-value discrepancies.

14 Private assets

14.1 Introduction

Accessing private assets (mostly equity, fixed income and real estate) through collective investment vehicles (making them investable private assets) implies the need to understand several important and peculiar issues associated with challenges regarding the value of the underlying assets and the performance of the asset manager in relation to the portfolio risk. Several econometric techniques have been developed to answer the legitimate interest, on the part of investors and society at large, in a periodic evaluation of a private asset class. Such techniques must face challenges associated with the heterogeneity of the portion of the stock that is traded in a certain period of time, implying changes in the quality of the underlying assets and the need to account for time-varying average quality. Hedonic indices and repeated sale indices are an econometric answer to the challenges.

Finally, there is a deep interest on the part of investors to jointly consider public assets and private assets in the same overall portfolio optimization logic. Private assets attract a lot of attention due to their being considered "alternative," that is, investments whose return has low correlation with that offered by financial markets (particularly equity markets). We have seen in the book that investors are willing to pay a premium to buy an alternative investment that may be able to stabilize the value of an overall portfolio over time. The problems associated with frequent valuation of the assets prevent a full comparison based on a unique definition of return and make it difficult to use the standard Markowitz optimization model relying on parameters of volatilities and correlations.

14.2 Private assets

Private assets are investment objects that are not traded (listed) in public markets. Their total value is unknown even though there are various attempts at estimating it (see a few studies discussed in Ilmanen, 2022). Some private assets are investable, while others are not. A small family business may produce earnings and dividends but is usually entirely owned by a family. An investor may think it would be a good idea to invest in a portfolio of small family businesses, but that is not possible if they are not investable. We refer to this part of private assets as non-investable private assets. Financial intermediaries help make private assets investable. When a fund buys a stake in a private company, the final investor acquires exposure to the private company by investing in the fund.

Figure 14.1 The assets

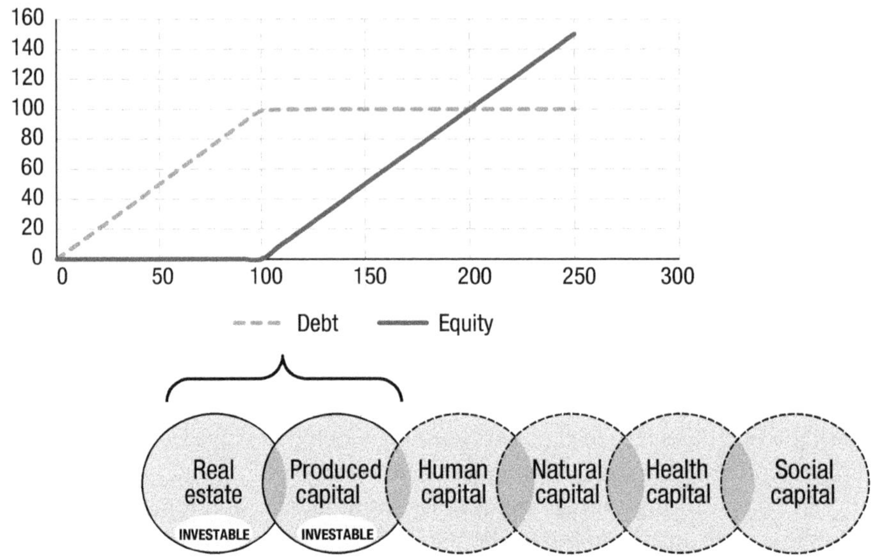

The assets in the circles in Figure 14.1 are mostly non-traded and are often neglected in national accounting systems (a point that will be reconsidered and discussed in Chapter 15). Technically speaking, real estate could be included in "produced capital" if the latter were defined as a collection of assets that have been created through the application of labor to raw materials, like for machinery, equipment, and infrastructure. However, given its relevance from a quantitative point of view, we have chosen to include real estate explicitly in the picture.

For any company, real estate and produced capital are included in the asset side of the balance sheet, whose value corresponds to that of the liability side, including debt and equity. For both assets, the investable portion is only a part of the total. Real estate and produced capital are accessible to investors due to the listing of companies that rely on such assets to produce earnings and dividends and through funds that invest in companies owning such assets. In the latter case, defined as investable private capital, investors can get exposure to real estate and produced capital through debt and equity contracts issued by vehicles provided by asset managers. Ilmanen (2022) uses Preqin data and estimates that investable private assets amounted to $7.3 trillion in mid-2020, divided into $4.5 trillion in private equity, $1.1 trillion in real estate, $0.9 trillion in infrastructure and natural resources, and $0.9 trillion in private debt. To understand the quantitative difference between "investable" and "non-investable" assets, Tostevin (2017) estimated a value of $228 trillion for all global real estate, of which $168 trillion is in residential real estate, $32 trillion in commercial real estate, and $27 trillion in agricultural land and forest. The ratio between the $1.1 trillion in private real estate and the total $228 trillion means that less than 0.5% of real estate assets are investable.

A ten-year closed-end fund is the typical solution offered by asset managers under the form of collective investment vehicles, one that is consistent with the liquidity of the underlying asset. For example, the private equity fund buys stakes in companies, holds them for a period, and then exits the investment (more on this in section 14.3). It would be difficult and unprofitable for the fund to liquidate the investment one year after building the position, because the fund manager is likely to have just started the complex operational and financing operations that might multiply the value of the company in the time horizon. A closed-end fund does not promise any liquidity (at least not on the part of the issuer) and as a result there is full alignment of interest between the fund manager and the fund investor. Only investors characterized by long horizons would invest in the fund.

Sometimes investments in private assets can be implemented through liquid structures such as an open-end fund, allowing for the possibility to redeem the shares either continuously or at least at given pre-specified intervals. Such vehicles seem to incentivize investors to acquire private assets by giving them the possibility to sell their holdings, even at the cost of making asset management much more challenging. This model works if only a small proportion of investors try to liquidate their investments. If the pressure to divest is too large and there are not enough buyers of new shares, the portfolio manager will be forced to sell the assets in the portfolio, and this may be difficult and unprofitable to do, creating negative externalities also for the investors who did not want to sell but were willing to hold on until the natural expiration of the fund.

A final note on the assets that are in dotted circles in Figure 14.1: human capital, natural capital, health capital, and social capital. Such assets are extremely important for consumption and production. Their relevance is implicitly valued by the stock market when setting the price of a listed company whose revenues are increased by the presence of a healthy and well-educated workforce, operating in an environment characterized by a high level of natural capital and by a cohesive social community. To some extent all these elements are included in the so-called level of intangibles often used to justify a market value much above the book value. For several reasons it is hard to think of diversified investment vehicles that could allow investors to have a direct and specific exposure to such assets.

14.3 Private equity

Private equity typically refers to investments in unlisted target companies. Fraser-Sampson (2010, p. 2) defines private equity as "any equity investment in a company which is not quoted on a stock exchange." Private equity funds are vehicles that invest in a portfolio of unlisted companies. In some cases, the investment takes place in listed companies but in the context of public-to-private transactions where the fund manager buys a listed company to make it private. Investors in private equity funds are characterized as limited partners (LPs) or general partners (GPs). GPs invest their capital but manage the fund at the same time, while LPs in general are purely external investors who do not participate in the fund's choices.

A relevant distinction is between "buyout" funds and "venture capital" funds. Buyout funds are interested in companies that are already established, often in traditional, medium-sized sectors. In these cases, the private equity fund tends to take on controlling positions and works together with the company's management team or a new management team that is newly integrated into the company. From a financial point of view, buyouts use financial resources obtained either as direct investments of the private equity (PE) fund that uses equity, or resources borrowed from banks or more often from private debt funds. In venture capital (VC) funds, the targets are young, typically small, high-tech companies. VC deals are more rarely controlled and generally only use equity.

Traditionally buyout funds are interested in low-growth, mature targets to improve their performance through operational improvements, financial restructuring, and governance and managerial optimization. A dominant strategy has become buy-and-build (B&B), where a fund objective is to scale up a platform company through smaller add-on acquisitions. Platform investments are companies that are regarded as a starting point for more acquisitions, or add-ons, to follow in the future. Normally, new platforms include companies in high-growth industries that are commanding a significant market share and may support add-ons. Add-on companies are typically followers and need operational and financial actions to improve their management and potential. The page from Symmetrical M&A Advisory, https://symmetricaladvisory.com/private-equity-101-new-platforms-vs-add-ons/, estimates that add-ons constitute 40–50% of buyout activity. Hammer at al. (2022) show that B&B platforms command a relevant premium associated with the option to grow through follow-on acquisitions: PE investors pay up to 28% higher enterprise value-to-sales multiples if the target serves as the platform for a B&B strategy.

Private equity funds are "closed-end" and have a fixed duration (often ten years). The capital raising therefore targets the "patient capital" that remains in the fund for the entire term. Investors contractually commit to pay a certain amount of money for the purchase of the fund's units (committed capital). The committed capital is "called" over time (over an initial time horizon, often a couple of years) by the GPs of the private equity fund (drawn down capital) and gradually invested (invested capital). The capital that has not been formally called, and is therefore committed and ready to be invested, is defined as "dry powder."

The private equity fund benefits from a management fee that is paid by investors on all committed capital for the life of the fund, regardless of its actual investment. In some cases, the fee may be levied partly on the capital committed and partly on the capital invested, with proportions unbalanced in favor of the former in the initial phase of the fund's life and in favor of the latter in the second part of the fund's life. However, the most consistent remuneration comes from incentive fees (carried interest), which can be withdrawn when the average return exceeds a minimum target (hurdle rate) and the proceeds paid to investors exceed the value of the invested capital capitalized at the hurdle rate. For example, the contract may stipulate that carried interest cannot be paid until the fund's internal rate of return exceeds the 7% hurdle rate, at which point an incentive fee of 20% is applied to the management company. There are also other profit margins for GPs linked to the costs incurred directly by the companies that are part of the portfolio for various types of advisory provided, at least in part, by the management company itself.

14.4 Private debt

14.4.1 Private debt and business development companies

Traditionally, only banks could lend to corporations. Regulation has opened the way for intervention of other licensed financial institutions that provide lending activity, known as "private debt" or "private credit." Private debt funds together with collateralized loan obligation funds (CLO) are the main types of non-bank intermediaries. The main difference is that the former mostly make senior loans directly to middle-market firms (conventionally defined as firms with revenues between $10 million and $1 billion), while the latter invest in syndicated loans that are usually arranged by large banks. According to Preqin (2023), in the United States private debt was worth $1.5 trillion as of 2023. Among the financial institutions that are active players in this space we find finance companies, investment banks, insurance companies, hedge funds, and private debt funds.

The main three categories of credit investments are liquid debt instruments (loans and bonds of companies that trade like equities), direct lending (loans directly made to companies with bespoke terms for maturity, interest, collateral, and seniority), and distressed debt (loans or bonds that are in distress). Direct lending is the main focus of private debt, and an important distinction in this regard is whether there is a sponsor to the borrower.

In sponsored financing the business is either wholly owned or majority owned by a PE firm, providing more safety to the lender due to its commitment, its ability and willingness to share some of the information created in the process of becoming shareholders, and an implicit availability to inject more equity in the future if needed. Non-sponsored financing requires more work and due diligence effort and more time to complete, and it may be riskier and compensated with higher remuneration for the lender.

Private debt funds can have an open-end or a closed-end structure. Open-end funds have been described in Chapter 1 and closed-end structures in section 14.3. Closed-end funds have a final date by which they must obtain the repayment of the loans and return the capital initially invested to LPs. The activities associated with raising capital, investing it, and returning it involve a lot of transaction costs: An asset management company that manages a closed-end fund must continuously devote resources to raise capital for the new funds proposed to investors and must manage the fund with a limited horizon.

To reduce transaction costs there is a lot of interest in permanent capital vehicles where capital must not be returned to investors by a fixed date. Particularly important cases of companies with permanent capital in private debt are business development companies (BDCs). Block, Young Soo, Kaplan, and Schulze (2023) survey institutional investors active in private debt in Europe and the United States, representing about 35% of the total value, and find that in the US 45% of the funds are BDCs. BDCs are financial institutions, often but not necessarily listed on the stock exchange, that make medium-term loans to companies, even small to medium-sized ones (for a very early academic paper studying BDCs, see Beltratti and Bock, 2018). To be recognized as a BDC it is necessary to:

- invest at least 70% of the assets in certain asset classes such as corporate bonds, equities, cash, and so forth;
- maintain leverage at a limited two dollars of debt for every dollar of equity;
- no investment may account for more than 25% of the total value of the assets;
- 50% of the value of the portfolio must represent no more than 5% of the assets;
- 90% of the income must be obtained from dividends and interest.

BDCs are generally listed on the stock exchange and therefore are useful for aiding liquid investment in illiquid assets. Liquidity, in other words, is sought through investors' frequent trades instead of pretending there is liquidity in assets that are not by their nature liquid. They also do not have a time horizon, allowing BDC managers to focus on lending and portfolio quality control (see Hedlund, 2019). Box 14.1 describes a case study regarding Ares Capital Corporation.

Box 14.1 Case study: Ares management and Ares Capital Corporation

Ares Capital Corporation (ARCC) is the largest (as of the end of 2023) publicly traded BDC focusing on the financing needs of private middle-market companies in the United States. ARCC invests primarily in senior secured loans but also in subordinated debt, sometimes including equity components, and preferred equity. ARCC's investment advisor is Ares Capital Management. As of April 2024, 99.3% of the shares are free-floating in the market. The main shareholders are Morgan Stanley Investment Management (2.255%), RBC Private Counsel (2.099%), van Eck Associates Corp. (1.365%), and J.P. Morgan Private Wealth Advisors (1.060%). Ares Management Corporation is a leading global alternative investment manager, founded in 1997, offering clients primary and secondary investment solutions across the credit, private equity, real estate, and infrastructure asset classes. Ares is active in five distinct sub-sectors, including direct lending (private loans or investments directly to sponsor-backed or management-owned companies primarily based on cash flows, corporate enterprise value, and assets), alternative credit (private asset-based credit that invests in diversified pools of assets that generate cash flows across a wide group of sectors, including auto and aviation, consumer, mortgages, equipment leasing, and fund finance), real estate debt (to finance the purchase or development of real estate assets), infrastructure debt, and opportunistic credit (private lending to healthy companies and businesses in need of transitional capital through flexible debt and/or non-control equity solutions).

14.4.2 Why private debt

Academic literature claims that private debt arises out of regulation-induced bank disintermediation, preventing banks from profitably lending to less creditworthy companies characterized by high levels of debt, as measured for example by the debt/EBITDA ratio. Irani, Iyer, Meisenzahl and Peydró, (2021) show that banks with weak regulatory capital positions have been more likely to reduce loan retention through secondary market activity, particularly non-performing loans.[1] Chernenko, Erel, and Prilmeier (2022) and Block, Young Soo, Kaplan and Schultze (2024) suggest that borrowers approach private debt funds when they are unable to obtain bank financing, and this is consistent with such firms being riskier than firms who get bank loans.

Private debt funds charge an annual management fee of about 1.5% and a carried interest of 15%. To compensate for such high fees, they need to provide expensive forms of financing. Davydiuk, Marchuk, and Rosen (2020) find that BDCs charge rates on their direct loans that are at least 4% higher than those on bank loans. Chernenko, Erel, and Prilmeier (2022) find that firms with negative EBITDA and higher debt are more likely to borrow from non-banks and pay higher interest rates.

If their existence is mainly due to regulatory arbitrage, then private loans may earn a higher interest rate due to the scarcity of cheaper funding from the point of view of borrowers. However, private debt funds may be more efficient than banks; for example, they are better able to understand firms' needs and can structure the best contracts in a short time, in which case the extra cost could be due to a better-quality service. For example, Ares (2024) shows that total annualized net returns over the period 2005–2023 as measured by the Cliffwater Direct Lending Index was 9.45%, about double the net return on the Morningstar LSTA US leveraged Loan Index and 50% larger than the Bloomberg High Yield Index, with similar annualized credit loss/charge off rates respectively equal to 1.02%, 0.84%, and 1.48%[2]. The paper also claims that the efficiency ratio (the amount of cost, including fees and expenses, to generate a dollar of return for investors) of banks is 62% while that of an average top BDC is 26%. While the comparison may not be appropriate, it suggests that the reason why private debt is popular may be due to the advantages of its own business model rather than the retreat of banks.

[1] They also point out that lending activity by non-banks is penalized in secondary markets during crises: The impossibility on the part of non-banks to access central bank liquidity may force them to cut new lending to meet their own liquidity needs.

[2] See Munday, True and Zhang (2018) for consistent results.

14.5 Real estate

14.5.1 How to invest in real estate

There are various possibilities for investing in real estate, one of which is direct investment into single buildings or projects, for example an institutional investor buying a building that is then rented out to provide offices to firms. The problem with direct investment lies in low diversification due to the large size of real estate investments, low liquidity, and the need to have expertise for understanding the risk and opportunities of the various possibilities.

Indirect investment may occur through purchasing shares in funds that in turn invest in the residential or commercial sector, and financial products. Financial products for real estate investment have a long tradition in the United States especially associated with the use of securitization techniques, in particular mortgage-backed securities (MBS) and collateralized mortgage obligations (CMO).

14.5.2 Indirect investment in real estate stocks

Real estate is a relevant asset for most corporate and financial institutions and therefore purchasing a stock or a bond issued by a listed entity involves an exposure to real estate assets. Such assets may be owned by the entity and may be instrumental to carrying out the primary business activity. In most cases their valuation is relevant for the corporate or financial institution and that is why indirect investment in real estate often takes place through the channel of securities listed on the stock exchange.

Among the companies listed on the stock exchange, we remember first those whose main business is precisely construction. However, there are other examples of companies that are sensitive to the real estate market, sometimes in a completely unexpected way. In addition to the interesting case of McDonald's and WeWork, described in Box 14.2, just think of the case of the banking system. Banks seem to be a sector with little exposure to real estate, but their secured lending operations generally involve a real estate collateral that wuld be repossessed if the borrower is unable to repay the debt. As a result, a crisis in the real estate sector reducing the value of collateral can increase banks' risk. This is even more true when, as is often the case, the crisis in real estate prices is correlated with a recession. In this case, banks face a "perfect storm": Companies to which they have lent financial resources have greater difficulty in honoring their debts and may be forced to sell or hand over real estate to banks at times when the value of the property is lowest. Thinking back to the models for determining risk analyzed in the book, banks are sensitive to real estate risk, with the aggravating circumstance that the phases in which risk manifests itself are precisely those in which the rest of the economy suffers—an example in which the covariance with the economy increases precisely in the worst phases!

Tuzel (2010) finds that the returns of companies most exposed to real estate are 3–6% higher on average per year than the returns of companies with little exposure to real estate, even after taking into account the exposure of securities to the risk factors (described in Chapter 10 such as size, value, and momentum. The explanation for the results is found in the high level of risk associated with real estate exposure, which increases the damage associated with negative shocks to company productivity due to the difficulty of reusing the input.

Box 14.2 Which company is most sensitive to real estate trends?

Sometimes it is hard to understand the drivers of corporate earnings. Take McDonald's and WeWork, for example, two very different companies. There is no need to describe the former. The second is a platform that promotes flexible working through space rental. Which of the two companies is more sensitive to real estate trends? The answer seems obvious if it is given using one of the behavioral biases described in Chapter 4, that is, if one associates the estimation of real estate sensitivity with the mental image of the product and service that seems predominant (hamburgers on the one hand, office spaces on the other). The real answer, however, is perhaps less simple than one might imagine. McDonald's over time has become the owner of land and buildings that are rented out to franchisees. The rent is partly fixed and partly linked to sales. Using the 2008 crisis, McDonald's has increased its ownership stake and owns 45% of the land and 70% of the buildings where the restaurants are located. McDonald's has a risk related to the proprietary exposure of buildings and land, but a low exposure to the risk of recession (indeed, as demonstrated in the US crisis in 2008, people consume more cheap food at times of crisis, which allows the company to maintain its value even when things go wrong). WeWork was founded as a platform, and in theory a change in real estate prices may not be particularly relevant, while a recession that reduces the demand for flexible work could cause much more significant damage. To add more conflicting evidence, in May 2019 WeWork created a subsidiary, Ark, to buy the properties rented by WeWork. This is an interesting case of how a platform can decide to move upstream in the value creation process and change its business model accordingly. Presumably, in the case at hand, the move depends both on the costs incurred for leasing contracts and on the importance of having real estate assets that can also constitute a tangible source of assets, useful in business relationships.

14.5.3 Funds and investment in real estate

Real estate investment trusts (REITs) were introduced in the 1960s in the United States to allow diversified investment in real estate properties of various types (residential, infrastructure, logistics, hotels, etc.), ensuring that investors are tax-neutral due to the possibility of deducting any cash flow paid to shareholders as remuneration from gross income. Most such collective investment vehicles buy real estate assets, lease them, and use the rents to pay dividends to their shareholders. To be defined as a REIT, the fund must observe a few rules:

- invest at least 75% of assets in real estate, government bonds, or cash;
- obtain at least 75% of gross income from real estate property rentals, interest on mortgages that finance properties, and sales of assets held in portfolios;
- pay a dividend each year on at least 90% of pre-tax income;

- have at least 100 shareholders; and
- the top five investors may not hold more than 50% of the capital.

In the United States, REITs hold over $3 trillion in assets, of which $2 trillion are held by publicly traded REITs. REITs are useful for aiding liquid investment in illiquid assets. Liquidity, in other words, is sought through investors' frequent trades of the vehicles rather than of the illiquid underlying assets. There is much attention to REITs on the part of academics.

Two examples are Ghent, Torous, and Valkanov (2019), showing that the type of properties purchased by REITs reflects the characteristics of commercial real estate in general, except for the larger size and younger age, and Muhlhofer (2013), showing that REITs tend to buy real estate more for their income than for capital gains prospects, given the previously exposed constraints that lead them to prioritize income.

14.6 Art

14.6.1 Art as an alternative asset

The fundamental value of art is largely based on preferences (see Technical Box 14.1), but factors such as interest rates and the business cycle may affect consumption and its marginal utility. It follows that art is an interesting asset class because the relevance of buyers' preferences may decrease the correlation with the business cycle and other asset class returns.

Technical Box 14.1 Pricing art objects

This box uses the consumption pricing model described in 13.4.2. If the collector derives utility from enjoying a work of art, we can extend the utility function to account for the contribution made by both consumption of general goods and services c_t and the service (pleasure) s_t obtained from the art object $u(c_t, s_t)$. We assume the existence of a simple linear relationship $s_t = \tau a_t$ where a_t is the stock of available artwork and denote the market price of art with P_t. The cost of buying art is the product of its price and the marginal utility of consumption, as measured by $u'_c(c_t, s_t) \times P_t$ where $u'_c(c_t, s_t)$ is the marginal utility of consumption. The benefit of buying art is provided by the sum of the expected future marginal utility of enjoying the art object, as measured by the marginal utility associated with art $u'_s(c_{t+1}, s_{t+1})$, and the expected marginal utility of consumption associated with the resale of the art object at the future price P_{t+1}. The present value of the expected future benefit is reduced by the discounting due to the rate of time preference δ. Balancing cost and revenue therefore implies $u'_c(c_t, s_t) \times P_t = \delta \times E_t\left[u'_c(c_{t+1}, s_{t+1}) \times \left(P_{t+1} + \tau \times u'_s(c_{t+1}, s_{t+1})\right)\right]$. Using the definition of the stochastic discount factor M and solving forward we obtain $P_t = E_t\left[\tau \times u'_s(c_{t+1}, s_{t+1}) \times M_{t+1} + \tau \times u'_s(c_{t+2}, s_{t+2}) \times M_{t+2} + \ldots\right]$. The fundamental price of art depends on the present discounted value of the stream of marginal utility associated with the pleasure provided by artistic creations. It can be affected by growth and interest rates to the extent these factors influence future consumption and the associated marginal utility, which in turn affects the expected present discounted value.

14.6.2 Investing in art

The prevailing instrument for investing in art is the direct purchase of works in venues such as auctions, galleries, or specialized sites. Arts Economics (2024) estimates sales in the art market in 2023 at $65 billion worldwide, with a decrease in both public auction and dealer sales relative to 2022, with 42% concentrated in the United States. Online sales reached almost $12 billion.

It is also possible to invest in a diversified manner through traditional vehicles such as art funds and new vehicles associated with technology platforms. The choice between direct investment in one or more art objects and a private fund or a platform has to do with the trade-off between the benefit of a diversified investment and the opportunity cost of not enjoying art pieces at home. Art funds work similarly to other private funds, clearly requiring specific knowledge of the market on the part of fund managers. According to Frye (2018), in 1904 a group of Parisian art collectors formed the first private art investment club, and many art funds were created in the 2000s.

Diversified investment made through funds has not become widespread, probably due to the peculiarity of the purchase of works of art, requiring physical possession of the same to enjoy the aesthetic benefits, which cannot be obtained by purchasing a share of a fund. In addition, the low liquidity of the market makes it very difficult to operate vehicles that manage the investment of several customers.

A recent addition is provided by art platforms that allow collectors to select art objects and directly purchase the objects. Some of these platforms also allow for a potential resale of art objects that have been purchased in the past, trying to create some liquidity. Arts Economics (2024) points out that in the period 2021–2023 there was a decline of interest in third-party platforms (platforms not managed directly by auction houses and dealers) including non-fungible tokens (NFTs).[3]

Technological and institutional convergence has created the possibility to invest in an art fund selling shares through crowdfunding platforms. For example, Masterworks sells shares in current art offerings and allows trading on the platform's secondary market, charging an annual fee of 1.5% and 20% of the profits.

More recent experiences allow for indirect investment in loans secured by works of art. In such a scheme, a collector obtains a loan from a financial intermediary, secured by one or more works of art. Depending on legislation and customs, works of art can be left in collectors' homes or transported to safe locations to prevent them from being damaged. The intermediary providing the loan can in turn invest capital from third-party investors, who have the benefit of obtaining the value of the under-

---

[3] According to Britannica (https://www.britannica.com/story/what-is-an-nft), "a non-fungible token is a digital asset that has been authenticated using blockchain technology. Digital assets are intangible objects that live on the Internet, including videos, GIFs, images, and collages. NFTs allow their makers not only to 'sign' digital assets but also to make money from them, often selling them on digital marketplaces using digital wallets holding cryptocurrency … A digital artist can authenticate one or more copies of an asset, each copy having its own unique token."

lying asset if the debtor cannot meet the payment of interest and principal. However, these new examples are still very limited, particularly in Europe, in part because of the high transaction costs necessary for all ancillary activities, from the valuation of works of art to their safekeeping.

14.7 Performance evaluation of private assets

14.7.1 The internal rate of return

A private fund involves a series of negative and positive cash flows. At the very beginning, LPs start paying fees on the amount of committed capital. Next, the committed capital is invested over time, with more outflows from the point of view of the investor. As the fund matures, there are distributions back to investors due to sales of or proceeds from portfolio companies. The situation is therefore different from what typically happens for a financial investor in public markets, investing a specific amount of money at a point in time and then measuring the return. The geometric rate of return r, defined in Chapter 2 as $(1+r)^T = (1+r_1)\times(1+r_2)\times\ldots\times(1+r_T)$, is known as the time-weighted return because all the different periods have the same relevance. The geometric average return cannot account for different cash flows (positive or negative) being invested at different times. The money-weighted rate of return r_{MW} is the solution to this need:

$$\sum_{t=1}^{T}\frac{CF_t}{(1+r_{MW})}=0\,.$$

The money-weighted rate of return is the internal rate of return (IRR)[4] of the cash flows. Assume, for example, that initially there is a payment of €30 that is used to pay for the €3 fee and for purchasing companies. The internal rate of return for the first year is computed as $-30+\frac{27}{(1+r_{MW})}=0$ providing $r_{MW}=-10\%$. We are therefore assuming that the €27 invested in private companies is paid to the investor even though no cash flows go to the investor at the end of the period.

For the first few years in the life of a fund, the IRR is negative since the investor incurs costs but the capital is not able yet to produce returns because it has just been invested. Positive cash flows are obtained when dividends are paid by portfolio com-

[4] The internal rate of return is the number y that satisfies the equation $\sum_{t=1}^{T}\frac{FP_t-FN_t}{(1+y)^t}=0$ where FP_t is the positive cash flow obtained by the investor from dividends and sales of the companies in the portfolio and FN_t is the negative flow related to the payment of commissions. There are critical issues regarding the interpretation of the IRR, including the assumption that all intermediate flows should be reinvested at exactly the same rate, a theme addressed in Chapter 5.

panies and/or when the companies themselves are sold to other investors, often other PE funds, or listed on the market. The presence of a typical trend characterized by a negative value of the annual IRR from the start of the fund's activities to the specific point in the fund's life is known as the "J curve," an example of which is represented in Figure 14.2.

The J curve represents the IRR of the investment from the beginning to each period considered in Figure 14.2. To continue with the previous example, assume that after the initial payment of €30 there is a second payment of €30, again allocated for €3 to fees and €27 to company purchases, in the third year there is a €3 payment for fees and the portfolio companies are kept at book value, while finally in the fourth year the overall portfolio is liquidated for €100. The IRRs in the different years are shown in Table 14.1.

Table 14.1 **IRR example**

Year	1	2	3	4
Outflow	30	30	3	
Book value	0	27	54	
Market value				100
IRR computation		$-30+\frac{27}{(1+r_{MW})}=0$	$-30-\frac{30}{(1+r_{MW})}+$ $+\frac{54}{(1+r_{MW})^2}=0$	$-30-\frac{30}{(1+r_{MW})}-$ $-\frac{3}{(1+r_{MW})^2}+$ $+\frac{100}{(1+r_{MW})^3}=0$
IRR result (r_{MW})		-10%	-6.82%	20.66%

Table 14.1 describes an example of a fund with a life of four years, with outflows (from the point of view of limited partners) that amount in total to 63, of which 9 is paid in fees. Portfolio companies are evaluated at their book value in years 2 and 3, where the book value corresponds to the amount spent to buy the company equal to the outflow of 30 minus the fee. In year 4, the portfolio is liquidated for a market value of 100. The true ex post IRR of the fund can only be computed at the end, equal in this example to 20.66%. Intermediate IRRs are obtained based on the assumption that portfolio companies could be instantaneously liquidated at their book value.

Charts representing the "return" of private assets, for example private equity funds, describe the median IRR across funds that were set up in the past and are included in the database. Figure 14.3 portrays a typical example (numbers invented for illustration only).

Figure 14.2 The J curve for a private equity fund

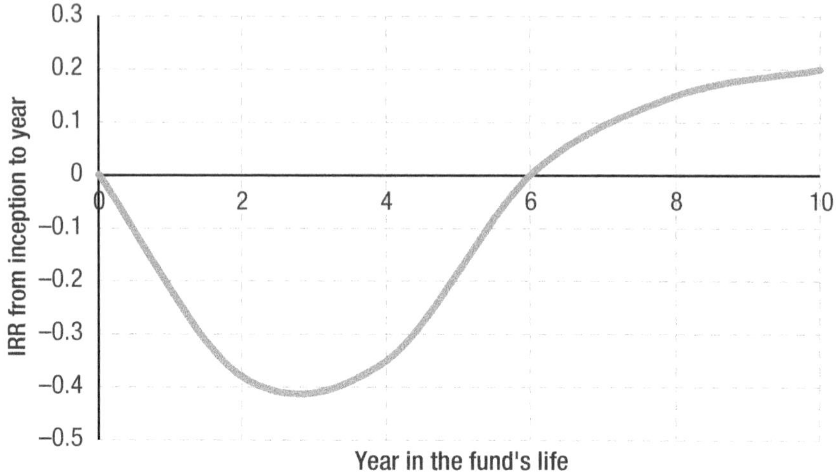

Figure 14.3 represents the time series of IRR from a sample of private equity funds. In the example, it is assumed that the sample includes all funds that are present in the database in the period 2010–2020. The 10% IRR for 2015 represented in Figure 14.3 is the median IRR across all funds that were alive in 2015. Some of these funds may have been founded in 2010 (they belong to the "2010 vintage")[5] and are characterized by an IRR computed over the period 2010–2015, some other funds belong to the 2011 vintage, and so forth up to funds in the 2014 vintage, whose IRR is computed with data for one year of their life. The 15% for the year 2016 is similarly computed as the median IRR across all funds that were founded in the period 2010–2015 and are still alive.

Before looking at other performance indicators, it is worth reiterating what has been already discussed in the context of bond pricing: The ex post IRR will be equal to the ex ante IRR only if intermediate cash flows are reinvested at the same IRR.

Ang (2014) observes that IRR maximization on the part of a PE GP may not necessarily be in the best interest of LPs. Compare an investment of 100 that can be divested the following year at 150 (50% IRR in one year) with one of 100 that can be divested after five years at 366 (30% IRR for five years). Many investors would prefer the latter but a GP may have an incentive to pursue short-term rather than long-term value. A way to boost IRR is for the PE fund to return cash to shareholders as soon as possible by paying early dividends.

---

[5] The year in which a private equity fund first draws down or calls committed capital is known as the fund's vintage year. Paid-in capital is the cumulative amount of capital that has been drawn down. The amount of paid-in capital that has actually been invested in the fund's portfolio companies is simply referred to as invested capital.

Figure 14.3 **Performance over time**

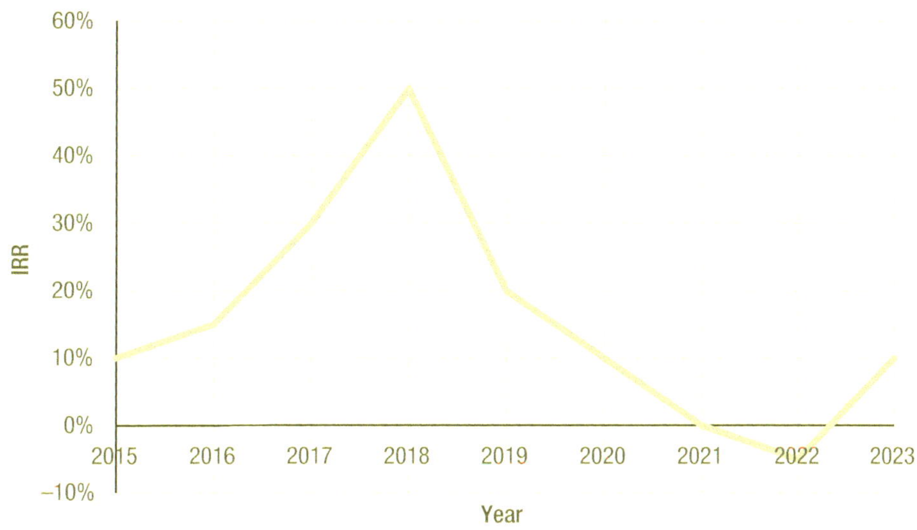

14.7.2 Other performance indicators

The calculation of the IRR is not the only indicator of performance for private assets. Another frequently used indicator is the calculation of the multiple $\frac{\sum_{t=1}^{T} CD_t}{\sum_{t=1}^{T} PI_t}$, represented by the ratio of the sum of the value of the cumulative distributions (CD) made by the fund and the sum of the value of the cash flows invested in the fund (paid-in capital, or PI). Such a multiple is defined as the "realization multiple" or "distributions to paid-in" (DPI). The multiple totally ignores the value of time and mixes cash flows that cannot even be compared with each other. Fraser-Sampson (2010) notes that this multiple cannot be computed unless the fund is at the end of its life and all cash flows have been distributed.

Another multiple is known as "total value to paid-in" (TVPI), obtained by dividing the fund's cumulative distributions and residual value by the paid-in capital $\frac{\sum_{t=1}^{T} (CD_t + RV_t)}{\sum_{t=1}^{T} PI_t}$. This multiple proxies for the ratio between the total value of the fund and its cost.

A multiple equal to 2 suggests investors have doubled their money; however, all the multiples (a) ignore the risk associated with the investment, like the IRR, and (b) ignore the time value of money and the time it takes to obtain the reported money increase.

Kaplan and Schoar (2005) propose a risk-adjusted multiple known as the public market equivalent (PME), $\frac{\sum_{t=1}^{T} CD_t}{\prod_{j=1}^{t}\left(1+r_{M,j}\right)} / \frac{\sum_{t=1}^{T} PI_t}{\prod_{j=1}^{t}\left(1+r_{M,j}\right)}$, where $r_{M,j}$ is the rate of return of the stock market (the public equivalent of private equity). The methodology discounts each cash inflow and outflow by the cumulative rate of return that would have been obtained by investing in the public equity market, implicitly assuming a unitary beta for the PE fund under evaluation.

There is extensive academic literature on the ability of PE funds to generate positive risk-adjusted returns. Negative results are reported by Phalippou and Gottschalg (2009) (underperformance of 3% compared with the S&P 500 index), Driessen, Lin, and Phalippou (2012) (underperformance of 0.4% per month for buyout funds and 1.1% per month for venture capital funds), Jegadeesh, Kraussl, and Pollet (2015) (underperformance of 6% on average per year for publicly tradeds PE funds), and Franzoni, Novak, and Phalippou (2012) (underperformance when the risk of illiquidity is also taken into account). Korteweg and Nagel (2016) generalize the PME (generalized PME, or GPME) by allowing for a beta sensitivity of each fund in a CAPM style. Unsurprisingly, they find that the GPME reduces the estimate of the value created by funds during times of increasing public equity markets, with an application mainly involving venture capital funds.

14.7.3 Value creation in private equity funds

Private equity funds create value for their partners directly through operational actions aimed at increasing portfolio company earnings growth, a goal toward which organizational and corporate governance improvements may contribute in a relevant way. A second important tool is financial engineering, associated with restructuring the liability side of the balance sheet, typically increasing leverage and improving the return on equity for partners due to fiscal optimization (an increase in debt also increases interest payments, which are deductible) and the possibility to return capital to investors already in the early phase of the fund life (these are called recapitalizations and consist of further reducing equity in portfolio companies replacing it with debt) with a positive impact on multiples and IRR.

Finally, external conditions may help if the portfolio companies are sold for a multiple (for example the ratio between enterprise value and EBITDA) that is larger than the one that was prevailing at the time of purchasing the company. Such multiples are often connected with general valuation situations in equity markets, which creates a positive correlation between public equity returns and private equity funds returns. The product of earnings growth and multiple increase represent a strong boost to performance.

Gupta and Van Nieuwerburgh (2021) propose a further methodological innovation in private equity fund performance evaluation and extend the replicating portfolio approach to the cash flows produced by private equity funds: The value of the replicating portfolio is interpreted as the cost of replicating the private equity fund strategy, and its return should be lower than the fund return if the latter does create value. The results are disappointing for the sample of private equity funds.

14.8 Private market price indices

14.8.1 Why is it difficult to measure the performance of private markets?

When no funds from investable funds are available, the measurement of the performance of private markets requires with building and maintaining an index representing an average valuation of the objects transacted in the market. The main challenges are the following:

- low representativeness of the objects that are exchanged relative to the dimension of the stock;
- heterogeneity of the objects exchanged over time;
- different detection frequencies of the individual objects; and
- lack of liquidity.

Let us consider real estate as a laboratory to better understand the sources of these problems. In each period, only a small part of real estate is exchanged, and the flow of objects that are exchanged in a certain period can be peculiar from the point of view of qualitative characteristics (number of rooms, location ecc.) and unrepresentative of the stock. If, say, in January most transacted apartments belonged to a luxury class located downtown and in February most transactions were in the periphery, we would observe a drop in average price that would not reflect a decrease in valuation of the overall stock but only two different samples, neither of which is representative of the universe. The problem due to heterogeneity of objects exchanged over time is magnified by different detection frequencies; for example an apartment may be held for decades before being resold. Lack of liquidity, meaning few transactions taking place in each period, is a further problem that is clearly associated with the previous three elements.

14.8.2 Unsmoothing

In markets characterized by little liquidity one can use appraisal value rather than transaction prices. However, the resulting appraisal-based indices are artificially smoothed because appraisals over a given period often refer to the value of the previous period adjusted for market conditions. Statistical methods of unsmoothing can be used to remedy this: If the performance measured with error r_t^* (smoothed return) is equal to true but unknown return r_t plus a component related to the measured return of the previous period, the relationship between measured and true return is described by the following equation:

$$r_t^* = (1 - \Phi)\, r_t + \Phi\, r_{t-1}^* \qquad (1)$$

An adjustment known as "unsmoothing" can then be made, proposed in real estate by Geltner (1993), in which the true return is estimated based on the average of the observed returns. The previous equation can be rewritten as:

$$r_t = \frac{r_t^* - \Phi r_{t-1}^*}{(1-\Phi)}$$

that is, the adjusted return is proportional to a moving average of the last two observed returns. The coefficient Φ is the auto-correlation coefficient of the series.

The unsmoothed variance is equal to $\left[(1-\Phi)^{-2}(1+\Phi^2)\right]$ times the smoothed variance. If the smoothing parameter is low, the correction is small (for example, if $\Phi = 10\%$ (30%), the correction is 1.25 (2.22)), which means that the unsmoothed variance is 25% (122%) higher than the smoothed variance.

Box 14.3 What is the impact of price smoothing?

Question: The real estate price index was 100 at the beginning of 2016, 102 at the beginning of 2017, and 101 at the beginning of 2018. Sara is a homeowner and wants to know if the value of her assets fell only 0.99% in 2018. She turns to the company A.F.I. to get its evaluation since she knows that the price index is calculated based on expert estimates.

Answer: A.F.I. estimates that the smoothing parameter is equal to $\Phi = 10\%$. To estimate the true percentage change in price during 2018, it uses the equation according to which the true return in 2018 is a weighted average of the returns recorded by the index over the last two years, respectively equal to 2% and -0.99%. It then obtains $(1-0.1)^{-1}(-0.99\%) - 0.1(0.9)^{-1}2\% = -1.32\%$. With this methodology, there would have been a return of -1.74% if the coefficient Φ was 20%. A.F.I. then explains to Sara that the real price change is between -1.32% and -1.74% and is therefore significantly lower than the one observed. Unfortunately, the tendency of experts to calculate the price based on the previous year's price plus an adjustment implies that the real change in 2018 is more negative than the official one.

In markets where indirect investment through funds is common, it is possible to leverage the available data and create price indices that combine the value of those funds. For example, in the United States, there are indices constructed from the observed prices of REITs. They are much more volatile than others and tend to anticipate market trends because they are based on the assessment of the future by investors who react by trying to anticipate the dynamics of fundamentals. In addition, they have the advantage of being available at high frequency and therefore comparable to financial asset class indices.

14.8.3 Hedonic prices

One of the reasons why it is difficult to accurately measure the dynamics of real estate prices is associated with the variability of the physical characteristics of the properties that are on the market. The "hedonic regressions" technique makes it possible to break down the price of each property into the assessment of its characteristics and then to attribute, based on the prices observed for the properties in the sample, a "shadow price" to each characteristic. This makes it possible to create a time series of aggregate prices valued on stable characteristics.

We start from a linear regression model in logarithmic form applied to the cross-section of the prices observed for a certain period t:

$$p_{n,t} = \beta_{0,t} + \sum_{k=1}^{K} \beta_{k,t} \times z_{n,k,t} + \varepsilon_{n,t} \; n = 1, 2 \ldots N$$

where $p_{n,t} = \ln\left(P_{n,t}\right)$ is the price of the n-th unit observed at time t, and $z_{n,k,t}$ is characteristic number k, out of K, of the n-th unit, for example, the number of rooms in the same building observed at time t. Based on the estimated coefficients, which vary from period to period and represent the estimate of the shadow prices of the various characteristics, an estimated price for the n-th unit is:

$$P_{n,t} = \frac{\exp\left(\beta_{0,t}\right)\exp\left(\sum_{k=1}^{K}\beta_{k,t} z_n\right)}{\exp\left(\beta_{0,0}\right)\exp\left(\sum_{k=1}^{K}\beta_{k,0} z_n\right)}$$

and the general price index is:

$$P_t = \sum_{n=1}^{N} P_{n,t}/N$$

in which the characteristics are maintained unchanged z_k on a "typical" property that is representative of the sample. In this way, the time dynamics of the price will only be affected by the change in shadow prices and not by the physical characteristics of the units that have been bought and sold in the various periods. If the "shadow price" of the characteristics is assumed to be constant over time, the calculation of the estimate is simplified to $P_{n,t} = \dfrac{\exp\left(\beta_{0,t}\right)}{\exp\left(\beta_{0,0}\right)}$. Silver (2016) presents an extensive overview of hedonic pricing models applied to real estate.[6]

Hedonic pricing can also be used for valuation purposes with a view to determining the benchmark of a certain asset based on the information contained in comparable assets. The coefficients estimated by the regression summarize the information contained in the prices of all the units that have been purchased and this may be used to compare the (log) price actually paid $p_{n,t}$ with the one "predicted" by the regression $\widehat{p_{n,t}} = \beta_{0,t} + \sum_{k=1}^{K}\beta_{k,t} \times z_{n,k,t}$ and estimate possible under/overvaluation compared with the prices of other properties. Finally, the model can also be used to calculate a potential transaction price for a unit whose characteristics are known but which has not yet been put up for sale.

The perspective of using regression equations for valuation in real estate is that of automated valuation models (AVMs) (for examples of their application and extension

[6] Such models often form the basis for the evaluation of individual properties. See Kok, Koponen, and Martinez-Barbosa (2017) for a comparison between the performance of such models and models using more sophisticated econometric techniques and larger datasets than those that are limited to the characteristics of individual properties.

to non-linear models typical of machine learning and deep learning, see Kok, Koponen, and Martinez-Barbosa, 2017).

Box 14.4 What is the true performance when controlling for quality?

Question: Elena wants to see how the value of her property is developing. Last year, she observed four transactions in the market. The prices of the four properties were €250,000, €300,000, €180,000, and €400,000. The number of rooms in the four buildings was two, two, one, and three, respectively. The third property was in the center, the others in the suburbs. This year, Elena is looking at four more transactions, characterized by the same prices recorded in the first year and by the following information:

Unit	Number of rooms	Location
1	3	Central Business District
2	2	Suburbs
3	2	Central Business District
4	3	Central Business District

A real estate agent tells Elena not to worry because the market is stable, but Elena turns to an independent financial advisory (A.F.I.) firm for a second opinion. Why does the real estate agent tell Elena that the market is stable? And what does A.F.I. conclude?

Answer: The real estate agent tells Elena that the market is stable because she calculates a price index equal to the average value. Since the prices of the four transactions were coincidentally the same as those of the previous year, the agent concludes that there was no change in the average price. However, the advisory firm analyzes the characteristics of the transactions and notes that, for the same price, the quality of the four properties is very different. In the second year of observations, the buildings are larger and more frequently located in the center. A.F.I. then decides to use the hedonic pricing methodology to estimate what the real estate price index would have been if the properties sold on the market in the second year had the same characteristics as the first. The regression for the first year yields the following estimated parameters: 25,000 (constant), 125,000 (shadow price of the number of rooms), and 30,000 (shadow price of being located downtown). The regression for the second year, yields estimated coefficients of 10,000, 130,000, and 10,000, respectively. A.F.I. then calculates a theoretical price for the four properties that were sold in the first year based on the estimated shadow prices for the second year. For example, the theoretical price of a property with the same characteristics as the first one sold in the first year is €270,000 (obtained from the sum of 10,000 and twice the shadow price of the number of rooms equal to 130,000). Using the same methodology, it found that the theoretical prices of the other three properties sold in the first year would have been €270,000, €150,000, and €400,000, respectively. The average of the three theoretical prices is €272,500, down 3.5% compared with the average value of the first year. A seemingly stable market hides a deterioration in value after controlling for the characteristics of the transactions. Elena is not happy with the result but prefers to know the real situation rather than retain the illusion that the value of her investment in real estate is constant.

14.8.4 Prices obtained from repeat sales

An alternative way to control for variability in the characteristics of the properties transacted is to consider only the prices of properties that are bought and sold at least twice in the sample. Their change in price is a reliable indicator of changing market preferences due to characteristics being constant over time. This method was introduced into the economic literature by Bailey, Muth, and Nourse (1963) and provides a "repeat sales index."[7] The model assumes that the price (expressed in logarithms in the following equation) of the $i-th$ unit at time t reflects the general market price γ_t and a unit-specific error $p_{i,t} = \gamma_t + e_{i,t}$. In general, the $i-th$ unit will be traded on the market on two specific dates t_i and $t_i + T_i$, which in terms of the above equation can be written as:

$$p_{i,t_i+T_i} - p_{i,t_i} = \gamma_{t_i+T} - \gamma_{t_i} + e_{i,t_i+T_i} - e_{i,t_i}$$

which shows that the change in the price of the i-th unit provides information about the change in the aggregate price index over the same period. The price index estimator then considers the prices of the various transactions as signals that measure (with error) the price index and derives the latter from the estimate of the regression (in vector notation form) $y = \gamma \times Z + u$ where the dependent variable is the change in the logarithmic prices of the various units, and the regressor matrix is composed of 0, except on the date of purchase of the unit, in which the value -1 appears in the matrix, and on the date of sale, on which +1 appears. The estimated vector γ represents the estimate of the log price index. If the initial log price index is set equal to log (1) = 0, then the various elements of the vector $\gamma = (\gamma_1, \gamma_2, \ldots \gamma_T)$ are to be interpreted as both index levels and index changes. For example, if γ_1 is estimated at 5%, then the initial index is equal to 0 and the index at time 1 become 0.05, also representing the estimated 5% increase in average prices.

Technical Box 14.2 What is the repeated-measure price index?

Question (from Shiller, 1993): Ten sales are observed over 3 periods of time. At time 0 we observe transactions regarding units 1, 2, 3 and 4. At time 1 we observe transactions regarding units 1, 2 and 5, and at time 2 we observe transactions of units 3, 4 and 5. The log of the price of the $i-th$ unit observed at time t is denoted with $p_{i,t}$. What index can be obtained from the repeated sales methodology?

Answer: Combine the observed transaction prices into a vector of first differences of the observed price relatively to the observed price of the first transaction $y = [p_{1,1} - p_{1,0}, p_{2,1} - p_{2,0}, p_{3,2} - p_{3,0}, p_{4,2} - p_{4,0}, p_{5,2} - p_{5,1}]'$. The matrix of regressors is defined as:

$$Z = \begin{bmatrix} 1 & 1 & 0 & 0 & -1 \\ 0 & 0 & 1 & 1 & 1 \end{bmatrix}',$$

[7] Shiller (1991) and Case and Shiller (1987) made improvements to the methodology, which eventually led to the Case–Shiller Index, now the S&P–Case–Shiller Index.

The model allows estimation of a (2,1) vector of estimated log prices $(\widehat{\gamma_1}\ \ \widehat{\gamma_2})$ which we can show are equal to:

$$\widehat{\gamma_1} = \frac{p_{1,1} + p_{2,1} + p_{5,1}}{3} - \frac{p_{1,0} + p_{2,0} + \left(p_{5,2} \widehat{-\gamma_2}\right)}{3}$$

$$\widehat{\gamma_2} = \frac{p_{3,2} + p_{4,2} + p_{5,2}}{3} - \frac{p_{3,0} + p_{4,0} + \left(p_{5,1} \widehat{-\gamma_1}\right)}{3}$$

Notice that in this example we do not need to estimate the index for the initial time 0 because we conventionally set it equal to log(1) = 0. The estimated log index at time 1 is the arithmetic average log price of all transactions taking place at time 1 minus an estimated average of the price of the same transacted properties at time 0. In two cases out of three, properties 1 and 2, there is an observed log price. However, property 5 was not transacted initially, and we impute an estimated initial value equal to the observed log price in period 2, when there was a transaction, minus the estimate of the average increase in prices between 2 and 0. Similar intuition applies to $\widehat{\gamma_2}$ to be interpreted as the change in price between time 2 and 0, where the observed price of property 5 at time 1 is brought back in time at 0 using the estimated price increase between 1 and 0. For example, if the vector of observed log prices in the three time periods is equal to:

Time 0	Time 1	Time 2
13.81551	13.8643	
13.59237	13.71015	
13.99783		14.07787
13.38473		13.52783
	14.50866	14.4033

then the vector of price change for the regression is equal to the log price changes of the five assets traded in the three time periods $y = [0.049, 0.118, 0.08, 0.143, -0.105]'$ where for example 0.049 is the difference between 13.8643 and 13.81551, and the ordinary least squares model will return $(Z'Z)^{-1}Z'y = (11.7\%\ \ \ 7.8\%)$. Average price went up 11.7% in period 1 due to the observed increases equal to 4.9% and 11.8% in the first two properties and due to the reconstructed log price at time 0 of the fifth property equal to 14.325 (obtained from 14.4033-0.078), which provides a theoretical increase in the price of the fifth property equal to 18.35% at time 1.The resulting average market price increase of 11.7% is the simple average of 0.049, 0.118 and 0.1835.

Shiller (1993) also shows how the repeated-measures index can be combined with the hedonic pricing methodology to provide a hedonic repeated-sale index. Essentially, the linear regression used to apply the simple repeat sales methodology is enriched with value relevant characteristics that allow the researcher to compute a time-varying contribution of each characteristic to the overall price of each unit.

14.8.5 Long-term average returns for real estate

Real estate has traditionally been considered a low-return asset. Recent research casts doubts on this view. Jorda, Knoll, Kuvshinov, Schularick and Taylor (2019) reconstruct time series of prices and rents for real estate investment around the world and find that over the period 1960–2020 real estate in the United States has offered an average real rate of return equal to 6.2%, fairly close to the 8% real return paid by the stock market. To better interpret the results, note that the rent component of the return must be adjusted for operational expenditures that are hard to estimate and that is typically considered about 30–40% of the yield. Moreover, we should consider the need for quality adjustment over time. Chambers, Spaenjers, and Steiner (2021) consider these two issues and find a real total return for the United Kingdom equal to 2.8%, 1.6% lower than that found by Jorda, Knoll, Kuvshinov, Schularick and Taylor (2019). Moreover, while Jorda, Knoll, Kuvshinov, Schularick and Taylor (2019) find a real capital gain equal to 0.7% for the United States in 1891–2015, in the same period Dimson, Marsh, and Staunton (2018) find 0.3%, which becomes -2.1% accounting for quality changes.

14.8.6 Long-term average returns for art investing

The calculation of price indices for the art market is based on the elements described for real estate, since the problems are very similar. The results presented below have been obtained by various researchers based on partially different databases, heterogeneous periods and fields, and sometimes different econometric models.

Goetzmann (1993) constructs an index of works of art for the period 1715–1986, recognizing the possible biases that tend to artificially push up returns. The use of the method of repeated sales in the long period does not include the prices of works of art that may have been sold only once due to the subsequent lack of demand, associated with a low or no price level. In addition, it is only associated with objects that are sold by owners who may well decide not to sell works whose price is lower than the purchase price. The results obtained show the existence of instability in the relationship between returns on investment in art and stocks in the context of strong volatility of the former and lead the author to believe that art is not a good investment from a financial point of view.

Dimson and Spaenjers (2014) analyze art, stamps, and violins and construct price indices for the United Kingdom, finding average returns of 2.4–2.8% per annum in real terms respectively over the period 1900–2012. Renneboog and Spaenjers (2013) construct a dataset that contains information on more than 1.1 million works of art sold by auction houses, which is used to construct a price index via hedonic regression. The results show that art prices grew by 4% per year (in dollars) in real terms between 1951 and 2007. Among the characteristics relevant to the determination of the price at the level of the individual work are the element "masterpiece," the reputation of the artist, and the subject. Korteweg, Kräussl, and Verwijmeren (2016) use a sample of 20,538 paintings sold at auction between 1972 and 2010 and find that the paintings with the highest prices are more likely to be sold multiple times and thus to have more influence on the calculated indices (upwards). A robust methodology for this element estimates a price index that has a return that is 3.5% (10% to 6.5%) lower on average per year than the return obtained by an index that ignores the effect of prices on transactions. Chambers, Dimson, and Spaenjers (2020) examine J.M. Keynes's collection of a hundred pieces by modern masters, acquired through various channels in the period 1917–1945 and entirely bequeathed to King's College London. The researchers estimate the value in the years 1946, 1959, 1981, 1988, 2000, 2013, and 2019 and show that the collection has appreciated strongly over time: Keynes's total expenditure amounted to less than £13,000, with an estimated value of £76 million at the start of 2019, corresponding to an internal rate of return of 10.4% (6.1% in real terms), slightly lower (0.2%) than the return on an investment in the UK stock exchange. The very high performance of one of the objects that is part of the collection was very important in determining such a high return, and higher than that typically obtained by the calculation of art indices.

14.9 Alternative assets

Some private assets are referred to as "alternative." The stress on "alternative" is intended to convey the idea of a lack of correlation with the equity market. In the context of the Markowitz model, an asset with a low correlation with the equity market is attractive from the point of view of its ability to reduce the overall portfolio volatility. Alternative assets include private assets and hedge funds, meaning that not all private assets are alternative. The possibility to understand whether a private asset is truly alternative or not relies on the possibility to measure its rate of return at a frequency consistent with the returns of other assets, and this effort is made difficult by measurement issues that have been highlighted.

14.9.1 Real estate and optimization

What is the share of real estate in a diversified portfolio? This is a key question for most investors. Unfortunately, in the case of real estate, it is difficult to find reliable parameters to use as inputs. Table 14.2 shows average return and volatility data for various asset classes and real estate.

Table 14.2 compares the parameters characterizing public (in instruments listed on the stock exchanges) and private (unlisted) investments, as well as those of leveraged and unleveraged investments, and investments on which the unsmoothing methodology described earlier has or has not been applied. The time frame is extremely short but useful precisely because of the possibility of comparing various asset classes.

Bond and equity volatilities for the United States are consistent with those seen in previous chapters and obtained from longer samples. Interestingly, public real estate has a volatility of 17.84%, similar to that of equity investing, 16.01%. In the UK, the volatility of public real estate is even higher. For both markets, volatility is halved when investments are considered in their unleveraged form. Real estate volatility is reduced even more when we consider private real estate, which, being based on expert opinions rather than market prices, has a strong persistence of valuations. The application of unsmoothing procedures significantly increases volatility, which comes close to that of

Table 14.2 **Average return and risk: equity, bonds, and real estate**

	US, 1978–2014			UK, 1978–2014		
	Average return	**Volatility**	**Sharpe ratio**	**Average return**	**Volatility**	**Sharpe ratio**
Bonds	7.39	6.21	0.4	9.3	8.97	0.49
Equities	12.63	16.01	0.48	9.06	15.03	0.28
Public real estate	14.06	17.84	0.51	7.61	20.66	0.13
Public real estate (unlevered)	11.19	8.99	0.7	8.02	11.58	0.27
Private real estate (smoothed)	9.01	4.31	0.96	7.46	3.76	0.69
Private real estate (unsmoothed)	9.01	7.08	0.58	7.46	7.49	0.37
Private real estate (transactions)	8.48	12.31	0.18	10.39	8.84	0.06

Source: Norges Bank Investment Management (2015)

public real estate. Even higher volatility is associated with private real estate in the case where price indices are based on actual transactions instead of expert ones.

As a further comparison, Ang (2014) reports the following quarterly results for the US, 1978–2011, comparing indices obtained from expert opinions (NCREIF) and those obtained from listed vehicles (REITs). The S&P 500 index serves as a benchmark for comparison. Table 14.3 shows the mean, volatility, and autocorrelation coefficient (the correlation between the returns of one period and those of the previous period), while Table 14.4 shows the correlations between the three indices.

Table 14.3 **Average return and risk, equity and real estate**

	Average return	**Volatility**	**Autocorrelation**
NCREIF	2.21	2.25	0.78
REIT	3.47	9.18	0.11
S&P500	3.01	8.23	0.07

Source: Ang (2014)

Table 14.4 **Correlations, equity and real estate**

Correlations	**NCREIF**	**REIT**	**S&P 500**
NCREIF	1	0.15	0.09
REIT		1	0.63
S&P500			1

Source: Ang (2014)

Some of the previous results are confirmed: The volatility of public real estate is fully comparable to the volatility of the stock market, while the volatility of real estate assessed by experts is very low. The autocorrelation coefficient, which is almost zero in the case of the equity index and the public real estate index, is very high for the NCREIF index. This is entirely consistent with the unsmoothing equation presented earlier because it illustrates the tendency of experts to modify their assessments in previous periods to a limited extent.

14.9.2 Does CAPM explain the expected return from real estate?

Can noisy historical real estate returns be turned into expected returns through a pricing model? The CAPM may be helpful here. To answer this question, it is first necessary to note that real estate should be included in the market portfolio, as predicted by the theory of the model, which suggests that the market portfolio should not be restricted to the stock market alone. Let's assume that real estate's share of the market portfolio is 50%, and that the equity and bond shares are 20% and 30%, respectively.

Let us consider parameters consistent with the time series of monthly returns for these three asset classes. The equity market return is measured by the MSCI Europe Total Return Index, the bond market by the BD Datastream ten-year benchmark index, and real estate by the MSCI Global Real Estate Index. The volatilities of the three markets are respectively 15%, 5%, and 7%. The correlation between equity and real estate over the period is 5%, between equity and bonds is -19%, and between bonds and real estate is 30%. With these parameters, the volatility of the market portfolio is 5.1% and its risk premium is 3.5%. The risk premiums predicted by the CAPM are equal to 5.8% for equity, 1.3% for bonds, and 3.8% for real estate against beta ratios of 1.67, 0.38, and 1.10, respectively. As can be seen, these results are not far from historical experience and common sense, and they informally confirm the possibility of applying CAPM to the determination of the expected return of real estate.

Geltner and Miller (2001) note that CAPM fails to explain the differential of average returns within the real estate asset class: The average returns of the various sectors (residential, office, tertiary, etc.) are not related to the heterogeneity of their beta coefficients, reminding us of what happens when the CAPM is used to explain the cross-section of average returns of equity portfolios. However, it is still important to account for the uncertainty in the estimation of the parameters highlighted earlier, particularly in the case of real estate, given the critical issues in the construction of price indices, which can affect any econometric estimate.

What if you want to apply the CAPM to have a starting point for determining the expected return of a single project? In this case, it is necessary to recognize the existence of an idiosyncratic risk that is, by definition, ignored by the CAPM, a model that, as we have stressed, is derived from the Markowitz optimization model and assumes the point of view of a diversified investor. The CAPM does not consider specific risk due to its being diversifiable in a large portfolio. Many investors, and most companies that develop projects, are so large that they can afford to invest a small share of their assets in a real estate project. As a result, there may be a divergence in the calculation of the expected return between diversified and non-diversified investors. Bearing in mind that the inverse relation between the price and the expected return has been discussed several times in this book, this divergence has an impact on the price an investor is willing to pay to acquire the project. Theoretically, investors who place the project in a diversified portfolio would be willing to pay more for each individual project, while those evaluating the project on its own would have to add an additional risk premium (see Massari and Zanetti, 2008), which would decrease the willingness to pay to acquire the project.

14.9.3 Real estate and optimization

Does including real estate help diversify the portfolio? To answer this question, we use the same time series used in section 14.9.2 and apply portfolio optimization methodologies assuming that the expected returns are 5%, 0.5%, and 4%, respectively. The volatilities of the three markets are respectively 12%, 6%, and 12%. The correlation between equity and real estate in the period is 57%, between equity and bonds is -20%, and between bonds and real estate is 30%. For simplicity, we use the analytical formulas for calculating the tangency portfolio and the global minimum variance portfolio, which also allow negative positions. As noted in Chapter 8, all efficient portfolios are linear combinations of the tangency portfolio and the minimal global variance portfolio.

Let's first look at the case where optimization considers all three assets, and then only the case, which is more common in practice, where real estate is ignored. Table 14.5 summarizes the composition of the tangency portfolio w_T and that of the portfolio with minimal variance w_{GMVP}.

Table 14.5 Global tangency and minimum variance portfolio

	Equity	Bond	Real estate
w_T	55%	41%	4%
w_{GMVP}	33%	83%	-16%
w_T	57%	43%	
w_{GMVP}	24%	76%	

Table 14.5 shows that real estate does not play an important role in optimized portfolios, as evidenced by the comparison between the efficient frontier that uses three assets (solid line) and the one that uses only two (dotted line) in Figure 14.4.

The reason for the result is related to the high volatility of real estate (it has already been noted that listed real estate tends to take on the same volatility as equity

Figure 14.4 Efficient frontier with and without real estate

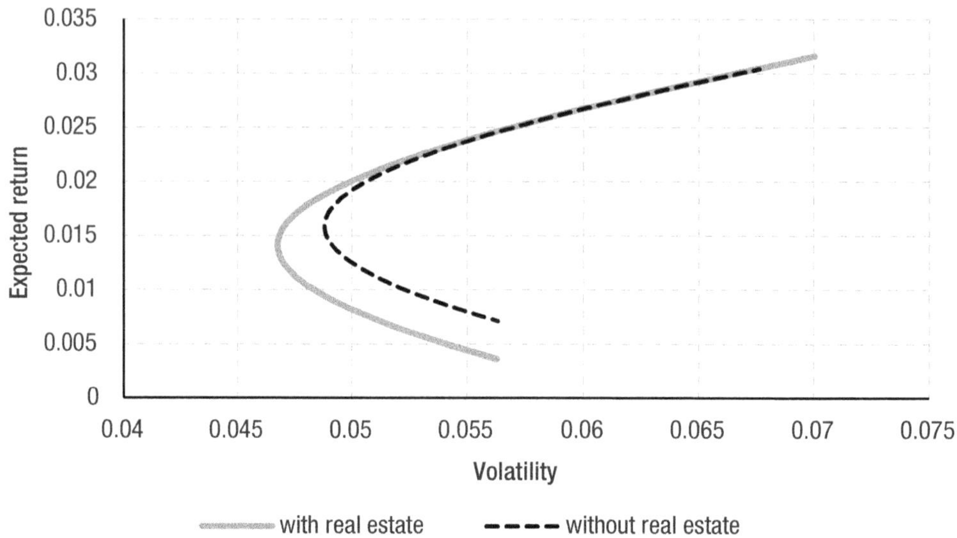

in general), the high correlation with equity and bonds, and the expected return lower than that of equity.

However, it is enough to change the correlation parameter between equity and real estate to radically change the results. If the correlation between equity and bonds is assumed to be equal to 5%, the relevant portfolios are as shown in Table 14.6.

Table 14.6 Global tangency and minimal variance portfolio, 5% correlation

	Equity	Bond	Real estate
w_T	49%	19%	32%
w_{GMVP}	23%	73%	4%

As can be seen in Figure 14.5, real estate now contributes significantly to both portfolios, and the two efficient frontiers are significantly different from each other.

These results confirm the extreme sensitivity of the optimization tool to the estimation of parameters, and the need to proceed with close attention to the estimation of these parameters, particularly in the case of assets, such as real estate, which are affected by strong, and inevitable, measurement errors. Listed real estate does not seem to be attractive in a diversified portfolio with US data due to large correlations with equities and bonds, a volatility almost as large as that of equity but a lower average return. Unlisted real estate seems on the contrary be extremely useful in a diversified portfolio due to low correlation and low volatility.

Figure 14.5 **Efficient frontier with and without real estate, 5% correlation**

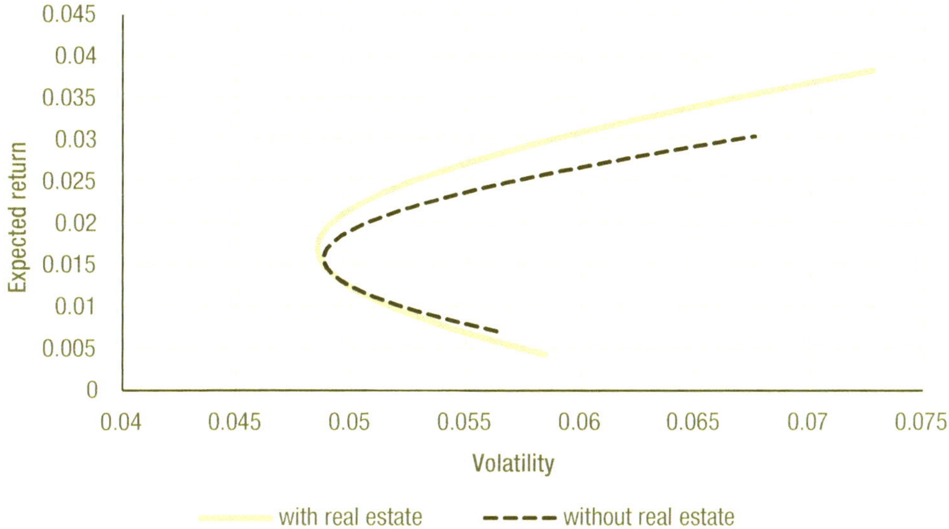

Summary

- Private assets are investment objects that are not traded (listed) in public markets. Their total value is unknown even though there are various attempts at estimating it.
- Investable private assets are accessible to investors through diversified investment vehicles, often of a closed-end structure to account for the low liquidity of underlying assets.
- Private equity funds are vehicles that invest in a portfolio of unlisted companies. General partners invest their capital but manage the fund at the same time, while limited partners in general are pure external investors who do not participate in the fund's choices.
- The private equity fund benefits from a management fee that is paid by investors on all committed capital for the life of the fund, regardless of its actual investment. The most consistent remuneration comes from incentive fees (carried interest), which can be withdrawn when the average return exceeds a minimum target (hurdle rate) and the proceeds paid to investors exceed the value of the invested capital capitalized at the hurdle rate.
- Traditionally, only banks could lend to corporations. Regulation has opened the way for the intervention of other licensed financial institutions that provide lending activity, known as "private debt" or "private credit."
- Private debt funds can have an open-end or a closed-end structure. The activities associated with raising capital, investing it, and returning it involves a lot of transaction costs: An asset management company that manages a closed-end fund must continuously devote resources to raise capital for the new funds proposed to investors and must manage the fund with a limited horizon. To reduce transaction costs there is a lot of interest in permanent capital vehicles where capital must not be returned to investors by a fixed date. Particularly important cases of companies with permanent capital in private debt are business development companies (BDCs).

- Private debt funds arise out of heavy regulation imposed on banks lending to riskier borrowers. However, it could be that private debt funds are more efficient than banks; for example, they are better able to understand firms' needs and can structure the best contracts in a short time, in which case the extra cost could be due to a better-quality service.
- Investors get exposure to real estate in most equity and bond investments due to the relevance of real estate assets in the productive organization of most companies. Real estate investment trusts (REITs) are very popular in the United States and other countries and allow investors the benefit of a diversified investment.
- Art is an alternative asset class: Theory tells us that art price movements over time should be less correlated than average correlations across asset classes due to the relevance of taste shocks that do not affect other assets. The data partially support this view.
- Performance evaluation for private assets is difficult due to lack of frequent valuation of investments. Private asset funds are typically evaluated using the internal rate of return in the context of strong assumptions about the value of portfolio companies and the use of the assets at book value. Recent developments try to mix the internal rate of return methodology with replicating portfolio techniques that estimate a portfolio of public assets that might replicate the cash flows offered by private equity and debt funds.
- It is difficult to measure the time dynamics of private markets due to trading taking place in each period only for a small portion of the available stock. Moreover, traded assets are very heterogeneous and quality changes need to be considered before constructing price indices. The typical techniques are the hedonic index methodology and the repeat sales methodology.
- It is challenging to study private and public assets in the context of a portfolio optimization exercise due to data problems and the relevance of risk elements that may not be fully accounted for by standard mean/variance optimization.

15 Sustainability and ESG investing

15.1 Introduction

Public opinion is increasingly worried about environmental and social issues, and financial investments are an activity of central importance within the overall signal generation mechanism that aims to guide the management of companies toward models that minimize negative externalities (e.g., pollution) and maximize positive impacts on society (e.g., education). The chapter begins with the debate that has existed for decades in economics and finance on the role of externalities in the management of companies, briefly recalling the various acronyms that have followed one another over time, starting from corporate social responsibility (CSR) and moving to environmental, social, and governance (ESG) factors. A new and interesting element concerns measurement aspects as the debate was very much linked to theoretical discussions, which, however, had difficulty deriving practical implications. The interest of the major international rating agencies in the evaluation of these aspects has triggered a significant debate on measurement, which is now also affecting accounting elements that promise to change the presentation and the corporate identity itself in the coming years. As highlighted in the previous chapters, in order to understand the impact on prices and expected returns, it is first necessary to describe the change in the demand function of the various assets resulting from the consideration of ESG factors, either for reasons related to preferences or because these factors serve to better estimate the parameters of expected return and risk. The theoretical relationships between ESG factors and average returns and risk are then evaluated in light of the data provided by a growing and now large empirical literature, which will be only partially considered to give the reader an idea of the main results, without claiming to be complete. The chapter closes with a section on climate change, an important topic that poses challenges for investors and companies. It describes the empirical evidence currently available and its relevance for investors' portfolios, with a nod to the measurement of climate risk, a topic that is currently in its infancy but which is easy to predict will be of great relevance in the coming years.

15.2 What is sustainability?

15.2.1 Sustainable development

The Brundtland Report (1987, page 8) defined sustainable development as "development that meets the needs of the present without compromising the ability of future generations to meet their own needs." There are several interesting keywords in this definition.

- Development stresses the qualitative, and not only the quantitative, process of creating goods and services in economic systems. Environmental and social goods are crucial for welfare but the pursuit of their improvement must be searched for in the context of a process of economic growth.
- Generations are characterized by needs that are not exactly defined either now or in the future, consistent with the evolution of needs over time and the heterogeneity of needs perceptions across the world.
- Current and future generations are equally important, with an implicit reference to Rawls' (1971) "veil of ignorance" methodology to judge the fairness of allocation arrangements.
- Not "compromising the ability" refers to the consumption and investment opportunity set that we leave to future generations. This idea refers to the financial concept of optionality: sustainability amounts to leaving enough resources to future generations to allow them to satisfy needs that may be very different from those of today. The principle is also associated with recent European legislation with reference to "do no significant harm," arising from the need to make choices among dimensions expressed in different units of measurement, in which case an action is taken if it has a positive impact on one dimension and does not reduce the level of other relevant dimensions.

This is still, after almost forty years, the most general definition of sustainable development. In a more theoretically oriented definition, Arrow, Dasgupta, Goulder, Mumford and Oleson (2012, p. 318) identify sustainable development "with economic paths along which intergenerational well-being does not decline … intergenerational well-being would not decline over a specified time-period if and only if a comprehensive measure of the economy's wealth were not to decline over the same period. By wealth we mean the social worth of an economy's entire productive base. Because the productive base consists of the entire range of factors that determine intergenerational wellbeing, we will sometimes refer to wealth as comprehensive wealth." Economic theorists use more specific requirements for measuring welfare and, most of all, define the condition for achieving sustainable development through the definition of comprehensive wealth.

Before elaborating on measurement issues, it is useful to discuss why this debate matters for finance. It is relevant because pursuing sustainable development requires making new economic decisions on several production and consumption activities, which need financing on the part of markets and intermediaries. Reasons for the unsustainability of our current economic growth include (a) private agents being affected by a form of tragedy of the commons, that is, they are unable to rationally manage common resources with ill-defined property rights, (b) markets producing distorted prices, (c) markets being unavailable for some relevant goods, and (d) bad economic policies. These reasons may be jointly at work and require changes in our framework for measuring economic activity and financing firms and individuals. Financial markets and intermediaries are the fundamental channels for resource allocation in a decentralized economy, and changing the structure of development requires changing the financing criteria.

15.2.2 Accounting for environmental and social goods and services

Arrow, Dasgupta, Goulder, Mumford and Oleson (2012) suggest that comprehensive wealth includes reproducible capital goods (roads, buildings, machinery and equipments), human capital (health, education, skills), and natural capital (ecosystems, minerals and fossil, fuels). Do we account for these characteristics in our accounting system? The short answer is that we do not, neither at the national accounting nor at the company accounting level. There are two main reasons for this. First, many environmental goods and services are not traded in markets and do not have a price, even though there is a long literature in public economics estimating value from costs. Second, the overall scheme for considering such goods and services may not be clear and well known even though it was discussed in the early 1990s in a theoretical context (see, e.g., Dasgupta and Maler, 2000).

The key observation is that in macroeconomic accounting, gross domestic product (GDP, also corresponding to gross income, that is, the sum of compensations paid to factors of production) equals the sum of consumption and gross investment, the latter being the change over time of the stock of produced capital. Income was defined by Hicks (1939) as the maximum amount of consumption that does not decrease the level of wealth. If, in a given time period, an income equal to €100 is totally consumed, the person expects to be as well off for the next time period as she was at the beginning if her wealth does not depreciate over time. If income is not totally consumed due to €10 of savings, so that income is larger than consumption, then the person may expect to be better off in the future as savings increase wealth. When consumption is larger than income, then the person dissaves and the situation will deteriorate in the future.

We can use a similar logic for macroeconomic accounting. If we save and invest at the aggregate level, then our stock of produced capital goes up and we have enlarged production possibility in the future. If we consume all our income, then the production possibility set does not change (neglecting the deterioration in the productivity of the stock of capital).

How should the framework change to account for sustainability? First, the definition suggests there are other things over and above produced capital that matter for the welfare of current and future generations. Therefore, we should also include in our definition of GDP the change in other relevant stocks of capital that may be useful for their amenity and/or productive value, including natural capital, social capital, health capital, and human capital. In terms of the Hicksian definition, income can be defined as the maximum consumption that maintains all relevant stocks of capital. If the relevant stocks of capital go beyond produced capital, then capital maintenance requires maintenance of environmental and social capital for future generations, as dictated by the definition provided in the Brundtland Report. If current consumption deteriorates the stock of environmental and social capital, then the maximum amount that can be consumed without decreasing the stocks of the relevant types of capital is lower than the amount that could be consumed without decreasing the stock of produced capital. If we recognized this in national accounts, then GDP and income would account for the change in the value of environmental and social capital. Say GDP is €100, consumption is €70, investment is €30, and the change in the value of environmental assets is -€10, then comprehensive GDP (to be defined in section 15.2.3) would be equal to €90, correctly reflecting the welfare loss associated with the decrease in the stock of environmental assets.

15.2.3 Challenges in accounting for environmental and social goods and services

There are good reasons why macroeconomic and company accounting do not include assets such as natural capital, health capital, and human capital. A common issue across these different assets is that they are typically not traded. Lack of trading means there are no observed market prices. We do not want to enter the long debate in accounting about the pros and cons of market value versus historical cost accounting, but we do notice that market prices usually help in recognizing the value of assets. To highlight avenues for future research, it is interesting to review some of the issues discussed in Arrow, Dasgupta, Goulder, Mumford and Oleson (2012).

In the case of natural capital (e.g., oil, natural gas, minerals, metals, timber) there are several items that do have a market price, and the main issue is to gather data on the net depletion of the stock. In such cases we can multiply the change in the stock by the market price and obtain a monetary value. This will provide a measure that does not account for externalities if the latter are not reflected in market prices (which is exactly what the definition of externality suggests). Arrow, Dasgupta, Goulder, Mumford and Oleson (2012) consider one type of environmental externality, climate-related damages, whose changes are estimated based on data on the amount of CO2 and an assumption about their value. Nowadays such estimates could be improved by using the price of CO2 emission permits traded in Europe. All such cases can easily be accommodated in the general framework to extend standard GDP to get a measure of the change in comprehensive wealth, which we can define as "comprehensive GDP."

Human capital is another important example. In theory, human capital for a worker is the present discounted value of future wages. Multiplying this forward-looking estimate by the number of workers would give a monetary measure of the value of human capital, and its change would be included in comprehensive GDP. The estimate is of course full of assumptions that need to be clarified, for example about the mortality of the existing workforce, the education of young people, and so forth. It is useful to think of human capital as connected with health capital. Arrow, Dasgupta, Goulder, Mumford and Oleson (2012) approach is based on life expectancy: An increase in life expectancy translates into an improvement in health, and to calculate the value of an additional life year, the paper uses estimates of the value of a statistical life (VSL), derived from differential wages for jobs involving differential risks of a fatal on-the-job accident.

15.3 CSR, ESG investing, and sustainability

15.3.1 CSR

Externalities generated by the functioning of economic activity may be negative or positive. An example of a negative externality is the effects on the quality of the water drunk by those who live near a river polluted by the production of a factory. A positive externality arises from companies that invest in technology and human capital and create agglomeration economies that favor the development of industrial districts. Externalities have always been at the center of the academic debate. But what can companies do about externalities?

In a *New York Times* column, Milton Friedman argued on September 13, 1970, that corporate social responsibility is to increase its profits, as it is the task of public policy and regulation to address any harm inflicted on the community. An alternative has been described in numerous research papers, such as Bowen (1953), which refer to corporate social responsibility, defined by the Commission of the European Union (2006) as "the voluntary integration by companies of social and environmental concerns into their business operations and their relations with stakeholders on a voluntary basis."

In the presence of a trade-off between the quantity and quality of environmental resources and economic growth, forcing companies to internalize negative externalities may reduce the level of production and therefore profits and value. Chichilnisky, Heal, and Beltratti (1995) show, for example, that the optimal level of long-run growth must be reduced when the community obtains well-being from the stock of environmental goods if the latter is damaged by production. Consistent with the idea of a trade-off between profit and social responsibility that must be managed by the public hand, Liang and Renneboog (2017) study the relevance of the legal system for a company's decision to behave in a way that is consistent with CSR, comparing the common law system typical of Anglo-Saxon systems (which is favorable to business activities, the freedom of managers, and the protection of shareholders), and the civil law system (which is more consistent with public intervention and the protection of various stakeholders). Analyzing data from more than 25,000 listed companies worldwide, they find that companies located in countries that use civil law perform better from an environmental and social perspective and tend to react more strongly to natural disasters and scandals related to food fraud and environmental accidents. In fact, these companies are more constrained by public intervention and regulation, which are important elements for managing externalities.

Growing attention by consumers and investors to the impacts generated by businesses. Such awareness can to some extent replace, or complement, economic policy and regulation. A few externality-conscious consumers may have little influence, but firms cannot ignore aggregated behaviors and may come to view CSR as one of several activities that serve to maximize their value. For example, the pursuit of social goals can lead to a higher selling price of products, thanks to increased demand from consumers who appreciate this company policy, and/or an increase in resource productivity, when people work harder for a greater sense of belonging to a responsible company. Empirical research suggests that firms may be "doing well by doing good" because of larger demand and/or higer internal productivity. This implies that "stakeholder value maximization" may dominate the traditional neoclassical view of "shareholder value maximization" as described by Milton Friedman.

15.3.2 SRI/ESG investing

Socially responsible investing (SRI) occurs when investors are concerned about the non-monetary consequences of their choices.[1] For example, in the 1960s, civil society asked university endowments to divest from the stocks of companies that produced weapons. In recent years, there have been well-known requests from student communities to universities to divest from the stocks of companies most responsible for CO2 emissions.

Today, the discussion about environmental, social, and governance factors represent, according to Kell (2018), the evolution of the SRI movement.[2] According to this source, the acronym ESG was introduced in 2005 in the report “Who cares wins: Connecting financial markets to a changing world,” attributed to a group of leading international financial institutions that, together with the United Nations’ “Freshfield report,” contributed to the launch of the principles for responsible investing (PRI). One way to understand the coexistence and complementarity between SRI and ESG is to consider SRI as the use of ESG factors in investment strategies, albeit primarily in a way that excludes those securities that are deemed to be most harmful to the community. Today’s focus on ESG-related investing is

[1] There are various historical reconstructions regarding the origins of the SRI movement that go back hundreds of years to people who believed in religious values that were opposed to personal enrichment linked, for example, to slavery and war (see, e.g., the cases of the slave trade, apartheid in South Africa, and the Vietnam War). According to some, the concern to heal the negative aspects of economic life goes back to Jewish law and the Bible.

[2] Definitions are not unanimous; for example, Gillan, Koch and Starks (2021) use the terms CSR and ESG interchangeably.

to some extent more general as it sees these factors as distinctive elements from the point of view of preferences but also as useful for better estimating the expected return and risk parameters of individual assets. ESG investing can therefore be defined as a portfolio selection methodology that considers environmental, social, and governance factors as useful elements for investment as they are associated with the return/risk ratio (value) and/or as they are linked to values and ethical elements (see Starks, 2023).

The empirical evidence obtained from the analysis of company financial statements in relation to ESG characteristics seems to highlight a relationship of complementarity and not substitution between individual effort and performance. Friede, Busch, and Bassen (2015) conduct a meta-analysis based on the results of more than 2,000 published studies and show that in 90% of cases there is a non-negative, and generally positive, relationship between ESG indicators and business results. A more recent meta-analysis conducted by Whelan, Ulrich, Van Holt and Clark (2021) argues that the results obtained from studies over the previous five years were even stronger: 58% identified a positive relationship between ESG indicators and the firm's accounting performance, and 59% found a positive relationship between ESG-related investment styles and market returns measured on the basis of the Sharpe ratio or Jensen's alpha. Khan, Serafeim, and Yoon (2016) confirm the existence of a relationship between ESG indicators and financial performance, but only for indicators that are relevant in the accounting sense as defined by the SASB. Giese, Lee, Melas, Nagy and Nishikawa (2019) argue, on the basis of bivariate analyses of the relationship between ESG ratings and relevant variables, that compliance with ESG factors allows for (a) greater productivity linked to elements such as people and innovation management, (b) lower tail risk thanks to the reduction of episodes such as environmental disasters and fraud, and (c) lower beta, thanks, for example, to better use of natural resources, which allows for less sensitivity to trends in commodity prices.

Finally, it is worth mentioning the existence of impact investing, defined by the Global Impact Investing Network (GIIN) as investments made with the intention of generating, in addition to financial returns, measurable and positive impacts from a social and environmental point of view. Impact investing therefore differs from ESG investing in the active search for a result in the social and environmental field, which is not limited to excluding investments associated with negative externalities from its portfolio but also includes companies that start from a lackluster situation in ESG terms to pursue direct intervention (engagement). The OECD (see Boffo and Patalano, 2020) further distinguishes between impact investing, carried out with the aim of measuring social and environmental implications, and social investing, where the social and environmental part takes on the greatest importance, even higher than the financial return. Philanthropy lies at the end of the spectrum as it completely neglects the aspect of financial performance.

15.3.3 Measurement and ratings

Externalities present challenges from a measurement point of view. A long literature has discussed the environmental impact of economic activity, highlighting that GDP is not a measure of well-being. The deterioration of water quality due to industrial production forces individuals to consume mineral water which generates economic activity that further contributes to the growth of the product but not to the well-being of individuals. The reduction of forests to allow land use is functional to economic growth but depletes the stock of natural resources. Even today, despite the debate of recent decades, we do not have a real alternative to GDP to better measure the consequences of economic activity on well-being, even if the indication of economic theory is to measure the change in the value of all relevant capital stocks (see Arrow, Dasgupta, Goulder, Mumford and Oleson, 2012). It is therefore very important that macroeconomic analyses on the creation of environmental indicators are complemented by studies that try to measure the effect on ESG elements at the company level.

Many ESG elements are hard to measure. The presence of these difficulties and the lack of a certain and unambiguous point of reference have favored the presence of a plurality of approaches followed by various specialized agencies calculating and selling environmental ratings. Over time, the demand for ratings of this type has expanded, especially from those who contribute capital to companies and want to look at account performance indicators that are not limited to the aspects traditionally contained in financial statements. The increase in demand has transformed the ratings industry by attracting larger players, all the way up to the well-known credit rating agencies. For example, Refinitiv starts with the analysis of more than 500 variables that are summarized in ten categories (emissions, innovation, and use of resources for the E; CSR strategy, management, and shareholders for the G; and impact on the community of reference, respect for human rights, product responsibility, and attention to employees for the S), whose weighted average helps define the value of an ESG rating for each company. Refinitiv evaluates each company in relation to its industry since the data must be placed in the context of the typical production process and the product/service.

MSCI considers the following items for the environmental dimension: CO2 emissions, ecological footprint of products, vulnerability to climate change, water stress, land use and biodiversity impact, environmental impact financing, toxic emissions, packaging waste management, clean technology approach, green real estate opportunities, and renewable energy opportunities. For the social aspect, it includes elements such as the management of labor relations, health and safety in the workplace, development of human capital, standards in the management of the value chain from the point of view of labor relations, safety and quality of products, consumer protection, privacy and data security, relations with local communities. Finally, governance is assessed through various indicators representative of the functioning of the board of directors, representing, among other things, ownership, remuneration structure, business ethics, and tax transparency.

How different are the indicators considered by the various specialized agencies, and how different are the ratings? Berg, Kölbel, and Rigobon (2020) group the 709 indicators used by the six ESG rating agencies studied into a taxonomy of sixty-five categories and highlights how the ESG ratings assigned by the main specialized operators are very divergent from each other, with a correlation of just over 50%. The main causes of this heterogeneity are the dispersion of the indicators and the different ways of measuring each of the indicators.

The dispersion of ratings is one of the elements underlying the current proposals to measure corporate behavior from balance sheet items rather than external ratings. Various companies have been producing environmental reports for years, but according to Kaplan and Ramanna (2021) these are very heterogeneous approaches and not integrated into ordinary accounting, and as such they are unable to resolve the perplexities associated with the heterogeneity of ratings. The Financial Accounting Standards Board (2021) is working on guidelines for better integration of material items into financial statements. The experience in this regard is very limited, but it can count on a robust effort being made since the 1990s at the international level to take into account elements such as pollution and the depletion of natural resources in national accounts.

15.4 ESG investing, portfolio choice and risk premia

15.4.1 Preferences for ESG factors

Do ESG elements influence investors' demand for assets? Dyck, Lins, Roth and Wagner (2019) show that the presence of institutional investors in the ownership of companies is associated with an improvement in their environmental and social performance, achieved through active interaction with the companies themselves. Dimson, Karakas, and Li (2015) analyze companies listed in the United States in the period 1999–2009 and highlight how the "active ownership" of institutional investors focuses on all ESG elements, generating both positive abnormal returns in case of success and an improvement in accounting results and increased interest from institutional investors.

Hartzmark and Sussman (2019) use a quasi-natural experiment to analyze the impact of ESG ratings on investor demand associated with Morningstar's introduction in 2016 of sustainability ratings for approximately 20,000 mutual funds. The authors find that in the year following the introduction of the ratings, mutual funds in the top 10% had net inflows of 4% of assets, while funds in the worst 10% had outflows of 6% of assets. The difference is not justified by different collection dynamics before the event or by changes in performance after the event. The preference for mutual funds perceived as attentive to sustainability and ESG elements is confirmed by Pástor and Vorsatz (2020) based on alpha and subscription flows during the Covid-19 pandemic period.

The behavior of investors who select funds defined as socially responsible is more stable than that of investors in other funds (Bollen, 2007), and surveys (see, e.g.,

Riedl and Smeets, 2017) find that SRI funds have lower expected returns than those of other funds and higher management costs. Barber, Morse and Yasuda (2021) present a study that is highly relevant from the point of view of understanding the role of ESG factors in the description of preferences. They analyze a large sample based on investments of 3,500 international investors in 4,649 venture capital funds in the period 1995–2014, of which 159 are defined as impact investing (II) protagonists. Applying various methodologies, Barber, Morse and Yasuda (2021) (2021) find that the average internal rate of return (IRR) of II funds is 4.7 percentage points lower than that of other funds, and that institutional investors are willing to pay up to 2.5–3.7 percentage points of lower return in order to invest in II funds.

One of the environmental issues that the community is most passionate about today is climate change. Sensitivity is higher in warmer periods, as highlighted by Choi, Zhenyu, and Wenxi (2020) based on data collected from seventy-four world cities, according to which, when the temperature rises in a certain area, the stock valuations of high-CO2-emitting companies fall compared with those of low-emission companies.

15.4.2 ESG factors, asset demand, and risk premia

Investors can consider ESG factors as relevant for the best determination of the parameters needed for optimization. For example, environmental performance is relevant because it can subject the company to regulatory risks and lawsuits that can be reflected in creditworthiness and equity value. There is also a reputational risk associated with financial exposure to a company that violates environmental standards. A relevant and recently much discussed case, regarding companies producing raw materials with a high CO2 emission content that could in the future be constrained by the market and/or regulators, is that of so-called "stranded assets," that is, assets losing value because of changes in business opportunities. Equally clear considerations can be made about corporate governance, which a long literature has shown to be important for the creation of value, while social elements are increasingly mentioned in debates, especially after the 2020 Covid-19 pandemic, but are more difficult to measure.

How should ESG factors be considered in the context of the portfolio choice model described in the previous chapters? Pedersen, Fitzgibbons, and Pomorski (2021) consider investors who include ESG factors in their preferences and select assets by evaluating the parameters of expected return and risk considering environmental, social, and governance characteristics.[3] To get a more general model than the traditional one, the utility function is written extensively as:

$$u(Er, \sigma^2, \mathrm{ESG}) = Er - 0.5 \times A \times \sigma^2 + f(ESG)$$

[3] In the terminology of Chapter 2, such investors condition their estimates of expected returns and volatilities to ESG information.

where $f(ESG)$ represents the impact of the portfolio's ESG characteristic on the overall utility, which in turn depends on the ESG characteristics of the individual securities and the portfolio selected by the investor. To maximize such function, the portfolio should be chosen not only to optimize the Sharpe ratio, that is, the ratio of expected return to risk, but also to meet preferences for non-monetary items. In addition, the characteristics summarized in ESG are useful for improving estimates of the expected return, variances, and covariances of each individual security. Investors are therefore divided into three classes:

- those who ignore ESG characteristics choose an inefficient portfolio because they incorrectly estimate the expected return and variance;
- those who use ESG characteristics but do not include ESG performance in the utility function maximize the Sharpe ratio according to traditional models; and
- those who assign a positive value to the ESG profile of the portfolio make a selection of stocks with a lower Sharpe ratio and suffer a damage offset by the additional utility due to non-strictly-financial elements.

Pedersen, Fitzgibbons, and Pomorski (2021) show that the portfolio demanded by investors considering ESG elements is as follows:

$$w = \frac{1}{A} V^{-1} \left[Er - r_f i + \pi(s - i\bar{s}) \right]$$

where π indicates the relevance of preferences for ESG factors, s is the vector of the ESG characteristics of the N securities, and $\bar{s}$ is the average value of the ESG indicator of the various securities. Demand for a stock therefore depends on its risk premium and relative strength in terms of ESG characteristics. A stock that has the same ESG characteristics as the average has a similar role in portfolios as it would on the basis of pure risk and expected return considerations, since the portfolio can be thought of as the ideal sum of a portfolio that maximizes the Sharpe ratio and one that reacts purely to the relevance of the various securities to investors' ESG preferences.

As Merton (1987) illustrated, financial decisions by capital contributors can create quantity effects that affect equilibrium prices. For example, the decision by a significant proportion of investors not to buy a certain security limits demand and can lower the equilibrium price and increase the expected return. In the context of lending, the decision by some banks not to lend resources to companies with certain characteristics may result in an increase in the rate by other banks.

Pedersen Fitzgibbons, and Pomorski (2021) derive the equilibrium implications and show that when investors take ESG elements into account, both the price and expected return of each security also depend on ESG characteristics. In particular, the expected return from the individual security generalizes the CAPM:

$$Er_i = r_f + \beta_i (Er_M - r_f) - \pi(s_i - s_M)$$

where s_M represents the value of the ESG indicator for the market as a whole. The expected return of the security is lower than that predicted by the CAPM in case the

ESG indicator of the security is higher than that of the market: Investors' preferences increase the demand for securities with the best ESG characteristics, increasing their price and decreasing their expected return, a result shared by Pástor, Stambaugh, and Taylor (2020), who highlight how reducing the cost of capital for the best companies from an ESG perspective allows them to develop further than companies that do not stand out for their compliance with ESG criteria

The relationship between demand and equilibrium price naturally affects not only the expected return but also the unexpected return, following the general rules discussed in Chapter 12. Stocks of ESG-conscious companies can positively surprise the market if they are able to generate higher cash flows and lower-than-expected discount rates. Pástor, Stambaugh, and Taylor (2022) find that over the period 2012-2020 green stocks overperformed brown stocks due to unexpectedly strong increases in environmental concerns and not due to higher expected returns. In fact, the opposite is true: consistent with theory, green stocks have lower expected returns than brown stocks. The expected return is lower for stocks clearly connected with ESG. Avramov, Cheng, Lioui, and Tarelli (2022) show that expected return increases with ESG uncertainty as measured from the standard deviation of ratings from six major providers.

15.4.3 Expected returns, volatilities, and ESG factors

Average returns on equities are higher for stocks that finance companies active in the sectors most harmful to the community, the so-called sin stocks related to tobacco, alcohol, and gambling, a phenomenon associated, according to Hong and Kacperczyk (2009), with the lower presence of these securities in the portfolios of institutional investors. Hsu, Lin and Tsou (2023) claim that the "pollution premium" equals 4.42% in the United States based on emission intensity factor (defined as total emissions divided by total assets) constructed using data from the Toxic Release Inventory database over the period 1991-2016. The premium is explained as a compensation for holding firms creating negative externalities in an economy characterized by environmental legislation uncertainty and increased attention to pollution with an association to activists protests and litigation risk. The paper shows that firms producing more toxic emissions are affected by larger profitability decline when regulation becomes tighter.

The environmental profile of companies is linked to the cost of capital. Chava (2014) points out that companies with poorer environmental performance, for example due to toxic waste emissions and revenues from the sale of high-CO2 fuels, have an expected return on equity (measured by the calculation of the valuation-implied cost described in Chapter 12) that is more than 1% higher and a cost of bank loans that is 0.25% higher than that of successful companies.[4] Flammer (2013) proposes an event study that starts with the study of daily news about new information on the environ-

[4] Speaking more broadly about CSR, the worst companies pay a 7–18 basis point higher cost of debt (Goss and Roberts, 2011).

mental behavior of companies surveyed in the period 1980–2009 and finds that stock prices react positively to news that illustrates a strong environmental commitment and negatively to news that is associated with little respect for the environment. The impact of positive news tends to decrease over time, while the impact of negative news tends to rise, consistent with a growing focus on corporate social responsibility by investors.

For some years now, "green bonds" have been present on the bond markets. These are fixed income securities purchased by investors on the basis of the issuer's commitment to use the resources obtained in investment projects with positive effects on the environmental side. Companies are interested in identifying funding requests as "green" to attract the interest of the ever-increasing number of investors who intend to implement forms of ESG investing. However, it is not clear ex ante whether the relationship between supply and demand may be such as to cause an impact on the price and therefore a reduction in the cost of capital (and investors' remuneration). Flammer (2021) analyzes all fixed income securities issued by companies defined as "green" on Bloomberg between 2013 and 2018 and, based on an event study, highlights the existence of an abnormal return that increases stock market capitalization by 0.49% when the issuance of a green bond is announced, especially if it is the first time for the company and if there is an independent certification. The author's interpretation concerns the signaling value of this issue, which is in fact supported by a subsequent improvement in environmental performance but is in no way associated, at the time of issuance, with a reduction in the cost of debt.

How do we account for the possibility that the environmental characteristics considered in the empirical analysis are relevant simply as a proxy for unmeasured variables? Returns and interest rates could depend on risk elements unobserved in the empirical analysis but positively correlated with environmental characteristics, and empirical results could be spurious. Or the results could be due to reverse causation, where higher-value companies are better able to pursue ESG investments. This is a common problem in empirical analyses in economics and finance, which in many cases is completely overlooked. To demonstrate that the results are not the result of measurement error, Chava (2014) shows that the least environmentally responsible companies are penalized both from the point of view of their inclusion in the portfolios of institutional investors and from the point of view of banks' participation in financing operations carried out by pools of financial intermediaries. Martins (2020) uses a methodology that exploits seemingly random variations in ESG variables to verify their impact (regression discontinuity design).

15.5 Finance and climate change

15.5.1 Climate change and financial risk

A distinction is made between physical risk and transition risk. Physical risk is characterized in chronic and acute terms: The former occurs in a predictable and gradual manner over time, while the latter is linked to extreme and unpredictable events, such as heat waves, periods of extreme cold, heavy rainfall, snowfall, and wind. Transition risk depends on the cost imposed by policymakers to companies for their CO2 emissions. A survey of 861 economic and financial experts working at financial institutions and central banks conducted by Stroebel and Wurgler (2021) shows that transition risk is the most important over a five-year horizon and physical risk the most relevant over a thirty-year horizon.

Risk measurement can use evidence on the returns produced by financial markets. In fact, if we assume that climate change risk is recognized by investors and therefore embedded in prices, we can use return data, making the necessary assumptions to move from total volatility risk (as done in the Value at Risk analysis) to the total risk component attributable to climate change, or use a multifactor model that allows us to attribute a share of the total risk. This class of models will be described in the next section. If, however, it is assumed that the market does not recognize this type of risk in prices, then it is necessary to use structural models that are based on various economic assumptions to estimate the impact of climate change.

For an example of a structural model, we can consider for example UNEP (2019), whose fundamental element is a simulation engine capable of creating scenarios for the elements of the climate that are most relevant for their economic impact, such as temperature dynamics, rainfall, and extreme events such as droughts and floods. The consequences of these scenarios are analyzed from the point of view of physical and transition risk over a fifteen-year horizon.

For each of these elements, a threshold is selected beyond which normal production operations cannot be maintained. The cost of chronic risk is given by the reduction of economic activity. Acute risks involve damage caused by physical impact to economic capital as well as damage associated with the interruption of economic activity. Risk is quantified as the difference between the ninety-fifth and fiftieth percentiles of the damage distribution. The transition risk mainly concerns the possibility that policymakers will force companies to pay for CO2 emissions, incurring a cost that is estimated according to the objectives of containing the temperature increase compared with the business-as-usual scenario, quantified as an increase of 1.5 degrees, 2 degrees, and 3 degrees. By adding the cost of the physical risk and of the transition risk, the estimate of the CVaR (Climate Value at Risk) given for each company is the ratio between the present value of the costs over the horizon considered and the value of the company.

15.5.2 Climate change and risk premia

Bolton and Kacperczyk (2021) estimate a multifactorial model to examine the presence of a risk premium specifically linked to company-wide observable indicators such as CO2 emissions: Companies with high emissions are more subject to the risk that policymakers will establish aggressive regulation aimed at limiting the average temperature increase by reducing CO2 emissions. The presence of transition risk is not the only relevant element, as companies with high CO2 emissions may be more exposed to the risk that technological innovation will further favor production processes that make use of renewable energy.

The analysis of this possibility requires first of all the availability of data on CO2 emissions, which the authors obtain from various sources, including mainly Trustcoast for a sample of more than 3,400 American companies in the period 2005–2017. To link emissions to yields, Bolton and Kacperczyk (2021) use a methodology based on Fama and MacBeth (1973) with a monthly regression of the return of the individual security returns on CO2 emissions and control characteristics:

$$r_{it} = \gamma_{0,t} + \gamma_{1,t} \ln(CO2_{it-1}) + \gamma'_{2,t} Z_{t-1} + \varepsilon_t$$

where Z_{t-1} is a vector of characteristics that can predict returns, including size, book-to-market, and others. The $\gamma_{1,t}$ is an estimate of the premium for CO2 exposure in period t. On average, the premium value ranges, across different econometric specifications, between 1.5% and 3.6% annualized. On the basis of further empirical analyses they show that institutional investors tend to reduce the weight in their portfolios of securities with high CO2 emission intensity.

Engle, Giglio, Kelly, Lee and Stroebel (2020) use a simplified version of the factor replicating portfolio methodology to construct portfolios of stocks that allow for the replication of new information on climate change. This requires first constructing the variable that serves as a proxy for climate change, measured by the monthly correlation between the content of *Wall Street Journal* articles and a predetermined vocabulary of terms associated with climate change. Second, the indicator thus calculated is regressed on the contemporary return of dynamically constructed portfolios:

$$CC_{t+1} = \gamma_0 + \gamma_1 r^{SUS}_{t+1} + \gamma_2 r^{S}_{t+1} + \gamma_3 r^{V}_{t+1} + \gamma_4 r^{M}_{t+1} + \varepsilon_{t+1}$$

where r^{SUS}_{t+1} is the return of a long portfolio in securities with a high ESG indicator and short in securities with a low ESG indicator, r^{S}_{t+1} is the return of a long portfolio in small companies and short in large companies, r^{V}_{t+1} is the return of a value portfolio, and r^{M}_{t+1} is the return of the market portfolio. The model is therefore a Fama–French regression extended to include an ESG portfolio. Estimated coefficients γ_1, γ_2, γ_3, and γ_4 are the weights of the four assets in the construction of the portfolio that replicates the social focus on climate change.

Can we use the climate change tracking portfolio in asset allocation? One possibility is to think of the model by Sharpe and Tint (1990), where the rate of return of the climate change replicating portfolio plays the role of the liability. The model suggests that investors form their portfolios also based on the covariance between the return on financial assets and the return on liabilities. Securities that have a positive covariance with the realization of the liability play a larger role in financial portfolios, in this case securities (e.g., those issued by companies active in the field of renewable energy) whose prices tend to rise whenever the perception of climate change increases. Pástor, Stambaugh, and Taylor (2020) note that ESG stocks may have an additional demand component due to their higher ability to hedge against climate risk elements.

15.5.3 Climate change and real estate

Real estate prices are expected to be sensitive to the prospects of climate change and the related rise in average sea level. Empirical evidence regarding the impact of climate change on residential prices is evident in many studies, although causality is difficult to estimate. As a result, the best studies use quasi-natural experiments that can identify the marginal impact of prospective temperature variation.

An example is Murfin and Spiegel (2020), according to which it is not enough to use the distance from the coast as a proxy for the potential climate effect on a property, as it is precisely the properties on the coast that benefit from other elements that increase the price for the same characteristics. The authors then use as a relevant characteristic the tendency of the land to descend (e.g., due to gas extraction) or rise (e.g., due to melting ice) over time, which can be projected forward to estimate sea level rise. Murfin and Spiegel (2020) do not find a material impact of climate change on prices using this hypothesis. Giglio, Maggiori and Stroebel (2021) estimate a climate change awareness index starting from the descriptions of the apartments for sale and considering the characteristics that illustrate the relevance of aspects related to climate change. They find a negative relationship between this index and housing prices while acknowledging the measurement error associated with the type of description of the apartment for sale, which is unlikely to emphasize the negative aspects associated with climate change, such as being located in an area prone to frequent flooding. Baldauf, Garlappi, and Yannelis (2020) combine transaction prices with projections of flood risk associated with sea level rise and surveys on belief in the existence of climate change, finding that an increase in a standard deviation in the percentage of climate change believers is associated with a 7% decrease in the price of homes most affected by rising waters. From a methodological point of view, they do not exploit the tendency of land to rise and fall or an index of perception of the existence of climate change but hypothesize that the hedonic regression used can encompass all aspects relevant to the determination of the price. With similar methodology, Bernstein, Gustafson, and Lewis (2019) find that the prices of homes most exposed to sea level rise are 7% lower than otherwise similar homes. The gap is particularly strong when there is a greater presence of institutional investors. Keys and Mulder (2020) jointly analyze the residential and mortgage markets with data related to Florida, finding that in the period 2013–2018 transactions of properties most exposed to climate change risk fell by 16–20% compared with those of less exposed properties There was no price impact in 2013-2018 but a 5% drop in 2018-2020. The authors interpret the evidence in light of the typical model of residential market functioning in which changes in price follow changes in volume. It is interesting to note the lack of reaction from the point of view of mortgages, which do not seem to be affected by the prospects of climate change, neither from the point of view of cost nor from that of the availability of financing.

Summary

- The corporate social responsibility (CSR) approach suggests that companies internalize some externalities and do not limit themselves to maximizing value through the pursuit of profit.
- The empirical evidence regarding the trade-off between earnings and CSR is unclear. Companies that adopt CSR objectives operate predominantly in legal systems that are more oriented toward public intervention in the economy, but at the same time the pursuit of CSR ensures benefits in terms of demand, productivity, and financing that positively affect economic value.
- The positive relationship between CSR and economic value may be due to the increasing attention paid by the community to problems that are exacerbated by consumption and production behaviors that are solely oriented toward individual interest. Regulators, policymakers, and investors are increasingly aware of the interest in the problems created by negative externalities.
- Social responsibility has extended to investors through socially responsible investment (SRI), which has been codified in environmental, social, and governance (ESG) criteria. Investors can pursue the improvement of ESG indicators through an exclusionary approach or through a focus on seeking improvements in the investee companies as part of impact investing.
- Recently, the theme of externality-taking investment has been focused on sustainability. Academic and institutional definitions of sustainability converge on the relevance of the comparison of well-being between generations in the long term, even if sustainability can be interpreted in different ways, either as a primary interest for economic activity limited by the excessive generation of negative externalities or as a primary interest for environmental and social elements that must be respected even at the cost of reducing the level of economic activity.
- The measurement of ESG elements attracts strong interest from specialist agencies, who sometimes see it as a service in its own right and sometimes as a useful element to further improve the credit rating. Empirical analyses show that there is a wide disparity between ESG ratings given to the same company by various providers, which converge on general concepts and indicators but diverge on specific measurement.
- ESG factors are important for portfolio selection both from the point of view of the direct impact on preferences, which can lead to a deviation from the optimal portfolio in a purely financial sense to favor better companies from the point of view of ESG measurement, and from the point of view of the relevance of ESG characteristics for determining the expected return and risk parameters that serve as inputs in the Markowitz model.
- As is always the case, when an element is important for the financial choice, market prices and risk premiums are also modified. Stocks that stand out for ESG characteristics therefore benefit from higher demand, higher capitalization, and lower risk premia.
- From the point of view of empirical analyses, the most consolidated results concern environmental and governance aspects. The evidence is quite clear. Good environmental performance and compliance with the best governance criteria are recognized by the market in higher prices and lower risk premia. Asset management companies that offer products that are characterized by high ESG and sustainability standards have greater attention and flows from investors, as well as better performance in terms of return and risk.
- Climate change is the last frontier of analysis. The results available so far begin to shape the frameworks for risk analysis and highlight the relationship between climate change sensitivity indicators and market assessments. Real estate is also influenced by expectations of rising temperatures and associated sea level rise.

Bibliography

Aggarwal, D., A.H. Choi, and Y.A. Lee, 2023. The meme stock frenzy: Origins and implications. Working paper, https://ssrn.com/abstract=4432824.

Ai, H., and R. Bansal, 2018. Risk preferences and the macroeconomic announcement premium. *Econometrica*, 86, 1383–1430.

Amihud, Y., and R.Y. Goyenco, 2013. Mutual fund's R2 as predictor of performance. *Review of Financial Studies*, 26, 667–694.

Amihud, Y., and H. Mendelson, 1986. Asset pricing and the bid-ask spread. *Journal of Financial Economics*, 17, 223–249.

Anarkulova, A., S. Cederburg, and M. O'Doherty, 2022. Stocks for the long run? Evidence from a broad sample of developed markets. *Journal of Financial Economics*, 143, 409-433.

Andonov, A., P. Eicholtz, and N. Kok, 2013. A global perspective on pension fund investments in real estate. *Journal of Portfolio Management*, 39, 32–42.

Ang, A., 2014. *Asset Management: A Systematic Approach to Factor Investing*. Oxford University Press

Ang, A., R. Hodrick, Y. Xing, and X. Zhang, 2006. The cross-section of volatility and expected returns. *Journal of Finance*, 61, 259–299.

Ares, 2024. Understanding private credit. Available at https://www.aresmgmt.com/sites/default/files/2024-04/Understanding-Private-Credit-2024.pdf.

Arrow, K.J., P. Dasgupta, L.H. Goulder, K.J. Mumford, and K. Oleson, 2012. Sustainability and the measurement of wealth. *Environment and Development Economics*, 17, 317–353.

Arts Economics, 2024. Art market report. Available at https://theartmarket.artbasel.com/.

Asch, S., 1952. *Social Psychology*. Prentice Hall.

Asness, C.S., A. Frazzini, and L.H. Pedersen, 2019. Quality minus junk. *Review of Accounting Studies*, 24, 34–112.

Asness, C.S., T.J. Moskowitz, and L.H. Pedersen, 2013. Value and momentum everywhere. *Journal of Finance*, 68, 929–985.

Asvanunt, A., and S. Richardson, 2017. The credit risk premium. *Journal of Fixed Income*, 26, 6–24.

Atmaz, A., and S. Basak, 2018. Belief dispersion in the stock market. *Journal of Finance*, 73, 1225–1279.

Avdis, E., and J.A. Wachter, 2017. Maximum likelihood estimation of the equity premium. *Journal of Financial Economics*, 125, 589–609.

Avramov, D., S., Cheng, A. Lioui, and A. Tarelli, 2022, Sustainable investing with ESG rating uncertainty, Journal of Financial Economics, 145, 642-664.

Bailey, M.J., R.F. Muth, and H.O. Nourse, 1963. A regression method for real estate price index construction. *Journal of American Statistical Association*, 58, 933–942.

Bain & Company, 2019. *Global Private Equity Report.*

Baker, M., and J. Wurgler, 2006. Investor sentiment and the cross-section of stock return. *Journal of Finance*, 51, 1645–1680.

Baker, S., N. Bloom, and S.J. Davis, 2016. Measuring economic policy uncertainty. *Quarterly Journal of Economics*, 131, 1593–1636.

Baldauf, M., L. Garlappi, and C. Yannelis, 2020. Does climate change affect real estate prices? Only if you believe in it. *Review of Financial Studies*, 33, 1256–1295.

Ballentine, C., 2021. How active ETFs are shaking up passive investing. Bloomberg News, August 26.

Bansal, R., and A. Yaron, 2009. Risks for the long run: A potential resolution of asset pricing puzzles. *Journal of Finance*, 59, 1481–1509.

Banz, R.W., 1981. The relationship between return and market value of common stocks. *Journal of Financial Economics*, 9, 3–18.

Barber, B.M., Y. Lee, Y. Liu, and T. Odean, 2009. Just how much do individual investors lose by trading? *Review of Financial Studies*, 22, 609–632.

Barber, B.M., Y. Lee, Y. Liu, T. Odean, and K. Zhang, 2020. Learning fast or slow? *Review of Asset Pricing Studies*, 10, 61–93.

Barber, B.M., A. Morse, and A. Yasuda, 2021. Impact investing. *Journal of Financial Economics*, 139, 162–185.

Barber, B.M., and T. Odean, 2000. Trading is hazardous to your wealth: The common stock investment performance of individual investors. *Journal of Finance*, 55, 773–807.

Barber, B.M., and T. Odean, 2008. All that glitters: the effect of attention and news on the buying behavior of individual and institutional investors. *Review of Financial Studies,* 21, 785–818.

Barber, B.M., and T. Odean, 2013. The behavior of individual investors. In *Handbook of the Economics of Finance*, Volume 2, part B, edited by G.M. Constantinides, M. Harris, R.M. Stulz, 1533–1570, Elsevier.

Barberis, N., 2018. Psychology-based models of asset prices and trading volume. In *Handbook of Behavioral Economics*, edited by D. Bernheim, S. DellaVigna, and D. Laibson. North Holland.

Barberis, N., and M. Huang, 2008. The loss aversion/narrow framing approach to the equity premium puzzle. In *Handbook of Finance: Handbook of the Equity Risk Premium*, edited by R. Mehra, Elsevier.

Barberis, N., M. Huang, and T. Santos, 2001. Prospect theory and asset prices. *Quarterly Journal of Economics*, 2001, 116, 1–53.

Bargh, J., 2017. *Before You Know It: The Unconscious Reasons We Do What We Do.* Simon & Schuster.

Barretto Garcia, M., G. de Hollander, M. Grueschow, R. Polania, M. Woodford, and C.C. Ruff, 2023., Individual risk attitudes arise from noise in neurocognitive magnitude representations. *Nature Human Behaviour,* 7, 1551–1567.

Barro, 2009. Rare disasters, asset prices, and welfare costs. *American Economic Review*, 99, 243–264.

Barroso, P., and P. Santa-Clara, 2015. Momentum has its moments. *Journal of Financial Economics*, 116, 111-120.

Bebchuk, L., A. Cohen, and A. Ferrell, 2009. What matters in corporate governance? *Review of Financial Studies*, 22, 783–287.

Bekaert, G., C.R. Harvey, and C. Lundblad, 2007. Liquidity and expected returns: Lessons from emerging markets. *Review of Financial Studies*, 20, 1783–1831.

Beltratti, A., and J. Bock, 2018. BDCs: The most important commercial lenders you've never heard about. *Journal of Alternative Investment*, 20, Spring, 8–20.

Beltratti, A, and R.M. Stulz, 2012. The credit crisis around the globe: Why did some banks perform better? *Journal of Financial Economics*, 105, 1–17.

Benartzi, S., and R.H. Thaler, 2013. Behavioral economics and the retirement savings crisis. *Science*, 339, 1152–1153.

Ben Dor, A., L. Dynkin, J. Hyman, P. Houweling, E. van Leeuwen, and O. Penninga, 2007. DTS (duration times spread). *Journal of Portfolio Management*, Winter, 77–100.

Berg, F., J.F. Kölbel, and R. Rigobon, 2022. Aggregate confusion: The divergence of ESG ratings. *Review of Finance*, 26, 1315–1344,

Berk, J.B., and R.C. Green, 2004. Mutual fund flows and performance in rational markets. *Journal of Political Economy*, 112, 1269–1295.

Bernard, V.L. and J.K. Thomas, 1990. Evidence that stock prices do not fully reflect the implications of current earnings for future earnings. *Journal of Accounting and Economics*, 13, 305–340.

Bernstein, A., M.T. Gustafson, and R. Lewis, 2019. Disaster on the horizon: The price effect of sea level rise. *Journal of Financial Economics*, 134, 253–272.

Bessembinder, H., 2018. Do stocks outperform Treasury bills? *Journal of Financial Economics*, 129, 440–457.

Best, M.J., and R.R. Grauer, 1991. On the sensitivity of mean-variance-efficient portfolios to changes in asset means: Some analytical and computational results. *The Review of Financial Studies*, 1991, 315–342.

Bhattarai, S., and C.J. Neely, 2022. An analysis of the literature on international unconventional monetary policy. *Journal of Economic Literature*, 60, 527–597.

Bianchi, M., 2018. Financial literacy and portfolio dynamics. *Journal of Finance*, 73, 831–859.

Black, F., 1986. Noise. *Journal of Finance*, 41, 528–543.

Blais, A., and E.U. Weber, 2006. A domain-specific risk-taking (DOSPERT) scale for adult populations. *Judgment and Decision Making*, 1, 33–47.

Blanchard, O., and M.W. Watson, 1982. Bubbles, rational expectations and financial markets. In *Crises in the Economic and Financial Structure*, edited by P. Wachtel, 295–316, Heath-and Company.

Block, J., J. Young Soo, S. Kaplan, and A. Schulze, 2024. A survey of private debt funds. *Review of Corporate Finance Studies*, 13, 335-383.

Boffo, R., and R. Patalano, 2020. *ESG Investing: Practices, Progress and Challenges*. OECD Paris, www.oecd.org/finance/ESG-Investing-Practices-Progress-and-Challenges.pdf.

Bollen, N.P.B., 2007. Mutual fund attributes and investor behavior, *Journal of Financial and Quantitative Analysis*, 42, 683–708.

Bollen, N.P.B., and J.A. Busse, 2004. Short-term persistence in mutual fund performance. *Review of Financial Studies*, 18, 569–597.

Bolton, P., and M. Kacperczyk, 2021. Do investors care about carbon risk? *Journal of Financial Economics*, 142, 517–549.

Bongaerts, D., F. de Jong, and J. Driessen, 2017. An asset pricing approach to liquidity ejects in corporate bond markets. *Review of Financial Studies*, 30, 1229–1269.

Bordalo, P., N. Gennaioli, R. La Porta, and A. Shleifer, 2024. Belief Overreaction and Stock Market Puzzles. *Journal of Political Economy*, 132, 1450-1484.

Bowen, H.R., 1953. *Social Responsibilities of the Businessman*. Harper.

Boyd J.H., J. Hu, and R. Jagannathan, 2005. The stock market's reaction to unemployment news: Why bad news is usually good for stocks. *Journal of Finance*, 60, 649–672.

Camerer, C., J. Cohen, E. Fehr, P. Glimcher, and D. Laibson, 2016. Neuroeconomics. *In Handbook of Experimental Economics*, Volume 2, edited by J.H. Kagel and A.E. Roth, Princeton University Press.

Campbell, J.Y., and L. Hentschel, 1992. No news is good news: An asymmetric model of changing volatility in stock returns. *Journal of Financial Economics*, 31, 281–318.

Campbell, J.Y., A.W. Lo, and A.C. MacKinlay, 1997. *The Econometrics of Financial Markets*. Princeton University Press.

Campbell, J.Y., and R.J. Shiller, 1987. Cointegration and tests of present value models. *Journal of Political Economy*, 95, 1062–1088.

Campbell, J.Y., and R.J. Shiller, 1988. The dividend–price ratio and expectations of future dividends and discount factors. *Review of Financial Studies*, 1, 195–228.

Campbell, J.Y., and L. Viceira, 2002. *Strategic Asset Allocation: Portfolio Choice for Long-Term Investors*. Oxford University Press

Campbell, J.Y., and T. Vuolteenaho, 2004. Bad beta, good beta. *American Economic Review*, 94, 1249–1275.

Campbell, R.A.J., 2008. Art as a financial investment. *Journal of Alternative Investments*, Spring, 64–81.

Canner, N., N.G. Mankiw, and D. Weil, 1997. An asset allocation puzzle. *American Economic Review*, 87, 181–191.

Carhart, M., 1997. On persistence in mutual fund performance. *Journal of Finance*, 52, 57–82.

Carosso, V.P., 1970. *Investment Banking in America: A History*. Harvard University Press.

Case, K.E., and R.J. Shiller, 1987. Prices of single family homes since 1970: New indexes for four cities. *New England Economic Review*, Sept./Oct., 45–56.

Chambers, D., E. Dimson, and C. Spaenjers, 2020. Art as an asset: Evidence from Keynes the collector. *Review of Asset Pricing Studies*, 10, 490–520.

Chambers, D., C. Spaenjers, and E. Steiner, 2021. The rate of return on real estate: Long-run mcro-level evidence. *Review of Financial Studies*, 34, 3572–3607.

Chan, L.K.C., J. Karceski, and J. Lakonishok, 2003. The level and persistence of growth rates. *Journal of Finance*, 58, 643–684.

Chava, S., 2014. Environmental externalities and cost of capital. *Management Science*, 60, 2223–2247.

Chava, S., and A. Purnanandam, 2010. Is default-risk negatively related to stock returns? *Review of Financial Studies*, 23, 2523–2559.

Chen, N., R. Roll, and S.A. Ross, 1986. Economic forces and the stock market. *Journal of Business*, 59, 383–403.

Chernenko, S., I. Erel, and R. Prilmeier, 2022. Why do firms borrow directly from nonbanks? *Review of Financial Studies*, 35, 4902–4947.

Chichilnisky, G., G. Heal, and A. Beltratti, 1995. The green golden rule. *Economics Letters*, 49, 175–179.

Choi, D., G. Zhenyu, and J. Wenxi, 2020. Attention to global warming. R*eview of Financial Studies*, 33, 1112–1146.

Chordia, T., and B. Swaminathan, 2000. Trading volume and cross-autocorrelations in stock returns. *Journal of Finance*, 55, 913–935.

Clark, R., A. Lusardi, and O.S. Mitchell, 2015. Financial knowledge and 401(k) performance. *Journal of Pension Economics and Finance*, 10, 1–24.

Coase, R.II., 1937. The nature of the firm. *Economica*, 4, 386–405.

Cochrane, J.H., 2005. *Asset Pricing*. Princeton University Press.

Cohen, R.B., C. Polk, and T. Vuolteenaho, 2003. The value spread. *Journal of Finance*, 58, 609–642.

Collin-Dufresne, P., R. Goldstein, and J. Martin, 2001. The determinants of credit spread changes. *Journal of Finance*, 56, 2177–2208.

Communication from the Commission to the European Parliament, the Council and the European Economic and Social Committee, 2006. Implementing the partnership for growth and jobs: Making Europe a pole of excellence on corporate social responsibility. Available at https://eur-lex.europa.eu/LexUriServ/LexUriServ.do?uri=CELEX%3A52006DC0136%3AEN%3AHTML.

Cremers, M., and A. Petajisto, 2009. How active is your fund manager? A new measure that predicts performance. *Review of Financial Studies*, 22, 3329–3365.

Cutler, D, J.M. Poterba, and L.H. Summers, 1989. What moves stock prices? *Journal of Portfolio Management*, 15, 4–12.

Damasio, A., 2003. *Looking for Spinoza*. Harcourt Books.

Dasgupta, P., and K. Maler, 2000. Net national product, wealth, and social well-being. *Environment and Development Economics*, 5, Special issue: *Advances in Green Accounting*, 69–93.

Davydiuk, T., T. Marchuk, and S. Rosen, 2020. Direct lending in the U.S. middle market. Carnegie Mellon University Working Paper.

Davydova, D., R. Fahlenbrach, L. Sanz, and R.M. Stulz, 2023. The unicorn puzzle. Fisher College of Business Working Paper No. 2022-03-012.

de Jong, F., and J. Driessen, 2012. Liquidity risk premia in corporate bond markets. *Quarterly Journal of Finance*, 2, 1–34.

Dennison, J.B., D. Sazhin, and D.V. Smith, 2022. Decision neuroscience and neuroeconomics: Recent progress and ongoing challenges. *Wiley Interdisciplinary Review of Cognitive Science*, 13.

Deutsch, M., and H.B. Gerard, 1955. A study of normative and informational social influences upon individual judgment. *Journal of Abnormal and Social Psychology*, 51, 629–636.

Dimson, E., 2011. Ex post: The investment performance of collectible stamps. *Journal of Financial Economics*, 100, 443–458.

Dimson, E., O. Karakaş, and X. Li, 2015. Active ownership. *Review of Financial Studies*, 28, 3225–3268.

Dimson, E., P. Marsh, and M. Staunton, 2002. *Triumph of the Optimists: 101 Years of Global Investment Returns*. Princeton University Press.

Dimson, E., P. Marsh, and M. Staunton, 2018. *Global Investment Returns Yearbook*. Credit Suisse Research Institute.

Dimson, E., P. Marsh, and M. Staunton, 2019. *Global Investment Returns Yearbook*. Credit Suisse Research Institute.

Dimson, E., P. Marsh, and M. Staunton, 2020. *Global Investment Returns Yearbook*. Credit Suisse Research Institute.

Dimson, E., P. Marsh, and M. Staunton, 2023. *Global Investment Returns Yearbook*. Credit Suisse Research Institute.

Dimson, E., and C. Spaenjers, 2014. The investment performance of art and other collectibles. In *Risk and Uncertainty in the Art World*, edited by Anna Dempster. Bloomsbury Publishing.

Driessen, J., T.-C. Lin, and L. Phalippou, 2012. A new method to estimate risk and return of non-traded assets from cash flows: The case of private equity funds. *Journal of Financial and Quantitative Analysis*, 47, 511–535.

Durand, R.B., R. Newby, L. Peggs, and M. Siekierka, 2013. Personality. *Journal of Behavioral Finance*, 14, 116–133.

Durand, R.B., R. Newby, and J. Sanghani, 2008. An intimate portrait of the individual investor. *Journal of Behavioral Finance*, 9, 193–208.

Dyck, A., K.V. Lins, L. Roth, and H.F. Wagner, 2019. Do institutional investors drive corporate social responsibility? International evidence. *Journal of Financial Economics*, 131, 693–714.

Ellsberg, D., 1961. Risk, ambiguity, and the Savage axioms. *Quarterly Journal of Economics*, 75, 643–669.

Elster, J., 1979. *Ulysses and the Sirens*. Cambridge University Press.

Elton, E.J., and M.J. Gruber, 1973. Estimating the dependence structure of share prices. *Journal of Finance*, 28, 1203–1232.

Elton, E.J., and M.J. Gruber, 2020. A review of the performance measurement of long-term mutual funds. *Financial Analyst Journal*, May, 22–37.

Elton, E.J., M.J. Gruber, and A. de Souza, 2019. Are passive funds really superior investments: An investor perspective. *Financial Analysts Journal*, 75, no. 3.

Engle, R.F., 1982. Autoregressive conditional heteroscedasticity with estimates of the variance of United Kingdom inflation. *Econometrica*, 50, 987–1007.

Engle, R.F., R. Ferstenberg, and J. Russell, 2012. Measuring and modeling execution cost and risk. *Journal of Portfolio Management*, 38, 14–28.

Engle, R.F., S. Giglio, B. Kelly, H. Lee, and J. Stroebel, 2020. Hedging climate change news. *Review of Financial Studies*, 33, 1184–1216.

Estrada, J., 2013. Stocks, bonds, risk and the holding period: An international perspective. *Journal of Portfolio Management*, Fall, 25–44.

Fama, E.F., 1965. Random walks in stock market prices. *Financial Analysts Journal*, 21, 55–59.

Fama, E.F., 1970. Efficient capital markets: a review of theory and empirical work. *Journal of Finance*, 25, 383–417.

Fama, E., 1998. Market efficiency, long-term returns, and behavioral finance. *Journal of Financial Economics*, 49, 283–306.

Fama, E.F., and K.R. French, 1988. Permanent and temporary components of stock prices. *Journal of Political Economy*, 96, 246–273.

Fama, E.F., and K.R. French, 1992. The cross section of expected returns. *Journal of Finance*, 47, 427–465.

Fama, E.F., and K.R. French, 1993. Common risk factors in the returns on stocks and bonds. *Journal of Financial Economics*, 33, 3–56.

Fama, E.F., and K.R. French, 2002. The equity premium. *Journal of Finance*, 2, 637–659.

Fama, E.F., and K.R. French, 2012. Size, value, and momentum in international stock returns. *Journal of Financial Economics*, 105, 457–472.

Fama, E.F., and K.R. French, 2004. New lists: Fundamentals and survival rates. *Journal of Financial Economics*, 73, 229–269.

Fama, E.F., and K.R. French, 2010. Luck versus skill in the cross-section of mutual fund returns. *Journal of Finance*, 65, 1915–1947.

Fama, E.F., and K.R. French, 2015. A five-factor asset pricing model. *Journal of Financial Economics*, 116, 1–22.

Fama, E.F., and K.R. French, 2017. International tests of a five-factor asset pricing model. *Journal of Financial Economics*, 123, 441–463.

Fama, E.F., and J.D. MacBeth, 1973. Risk, return, and equilibrium: Empirical tests. *Journal of Political Economy*, 81, 607–636.

Feld, L., and M.Lowry, 2022. Why do IPOs choose controversial governance structures and why do investors let them. *Journal of Financial Economics*, 146, 27–54.

Ferguson, N., 2017. *The Square and the Tower.* Penguin.

Festinger, L. 1957. *A Theory of Cognitive Dissonance.* Stanford University Press.

Financial Accounting Standards Board, 2021. Intersection of environmental, social and governance matters with financial accounting standards. FASB Staff Educational Paper.

Fink, J., 2021. A review of the post-earnings announcement drift. *Journal of Behavioral and Experimental Finance*, 29, 1–13.

Flammer, C., 2013. Corporate social responsibility and shareholder reaction: The environmental awareness of investors. *Academy of Management Journal*, 56, 758–781.

Flammer, C., 2021. Corporate green bonds. *Journal of Financial Economics*, 142, 499-516.

Flannery, M.J., and A.A. Protopapadakis, 2002. Macroeconomic factors do influence aggregate stock returns. *Review of Financial Studies*, 15, 751–782.

Franzoni, F., E. Novak, and L. Phalippou, 2012. Private equity performance and liquidity risk. *Journal of Finance*, 67, 2341–2373.

Fraser-Sampson, G., 2010. *Private Equity as an Asset Class.* Wiley Finance.

Frazzini, A., and L. Pedersen, 2014. Betting against beta. *Journal of Financial Economics*, 111, 1–25.

French, K.R., 2008. The cost of active investing. *Journal of Finance*, 63, 1537–1573.

Friede, G., T. Busch, and A. Bassen, 2015. ESG and financial performance: Aggregated evidence from more than 2000 empirical studies. *Journal of Sustainable Finance & Investment*, 5, 210–233.

Friedman, M., 1970. The social responsibility of business is to increase its profits. *New York Times*, September 13.

Frydman, C., N. Barberis, C.F. Camerer, P. Bossaerts, and A. Rangel, 2013. Using neural data to test a theory of investor behavior: An application to realization utility. *Journal of Finance*, 69, 907–946.

Frye, B.L., 2018. New art for the people: Art funds & financial technology. *Chicago-Kent Law Review*, 93, 113–139.

Gaar, E., D. Scherer, and D. Schiereck, 2022. The home bias and the local bias: A survey. *Management Review Quarterly*, 72, 21–57.

Galbraith, J.K., 1954. *The Great Crash 1929.* Houghton Mifflin.

Geczy, C.C., J. Jeffers, D.k. Musto, and A.M Tucker, 2021. Contracts with (social) benefits: The implementation of impact investing. *Journal of Financial Economics*, 142, 697–718.

Geltner, D., 1993. Estimating market values from appraised values without assuming an efficient market. *Journal of Real Estate Research*, 8, 325–345.

Geltner, D., and N. Miller, 2001. *Commercial Real Estate Analysis and Investments.* West Group.

Gervais, S., R. Kaniel, and D.H. Mingelgrin, 2001. The high-volume return premium. *Journal of Finance*, 56, 877–919.

Getmanski, M., P.A. Lee, and A. Lo, 2015. Hedge funds: A dynamic industry in transition. *Annual Review of Financial Economics*, 7, 483–577.

Ghent, A.C., W.N. Torous, and R.I. Valkanov, 2019. Commercial Real Estate as an Asset Class. *Annual Review of Financial Economics*, 11, 153-171..

Giese, G., L. Lee, D. MeLas, Z. Nagy, and L. Nishikawa, 2019. Foundations of ESG investing: How ESG affects equity valuation, risk, and performance. *Journal of Portfolio Management*, 45, 1–15.

Giesecke, K., F.A. Longstaff, S. Schaefer, and I. Strebulaev, 2011. Corporate bond default risk: A 150-year perspective. *Journal of Financial Economics*, 102, 233–250.

Giglio, S., M. Maggiori, and J. Stroebel, 2016. No-bubble condition: Model-free tests in housing markets. *Econometrica*, 84, 1047–1091.

Giglio, S., M. Maggiori, J. Ströbel, and A. Weber, 2021. Climate change and long-run discount rates: Evidence from real estate. *Review of Financial Studies*, 34, 3527–3571.

Gillan, S.L., A. Koch, and L.T. Starks, 2021. Firms and social responsibility: A review of ESG and CSR research in corporate finance. *Journal of Corporate Finance*, 66, 10189.

Goetzmann, W.N., 1993. Accounting for taste: Art and the financial markets over three centuries. *American Economic Review*, 83, 1370–1376.

Goetzmann, W.N., 2016, *Money changes everything: How finance made civilization possible.* Princeton University Press.

Gompers, A., J.L. Ishii, and A. Metrick, 2003. Corporate governance and equity prices. *Quarterly Journal of Economics*, 118, 107–155.

Goss, A., and G.S. Roberts, 2011. The impact of corporate social responsibility on the cost of bank loans. *Journal of Banking and Finance*, 35, 1794–1810.

Graham, B., and D. Dodd, 1934. *Security Analysis.* Mc-Graw Hill.

Greenwood, R., A. Shleifer, and Y. You, 2018. Bubbles for Fama. *Journal of Financial Economics*, 131, 20–43.

Grossman, S., and R.J. Shiller, 1981. The determinants of the variability of stock market prices. *American Economic Review*, 71, 222–227.

Grossman, S.J., and J.E. Stiglitz. 1980. On the impossibility of informationally efficient markets. *American Economic Review*, 70, 393–408.

Gruber, M.J., 1996. Another puzzle: The growth in actively managed mutual funds. Journal of Finance, 51, 783–810.

Guiso, L., and P. Sodini, 2013. Household finance: An emerging field. In *Handbook of the Economics of Finance*, Volume 2, Elsevier, edited by G.M. Constantinides, M. Harris, R.M. Stulz, 1397–1532.

Gupta, A., and S. Van Nieuwerburgh, 2021. Valuing private equity investments strip by strip. *Journal of Finance*, 76, 3255–3307.

Haliassos, M., and C.C. Bertaut, 1995. Why do so few hold stocks? *Economic Journal*, 105, 1110–1129.

Hammer, B., N. Markotty-Dehm, D. Schweizwer, and B. Schwetzler, 2022. Pricing and value-creation in private equity-backed buy-and-build strategies. *Journal of Corporate Finance*, 77, 102285.

Han, Y., D. Huang, D. Huang, and G. Zhou, 2022. Expected return, volume, and mispricing. *Journal of Financial Economics*, 143, 1295–1315.

Harari, Y.N., 2017. *Homo Deus. A brief history of tomorrow.* Vintage Publishing.

Hartzmark, S.M., and A.B. Sussman, 2019. Do investors value sustainability? A natural experiment examining ranking and fund flows. *Journal of Finance*, 74, 2789–2837.

Harvey, C.R., 2017. Presidential address: The scientific outlook in financial economics. *Journal of Finance*, 72, 1399–1440.

Harvey, C.R., Y. Liu, and H. Zhu, 2016. ... And the cross-section of expected returns. *Review of Financial Studies* 29, 5–68.

Hedlund, A., 2019. The time is right for permanent capital. *Private Debt Investor*, September 2.

Henriksson, R.D., 1984. Market timing and mutual fund performance: An empirical investigation. *Journal of Business*, 57, 73–96.

Hicks, J.R., 1939. The foundations of welfare economic. *The Economic Journal*, 49, 696–712.

Hong, H., and M. Kacperczyk, 2009. The price of sin: The effects of social norms on markets. *Journal of Financial Economics*, 93, 15–36.

Hsu, P., K. Li, and C. Tsou, 2023, The pollution premium. *Journal of Finance*, 78, 1343-1392.

Huang, J., and M. Huang, 2012. How much of the corporate–Treasury yield spread is due to credit risk? *The Review of Asset Pricing Studies*, 2, 153–202.

Ilmanen, A., 2011. *Expected Returns.* Wiley Finance.

Ilmanen, A., 2022. *Investing amid Low Expected Returns.* Wiley.

Ingersoll, J., 1987. *Theory of Financial Decision Making.* Rowman & Littlefield.

Irani, R.M., R. Iyer, R.R. Meisenzahl, J. Peydró, 2021, The Rise of Shadow Banking: Evidence from Capital Regulation, The Review of Financial Studies, 34, 2181–2235,

Ivkovic, Z., and S. Weisbenner, 2005. Local does as local is: information content of the geography of individual investors' common stock. *Journal of Finance*, 60, 267–306.

Jacobs, H., and S. Muller, 2020. Anomalies across the globe: Once public, no longer existent? *Journal of Financial Economics*, 135, 213–230.

Jagannathan, R., and T. Ma, 2003. Risk reduction in large portfolios: Why imposing the wrong constraints helps. *Journal of Finance, American Finance Association*, 58, 1651–1684.

Jappelli, T., and M. Padula, 2013. Investment in financial literacy and savings decisions. *Journal of Banking and Finance*, 37, 2779–2792.

Jegadeesh, N., R. Kraussl, and J. Pollet, 2015. Risk and expected returns of private equity investments: Evidence based on market prices. *Review of Financial Studies*, 28, 3269–3302.

Jegadeesh, N. and S. Titman, 1993. Returns to buying winners and selling losers: Implications for stock market efficiency. *Journal of Finance*, 48, 65–91.

Jensen, M.C., 1968. The performance of mutual funds in the period 1945–1964. *Journal of Finance*, 23, 389–416.

Jensen, M.C. and W.H. Meckling, 1976, Theory of the firm: Managerial behavior, agency costs and ownership structure. *Journal of Financial Economics*, 3, 305–360.

Jorda, O., K. Knoll, D. Kuvshinov, M. Schularick, and A.M. Taylor, 2019. The rate of return on everything, 1870–2015. *Quarterly Journal of Economics*, 134, 1225–1298.

Jorion, P., 1985. International portfolio diversification with estimation risk. *The Journal of Business*, 58, 259–278.

Jorion, P., and W.N. Goetzmann, 1999. Global stock markets in the twentieth century. *Journal of Finance*, 54, 953–980.

J.P. Morgan/Reuters, 1996. Risk metrics technical document.

Jung, J., and R.J. Shiller, 2005. Samuelson's dictum and the stock market. *Economic Inquiry*, 43, 221–228.

Kacperczyk, M., S.V. Nieuwerburgh, and L. Veldkamp, 2014. Time-varying fund manager skill. *Journal of Finance*, 69, 1455–1484.

Kahneman, D., 2011. *Thinking, Fast and Slow.* Penguin.

Kahneman, D., J.L. Knetsch, and R.H. Thaler, 1991. The endowment effect, loss aversion, and status quo bias. *Journal of Economic Perspectives*, 5, 193–206.

Kaiser, T., A. Lusardi, L. Menkhoff, and C. Urban, 2022. Financial education affects financial knowledge and downstream behaviors. *Journal of Financial Economics*, 145, 255–272.

Kaplan, R.S., and K. Ramanna, 2021. How to fix ESG reporting. University of Oxford Blavatnik School of Government, BSG Working Paper Series BSG-WP-2021/043.

Kaplan, S.N., and A. Schoar, 2005. Private equity performance: Returns, performance, and capital flows. *Journal of Finance*, 60, 1791–1823.

Kaustia, M., A. Conlin, and N. Luotonen, 2023. What drives stock market participation? The role of institutional, traditional, and behavioral factors. *Journal of Banking and Finance*, 148, 106743.

Kell, G., 2018. The remarkable rise of ESG. *Forbes,* July 11.

Keloharju, M., J.T. Linnainmaa, and P. Nyberg, 2021. Long-term discount rates do not vary across firms. *Journal of Financial Economics*, 141, 946–967.

Keynes, J.M., 1921. *A Treatise on Probability*. Dover Publications.

Keynes, J.M., 1936. *The General Theory of Employment, Interest and Money*. Macmillan.

Keys, B.J., and P. Mulder, 2020. Neglected no more: Housing markets, mortgage lending, and sea level rise. Jacobs Levy Equity Management Center for Quantitative Financial Research Paper, http://dx.doi.org/10.2139/ssrn.3906066.

Khan, M., G. Serafeim, and A. Yoon, 2016. Corporate sustainability: First evidence on materiality. *Accounting Review*, 91, 1697–1724.

Klapper L., A. Lusardi, and P. Van Oudheusden, 2015. Financial literacy around the world (2015): Insights from the Standard & Poor's ratings services Global Financial Literacy Survey.

Knight, F. H., 1921. *Risk, Uncertainty and Profit*. Sentry Press.

Kok, N., E. Koponen, and C.A. Martinez-Barbosa, 2017. Big data in real estate? From manual appraisal to automated valuation. *Journal of Portfolio Management*, 2017, Special Real Estate Issue, 202–211.

Korteweg, A.G., R. Kräussl, and P. Verwijmeren, 2016. Does it pay to invest in art? A selection-corrected returns perspective. *Review of Financial Studies*, 29, 1007–1038.

Kosowski, R., 2011. Do mutual funds perform when it matters most to investors? US mutual fund performance and risk in recessions and expansions. *Quarterly Journal of Finance*, 1, 607–664.

Lakonishok, J., A. Shleifer, and R.W. Vishny, 1994. Contrarian investment, extrapolation, and risk. *Journal of Finance*, 49, 1541–1578.

Lamont, O., 2001. Economic tracking portfolios. *Journal of Econometrics*, 105, 161–184.

La Porta, R., 1996. Expectations and the cross-section of stock returns. *Journal of Finance*, 51, 1715–1742.

La Porta, R., F. Lopez-de-Silanes, A. Shleifer, and R.W. Vishny, 1997. Legal determinants of external finance. *Journal of Finance*, 52, 1131–1150.

La Porta, R., F. Lopez-de-Silanes, A. Shleifer, and R.W. Vishny, 1998. Law and finance. *Journal of Political Economy*, 106, 1113–1155.

La Porta, R., F. Lopez-de-Silanes, A. Shleifer, and R.W. Vishny, 2000. Investor protection and corporate governance. *Journal of Financial Economics*, 58, 3–27.

Laux, C., and C. Leuz, 2010. Did fair-value accounting contribute to the financial crisis? *Journal of Economic Perspectives*, 24, 93–118.

Ledoit, O., and M. Wolf, 2003. Improved estimation of the covariance matrix of stock returns with an application to portfolio selection. *Journal of Empirical Finance*, 10, 603–621.

Levine, R., 2005. Finance and growth: Theory and evidence. In *Handbook of Economic Growth*, edited by Philippe Aghion and Steven Durlauf, Volume 1, Elsevier, 865–934.

Li, H., R. Novy-Marx, and M. Velikov, 2019, Liquidity risk and asset pricing, Critical Finance Review, 33, 223-255.

Liang, H., and L. Renneboog, 2017. On the foundations of corporate social responsibility. *Journal of Finance*, 72, 853–910.

Longstaff, F.A., S. Mithal, and E. Neis, 2005. Corporate yield spreads: Default risk or liquidity? New evidence from the credit default swap market. *Journal of Finance*, 60, 2213–2253.

Lucas, R.J., 1978. Asset prices in an exchange economy. *Econometrica*, 46, 1429–1445.

Lusardi, A., and O.S. Mitchell, 2008. Planning and financial literacy: How do women fare? *American Economic Review*, 98, 413–17.

Lusardi, A., and O.S. Mitchell, 2011a. Financial literacy and planning: Implications for retirement well-being. In *Financial Literacy: Implications for Retirement Security and the Financial Marketplace*, edited by O.S. Mitchell and A. Lusardi, Oxford University Press, 17–39.

Lusardi, A., and O.S. Mitchell, 2011b. Financial literacy around the world: An overview. *Journal of Pension Economics and Finance*, 10, 497–508.

Lusardi, A., and O.S. Mitchell, 2014. The economic importance of financial literacy. Theory and evidence. *Journal of Economic Literature*, 52, 5–44.

Markiewicz, L., and E.U. Weber, 2013. DOSPERTS's gambling risk-taking propensity scale predicts excessive stock trading. *Journal of Behavioral Finance*, 14, 65–78.

Markowitz, H., 1952. Portfolio selection, Journal of Finance, 7, 77–91

Martin, G.N., N.R. Carlson, and W. Buskist, 2013. *Psychology*, 5th ed. Pearson.

Martins, F., 2020. Corporate social responsibility, shareholder value, and competition. SSRN: https://ssrn.com/abstract=3651240 or http://dx.doi.org/10.2139/ssrn.3651240

Massa, M., and A. Simonov, 2006. Hedging, familiarity, and portfolio choice. *Review of Financial Studies*, 19, 633–685.

Massari, M., and L. Zanetti, 2008. *Valutazione. Fondamenti teorici e best practice nel settore industriale e finanziario*. McGraw Hill.

McLean, R.D., and J. Pontiff, 2016. Does academic research destroy stock return predictability? *Journal of Finance*, 71, 5–32.

Mehra, R., and E.C. Prescott, 1985. The equity premium: A puzzle. *Journal of Monetary Economics*, 15, 145–161.

Merton, R.C., 1969. Lifetime portfolio selection under uncertainty: The continuous-time case. *Review of Economics and Statistics*, 51, 247–257.

Merton, R.C., 1974. On the pricing of corporate debt: The risk structure of interest rates. *Journal of Finance*, 29, 449–470.

Merton, R.C., 1987. A simple model of capital market equilibrium with incomplete information. *Journal of Finance*, 42, 483–510.

Michaely, R., and A. Moin, 2022. Disappearing and reappearing dividends. *Journal of Financial Economics*, 143, 207-226.

Mischel, W., Y. Shoda, and M.L. Rodriguez, 1989. Delay of gratification in children. *Science*, 244, 933–938.

Moskowitz, T.J., 2000. Mutual fund performance: An empirical decomposition into stock-picking talent, style, transactions costs, and expenses: Discussion. *Journal of Finance*, 55, 1695–1703.

Moskowitz, T.J., Y.H. Ooi, and L.H. Pedersen, 2012. Time series momentum. *Journal of Financial Economics*, 104, 228–250.

Muhlhofer, T., 2013. Why do REIT returns poorly reflect property returns? Unrealizable appreciation gains due to trading constraints as the solution to the short-term disparity. *Real Estate Economics*, 41, 814–857.

Munday, S., W. Hu, T. True, and J. Zhang, 2018. Performance of private credit funds: A first look. *The Journal of Alternative Investments*, 21, 31–51.

Murfin, J., and M. Spiegel, 2020. Is the risk of sea level rise capitalized in residential real estate? *Review of Financial Studies*, 33, 1217–1255.

Muth, J.F., 1961. Rational expectations and the theory of price movements. *Econometrica*, 29, 315–335.

Norges Bank Investment Management, 2015. The diversification potential of real estate.

Novy-Marx, R., 2012. Is momentum really momentum? *Journal of Financial Economics*, 103, 429–453.

Novy-Marx, R., 2014. Predicting anomaly performance with politics, the weather, global warming, sunspots, and the stars. *Journal of Financial Economics*, 112, 137–146.

Novy-Marx, R., and M. Velikov, 2016. A taxonomy of anomalies and their trading costs. *Review of Financial Studies*, 29, 104–147.

Odean, T., 1999. Do investors trade too much? *American Economic Review*, 89, 1279–1299.

Pagano, M., F. Panetta, and L. Zingales, 1998. Why do companies go public? An empirical analysis. *Journal of Finance*, 53, 27–64.

Pagano, M., A. Sánchez Serrano, and J. Zechner, 2019. Can ETFs contribute to systemic risk? Reports of the Advisory Scientific Committee, No. 9.

Parker, J.A., A. Schoar, and Y. Sun, 2023. Retail financial innovation and stock market dynamics: The case of target date funds. *Journal of Finance*, 78, 2673-2723.

Pástor, L., and R.F. Stambaugh, 2003. Liquidity risk and expected stock returns. *Journal of Political Economy*, 111, 642–685.

Pástor, L., and R.F. Stambaugh, 2012. Are stocks really less volatile in the long run? *Journal of Finance*, 67, 431–478.

Pástor, L., and R.F. Stambaugh, 2019. Liquidity risk after 20 years. *Critical Finance Review*, 8, 277-299.

Pástor, L., R.F. Stambaugh, and L.A. Taylor, 2020. Sustainable investing in equilibrium. *Journal of Financial Economics*, 142, 550-571.

Pástor, L., R.F. Stambaugh, and L.A. Taylor, 2022. Dissecting green returns. *Journal of Financial Economics*, 146, 403-424.

Pástor, L., and M.B. Vorsatz, 2020. Mutual fund performance and flows ruring the COVID-19 crisis. *Review of Asset Pricing Studies*,10, 791–833.

Patton, A., and B. Weller, 2020. What you see is not what you get: The costs of trading market anomalies. *Journal of Financial Economics*, 137, 515–549.

Pedersen, L. 2015. *Efficiently Inefficient*. Princeton University Press.

Pedersen, L.H., S. Fitzgibbons, and L. Pomorski, 2021. Responsible investing: The ESG-efficient frontier. *Journal of Financial Economics*, 142, 572–597.

Petkova, R., and L. Zhang, 2005. Is value riskier than growth? *Journal of Financial Economics*, 78, 187–202.

Phalippou, L., and O. Gottschalg, 2009. The performance of private equity funds. *Review of Financial Studies*, 22, 1747–1776.

Preqin, 2023, *The 2023 Preqin Global Private Equity and Venture Capital Report.*

Rawls, J., 1971. *A Theory of Justice*. Harvard University Press.

Renneboog, L., and C. Spaenjers, 2013. Buying beauty: on prices and returns in the art market. *Management Science*, 59, 36–53.

Riedl, A., and P. Smeets, 2017. Why do investors hold socially responsible mutual funds? *Journal of Finance*, 72, 2505–2550.

Rietz, T., 1988. The equity risk premium: A solution. *Journal of Monetary Economics*, 22, 117–131.

Risk Metrics Group, 2007. Credit metrics technical document.

Roll, R., 1977. A critique of the asset pricing theory's test; part I: On past and potential testability of the theory. *Journal of Financial Economics*, 4, 129–176.

Ross, S. A., 1976. The arbitrage theory of capital asset pricing. *Journal of Economic Theory*, 13, 341–360.

Sadka, R., 2010. Liquidity risk and the cross-section of hedge-fund returns. *Journal of Financial Economics*, 98, 54–71.

Samuelson, W., and R. Zeckhauser, 1988. Status quo bias in decision making. *Journal of Risk and Uncertainty*, 1, 7–59.

Starks, L., 2023. Sustainable finance and ESG issues: Value versus values (Presidential address). *Journal of Finance*, 78, 1837–1872.

Sharot, T., 2011. *The optimism bias: A tour of the irrationally positive brain*. Pantheon/Random House.

Sharot, T., 2017. *The Influential Mind: What the Brain Reveals About Our Power to Change Others*. Henry Holt and Co.

Sharpe, W.F., 1964. Capital asset prices: A theory of market equilibrium under conditions of risk. *Journal of Finance*, 19, 425–442.

Sharpe, W.F., and L.G. Tint, 1990. Liabilities – a new approach. *Journal of Portfolio Management*, Winter, 5–10.

Shefrin, H.M., and M. Statman, 1985. The disposition to sell winners too early and ride losers too long: Thery and evidence. *Journal of Finance*, 60, 777–790.

Shefrin, H.M., and R.H. Thaler, 1988. The behavioral life-cycle hypothesis. *Economic Inquiry*, 26, 609–643.

Shiller, R.J., 1981. Do stock prices move too much to be justified by subsequent changes in dividends? *American Economic Review*, 71, 421–436.

Shiller, R.J., 1991. Arithmetic repeat sales price estimators. *Journal of Housing Economics*, 1, 110–126.

Shiller, R.J., 1993. *Macro Markets*. Oxford University Press.

Shiller, R.J., 1999. *Irrational Exuberance*. Princeton University Press.

Shiller, R.J., 2005. *Irrational Exuberance*, 2nd ed. Princeton University Press.

Shiller, R.J., 2013a. *Finance and the Good Society*. Princeton University Press.

Shiller, R.J., 2013b. Speculative asset prices. Prize Lecture, December 8. Available at https://www.nobelprize.org/uploads/2018/06/shiller-lecture.pdf.

Shiller, R.J., 2019. *Narrative Economics*. Princeton University Press.

Shiller, R.J., and A. Beltratti, 1992, Stock prices and bond yields, *Journal of Monetary Economics*, 30, 25-46.

Shleifer, A., and R. Vishny, 1997. A survey of corporate governance. *Journal of Finance*, 52, 737–783.

Silver, M., 2016. How to better measure hedonic residential property price indexes. IMF WP/16/213.

Simon, H.A., 1955. A behavioral model of rational choice. *The Quarterly Journal of Economics*, 69, 99–118.

Solnik, B., and L. Zuo, 2010. A global equilibrium asset pricing model with home preference. *Management Science*, 58, 273–292.

Statman, M., 2010. What investors really want. *Financial Analysts Journal*, 66, 8–10.

Stroebel, J., and J. Wurgler, 2021. What do you think about climate finance? Cesifo Working Paper 9350.

Surowiecki, J., 2004. *The Wisdom of Crowds: Why the Many Are Smarter than the Few and How Collective Wisdom Shapes Business, Economies, Societies, and Nations*. Doubleday.

Tetlock, P.C., 2007. Giving content to investor sentiment: The role of media in the stock market. *Journal of Finance*, 62, 1139–1168 .

Thaler, R.H. 1980. Toward a positive theory of consumer choice, Journal of Economic Behavior & Organization, 1, 39-60.

Thaler, R.H., 2016. Behavioral economics: past, present, and future. *American Economic Review*, 106, 1577–1600.

Thaler, R.H., and C.R. Sunstein, 2008. *Nudge: Improving Decisions about Health, Wealth, and Happiness*. Yale University Press.

Tostevin, P. 2017. How much is the world worth? The Savills Blog.

Tracy Ke, Z., B.T. Kelly, and D. Xiu, 2019. Predicting returns with text data. Yale ICF Working Paper No. 2019–10.

Treynor, J.L., and F. Black, 1973. How to use security analysis to improve portfolio selection. *Journal of Business*, 46, 66–86.

Treynor, J., and K. Mazuy, 1966. Can mutual funds outguess the market? *Harvard Business Review*, 44, 131–136.

Tuzel, S., 2010. Corporate real estate holdings and the cross-section of stock returns. *Review of Financial Studies*, 23, 2268–2302.

Tversky, A., and D. Kahneman, 1974. Judgment under uncertainty: Heuristics and biases. *Science*, 185, 1124–1131.

UNEP (United Nations Environment Programme), 2019. Changing course. Available at https://www.unepfi.org/wordpress/wp-content/uploads/2019/05/TCFD-Changing-Course-Oct-19.pdf.

UNWCED (United Nations World Commission on Environment and Development), 1987. Our Common Future. Oxford University Press.

Van Rooij, M.C.J., A. Lusardi, and R.J.M. Alessie, 2012. Financial literacy, retirement planning and household wealth. *Economic Journal*, 122, 449–478 .

Von Gaudecker, H.M., 2015. How does household portfolio diversification vary with financial literacy and financial advice? *Journal of Finance*, 70, 489–507.

Vuolteenaho, T., 2002. What drives firm-level stock returns? *Journal of Finance*, 57, 233–264.

Watson, J.B., 1919. *Psychology from the Standpoint of a Beheviorist*. Lippincott.

Weber, E.U., A.R. Blais, and N.E. Betz, 2002. A domain-specific risk-attitude scale: Measuring risk perceptions and risk behaviors. *Journal of Behavioral Decision Making*, 15, 263–290.

Wermers, R., 2002. Mutual fund performance: An empirical decomposition into stock-picking talent, style, transactions costs, and expenses. *Journal of Finance*, 55, 1655–1695.

Whelan, T., A. Ulrich, T. Van Holt, and C. Clark, 2021. ESG and financial performance: Uncovering the relationship by aggregating evidence from 1,000 plus studies published between 2015–2020. Rockefeller Asset Management and NYU Stern Center for Sustainable Business.

Woodford, M. , 2020. Modeling imprecision in perception, valuation and choice. *Annual Review of Economics*, 12, 579–601.

Yoong, J., 2011. Financial illiteracy and stock market participation: Evidence from the RAND American life panel. In *Financial Literacy: Implications for Retirement Security and the Financial Marketplace*, edited by O.S. Mitchell and A. Lusardi, Oxford University Press, 76–97.

www.ingramcontent.com/pod-product-compliance
Ingram Content Group UK Ltd.
Pitfield, Milton Keynes, MK11 3LW, UK
UKHW051447290926
15471UKWH00008B/1062

9 791281 627185